Event Management Blueprint

Creating and Managing Successful Sports Events

Heather Lawrence • Michelle Wells

Kendall Hunt
publishing company

Cover image © Shutterstock

Kendall Hunt
p u b l i s h i n g c o m p a n y

www.kendallhunt.com
Send all inquiries to:
4050 Westmark Drive
Dubuque, IA 52004-1840

CONTENTS

EVENT MANAGEMENT OVERVIEW

Heather Lawrence, Athena Yiamouyiannis, and Michelle Wells

Heather Lawrence, Ph.D., is an Associate Professor of Sports Administration and AECOM Professor of Sport Business at Ohio University. She earned her Ph.D. from the University of Florida, and also received bachelor's and master's degrees from Florida. Dr. Lawrence primarily teaches in the area of Event and Facility Management. In addition to her role at Ohio University, she has led event and facility courses in Spain, China, and Dubai. Prior to beginning her academic career, Heather worked in various administrative positions within intercollegiate athletics at Southeastern Louisiana University and the University of Florida. Her sport industry responsibilities have included working in NCAA compliance, facility management and construction/renovation management, event management, and general administration.

Athena Yiamouyiannis, Ed.D., is the former Executive Director of the National Association for Girls and Women in Sport (NAGWS). Since fall 2006, she has taught both full-time, and as an Adjunct Professor, on Ohio University's Sports Administration faculty bringing more than 15 years of industry experience to the classroom. She currently serves as an Administrator in the College of Arts and Sciences at the Ohio State University. Previously, she worked at the National Collegiate Athletics Association (NCAA) as the Director of Membership Services overseeing NCAA rules education operations and serving as liaison to the NCAA's Committee on Women's Athletics. Dr. Yiamouyiannis received a bachelor's in math and a master's in sports management from the Ohio State University, in addition to earning an Ed.D. in higher education administration from George Washington University.

Michelle Wells is a Visiting Instructor of Sport Studies at Guilford College in Greensboro, NC. She began teaching undergraduate students in 2008 and has taught event management, sports marketing, sports communication, sports law, and international sports. Prior to teaching, Michelle worked in event management for various organizations, including ESPN (Disney's) Wide World of Sports, Disney's Animal Kingdom, and New York Road Runners. She has managed and/or worked over 200 sports and entertainment events throughout her career. She received her bachelor's degree in business administration (marketing) from the University of Florida and a master's degree in sports administration and facility management from Ohio University.

Whether planning and executing a youth baseball tournament, college wrestling match, downhill ski race, triathlon, or any other variety of sporting event—there are strategies and tools available to event managers to help ensure the event is a success. This chapter sets the stage for the production and execution of a successful sport event. It focuses on the definition of event management, the role of event managers, different types of sport-governing bodies, and introduces event categories. It also describes the characteristics of effective event managers and provides insight into the job market. Becoming aware of core concepts of successful events and establishing the goals, objectives, tactics, and measures for the event are necessary first steps in the planning process. With a solid foundation, event management success is likely.

Event Management

Sport event management has become a highly sought after career path for those with business skills, an interest in sports, and the ability to combine the two through the management of events. Event management is unique in the sport industry because it requires the managers to have a broad base of knowledge in many different areas of the sport industry. For example, event managers for a minor league baseball team have to have an understanding of the principles of event management as well as being educated in the areas of customer service, marketing, tickets, budgeting, grounds maintenance, risk management, and many other areas. The individual will also be working with all of the aforementioned departments to ensure each knows, understands, and executes its role toward the overall success of the event.

The process of event management is not entirely linear which can make the planning process complex. There are four large categories that must be addressed for all events including the Foundation, Marketing and Sponsorship, Operations, and Ancillary Revenue. Within each of these areas, there are processes that occur while conceptualizing the event, developing the event, and executing the event. Many processes crossover between categories or are simultaneously occurring and impacting multiple categories. If it is already sounding a little confusing, that is because it is confusing. To provide an example from an open-water swimming race, consider the athlete registration process.

Getting to "event day" requires a lot of planning.

- The cost of participation is established.
- Athlete registration is marketed to a target group of potential participants.
- Various technologies are considered to make the registration process as easy as possible for the participants and as cost effective as possible for the event organizers.
- The waiver is written.

- Logistics of prerace and on-site registration are determined.
- Registration data is captured for future marketing efforts.
- On-site registration (and timing equipment pick-up) athlete and spectator flow is established.
- Data from on-site registration is merged with preregistrations for the public address announcer and timing equipment.
- Post-race evaluative surveys are sent using registration data.

As shown, one task that sounds small, like an athlete registration process, will impact everything from the layout of the venue to the budget to the quality of the public address announcements. The details of each of the areas previously listed make the process even more complex.

Event management is an exciting emerging industry. Based upon the complexity of some events and the economic impact to locales in which major events occur, it is also rapidly becoming known as a stand-alone industry. Author and event manager Julia Rutherford Silvers provides one of the best definitions of **event management** available:

> *Event management is the process by which an event is planned, prepared, and produced. As with any other form of management, it encompasses the assessment, definition, acquisition, allocation, direction, control, and analysis of time, finances, people, products, services, and other resources to achieve objectives.* (Silvers, 2003, para. 2)

From this definition, it is clear that the management of events encompasses a variety of business-related tasks; it is like managing a small business. These management functions often occur simultaneously, which creates challenges for all involved because change in one area may impact change in other areas. For example, if the budget is reduced, the organization's ability to pay staff and provide services is also limited. As in any business, the overall objectives are reached through the leadership and work of the people involved. In the case of event management, the event managers are ultimately responsible.

The Event Manager

Event managers are responsible for making the event "come to life." From conceptualization to execution, the event managers follow business functions in defining event management in a variety of specific areas that are part of the event. Additionally, there are certain personal characteristics that event managers must recognize as keys to success in the industry.

Beyond the business functions noted in Silvers' definition of event management, there are specific areas of knowledge in which event managers must be educated.

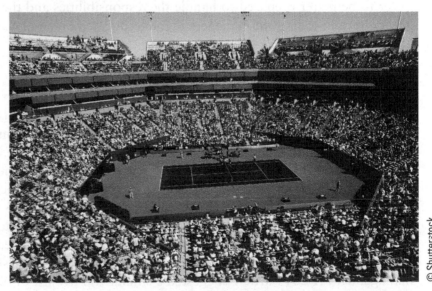

Event managers must manage a lot of different areas to reach the event day.

© Shutterstock

According to Ammon and Stotlar (2003, p. 258), successful event management requires attention to the following content areas:

- Recruitment and Training of Personnel
- Planning Emergency Medical Services
- Risk Management
- Facility Rental and Venue Logistics
- Alcohol Management and Training
- Box Office Management and Ticketing
- Food Services Management and Catering
- Building Maintenance
- Marketing, Advertising, and Public Relations
- Hospitality and VIP Protocol
- Securing Proper Permits and Licenses
- Contract Negotiations with Promoters
- Merchandise, Concessions, and Novelty Sales
- Crowd Management
- Parking and Traffic Control
- Evaluating the Final Result

Event managers need to have a broader understanding of the sports organization than many other staff. For example, a box office manager must be an excellent salesperson, have customer service skills, be detail oriented, and have a comprehensive understanding of ticketing. But the event managers have to be jacks-of-all-trades. They need to have the competencies associated with the box office manager (not quite to the level of a ticketing professional), and also excel in facility management, marketing, finance, logistics, food and beverage (F&B), building maintenance, and other areas.

Event managers find out quickly that their job responsibilities encompass a wide spectrum of duties without a typical day. Job descriptions will vary substantially depending on the type of organization, objectives of the position, number of events the organization produces, and level of employment. In order to be better prepared to handle the responsibilities and the variety of situations that may arise, it is important that event managers become educated on all of the areas that are related to the event.

Personal Characteristics

Knowledge of the functional areas related to event management is critical, but so is being able to lead, effectively communicate, and consistently act in an ethical manner. High-achieving event managers must possess many of the same leadership characteristics that are valued in other aspects of life such as compassion, good listening skills, the ability to make decisions, and an understanding of the profession. Regardless of proficiency level, event managers can improve their leadership skills to become more effective and efficient in their position.

There is agreement on some of the fundamental characteristics needed to succeed in this industry. Based on candid responses of current event managers via the Event Manager Blog (2008), the top five qualities for successful event managers include flexibility, people skills, organization, passion, and time management. A 2014 article suggested a similar top five list of qualities demonstrated by great event mangers, noting great interpersonal skills, flexibility, high energy, creativity and innovation, and a keen eye for detail (Evvnt, 2014). Event managers are faced with many tasks and responsibilities. Successful event managers must be flexible as things change around them. In many instances, event managers will have to handle multiple projects simultaneously. They need to be solution providers to problems that arise, because problems will arise during all phases of the event. Being a solution provider requires flexibility, energy, and resourcefulness, all while maintaining a positive outlook. Addressing challenges and changes promptly is vital because that is an inevitable part of the event-management process. This will keep the event moving forward and on-track.

Communication skills, particularly the development of interpersonal skills and the ability to interact well with others at any level, are contributors to success. Networking with vendors, being customer friendly, exuding a positive attitude, demonstrating enthusiasm and passion for one's job, and creating positive interactions with others are examples through which event managers can serve as positive role models for their staff. These interpersonal skills will help to create new relationships and strengthen existing relationships with all of those involved in the event. Being able to communicate effectively is essential in the event managers' role of supervisor to other staff. As supervisor, the event managers are responsible for training staff, delegating work responsibilities, and evaluating/providing feedback to the staff. The event managers will also become responsible for conflict resolution and workforce motivation. Event managers who utilize good communication strategies will be more effective in getting event staff to work together and adapt as changes occur on projects and events.

Organizational skills are also essential. Event managers need to manage time effectively, be able to meet deadlines, and be committed to excellence. This requires the ability to think ahead, develop plans, pay attention to details, develop timelines, stick to deadlines, and execute events.

Event managers as leaders also make a habit of reflecting upon the ethical nature of their actions. One way sport professionals can evaluate themselves is through the use of the Six Pillars of Character as identified by the Josephson Institute Center for Sports Ethics (2015). The Six Pillars of Character include trustworthiness, respect, responsibility, fairness, caring, and citizenship. Conducting an honest self-evaluation in these areas and developing a personal plan for improvement can contribute to individuals becoming more effective and ethical event managers and leaders in the sports industry. As in other areas of life, ethical behavior is valued in event management. The sports industry continues to grow; it is a profession where everyone seems to know everyone. As a result, one unethical decision and/or action by an event manager could follow someone throughout her career. By using the Six Pillars of Character as a guide to decision making, event managers are sure to act ethically when faced with tough decisions.

A solid knowledge base in a large number of content areas along with personal characteristics that are desirable to the industry is a good combination to have for anyone interested in working in event management. From a more macro perspective, event managers must also understand the sport industry as a whole as well as general information about a lot of specific sports. Keeping abreast of sport business stories, human-interest stories about athletes, developing controversies, and recent scores and stats is important for event managers. But even more essential is a true understanding of sports as a business. Central to this understanding is the idea of sport governance and the role of governing bodies in sport.

Sport Governance

It is important to realize that sporting events do not take place in a vacuum. They are usually part of a larger sport entity or sport governing body. Let's use the Mid-American Conference (MAC) Track and Field Championship as an example. The event is a subset of the MAC and the National Collegiate Athletic Association (NCAA). Therefore, sport event managers need to be aware of the organizational structure that governs each event. Events are not stand-alone operations. They are part of a larger industry. Whether the event is related to college athletics, professional sports, or a community sports organization, understanding sport governance is important for event managers.

Hums and McLean (2008, p. 4) defined **sport governance** as "the exercise of power and authority in sport organizations, including policy making, to determine organizational mission, membership, eligibility, and regulatory power, with the organization's appropriate local, national or international scope." How the governing organization operates, the staff reporting lines, and where the power lies within that organization are key pieces of information event managers must learn to discern to be successful. An understanding of the policies and procedures of the governing body is also required. Knowing who has final authority in the decision-making process and establishing good relationships with these key individuals will benefit event managers, particularly if problems arise.

Governing Bodies

Governing bodies are organizations charged with setting the rules for the sports they oversee. Adopting playing rules, selecting championship sites, certifying officials, and sanctioning events are all under their purview. They exist at many different levels, from local youth sports to elite international competition.

Youth Sport

There are too many youth sport governing bodies to mention here, but some of the most recognizable national organizations include the Amateur Athletic Union, Inc. (AAU), the United States Specialty Sports Association (USSSA), Little League Baseball, and Little League Softball. These governing bodies provide support to their regional, district, state, or local office through leadership, organization, and the creation of competitive sport opportunities. There are some youth sport governing bodies that extend beyond the borders of the United States such as Little League, which has more than 6,500 teams operating in almost 90 countries (Little League, n.d., para. 3). At the local level, additional governing bodies develop as a result of a need in the community for organized sports participation and competition opportunities. These governing bodies are not nearly as sophisticated as those at the national level, but they still provide structure and guidance for youth sport in the area. Often times, these organizations take the form of leagues run from the city or community recreation department.

Interscholastic Sport

The National Federation of State High School Associations provides oversight to 50 state associations (plus the District of Columbia) for athletics and other activities, and it also publishes playing rules for all 16 of their sports (National Federation of State High School Associations, n.d.). In addition, in North America, individual states and provinces have direct authority over public high school sports. Private schools, religiously affiliated or not, have many choices in selecting athletic governing bodies.

Intercollegiate Athletics

For intercollegiate athletics competition, the NCAA is the largest and most powerful governing body with 1,089 institutional members (NCAA, n.d.a.). However, there are other entities that govern intercollegiate athletics. The National Junior College Athletic Association (NJCAA) and the National Association of Intercollegiate Athletics (NAIA) both govern their member institutions' athletic competitions. All of these organizations offer structure to the intercollegiate athletic operations of their member institutions.

Professional Sport

In professional sports in the United States, sport-specific leagues (e.g., National Basketball Association [NBA] and Major League Baseball) are generally responsible for all aspects of the sport, including rules related to trading and payment of players. There is not one **national governing body** (**NGB**) for all professional sports in the United States. There are a variety of models for professional sport around the world ranging from models similar to the United States to countries where athletes with elite potential are identified at a young age and enter the club system or a government run training system.

National and International Governing Bodies

Most amateur sports in the United States have an NGB (e.g., USA Volleyball, USA Swimming, and USA Table Tennis) recognized by the United States Olympic Committee (USOC) to oversee that particular sport. What separates an NGB from other governing bodies previously discussed that oversee aspects of amateur sport is that the NGB has a formal relationship with the USOC and thus the International Olympic Committee (IOC). However, the NCAA and many of the governing bodies work together closely with NGBs on competition schedules, sport competition and eligibility rules, and policies that impact athletes. Many times, a member of the United States National Team is also a student-athlete at an NCAA institution and thus, care must be taken for NCAA rules not to conflict with NGB's rules.

NGBs also have **international governing body** (IGB) counterparts (e.g., Fédération Internationale de Natation [FINA] for many aquatic sports, and International Federation of Associated Wrestling Styles [IFAWS] for wrestling) that are responsible for international and Olympic playing rules and competitions in specific sports. The IOC is the international umbrella organization for all the sports specific to the various international federations. In addition, the IOC is responsible for the bid process and site selection for the Olympic Games.

Rights Holders

Rights holders are organizations or businesses that control and own the rights to an event. In many cases, the rights holder is also the NGB or governing body, but in other cases, the rights holder is a corporation or business. For example, ESPN owns the X Games and controls everything associated with the event. Permission would be required from ESPN if another organization wanted to use the X Games name, logo, or brand. Because ESPN does not govern the sports that are contested as part of the X Games, it is not a governing body, but its ownership of the event makes it the rights holder.

Although governance structures vary between various segments in the industry, it is clear that some form of governance structure is needed to establish policies and procedures as well as competition rules. To ensure that competitions are conducted in keeping with expectations of the rights holder and within established sport rules, event sanctions are required for many sporting events. In this case, a "sanction" is not a "punishment," but rather the official recognition by the rights holder.

Event Sanctions

Event sanctions ensure consistency between sports events and provide standards related to competition. Almost any event that seeks to be associated with an NGB, IGB, or collegiate governing body will be required to acquire a sanction. **Event sanctions** are considered an official approval for the event and are granted by the governing body associated with the sport (Solomon, 2002). "The sanctioning process allows the governing body to control the game ... so that it is played under authorized rules with approved equipment" (p. 9). There is usually a fee associated with obtaining the sanction, but in return the host organization has proof it has met the standards of the governing body.

Sanctions are also important because they help to ensure fairness, safety, and consistency among competitions held under the auspices of the governing body. It would be unfair for a swimmer to set a national record in a pool that was a few inches shorter than it should be. The sanction will provide for course certifications for swimming, running, cycling, and multisport events to ensure consistency across venues. Often sanctions also require a certain amount of medical personnel to be available as well as the provision of insurance coverage for the event operators and the participants.

Happy participants indicate a well managed event.

USA Triathlon (USAT) is one example of an NGB that sanctions events. USAT annually sanctions over 4,300 events (e.g., triathlons, duathlons, and aquathlons, and aquabike) ranging in cost from $200 to $450 depending upon how early the request is submitted (USAT, n.d.a.; USAT, 2014). When USAT (2014) sanctions an event, it means they are confirming that certain conditions have been met. A USAT-sanctioned event signifies, "that the race director has completed a thorough review of the swim, bike, and run courses, has evaluated and planned for medical, emergency, safety and volunteer support and will conduct the event according to the USA Triathlon Competitive Rules" (para. 1). The benefits to being a USAT-sanctioned event include insurance coverage for event staff, volunteers, and participants; inclusion in the USA Triathlon National Ranking System for participants; access to USAT officials; access to the USAT membership mailing list; and access to sponsor programs and benefits (USAT, n.d.a.).

The type of event will impact whether a sanction is needed, and not all competitions need to be sanctioned. Event planners interested in starting a new event should investigate opportunities for sanctioning the event with the appropriate governing body. Then a determination can be made whether sanctioning is needed and the benefits to sanctioning the event. The variety of sports related events that can be created and executed is endless. But, most events can be categorized into one of four main types, which helps in making event-related decisions in the event management process.

The Harlem Globetrotters

Brian Brantley, Former Marketing Director, Harlem Globetrotters

The Harlem Globetrotters have been around for 82 years and are still going strong. What started as a small basketball team in Chicago has turned into one of the longest running entertainment events in the world. Because of the ever-changing nature of the sports and entertainment industry, managing the events of the Globetrotters and other traveling shows has become more complicated.

When putting on a family show that travels across the country, finding a suitable site for the event comes first. The great thing about the Harlem Globetrotters is the fact that they will play, and have played, in all types of facilities. They have played in recreation halls, high school gymnasiums, small arenas, mid-size arenas, large arenas, and even on the deck of an aircraft carrier. To play a broad spectrum of venues, there has to be a lot of coordination between individuals responsible for scheduling, marketing, community involvement, public relations, media, operations, ticketing, and facility management.

Because of the variety of locales the Globetrotters play in, the goals of each show vary somewhat. If the Globetrotters are exploring a new, small market, the goal of the event might be exposure and brand awareness in that area. However, in a major market, goals tend to be more directly tied to revenue generation. But whatever the goals of the organization are for a specific show, the underlying theme is one of community fun. If the event is entertaining and the fans enjoy it, then the secondary goals are sure to be accomplished.

For example, let's examine the Harlem Globetrotters playing in Athens, Ohio. First, it must be clear who is hosting the event. Is it the building that would like to bring the Globetrotters to the arena (Convocation Center), or is it the Globetrotters that would like to play the Convocation Center? Sometimes, it may be an outside group that would like to host an event and bring a family show like the Globetrotters to their community. In this scenario, suppose it is the Convocation Center that would like to bring the Globetrotters to Athens. The building probably has open dates (days/nights without events) and wants to fill its event schedule. Timing, of course, is a key here. Many scheduling conflicts such as other athletic events, other traveling family shows, university events, and community events can potentially arise and make scheduling an event a challenge. In a small college town like Athens where the Globetrotters have played before, the primary goal of all involved might be to provide entertainment to the community while generating revenue for the venue and the Globetrotters. Achieving these goals would ensure that the show would return to Athens in the future.

Marketing of such family shows also evolves with each show and city. No matter who is putting on the show, all parties want a show that reaches as many people as possible and brings a positive experience to the community. Marketing can take many forms, including TV, radio, print advertisements, and local and national sponsorships. Because the show is usually in town for only one night before heading to a new area, the marketing is done way in advance of the show. This ensures that the maximum number of people have been reached. Creativity in marketing is extremely important. An example of a promotion related to our previous example would be having a local grocery store sell discounted tickets to shoppers. The store would then be mentioned in other publicity events about the show such as print, TV, and radio advertising.

When all of these elements are put together, the result is a show that is unforgettable and will have people ready to come back for more the next time the show is in town. For event managers and marketing professionals, the Harlem Globetrotters family show brings many different elements to the forefront. From a public relations standpoint, there is the famous song "Sweet Georgia Brown" and memorable former players such as Meadowlark Lemon, Curly Neal, and Sweet Lou Dunbar. From an event management perspective, the unique elements of the Harlem Globetrotters show are merely opportunities to enhance the event experience for all. Event managers who are able to set realistic goals, use creativity throughout the planning process, and create a memorable experience for fans will, like the Globetrotters, find success in the sports and entertainment industry.

Types of Events

It would be great if sports events all fit neatly into a certain category and the management of each event within a category was standard. But, if that were the case, there would be no need for an entire book on event management, nor would competent event managers be in such high demand. It is the diversity of sporting events that makes the field an exciting and challenging place to work.

That being noted, there are four broad categories in which most events will fit and will aid in the discussion of event management throughout this book. The four categories include the following:

- Recurring Events
- Traveling Events
- Mega Events
- Ancillary Events

Determining which category is most like a specific event includes careful consideration of the event goals and objectives, the event frequency, the perceived importance of the event, the number of participants and spectators, media presence, and the extent of involvement by a sport governing body or the rights holder.

Recurring Events

The most common event for sport managers is the recurring event. A **recurring event** is one that happens on a regular basis (e.g., university basketball game or youth soccer game). Although these events may vary in the number of participants and spectators, many of the operating characteristics are consistent each time the event takes place. Most recurring events appeal to local or regional spectators, but there are recurring events of national magnitude (e.g., college football rivalry games). Recurring events are very common in community organizations, universities, and professional sports.

A community organization may provide opportunities for local youth to participate in a soccer league, offering the kids multiple games throughout the season. A local community might also host a 5K run each year to promote fitness within the locale. Both of these types of events are grassroots efforts where local event managers organize and operate the recurring events.

© Shutterstock

Event managers at colleges may manage many different sports events.

Within a university setting, a sport event manager will likely supervise upward of 6 football games, 10 soccer games, 10 volleyball games, 30 basketball games (men's and women's), 10 swimming and diving meets, 15 softball games, 20 baseball games, 15 ice hockey games, and many other sports depending on what the schedule requires. It is common for intercollegiate athletics event managers to average four to five events per week during the academic year at institutions that sponsor a full complement of competitive teams. The University of Florida reported that over 1 million fans attended 172 home events in the 2013–2014 season (University of Florida Athletic Association, 2013). A small event such as a cross-country meet may have mostly friends and families of the student-athletes in attendance with only a few personnel working the event. A much larger event such as an NCAA division I football game may have a championship title at stake, millions of dollars in potential revenue, and over 100,000 fans in attendance. But each cross-country meet is managed in a similar manner to a football game.

In professional sports, the events are usually larger in scope than most sports events in colleges and universities. However, in professional sports the event managers are commonly only dealing with one specific sport. This allows for consistency in operations from one event to the next. There will always be some variation in planning, depending on the opponent, the importance of the game, marketing and promotions activities, and other variables. But just as in the university sector, each game begins with a similar plan and structure for its operations.

Generally, recurring events share the following characteristics: (a) a set schedule; (b) a known facility; (c) employees and participants familiar to the event managers; and (d) an existing event management template. The common theme throughout recurring events is that the basic planning and processes are similar each time the event occurs. Whether it is the first or twentieth Major League Baseball game of the season, the planning template is similar.

Traveling Events

A **traveling event** is one that does not occur on a regular basis at a consistent location, but a traveling event may either occur on a regular basis or at a set location. For example, the NCAA Women's Basketball Final Four occurs every year but not in the same location, thus making it a traveling event. Conversely, the Harlem Globetrotters (see sidebar in this chapter) visit some venues more than once in a multi-year period, but not on a regular basis, thus making it a traveling event. Traveling events require more up-front planning than recurring events because event managers do not have the benefit of hosting the event on a consistent basis in the venue. Many of these types of events use a bid process to secure locations or a booking agency to handle scheduling.

Traveling events can vary substantially from one another and coming up with a list of similarities is impossible. Goals for traveling events can range from providing an opportunity for athletes to qualify for the Olympic Games to providing an opportunity for youth to experience competition in a fun environment. Most traveling events have a rights holder or governing body that requires specific aspects of the event to occur within its established framework. Event managers are required to ensure that the needs of the event can be met in the available facility and that appropriate financial and personnel resources are available. For example, for NCAA Championships, the NCAA provides sponsor banners that must be displayed throughout the venue. In most cases, existing sponsor signage must be covered up to ensure there are no conflicts between NCAA sponsors and existing venue sponsors. Event managers who have not given careful consideration to NCAA requirements may have to scramble unnecessarily at the last minute to comply with this regulation.

Mega Events

Mega events are the most complex category as they often take years of planning. Mega events are often international in nature (whether through media exposure, participation, or location) and are easily identifiable to sports consumers because the event has become a brand. Budgets can be in the multi-millions of dollars, as can the economic impact on the location. These events become stand-alone business ventures because many of them have organizing committees composed of full- and part-time personnel dedicated solely to the execution of the event. Although the Olympic Games is the ultimate example of a mega event, there are many others such as world championships, major international marathons and bicycle races, World Cup Soccer, the Asian Games, and the Commonwealth Games.

Mega events are some of the largest and most complex events to manage.

© Shutterstock

The bid process for hosting mega events is complex, lengthy, expensive, and has multiple phases. Hosting a mega event is a huge undertaking that requires the cooperation of many entities (i.e., governments, organizing committees, national governing bodies, international governing bodies, military, and police). National and international sports governing bodies are heavily involved in the planning and execution of mega events because the integrity of the sport is on display for an international audience during the competitions. Additionally, many of these events encompass multiple competition days, venues, and sports, resulting in many special events within the mega event. Another common feature of mega events is the presence of ancillary events (e.g., opening ceremonies, concerts, fan experience exhibits) that enhance and support the core sports event.

Ancillary Events

Ancillary events have become an increasingly common aspect of event planning and management. They commonly supplement and surround the predefined core sport events and can range from a spaghetti dinner the night before a 5K road race to a 10,000-person VIP tailgate party before the Super Bowl. Ancillary events provide event managers the opportunity to generate additional revenue through sponsorships, ticket sales, media contracts, and merchandise. Ancillary events promote brand awareness of the event, create excitement, and give fans a unique experience. They can also increase economic impact of the events because people may attend ancillary events that do not attend the core event and spectators attending the core event end up spending more time in the host area.

Courtesy of Michael Stephens

A cornhole tournament as an ancillary event at Ohio University.

Some sport events fit neatly into one of the four categories mentioned above, and others have characteristics that cross categories. In either case, event managers are charged with ensuring that all of the stakeholders (i.e., participants, spectators, sponsors, and media) experience the best event possible, given the objectives and parameters of the event. The goals and limitations of an event are often the result of the actions of various governing bodies associated with the event.

Goals of Events

Sports events take place for a multitude of reasons. As event managers begin to plan, understanding the overall goals for the event will assist them as they move forward. One obvious reason to hold an event is to make money for an organization or municipality. A city may want to create an event that will help establish itself as a travel destination or the goal might be to drive economic impact for a city. The locations of summer youth championship tournaments often turn into locations where families spend summer vacations. **Sports commissions** exist specifically to attract sports events to the area and assist in hosting the events. They know that hosting these tournaments can draw hundreds or thousands of people, all of whom will spend money at local hotels, restaurants, and shops. On the other hand, some events are driven by charity or by the goal to create awareness about a topic. The Susan G. Komen Race for the Cure is held to raise awareness about breast cancer and to fund research. Some events are even created to further establish brand awareness. A multisport complex may target youth sports as its key demographic, yet may hold several pro sports events to get its brand in the market. The cost of the event in exchange for the awareness created by broadcast exposure may be seen as a fair trade-off.

Event Purpose

The **purpose statement** is a short, to-the-point acknowledgment of the overall motivation for holding the event. For a high-level adult triathlon, the purpose statement might read, "To host an elite level triathlon sanctioned by USAT with national rankings implication for the participants." Another event may target local recreational cycling athletes where socializing with other participants is an important part of the event. The purpose statement for the cycling event might be, "To provide a fun community bike ride while providing opportunities for personal connections." Whatever the purpose statement is, it should be the driving force behind the goal-setting process.

Event Goals-Objectives-Tactics-Metrics

Establishing the goals, objectives, tactics, and metrics or measures of success of the event first will ensure that everyone in the organization is on the same page and moving in the same direction. **Goals** are the items an event wants to accomplish with a given strategy and aligned with its purpose. The purpose statement serves to frame the goals, objectives, tactics, and metrics and should be revisited throughout the process. For example, the goals of the previously mentioned elite level triathlon might be threefold: (1) to attract nationally competitive athletes (2) to expose participants to the great training facilities in the area; and (3) to generate interest in the area so participants might return for vacations and/or to buy a second home (because they know that they can continue with their sports in the area). The community cycling event, on the other hand, might have entirely different goals that might include: (1) to provide a safe bike route where cyclists of all levels can participate; (2) to create a reasonable schedule, with participant socializing being a priority; (3) to provide a physical setting that encourages socializing.

Objectives are connected directly to their explicit, related goals. They are specific and measurable, enabling event managers to determine success. Each goal will have one or more objectives associated with it. The elite level triathlon has one goal of attracting nationally competitive athletes. One objective for this goal could be to have a 30% increase from the previous year in nationally ranked participants. **Tactics** are the actions used to accomplish the objectives. They can take a variety of forms, but must relate directly to the objectives with which they are connected. A tactic answers the question of how the objective will be achieved. In this example, one tactic to increase by 30% the nationally ranked participants might be to contact all nationally ranked triathletes and offer them a free hotel stay for the race weekend. Finally, **measures** or **metrics** are the methods used to determine the success of tactics, and subsequently, the goals and the objectives. Continuing with the triathlon example, the triathlon organizers could simply count how many entrants are nationally ranked as compared with the previous year to calculate whether the increase of 30% was met. The key is that the metric or measure must relate to the tactic so the data gathered can be compared with the objective for the relevant tactic.

Reviewing the two different events (elite triathlon and community bike ride), they would be very different based first on the purpose statement and then on the established goals, objectives, tactics, and metrics. The triathlon registration packets may include discounts to other elite events and special high-level coaching sessions and the nationally ranked athletes could receive their own starting time and other benefits to help them succeed. The schedule for the community-cycling event would include plenty of down time and a social setting nearby (e.g., a beer garden) where participants could sit and talk. A lot of bells and whistles can be added to events that will impress people—opening ceremonies, free meals, clinics—but if the money spent is unrelated to achieving the goals, it is not money well spent.

Creativity in Event Management

The word *creative* is not one that immediately comes to mind with sports event management. However, when working on all types of sports events addressed in this book—recurring, traveling, mega, and ancillary—creativity becomes particularly important. The opportunity to be inventive in the planning of sports events is also one of the fun parts of working on them. It allows event managers to have a blank slate to ask the limitless question—what if …?—that can lead to new types of events that could be major money earners for an organization. Creativity in developing events can reveal itself in several ways. It can involve coming up with a new theme for a pre-existing event format (e.g., Rock 'n' Roll Marathon created in the 1990s), or developing an entire bid package and theme for a multisport event (e.g., National Senior Games), or generating ancillary events that tie in well with existing ones (a music concert or barbecue held the night before a big rivalry game).

© Shutterstock

Color runs are a recent creative trend in road races.

Ancillary events particularly allow creativity to come into play. Event managers often work on sporting events that have been in existence for many years. Creating new ancillary events can add both a novel perspective and a new revenue stream. These are the types of events where event managers can use their creativity to explore new ideas. It may not be feasible for an organization to take on the financial risk for a new large-scale event. It is often easier to add on to existing events and expand their reach. Ancillary events may be created to complement an existing theme or to add another related theme. They can help expand the overall brand of the event and create a longer timeframe. For the TCS New York City Marathon, marathon week begins the Sunday before the actual event with the six-mile Poland Spring Marathon Kickoff race in Central Park. During the week, there are press conferences, fireworks, pasta dinners, and other races that lead up to marathon day.

For the NBA All-Star Game, the NBA puts on events such as the All-Star Jam Session, the Slam Dunk Contest, and many others. Sometimes ancillary events are creatively designed to alleviate traffic pressure by trying to entice spectators to delay their departure from the event. A free concert after an MLB baseball game is one example. Developing events that are fun and innovative helps ensure they will be successful. These types of events allow event managers to use their full range of imagination and expand the organization's brand identity.

Event Themes

Take a look at any major sports event—Super Bowl, NCAA Final Four, Olympic Games—and it is noticeable that each has a consistent theme running throughout it. The **event theme** helps establish an identity that people will associate with it and should be a part of every aspect of the event. Much of the discussion of themes has to do with branding the event. Take, for example, the Ohio University Race for a Reason event consisting of a 3K walk, 5K run, mud run, and triathlon/duathlon, The event goal is to raise money for charitable organizations ($115,000 benefiting 107 charities in 2014) get encourage people to be active (1,050 participants in 2014.). The event theme has been consistent asking the question, "What's your reason?" and using #WhatsYourReason on social media. This branding is directed at the receiver of the message, clearly shows the tie to charitable giving, differentiates the event from dozens of other local races, and is consistent throughout the year. This message should not deviate and it should be nearly omnipresent for the event—on letterhead, in PA announcements, in commercials, on promotional give-aways, on invitations, on signage, on T-shirts, and so on. All of the areas should complement each other to create the theme and brand image for the entire event. The event stays the same each year, but the application of the theme can change and distinguish one year's event from another.

Breaking into Event Management

Even students that have event management experience understand the various responsibilities of event management, and have a strong desire to work in the industry that is sometimes difficult to break into. This is not an industry where people can wait for the jobs to come to them. Conversely, those interested in event management must understand the market, develop their professional network, and actively seek out positions.

An Interview with Paul Ortolano

Director, Event Management and Logistics, New York Road Runners

The following interview was conducted with Paul Ortolano, Director, Event Development and Production, New York Road Runners. Celebrating its 50th anniversary in 2008, the New York Road Runners (www.nyrr.org) continues to promote the sport of distance running, enhancing health and fitness for all, and responding to community needs. Their road races and other fitness programs draw upward of 300,000 runners annually, and together with their magazine and Web site support and promote professional and recreational running. Annually, Mr. Ortolano, in his capacity as the leader of the department that manages over 55 road races per year, such as the TCS New York City Marathon, reviews hundreds of resumes of aspiring event managers. Paul provided some insight on the attributes he looks for in event managers.

What qualities do you look for in event managers?

I think communication skills are *the* most important thing in event management, absolutely the number one thing. The reason communication skills are number one is because a significant part of this type of work revolves around the ability to communicate well. The relationships with my agency partners, the relationships with my team members (other New York Road Runners employees), the relationships with vendors, and the relationships with facilities are critical to success in managing road races.

Looking at a resume, how do you determine if a person has good communication skills?

I look at how well the resume is written and ask myself two questions: (1) How articulate are they? and (2) Are they specific in expressing what they have done professionally? What I mean by being specific is not just listing activities, but being specific about revenue generation, size of budgets, and how they impacted the organization or event.

What other areas are you assessing in potential event managers?

Other things that are also extremely important include how they have utilized the experiences they have had. Just because an undergraduate student recently graduates does not mean they have not had valuable experiences. There could be things they did while in school (i.e., internships, working events, or volunteering) that gave them a feel for event management and an understanding of what it takes to succeed. If job candidates have no experience and want to work in sports event management, how do they really know it is the right career for them? If a person is changing careers to come into sports event management, I prefer they have at least a little experience in planning projects. My background is in project management and I was always planning things. I developed very long-term information systems and that is how I got into sports event management because I was utilizing my project management skills from a prior career. Again, it is all about how they have used their time so far in their career.

Are there different things you look for, depending on the level of the job?

Communication skills are going to cover all levels of jobs. At the coordinator level, I am looking for eagerness, someone who really is passionate and wants it. But, it is not just about wanting the job; it is also about having a joy for doing the job. In the case of the New York Road Runners, candidates do not have to be runners; it can be the idea of "I've always loved sporting events and the reason that running is compelling to me is ..." and then they go into that. I am looking for the passion in reference to that at the lower level because typically when coming straight from undergraduate work, or even straight from graduate school, it should be all about eagerness to learn and wanting to be mentored and developed. They should want to be a sponge and absorb everything. That is what I look for at entry-level positions.

When I get up to a manager level, I am looking for 2–4 years of experience. They have been out there in the industry, even if it is just working a small component of an event, maybe as a support person for a production company working on the production of a major event. Or maybe they were the administrative assistant for an executive at a sports league or something similar. I am usually looking for something related to sports and event planning and their core components.

At the senior management level, I am looking for people with 4–7 years of experience who have gone through the full event life cycle multiple times. They should have planned on-going events and maybe even created new events. In creating new events it demonstrates that they had this idea and then they created it, they developed it, they executed it, and they can discuss the outcome. Sometimes the event is not successful, but it shows their eagerness and that they have tried to take a concept and bring it to life. Maybe it did not work, but they learned something from it. At the senior level, I'm concerned with, What did they learn and how did it make the next thing they did better?

Once you hire a person with the ideal characteristics and they are out there managing events, what do you think are some of the most important traits to have as an event manager?

What I look for and what I try to teach is to go out and do it. Do not just be a pencil pusher and stand on the sidelines with a clipboard and tell people what to do. They should go out there and show the people that they are working with that they will do everything that they ask their event staff to do. This is one of the things that is really important—to get their hands dirty and be hands on. Show the people that they are working with that no one is better than anyone else. Everyone is trying to get to the same goal, and doing whatever it takes to achieve the best event is how to get there.

The other thing is to have a plan in place. The worst thing an event manager can do is go out on an event day without a plan. If they do not have a plan, things are going to fall through the cracks. Have a plan early and review the plan over and over, especially with the people who are working the plan. This will ensure that when the event manager gets to the event day and surprises come up, the basic event plan remains without major adjustments as the surprise is handled. Along with event plans, a contingency plan should also be developed. Always having the brain in the background asking the questions such as, What if a lightning storm comes through?, or What if new construction is in the way of one of the road race courses?, or What if we mistakenly oversold the bleacher seats at a particular event? will help them plan ahead for the surprises that are inevitable in this profession.

What do you think are some of the biggest misconceptions that people have about being a sports event manager?

I think the biggest misconception is that it is all about the glitz and glamour of putting on sports events. I would say that 99.9% of the events and 99.9% of the time we are planning events for someone other than professional caliber athletes. It is only that small amount that is the glitz and glamour, but what we have to do is to always focus on the target audience, and that target audience is the 10 minute milers or 15 minute milers or weekend warriors who are out there and supporting the events. This is really who we most often plan events for and people should not expect the glitz and glamour.

Trying to get a first job in sports is a difficult and frustrating time for many people attempting to break into the industry. With 330 academic programs in sport management in the United States, there are plenty of applicants and not enough jobs (North American Society for Sport Management, n.d.). For example, the Red Sox annually hire fewer than 10 new employees, but receive 2,500 resumes for those 10 positions (Kladko, 2008). However, for those individuals who put extra effort into preparing themselves for their career and take time to understand the needs of employers and what they are looking for, a job in sports and event management is sure to become a reality.

Other realities of the sport industry are low starting pay and long hours. Entry-level jobs in sports generally do not pay as well as job seekers anticipate (starting salaries range between $20,000 and $40,000) and sometimes multiple internships are required before one can obtain a full-time job. The hours are also long because sports managers (especially event managers) are working when everyone else is playing. For example, a local 10K road race would never happen on a Tuesday afternoon around 2 pm because that is when most people are at work. Event managers are at work all week planning the race and then back at work Saturday morning to execute the race. Then the teardown and cleanup occur after the race and could last well into Saturday afternoon. So it is likely that the race manager will work in excess of 50 hours per week during the events. But for those who are truly passionate about sports, business, and entertainment, the job will be enjoyable and will not feel like work. By working hard, gaining experience, and working toward having the content knowledge and personal characteristics explored in this chapter, event managers will quickly work their way up the organizational hierarchy. An example of a mid-level event manager position for a university is provided in the box on page 16 to demonstrate the responsibilities one might find while moving up in the industry.

Given the current ultracompetitive landscape in the sports industry, job seekers must strategically separate themselves from the competition. Recently, some sports management degree programs have been criticized for not providing a diversity of skill sets to students (Kladko, 2008). This is pointed out not to be negative, but to make readers aware of the reality of the needs of sports employers. Students seeking a job in the sports industry must take it upon themselves to go above and beyond the work in the classroom and gain real-life experiences in sport. The goal of obtaining these extra experiences should be to develop all of the competencies identified throughout this chapter. As demonstrated in the interview with Paul Ortolano, Director, Event Development and Production, New York Road Runners (see the box on page 13), individuals who make good use of their time are more likely to be hired than those who have simply completed their academic requirements. The interview with Mr. Ortolano provides detailed information of what a sports employer looks for when hiring event managers, and it provides an excellent starting point for students looking to make themselves more marketable to employers.

Another way to become more marketable is to know more people. If people in the industry are aware of a talented person, it is likely that when a job does become available, those "in the loop" will be contacted first. Professional organizations are a good way for new event managers to get involved and begin to create their own professional network.

Professional Organizations

In the world of sports, building a professional networking system is essential to functioning and excelling in the industry. Whether looking for a new job, seeking information on a specific challenge being faced, or taking advantage of professional development opportunities, professional organizations are a good place to start. For sports event managers, there are multiple organizations that relate to specific types of event management. The National Association of Collegiate Directors of Athletics (NACDA) has a subdivision for event managers in college athletics called the Collegiate Event and Facility Management Association (CEFMA) (http://nacda.cstv.com/cefma/nacda-cefma.html). For those interested in event or facility management within college athletics, membership in this organization provides access to current information, top professionals in the industry, and networking opportunities.

The International Association of Venue Managers (IAVM) (www.iavm.org) is another well-known industry organization. IAVM provides opportunities for public assembly facility managers of all types. Often, industry segments are grouped together in professional organizations and IAVM is one example of that. IAVM is broad in scope and targets those individuals involved in managing facilities such as sports stadiums, sports arenas, performing arts centers, convention centers, exhibit halls, and amphitheaters. The organization is also dedicated to providing opportunities for students through volunteer opportunities at its annual conference and professional development programming through its institutes and certification programs.

The Stadium Managers Association (SMA) (www.stadiummanagers.org) includes members who are involved with administration and operations of sports stadiums. SMA holds annual meetings where information is shared between vendors and stadium managers. SMA was formed in 1974 and its purpose and membership groups are as follows:

> *SMA promotes the professional, efficient, and state-of-the-art management of stadiums around the world. Our members are administrators, operators, and marketing personnel from teams, government entities, colleges and universities, and suppliers to the industry.* (n.d., para. 2)

SMA is a niche organization focusing on specific issues related to sports stadium managers. As such, future event managers interested in this segment of the industry should consider membership in this organization.

These are just a few examples of organizations related to event and facility management in sport. There are hundreds of others associated with job function (e.g., Sport Marketing Association), type of sport (e.g., Road Runners Club of America), or a combination of characteristics (e.g., National Association of Collegiate Women Athletic Administrators). The authors have compiled a list of professional organizations (see Appendix A) as a starting point for those looking to affiliate with one. The organizations highlighted are related to aspects of event management and readers are encouraged to explore them by evaluating the objectives, professional development opportunities, information sharing opportunities, annual conference content, and the cost of membership compared with anticipated benefits.

Sample Job Posting for a University Event Management Position

Function

The event manager will report to the Senior Associate Director of Athletics and provide support in the areas of event management, facility operations, new construction and renovations, special events, and general administration.

Duties

1. Responsible for all athletic events.
2. Effectively and efficiently direct all event staff.
3. Responsible for assisting in the design, bidding, and construction of new softball stadium and new basketball practice facility.
4. Responsible for all athletic department special events (i.e., student-athlete banquet, alumni BBQ, and football booster auction).
5. Additional duties as assigned by the Senior Associate Director of Athletics and Director of Athletics.

Knowledge and Abilities

1. Knowledge of principles of athletic management (i.e., customer service, budgeting, contracts, sponsorship, marketing, and risk management).
2. Understanding of turf management, athletic surfaces, facility maintenance, custodial considerations, and construction processes.
3. Knowledge of NCAA rules and regulations.

Qualifications

1. Bachelor's degree in Sport Administration required (Master's Degree preferred), Management, Communications or related field.
2. Previous experience in a facility management or collegiate athletic department.
3. Excellent communication skills, work ethic, and a record of dependability and reliability required.
4. Proven ability to interact with coaches and staff in a positive manner.
5. Ability to work nights and weekends.

Salary

1. Commensurate with experience and education.

SUMMARY

The main purposes of this chapter were to discuss what event management is, the role of event managers, and to establish the competencies needed to be a successful event manager. Information was also provided on breaking into the event management industry as well as the realities of the occupation. As discussed, the challenges that event managers face (i.e., tasks changing daily, a solid base of knowledge in many areas) are the same things that make the job fun and exciting. Those interested in getting started in event management need to educate themselves on all aspects of event management, assess their own abilities, acquire an understanding of what employers are looking for in the field, and be ready for a competitive job search.

Another purpose of this chapter was to provide an overview of some of the core event management concepts that come into play during the event planning and management process. From defining the event purpose and goals to understanding how governing bodies are involved, event managers must be well versed in a variety of areas internal and external to their event. Those event managers that understand the creative aspects of event management and how to leverage them to generate revenue will certainly be successful. It is not enough to simply put on an event in the current sports culture; participants, spectators, media, and sponsors all expect something more than the core sports product. It is the ability to conceptualize and execute this "something more" idea that will separate the good event managers from the great ones.

Student Challenges

Event Management and the Event Manager

NAME _____ DATE _____

Question 1.1

Explore two current job postings in the field of event management and respond to the questions about each position. Organizations such as IAVM (http://www.iavm.org/), The NCAA (http://ncaamarket.ncaa.org/jobseekers/index.cfm), and TeamWork Online (http://www.teamworkonline.com/) often have event management jobs posted.

Job #1 Title:
- Responsibilities:

- Education Required:

- Other knowledge/skills required:

Job #2 Title:
- Responsibilities:

- Education Required:

- Other knowledge/skills required:

Evaluation:

- What similarities did you find between the two jobs?

- What differences did you find between the two jobs?

Question 1.2

Conduct research on five events and determine whether the event is recurring, traveling, mega, ancillary, or a combination. Each category (recurring, traveling, mega, and ancillary) must be represented at least once. Use the event websites to determine what the event theme is and how creativity was integrated into the event.

Event #1:
- Type of Event:
- Theme:
- Creativity:

Event #2:
- Type of Event:
- Theme:
- Creativity:

Event #3:
- Type of Event:
- Theme:
- Creativity:

Event #4:
- Type of Event:
- Theme:
- Creativity:

Event #5:
- Type of Event:
- Theme:
- Creativity:

Question 1.3

Brainstorm for 5 minutes. If you could create any event you wanted, what would it be? During the 5 minutes, write down as many ideas as possible.

EVENT FEASIBILITY

Heather Lawrence

Heather Lawrence, Ph.D., is an Associate Professor of Sports Administration and AECOM Professor of Sport Business at Ohio University. She earned her Ph.D. degree from the University of Florida, and also received bachelor's and master's degrees from Florida. Dr. Lawrence primarily teaches in the area of Event and Facility Management. In addition to her role at Ohio University, she has led event and facility courses in Spain, China, and Dubai. Prior to beginning her academic career, Heather worked in various administrative positions within intercollegiate athletics at Southeastern Louisiana University and the University of Florida. Her sport industry responsibilities have included working in NCAA compliance, facility management and construction/renovation management, event management, and general administration.

When evaluating the **feasibility** of an event, the event managers are figuring out whether or not the event can be produced successfully. The potential for success is not easy to gauge and requires extensive analysis of what it takes to produce the event being considered. Exploring event feasibility also includes determining the likelihood of achieving the established goals, objectives, and tactics. To decide if the event should be held, an honest assessment of many aspects of the event is conducted. To begin, event managers should research the following areas of the event:

- Does hosting this event require a bid submission?
- Is an event sanction needed? If so, can it be obtained and at what cost?
- Where will the primary event be held?
- Is the facility available and adequate?
- Are ancillary facilities needed?
- What competing events are taking place (sport and nonsport)?
- Are permits required?
- Is lodging available?
- What type of transportation exists for participants, spectators, officials, and volunteers?
- What is the media interest?
- Are there potential sponsors?
- What are the security needs?
- What are the staffing needs?
- What are the estimated costs?

These questions will guide the decision-making process as to whether the event managers should move forward with the event or not. Many of these topics are discussed in detail in later chapters, but an introduction to some of them is presented here to assist event managers in their initial assessment of an event.

Event Bidding

Bidding on an event involves competing with other potential host sites for the right to host an event. The process can range in scope from filling out a one-page document to a multiyear, multimillion-dollar endeavour. The bid process allows rights holders to screen sites and organizers to ensure that the host site can successfully meet the requirements of the event. For those events that are attractive to many locations, the bid process is also used to generate the most revenue possible through guarantees and sponsorships offered by the potential host.

Not all events require a bid, but early in the feasibility evaluation process the event organizers should determine whether or not the event they are interested in hosting requires one. For most recurring events, there is not a bid process. Traveling and mega events will most likely have some sort of bid process and require that an organizing committee be established. In some cases, a venue may choose to bid on an event independently and thus function the same way an organizing committee would.

Depending on the sport and the rights holder, different criteria exist for selecting a host site. In some cases the rights holder might be looking to attract new participants to the sport, while in other cases the goal is purely revenue generation. Still other rights holders may be focused only on providing a good experience for the participating athletes. Understanding the objectives of the rights holder is critical to a successful bid submission. One of the best ways to prepare for the bid process is to attend the event the year or two prior to bidding. If that is not possible, bidders should at least contact previous hosts of the event. Through attendance at the event and discussions with former hosts, event managers can gather information on bid expectations, event goals and objectives, budget, attendance, and the working relationship with the rights holder.

If the event organizers are creating a new event from scratch, then there will not be a bid process, but the organizers will often need the approval of the sport National Governing Body (NGB) through an event sanction to create the event. The event sanction is often tied to the bid process. A host that is awarded an event by a rights holder is generally required to also complete the paperwork and pay the fees associated with the NGB event sanction. As discussed in Chapter 1, the event sanction is considered an official approval for the event and is granted by the governing body associated with the sport (Solomon, 2002). There are few competitive sports events today that are exempt from sanctions.

The Role of Organizing Committees

Organizing committees consist of a group of people, representing the host, that take on the bidding, planning, and management. Many cities have convention and visitors bureaus (CVBs) that assist in attracting various events, tourism, and business to the local area. In some communities, a **sports commission** exists specifically to attract sports events to the area and assist in hosting (see Chapter 10 for more on CVBs and sports commissions). In conjunction with the CVB and/or sports commission, there might also be a sport specific group that has a vested interest in attracting an event. For example, a local track club might be interested in bidding on the Junior National Track and Field Championships to generate revenue, increase the profile of their club, and give their athletes a home track advantage. Any combination of these organizations may be involved in the bid process.

Representatives from these groups along with other influential individuals in the community will make up the organizing committee. Local politicians, community leaders, members of the media, business leaders, representatives of special interest groups, and prominent sports figures should be considered for membership on the organizing committee. Conducting research and building relationships with successful sports coaches, teams, and individual athletes can have a positive impact on the success of a bid. If an Olympic gold medallist is coaching in the community, it benefits the organizers to recruit them to the organizing committee. Then, the Olympian can emphasize the accomplishments of athletes, the importance of hosting the event, and their role in potentially hosting the event. Having a diverse and interested group of people serve on the organizing committee will help in submitting a strong and informed bid, as well as helping to generate excitement for the event.

© Shutterstock

The Olympic Games are the most complex bid in sport.

The Roles of Sports Commissions and CVBs

Don Schumacher, Executive Director National Association of Sports Commissions

It is a fortunate community that has both a CVB and sports commission. The combination provides the best of both worlds. The ability to combine strengths can produce an effective strategic plan and agreement on role sharing. Historically, convention bureaus have billed themselves as "one stop shopping" for visitors while sports commissions are exclusively focused on attracting sport events. Both, however, look to generate economic impact in the community. CVBs need to work with sports commissions to establish partnerships that will provide the sport event assistance needed. Conversely, sports commissions offer the knowledge, expertise, and relationships that it takes to obtain and produce a sports event.

Sports commissions have relationships with venues and most of the rights holders/event owners who have events that might be a good fit for these venues. Sports commission leaders know what types of sports facilities are available, amenities offered, and other details of the venues in the area. They will also know how many of these facilities are "tournament friendly." It is not enough to know the number of baseball fields in the destination. It is necessary to know how many are suitable for the level of play of the event, how many fields the event requires, and where the fields are in relation to each other and overnight accommodations. The sports commission can use their working knowledge of the destination to bring the venues together with rights holders resulting in beneficial partnerships.

CVBs may not have specific sport knowledge, but they do have a variety of important strengths. CVBs have relationships with hotels, intimate and detailed knowledge of the number and kind of hotel rooms available, and an understanding of various prices throughout the year. They also have expertise associated with other entertainment and recreation options in the area and are able to provide a variety of promotional materials about the locale that can be helpful to sport event managers.

CVBs are supported completely or in very large measure by the room tax in the city in which they operate. This means that CVBs focus on generating room nights to increase their revenue. Sport events can generate large numbers of room nights and the CVB will often provide financial support to a sports commission in an effort to attract more events with the end result being more room nights.

Sports commissions share interest with CVBs in attracting visitors, but they are also concerned with additional measures of success. As a general rule, sports commissions are interested in attracting and producing sports events. The generation of economic impact through visitor spending is an important element for any commission. Since a sports commission is not primarily funded by a room tax (except in those cases where the commission is a department of the CVB), they are also concerned with quality of life issues for the community (i.e., getting kids moving to keep them healthy, creating community pride through hosting nationally televised sport events, etc.). This interest stems in part from their primary source of funding: the corporate community. Corporate supporters want sports commissions to find events that are exciting and beneficial to the community.

In sum, CVBs strive to generate room nights whereas sports commissions focus on attracting sports events that have a positive economic impact, increase the quality of life in the community, and attract visitors. The best scenario is that the CVB and sports commission work together in a community to create partnerships and attract events that are in the best interest of their locale.

Source: NASC Report on the Sports Travel Industry (2012). Edited and reprinted with permission.

Economic Impact Through Events

CVBs and sports commissions have a shared goal in generating economic impact. Many times, these groups are the driving force in a locale seeking events on which to bid. A more detailed explanation of economic impact can be found in Chapter 10—Event Travel Packages and Sports Tourism. **Economic impact** in sports refers to new money entering a region resulting in a change in regional output, earnings, and employment (Humphreys & Plummer, 1995). When an event is hosted in a city, the result is an infusion of money during the time of the event, as well as a lingering impact on the location as the new money recirculates within the community. For example, an out-of-town visitor will attend an event at a stadium and spend money on tickets, concessions, and parking. A stadium worker will earn wages for working the event and be paid by the stadium owners using the money spent by the out-of-town spectator. The stadium worker then will have money to spend on other items in the community (e.g., groceries, entertainment) and the cycle of spending may repeat again in the same locale, creating an impact well beyond the actual event.

Economic impact is measured for single day events and multiple day events. There are various calculation methods for determining economic impact and differing opinions as to which method is best. Some events, such as the TCS New York City Marathon, only occur on one day while others, like the Olympic Games or Commonwealth Games, occur over many days. The economic impact for the 2010 TCS New York City Marathon was estimated at $340 million (up from $220 million in 2008 and $205 million in 2006) (New York Road Runners, n.d.; New York City Sports Commission and New York Road Runners, 2007). In America's largest city, with many sizeable sports events, this is the largest economic impact for any one-day sports event in New York City (Goldenberg, 2011). Many high profile events that may have only 1 day of focused activity have built up an entire week of related or ancillary events. In a press release from New York City Mayor Michael Bloomberg's office on January 31, 2007, the city announced that the 2008 MLB All-Star Game at Yankee Stadium and its activities for the week were estimated to generate $148 million for New York City (NYC.gov, 2007).

The event does not have to be something that attracts a large national television audience to impact the community. In 2007, Ohio University hosted the first round of the NCAA Women's Volleyball tournament. The University found out it was hosting just 3 days prior to the participating teams (Ohio University, Xavier University, Purdue, and Cal Poly) arriving for their matches (Corriher, 2007). Overall, the Visitor's Bureau estimated that the tournament resulted in $283,318 of economic impact to the area through money spent on lodging, meals, entertainment, and shopping (Corriher, 2007). Events in larger cities and those that attract thousands of tourists to a location generate huge economic impact. For example, the economic impact of the Super Bowl in 2014 was an estimated $600 million for New York (Rice-Jones, 2014) and the 2012 Olympic Games in London were estimated to surpass $20 billion (Weir, 2013).

Often it is the economic impact of events that makes hosting sports events appealing to communities. It is also why there is a competitive bid process for so many events. However, event managers should be wary of the numbers seen in many calculations of economic impact because of the variety of methodologies used by economists. High economic impact numbers generally look great to event organizers and especially to cities, but they should be evaluated with caution. Reporting that economic impact will occur is easy, but showing hard numbers to prove it may be more challenging. For example, some research of the economic impact of the Super Bowl by economist Philip Porter from the University of South Florida has shown that the average sales tax revenue in a city that hosts the game is not significantly different from the year before or the year after the city hosts the Super Bowl (Deeson, n.d.). Cities may still want to host events such as the Super Bowl for the prestige or for other reasons, but if economic impact is one of the major determining factors, it should be assessed with care. Event organizers that are asked to provide estimated economic impact figures should remember the rule, "under promise and over deliver."

The Bid Submission

Bidding for an event requires extensive knowledge of the community, venue, hotels, transportation, and the availability of financial resources. A list of possible bid components has been provided within this chapter. Generally, the rights holder will require answers to questions related to the facility location, availability, size, and amenities to ensure it meets the needs of the event. Oftentimes the venue must be available days prior to the event for setup and practices. Spaces for hospitality, locker rooms, and storage may also be required. Information on media accommodations is critical for those events that will attract a media presence. Modern media amenities such as broadcast compounds, adequate internet/Wi-Fi connections, and workspaces are expected for major events. Additionally, it is customary to provide meals to members of the media, volunteers, and sometimes participants. Something as seemingly small like the ability or inability to provide meals could impact the strength of the bid. External to the facility, the number, availability, quality, and price of hotels close to the venue will be important to the organizing committee so they know that all parties involved in the event will have access to adequate accommodations.

Having qualified, competent, and dedicated people on the organizing committee will also help to inspire confidence in the bid submission. The rights holder will have to trust that the event organizers can execute the event as described in the bid submission. Thus, having organizing committee members with a background in the sport and in executing similar events is an asset to the submission. If allowed by the rights holder, ancillary events can be used to enhance a bid package. Ancillary events provide additional excitement about the event and can also generate revenue. Other areas where a bidder might enhance the offerings to the rights holder are in free hotel rooms and workspace to the governing body, hosting a participant banquet as part of the event, securing potential sponsors prior to bid submission, guarantees of media presence, and offering creative cross-promotions with other businesses.

Even though the bid process is a competition between potential sites, it is important that the bid focuses on the abilities and dedication of the bid location, and is not critical of competing bidders. Most rights holders are experts in evaluating potential host sites and anything that varies from concise, accurate, and professional presentation will not be well received.

Events Without Bidding

For those events without a formal bid process, event managers must still evaluate event feasibility by answering many of the common questions for themselves that would be posed in the bid. With no set formula to evaluate the potential success of the event, this step is sometimes overlooked. To find answers to these questions, event managers must conduct a lot of research and get out of their offices and meet the participants, potential sponsors, or local government officials that will be impacted by the event. It is beneficial to attend similar events and talk to event managers to gather as much information as possible.

Existing events are also a concern when considering new events. Longstanding relationships deserve attention, and the economic impact provided by repeat business should not be taken for granted. Any time a new event enters the marketplace, the business space becomes more cluttered and competition for spectators, sponsors, and media increases. Integrating a new event into an area that already hosts successful, well-recognized events should be approached carefully because it could negatively impact existing relationships. With either the bid process or an independent evaluation of an event, there must be a positive working relationship with all of the stakeholders.

The following list illustrates the type of content required for a bid submission. This example includes the type of possible questions a governing body might ask on a bid document for a traveling event to be held in a stadium. Even with these specific questions being asked, there is usually an opportunity for the bidders to use some creativity to influence the selection committee. A **unique selling proposition** is a point of differentiation from all other brands in the sales and marketing process. In the case of event bidding, a unique selling proposition differentiates the bid from all of the other bids submitted. By viewing the organizing committee and locale as a brand, it will help bidders create the right unique selling proposition emphasizing selling points and why they are the best host for the event. For example, if a city with 30% of kids interested in skateboarding is bidding on a national level skateboarding competition, there is an opportunity to sell the uniqueness of this high level of youth interest to the rights holder. The city could host a parallel youth skateboard competition to inspire talent to continue to compete, could leverage the event and offer skateboarding clinics and camps partnering with the rights holder, and can highlight that 30% interest is substantially above average ensuring great attendance at the event.

I. General Stadium Information
  A. Owner/address
  B. Management
  C. Year opened
  D. Renovation information

II. Stadium Specifics
  A. Size of main stadium floor
  B. Storage space for equipment
  C. Field surface
  D. Field lighting
    i. Foot candles
    ii. Warm-up time of lights
    iii. Shutters availability
    iv. In-stand spotlight locations
  E. Number of Seats
    i. Permanent seating in main seating bowl (nonpremium)
    ii. Permanent club seats
    iii. Suites (number and seats in each)
    iv. Ability to add temporary suites/club seats
    v. ADA seats available and location in stadium
  F. Stadium availability for practice
  G. Wi-Fi capabilities (general seating area, premium areas, ancillary areas)
  H. Description of union contracts

III. Media
  A. Number of working media seats in press box
    i. Type of work setup (Internet access, telephone, power)
  B. Number and location of working media seating
    i. Type of work setup (Internet access, telephone, power)
  C. Size and location of postevent press conference room
  D. Size and location of postevent media work room
    i. Type of work setup (Internet access, telephone, power)
  E. Media lunch/dinner location

IV. Television/Radio
  A. Domestic broadcast abilities/compound
  B. Network broadcast abilities/compound
  C. Interview areas
  D. Photographers' areas

V. Sound/Scoreboards/Signage
  A. Press box sound system
  B. Stadium scoreboard screens (number, location, and size)
  C. In-stadium electronic message boards (number, location, and size)
  D. Exterior stadium electronic message boards (number, location, and size)
  E. Nature of all existing advertising and/or sponsorship contracts (including naming rights)

VI. Hotels
   A. Number of available rooms in vicinity
   B. Anti-gouging agreements
   C. Headquarters hotel for rights holders
   D. Headquarters hotel for media
   E. Headquarters hotel for participants
VII. Ancillaries
   A. Club/restaurants in stadium
   B. Existing stadium stores
   C. Novelty vending
   D. Concessionaire
      i. Name and contact
      ii. Terms of agreement
      iii. Other relevant information
      iv. Any differences with suite catering
   E. Security
      i. Name and contact
      ii. Terms of agreement
      iii. Other relevant information
   F. Relevant alcohol laws
   G. Parking
      i. Stadium owned/controlled spaces (number and location)
      ii. Regular prices charged
      iii. Availability of disabled parking spaces
   H. Sponsor tent location
VIII. Host committee description
   A. Members
   B. Mission

Location and Venue

Choosing the right location and venue might be the most important aspect of event planning. The city or locale of the event is the first decision that must be made in the conceptualization process. If the event organizers represent a community, then it is only logical that the event be held within the community. If the event is a recurring event with spectators used to a certain location it may not make sense to explore new locations. However, there could be some circumstances where moving a recurring event to a different location is a great idea. For example, colleges and universities occasionally schedule basketball games at neutral locations to expose a different fan base to the team and create excitement somewhere new. For traveling and mega events, the decision of a location is critical and much more difficult to determine.

Considerations for choosing a location vary by the type of event. Event managers should rely on their purpose, goals, objectives, and tactics for their event when examining location and venue options. For many events, demographic and psychographic research should also be conducted to ensure that the locale is a good fit with the event. United States Census data is available online (http://factfinder.census.gov) and can help event managers analyze demographics such as population size, population centers, age, sex, educational level, and income.

Understanding the community is important during the feasibility analysis process and also later when marketing for the event begins. Many non-traditional sports such as skateboarding are popular with younger age groups. If a skateboarding event is being planned, it makes sense to examine the types of individuals interested in skateboarding (i.e., age, sex, income level) and then look for a community mirroring those characteristics. Basic online research will provide event managers a variety of market research reports in sports that are available for purchase, or occasionally free. Local and university libraries can also be a valuable resource for event managers. Librarians are trained to help people find information and finding market research reports is an area that many are highly skilled in.

Emerging sports such as CrossFit have different venue needs as compared to more traditional sports.

Courtesy of MariaPaz Hermosilla

The appropriateness and quality of the venue should also be of paramount concern. For participant-driven events, the location and facility should accommodate participant needs and provide a chance for everyone to perform at their best. A beginner's triathlon that is held in a location with unsuitable weather (e.g., average winter temperature of 20°F) for the strenuous event or that routinely has very choppy water for swimming will not be a good experience for participants. For spectator-driven events, the participant needs must be met, but spectator accommodations enter the equation. The NBA All-Star Game accommodates a large number of in-person spectators for the game, but also needs to attract visitors to the city for the entire weekend of ancillary events. Television is also a key factor for the NBA All-Star Game, although regardless of the host site the television audience will be attracted to this event.

Convenient parking is vital to spectators and participants starting their event experience on a positive note. For many, it is the first thing they associate with the event upon arrival. The availability of parking at some locations may vary by day and time. Normal traffic patterns around the venue should be reviewed to ensure that the parking lot that is empty on Sundays will also be empty for the day of the event. If parking is part of the venue rental agreement, it should be clearly communicated and understood during the feasibility assessment process whether or not there is a fee to park, who retains that revenue, and who is responsible for staffing the parking areas.

If ancillary events are associated with the primary event, there are additional considerations for the location. Tailgating parties, interactive sponsor tents, and concerts all need their own space if they are planned as part of the event. Since event managers may not be sure of ancillary event needs at this point in the process, every effort should be made to secure a venue with extra space in case it is needed.

Once the location and venue options have been narrowed to a few, inquiry into available open dates for the venue begins. Many facilities begin the process with a Rental Application procedure to gather the pertinent information for the event (see Figure 2.1). This form tracks the event from inquiry up until the point a contract is executed. Simple items such as the date, time, ticket prices (if applicable), contact information, space needs, and early cost estimates are part of the Rental Application. Sometimes the event manager has control of the event date and other times it is set by the rights holder with no flexibility. In addition to competition dates, the venue must also be available for practice times, warm-up, equipment setup, and equipment teardown. In the case of outdoor events, weather can significantly impact attendance at the event and thus impact revenue. Event managers should research weather patterns on that date for past years to help in predicting good weather on the event day.

© Shutterstock

Parking is often one of the first experiences spectators will have with an event.

Figure 2.1

Stephen C. O'Connell Center

RENTAL APPLICATION

CHECK: ☐ Inquiry ☐ Follow Up ☐ Tentative Reservation ☐ Confirmed Need Contract

EVENT INFORMATION:

_____

Name of Event   *Estimated Attendance*

Date(s) Desired: _____

Day of Week   Month   Date   Year   *ShowTime(s)*

Type of Event: _____

Ticket Prices: _____ On Sale: _____ ☐ General Admission ☐ Reserved

ORGANIZER:

_____

Name   *Phone #*   *Email Address*

_____

Address   *City*   *State*   *Zip*

BILL TO: ☐ Check if Same as Above

_____

Name   *Phone #*   *Fax #*

Address   _City_   _State_   _Zip_

SPECIFIC AREAS DESIRED:

☐ Main Arena   ☐ Martial Arts Room   ☐ Practice Court

☐ Performer's Dressing Rooms   ☐ Pool   ☐ Dance Studio

☐ Other (Please List) _____

QUOTED FEES/REQUESTED SERVICES:

Rental: _____

Personnel: _____

Equipment:_____

Set/Strike: _____

Deposit Amt.: $_____   Date Due: _____   Date Received: _____

Insurance Amt.: $_____   Date Due: _____   Date Received: _____

MISCELLANEOUS INFORMATION:

_____

_____

_____

Contract Number: _____

Date Reservation Made: _____   Handled By: _____

*Thank you to the Stephen C. O'Connell Center at the University of Florida for providing this example

Date and Time

The idea of choosing a date for an event might seem simple at first, but much more goes into choosing a date than simply venue availability. No similar events should be going on in the region on the same day, other entertainment events on the day should be considered, and the time should align with spectator and participant availability. In some instances, the governing body might have established dates and event timelines that cannot be altered. Dates that are dictated by a rights holder have been established because they make sense for the sport and the competition season. Generally, the national championship in a particular sport follows the regular season competition season and precedes important international events.

Flexible Dates and Times

The first consideration when choosing a date for an event without an established date is participant availability. The date chosen should coincide with participant interest. Not only does this premise hold true for the time of the year chosen, but also the day of the week. Many youth sports have their heaviest travel competition season during the summer because that is when parents are able to transports kids to competitions without missing school. When dealing with a participant-driven event, weekend dates are essential to participation. A youth soccer tournament that is scheduled for Tuesday through Thursday in October is not a good fit with participant needs because many adults cannot take time off from work to take their kids to a midweek event. Additionally, the kids would miss a full week of school with travel.

In some cases, event managers might consider if opportunity scheduling makes sense for an event. **Opportunity scheduling,** in this context, refers to those times during the year where venues and hotels struggle to find occupants. For example, the Thanksgiving holiday may be a busy travel week, but often travellers often stay with family or friends and are focused on activities at home. There is very little business travel Thanksgiving week in the United States. Therefore, it leaves sport and entertainment venues and hotels seeking revenue streams. As a result, opportunity scheduling can result in deep discounts on hotel and venue rates.

If the event is spectator driven, times outside of normal working and school hours, Friday and Saturday evenings, and Sunday afternoons, tend to be good times. A recent phenomenon is that more and more event dates and times are dictated by live television scheduling. In some circumstances, the availability of television revenue and the exposure provided by television will supersede the value of scheduling to maximize spectator attendance. This has become especially apparent in college football, where revenue is of paramount importance. The challenges of midweek games on college campuses are many and they come from all constituent groups. Zullo (2005) discusses the struggle of athletic directors related to scheduling of football games.

> Faculty sometimes complain that a mid-week game hurts the academic progress of both student-athletes and student fans, and it sends the message that athletics takes precedence over academics on campus. Students lose focus in the classroom the day of the game, then often neglect their classes the day after (15).

Zullo (2005) goes on to discuss the impact on other areas of the campus such as parking, security, and night classes that may have to be cancelled, rescheduled, or are disrupted. There are operational as well as public perception issues with midweek college football games. These are the types of issues that event managers must consider before choosing a date and time for their event.

Competing events in the area are another scheduling consideration. A small community that is already hosting a road race on a particular Saturday probably cannot support another one the following weekend. If high school football is a big community event on Friday nights in the fall, then another sports event in the area should try to avoid Friday night competitions. Non-sports events should also be considered here. Even in urban locations, it is difficult to support more than one major event on a given day. To schedule a monster truck event the same evening in the same city as an NHL game forces people to choose one event over the other. If the monster truck show is scheduled on a week when the NHL team is on the road, there would be less competition for spectators.

Established Dates and Times

For events with more guidance provided by the rights holder, it is the responsibility of the event managers to ensure that the event fits the timeline. For example, along with many facility requirements, United States Diving has an established order of events for their National Championships and stipulations for needed schedule changes in the event of inclement weather (USA Diving, 2014). The specifics listed by the rights holder are important for event managers to know early in the event feasibility evaluation process. If an aquatics venue is unable to meet the extensive requirements for these national championships for diving, it is better to know early in the process as opposed to after planning has begun and a financial investment has been made. Overall, the selection of the date and time of an event is critical to its success.

Permits

Events that are held outside of a traditional venue will most likely need a permit from city, county, or federal authorities to allow the event to occur. **Permits** are generally required for road races, bike races, open water swims, to serve food, to hold concerts, and for ancillary events in parks or on roadways. City and county permits are the most common that event managers will need to acquire, but occasionally a federal permit is warranted (i.e., National Parks and/or events held in Washington, DC). When a permit is required, it should be investigated and obtained early so that organizers have the date held and meet any requirements for submission dates that might be in place. Generally, the information is located on the city website and is called a special event, public assembly, parade, parks, road race, or bicycle race permit. Vending, food and beverage, and sound permits may also be required, depending on the scope of the event. It is not uncommon for municipalities to require 90 days or more lead time for permit applications. There also may be other stipulations in the permit such as paying for overtime police officers, participant limits, escort vehicle requirements, signage parameters, allowable road closures for races, or insurance coverage.

Lodging and Transportation

Depending on the purpose of the event, the lodging and transportation needs will vary. For single day events featuring local participants and spectators, lodging and transportation may not even factor into the decision-making process (except for parking). However, for mega events such as the Super Bowl, requirements in these areas are extensive. The National Football League (NFL) Host City Bid Specification Requirements consist of 153 pages of detail about the relationship between the host committee and NFL for the Super Bowl (National Football League, 2013). For example, in 2018, the NFL requires the host to provide 53,000 free parking spaces at no cost to the NFL (National Football League, 2013). Additionally, there are a variety of stipulations about tens of thousands of available hotel rooms in the vicinity, NFL headquarters hotel requirements such as 150 complimentary hotel nights to the NFL prior to the Super Bowl for planning purposes, and hundreds of free hotel rooms at team headquarters hotels (including presidential suites) (National Football League, 2013). These parameters are common among mega events, and transportation and hotel requirements alone exclude many locations from hosting events such as the Super Bowl.

When calculating the number of hotel rooms needed for an event, research can be conducted to assist in planning. Event organizers can contact hosts of past events, or oftentimes CVBs and sports commissions have access to national databases with information on past event hotel usage rates. For new events, it is important that organizers do not underestimate the number of rooms needed. It is better to have too many rooms than too few.

In addition to making sure there are enough hotels in the area to accommodate the event, it is important that they meet the specific needs of the event. This will include accommodating any participants or spectators with special needs (e.g., wheelchair access). Organizers should leverage their event to negotiate special prices for participants and spectators and even free rooms for event officials. It is common that one hotel room is provided free for every 50 rooms booked and some hotels will provide as many as one free room for every 10 or 20 booked. Event managers have significant negotiating leverage when they can guarantee that the hotel will be touted the "official host hotel" and that they will drive business to the property. Beyond room rates, event managers can ask hotels for perks such as free breakfast for participants or transportation to and from the competition venue. Many hotels already own vans or small buses for airport transportation. These vehicles are perfect for transporting participants and spectators to and from the competition venue and will enhance the event experience. Consideration should also be given to confirming the transportation can accommodate those with disabilities so as to not exclude some spectators or participants from using the provided services. Additionally, this is a nice bonus to include in the bid. For events requiring bids, rates and perks should be negotiated and a tentative hold put on blocks of rooms early in the bidding process. This will guarantee that the rooms are available if the bid is awarded.

Event organizers may or may not choose to get involved with transportation for their event. For many events it is not necessary, but for those located far from an airport or for team events, transportation may become an issue. As with hotels, negotiating rates and benefits for rental cars are part of organizing a successful event. Events that feature teams often need 15-passenger vans or buses. In some locales these types of vehicles are scarce, so event organizers may need to work with rental car agencies to have additional 15-passenger vans available, or with bus companies to make sure an adequate number of buses are available during the event dates. Event mangers should also consider that for some events, athletes need to transport large pieces of equipment (e.g., poles for pole vault), may need to move wheelchairs, may not speak English, or may need other special accommodations. Each of these situations requires a different type of research on available transportation in the area.

High profile athletes will expect transportation to be provided for them. Cars are borrowed or rented and event staff assigned to airport runs to pick up and drop off athletes as they come and go. Golf and tennis events regularly work with car dealers and manufacturers as part of their partnerships to provide cars for athletes to use while they are in town at the event, or for organizers to use to transport the athletes.

While researching lodging and transportation, event organizers may find that other events (e.g., conventions, conferences, or entertainment events) are planned for the same time period. This

Providing transportation is sometimes required for larger events, and may start with pick up from the airport.

© Shutterstock

could be a deal breaker for the event. Major conferences and conventions can take over small and midsize cities and make it difficult to hold a sports event, even if it is not a direct competitor. It is better to know about problems such as a lack of hotel rooms or other events early in the process, prior to event organizers signing contracts.

The Olympic Bid Process

Maria Solomon, Sports Marketing & Sponsorship Consultant

The magnitude of the Olympic bid process is difficult to explain, but the timeline should provide an idea of what a massive undertaking bidding on the Olympics is. It is a multi-phased process beginning at the National Olympic Committee (NOC) level and then moving to the International Olympic Committee (IOC). The 2016 Olympic bid process began with countries interested in bidding putting forward a city as a potential host by September 2007. In the United States, Chicago was chosen to move forward by the United States Olympic Committee (USOC) (IOC, 2007a). Other candidates submitting bids to the IOC included Baku (Azerbaijan), Doha (Qatar), Madrid (Spain), Prague (Czech Republic), Rio de Janeiro (Brazil), and Tokyo (Japan).

There is then a two-phase process during which the IOC reviews the bid, visits the potential host sites, and evaluates each city's potential to successfully organize the Olympic Games (IOC, 2007b). Phase I (candidature acceptance procedure) involves about a year of evaluation of the potential host city by the IOC (IOC, 2007b). If a city advances through phase I, it then moves into phase II (candidature procedure), which takes another year. Phase II involves submission of an in-depth report on the city's Olympic project, a visit from city representatives to observe the current Olympic Games (8 years prior), a visit to the potential host city by the IOC Evaluation Commission, and a full report published by the IOC Evaluation Commission prior to final bid award (IOC, 2007b). Finally, the IOC selects a host and announces a winner. The entire process takes approximately 2 years at the IOC level, but many Olympic Bid Organizing Committees work years in advance just to be the city representing its country in the Olympic Bid process.

The Road to the 2016 Summer Olympic Games Selection:

Phase I

1. NOCs to inform the IOC of the name of an Applicant City (September 13, 2007)
2. Signature of the Candidature Acceptance Procedure (October 1, 2007)
3. Payment of the Candidature Acceptance Fee ($150,000) (October 1, 2007)
4. Creation of a logo to represent the application (no date)
5. IOC information seminar for 2016 Applicant Cities (week commencing October 15, 2007)
6. Submission of the Application File and guarantee letters to the IOC (January 14, 2008)
7. Examination of replies by the IOC and experts (January–June 2008)

Phase II

1. IOC Executive Board meeting to accept Candidate Cities for the Games of the XXXI Olympiad in 2016 (June 2008)
2. Payment of the Candidature Fee ($500,000) (no date)
3. Creation of an emblem to represent the candidature (no date)
4. Olympic Games Observer Programme—Beijing 2008 (August 8–24, 2008)
5. Submission of Candidature File to the IOC (February 12, 2009)

6. Report of the 2016 IOC Evaluation Commission (1 month before the election of the Host City)

7. Election of the Host City of the Games of the XXXI Olympiad in 2016 (October 2, 2009)

Not only is the time commitment extensive for Olympic Bid Organizing Committees, but so is the financial investment. The bid process alone for the 2010 Winter Olympics cost $34 million (BC 2010 Olympic Bid, n.d.) and cost the Chicago organizing committee $70.6 in its losing bid to host the 2016 Summer Olympics (Pletz, 2010). With only one city lucky enough to host a Summer Olympic Games every 4 years, the competition is intense. The actual cost of winning the bid is even larger. London, host of the 2012 Summer Olympic Games, originally estimated hosting the Olympics to cost approximately $4.6 billion (Quinn, 2008). Cost estimates tripled to $13.8 billion 4 years prior to the games in 2008 (Quinn, 2008). However, the rewards are great for those cities hosting successful Olympic Games. The international spotlight is on the country and city for an extended period of time during the Games as well as the years leading up to the Olympics. Athletes from the host country are able to represent their country at home, and the national pride associated with hosting the Olympic Games is great.

Note: Timeline bidding information compiled from www.olympic.org and the IOC Candidature Acceptance Procedure and Questionnaire.

Media and Sponsorships

Many marketing details can be left until after it is decided whether to host the event or not, but it is beneficial to gauge the media and sponsorship climate prior to making the decision to host an event. Having a member of the local media on the organizing committee can help organizers figure out whether or not the event is interesting to media outlets. For local and youth events, media attention may not matter when assessing event feasibility. However, when considering a major event, television revenue can be critical to a financially successful event. Most rights holders retain the television rights and revenue associated with their major events, but for new events, securing a television deal could mean the difference between success and failure.

It is likely that organizers will be actively seeking potential sponsors very early in the event planning process. For all sizes of events, sponsors can impact the viability of the event. The challenge is finding sponsors that align the needs of the event with the needs of the company. When dealing with community or high school events there might be businesses willing to sponsor the event primarily to help a local group without expectation of return for their investment. Technically, this type of sponsorship is philanthropic on the part of the local business as they look to support the community. For larger events, the sponsorship prospecting and acquisition process is much more complex. Securing sponsors and creating partnerships with companies can be a fantastic win–win situation for both the event organizers and the sponsor.

The specifics of sponsorship are discussed in Chapter 8, but potential sponsors should be approached prior to deciding to host the event if they are needed to make the event a success. For example, a community examining the feasibility of hosting a 10K charity road race might need to secure a corporate title sponsor to offset the costs of the event and ensure that as much money as possible goes to the specified charity. It would not make sense to plan the race, advertise, and register participants without first knowing if a sponsor was willing to be involved. In this scenario, without the sponsor, the event will not achieve the goal of raising money for a charity. If the goals cannot be met, then the event should not take place. If the event organizers discuss the race with potential sponsors early in the process, the sponsor can then be an integral part of the planning and execution of the event, resulting in a better event and more benefit to the sponsor.

Staffing and Security

Staffing and security needs are dependent upon the type and size of event being considered. Whether or not the event is ticketed, the type of crowd expected, and the history of the event should all be considered when evaluating staffing and security. Organizers decide whether or not staffing and/or security needs are a big enough job to outsource to a professional staffing company, or if security needs can be met by part-time employees and volunteers. If the event is in a traditional sports venue, the facility may provide these services as part of the rental agreement. For events that are being held in parks, on roadways, or on waterways, the permitting process often requires a certain level of police and security presence. Organizers should also consider any unique aspects to the event that may require additional security or staffing. For example, anytime alcohol is part of an event, the security needs are increased. The exact numbers of staff needed are not required at this point in planning, but the availability of people (through part-time employees and volunteers or through outsourcing) should be evaluated.

Security staffing may be provided by a venue or may need to be outsourced for non-venue events.

Equipment

Common equipment is usually either owned by sports facilities or can be rented. If there are unusual needs that the event has, it is critical that the equipment can be attained prior to making the final decision to hold the event. For example, it may sound like a great idea to have an indoor skateboarding competition. However, the ramps needed for the athletes may not be available for the date/time of the event, unavailable in the local area, or shipping costs might make it cost prohibitive. To schedule the event without 100% certainty that the ramps are available would be embarrassing for the organizers. The event would be forced to cancel or the ramps would have to be built at a very high cost.

Specialized equipment for sports such as gymnastics can be expensive to purchase or rent.

Finances

Understanding the budget can make or break the event. There are costs associated with almost everything related to hosting an event. The venue, officials, staff, security, medical personnel, marketing, equipment, sponsor activation, hospitality, ticket stock, insurance, awards, and office supplies are a partial list of what will be part of the overall event budget. Some of these expenses will require payment or partial payment prior to the event. If organizers are relying on ticket revenue to pay expenses, it could result in cash flow problems because a lot of the ticket revenue will not be available until after the event concludes. Marketing and sponsor activation are just two of the areas that will cost money prior to and during the event. During the feasibility assessment stage, organizers should begin to get a handle on the major costs and potential revenues. Seeking out information on past event budgets from other hosts and conducting research into the major operational costs will begin to bring the overall budget into focus. A detailed explanation of how to create and manage an event budget is provided in Chapter 6.

More Is Not Always Better

Some event managers fall into the "more is better" trap of hosting events. However, more is only better if each and every aspect of the event is feasible, aligns with the purpose and goals, has the potential to succeed, and does not cannibalize existing parts of the event. Sticking to the purpose, goals, and objectives of the event is important when beginning to explore the feasibility of the event. For example, if one goal of a youth fun walk is to get kids moving and fit, a donut company sponsor providing donut samples does not fit. In this case, the sponsor might be attractive because they can provide cash to offset expenses, but it does not fit within the purpose and goals and therefore should be avoided. All decisions must keep the purpose, goals, and objectives of the event in mind.

Over-committing is another common pitfall in the planning process. It is easy to get caught up in the excitement of all of the possibilities surrounding an event. But, when it comes down to executing all aspects of the event, everything takes time and energy, and probably more time and energy than anticipated. If the event management team consists of three volunteers, the team needs to be realistic about what can be accomplished. Planning to set up an entire downhill ski course and manage a race with three people is not realistic. The feasibility analysis is the time to examine and gain an understanding of the limitations related to human, financial, and facility resources.

SUMMARY

The feasibility analysis process varies in depth based upon the type of event being considered. A potential Olympic Games bid will involve a multiyear feasibility study, while a high school track and field meet only requires a few hours or days to think through all the areas discussed. A comprehensive evaluation of the event will help organizers decide whether or not accomplishing the event goals is feasible. For events with a bid process, organizers will work to position their location as the best host for the event. CVBs and sports commissions often take the lead in seeking out possible events that will result in economic impact to an area. By establishing a qualified organizing committee and submitting a well thought out bid package, the host location is able to highlight what they have to offer the rights holder. Whether through a bid process or independently, event organizers should evaluate the location, venue, date and time, lodging, transportation, permits, media, sponsorships, staffing, security, equipment, finances, and all unique aspects of the event when deciding whether or not to proceed. Results of this research will provide information not readily apparent, but nonetheless critical, to gauge the potential to host a successful event.

Student Challenges

NAME _____ DATE _____

In this challenge, examine the governing bodies that are involved with sport events. Additionally, complete an exercise to examine the feasibility of a new event.

Question 2.1

Choose a sport governing body to research. Be sure to visit the official website of the governing body and then respond to the following questions.

a.   List the governing body and website:
b.   List the events the governing body hosts (or selects a host for):
c.   How does the governing body select a host site for the events?
d.   Are there any special or unique aspects to the process of host site selection for events?

Choose a new sport event for your campus or city. Conduct a few aspects of the feasibility study for the potential event and decide whether or not the event should be held. Revisit Chapter 1 for a review of goals, objectives, tactics, and measures.

a.   What is the purpose of the event? List 1 goal, 2 objectives, 1 tactic for each objective, and 1 measure for each tactic.
b.   Is there a bid process?
c.   Is there a rights holder?
d.   List potential organizing committee members.
e.   What are the facility needs?
f.   Is a facility available that meets the event needs? If so, which one?
g.   When will the event be held? Why was that date/time selected?
h.   Are permits required?
i.   Approximately how many hotel rooms are needed? Are there enough in the area?
j.   What are the transportation needs?

k. What type of media will the event attract?

l. List potential sponsors.

m. Can staffing and security be done in-house or will it be outsourced?

n. Are there any special equipment needs?

o. List the major cost categories associated with the event.

p. Should this event be held or not? Why?

EVENT CONTRACTS

B. David Ridpath and Kelley K. Walton

B. David Ridpath, EdD, is an Associate Professor of Sports Administration and the Kahandas Nandola Professor of Sport Management at Ohio University where he also earned his master's in Sports Administration. Prior to returning to Ohio University as a member of the faculty, Dr. Ridpath spent 2 years directing the graduate Sports Administration Program at Mississippi State University. He also worked at Marshall University in Huntington, West Virginia, where he served as an Adjunct Professor of Sport Management and Marketing, Director of Judicial Programs, and Assistant Athletic Director for Compliance and Student Services. His research interests include intercollegiate athletics academic standards, reform, enforcement and infractions, and governance.

Kelley K. Walton, JD, SPHR, is an Instructor for the Department of Sports Administration at Ohio University. She holds a bachelor of science degree from Eastern Michigan University and a juris doctor from Capital University Law School. Prior to joining Ohio University, Ms. Walton served as the Director of human resources for the Columbus Blue Jackets of the National Hockey League. She is an Attorney and Consultant specializing in career counseling and human resources consulting in the sport industry. She is the author of *Prepare for Opportunity: A Practical Guide for Applying for a Job in Sports.* Her research interests include best practices in human resources management, legal issues affecting the sport industry, and recruitment and selection in the sport industry. In addition to her role as Instructor, Ms. Walton provides significant administrative support to the Professional Master of Sports Administration program, which is a master of sports administration degree offered in a primarily online format for working sport industry professionals.

This chapter introduces some of the major concepts related to contracts and legal considerations related to event management. Contracts are a necessary part of business and outline the agreements made for events, services, and other business relationships. Contracts are important because they provide a guideline for the parties involved as to what each has agreed to do in a given situation. Contracts are used in a variety of situations: events, sponsorship, facilities, and so on. It is important to understand the basic concepts of contracts, as well as understand the legal considerations surrounding those contracts as they apply to event management.

A contract is an agreement between two (or more) parties. Understanding contract principles is important for all event managers. In this chapter, the following will be addressed: contract elements, components of a valid contract, relevance of contracts in event management, and examples of common event management contracts.

What I Wish I Had Known

B. David Ridpath, Associate Professor, Ohio University

Much of what I know about event contracts, I learned the hard way. In the mid-1990s, I was a young athletic administrator at Weber State University in Ogden, Utah, hoping to prove myself and move up in the ranks of college athletics administration. I had just finished a 1-year internship and a short time as the Assistant Director of Marketing/Director of Compliance when the Associate Athletic Director left Weber for a new job. I was immediately asked to step in and take on responsibilities in event management to fill in for the newly vacated duties. Of course I agreed and was thrust into action.

The first event I managed was a football game and it was one I will always remember for many reasons. Prior to entering my career in college athletics administration, I had been in the Army and was responsible for hundreds of troops and million dollar budgets. I thought my Army experience would make managing a football game a breeze, but I was wrong. What I quickly learned is that there is a variety of competing constituency groups involved in presenting a successful football event and my "militarism" was not going to work to get things done.

All of the different groups had different understandings of what needed to be done and what they got in return for providing a service. As with most sports events, a major challenge is organizing and motivating volunteers and part-time employees. From the side-line chain gang and ball boys to the referees and press box personnel, all had different understandings of what the expectations were and what they received for doing their job. The week prior to the game, I sent out a memo to all personnel, followed by phone calls and emails informing them to be "on station" at least 1 hour prior to kickoff. But it seemed to fall on deaf ears. For example, the chain gang showed up so late that I was not even sure they were going to make it for kickoff. By the time they arrived, I was upset and nervous. I immediately went to the head of the chain gang crew and asked why they were so late. His response was that they never had to show up at a specific time. He then added, "Where's our pizza and Coke?" To which I simply replied, "What?" He then went on to inform me that chain gang was always provided with pizza and Coke, as were the ushers and others. Well, this was the first I had heard of it and I was not sure if I could or would provide the snacks.

As the game progressed, more challenges began to crop up and other groups were asking for things they "always got" from the previous game manager. The band also threatened to head home because I had not given them any food. Thankfully, I was able to quickly get some free hotdog coupons to prevent an uprising, but things were spiraling out of control and it became my goal to merely survive the game.

Even after the game ended, I was still being surprised by things. The stadium maintenance workers informed me that union rules had them waiting until Monday morning to begin trash clean up. Between Saturday night and Monday morning there was plenty of time for trash to blow all over campus and create a bigger mess than there needed to be. The concessionaire had generated thousands of pounds of trash, and I figured they would clean up after themselves. But I was wrong. The concessionaire supervisor let me know that it was not in their contract to pick up trash and it was the stadium staff's responsibility. It was then that I nearly quit my job!

While quitting was only a passing thought, I was determined to improve the event management system and begin to hold staff accountable for their jobs to make the event a better experience for participants, spectators, and employees. The next week, I began to prepare an operations manual, and I created a specific employment contract for each and every person that worked at the game. I had decided that having a group supervisor would be my first step in organizing my staff. The group supervisor would be responsible for carrying out the duties outlined in the game management manual. The manual was reinforced by a contract outlining his or her specific areas of responsibility. I was determined to get rid of the handshake agreements of the past and set clear expectations for all event staff. I also needed to clarify what people received for their service (i.e., payment, snacks, game tickets). The use of contracts made my job much easier and provided a template for what needed to be done, by whom, and when.

While the responsibility of facility and event manager was probably the most enjoyable part of all my jobs during my intercollegiate athletic administrative career, it was also extremely challenging. I learned a lot through my experiences at Weber State, and specifically learned the value of well-written contracts. I was able to prove that with a written policy and procedure manual in place, backed up by comprehensive and specific contractual agreements, an event can be run efficiently and professionally.

Contract Basics

It is important when discussing contracts specific to event management, or any contract, to define what a contract is and how it is used. A **contract** is a legally enforceable promise or set of promises. Event managers must have an understanding of contracts and how contracts fit into the overall scheme of managing a sport or entertainment event. In addition, penalties associated with noncompletion of the terms of a contract should be understood. The failure of any party (e.g., event manager, vendor, auxiliary entity) to meet the terms of the contract can have a major impact on the execution of an event as well as the possibility of causing financial hardship to all involved.

At its most basic level, a contract is an agreement between parties.

Contract principles and the process of entering into a contract in sports and events are similar to those of other business contracts. Typically, negotiations between parties occur and revisions are made prior to a contract being finalized. The goal of any contract negotiation is to provide a document that outlines the promises and expectations of both parties.

Under ideal situations, a lawyer is consulted when a contract is involved. During the process of drafting the contract, negotiating the terms, and final agreement to the contract; a lawyer is essential.

If a manager is entering into a legally binding agreement, it is advisable to have legal counsel review it. Many organizations, teams, and facilities have in-house legal representation or outside counsel who regularly assists with legal affairs. While there is no legal requirement to have a contract reviewed by a lawyer to be valid, it is recommended that event managers do so.

Elements of a Valid Contract

The basic concepts of contracts are the same regardless of the type of contract. Although there is room for creativity with respect to areas of performance indicated in the contract, there is less room for creativity when dealing with the contract components and structure. Specifically, there are certain elements that must be met in order for a contract to be valid.

The elements are:

- Offer
- Acceptance
- Consideration
- Capacity
- Legality
- Writing (in certain situations)

Each of the elements must be present to create a valid, legally binding agreement.

Offer

An offer is an act or statement made to another party. This is the proposal that begins the process of the formation of a contract.

An offer must be:

- Communicated by the offeror (the party who initiates the offer) to the offeree (the party to whom the offer is made)
- Sufficiently definite and certain in its terms
- Show intent to enter into a contract

Communication of the offer is usually a straightforward process. The offeror must communicate the offer to the offeree. The method of communication is not as important as the fact that it is actually communicated to the offeree.

The contract must also be sufficiently definite and certain in its terms. This means that terms cannot be left open to interpretation. To put it simply, the language used must be definite enough so that both parties are able to determine their legal obligations. Another way to look at it is that the terms must be definite and certain enough so that a court can understand what the parties agreed to. If you want a contract to be enforceable, you need to make sure that someone outside of the negotiations, event or situation would be able to read the contract and understand the obligations of the party.

Typically, the communication of an offer is sufficient to show that there is intent to enter into a contract. Intent is also often easily proven by a Letter of Intent signed by both parties, which is an agreement to enter into an agreement. These are not necessary for many contractual situations, but if a party wants to gain an agreement before all of the terms can be hashed out, then a Letter of Intent is an effective tool to prove intent to enter a contract.

Example: A local running organization may put forth an offer to a city to put on a marathon. Event managers may solicit arenas, communities, or sports commissions to hold events. Conversely, a city, municipality, or other organization may approach event managers asking them to host an event or putting forth the offer. In many cases, a formal bid process would follow. Regardless of which entity initiates the discussion about hosting an event, to start the contractual process an offer to host must be made.

Acceptance

The next part in forming a contract is acceptance. **Acceptance** is when the offeree (the party to whom the offer is made) accepts the offer. It is when the offeree accepts the terms of the offer for the purposes of fulfilling the contract.

An offer must be accepted as it was communicated by the offeror. If it is not, then a new offer is made. In terms of formation of a contract, a counteroffer is not an acceptance but is a new offer.

Example: A local running organization sends forth a letter to a municipality offering to manage a running event if the municipality is willing to host it. Potential dates, times, and a general idea of the course are put forth in the letter. The municipality likes the idea of hosting an event and agrees to host by sending a letter back to the running organization agreeing to host and that the proposed dates, times, and routes will need to be worked out prior to an official agreement. This is the beginning of the formation of a contract. A general agreement has been made to host, but there is no contract yet as the terms of the contract are not yet agreed to. If the municipality were to respond that the dates, times, and routes are acceptable, then the offer is accepted.

Details such as when the marathon will be run, the course, which city offices will be involved, and costs enter the contract at this stage. For large events such as a major marathon, hotel space, ancillary events, ticketing, required permits, hospitality, and security all might be addressed in the contract. There can be as many, or as few, details as all parties want. But it is important that both parties agree to the terms of the agreement.

Consideration

Consideration is necessary for the formation and validity of the contract. There must be an exchange of value between the parties involved in the contract. While this exchange of value is a vague explanation compared to the other contract elements with clearer explanations, the simplest way to understand consideration is that contracts are a two way street. Both sides must get some benefit from the contract. There is no minimum or maximum value requirement, it does not have to be of equal value, but there must be some value.

Example: A local running company and a municipality have agreed to the dates, times, and location of a marathon to be managed by the local running company and to be hosted by the municipality. As part of the contract, the event company promises to provide payment to the municipality. In turn, the municipality will allow the use of roads and will allow police presence. (There will be many more details in an agreement, but this is sufficient for example purposes.) Each side promises to do something in order for the event to occur and each side gets a benefit from the contract. The event company has the right to use the roads during the event and the municipality is paid for that use. This is an example of consideration.

Capacity/Authority

Capacity means that the parties involved in the contract must have the legal ability to enter into a contract. Capacity means that the person signing the contract is of legal age (18 years or older), is mentally competent, and is not under the influence of drugs or alcohol. The person who agrees to the contract must also have the authority to enter into a contract. In event management, there are only certain people, such as event managers, facility managers, and athletic directors that are designated as signing authorities. Event managers must make sure that the person signing the contract is authorized to do so.

Example: Using the marathon example, both parties must have the capacity to enter into the contract. It must be confirmed that the individual signing on behalf of the city is authorized to enter into agreements on behalf of the city (e.g., City Recreation Director) and the representative of the running company (e.g., CEO) must also be someone authorized to enter into such agreements. All signatories must also be over the age of 18.

Legality

To be valid, a contract must be for legal purposes. A contract that is for illegal purposes is void and unenforceable. This might seem straight forward, but city, county, and state laws vary greatly so having an understanding of local laws is critical in event management.

Example: The management and hosting of a marathon is agreed to in a state that does not allow gambling on sporting events. If the contract contains language related to managing betting on race winners, then the contract contains an agreement for illegal purposes and will not be upheld.

Writing

Not all legally binding contracts have to be in writing. Even if law does not require a written contract, it is a good business practice and highly recommended to create a written agreement that outlines the expectations and responsibilities of both parties. If both parties clearly state expectations in a written document, it is much easier to hold the other party accountable for meeting expectations.

However, there are several types of contracts that require the agreement to be in writing in order to be enforceable. Those contracts are those agreements:

- That cannot be performed within 1 year
- To pay the debt of another
- For any interest in land
- Made by an executor of an estate
- For the sale of goods over $500

Most of these concepts are fairly self-explanatory. Moreover, the concept of whether or not a contract can be completed within 1 year is a bit more difficult to understand. There are a variety of circumstances where an event contract would not be able to be completed within 1 year. Most major intercollegiate athletic game contracts would fall into this category. Generally, these events are scheduled years in advance. In cases such as a college football game scheduled 5 years in advance, a written contract would be required. Many other traveling, mega, and ancillary events are also scheduled more than a year in advance. In these instances, contracts related to the venue for the event, execution of the event, television agreements, or sponsorship of the event would need to be in writing.

While a written contract is not always required, it is always recommended. Verbal agreements can be enforceable and legally binding, but it is much more difficult to hold a party accountable for what they have agreed to if that agreement is done verbally instead of written down in a signed agreement. In order to hold a party accountable for a verbal contract, it would be necessary to first prove that there was an agreement. Witnesses or the other party starting performance on the agreement are good examples of evidence of a contractual agreement. However, in order for an agreement or understanding to rise to the level of a contractual agreement; all the contract elements have to be met. The best way to prove those elements have been met is to have a written, signed agreement that outlines the obligations of both parties.

Electronic Signatures

In 2000, the **Electronic Signatures in Global and International Commerce Act (ESGICA)** was enacted to provide guidance on electronic contracts and electronic signatures. Electronic contracts and signatures are valid contracts. No paper or hard copies are required to create a valid contract. Digital signatures can be in a variety of forms, including clicking an "accept" button or providing a photo of a signature on a signature line.

Electronic signatures have become standard and accepted practice.

There are some contracts that are not protected by ESGICA and therefore a written signature must be obtained in order for the contract to be valid, but most of those are unrelated to event management or sport industry contracts; such as documents related to wills and trusts, documents related to adoption or divorce, documents involved in court proceedings (orders, notices, motions, etc.), and cancellation or termination of health/life insurance.

Basic Provisions

The **basic provisions** section of a contract includes the basic information that is the foundation of the agreement that includes the parties, locations, and general information about each. The basic provisions usually begin on the first page of a contract and differ from event to event. The opening paragraph identifies the parties and the contact information of each. The remainder of the information is broken down into smaller sections within the agreement. Following is a simple example of a basic provisions section using fictitious organizations:

This letter confirms the terms of the agreement in connection with XYZ Tournament between **ABC DOME AT THE ORANGE REGIONAL SPORTS COMPLEX** ("Complex") authorized to do business in the state of Ohio, whose mailing address is 1010 Championship Way, Anytown, OII 99999 and **XYZ SPORTS, INC.,** ("Licensee") a Delaware corporation whose mailing address is 890 Regents Blvd, Anytown, FL, 99991.

The terms of our agreement, consisting of the BASIC PROVISIONS and GENERAL TERMS AND CONDITIONS, are as follows:

I. EVENT

XYZ Tournament in 2009 and 2010

II. EVENT VENUE

ABC Dome at the Orange Regional Sports Complex

III. EVENT SCHEDULE

June 1–7, 2016; Dates for 2017 to be mutually determined. These dates include load in, competition, and load out.

IV. TERM

Subject to paragraph 20 in the General Terms and Conditions, the term of this agreement will be for a period of 2 years, commencing as of the date of this Agreement and terminating on the last day of the Event in 2017, or such later date as required in order for both parties to comply with the obligations of this Agreement.

V. LICENSEE RESPONSIBILITIES

Licensee shall provide, at its sole expense, the following:

a. All event participants, staff, and equipment necessary to conduct the Event, except as otherwise set forth in this Agreement.

b. All officials and judges necessary to conduct the Event.

c. Selection and management of volunteers.

d. Assistance to Complex with field of play security.

e. Promotion of the Event through newsletters, mailings, email, and the Internet to possible event participants.

VI. COMPLEX RESPONSIBILITIES

Complex shall provide:

a. Field markings and equipment; tables for awards; water cooler and cups for participants; seating at each field of play.

b. Awards for each age division, number and type to be mutually agreed upon.

c. On-site emergency medical and first aid services.

d. Audio equipment and announcers for the Event.

e. Assistance to Licensee with field of play security.

VII. LICENSEE'S CURRENT CONTRACTUAL EVENT SPONSORS

Licensee shall present potential Event sponsors to Complex for approval no less than 90 days prior to the Event. Event sponsors will be mutually agreed upon in advance, subject to any conflicts with existing Complex corporate sponsors.

VIII. LICENSEE CONTACT

Jane Smith

President

XYZ Sports, Inc.

890 Regents Blvd

Anytown, FL 99991

VIII. COMPLEX CONTACT

David Brown

Vice President, Business Development

Orange Regional Sports Complex

1010 Championship Way

Anytown, OH 99999

The basic provisions set the stage for those items that are specific to the event being contracted. As with any contract, additional areas can be written into the contract depending on the needs of both parties.

General Terms and Conditions

In addition to the basic provisions, most event contracts will have the general terms and conditions as another section. General terms and conditions provide the details of the promises of each of the parties. This can include almost anything else not mentioned in the basic provisions and further expansion on the basic provisions. It can be as much, or as little, as needed. Some items commonly mentioned in terms and conditions sections include approval clauses for cosponsors, cancellation clauses, indemnification agreements, fees and expenses, performance incentives, and buy-out provisions, among a litany of other possibilities. Because of the detail involved in this section, it is common for organizations to put the general terms and conditions of their agreements in a boilerplate. With regard to contracts, a **boilerplate** is a standard or template contract that includes the typical language used by a company for a contract. The boilerplate will remain the same for all clients unless all parties agree to specific changes. Having a boilerplate can make the writing and execution of a contract more efficient and provide a basic organizational structure for the various sections. Having a clear and consistent structure helps both parties understand the terms and ensure that the content order makes logical sense. It also gives the event manager piece of mind knowing that the boilerplate language has been approved by legal counsel without having to have a lawyer review a contract every time a similar contractual situation arises. That does not negate the need for counsel; as each situation brings with it different parties, different terms, and different legal needs; but it does provide a template that can be used in various situations.

General business contracts will not have the same types of terms as an event contract, and event managers should be cautious to choose legal counsel with expertise in sports and entertainment. Specific to event management are terms related to event administration, merchandise, food and beverage, promotional rights, and insurance. Following are some of the sections that a sport organization may include in the general terms and conditions boilerplate. As with any aspect of contracts, legal counsel should be sought in the generation of a specific contract as well as for contract review.

1. Definition of Terms: Lists and describes certain words that are routinely used in the rest of the contract.

2. License: General statement allowing event organizers access to the facility for the purposes of executing the contract. Some contracts will be more specific than others in this area.

3. Event Administration: Defines which party is responsible for which event management functions.

4. Organization Standard: A statement noting that because of the organization's current positive reputation, a certain standard will be expected for the event, and the party signing the contract agrees to adhere to that standard.

5. Exclusivity: Prohibits those involved in the event from copying the theme and other attributes of the event.

6. Merchandise: Artwork, event logo, and event merchandise development, approval, sales, and revenue sharing process.

7. Food and Beverage: Catering and concessions rights, sales, and revenue sharing agreement.

8. Promotional Rights and Responsibilities: Which party will be responsible for developing and implementing specific promotional aspects, and which party is responsible for paying for them.

9. Reserved Rights: Outlines which party will retain the rights to filming, videotaping, audio recording, photographing, or any other manner of recording, and which party has the right to exploit the material. Both parties may mutually retain these rights rather than just one party retaining them.

10. Sponsorship: Specifies what rights existing sponsors of both parties have, if any. Also specifies what sponsorship sales rights each party has and the revenue sharing of those sales.

11. Right to Photograph: A party's right to take and use photographs of the event for commercial or other purposes, during the contract period and beyond, without paying compensation to the event.

12. Waivers/Consents: Requirements related to whether or not participant waivers are required.

13. Insurance: General liability required limits for venue users and any workers compensation insurance is also often mentioned here, if relevant

14. Indemnification: An indemnification section provides that one of the contractual parties will indemnify (or hold harmless) the other party for specific actions that may cause damage to the other party. Do not overlook this section as just a formality. Make sure that you agree to the language of holding the other party harmless for certain actions.

15. Warranties: Promises made by a seller who may be liable if promises are broken.

16. Force Majeure: Specifies that certain conditions may allow for nonperformance of the contract. Conditions generally include those deemed an "act of God" or other conditions out of the control of those involved in the event.

17. Alterations: Notes allowable changes to the venue (e.g., drilling, hanging posters).

18. Risk of Loss: Defines which party is responsible for loss or damage of equipment/personal belongings during the event.

19. Rules and Regulations: States which party has authority to create venue rules.

20. Termination: Describes under which circumstances the event may be cancelled and under which circumstances the agreement may be terminated.

21. Joint Venture/Partnership Disclaimer: Disclaimer that the parties entering into the contract do not wish to form a legal formal relationship.

22. Signatory's Warranty: States that the person signing the contract has the authority to do so.

23. Confidentiality: Explains what is confidential and to whom.
24. Governing Law and Waiver of Jury Trial: Specifies which State has jurisdiction over legal proceedings.
25. Entire Agreement: Waiver/Modification: Confirms that the contract replaces any previous agreements and outlines the conditions under which aspects of the contract could be changed.
26. Notice: Provides for the specifics of mail communication (i.e., address on front of contract will be used for mail).
27. Signature Lines: The end of the contract should have lines for both a signature and a date for the parties authorized to sign the contract. Often signatures must be notarized, depending on the nature and amount of money involved in the contract.
28. Addendum(s): An addendum or addendums may be added with specific details of the agreement that may not be appropriate in the main boilerplate portion of the contract.

It is apparent from the above list that the general terms and conditions section of a contract covers many aspects of the event. Issues such as merchandising, sponsorship, rules and regulations of the facility, insurance requirements, and confidentiality are all important information to include in a contract.

Breach of Contract

Often, all the terms of an agreement are completed and the contract is successfully completed. However, sometimes some or none of the agreed upon terms are completed. This may be intentional or it may be unintentional. Regardless of intent, if a party does not complete the terms of a contract, it may be deemed a **breach of contract.**

A breach of contract is either a minor breach or a material breach. A minor breach of contract is where most of the contract has been performed (substantial performance has been made) and therefore the nonbreaching party can sue for damages. A material breach is when the breaching party's failure to perform or the performance is substantially different from what the contract specified. In the case of a material breach, the nonbreaching party is no longer required to perform under that contract and can seek legal recourse to remedy the breach.

Why Contracts Are Used in Event Management

The reason contracts are used in event management is to provide a written agreement of terms, expectations, and responsibilities of the parties involved. Event managers can use contracts as an outline to ensure that obligations are met. For any given event, there are a multitude of groups and individuals that need to be under contract with the host organization or venue (McMillen, 2003). Misunderstandings and miscommunications are avoided though the use of a well-drafted, legally binding contract. Sport events can involve large sums of money, thousands of people, safety concerns, and have many potential pitfalls. Thus, protection through various types of contracts is important. If event managers are in charge of an event bringing in thousands of people, they have needs in the area of customer service, security, food and beverage service, logistics, parking, sponsorship, and merchandise. The massive list of what needs to be done, which people need to do it, how it needs to be done, and when it needs to be done can be daunting for new event managers. The use of contracts is one way to ensure that all involved understand their roles and responsibilities.

Besides the who, what, when, and where aspects of contracts related to events, contracts also commonly contain language that provides for legal liability protection for individuals and groups working the event (McMillen, 2003). Individuals working events have a reasonable expectation that they receive a contract in writing specifying their formal working relationship with the sport organization and the expectations of the organization. In rare circumstances, breach of contract may occur and the contract will be the primary documentation used by the legal system to determine if there was nonfulfillment of any aspect of the contract and what the remedy will be.

Common Event Management Contracts

Organizations that enter into contracts for sporting events include vendors, concessionaires, game officials, sponsors, insurance agents, mascots, entertainment, promotional activities, essential personnel, and media (specifically television and radio). There are four main types of contracts (plus employment contracts discussed in the Event Staffing Chapter) that event managers should be familiar with. The type of contract will determine the specific consideration of the contract. These types of contracts are:

- Game Contracts
- Event Contracts
- Venue and Facility Contracts
- Sponsorship Contracts

Game Contracts

A **game contract** (Figure 3.1) is a contractual agreement that arranges a contest or contests between two organizations. The focus of a game contract is on time and place for the game and the financial considerations of the event. If a **game guarantee**, payment for one team to play another team, is part of the agreement, it will be specified in the contract. Travel (which may include payment for a team to travel to a certain location), housing (which may include some complimentary hotel rooms), officials and officials' pay scales, concessionaires, television and radio broadcast rights, sponsorship exclusivity, potential escape clauses, and breach of contract provisions also will be addressed in a game contract.

For example, it is customary in college athletics to schedule games many years in advance in football, men's basketball, and women's basketball. Every year, some institutions jockey for more lucrative guarantees, or try to get out of a game that was more highly regarded when the game contract was originally agreed upon. It is common for game contracts have escape clauses, predetermined buyout clauses, or language allowing for mutual agreed upon termination of the contract.

Event Contracts

Event contracts (Figure 3.2) are very similar to game contracts in that the time and place are paramount. Many times, an event contract will also address an athletic contest between two parties. The key term is the word "event." An event, in a sporting context, can include a contest, a single special event like the Super Bowl, or multiple events like the Olympics or Amateur Athletic Union (AAU), Inc. Junior Olympics. Event contracts differ from game contracts in that they often include ancillary event stipulations. Ancillary events might include athlete banquets, a related sponsor tailgate, a vendor village, or a concert associated with the main sporting event.

It would be advisable to have a written contract for any special event. From a local 5K run to a pro-am charitable ski race, this is where an event contract or several event contracts would be beneficial to outline expectations and responsibilities. Figure 3.2 provides an example of a traveling family show (The Harlem Globetrotters) contract. Not only does the contract address the main event (Harlem Globetrotters), but specific ancillary items are also addressed including an autograph session, and stipulations regarding load in/load out, merchandise, ticketing, marketing, advertising, sponsorships, and insurance.

Venue/Facility Contracts

While many states will enforce short-term rental agreements that are not in writing, it is advisable for any venue or **facility contract** to be in writing. The agreement should include the specific terms of the lease including time, length of event, how much rent is to be paid, maintenance, custodial, grounds, security, medical support, and any other relevant terms. In addition, individuals or groups renting and using a venue for an event usually must present evidence of a certificate of insurance with minimum policy limits often set at $1 million. Even though venue/facility contracts can be specific to the event, many venues use a basic boilerplate contract for almost every group coming into their venue.

The Ohio University Facility Rental Agreement (Figure 3.3), covers all of the above items and is a good example of a standard venue or facility contract. While many venue contracts may have more terms and consideration, this example is sufficient for most any venue or facility rental situations. Also, the Harlem Globetrotter contract (Figure 3.2) example contains some facility contract information within an event contract, and many times these two types of contracts are combined.

Sponsorship Contracts (May Also Include Trade and/or Gift-in-Kind in Lieu of Cash)

A **sponsorship contract** (Figure 3.4) is a legal agreement that binds two or more parties to agreed-upon obligations related to the sponsorship of an event, facility, team or other related sports entity. Sponsorship contracts can be relatively simple, covering signage, media advertising, and public address announcements. Alternately, they can be extensive and require substantial consideration of both of the parties. A sponsorship contract is not a one-sided relationship. It should be a mutually beneficial partnership in which each organization is helping to activate the sponsorship to achieve its goals. For example, a high-profile naming rights deal like Nationwide Arena in Columbus, Ohio, includes much more than the name on the arena. Since Nationwide is an insurance company and spent millions of dollars on the rights to have its name on the outside of the arena, it needs to be able to leverage that sponsorship into new business. Most sponsors need leads and sales contacts to generate business and stay ahead of their competitors. The benefits and activation plans agreed to by both parties are geared toward helping the sponsor achieve its goals (Figure 3.5).

SUMMARY

The purpose of this chapter was to provide an overview of contracts and contract law specifically applied to the event management industry. Basic contract knowledge is essential in that contracts are a set of promises made in some type of a bargained exchange. A valid and enforceable contract is one that has the following elements: offer, acceptance, consideration, capacity, legality, and in writing (if required). Elements of a contract are applied in event management through game, event, venue, and sponsorship contracts. These types of contracts are the primary types used in event management and examples of each are included following this summary. The sample contracts provided should assist event managers in preparing contracts for future events. Of course, in all contract dealings it is recommended to use legal counsel to ensure the contract passes legal standards and provides for adequate insurance coverage in the event of unforeseen circumstances. However, legal counsel is not always available for an event manager. Therefore, it is important to understand the basics of forming a valid contract and the types of contracts that you may encounter so you are aware of the important elements needed to create a valid contract. As discussed using examples throughout the chapter, well-written contracts are essential to successful event planning and management.

Acknowledgments

Special thanks to Ohio University Athletic Department, Jason Farmer, Assistant Athletic Director—Facilities, Jim Schaus, Director of Athletics, and Amy Dean, Executive Senior Association Athletic Director/Administration and Sport Programs (SWA).

Figure 3.1 Example of a Game Contract.

Ohio University

Department of Intercollegiate Athletics

Athens, Ohio 45701

Phone (740) 593-0982 Fax (740) 597-0798

Ohio Athletic Participation Agreement with Visiting Team

This agreement made and entered into this <u>\<Insert Date\></u> day of <u>\<Insert Date\></u>, <u>\<Insert Date\></u> by and between <u>\<Insert College/University\></u> ("Visitors") and Ohio University ("Ohio"), by their duly authorized agents:

1. That the teams representing the above named institutions agree to meet in the sport of <u>\<Insert Sport\></u>.

2. That each party shall agree in principle to adhere to the rules of the sport of <u>\<Insert Sport\></u> in accordance with the terms of this agreement. The game(s) shall be held as set forth below:

    Date (s): \<Insert Game Date\>

    Site (s): \<Insert Location/Venue\>

    Time (s) to be determined by host institution

3. That the contest shall be played under eligibility rules of the NCAA.

4. The officials are to be secured by the host institution and the expenses are to be borne by the host institution, unless otherwise stipulated. The Mid-American Conference Office will assign MAC officials for the game scheduled in Athens, OH.

5. That in consideration of playing the above named contest, the host institution shall pay the Visitors in the sum of \<Insert Dollar Amount\>. The payment of \<Insert Dollar Amount\> should be paid no later than \<Insert Payment Date\>.

6. The host institution shall provide \<Insert Number of Tickets\> complimentary tickets to the Visitors.

    a. The host institution shall extend <u>\<Insert Number of Tickets\></u> reserved tickets for the Visitors to purchase on consignment. All unsold tickets must be returned to the host institution no later than 15 days before the contest. All unsold tickets not returned will result in payment by the Visitors to the host institution.

7. The host institution shall have the exclusive right to sell game programs and operate concessions and parking. All income from game program sales, concessions, and parking shall be the sole property of the host institution.

8. The host institution shall provide a medical doctor and an emergency ambulance to the game site throughout the entirety of the game.

9. The Visitors shall present themselves at the site of the game in condition to play at least 60 minutes before the time set as the starting time of the game.

10. Each party shall have the right to its own radio broadcast of the contest and shall retain all revenue from these broadcasts. Accommodations include press row space for three persons.

11. The host institution shall control all television broadcast rights to the game according to the following, including MAC operations.

    a. If the game is not televised by a national network, the host institution may cause the game to be cablecast on a national/regional cable television network or to be broadcast on an over-the-air television station, and the host institution shall be entitled to retain the negotiated rights fee.

    b. The host school shall retain all television and new media rights for each contest.

    c. Each party shall have the right to produce films and/or video tapes of the game for use in a coach's show or locally originated delayed television broadcast of the game subject to compliance with the rules governing delayed television broadcast by the NCAA or other agencies of which either or both institutions are members. Each party may retain all income received from such commercial opportunities.

    d. The host institution agrees to provide reasonable facilities and production accommodations for the origination of programs herein. The Visitors shall reimburse the host institution for costs associated with and incurred on the Visitors' behalf, or the Visitors will be responsible for such services individually contracted.

    e. Each party shall be solely responsible for payment of any assessments due its own conference or other governing body.

    f. Any discussion regarding the conditions of MAC television products should be directed to the MAC offices.

12. It is recognized that neither party can foresee the exigencies, which may hereafter arise by reason of emergency, catastrophe or epidemic making it necessary or desirable, in sole judgment of the host institution, to cancel this Agreement.

13. If either party, for any reason other than those stated in paragraph 12 above, breaches the Agreement by failing to appear at the time and place scheduled herein for the game, they shall pay liquidated damages in the amount of <u><Insert Dollar Amount></u>, unless otherwise agreed upon.

14. This Agreement shall be governed, construed and enforced in accordance with the laws of the state of Ohio, regardless of its place of execution. Any legal action arising under this Agreement shall be brought in a Court of Claims in the State of Ohio.

15. This Agreement is the whole agreement between the two parties with respect to the subject matter hereof and supersedes in all respects all other agreements either written or oral. Any additions or modifications must be in writing and must be signed by both parties.

16. Ohio has a pre-existing agreement that contractually binds Ohio to place and utilize Gatorade-identified cups, coolers, ice chests, squeeze bottles, towels and product ("Branded Items") exclusively within the players' bench area during the event. The Visitor hereby acknowledges Ohio's obligation to exclusively place Branded Items in the Visitors' bench area and agrees that Ohio shall have the right to place such Branded Items at the Visitor's game activities.

The parties hereto by their respective offices duly authorized, have caused this Agreement to be executed as of the day, month, and year first written above.

Ohio University	College XYZ
By: _____	By: _____
Name: Jim Schaus	Name: _____
Title: Director of Athletics	Title: _____
Date: _____	Date: _____

Please sign both copies and return one to:

Jim Schaus

Director of Athletics

Ohio Athletics

S130 Convocation Center

Athens, Ohio 45701

Figure 3.2 Example of an Event Contract.

HARLEM GLOBETROTTERS STANDARD CO-PROMOTION AGREEMENT

This AGREEMENT dated August 6, 2007 by and between **HARLEM GLOBETROTTERS INTERNATIONAL, INC.**, a Nevada corporation, One Arizona, 400 E. Van Buren Street, Suite 300, Phoenix, Arizona, 85004 ("**Producer**") and **OHIO UNIVERSITY, ATHENS OHIO 45701** ("**Operator**").

Operator hereby agrees to furnish facilities (the "Arena") for the presentation of a Harlem Globetrotters Basketball Show (the "Performance"), and to make said facilities available to the Producer from 6:00 A.M. until 11:00 P.M. on the Performance date listed below, and Producer hereby agrees to use the Arena, upon and subject to all of the provisions set forth below and attached hereto.

ARENA NAME AND LOCATION:

CONVOCATION CENTER

OHIO UNIVERSITY

ATHENS, OHIO 45701

740-593-4666

PERFORMANCE:

DATE: WEDNESDAY, JANUARY 16, 2008 at 7PM

NUMBER OF SEATS Operator certifies that capacity for this performance is **13,000**. If such capacity is reduced following the full execution of this contract, Operator shall reimburse the Producer for the number of the reduced seats at the average ticket price.

TIME LINE:

- **Move In:** Approximately 4 hours prior to Performance, unless otherwise notified.
- **Globetrotter University:** Operator agrees to open one single entrance, mutually agreeable to both parties, for Globetrotter University will begin approximately 30 minutes prior to doors opening to the general public and last approximately 15–20 minutes.

- **Doors Open to General Public: 6pm;** approximately 1 hour prior to start of Performance.
- **Start of Performance: 7pm**
- **Length of Performance:** Approximately 2 hours. The performance has four 10-minute quarters with a half-time intermission; (occasionally, a running clock may be used during game time).
- Autograph Session: Immediately following game. There shall be an autograph session lasting no more than 30 minutes.
- **Move Out:** Approximately 3 hours after scheduled start of Performance.

CREDIT CARD FEES: All fees to be paid by operator.

HARLEM GLOBETROTTER SURCHARGE: It is agreed that a $1.00 surcharge shall be added to the Producer's established ticket price, and added to the gross ticket sales amount. After deduction of all applicable admission taxes, if any, Producer shall receive the remainder. The surcharge is as stated above for each performance and is not subject to change without the prior written consent of Producer. A Surcharge shall not be added on complimentary tickets.

GROUP SALES COMMISSION: All commissions paid for Group Sales must be approved by Producer's Marketing Department and said commissions shall be paid after applicable facility fees and taxes.

ADMISSIONS TAX:

It is agreed by both parties that the following taxes shall be assessed on Gross Ticket Sales only, and deducted from Gross Sales before any and all divisions of Proceeds (as defined below):

State- N/A   City-N/A   Other-N/A

Operator shall be responsible for collection and submitting payment for all admission taxes (and other such taxes) and for the filing of any reports and returns with respect thereto. Operator shall hereby indemnify and hold Producer harmless from any and all cost and liability with respect thereto. Operator agrees to furnish to Producer receipts for the payment of all such taxes.

FACILITY FEE: NONE

I. DIVISION OF PROCEEDS:

The "Adjusted Gross Admission Proceeds" defined as all proceeds derived from the sale of all tickets, including but not limited to Main Concourse seating, Club Level seating and Mezzanine seating, Sponsorship revenue(as defined in Section VIII), etc., less:

1. Any applicable admission taxes;
2. $1.00 HGI Surcharge as defined above;
3. The advertising, publicity and Group Sales commission and materials expense billed at Net as defined in Section VII;

Shall be divided in accordance with the percentages as set forth below:

<u>Share to Producer</u>	<u>Share to Operator</u>
80%	20%

II. MERCHANDISE:

Producer and/or designee, ("Merchandiser"), shall have the exclusive right to furnish and distribute all programs, novelties, and souvenirs, ("Merchandise"), in connection with the Harlem Globetrotters or the Performance(s). Such Merchandise, the nature of which shall be determined at the sole discretion of Producer, shall be the only Merchandise items sold and displayed before, during and after the Performance(s).

1. All Gross proceeds received from the sale of Merchandise, less the payment of sales taxes and credit card fees, shall be called Net Merchandising Proceeds. **Producer** shall retain 100% of the proceeds from said Merchandise

PRODUCER SHALL SELL PRODUCER'S MERCHANDISE

2. Operator shall provide prominent and adequate space for Merchandiser or Concessionaire to vend such Merchandise and Operator agrees that Merchandiser shall, as it may require, have reasonable access to appropriate hall facilities and areas adjacent to the venue.

3. It is understood that the term "Merchandise" as used herein shall not include food, such as hot dogs, burgers or nachos, refreshments, parking or checkroom services.

4. Operator shall retain all proceeds from the sale of food concessions.

III. THE ARENA

A. Operator shall, at its sole expense, furnish the Arena to include the following:

1. Audience seats of a number no less than as specified on the cover page;

2. Facilities, supplies, equipment (including, but not limited to, general house lighting, two (2) spotlights, Jumbotron/video board and Clearcom communication), team dressing room requirements (including, but not limited to, locker room refreshments as specified in the Harlem Globetrotters Technical Rider, and staffing/stagehands (including, but not limited to, a scoreboard operator, a house person to turn house lights off and on, Jumbotron/video operator and two (2) spotlight operators) as specified in the Harlem Globetrotter Technical Rider attached hereto and made part of this Agreement as required for the professional presentation of Producer;

   a. Any items, equipment or staffing/stagehands which Operator cannot supply shall be mutually agreed upon by both parties.

3. 10' X 10' space, in high traffic area, for each of the Producer's sponsors. Producer's sponsors shall not conflict with Operator's sponsors. There shall be no fees or commissions paid to Operator for said space;

4. Storage space in the Arena sufficient for the equipment required for the Performance(s);

5. The Arena and all other facilities included therein, in good, clean and safe condition;

6. Parking for two (2) 40-foot Globetrotters coach-style tour buses, one (1) 25-foot Ryder truck for merchandise and one (1) 25-foot Ryder truck for equipment, as close to artist entrance as possible;

7. A clean professional or collegiate basketball floor, with a 3-point line and professional breakaway rims, permanent and temporary seating, and ample lighting for the presentation of the Performance, installed in a safe and professional manner by Operator, and according to all current industry standards;

8. Full compliance with all applicable governmental statues, regulations, ordinances and codes relating to health, safety, maintenance, fire or otherwise, with respect to the Arena building and any part thereof, any equipment or facility contained therein and any activity carried on therein, whether by Operator or others;

9. Heated and ventilated dressing rooms, audience seating areas, and such other parts of the Arena as may be necessary for the proper comfort of the audience and the performers;

10. All licensed required under any applicable governmental statues, regulations, ordinances or codes with respect to the operation of the Arena and the hosting of the Performance; (excluding rights of music for the Performance)

11. Discharge all obligations imposed on Operator by any federal, state or local law, regulation, ordinance, code or order now or hereafter in force with respect to employees, including, but not limited to, taxes, unemployment compensation or insurance, disability insurance, social security and workers' compensation, and Operator shall file all returns and reports and pay all assessments, taxes, contributions and other sums required in connection therewith;

12. All personnel, equipment and facilities necessary to adequately safeguard Producer and its employees from thefts of personal property, and any other damage or injury to their person or property;

13. Ushers, door keepers, electricians, ticker sellers, telephone operators, cleaners, watchmen, security guards, firemen, and all other personnel to operate the Arena and to carry out the obligations of Operator under this Agreement;

14. Conform to, comply with and abide by all applicable labor or collective bargaining agreements to which Producer and/or Operator are or may become a party, as the same now exist or may be amended; and

15. Reimburse Producer for fees and expenses which may be incurred by Producer as a result of Operator's default or failure to provide any of the foregoing.

B. Operator shall not permit the use of the Arena, or any part thereof, for the presentation of any basketball exhibition for a period of 8 weeks prior to the Performance and 6 weeks subsequent to the Performance and warrants and represents that no such presentation will be made. A professional league, collegiate, high school or local amateur basketball game shall not be considered a basketball exhibition.

IV. HARLEM GLOBETROTTERS INTERNATIONAL, INC.

A. As between Producer and Operator, Producer retains sole and exclusive ownership and control of all of the properties, materials and rights of Harlem Globetrotters International, Inc. and any other third party marks used by the Harlem Globetrotters in connection with its basketball exhibitions, including certain service marks, trademark registrations and attendant goodwill relating to, inter alia, the unique entertainment services in the nature of basketball exhibitions performed in the United States and the world (such marks including, but not limited to the following registered trademarks: "Harlem Globetrotters," "Globetrotters," "Magicians of Basketball," "Magic Circle," and "Globie") and certain designs, characters, symbols, logos, musical renditions, likenesses and visual representations heretofore used in connection with said marks. Operator is licensed to use the aforesaid marks and the names and likenesses of the performers only during the period beginning with the group sales and/or advertising campaign through **January 16, 2008** and to the event expressly authorized by Producer.

B. The Arena shall insure that the Performance(s) shall not, in whole or in part, be recorded or carried by any mean outside the Arena, without the prior, written consent of Producer, except for bona fide news coverage.

C. If Producer authorizes broadcast coverage, phonograph or tape recordings, motion pictures or other commercial tie-ups of the Performance(s) hereunder, any and all proceeds therefrom shall belong to Producer.

D. The "Magic Circle" shall not be video taped, filmed or broadcast by anyone other than Producer. There shall be no exceptions.

E. The rights to any and all audio and/or visual transmission, reproduction or recording of the Performance in the Arena, or any part thereof, shall be the sole and exclusive property of the

Producer, whether the same be for simultaneous, in-house or subsequent use, except for bona fide news coverage by local media as set forth in Section III.B. above.

V. SALE OF TICKETS

A. **Printing**. Operator shall, prior to the commencement of the advanced sale of tickets, and subsequent to mutual determination by Operator and Producer of ticket prices and locations:

1. Cause to be printed tickets for all audience seats in the Arena or arrange for sale of tickets through a computers ticket service, and

2. Furnish to Producer a certified printer's manifest or a certified computer program manifest of all tickets, together with a summary showing the number of seats at each price for each Performance.

B. **Sale**.

1. Prior to the Performance:

   a. Producer shall solely determine a date to place tickets for the Performance(s) on sale and Operator shall from that time until the end of the Performance furnish the facilities and personnel (including box offices, ticket sellers, telephone lines and operators) required for the proper sale of tickets at the Arena and at such other places as may customarily be utilized by the Operator for such purposes.

   b. The box office at the Arena shall remain open at least 6 hours per day during normal box office hours, including the last 7 days leading up to the day of the Performance, and must be open for business from 10:00 AM through halftime of the Performance. **Normal box office hours shall be: Day(s) Time.**

   c. On weekends and holidays, Operator shall designate hours of operation at the box office for those days and make tickets available to the public during those times. If Operator is unable to perform this function, they must notify Producer in writing at signing of Agreement.

   d. Operator will insure that ticket information will be readily available to the public by supplying adequate telephone lines and operators during the time the box office is open.

   e. Operator shall provide sufficient ticket sellers in a sufficient number to properly service the public 2 hours prior and throughout each Performance.

2. Operator shall furnish Producer with complete daily reports of tickets sold and other ticket sales information beginning the say after Performance tickets have gone on sale. Ticket sales information shall include such information as ticket outlet, telephone/credit card, discount and cumulative ticket sales.

3. Immediately after each Performance, Operator shall furnish Producer with a complete report showing the number of tickets sold and unsold, complimentary tickets issued for said Performance, and all other information relevant to the proceeds from the sale of tickets for said Performance, including a box count of all tickets collected for said Performance, and shall at such time have all unsold tickets available for inspection by Producer. Operator shall grant Producer approval to directly access TicketMaster for all ticket sales pertaining to Harlem Globetrotters International.

4. All ticket sales and/or box office reports are **public records under Ohio law**.

C. **Gross Admission Proceeds**. Gross Admission Proceeds as used herein is defined as all proceeds derived from the sale of tickets and local sponsorship revenue (as defined in

Section VIII(B)), including applicable taxes and excluding any facility fees, parking, concessions, and merchandise, etc. shall not be included in the Gross Admission Proceeds. Operator shall be responsible for the collection of all monies and proceeds of sale of tickets, including Main Concourse seating, Club Level seating and Mezzanine seating and shall, at its own expense:

1. Bond all ticket sellers and other persons handling such monies and proceeds of an amount sufficient to cover the value of the monies and proceeds handled by them, and

2. Insure such monies and proceeds against all other risks which might result in a loss thereof. The Gross Admission Proceeds shall be a confidential matter between Producer and Operator and this information shall not be disclosed to any unauthorized individual(s) without the written consent of the other part.

3. In addition to above, Gross Admission Proceeds does/does not include all Suite sales which represents a total of n/a ticket and a total of Suites.

D. **Complimentary Tickets.**

1. Operator shall set aside for the exclusive use of Producer's Team Tour Manager sixty (60) complementary seats for each Performance at the highest prices (**shall not be MAGIC CIRCLE COURTSIDE seats**) located behind the Harlem Globetrotters player's bench. The specific location of these seats must be approved by Producer.

2. Operator shall set aside for the exclusive use of Harlem Globetrotters Corporate Office sixty (60) complimentary seats for each Performance at the highest prices (**shall not be MAGIC CIRCLE COURTSIDE seats**) located in the Center Section. The specific location of these seats must be approved by Producer.

3. Operator shall honor all written requests for complimentary tickets by Producer. In addition Operator shall honor all official complimentary ticket coupons used in Producer's advertising, promotional campaign, and sponsorship ticket requirement.

4. **MAGIC CIRCLE COURSIDE and VIP tickets shall not be issued or used as complimentary, discounted or Group Sales tickets without the express written consent of the Producer.** MAGIC CIRCLE COURSIDE ad VIP tickets issued without the express written consent of the Producer shall be deemed paid admissions valued at the manifested ticket price per ticket for the purpose of computing the Gross Admissions Proceeds to the Performance hereunder.

5. Trade tickets used in the Advertising, Publicity & Group Sales campaign must be approved by Producer's Marketing Department prior to distribution.

6. Operator will be entitled to the following number of complimentary tickets: <u>One percent (1%) of manifested seating capacity</u>. Such complimentary tickets **shall not include Magic Circle or VIP tickets** without written approval of Producer. Accurate records and accounting of these complimentary tickets shall be provided by Operator to Producer at the time of settlement.

E. **Records and Inspection.** Operator shall maintain full and complete accounting and other records with respect to the sale of tickets and the proceeds thereof and Producer and accountants of Producer shall have the right at all reasonable times to examine all such records or to verify the program of the computer ticket service. Throughout the duration of this Agreement and for a period not exceeding 6 months following the completion of the Performance Producer or it's authorized representatives shall have the right to audit any and all accounting and other records relating to this Agreement including, but not limited to, box office and admission proceeds, unsold tickets, the drop count, any and all other ticket proceeds, advertising expenses and agreements, and admission taxes. Such right to audit may be exercised upon reasonable notice to the Operator.

VI. ADVERTISING, PUBLICITY & GROUP SALES

A. The advertising, publicity and Group Sales budget shall be mutually agreed upon at Net by the Producer and the Operator. "Net" is hereby defined as the gross advertising, publicity and Group Sales material expense, less any media commission, Group Sales commission and any marketing company's fee or commission,. The budget shall itemize advertising expense, publicity/advance ambassador expenses, and Group Sales material expenses. Any media commission, group sales commission, any marketing company's fee or any other commission shall not be included in the budget and shall be at the sole expense of the Operator.

B. With respect to the billing of advertising, publicity and Group Sales material expense, all advertising, publicity and Group Sales material expense shall be billed at Net. All such billing shall be completed at the offices of the Operator (or Arena) and Operator (or Arena) shall draw and issue checks for all such media expenses without any commission resulting there from being billed to Producer.

C. Operator shall, at its sole cost and expense, unless specified in Division of Proceeds on Page 3, provide for an advertising, publicity, and Group Sales campaign billed at Net for the Performance(s) under the supervision of Producer and shall, in connection with said campaign, expend no more or no less than the amount mutually agreed upon, between Producer and Operator, without the prior written consent of Producer. Twelve weeks prior to the Performance, Operator shall furnish Producer with proposed budget allocations of advertising, publicity, and Group Sales expenses. Detailed schedules of newspaper advertisements, radio and television commercials shall be furnished to Producer not less than 8 weeks in advance of the first Performance. The campaign shall commence at least 4 weeks prior to the first Performance at the Arena and shall continue through the date of the last Performance.

D. The objective of the campaign shall be to attain the greatest possible amount of ticker sales for the Performance(s) at the Arena using various forms of advertising media, including radio and television broadcasting, outdoor and transit advertising, and newspapers of general circulation. Operator shall utilize the advertising and promotional materials, designs and forms designated by Producer without modification and shall use no other advertising or promotional materials, designs and forms without the prior written consent of Producer. Production costs incurred by Operator for radio, television newspaper or other advertising materials shall not be included in the advertising or publicity expenses unless otherwise agreed by Producer. The campaign shall feature the name "Harlem Globetrotters." Producer shall furnish Operator with advertising ad promotional materials prior to the Performance. Such materials shall include a press kit and one set of photographs of performers.

E. Any promotional materials or merchandise that Producer and Operator deem appropriate to the campaign shall be paid for according to the Producer's price schedule. Operator shall not utilize the advertising and promotional materials, designs and forms designated by Producer subsequent to the advertising campaign without the prior written consent of Producer.

F. With respect to Magic Circle Courtside seating in the Arena for the event hereunder there shall be no promotional item ("Premium") with the purchase of a Magic Circle Courtside admission ticket.

VII. SPONSORSHIP(S)

A. All sponsorship revenue derived from any designated local sponsor(s) secured by operator and or producer shall be shared by adding said sponsorship revenue to the gross admission proceeds prior to its division.

B. If operator obtains sponsorship revenue from a single local sponsor, operator shall be entitled to receive a commission of 20% of said sponsorship revenue. The remainder of the sponsorship funds shall be added to Gross Admission Proceeds prior to division. In no other instance shall the Operator or Producer be entitled to any other fee or commission with respect to sponsorship revenue.

C. Any expense associated with sponsorship agreements such as, but not limited to, banners, floor decals, pre/post game parties shall be included in advertising, publicity and Group Sales materials expense budget and deducted from the Gross Admission Proceeds.

D. Producer shall retain one hundred percent (100%) of any sponsorship revenue derived from any regional, national, and international, corporate sponsor(s) secured solely by Producer.

E. Producer shall be allowed to display any of the Producer's regional, national, and international sponsors' banners, and/or signage in the Arena during the performance, at Producer's press conferences, and at events promoting performance(s). Also, Operator shall supply, upon request, a 10' x 10' space, in a high traffic area, for each of the Producers' sponsors. Producer's sponsors shall not conflict with Operator's sponsors. There shall be no fees or commissions paid to Operator for said space.

F. Producer must approve in writing all local sponsors secured by Operator. In addition Producer must approve in writing the use and placement of all logos and the copy of local sponsors in all advertising for the Performance.

VIII. ADA

Operator ids responsible for the compliance with Title II of the Americans with Disabilities Act of 1990 or as amended and all regulations thereunder as they shall or may relate to permanent Arena access accommodations such as, but not limited to, wheelchair ramps, elevator standards, door width standards, and restroom accessibility. In addition, Operator should be prepared to respond to reasonable request for auxiliary aids from patrons with disabilities and shall bear the financial cost of providing auxiliary aids such as assistive listening device rental, readers, and interpreters.

IX. INSURANCE AND INDEMNIFICATION

Thirty days prior to the Performance, Operator shall provide Producer with certificate(s) of insurance evidencing that insurance policies covered by this paragraph are with an insurance company recognized as an authorized carrier in the state where the Arena is located, and acceptable to Producer.

Said certificate(s) and policy shall be in a form and content satisfactory to Producer, which shall:

1. Provide Commercial General Liability having a combined single limit (bodily injury, property damage and personal injury) of at least $1,000,000.00 per occurrence ($2,000,000.00 aggregate);

2. Provide Workers' Compensation insurance coverage and Employer's Liability for Operator's employees;

3. Specify as additional insureds; **Harlem Globetrotters International, Inc.**;

4. Indemnify and hold Producer harmless **in accordance with Ohio law if possible** during the term of this Agreement from any and all claims, demands, judgments, losses and

expenses, including reasonable attorney's fees, which may be made against Producer and which is in any way related to the Arena or to the Performance in the Arena, except those claims which may arise through the negligence of the Producer or its employees;

5. To the extent not covered by insurance, Operator shall and does hereby indemnify and hold Producer harmless **in accordance with Ohio law** from and against any loss, damage, cost or expense arising out of or in any way related to Producer's occupancy of the premises or use of the Arena (except in any case where such loss, damage, cost or expense is caused by the negligence of the Producer or its employees);

6. When timely requested, Producer shall furnish to the Operator or facility a certificate of insurance evidencing a policy of comprehensive general liability insurance having limits not to exceed a combined single limit of $1,000,00.00 per occurrence, ($2,000,000.00 aggregate) which will name Operator as additional insured thereunder, but only or liability arising out of the negligence of the Producer its agents, servants, licensees or employees with respect to the operations of Producer in the Arena.

7. It is agreed that neither of the parties shall be deemed to have accepted the obligation of the other, whether by reason of loss hereunder or otherwise. Producer and Operator agree to assume responsibility for its own negligence in situations involving joint negligence. It is not intended that Producer assumer protection for sole negligence on the part of the Operator or vice-versa.

X. GENERAL

A. Operator and Producer each represent and warrant to the other that they have full right and power to enter into and perform this Agreement according to its terms.

B. Neither party to this Agreement shall be liable to the other for nay failure to perform any of the terms or conditions of this Agreement which is attributable to war, an act of God, a strike, a lockout, or any other cause beyond the control of such party.

C. This Agreement shall remain binding and in full force and effect and constitutes the entire understanding between the parties and supersedes all prior and contemporaneous written or oral agreements pertaining thereto and can only be modified by a writing signed on behalf of both parties hereto. This Agreement shall be governed by and construed in accordance with the laws of the state of **Ohio** applicable to contracts entered into and fully performed therein. In the event of any breach, termination or cancellation of this Agreement by Producer, Operator's sole and exclusive remedy shall be an action at law for damages. Operator hereby waives any right to seek and/or obtain rescission and/or equitable and/or injunctive relief.

D. Neither this Agreement nor nay of the duties, obligations or rights hereunder may be assigned by either of the parties hereto without the express written consent of the other, provided that Producer may at any time this Agreement, and all or any part of its rights hereunder, to any person, firm, or corporation controlling, controlled by or under a common control with Producer or with which Producer may be merged or consolidated.

E. The delay or failure of either party to asset or exercise any right, remedy or privilege hereunder, with actual or constructive notice or knowledge of the breach of any representation, warranty or provision herein, shall not constitute a waiver of any such right, remedy, privilege or breach. No waiver shall in any even be effective unless in writing, and then it shall be effective only in the specific instance for which given.

F. This Agreement shall inure to the benefit of and be binding upon Producer and Operator and their respective successors and assigns.

G. The Arena and facilities being furnished by Operator to Producer pursuant to this Agreement are of a special, unique and extraordinary character and accordingly in the event of a default, threatened default or cancellation by Operator under this Agreement, Producer shall be entitled, in addition to any other remedies it may have, to equitable relief by way of injunction, specific performance or otherwise.

H. Nothing herein contained shall constitute a partnership between or joint venture by the parties hereto, or constitute either party the agent of the other. Neither party shall hold itself out contrary to the terms of this paragraph, and neither party shall become liable of the representation, act or omission of the other contrary to the provisions hereof. This Agreement is not for the benefit of any third party and shall not be deemed to give any right or remedy to any third party, whether referred to herein or not.

I. This instrument shall be and become a binding Agreement when executed by authorized officials of Producer and Operator and until then shall have no force or effect.

J. If language in this agreement conflicts with any agreement provided by the Operator, the language in Harlem Globetrotters Standard Co-Promotion Agreement shall govern.

SPECIAL CONDITIONS:

1. Operator pays all other direct game related expenses.
2. **HARLEM GLOBETROTTERS TECHNICAL RIDER** shall be attached to, or otherwise made a part of, the Harlem Globetrotters Standard Co-Promotion Agreement.

ACCEPTED AND AGREED:

OPERATOR:	**PRODUCER:**
CONVOCATION CENTER GLOBTROTTERS	**HARLEM**
OHIO UNIVERISTY:	**INTERNATIONAL, INC.:**
By: _____	By: _____

Figure 3.3 Example of a venue contract.

FACILITY RENTAL AGREEMENT

This facility rental agreement is entered into between Ohio University Department of Intercollegiate Athletics (hereinafter, Ohio) and

(hereinafter, Lessee) under the following terms and conditions:

1. Beginning Date: _____ Concluding Date: _____

   Purpose of Activity: _____

2. Person in Charge: _____

   Phone: _____ Email: _____

Ohio agrees that Lessee shall have use of the during the time and for the purpose listed above. No alcohol may be sold, given away, or consumed on Ohio property during the Lessee's use of said facility.

Ohio agrees to make the following arrangements on behalf of Lessee:

Special Arrangements: _____

_____

_____

_____

The Ohio athletic department reserves the right to charge for parking. If this process is instituted for the event, the Ohio athletic department will make all arrangements and benefit from the proceeds.

In consideration for said use of Ohio's facilities, the Lessee agrees to pay Ohio the following charges:

$ _____ Rental

$ _____ Maintenance Support

$ _____ Custodial Support

$ _____ Grounds Support

$ _____ Video Board Rental/Production

$ _____ Event Manager (from Ohio staff)

Lessee agrees to provide upon request of Ohio a public liability insurance policy, in which, Ohio University, its trustee directors, officers, employees, agents, and contractors are named as insurers, and an acceptable Certificate of Insurance, with minimum policy limits of:

- $1,000,000 for injuries, including death, sustained by one person.
- $2,000,000 for injuries, including death, sustained by two or more persons from a single occurrence.
- $500,000 for property damage.

Lessee indemnifies and holds harmless Ohio from any and all claims, demands, actions, liabilities, and attorney fees arising out of, claimed on account of, or in death of, and all persons whatsoever, in any manner caused or contributed to by the Lessee while in, upon, or about the property and/or facility, or while going to or departing from the same.

Any property of Ohio damaged or destroyed by the Lessee incident to the exercise of privileges herein granted shall be promptly prepared or replaced by the Lessee to the satisfaction of Ohio, or in lieu of such repair or replacement, the Lessee shall, if so required, pay to Ohio money in the amount sufficient to compensate for the loss sustained by Ohio.

In occupying the building, property, and/or grounds at the site/facility, the Lessee understands that Ohio does not relinquish the right to control the management thereof, and to enforce all necessary laws, rules, and regulations.

All labor, administrative fees, maintenance, and services not specifically mentioned, but required for the execution of the Lessees' event shall be secured by Ohio and be considered reimbursable costs payable to Ohio by Lessee. Make check payable to the Ohio Athletics Department.

Lessee shall not discriminate in any manner whatsoever on the basis of race, sex, creed, national origin, age, handicap, or sexual preference and shall only use the stated facility for lawful purposes.

This Facility Rental Agreement is neither assignable nor transferable by the Lessee. Ohio reserves the right to determine facility and/or property usage and playability.

In witness whereof, the parties hereto have executed this Facility Rental Agreement on this _____ day of _____, 2016.

_____

Director of Athletics

Lessee:

By _____

_____

Signed By

Figure 3.4 Sample sponsorship contract #1.

<u>Offer to the sponsor (Sponsor Redacted)</u>

Video Board Feature $7,000

Entitlement of one (1) exclusive video board feature per game.

Opportunity beings with 2009 season.

Game Day Promotion at Home Football Stadium $2,000

Opportunity to sponsor Exclusive Day at Home Football Games

<INSERT DATES>

Promotion includes table in the North end zone, ability to distribute materials, exit couponing for upcoming events, and ability to showcase products.

Includes opportunity for Company Trivia at game in which we would take one fan and ask them a multiple choice question about your business animal OR PA announcer could read a Company Trivia Question to all fans and encourage them to submit their answer to the Company table in the endzone.

Successful fan would win a gift from the Company

Also includes two (2) PA announcements during the game

Game Day Promotion at Home Basketball Arena $2,750

Opportunity to sponsor Company Day at Home Basketball Games

Promotion includes table in the concourse, ability to distribute materials, exit couponing for upcoming events and ability to showcase Product.

Includes opportunity for Company Trivia at game in which we would take one fan and ask them a multiple choice question about Company animal OR PA announcer could read a Company Trivia Question to all fans and encourage them to submit their answer to the Company table in the endzone. Successful fan would win a gift from the Company.

Also includes two (2) PA announcements during the game

Video Board Feature $3,000

Entitlement of one (1) exclusive video board feature per game – Company Trivia

Coupon Book $1,000

One (1) ad in 20,000 coupon books to be distributed in at <INSERT DATE> football game and distributed in all football season tickets. Artwork deadline <INSERT DATE>.

Football Game Program $1,500

One (1) half page, black and white program ad

Circulation of 1,000 at each game

Basketball Season Yearbook $1,000

One (1) half page, black and white program ad

Circulation of 2,000 per season

<u>TERMS AND CONDITIONS</u>

1. This proposal is effective through <INSERT DATE>, or until described inventory is sold.
2. The term of this agreement shall be from <INSERT DATES>. Neither party shall have rights defined in this agreement after contract expiration.
3. Payment terms

    CASH:

    BILLING TERMS: Net due upon receipt of invoice. Late payment(s) are subject to interest charges of 1.5% per month (18% APR).
4. In the event that the Company produces a football bowl guide, sponsor would have the choice to participate in the publication at the rate of $1,000 for a full-page ad each year of this agreement. Sponsor will have the opportunity to change the artwork for the football bowl program ad.
5. As used herein, Sponsor includes any successor in interest thereto. This contract is non-cancelable.
6. This agreement is governed by the laws of the state of Ohio.

ACCEPTED AND AGREED:

Sponsor

Anytown University

Phone:

Fax:

By: _____

       Jane Doe

       Vice President

Date: _____

       Company

       107 Main Street

       Anytown, USA

Phone:

By: _____

       John Doe

       General Sales Manager

Date: _____

Phone:

Fax:

Payment Remittance Address:

University Sponsorship Inc.

PO Box 1000

Anytown, USA

Figure 3.5 Sample sponsorship contract #2.

ABC Cycle

100 West Northwest Street

Athens, OH 45701

RE: Letter of Agreement for Sponsorship

This letter of agreement (the *"Agreement"*) by and between ABC Cycle and Ohio University Athletes in Action (OU AIA) sets forth the terms and conditions governing your sponsorship of the O'Bleness Health System Race for a Reason from Feb 22, 2016 to December 31, 2016.

1. <u>SPONSORSHIP EXPOSURE and RACE DAY BENEFITS</u>: OU AIA agrees to provide ABC Cycle with the following:

   - ABC Cycle is the Presenting Sponsor of Family and Student Organizational Triathlon Relay Categories of the O'Bleness Race for a Reason event and will be recognized as such during the Awards Ceremony and other promotional material.
   - ABC Cycle is entitled to set up a tent in the Hospitality Area in Tailgreat Park
   - ABC Cycle is entitled to provide an insert/handout/form of memorabilia to place in all participant race bags.
   - ABC Cycle logo will be placed on the back of all Race For A Reason T-Shirts, to include the Triathlon and Duathlon, 5k Run, 3K Walk, and Mud Run.

2. <u>SPONSORSHIP FEE:</u> ABC Cycle agrees to provide OU AIA with the following:

   - Thirty-four (34) $10 gift certificates from ABC Cycle to OU AIA for use in promoting the Race for a Reason event to be given to participants in the WellWorks triathlon classes and/or promotional incentives for post race surveys.
   - $300 cash sponsorship
   - Six (6) $10 gift certificates to present to the winning Family and Student Organizational Triathlon Relay

By signing below both parties agree to the terms set forth in this agreement.

Signed _____   Signed _____

Johnny Bicycle   **Tri Athlon**

Owner   2015 Race for a Reason Director

ABC Cycle

Student Challenges

NAME _____ DATE_____

Question 3.1

Prepare the Basic Provisions section of an event contract for the following scenario:

Top Ten Entertainment Company produces family ice skating shows called "Ice Games" that are performed in arenas throughout the world. Top Ten Entertainment Company is located at 9500 North Way, New York, New York. Worldwide Arena has agreed to host "Ice Games" this year from February 10th–20th. Worldwide Arena is located at 1000 Union Street, Chicago, Illinois.

Question 3.2

Amy and Brian have been working together for several years. Amy works for an event company that puts on an annual event each year at a venue where Brian works.

Neither Amy's company nor Brian's company requires a formal written agreement for venue rental and this has worked well for the last 5 years as both parties have fulfilled their promises without any problems. Each of the last 3 years has been better than the previous year in terms of revenue and operation of the event.

Four months ago Amy talked with Brian about the event and everyone agreed on the costs, terms, and operating procedures. Today; Amy, her staff and two semitrucks full of event materials pull up to the venue only to find that Brian quit 4 weeks ago and the new venue manager booked a different event during the time Amy had booked for her event.

What recourse does Amy's company have and how likely is she to recover any damages or obtain performance under a contract?

What advice would you give Amy to prevent this situation from happening again in the future?

CHAPTER

4

EVENT SUSTAINABILITY

Michael E. Pfahl, Colleen Theron, and Larissa Prevett

Michael Pfahl, Ph.D., is an Associate Professor of Sport Administration at Ohio University. Previously, Dr. Pfahl was on the Management and Marketing faculties in the International Colleges of Yonok College (Thailand) and Bangkok University (Thailand), respectively. He worked in various management and sales positions with the Cleveland Cavaliers and the Cleveland Lumberjacks during his career. Dr. Pfahl was also the Cofounder and President of Players Management, Inc., a sport marketing and athletic representation firm. Current research interests include the convergence of media, technology and sport, environmentalism and sport, and human resource issues in sport organizations. Dr. Pfahl earned a master in business administration from the University of Toledo along with bachelor, master, and doctorate degrees from Ohio University.

Colleen Theron is qualified as a solicitor in England, Wales, Scotland, and South Africa and holds an LLM in environmental law from the University of Aberdeen (with distinction). Colleen is also the Founder and Director of CLT envirolaw, a niche sustainability company providing specialist advice to companies and directors on sustainability issues. She lectures at Birkbeck University and is a Director of Finance against Trafficking. Colleen is the coauthor of *Strategic Sustainable Procurement: Law and Best Practice for the Private and Public Sectors* and has published broadly on corporate social responsibility (CSR) issues. She also conducts research in the sport sector related to sustainability return on investment.

Larissa Prevett joined CLT envirolaw as a Junior Associate in 2013 and assists clients in the development and implementation of strategic sustainability solutions, including the sustainable management system for the events sector, ISO 20121. She holds an LLB in English law with Hispanic law and an LLM specializing in competition law, both from University College London. Previously, Larissa gained experience in procurement operations at multinational Tata Consultancy Services based in Latin America and she has also worked in London at the British Association for Sustainable Sport (BASIS).

The need to incorporate more environmentally aware operating processes in sport requires sport organization personnel to balance organizational needs with environmental needs. Sustainability and the environment are contested terms that have different meanings for people. In this chapter, **environment** refers to the natural environment and **sustainability** refers to the practices to account for, and as often as possible, to protect the environment in the course of event planning and management operations. Sport event managers, like their counterparts in facility management or front office operations, are important stakeholders in environmental operations of sport events and organizations. They are

© Shutterstock

Event managers should work to protect the environment when planning events.

located at a connecting point between organizational planning and action, in touch with relevant stakeholders and able to influence attitudes, values, and behaviors.

Sport events run across all levels of society, but all impact the environment (Collins, Flynn, Munday, & Roberts, 2007; Collins, Jones, & Munday, 2009; Thibault, 2009). From the substantial and highly visible environmental footprint of the Olympic Games to the local golf course and Little League playing fields, the environment is affected by leisure and recreation. While there is a growing recognition that sport can contribute to economic and social regeneration, there is also a need to recognize its potential and actual detriment to the environment. The detrimental impact could be the construction and management of facilities (Scharfenort, 2012), the costs of transportation, unsustainable water or energy usage, or the manufacturing of equipment and merchandise among many other possibilities.

For example, the estimated carbon impact of the 2010 FIFA World Cup in South Africa, which is estimated to have been the largest emissions of any international sporting event in history, with a carbon footprint of around 1.5–2.5 million tons, depending on the metrics used to calculate it (i.e., actual versus projected) (Environmental Leader, 2010; United Nations Environmental Programme, 2012). Another recent, but significantly different effort, in terms of size and scope, was conducted by the Edmonton Oilers of the National Hockey League (NHL) where unserved food from Rexall Place events (e.g., Oilers, Oil Kings) was donated to a local food bank. The donation to Edmonton's Food Bank included over 1,200 pounds of prepared hamburgers, sausages, pastas, and chicken (Rutt, 2014). The program is the result of a partnership that includes the Edmonton Oilers Community Foundation (EOCF), Northlands (Rexall Place management company), and Dominion Sports Service (DSS, venue food supplier). The partnership assists in the fight against hunger by donating prepared, but unserved food from Oilers, Oil Kings games, and other events at Rexall Place. From this donation alone, Edmonton's Food Bank will be able to provide over 950 meals for its agencies—an opportunity local nonprofit groups jump at to ensure their clients are fed (Rutt, 2014). From this one effort in Edmonton, 5,747 pounds of food was donated during the 2013–2014 season allowing 4,416 meals to be prepared (Rutt, 2014). Many more examples like this take place every day at sporting events around the world.

Exactly how sport personnel at each of these levels undertake environmental planning and action varies by context, but there are several key principles that affect all sport and the natural environment issues (Pfahl, 2011a). The first of these is the fact that there is no end point to environmental issues. The environment will never be free from the influence of humans and all other living organisms that dwell within it. Thus, a strategic focus of continuous improvement and care are needed. Environmental efforts can always stop, but they can never be finished. Second, there is constant tension between individual and group level awareness of environmental issues, knowledge about the intricacies of the issues, and the variety of actions that can be taken across contexts. No single solution will work in all contexts and all contexts are ever changing, hence the need to incorporate the environment into strategic, and not just tactical, processes. Third, sport organizational personnel can only do what they can do. Each sport organization is different across a variety of levels (e.g., fan base, environmental issues, resource availability) and need to accept this as a foundation for environmental work. The importance of this issue is that each case is unique and, while there might be standards to meet or objectives to accomplish, environmental work is related to what can be controlled (Porter & Reinhardt, 2007). Taking a strategic approach and incorporating environmental issues into planning and actions across all organizational units help to keep the issue from becoming purely a marketing exercise or a short-term event campaign without substance. At worst, it grounds sport managers in their actions and focuses them on real action that is less likely to be open to *greenwashing* and other types of negative assessment and commentary.

While not all encompassing of the sport and natural environment context, these principles do provide a philosophical and foundational strategic perspective for sport personnel (Pfahl, 2013). They also help to minimize the challenge of the environmental issue as is it can be considered overwhelming at times. This chapter builds upon this foundation by providing an overview of the sport and natural environment context and the issues associated with it. It also provides a general guide for planning for environmental actions and tactics at events and venues. This chapter should be considered a starting point rather than a comprehensive guide for event management practitioners.

Primary Issues

Events have their own unique issues in terms of content and conduct. The environmental issues associated with them are also unique even if the general idea is similar to other events (e.g., water usage at a stadium) (Schmidt, 2006). Whether an event is a local fun run or a major international competition, environmental impacts are created. Dealing with them in the overall planning and evaluation of the event is crucial. This section provides a general overview of the areas of environmental impact that many, if not most, events have to manage.

Strategic Framework

Goals-Objectives-Tactics-Measures

As noted throughout the book, the foundation of strategic aspects of a sport event or organization is goals, objectives, tactics, and metrics or measures of success (GOTM), and sustainability is no exception. In the case of sustainable events, there are many levels of GOTM, all beginning with the main goals and objectives of the event itself. With so many GOTM elements across the marketing, operations, promotions, and other areas of an event, careful planning is required to make sure they all tie together and support the overall strategic level planning of the event (i.e., why you are holding an event in the first place). This section will focus only on key aspects of planning and managing an event that have a significant impact on the environment in which the event is held. While not comprehensive, these key elements must be integrated with the overall strategic level GOTM elements while simultaneously being comprised of GOTM elements themselves.

Transportation

The first of these key planning and management aspects of an event is the transportation-related issues of events. This issue encompasses all travel before, during, and after an event. Fans have to come to the games, some even for just the experience of being near a game (e.g., tailgating), making transportation and traffic issues a significant environmental area to address. Some venues were able to take travel and traffic issues into consideration when building facilities by virtue of incorporating mass/public transit into the overall venue footprint (e.g., AT&T Park, Candlestick Park in San Francisco). At multiday events (e.g., golf tournaments, motorsport), managing internal traffic flow to and from venue traffic is even more complicated. Some event personnel use carbon offset practices to compensate for limitations in controlling transportation emissions when they cannot effect change of driving to an event. Air quality and emissions is a difficult area for event personnel to control. Much of the issue centers on the transportation surrounding and within events. Working with municipal and private organizations to provide alternative transportation is one step. For example, the Seattle Seahawks, like many teams, post public transportation options and schedules on the team's website. The Seahawks also work with the local airport to provide a discount on parking at the airport's garage for fans who then take the light rail to the stadium on weekends. Encouraging alternative fan behaviors (e.g., carpooling, using bicycles or walking to the event) is another. When the sport itself produces emissions (e.g., motor sport) or the venues (e.g., heating, air condition), **offset programs** help. Offset programs might include buying carbon offset that are linked to renewable energy generation efforts (e.g., through a power provider) that work to balance the emissions from an event with efforts to reduce emissions elsewhere. Sport leagues and teams themselves take steps to reduce air quality and emissions problems. For example, in Formula 1, the teams participating in the sport worked with the Fedération Internationale l'Autombile (FIA) to develop technologies and rules to reduce emissions problems and foster advances in this area in road car technology (FIA, 2013; Formula 1, 2010). The FIA worked with Scolel Te project (Mexico) since 1997 in order to offset emissions from races in the Formula One World Championship (F1) and the World Rally Championship (WRC) through energy credits and tree plantations (Noble, 2007). The WRC, saw the 2013 Rally Australia become the first carbon neutral rally as it "achieved Carbon Neutral Status after offsetting 650 tons of CO_2 (carbon dioxide)" (Event, 2013, para. 2).

Food Waste

As noted earlier, food waste is a concern for event management staff. Sport venues, especially for major events, prepare a great deal of food, much of which is not eaten. Additionally, there is the disposal issue. Food waste and containers need to be managed so compost and recycling can be implemented to the greatest extent possible. Personnel from Waste Management Corporation and the Phoenix Open (golf) worked together to facilitate Waste Management's plan to make events it partners with more sustainable. In this case, "Waste Management will publish a list of sustainable restaurant option for attendees and strive to provide options at every meal that are locally sourced, Certified Organic, or recognized by another third party sustainable food certification" (Phoenix Open, 2014, para. 9). The Natural Resources Defense Council (NRDC), a partner to many sport organizations, leagues, and teams (e.g., National Basketball Association, Major League Baseball, Green Sport Alliance) has its own guide to composting at sporting events that seeks to achieve better preparation and conduct of food waste management as well as influence public and private policy on the issue (e.g., vending practices) (Natural Resources Defense Council, 2014a).

Lighting

The advent of stadium lighting meant games did not have to be confined to the daytime. Over the years, changes to society and sport made night games more attractive for participation, viewing, and revenue generation (e.g., television coverage). The amount of electricity used to power lights at sport events is an important consideration in planning and conducting an event. While simple actions, such as turning off lights when they are not in use, are common sense, significant issues arise in terms of how to build venues with efficient lighting and how to keep the maintenance and replacement costs of lighting to a minimum without sacrificing utility (McClung, 2008). Within sport, there is a shift from considering only initial costs associated with lighting toward more focus on heating, ventilation, and air condition (HVAC) and lighting concerns that account for life-cycle cost analysis to find integrated lighting solutions for different sporting events (McClung, 2008).

Water Usage

Water use has been an area of success in modern sporting venues as new buildings utilize the latest water saving techniques. In event planning, water use ranges from individual consumption to the management of playing surfaces (e.g., golf course). Innovative systems to manage water use are finding their way into venue management and design such as that by the St. Paul Saints in Minnesota (Kimball, 2014). Traditional major events such as a college football game hosting upward of 80,000 spectators requires a shift in water resources for the locale. Water providers in the area direct additional water to the stadium on game days to ensure event needs are met. Water reclamation and treatment at newer venues can reduce in the need for local water to be allocated to the stadium on event days. Of course, the issue of water (and other drinks) served at events is important as the containers and bottles used will contribute to the overall, nonfood waste aspect of events.

Nonfood Waste

General, nonfood waste, is an issue at events too. The more material goods provided or given away to fans, the greater the waste issue becomes. While sport personnel work to reduce or to recycle much of this waste (e.g., cardboard containers), they have to provide a fun and enjoyable event experience (Mallen & Chard, 2011). Reduction and recycling can be incorporated into event operations through stakeholder management practices (e.g., requiring vendors to reduce packaging) or through encouragement programs within event venues (e.g., recycling bins, announcements) (Casper, Pfahl, & McCullough, in press; Hart & Milstein, 2003).

Supply Chain/Vendors

The concept of a **green supply chain** is not a new one, but it is an important one. Sport personnel can utilize the appeal of events to request, and if needed, require, suppliers and vendors to change their parties to become more sustainable (Mamic, 2005; Sarkis, 2007; Walton, Handfield, & Melnyk, 1998). Many aspects of an event require stakeholder, supplier, and/or vendor assistance (e.g., food, waste removal, ticketing). Finding ways to integrate these stakeholders into event planning and to bring environmental concerns to the forefront of planning are a way to address supply chain and vendor issues related to the environment. Clear communication, understanding of separate and shared goals and objectives, and clear measures of success (i.e., metrics) are needed to form partnerships to address environmental issues (Gold, Seuring, & Beske, 2010).

Challenges Ahead

These areas are foundational aspects for most sport events. Planning for ways to address the environmental issues inherent in them is critical for success in greening sporting events. As the future is revealed, Mallen, Adams, Stevens, and Thompson (2010) noted several key challenges for event and facility management. These are described here as examples of future considerations, but they are not the totality of the environmental challenges facing sport personnel today (and tomorrow). They found a need for robust strategies and tools to reduce use of resources in daily operations, training of sport personnel, improved relationships with stakeholders and vendors (e.g., sourcing), and the development for useful measures of success (i.e., metrics) to bring strategic planning and action into a holistic system (see also Hart, 1995; Hart & Dowell, 2011; Hart & Milstein, 2003). As always, the right people must be in place and provided with the support, guidance, and resources needed to address environmental problems … in perpetuity (Mallen, et al., 2010; Pfahl, 2011b). Since there is no end point to sustainability efforts, environmental efforts must become part of the organization's DNA. The next section of the chapter examines the importance of these issues in relation to key business case points.

Macro Issues of Importance to Sport Events

Legal Issues

When planning for a sporting event, it is important to understand all legal requirements for hosting an event. Requirements related to environmental issues must be considered in this process. While fewer national level requirements exist compared with the local level, it is important to know what the requirements are and develop plans to address them. When events are planned, legal issues are at the forefront, but there are also legal issues related to environmental problems that pose liability issues for event organizers (e.g., pollution, waste disposal) (Judge & Douglas, 1998).

In some cases, organizations like the NRDC work with sport personnel to develop and to implement events. The NRDC works with Major League Baseball, the NCAA, and the National Basketball Association, among others, to assist in preparing strategic approaches to environmental work. The NRDC works with these organizations on "everything ranging from their purchasing decisions to transportation choices, energy use, and waste management policies, looking for ways to reduce their environmental impact. And they're encouraging fans to do the same online and in their stadiums and arenas" (Natural Resources Defense Council, 2014b, para. 3). The US Environmental Protection Agency (EPA) also has a range of topics, each with strict regulations regarding the environment. They include regulations related to air, emergencies, cross cutting issues, land and cleanup, pesticides, toxic substances, waste, and water (EPA, 2014b). Many of the regulations are targeted at nonsport activities (e.g., agriculture, electric utilities), but they do provide a departure point for sport event personnel to think through the environmental impacts and legal requirements of their events. However, it is important to remember these regulations are federal, and local and state agencies and governments have their own regulations. Finally, the EPA recognizes the contributions of sport as a platform for environmental awareness and change efforts at the same time it works to regulate sport. To this end, it was founding member of the Green Sport Alliance (Alliance) and produced a set of green sport guidelines and information to help sport personnel assess the environmental impact of their events (EPA, 2014a).

Sport and the Natural Environment Websites

Please visit the following websites to learn more about sport and the natural environment.

1. Green Sport Alliance: http://greensportsalliance.org/
2. Environmental Protection Agency Sport Guide: http://www2.epa.gov/green-sports
3. Natural Resources Defense Council: http://www.nrdc.org/greenbusiness/guides/sports/

Event rights holders and leagues also provide guidelines for events. At the international level, both FIFA and the International Olympic Committee have environmental guidelines for hosting World Cup and Olympic Games, respectively (FIFA, 2014; Samuel & Stubbs, 2013). League personnel are working to bridge the information— practice gap by working with organizations like the NRDC and teams (e.g., green weeks, stadium construction, operations, and maintenance). The Green Sport Alliance has "a mission to help sports teams, venues and leagues enhance their environmental performance. Alliance members represent over 220 sports teams and venues from 16 different sports leagues" (2014, para. 1). Green Sport Alliance personnel facilitate communication and information sharing among its members, which includes sport teams, leagues, and external partners such as the NRDC (Pfahl, 2013).

Codes and Standards

Codes and standards play an important role in encouraging companies to adopt sustainable practices. They can provide a common understanding of **corporate social responsibility (CSR)** issues and a more uniform approach to managing environmental, social, and economic risks. CSR efforts are the ways organizational personnel demonstrate a concern for society through a variety of activities including efforts toward sustainability and caring for the natural environment (Paramio-Salcines, Babiak, & Walters, 2013).

Events can show a concern for the environment and demonstrate corporate social responsibility.

The International Organization for Standardization (ISO) has long been a leader in evaluating quality of processes for products and services. Specifically, ISO 26000 and ISO 20121, with their emphasis on sustainable development principles, have changed the way organizations think about social and environmental impacts. Leadership in Energy and Environmental Design (LEED) is a certification program for buildings developed by the US Green Building Council. As a global certification standard, it uses a four level certification system for existing and new buildings and provides helpful tools and metrics to assist in planning, implementation, and review efforts. Certification also informs customers that a supplier (e.g., food caterers to a venue, such as Sodexho) implemented a management system conforming to certain standards (Theron & McKenzie, 2012).

Some examples of codes and standards tailored toward events industries, along with links for additional information, include:

- The American Standard for Testing and Materials (ASTM) (previously known as the American Society for Testing and Materials), General Meetings Standards
- Global Reporting Initiative G4 Reporting Framework and the Events Organizers Sector Supplement (https://www.globalreporting.org/Pages/default.aspx);
- ISO 20121 (http://www.iso.org/iso/iso20121)

What is ISO 20121?

ISO 20121 is one example of a framework for the implementation of a sustainable management system and is a standard designed to help the events industry improve the sustainability of their activities, products, and services. It is intended to integrate sustainability into the management practices of events, sports, and hospitality industries—operationally and strategically. It can be applied by any organization in the events sector, including organizers, venues, and suppliers (ISO n.d.).

It is based on a British predecessor from 2007, the *BS901 Specification for a Sustainability Management System for Events* and was formally launched for the London Olympics in 2012 (International Standards Organization, 2012) The involvement of the London Organizing Committee of the Olympic and Paralympic Games (LOCOG) (London Legacy Development Corporation, 2012) in developing the standard means it is an important part of the London 2012 legacy. A few years on from the event and its proliferation in the sporting sector it is beginning to take off. ISO 20121 requires organizational personnel to focus on the following aspects (London Legacy Development Corporation, 2012):

- Economic—operating in a way that is financially viable for the organization, its customers and suppliers
- Environmental—minimizing the use of resources and reducing waste
- Social—considering the needs and expectations of those affected by the organization or event

Although it follows the same formula as other ISO standards, namely a PLAN, DO, CHECK, ACT process grounded in relevant goals, objectives, tactics, and measures (GOTM), it is not a checklist. This distinguishes it from the abovementioned ASTM General Meetings Standards, too. Through the implementation of ISO 20121, an organization involved in the events sectors can innovate, drive continuous improvement and add value. These are broader business benefits, which should translate into financial gain, as well as cultural and performance gains. This means that ISO 20121 is not simply about environmental or green issues and is not the same as ISO 14001, which is an international standard for environmental management not specific to the events sector. ISO 14001 only deals with environmental impacts, whereas ISO 20121 is a holistic standard, which requires leadership, understanding internal and external risks to the organization, and emphasizes communication and supply chain awareness. These are all critical elements of a comprehensive and systematic sustainability strategy (Introductory Guide on ISO 20121, CLT envirolaw, 2014; Theron & Prevett, in press).

Getting certified to a standard, such as ISO 20121, or having an organization's sustainability credentials assured by an independent third party has its advantages. From data verification to report assurance, such independent assessments of an organization's sustainability performance increases a brand's credibility, accountability, and transparency and is particularly valuable for attracting investment. Moreover, a robust assurance process can create a benchmark and highlight opportunities for continuous improvement (iCompli Sustainability, 2014). The AA1000 Assurance Standard was specifically developed by sustainability professionals in response to stakeholder concerns that accounting standards such as the ISAE 3000 were too narrow in focus. The AA1000 Assurance Standard looks at inclusivity, materiality, and responsiveness and considers whether organization personnel are targeting the most significant sustainability challenges and opportunities. In contrast an ISAE 3000 engagement only looks at verifying specific numbers and not the holistic picture, which can result in a lengthy, cumbersome, and costly process (London Legacy Development Corporation, 2012).

Cost Reduction

Questions are often asked as to whether environmental initiatives are worth the cost. While this issue is contingent on many variables, especially the ability to plan and to implement environmental initiatives, there are ways to examine the direct and indirect costs of environmental efforts (Whistler, 2020, 2015). Further, interviews from a pilot study conducted by CLT envirolaw demonstrated that those implementing sustainability in sports organizations mainly view it as being green and also being costly. The principal findings can be summarized as follows (Theron and Prevett in press):

- Cost reduction was the only driver, and lack of budget the only barrier, cited by more than half the organizations in the survey.
- Sustainability measures focused on those areas with the highest potential for cost reductions, particularly in energy management. These were the same measures for which some participants were able to provide return on investment (ROI) figures.
- Venues that are competing for both sporting and commercial events (e.g., ExCel and Millennium Stadium) used their sustainability credentials to attract these customers. Other venues, particularly those associated with well-known brands linked to a single sport (e.g., Lord's and Emirates), did not feel this was a driver.
- Stakeholder engagement was undertaken by all venues as part of their sustainability strategies. All organizations stated that the engagement process has been beneficial.
- Difficulty in projecting direct financial returns for a measure can be a barrier to getting a budget for its implementation. This is particularly the case for social measures such as community engagement.
- The drivers and benefits for ISO 20121 for the participating venues were varied. Some saw it as a seal of approval whilst others used it as a framework for delivering other benefits. All certified or soon-to-be certified venues believe the standard has overcome the barrier of showing where sustainability fits within the broader strategy of the organization (i.e., overall GOTM).
- The majority of organizations stated that improved supply chain management and/or understanding of legal compliance issues were a benefit resulting from implementing a sustainability strategy. However, no participant provided ROI figures for these benefits.

Further, Willard (2012) refers to the executive mindset having to evolve from seeing early sustainability initiatives, those labeled green, environmental, and sustainable, as an expensive and bureaucratic impediment to success. However, the business case for sustainability is growing as many organizations are beginning to see the value in implementing either a sustainability management standard or committing to a sustainability standard. In some cases, returns have even been identified or measured. For example, the costs saved by the personnel at Aviva Stadium in Dublin, Ireland, who adopted BS9801, the predecessor for ISO 20121, demonstrates the business case for implementing a sustainability management system through its significantly improved processes and operations.

Case Study : The Value of Standards

The Aviva Stadium in Dublin, Ireland is BS901 certified. The venue's business case (Kirwin, 2013) demonstrates the broad benefits of implementing a sustainability management system, as a result of improved processes and operations. Effective waste and resources management strategies have led to the following:

- 400,000 liters of water saved annually
- Use of low impact materials such as GGBS concrete, a strengthening material used in the creation of concrete, saved approximately 4000 tCO_2 in embodied energy
- CO_2 savings equate to removing 1,280 automobiles from the road for 1 year
- 62% of all waste generated was recycled in 2012
- Diesel oil generator reduced carbon emissions by 50%
- Between 2010 and 2011, electrical usage was reduced by 26%
- **The significant savings have released €100,000 to be spent on an annual community fund (approximately US$135,000).**

Future Thinking: From Process Improvement to Innovation

Nike personnel stated that a key part of their sustainability strategy is not just about improving existing products through streamlined processes, but that it is also about innovation. That is, inventing better products (Nike, 2014). However, not many sport organizations are as far advanced in their thinking as Nike. Driving innovation constitutes the ultimate value add; however, many sporting clubs, venues, brands, and even apparel and equipment manufacturers are only now beginning to focus on process improvement as a means of reducing costs. In event management terms, this might mean finding ways to routinize aspects of the event planning process throughout the various events held by a sport organization. Use of a single, digital registration website, for example, might help to streamline operations and to alleviate certain resource usage. Larger scale events and those held often can benefit from the process elements, but it is the smaller events that might be held once per year, that are difficult to find continuous innovation in sustainability.

Sponsorship Opportunities

Major sporting events bring benefits to the represented sport and the local communities where they are held (e.g., media coverage, tourist spending). McKinsey & Company (2014) reported that sponsorship revenue for the World Cup in Brazil will have increased by 10% over that of the World Cup in South Africa, standing at an estimated $1.4 billion in sponsorship deals. This is still far below the US corporate spending on sports sponsorships, which was estimated to grow to $20.6 billion in 2014 (Schultz, 2014). Figures such as these reinforce the notion that brands are eager to associate themselves with sports, especially by leveraging the excitement of competition and the emotional connection fans have with their teams and each other. A recent development in the world of sports sponsorships is the interest companies are showing in the industry's sustainability works. For example, Dow, a packaging solutions company, decided to partner with the Sochi Winter Olympic Games in 2014 in order to increase its brand loyalty and raise awareness of its products range that can contribute to the improved sustainability performance of organizations (Dow, 2014; University of Pennsylvania, 2013).

The success of such sponsorships depends, to a large extent, on the alignment between a company's message and the green sports initiative it sponsors. What is surprising from the McKinsey & Company (2014) report is that about a third of US companies do not have a system in place to measure sponsorship ROI comprehensively let alone for environmentally related opportunities.

Case Study : Sustainability as Part of the Game Plan

Sustainability was given a prominent role in the build up toward, and throughout the duration of, the 2012 Olympic Games. In many ways, the event created a platform for promoting sustainability leadership in the sports sector by making it a priority of the Games and elevating its exposure in the public eye. The event has undoubtedly shaped the entire sporting community's attitude toward the importance of its own sustainability, but to what end and extent is not clear.

Obtaining Sponsorship

Above all, the event confirmed the marketing value of sustainability strategies. In particular, the LOCOG was able to use its sustainability strategy to engage with sponsors, many of whom wanted to improve their own sustainability credentials by collaborating with Olympia and becoming associated with London 2012.

Legacy

LOCOG personnel sought to demonstrate strong sustainability leadership and did so to great effect. For many sporting organizations, the event is likely to have put sustainability on the map for the first time. However, there is also a question of whether the Olympics can be criticized for overshadowing the achievements of venues who have been pursuing a sustainability strategy for longer term and whose practices have been developed to a higher standard than those adopted by LOCOG during London 2012.

Context

Undeniably the Olympics raised the profile of sustainability in the sport and event sector significantly and this merits special recognition as there may be less motivation to implement a sustainability strategy when there is no long-term gain involved. Contrastingly, ensuring good sustainability credentials is easier when limited to a particular event, albeit very complex and large-scale, and for a set duration. Although desirable, it is perhaps less realistic for venues to fervently prioritize sustainability habitually and it is more interesting to see how venues used during the Olympics, such as ExCel, continue to demonstrate leadership and make sustainability core to its business on an on-going basis.

Stakeholder Engagement

Stakeholder engagement and participation practices are increasingly becoming part of mainstream business. There are many advantages to implementing engagement programs, including:

- Improving communication
- Building wider community support and buy-in for projects
- Gathering useful data and ideas

Stakeholders are those groups who affect and/or could be affected by an organization's activities, products and services, and associated performance (Sport + Recreation Alliance, 2014). At a sports club (i.e., team), for example, there are many stakeholders, including managers and directors, athletes, employees, fans, local community, media, suppliers, and any relevant governing bodies.

Assessing and Measuring Sustainability of Events

There is limited information on measuring and assessing the impact of sports events. This is primarily because many metrics and measures have historically been built for the issues at hand. There are a various set of inputs represented by financial, human, infrastructure, plans, and policies to ensure that an event is carried out and completed. The outputs can be both direct and indirect. Direct outputs include financial outputs in the form of ticket sales, sponsorship, and media (Raj & Musgrave, 2009). Indirect outputs include visitor satisfaction, and brand management along with the impact on linked industries such as hotels, bars, and cities where visitors may spend time and money (Raj & Musgrave, 2009).

Professional Career Impact

For sport personnel, environmental issues can provide an important career path. While it is difficult to say how sport organizations and events will ultimately incorporate management and oversight of environmental issues (e.g., green teams, sustainability coordinators), this area of sport has a variety of impacts on daily sport jobs (Casper & Pfahl, 2012; Pfahl, 2011a, 2011b). This might take the form of working on a green team for a sports organization or having a person in charge of finding an environmental partner for an event. It might just simply be a person who is asked to recycle in the office.

Mallen, et al. (2010) examined the breadth of environmental issues in sport and raised several key points as to the skills future sport managers will need in relation to sport and the environment. While these issues are related primarily to facility management positions, they do have links to other aspects of sport organization and event management (e.g., marketing). The skills include awareness of environmental issues (see also Casper, Pfahl, & McSherry, 2012), the capacity to understand and evaluate procurement issues related to environmentally friendly options (e.g., cleaning products), understanding of environmental technologies (e.g., solar panels, HVAC), leadership skills related to environmental efforts, LEED and other standardization and guidelines programs, and overall strategic understanding of environmental issues and initiatives within organizational and event contexts (e.g., environmental implications of facility management). Academic preparation for sport organizations and event personnel is incorporating content related to sport and the environment to meet industry needs for students (i.e., premanagers) as a way to understand and to influence future practices (Casper & Pfahl, 2012; Mallen & Chard, 2011).

SUMMARY

This chapter provided an overview of the issues and processes associated with making sport events more environmentally friendly and sustainable. While it is not prescriptive, it provided a way to understand the issues involved in greening sport events as well as laid a foundation for individual sport managers to understand and to evaluate their events. In the end, the contextuality and uniqueness of each event means that custom approaches to going green are needed. Even within the same event history, last year's issues are not necessarily those of the following year. Sport plays a significant role in the lives of people around the world making the environmental side of sport events both important to our lives and to the future continuation of the sport events we enjoy.

Student Challenges
Event Sustainability

NAME _____ DATE_____

Question 4.1

Please examine the information found at the Whistler 2020 webpage that explores the cost argument for environmental efforts (http://www.whistler2020.ca/whistler/site/genericPage.acds?instanceid=196 7867&context=1967866) and the Natural Resources Defense Council's *GameChanger* reports (http:// www.nrdc.org/greenbusiness/guides/sports/game-changer.asp). Below, you will find a series of strategic questions designed to improve your strategic thinking processes about and understanding of direct and indirect environmental costs related to sporting events. From an event manager's perspective, think about a recent sport event that you watched, attended, or participated in. You can then work to find answers to these important questions as they would be integral to strategic thinking and planning for an event.

- What products were used that were made from nonsustainable materials or made from nonsustainable practices, including venues or event locations? What products were made from sustainable materials or made from sustainable practices?
- What are associated environmental and/or health impacts felt from the use of these products?
- What are the associated costs from the use of the nonsustainable and sustainable products?
- In what ways might the event in question have left a better or worse environment than before it was held?

Question 4.2

Motorsport is not often thought to be at the forefront of environmental efforts. However, the highest levels of motorsport are undertaking efforts to become environmentally responsible events. The Federation Internationale de l'Automobile (FIA), the governing body for many of the world's motorsport series, enacted new environmental initiatives and guidelines designed to improve motorsports' environmental footprint (http://www.fiainstitute.com/sustainability-programme/Pages/ home.aspx.htm). Like the International Olympic Committee, the FIA made the environment one of its cornerstone pillars (along with road safety). The FIA's efforts can be seen at events such as the Wales Rally GB (http://www.walesrallygb.com/about/carbonneutral_r_event.php) and Rally Australia (http://www.rallysportmag.com.au/home/wrc/9295-rally-australia-claims-another-world-first). Please review these areas and answer the following questions.

- Please review the chapter's key planning and management aspects of sustainable events. In what ways did the organizers of these two events address the key elements discussed?
- How did the event planners utilize the goals, objectives, tactics, and measures (GOTM) framework outlined in this book and chapter?
- In what ways might the public relations (e.g., *greenwashing* charges) need to be handled for motorsport events like these given the seemingly contradictory messages of the event planner's efforts with the type of event held?
- Please review and evaluate the FIA's environmental efforts. What role can this governing body continue to play in environmental efforts in motorsport?
- NASCAR is another, although North American-based, governing body like the FIA. Please review NASCAR's environmental information (http://green.nascar.com/). How do the efforts of NASCAR compare with those of the FIA?

EVENT BUDGET

Michelle Wells

Michelle Wells is a Visiting Instructor of Sport Studies at Guilford College in Greensboro, NC. She began teaching undergraduate students in 2008 and has taught event management, sports marketing, sports communication, sports law, and international sports. Prior to teaching, Michelle worked in event management for various organizations, including ESPN (Disney's) Wide World of Sports, Disney's Animal Kingdom, and New York Road Runners. She has managed and/or worked over 200 sports and entertainment events throughout her career. She received her bachelor's degree in business administration (marketing) from the University of Florida and a master's degree in sports administration and facility management from Ohio University.

One of the most essential aspects of creating any event is the budget: how much is it going to cost and how much money can the event make? Creating a budget is one of the areas that allow event managers to determine the scope of the event. They can add specific items that can take the event from a mere well-organized and functioning event to an over-the-top festivity that creates a WOW factor for everyone involved. Conversely, the budget may require scaling back on certain areas to ensure it meets the financial goals of the organizers. Creating the initial budget when assessing feasibility is one of the factors that will help event managers determine if an event gets the signal to go or no-go. This chapter provides a framework for drilling down into the budget detail that is necessary as the event is developed. **So that it does not have to be noted in each of the following sections, every budget item presented is going to vary by event depending on the type and scope of the event.**

Revenue Streams

In most cases, sports are a business and events are usually in business to make money. Hopefully that is not a surprise at this point. In order to make money, an event must have revenue streams that exceed costs to put on the event. The exception relates to those events that have a mission that is nonrevenue related (e.g., participatory in nature, charity, or community involvement), or those that are focused on generating economic impact to the locale. If a community believes that an event that is brought into a community will generate a significant amount of money via economic impact, they may be willing to cover the cost of producing the event. The event makes money, but in a slightly different way that is not direct revenue.

Registration and Processing Fees

For participation-driven events, the obvious revenue stream is the fee that participants pay to enter competition, or **registration fee**. This amount may determine whether an event should occur; it depends on how confident the event organizers are that they can bring in money from other revenue sources, especially sponsorship. If an event is very popular and has a cap on the number of participants, there is another revenue stream that an event may charge—a processing fee. A **processing fee** is the amount charged to participants for the right to enter the lottery or other selection process associated with the event. Some events will accept a large number of applications and then have a drawing or lottery to determine which registered participants gain entrance to the event. The event still has to process those prospective entrants' applications and all of their information, and there are costs associated with that work. If the event managers are using a third-party company for online registration, part of that fee will likely go to the registration company as part of their payment. It is money that the event will bill immediately and it may be $5–$10 for the fee, for example. An event in this situation of having a waiting list will not bill the participant for the actual registration fee unless or until that person is chosen in the lottery. They would not want to incur the administrative cost of refunding the fee to the person, plus the event probably would have already paid the processing fee to the credit card company, hence in net, they could lose money. The processing fee, however, is billed immediately when a participant registers. The lottery selection could be several months after a participant registers, which means that it will impact the event's cash flow. The processing fee is charged at the time that a person registers and is nonrefundable. This allows the organization to increase cash flow in the build-up to the lottery selection. For example, if a marathon has a cap of 20,000 runners, the event may get 35,000 applicants. With a $5 processing fee, that is an additional $175,000 of revenue for the event, and with a $10 fee it is an additional $350,000 of revenue.

Merchandise and Concession Sales

Merchandise sales can be a significant contribution to an event's revenue. Well-designed souvenir T-shirts, hats, jackets, and pins can bring in large amounts of money. People often want a souvenir to show where they have been and where they have competed (or where their family member has competed).

Along with merchandise sales, concessions can be a lucrative revenue stream. Generally, people purchase food and beverages when they attend sports events. A trend in food and beverage over the last decade has been to offer healthier options and regionalized selections. This is a plus for participant-driven events whose customers may be seeking something healthier than hot dogs and potato chips. When reading through the merchandise information, be aware that a lot of the information is similar for concessions.

Per Caps

When a new event is created, it is often hard to determine what the merchandise sales will be. The only likely possibility is to compare the new event with other similar events, if the organizers have access to that information. For existing events, the rights holder should be able to provide the event organizer with data on past merchandise sales. Taking the amount of merchandise sales and dividing by the number of participants gives the per capita amount of merchandise sales, or merchandise per cap. **Per capita spending, or per cap,** is the amount of money spent per person during an event. Per caps for concessions are calculated the same way. Most times, though, it is important to also know the ratio of spectators or family members to participants. This total ratio of people attending to the amount of merchandise sold will give the best number for merchandise per cap. For the event's rights holder, this is an important number to track for each event. When the event is up for bid, merchandise sales is a significant figure for the rights holder to be able to relay to the bidder. Often, percentage of gross sales agreements are made, and both parties will receive a percentage of merchandise sales. The revenue generated by each party depends on the agreement between the two parties. The bidding city may even have a third-party vendor provide the merchandise sales, but they would still have to honor the split in the agreement with the city. Even with the lower amount that the city will receive because of its agreement with a third-party vendor, this may be the best choice if the venue does not have merchandise sales capability. Merchandise revenue split percentages with third-party companies are going to vary from deal to deal, depending on the negotiated terms.

Types of Financial Agreements

There are three main types of financial agreements with respect to merchandise: flat fee, per person fee, or percentage of gross sales. In a **flat fee agreement,** the facility or city charges the event a flat fee for the right to set up and sell products. This arrangement is the easiest for both the venue and the event manager to keep track of, since it is a one-time payment. A **per person fee** agreement is structured so that the event is charged a small amount for each person in attendance. The rationale is that the larger the event, the more likely it is that the event will generate more revenue from sales. This is difficult for events such as a road race, where accurate attendance figures may not be available and the main purchasers will be participants and not spectators. Any time a per-person fee is being considered, research into past events related to per cap spending is critical. Event managers should not enter into these agreements without a solid understanding of expected sales. In both the flat fee agreement and the per-person fee, the venue has little involvement in the operation and accounting related to sale. These functions are passed on to those involved in the event. In a percentage of gross sales agreement, this changes a bit. Percentage of gross sales is the most popular type of agreement for sports events. In **percentage of gross sales** agreements, the event splits their gross revenue with the venue (or city in the case of many nontraditional venues). Common splits can be 70% to the event and 30% to the venue, or 80% to the event and 20% to the venue. Since the amount earned by each party is determined by sales figures, this type of agreement requires involvement of both venue or city personnel and event personnel in accounting for and reconciling sales figures to ensure agreement.

Specialty Merchandise Types

Souvenirs to "prove" that a person attended or participated in an event can amount to significant sales with the right type of products available. Merchandise pieces are also great souvenirs to allow people to hold on to the memories associated with the event. The obvious sales are at the event itself and of gear associated with the event, merchandise that simply has the event name on it. There are other merchandise revenue streams. For road races and triathlons, events that in most cases only require a person to register for the event rather than qualify for it, an event can create "In Training" gear. This line will often only be a couple of pieces, such as a T-shirt and maybe a cap or jacket. This can be sold beginning when registration opens. It allows participants to let others know of their commitment and intention to participate. Another line of gear is "Finisher Gear." Particularly for notoriously challenging events, being a finisher is a significant accomplishment. A similar merchandise line for team events are products with the score on them or "champion" title. These special lines of merchandise are completely different lines of merchandise and should not cannibalize the sales of the regular merchandise. Limited edition or collectors' items may not be as popular as general merchandise, but can still generate revenue. Items that may fall into this category include such things as trading pins and artwork. For more traditional sports events that have extraordinary importance, ticket display frames or acrylics are very popular with spectators. T-shirts and/or signs available immediately after the event noting the final score or the winning team also sell well as exuberant fans are eager to spend money on their way out of the venue.

Transportation

Another potential revenue stream, dependent upon the event, is transportation. If the event has to provide any sort of transportation or shuttle, the event may choose to charge a fee for the service. This fee may not cover the entire cost, but it can help offset what may be a huge expense.

Ancillary Events

Ancillary events add to the atmosphere of an overall event and are a great way to include family and friends in the festivities. They can also be additional revenue streams. Some events may require a ticket for admission, such as a pasta party, a concert, or an after-party celebration. Others may collect a registration fee, such as a fun run, slam dunk contest, or kids' race. Some events add ancillary events without the expectation of making money. The organizers may view them as benefits to the participants and consider them a success as long as the costs are covered, or they may even absorb the costs in the overall event.

Tickets

Chapter 12 covers Event Ticketing in depth, but there are parts of ticketing that relate to the budget that event managers should bear in mind. If the event managers are not responsible for managing ticket sales, it is important for them to work closely with the ticketing manager to determine the ticket prices for the event. Good ticket managers can provide valuable input to make sure the event does not price itself out of the market. They will also make sure event managers are aware of the associated costs of ticketing, such as staffing, printing, technology equipment, and so on.

Sponsorship

While there are costs associated with fulfilling the sponsorship, for many events sponsorship is a primary revenue stream. The percentage of the revenue spent on fulfillment varies, but the majority of the sponsorship is usually revenue to the event. Pricing a sponsorship and fulfillment are covered in Chapter 7, but event managers need to know that not all of the sponsorship amount will be revenue to the event. The entire amount will be entered as revenue for the event, but the corresponding costs of fulfilling the sponsorship (e.g., printing signage, activating the sponsorship) will be tracked in expenses. The net difference between the sponsorship amount and the fulfillment costs will be the sponsorship revenue for the event. As with ticketing, event managers will partner with their sponsorship sales team if the event managers are not selling the sponsorships themselves.

Travel packages are another area that some events, particularly larger events, may have as revenue streams, but they're not necessarily common for small or medium events. Because of this, they are covered in more depth in Chapter 10 Event Travel Packages and Sports Tourism.

Expenses

Expenses are something that every event has to balance with revenue. There may be a lot of great ideas for events and various add-ons for events, but if the money is not there to pay for them, they are not going to be put in place. Calculating and managing expenses is one of the necessary, but not always fun, parts of event management. Being fiscally responsible can help boost event managers' careers. Several big-ticket categories are going to make up a vast majority of an event's budget. Those categories include: venue rental, accommodations (hotels), meals, transportation, ancillary events, equipment, and staff salaries. Big-ticket items, though, are not the only items that go into an event budget. Some of those additional cost areas are covered with a few notes that may be helpful to event managers as they create their budgets.

Venue Rental

Whether an event takes place in a shopping mall parking lot or a multimillion dollar arena, the venue where it is held is more than likely going to charge a rental fee. This amount could not only take up a significant piece of the budget, but could also impact cash flow for the event. Depending on when the contract with the venue states that deposits and/or payments have to be made, the event could be required to pay out cash before revenue streams come into the budget. Those details of the rental contract are important for event managers to know and understand as they work on the budget so they can calculate how much up-front money will be required to be spent on the event.

Housing/Accommodations

Various groups require housing and accommodations. If elite athletes participate in the event, the organizers often pay for their hotel rooms and travel. When a National Governing Body (NGB) or rights holder puts an event out for bid, part of the contract with the host location will include receiving complimentary room nights based on the number purchased by attendees. The travel partner will often include in the contract that they keep a small amount that is used to house their staff on-site during the event. In the contract with the rights holder, the rights holder will usually require a certain number of complimentary room nights that must be at one or two of the host hotels and cannot be split between more than two hotels.

Large events may have costs before they even know whether they will be selected to host the event. For a city that bids to host events owned by rights holders, there are expenses associated with the bid. Depending on the rights holder's specific bid requirements, the city may have to pay for travel, accommodations, meals, or some combination for rights holder representatives to tour the proposed event location(s) and meet city officials. The bidding process could encompass several trips. Once a city is selected, the event organizers may still be required to pay for regular planning trips for the rights holder's staff.

For events that require hotel rooms, the event selects one or two host hotels, but may also block rooms in several additional hotels that aren't designated as "host" locations. The deal they, or more likely their travel partner, negotiate with the hotel is to give the event organizer a certain number of complimentary room nights (comp rooms) for every "x" room nights booked that are associated with the event. The general ratio ranges anywhere from one comp room per twenty (1:20) to fifty (1:50) room nights booked, depending on the city, the hotel, and the event. This ratio applies to all hotels where the event has blocked rooms. The sports commission or event organizer either has to pay for the rooms they have agreed to give various groups or they will have to use comp rooms.

If the number of comp rooms received is not large enough to cover the allotted rooms, the event will have to pay for the additional rooms out of its budget. They may be able to negotiate a rate that is lower than the rate provided to participants. Often, events agree to pay for rooms for rights holders, officials, and some out-of-town staff. The event may also pay for rooms for its own staff. For multiday events, staff members are usually required to be available for long hours. It is beneficial to have them near the event site rather than worry about them commuting on little sleep or getting stuck in traffic.

Meals

Meals can be a difficult item to justify, but create a lot of goodwill. They are often a necessity during planning meetings, especially with the rights holder. There may be several people in both groups and several meals over a number of days. Do not overlook these in the budget. With event planning meetings, it is important to realize that if the first planning meeting has food, even if it is only snacks and soda, the expectation will be that all of them will have food provided. These various items will start to add up and must be accounted for in the budget or they will use up the contingency money.

During the event, staff members have to eat and it is not easy for them to break away to go get food. Even when they can, the cost often comes back to the event when employees charge the meals on their expense report. It is easier for the event to pay for their food by providing catering or boxed sandwiches. One area where food is going to be required is for volunteers. Volunteers are covered more thoroughly in the Chapter 15 Event Volunteer Management, but remember that volunteers are not "free," they are just less expensive than part-time staff. Meals are usually one of the expense areas related to utilizing volunteers. Another food cost may be for participants. For long races, such as marathons, half-marathons, or triathlons, runners usually expect some type of food at the end. Even for many youth events, the competition days are very long and participants should have access to water and possibly high-energy snacks throughout the day. The goal for an event is to have a sponsor provide the product, but if that does not happen, the event will have to pay for it. The best practice is to put the amount in the budget at the beginning. If a sponsor provides the product, that amount will be a budget savings.

Transportation

Transportation is not something that every event supplies, but when it is provided, it costs the organizers a great deal of money. In addition to the obvious cost of paying for the vans/buses, it is also necessary to pay for the staff that helps to manage the transportation during the event. Companies that manage transportation have the expertise required to plan and manage the routes. Different transportation plans are often needed for different groups. Staff may be asked to park at a distant location and take a shuttle to the site. At an event like the Daytona 500, spectators park in many different lots and take buses to the track. Even a college football game may provide ancillary parking at a local mall with shuttle service to campus in an effort to alleviate game day traffic. Participants may be provided with transportation from host hotels to a marathon starting line. Elite-level participants, sponsors, and VIPs may all have separate transportation. For team events, police escorts may be needed to help buses to negotiate game day traffic in a timely manner. Some municipalities will provide this service at no cost, while others will charge for it. There are multiple combinations, and they can all be very complicated to execute. Having the right plans developed by professionals is vital, but as with the buses themselves, they are part of expenses.

Ceremonies

Ceremonies and special activities or parties add a great deal to the atmosphere and image of an event. Along with those great benefits, though, come the costs of putting on the activities. Ceremonies could be large, entertainment-filled productions such as the opening ceremonies of the Special Olympics World Games and a Super Bowl half-time show, or smaller, straightforward affairs such as trophy presentations after a soccer tournament. For a party or ceremony, the three biggest cost items are usually the food and beverage (especially if alcohol is involved), entertainment, and labor.

At first thought, it may seem that the venue would be one of the largest expenses. For large ceremonies, that may be the case and the venue will need to be booked for rehearsal (and the rehearsal included in the entertainers' schedules). For most venues that host special events, the venue is free as long as a certain amount of food and beverage are purchased. If an event has sponsors who provide beverages in-kind (alcoholic and/or nonalcoholic) as part of their sponsorship, event managers need to be certain to ask the venue what companies have pouring rights at the venue. This also goes for hotels where an event might host a lounge or suite for VIPs, sponsors, entertainers, and/or elite athletes.

Just because an event's sponsor(s) has pouring rights at a venue does not mean that the event will not be charged. A key factor to determine is whether the venue will charge corkage fees on sponsor products and how much. **Corkage fee** is a charge exacted at a hotel/venue/restaurant for every bottle of beverage (liquor, water, soda, isotonic drink, juice, etc.) served that was not bought on the premises. If sponsor food products are approved by the venue to be brought in, the event may still be required to purchase a certain amount of catering from the venue or pay a venue rental fee.

Expo

Some events hold an expo (short for exposition) as part of their activities, particularly larger road races, cycling events, and triathlons. An **expo** is a sponsor and/or vendor display that often ties into a larger event. It offers an additional way for sponsors and/or vendors to connect with their expanded target audience. An expo is going to be an expense, but could also potentially be a revenue stream. The biggest expense categories are going to be the venue, drayage, labor for the build out, shipping, and the design, artwork, and signage. **Drayage** is the monetary charge for pick-up and hauling of containers. As it relates to an expo, the containers usually hold the display equipment that exhibitors set up at expos. When event managers evaluate whether to have an expo, they need to first determine the purpose for their expo. If they determine that it is a fit for their event, the next step is to determine where to hold it. The venue selection, location, accessibility, flexibility, and number of booths it can accommodate will all impact the cost of the expo and contribute to its revenue generation potential.

Equipment

Equipment is going to be a big expense for most events. There are several considerations that will impact equipment expenses. One of them is whether to rent or buy equipment. This is covered in more depth in Chapter 18, Event Operations. For this chapter it is more important to know that equipment costs could be one of the event's major category expenses. Chapter 13 Event Documents contains a detailed list of possible items that event managers may need to have for events. This list is not exhaustive, but it is a start to help event managers as they begin to plan and create their event budget.

Staff Salaries

Full-time, part-time, or intern, staff must be paid. The regular schedule of their pay will impact the cash flow of the event organizers and require that money is on-hand and/or regularly available to meet these payment demands. In addition to the salary, benefits have to be calculated into the cost for the employees receiving benefits (generally this only applies to full-time employees). As a guideline, the cost of benefits above salary is about 30%–35%. As an example, if an employee earns an annual salary of $40,000, the actual cost of that employee to the company is $52,000–$54,000 ($40,000 × .3 = $12,000 and $40,000 + 12,000 = $52,000 or $40,000 × 1.3 = $52,000 and $40,000 × 1.35 = $54,000).

Staffing Areas

Chapter 14, Event Staffing, will cover the details of the actual staffing. This section will highlight staffing related to the event's budget and what items event managers may need to include in a budget. The quantity will be determined by the specific characteristics of each event and the contract with the venue.

Officials

There are various levels of officials. This category may include referees for actual events, master schedulers, tournament oversight officials, and/or NGB officials. Costs may be set per game, per day, or a flat fee for the event. Either separately or in conjunction with those costs, the officials my require travel, housing, parking, and/or food compensation. The event will also usually provide officials with the appropriate attire (e.g., shirt, hat, and/or jacket). In the case of officials for sports that have standard uniforms (e.g., basketball and football), they will usually at least receive a T-shirt or other attire as a souvenir.

It is important to know the format for the competition when preparing the budget. Otherwise, there is no way to know how many officials to budget. In a multigame tournament, officials will generally be scheduled to officiate more than one match/game/event. If it is a sport that the event managers are not familiar with, it may be beneficial to hire a master scheduler for officiating who can determine how many games one official can work on a given day and schedule accordingly. As examples:

- An inline hockey tournament may only require one official for the U8 age group, but two officials for all older age groups.
- A 3-on-3 basketball tournament may be self-officiating until the semi-finals and then have one official for each game from the semi-finals through the finals.
- A tennis tournament may be self-officiating for all rounds of each age group until the quarterfinals. For the quarterfinals and semi-finals it may have a chair umpire and for the finals it may have a chair umpire and two linesmen.

General Labor

Staff from any number of areas can be represented in this category. Setup and strike crew (also often called teardown, changeover, logistics crew) is going to be a main area. For hourly staff, plan for some of their hours to be overtime pay. Event managers should try to keep the costs down, but overtime may be unavoidable, especially if there are not a lot of staff members. When scheduling hours, a general rule of thumb is that it takes about half as much time for teardown as it does for setup. When working with a facility that is providing the general labor, event managers should work closely with the facility manager to ensure costs are managed appropriately.

Volunteers

Contrary to what logic might imply, volunteers are not free; they are just less expensive. Someone on the staff is going to have to work to recruit the volunteers, manage the communication and assignments, and then manage the volunteers during the event. This is an expense to the event. In exchange for their assistance, it is customary that volunteers receive at least a T-shirt. At many events, volunteers receive a meal coupon to use at a concession area or a meal for volunteering. If events have sponsors in attire, food, and/or drink categories, the contracts can be negotiated for the sponsors to provide these items for volunteers as well as participants. If not, they have to be budgeted.

Marketing and Creative Materials

Various pieces of marketing collateral are created for events, both printed and electronic. Each of these different pieces has an associated cost.

Print Collateral

Most events are moving away from paper, but there may be some print materials that are still needed. It can include promotional materials, participant instructions/handbooks, and ticket printing, but even these can all be electronic. Regardless of whether there are actual printing costs or these items are electronic, event managers must budget for the services of the creative staff designing the pieces.

Photography

Multiple areas within an event will need to have useful photos, and event managers have to budget for the appropriate number of photographers to get those photos. For small events, it may be adequate for volunteers to take photos to avoid the cost of a professional. The marketing department uses photos for collateral pieces to advertise and promote future events. Sponsor account service managers need them for sponsor recap reports to document the fact that items agreed to in the contract actually happened. The external relations and media staff are able to provide them to media outlets and the web master posts them on the website. For event managers, photos are useful to record the setup, look, and flow of the event.

If the event is a multiday event, it is helpful for future years if photos are taken each day of setup to document the progress by day. Photos taken on event day keep a record of the setup and are especially valuable to show spacing. Photos to document flow will not be necessary for every event, but for mega events, they can provide very valuable information to event managers. To document flow, photos are taken at a designated location(s) at set time intervals to detail the size of the crowd and/or number of vehicles. Another option is to set up video cameras in these locations to capture flow. This helps to establish arrival and departure patterns and provide information on crowd size and space utilization.

It is important to have (or hire) a photographer who can take the type of pictures that specific functional areas request. The view the marketing team needs is going to be different than what event management needs. Marketing will likely want to show people participating and enjoying the event. The event managers may be fine with photos taken hours before the event even starts. One way to ensure that everyone gets what is needed is by creating a shot list. A **shot list** is a document registering each photo/view that should be captured during an event by a photographer(s). When event managers hire a photographer, it is important to agree on certain requirements and get them in writing, preferably in a formal contract after consulting an attorney. Event managers should specify:

- Who owns the photographs (usually the event)
- Whether the photographer is allowed to use the photos for advertising of his/her services
- If so, whether advance approval is required from the event
- The timeframe required for advance approval (e.g., 2 weeks before needed)
- The format in which they will be given to the event (e.g., JPG, TIFF) and in what medium (e.g., uploaded to a server, external drive, both)

Whatever the size of the event, photos are going to be a valuable asset whether for historical, promotional, or revenue sources. With the advent of high quality digital cameras in phones, a tight budget might mean that volunteers are given the responsibility of photographer.

Website

Most events today cannot function if they do not have a useful and attractive website. The website may only be informational, or it may serve additional purposes, such as event registration. Whether the person creating the website is internal or the work is contracted to a third party, event managers have to budget for the creation and actual hosting. If the website is created and updated by a third party, any changes to the website are usually charged on an hourly basis. Event managers will have to conduct research to determine the cost and possible hours involved. It is also necessary to make sure the servers hosting the website can handle any anticipated traffic spikes, such as if the event is one where people rush to register on the opening day of registration.

Apps

With the ubiquitous use of cell phones and tablets, paying someone to develop an app has become a mandatory expenditure for larger events. While small events may easily survive without an app, major events without one may be viewed as fossils.

Communications Equipment

One of the most important things event managers do in both the planning and execution of sports events is to properly communicate. During the event, this communication can be imperative to the event's success. Having the proper equipment to do this is not an option, but a requirement. Depending on the number of people working the event and the size of the event, communication equipment could be its own category in the event budget.

Cell Phones/Tablets

Connection today is 24/7. During event time, event managers are often expected to be available at all times. Cell phones and tablets have become universal. They are an easy way to reach event staff, whether via voice, video, text message, or email. Sometimes it is best to let the event staff use their own phones and simply reimburse them for their expenses. For large events, it is often easiest from a budgeting perspective to rent phones and pay the services. This way, the event does not have to account for the different cell phone plans and rates that staff may have. It is one consistent and standard amount for service and equipment.

Phones/Landlines

Not every event will need landlines. Events that set up temporary offices or a communications center, though, may want to have landlines. When budgeting for this, what is not often obvious is to include the phone. Do not assume that because a landline is connected the phone company will automatically provide a phone. The event will need to rent or purchase the actual phones to connect to the landlines. One of the additional elements to include is voicemail. Another piece that may be required is setting up a phone tree where callers can access recorded messages about specific areas without needing to speak to one central person (e.g., for Volunteers press 1, for Logistics press 2).

Two-Way Radios

With the pervasive presence of cell phones and direct-connect communication devices, many events may move away from the use of two-way radios. If event managers decide to use two-way radios, some of the key items to include in the budget are extra batteries (at least one extra per event manager), individual chargers, adequate accessories (e.g., headsets, earpieces, microphones), and multibank charging stations.

Awards

Each event has its own requirements for awards, whether established by the event itself or the rights holder. If an event can create a unique award, it can become a fixture—and sometimes even a marketing piece—for the event. When working with an NGB, though, they may have specific requirements that the event must follow or they may order their own.

Trophies and Medals

If sanctioned by an NGB, the event may be required to use—or more likely purchase—awards that are standard for the NGB. If an event creates them, one of the ways to reduce per unit costs is to create a medal, plaque, or trophy that is consistent from event to event or from year to year. The specialization can be created for less money by making the medal's ribbon or trophy's plate specific to the date and/or location.

Prize Money

Events establish and state in advance, the amount for prize money, the requirements to win the prize money, and the collection procedures. If checks will be written on-site, a member of the finance staff, or other designated staff member with the proper authority, will need to be available to write the check.

Insurance

For many organizations, cancellation insurance could be something that saves their livelihood. It is something that is at least worth investigating for medium to large events. In 2012, the New York City Marathon was called off only 2 days before the race was scheduled to be run. This was because of the aftereffects of Hurricane Sandy which had hit the New York/New Jersey metropolitan area just 5 days before the race. That cancellation cost the owners of the race, New York Road Runners, nearly $19 million. Their insurance ended up paying for $15 million of that loss (Marcus, 2014).

Broadcast

Broadcast costs can be significant if an event has television coverage or records the event to create a broadcast production. The details of broadcast production costs are beyond the scope of this book, but event managers should be aware that they might have to be factored into the event budget.

Contingency

Contingency plans are created for all different areas of sports events. Contingency is a future event or circumstance that is possible, but cannot be predicted with certainty. With regard to budgets, contingency is money set aside in a coded account, called a **contingency account,** to cover costs that may arise due to an unexpected event or circumstance. While 10% of the total budget amount would be an ideal amount to set aside, for a large event or mega event budget that may be several million dollars, it will likely not be possible to receive sign-off for a 10% contingency account. In the case of most events, 5% of the total budget is more probable to be approved or available.

Using Excel to Create a Budget

There are various event software programs that have many useful features for planning aspects of events, including the budget. For events that do not have event software, Excel is a very useful program. Excel has the capability to do so many things that if event managers could only choose one piece of software for their computers, Excel would be a good choice. Many of Excel's uses for event managers are covered in Chapter 13, Event Documents. This section will look at Excel's use in creating and managing an event's budget. Many of the items in this section will be "how-to" items related to formatting and formulas. Basic assumptions have been made that readers know how to copy, cut, paste, and perform some other basic tasks. The same action in Microsoft products can often be performed by several different methods: drop-down menus, shortcut keys, and/or right-mouse click menus are some of the most common. How each action is accomplished is the choice of the reader. The method stated in this section may be just one way. Readers may know other ways to perform the functions addressed here. This section only covers a few of the things that event managers will likely use in Excel. As with any software program, the best way to become familiar with what it can do is by using it.

Workbooks and Worksheets

An Excel file is also known as a workbook, while each tab at the bottom of the screen is a worksheet or sheet. According to Microsoft, the number of worksheets that a workbook can contain is only limited by the amount of available computer memory. For various areas of a budget, each worksheet can serve as a specific section of a budget (e.g., equipment or labor) rather than having the entire budget in one worksheet.

Worksheets can be renamed by double-clicking the tab. This activates the tab to allow changes, and event managers can then type in the new name, up to 31 characters. Right-clicking on the tab and selecting "Tab Color" can change the color of the tab. Event managers may want to use color to show summary sheets in one color, revenues in a second color, and expenses in a third color, color-code them by which event managers are responsible for each area, or for other reasons (see Figure 5.1). The order of the worksheets in a workbook can be changed very easily. Simply click on the worksheet tab and drag it to the preferred location in the sequence.

Worksheets are an easy way to keep a lot of information in one file. If different sections have different budgets, they can be set up individually, but all of the information can be set up in one location.

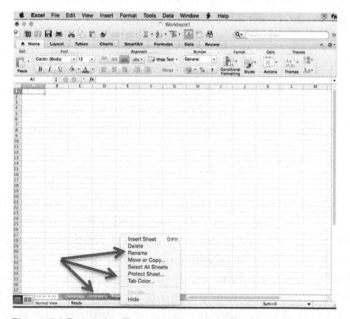

Figure 5.1 Renaming Tabs and Changing Tab Colors in Excel.

Budget Sections

When creating a budget, there will be three areas or columns that event managers will create and monitor: budget, forecast, and actual. The **budgeted amount** is the expenses and revenues that the event managers think the event will have. At a time when everyone agrees to the budgeted amount (usually at the go/no-go decision point), the budget will be locked down, meaning that no changes can be made to the budget moving forward. From that point, event managers will use the event forecast to note any variances in the projected revenues and/or expenses. The **forecast** should be updated regularly in order to show any positive or negative variances. A positive variance may be earning more in sponsorship sales than budgeted or equipment costing less than originally anticipated, and negative variances would be the opposite of those examples. The third area will be the actual costs. When concrete expenses or revenues begin to occur, such as invoices coming in and being paid, those amounts will be entered into the event **actual** section.

Each of these sections should also have columns denoting variances—variance of budget to forecast amounts and budget to actual amounts. Some event managers may also choose to note variance of forecast to actual. It is useful to include an explanation section or column after both the forecast and budget columns, clarifying why the variance is projected to occur or why it did occur.

Budget Summary

An event budget is going to be made up of several different segments, those segments mentioned earlier in the chapter and possibly others. The first worksheet in a budget should be a **budget summary,** or one-page synopsis showing the total from each segment of the budget (e.g., equipment, labor, marketing) and the grand total of those segments. It should show the budgeted, forecast, and actual amounts (see Figure 5.2). When evaluating a budget, having this high-level snapshot will give event managers a

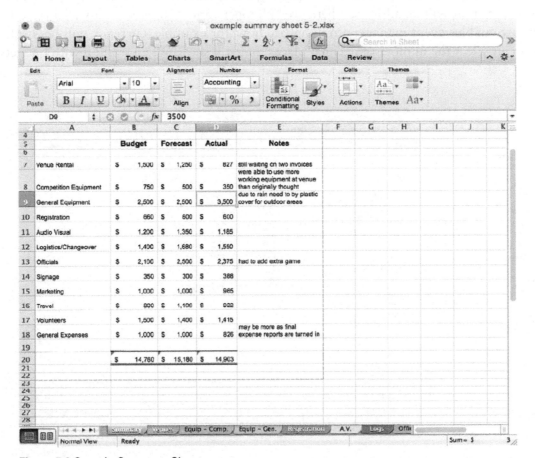

Figure 5.2 Sample Summary Sheet.

quick glance as to where the event stands compared with what was planned. To see the details, event managers can look at the information on the individual segment worksheets. With links from each of these specific worksheets, any changes in the detailed numbers will be reflected on the summary sheet.

Accounting Codes

On the budget summary sheet, accounting codes may be included next to the segment names. **Accounting codes, or a chart of accounts,** are identification numbers assigned to specific categories (accounts) of revenues and expenses and are used for record keeping. They allow event managers to monitor the budget by account. In addition to viewing the column of actual costs that should be updated, event managers can check the accounting software to see what dollar amounts have hit the event or organization's books. They will know exactly how much is spent or yet to be spent in that category. Established organizations will already have these codes set up as part of their general accounting system, and the number of accounts could be extensive. For smaller events or companies, 20–30 accounts are usually enough.

Formatting Cells

The formatting functions covered in this section can be performed on an individual cell, a row, a column, a group of cells, or an entire worksheet, depending on what the user selects. Formatting these areas with one look creates uniformity for the budget, allowing event managers to review the budget without being distracted by aesthetic inconsistencies.

Right-clicking and then selecting "Format Cells" opens a window that allows event managers to set up the format for a myriad of different items (see Figure 5.3). In the bar across the top of this window the two main areas that will be addressed here are "Number" and "Alignment." By clicking on "Number," this window enables event managers to designate how, for example, currency will be displayed. Event managers can select the number of decimal places that will show. When dealing with budgets and large

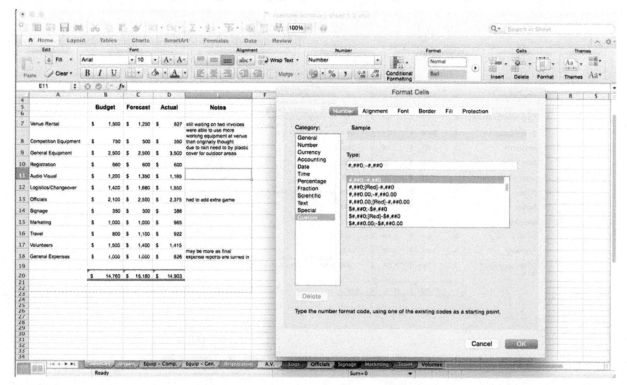

Figure 5.3 Formatting Cells.

numbers, it is too detailed to have cents displayed. The exact dollar and cents can be entered for Excel to calculate, but Excel can show the amount rounded to the nearest dollar. They can also select whether to show dollar signs ($) with the number or not. How a negative number, or loss, will show can also be set up from this window. In order to highlight the significance of such a number to the event budget, it is often useful to select the format that shows negative numbers in red and in parentheses.

The "Alignment" window can help with many items, but for budget formatting purposes this window is important because it enables event managers to wrap text or shrink it to fit in a cell. These features become relevant when entering the names of budgeted items or the names at the top of the columns. Rather than stretching out columns to fit a long name, simply click "Wrap text" to get the text to flow to the next line(s). The cell will expand and the words will fit within the existing width of a column. Another options is to click "Shrink to fit" to reduce the text size to fit within the given space. With this feature, though, the text could end up too small for most people to be able to read. Each of these features is also available on the general Excel tool bar.

Formatting Worksheets

Different event managers will have their own preferences for the specific format of their budgets, but whatever the format of the worksheet, there are easy ways to copy that format to the rest of the document rather than setting up worksheets individually. To insert an additional worksheet, place the cursor over a worksheet tab and right-click. From the right-click menu, select "Insert" and then select "Worksheet." Set up the format of the worksheet. Once the user likes the format, including column width, number format, and so on, click on the diamond in the top left corner of the workbook display (to the left of column A and above row 1) (see Figure 5.4). Clicking the diamond selects the entire worksheet. Select copy, click on the worksheet tab where the information is to be copied, select either the diamond or the topmost left cell (cell A1), and click paste. The content from the original worksheet will be copied to the new one, but so will all of the formatting. If only the content cells had been selected and copied rather than the diamond selected, the content would have been copied, but none of the formatting.

An additional way to format the entire workbook is to format one worksheet and then right-click on the worksheet tab and select "Move or Copy." Once "Move or Copy" is selected, a drop-down list will show the file name to which the worksheet is to be moved or copied (see Figure 5.5). By default, the name listed is of the current file (the worksheet can be moved or copied to an entirely different file). Below this is a list of the names of the worksheet tabs. Select the name of the sheet before which the

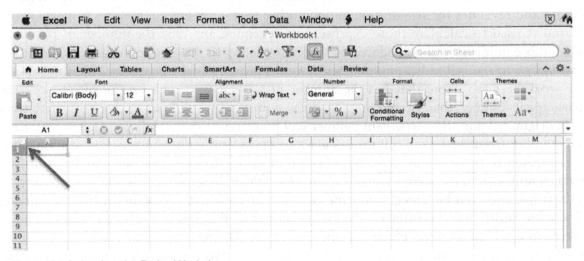

Figure 5.4 Selecting the Entire Worksheet.

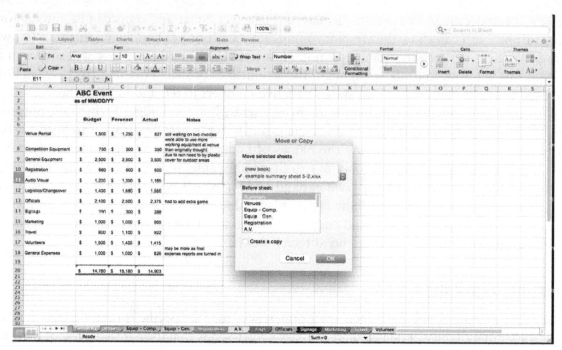

Figure 5.5 Move/Copy A Worksheet.

copy should appear, check the box "Create a copy," and the worksheet will be copied. The name of the worksheet will be the same with (#) after that name, with the number in parentheses depending on how many copies have been made.

Linking Worksheets

One of the most useful features of Excel (and any spreadsheet) is the fact that cells can be linked throughout the file and with other Excel files. This ensures that when changes are made to numbers, any related information in linked cells or formulas that use that number are updated throughout the workbook. This text will not cover formulas in Excel, but they are vital to creating any budget. Readers should use the Help menu on Excel or read through a text on Excel if they are not familiar with how to use formulas in Excel.

As an example, if event managers are looking at different scenarios for possible number of entrants for a tennis tournament, that number will impact expenses for T-shirts, courts, tennis balls, awards, and so on and revenues for registration (among other items). By linking number of participants into the formulas used to calculate those expenses and revenues, any time the number of participants is changed, those numbers will be updated. In this example, when the event managers create the budget, they would go to the cell indicating number of items, put an equal sign to start the formula, =, click on the worksheet tab name that has the number of participants, click on the specific cell that has the participant number, then press Enter. The view will then switch back to the worksheet where the formula originated and the participant number will now appear in this cell (see Figure 5.6). Excel will use the number from the linked cell for calculations that identify the number of items. Links to other files are created in the same manner. With both files open, after entering the equal sign to start the formula, simply switch the view to the file from which the number will come, click on the appropriate cell in that file, and then hit Enter. Again, the view will go back to the view in the original spreadsheet.

There are entire books written on the many features of Excel. It is a program that can help event managers to calculate budgets efficiently and accurately. The few topics covered here will hopefully allow event managers begin to explore the many facets of Excel. A final sample, Figure 5.7 shows a sample event budget.

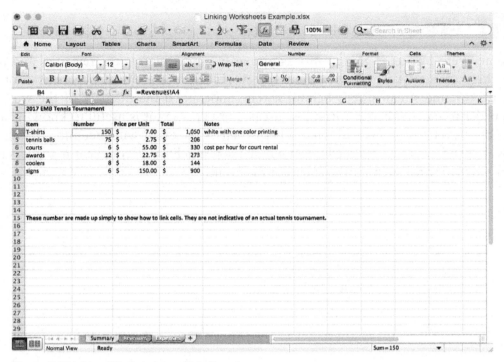

Figure 5.6 Linking Worksheets within Excel.

2017 EMB Basketball Festival	Budget (Locked as of Oct 1, 2016)	Forecast	Actual	Budget Variance	Comments
REVENUES:					
Entry Fees	$ 72,500	$ 37,500		$ (37,500)	
Merchandise	$ 30,000	$ 18,000		$ (18,000)	
Photography	$ 20,000	$ 12,000		$ (12,000)	
Total Revenues	**$ 122,500**	**$ 67,500**		**$ (67,500)**	
EXPENSES:					
Audio	$ 1,200	$ 1,362		$ (1,362)	
Balls	$ 800	$ 719		$ (719)	
Bleachers / Stage	$ 5,000	$ 4,300		$ (4,300)	
Carts	$ 1,200	$ 1,250		$ (1,250)	
Drivers	$ 3,000			$ -	
Equipment preparation	$ 1,000	$ -		$ -	
First aid	$ 2,000	$ 1,500		$ (1,500)	
Forklift	$ 900	$ 1,180		$ (1,180)	
Generator gas	$ 750	$ 928		$ (928)	
Generator Rental	$ 200	$ 450		$ (450)	
Gifts-Sponsor/VIP/Refs	$ 2,500	$ 1,350		$ (1,350)	
Hospitality functions	$ 3,500	$ 4,100		$ (4,100)	
Hospitality/Photography tent	$ 2,200	$ 1,922		$ (1,922)	
Ice	$ 500	$ 325		$ (325)	
Marketing Misc.	$ 8,500	$ 8,000		$ (8,000)	
Misc. administrative	$ 1,000	$ 810		$ (810)	
Photography	$ 1,200	$ 1,200		$ (1,200)	
Player Bags	$ 3,500	$ 3,968		$ (3,968)	
Portable lights	$ 750	$ -		$ -	
Portable toilets	$ 2,000	$ 1,660		$ (1,660)	
Printed Forms	$ 1,000	$ 370		$ (370)	
Prizes	$ 7,500	$ 7,385		$ (7,385)	
Promotions	$ 2,000	$ 427		$ (427)	
Referee fees	$ 8,000	$ 11,000		$ (11,000)	
Referee Uniforms	$ 1,000	$ 964		$ (964)	
Road Crew	$ 3,000	$ 4,320		$ (4,320)	
Scaffolding	$ 3,000	$ -		$ -	
Scissor lifts	$ 350	$ 450		$ (450)	
Scorecards	$ 1,100	$ 500		$ (500)	
Security - event	$ 1,500	$ 4,500		$ (4,500)	
Security - overnight	$ 1,000	$ 1,734		$ (1,734)	
Shipping	$ 500	$ 369		$ (369)	
Signage	$ 10,000	$ 6,119		$ (6,119)	
Site fees & permits	$ 1,500	$ 250		$ (250)	
Storage Facility	$ 15,000	$ 10,500		$ (10,500)	
Temporary labor	$ 3,000	$ 3,030		$ (3,030)	
Transportaion (Bus Rental)				$ -	
Transportation	$ 6,500	$ 6,175		$ (6,175)	
Trash maintenance	$ 750	$ 1,295		$ (1,295)	
VIP catering	$ 1,800	$ 2,150		$ (2,150)	
Volunteer meals	$ 3,500	$ 3,200		$ (3,200)	
Wardrobe	$ 7,000	$ 6,657		$ (6,657)	
Contingency	$ 6,000	$ 1,299		$ (1,299)	
Total Expenses	**$ 126,700**	**$ 107,717**	**$ -**	**$ (107,717)**	

Figure 5.7 Sample Event Budget.

SUMMARY

Generating an event budget is going to focus primarily on calculating the revenues and expenses for the event. There are various sources of both for events. Even if event managers are not responsible for managing revenue streams, it is helpful if they understand the nuances of the various types of revenue in order to partner better with those areas. For expenses, it is useful to know what categories may be the big-ticket cost items and what other expenses the event will encounter. Using Excel or an event software program to create the budget will make it much easier for event managers to create the budget and monitor it throughout the stages of the event.

Student Challenges

NAME _____ DATE _____

In this Challenge create the financial pieces associated with an event. Establish both the revenue and expense categories associated with each side of the budget. Also, use Excel to create a full and detailed budget for the event. If you cannot think of an event, use a weekend 3-v-3 basketball tournament with 12 courts, 48 teams, and a three-game guarantee.

Question 5.1

List all of the (realistic) probable revenue streams for the event, detailing the anticipated revenue for each item and category.

Question 5.2

List all of the expense items for the event detailing the anticipated cost for each item and category.

Item	Quantity	Cost per Unit	Total Cost

Question 5.3

Using Excel, create a budget detailing the revenues and expenses (breaking down the items on individual category sheets). Using links, produce a summary sheet with the individual total of revenue and expense categories.

EVENT MARKETING

Jim Kahler and Mark Rossi

James Kahler is the Executive Director of the Center of Sports Administration at Ohio University. Previously, he helped develop the MBA Sports Business Program at the W.P. Carey School of Business at Arizona State University and was the Senior Vice President of Sales and Marketing for the Cleveland Cavaliers (NBA) and Rockers (WNBA). Mr. Kahler has over 20 years of experience in sales and marketing in sport. He has also served on the NBA's Marketing Advisory Committee and is currently on the Advisory Board for a number of sports business organizations, including the National Sports Forum (San Diego, California), Navigate Research, and In Stadium Advertising (Chicago, Illinois). He also sits on the Board of Directors for US Table Tennis.

Mark Rossi is the Vice President of Sales and Marketing for Dover Motorsports, Inc., Mr. Rossi is responsible for coordinating the overall sales and marketing initiatives for the entire company. Dover Motorsports, Inc. owns and operates Dover International Speedway in Dover, Del. The legendary "Monster Mile" in Dover is known for being tough on drivers and their equipment, and has been hosting two NASCAR Sprint Cup Series race weekends each year for over 40 years. Rossi joined Dover Motorsports on January 1, 2002 and has helped to restructure and focus the sales and marketing efforts of the company on improving the fan experience and increasing partnership value. During his tenure, the company has experienced steady growth in group and season ticket sales, as well as strong results in sponsorship and secondary asset sales.

Prior to working for Dover Motorsports, Rossi spent over 16 years in the Consumer Packaged Goods industry with Nestle USA and Sara Lee. He worked to develop and execute a wide variety of sponsorship and branding initiatives, ranging from local and regional programs to full-scale national events, several of which involved racing and NASCAR.

This chapter is intended to provide students with an understanding of the process required to develop an event marketing plan, and the various types of advertising mediums that are available to market an event. To get started, a basic definition for an event marketing plan is needed. The **event marketing plan** includes the production and coordination of all advertising, promotional, and public relations campaigns for the event with the goal of maximizing revenue generation and event attendance.

It is important for the event manager to realize that technology has ushered in a brave new world of marketing. In contemporary event management, the consumer has an increasing level of control over content consumption coupled with a sophisticated knowledge of how to navigate across mediums to find it. There is a rapidly changing network of devices across a growing spectrum of platforms for information consumption.

Prior to building the marketing plan the marketing manager must have an understanding of the marketing area that is to be targeted, as well as the demographic and psychographic characteristics of the target audience. Sadly, when it comes to advertising, too often, event managers and promoters do not possess enough information about the market they are competing in, the audience they are marketing to, and thus, the most efficient way to reach them. This chapter will present a variety of options available to the marketing manager and how leveraged different forms of media can be leveraged to obtain the exposure needed to adequately promote the event. It will show a number of ways to make advertising more cost efficient and measurable.

The Marketing Plan

The promoter for any event is typically responsible for developing and implementing an event marketing plan that should include three basic campaigns; the advertising campaign, the promotional campaign, and the public relations campaign. Even though these duties likely will not fall directly on the event manager, the event manager should have an understanding of each aspect of the marketing plan.

The Advertising Campaign

The **advertising campaign** for an event can utilize any combination of one or more forms of media, including, but not limited to, television, radio, print, outdoor, direct mail, mobile, and digital. Choosing the appropriate mix of media is dependent upon the target demographic, event goals and objectives, and specific marketing goals. It is vital for today's marketing manager to understand the consumption habits of their target audience. The landscape today is so much different that it was even 10 short years ago. Rapidly growing penetrations of digital devices and subscription based streaming services have altered the consumption habits of consumers, especially those under the age of 45. There are a variety of ways to collect data on consumption habits depending on the how granular the information, the amount of time, and size of the available budget to secure the data. Data can be found in a variety of ways including Government reports, commissioned studies, focus groups, and online surveys.

The media advertising budget typically represents anywhere from 10% to 15% of projected gross ticket sales (sales before any entertainment or sales tax). For example, the Harlem Globetrotters might project $200,000 in gross ticket sales for a game and set aside a cash advertising budget of $30,000 (15%). Any time cash is spent in return for a specified form of advertising, it is considered **paid advertising**. In addition to paid advertising budgets, acquiring additional media through trade or in-kind advertising can extend the event media reach.

Trade or in-kind advertising represents any additional media advertising that is secured in exchange for desired event assets such as event tickets, VIP hospitality or pre-event meet and greets, and is generally a dollar-for-dollar trade. For example, a radio station agrees to run a $2,000 radio campaign (40/30-second spots with a value of $50 each) in exchange for $ 2,000 worth of tickets. Many media outlets (radio stations, television stations, and print) will use event assets to build brand equity, increase exposure, or entertain customers. Media providers can afford to run trade advertisements when they are not sold out of their advertising inventory, and will often make good use of the assets provided by the event manager.

The Promotional Campaign

The **promotional campaign** is an opportunity to demonstrate creativity, while simultaneously supporting partnerships and increasing event awareness and ultimately attendance. It can consist of special ticket discounts, premium giveaways, theme nights, and any number of other program elements. These are developed in conjunction with an event partner (media or sponsor) as part of a partnership agreement. The elements included in any promotional campaign are based on the defined goals of the partners and the creativity of the event manager.

Student promotions are important pieces of intercollegiate athletics and add excitement to the game atmosphere.

Promotional programs are not a part of the paid advertising campaign, but could be a part of the original marketing budget depending on how the event budget was constructed. In the Harlem Globetrotters example from above, if the event manager had a cash adverting budget of $30,000, their regional promoter would try to leverage the investment and secure another $20,000–$30,000 worth of measurable media for the game. They might do this by working with all media outlets that received a portion of the paid advertising budget. For example, WUAB TV agrees to be the presenting sponsor of the Harlem Globetrotters game in Cleveland, Ohio. In exchange for being the primary television station and receiving $15,000 of the $30,000 advertising budget for the event, the station gains the right to be the presenting media sponsor and will run an incremental 100, 30-second promotional spots in support of the game.

In this example, the Globetrotters and WUAB TV might offer a $3.00 discount on tickets to the game with coupons being made available at a mutually agreeable third-party (i.e., Subway). Subway is a paid advertiser of the station and also a promotional partner or local sponsor of the Globetrotters. If Subway becomes the third-party sponsor of the discount, and has 45 locations in northeast Ohio, the Globetrotters have extended their reach. Additionally, Subway also provides extra visibility with in-store posters promoting the event and distribution of the $3.00 discount coupons as early as 4 weeks prior to the event.

An example of a program that is built into the marketing plan is one at Dover International Speedway, a NASCAR, track in Dover Delaware. Dover International Speedway executes a sponsored direct mail program in its spring and fall event campaigns. The goal of this program is to deliver a valuable direct to consumer offer to Dover race fans from one of its sponsors and strengthen the bond between the track and the race fan. These programs are executed only when the business development team includes this offer as one of the elements of a sponsorship package to a new sponsor partner, the main promotional element of the program centers around a direct mail piece with an event discount offer and bounce back coupon driving traffic to the sponsor. A bounce back coupon is a discount coupon that is redeemable at some time in the future. The direct mail piece goes to between 5,000 and 8,000 accounts for each event.

Creativity with Caution

Dan Hauser, Athletic Director, High Point University

Annie Valeant Brackley, Instructor, Ohio University

Creativity and excitement are important elements that every sport entity attempts to accomplish in the execution of sporting events. A primary goal for event managers is for their customers to have a great time and a positive experience at their events. The fan experience is the one element that event managers can control and influence. Wins and losses are out of their control, but they can have an influence on the environment. Sport is entertainment, and in the competitive consumer environment creativity is one tool event managers can use to gain an edge.

Creativity can be very powerful, but event managers must use this power with caution. When creativity goes wrong it can result in a very public and enduring embarrassment for event managers. To illustrate this, let's investigate two examples in professional sport.

Chicago Blackhawks vs. Pittsburgh Penguins—February 28, 2009

The Blackhawks decided to show their appreciation for their "hard-working fans" on rivalry night by handing out hardhats to the first 10,000 people who entered the United Center. The promotion seemed to go well until Blackhawks player, Jonathan Toews scored what appeared to be his third goal of the game giving him his first career hat trick.

The tradition in hockey is that fans pay respect by throwing their hats onto the ice whenever a player scores three goals. Blackhawk fans immediately started throwing their hardhats onto the ice in celebration of Toews' shot.

Unfortunately, the goal was disallowed and hundreds of fans were left without hardhats. Ironically, Toews would end up scoring a third goal later in the game causing the remaining hard hats to be thrown on the ice. The game-day staff was forced to rush on the ice not once but twice and sweep up the hats as fast as possible. The promotion was creative but caused a lot of chaos during the game.

Villanova vs. #7 Pittsburgh—January 29, 2007

The game was a huge Big East men's basketball battle that was broadcast live on ESPN Big Monday, the type of game that gets every event manager excited. The game was very close and filled with a lot of excitement through halftime. With around 11 minutes left in the second half, the horn sounded for a media time out. Out came the event managers to the floor, setting up a promotion for a regional grocery store chain. There were two contestants located at half court and two grocery carts located around the free-throw line. The objective of the contest was for the contestants to attempt to throw a grocery item and land it in the shopping cart. The contestant who got the most items into the cart won.

It was a creative contest with strong sponsorship branding until the event managers provided the contestants with heads of lettuce as the item to throw. For 2 minutes, contestants threw heads of lettuce that exploded on impact with the floor and shredded into pieces when they hit the grocery cart. Lettuce was everywhere when the horn sounded for the end of the time out. Dust brooms were brought out to get all the lettuce off the floor, but the lettuce was stuck to the floor. An army of event managers and referees had to scour the court, picking up every piece of lettuce. The game was delayed for 5–10 minutes while ESPN broadcasted images and comments about the debacle to a national audience.

Texas Rangers vs. Cleveland Indians —June 4, 1974

Indians attendance was down 85% in 1974, forcing the Cleveland front office to get creative with its promotions. The organization came up with "10-cent beer night" offering fans an inexpensive way to party and enjoy baseball.

Over 25,000 fans showed up for the promotion, more than double the attendance at any other game. The organization's 10-cent pricing for beer seemed to be too good of a deal for many of its customers who later stumbled through the stadium.

The fans became so intoxicated and riled up over the rivalry between the Indians and the Rangers that one woman jumped on the Indians on-deck circle and a man went streaking into second base during a Rangers homerun. The game would eventually be called in the bottom of the ninth when drunken fans started throwing golf balls and rocks onto the field. The Rangers won because the Indians had to forfeit.

Western Michigan White Caps vs. Southwest Michigan Devil Rays—April 15, 2006

The majority of sports fans have probably attended a minor league baseball game. Event managers in minor leagues are the kings and queens of creativity and entertainment. They have to be, because the majority of their customers cannot name a player on their team or the team's current record. Minor league baseball fans want to be entertained, and this game was like most typical Saturday games—with one twist. At the conclusion of the game, there would be a $1,000 cash giveaway for kids. The promotion was set up with children lined up on the outfield fence. The cash was dropped from a helicopter over the ballpark, and the kids scrambled to pick up as much cash as possible. It was a very creative game day promotion to attract families to a minor league game, but with the excitement of the cash, the promotion turned dangerous. The kids' ages ranged from 5 to 12, and the old adage "the strong will survive" prevailed. In the mayhem, a 7-year-old boy was trampled and taken to a hospital. Additionally, many children left the outfield with bloody faces. The news was a national story picked up by ESPN; luckily the events were not more tragic.

The aforementioned examples were not provided to stifle event managers' creativity. Instead, each was presented to show the importance of using caution when being creative. Here are 10 creativity control measures to assist event managers with their event management:

1. *Practice:* Always execute a promotion on the court or field with staff before it is performed live at an event. Event managers should never roll out a promotion that they have not executed or practiced.

2. *Control:* Event managers have control of everything. Control the number of contestants, ages of participants, apparatus, rules, and so on. Review every detail with the contestants so they know what they are to do during the promotion. A great tip is to draw out the contest on paper to the contestants.

3. *Questions:* Create a think tank with the rest of the event staff and ask questions. Are there health and safety risks? What could go wrong with this promotion?

4. *Sell Contests:* The event managers are the experts. Sell contests to sponsors; do not let the sponsor make up the contest. What may seem creative to sponsors may put event managers and/or contestants in danger.

5. *Steal:* Observe what works with promotions and contests at other sporting events and implement these ideas at your events. If it works for their fans, then be creative and steal

▶

the idea. In an academic setting this might be plagiarism, but in the sports industry it is called benchmarking best practices.

6. *Adjustments:* A promotion or contest is never perfect. Always evaluate, make adjustments, and observe fan reaction.

7. *End:* Make sure there is an end to your promotion: time, number of attempts, tie breaker situation.

8. *Fresh:* Keep the promotions and contests fresh. Change the contests annually. Do not sell season-long promotions; instead, sell opportunities (10 out of 15 games) so the promotions are rotated and the event has variety. Fans want variety and new elements.

9. *Complement:* Use creatively matched music, video board displays, or lights to complement the promotions and contests.

10. *Go:* A common mistake is to spend too much time talking or telling the rules of a promotion or contest. Fans are smart and they can figure it out. Always keep a fast mentality: Ready … Set … Go!

The Public Relations Campaign

Once the paid advertising and promotional campaigns are put together, it is time to generate as much publicity as possible. **Publicity** is any news coverage for the event that is generated with some type of announcement, market tour, or interview. Public Relations events may have cost associated with them, but they are not part of paid advertising and the media gained is not paid for. Announcements come in the form of press releases and the resulting media coverage gained for the event. It is important to always be looking to make these campaigns newsworthy and genuine to maximize attendance, rebroadcast, or print coverage. In the past, event promoters hired local publicists to put together the publicity plan. Hiring a local PR agency made sense because of the working relationships that exist within given cities, especially when the event or attraction is traveling and does not have a year-round local presence in the market.

Today, most major arenas, stadiums, and convention centers have a full-time director of public relations and work closely with the event promoter to maximize publicity for the event. Referring back to the Globetrotters example, they will collaborate with the Sr. Director of Public Relations at the venue to generate publicity for the game in, and around, Cleveland.

The Sr. Director of Public Relations had over 20 years of experience working with the media in Cleveland and her plan included taking a former Globetrotter, who is serving as the advance ambassador for the team, out into the community for a day of promotional appearances. The advance ambassador arrives 1 week before the game and makes several school visits to reinforce the importance of teamwork. The Cleveland Public School System is happy to have a former NBA player and Globetrotter deliver the message on teamwork, and the local news media turns out in strong numbers to cover the clinic. The result of this community outreach effort is free publicity for the upcoming event.

Pulling all three components together (the advertising, promotional, and publicity campaigns) requires a lot of work and expertise. Today, many facilities have an in-house advertising and public relations agency that provides this type of service for the promoter. An in-house agency will also take the lead on any events that are produced and promoted by the facility.

Guerrilla and Grassroots Marketing

Guerrilla marketing is an aggressive way to market an event and is best be defined as "taking the message to the streets." **Grassroots marketing** is marketing an event on a local and personal level as a way to get the word out on the event. The method usually relies on a street team or group of volunteers to help promote the event. Often these two methods are combined for maximum impact. Event managers have the ability to do the following:

- Hand out flyers and, in some cases, discount coupons for the event in high traffic areas, including other events, shopping malls, and university campuses.
- Display mini posters for the event with area merchants willing to provide exposure in their window fronts.

Considerations when "taking the message to the streets" via guerrilla marketing.

Event managers need to be careful where they hand out flyers, as they may need permission ahead of time to distribute materials outside another event or on private property. In many instances promoters and street teams will ask for forgiveness as opposed to permission, hence the reference above to guerrilla marketing. With permission from the business owner, displaying mini posters that are typically 22″ high by 16″ wide in store windows along high traffic areas has proven to be a very successful way to increase exposure for events. This strategy works better with independent shop owners as opposed to shopping malls with nationally owned stores.

Major League Soccer (MLS) does an excellent job of leveraging grassroots marketing as the core of its advertising platform. MLS teams spend time in the community securing agreements with community soccer organizations. The MLS teams provide training, club nights, skills demonstrations, and a variety of other assets in exchange for promotional rights with the community soccer clubs. For example, the Philadelphia Union of MLS has developed strategic partnerships with the state soccer associations and individual youth soccer clubs within the Philadelphia designated marketing area (DMA) in an effort to capture the attention of an audience with a built-in affinity to the sport while providing the teams family of corporate partners a grass roots marketing platform that reaches deep into the communities in which they serve. These initiatives give MLS team promotional opportunities with a passionate constituency. Many of these youth soccer organizations have thousands children in a single club, so it is an incredibly effective tool.

From Personal Experience

Jim Kahler, Executive Director of the Center for Sports Administration, Ohio University

I was fortunate in my career to become the Director of Marketing at Cincinnati's Riverfront Coliseum at the young age of 25, and had the opportunity to run Coliseum Productions, the facility's in-house advertising and public relations agency. I believe the experience that I gained in this position helped me later in my career when I became the Sr. Vice President of Sales and Marketing with the Cleveland Cavaliers and Gund Arena. Much of what I learned in Cincinnati was garnered by working closely with a wide variety of family shows and regional promoters for such events as Ringling Brothers Barnum and Bailey Circus, Disney on Ice, Longhorn World Championship Rodeo, Sesame Street Live, the US Hot Rod Association, the Harlem Globetrotters, and the Ice Capades. Each of these events, with the exception of the Harlem Globetrotters, was a show with multiple performances that made up a large percentage of our 100+ events per year. Each event required Coliseum Productions to handle the advertising, promotional, and publicity campaigns.

One example from my time with Coliseum Productions was a discount program that I developed with a diaper service company in Cincinnati. When our first son was born, we received a 3 month supply of diapers and I was impressed with the delivery and pickup service that this company offered to our doorstep on weekly basis. As a satisfied customer, I called the owner of the company and asked him if he would be interested in giving his customers a special $2.50 discount coupon (via a simple mail-in order form) to our upcoming engagement with Sesame Street Live. I explained my position with Coliseum Productions and told him we would be happy to print the forms with his company's logo included. He jumped at the opportunity and we sold over 800 tickets to the event. Apparently there were other satisfied customers with young children and they were excited to receive this special discount.

Choosing the Right Media — Traditional Media

While strong promotional and publicity campaigns will enhance awareness for the event, strategic decisions will also have to be made about the best way to utilize the cash advertising budget established for the event. Event promoters are faced with three key questions as they begin to put together their advertising campaign:

1. What is the best media to use for the particular event?
2. How important is creativity to get the message across to the targeted audience?
3. Is there a way to buy space and time that will stretch the advertising budget?

Advertising is ultimately an investment in the success of the event, and like any investment, it is important for event managers to understand as much as they can about how to reach their target audience. This should be done before they start committing advertising dollars to specific mediums.

Purchasing advertising is like buying many commodities, as there is only so much television, radio, newspaper, and online advertising available at any one given point in time. It is important to point out that all electronic advertising (television, radio, and online) becomes very negotiable, and that the rate card used in each of these mediums is just the starting point when putting together your advertising plan. A radio or television station's **rate card** is simply the rates charged for advertising during different day parts or during specific programming on the station. It is important to understand where there is negotiating leverage, the minimum acceptable exposure by medium, and to have more than one scenario of how the budget might be segmented across platforms. The better the plan going in, the stronger the negotiating position will be.

So how do television and radio stations come up with different rates for different programming? The two most common methods of establishing rates for television and radio advertising are based on a **cost per thousand (CPM)** or **cost per rating point (CPP)**. Both the radio and television industry are monitored and measured by a company called Arbitron (www.arbitron.com). Through its research methodology, Arbitron can determine the demographics of the audiences that are watching and listening to advertisements. The boxed glossary of terms on page 110 provides some other key terms as they relate to radio advertising.

Traditionally, events have used three main staples of advertising (television, radio, and newspaper) to promote ticket and admission sales. Each medium offers advantages and disadvantages for promoters to consider when putting together their actual advertising campaign.

Television Advertising

For the better part of the past half century Television advertising is often referred to as the "king" of all advertising because the majority of people spend more time watching television than listening to radio or reading newspapers combined. This is about to change and most experts predict by 2017 more advertising will be spent on the internet than television, however TV advertising will still be a very important medium to reach a core audience. TV allows event promoters the ability to combine the use of sight, color, sound, and motion to get their message across to a targeted audience. According to the latest research from The Nielsen Company, a global marketing research firm that specializes in measuring TV, radio, and newspaper audiences (2014), the average American spends just under 5 hours (4 hours, 51 minutes) a day watching television. This ends up being close to 35 hours per week, or 2.5 months of television viewing per year. It is good to know that there are two types of television broadcast, one is called Network (or over air) Broadcast, and the other is Cable Broadcast. Network broadcast can be picked up with an antenna and does not need a subscription to view. This form has the largest viewership universe. Cable is subscription based and really has two main players—Cable Networks and Satellite TV Broadcasters. The biggest difference is that there is cost to the viewer associated with cable and satellite services. It is also important to understand the changing dynamic in television advertising today, with the ever increasing number of cable stations, and the proliferation of alternative viewing mediums offered as a result of digital and mobile technology, there is downward pressure on ratings, attention is divided across more content sources. The event manager's ability to understand the landscape will play a big role in their ability to negotiate a fair advertising deal and maximize reach, frequency, and return on investment (ROI).

Reach

While television advertising has proven to be an influencer in driving ticket sales for events, it is also the most expensive form of media available to promoters. One television commercial during prime time viewing in a market like Cleveland (8:00 pm until 11:00 pm) can cost $3,000 and 10 times more than one radio spot during morning drive on the most popular radio station in any given city. For example, one 30-second commercial during American Idol could cost Ringling Brothers Barnum and Bailey Circus $3,000 in Cleveland. Conversely, one 30-second radio commercial on WTAM, Cleveland's number-one-ranked AM radio station, might cost $300 during the morning drive spot. However, the television commercial can reach 10 times (or more) as many prospective customers. You will also find that your cost to advertise on TV will vary based on the size of the market you want to advertise in. So for example, to advertise in the same time slot in New York City, it will cost more than it will in the Cleveland market.

Production Quality

Generating a quality television commercial becomes an important variable for any event producer to consider. Many of the events enjoy an economy of scale by producing generic commercials that can be distributed across a multiple-city tour schedule and simply be tagged at the end of the commercial with pertinent information on the dates, venue, and ticket information for the event. This would allow a touring event like Ringling Brothers Barnum and Bailey Circus the ability to invest more money into a series of three or four standard commercials that could be divided over a 40-city tour, as opposed to a shooting a new commercial for every single event that only plays in a particular city.

Today's television audience is very sophisticated and has come to expect quality commercials. A poorly produced commercial could adversely impact ticket sales for a single event and leave a bad image in the mind of a prospective ticket buyer.

Cable

Cable advertising is a lower-cost alternative to traditional broadcast television, as it does not reach as broad an audience. However, it can often deliver a targeted audience that has real interest in an event. For example, the Gatorade Rock-N-Roll Shootout is a major college basketball doubleheader in Cleveland. The event relied heavily on the purchase of cable advertising on ESPN and Fox Sports Ohio to reach the college basketball crowd in northeast Ohio.

The biggest downside to cable is that it will not reach every household with a television set and the viewing audience can be slightly smaller. Cable and satellite TV reaches almost 100 million households in the United States, but many consumers are opting for cheaper TV packages (Hagey & Ramachandran, 2015) or joining the already 7.3% of homes that no longer pay for TV known as "cord-cutters" (Fetto, 2015). Even if consumers do not take these actions, event marketers should be aware of television viewing trends. In the case of the Gatorade Rock-N-Roll Shootout, the event organizers felt that the cable audience watching college basketball was a perfect fit for the doubleheader and the teams playing in the shootout. The approximate cost of a cable spot for a medium-sized market during an early season college basketball game is much more affordable than a radio spot on morning drive radio in Cleveland (estimated at $50–$100 per cable spot vs. $200 for an average radio commercial). While the size of audience reached with a 30-second commercial on cable was much lower than the radio audience, it certainly was much more targeted for the event the organizers were promoting.

Cost

For event promoters to generate positive results and ticket sales with television advertising, they must have enough money to cover the cost of producing a good commercial. The Cleveland Cavaliers, for example, have their own in-house broadcast production crew and could produce a quality commercial for under $2,500. Using an outside agency to produce the same commercial could have cost the organization two to three times that amount.

For commercials that run in the Super Bowl, it would not be uncommon for an advertiser to spend in excess of $250,000 in production cost. With the average cost of a 30-second commercial in the 2008 Super Bowl at $3 million, the ratings and stakes are high for advertisers to get their message across in a very competitive environment (Sports Business Daily, 2008).

In addition to covering production costs, the promoters need to have a large enough budget to reach their targeted audience multiple times during their advertising campaign to be effective. Properly done television and cable advertising is the most effective medium available for an event. However, it is major league advertising and should not be included in the plan unless enough money is projected in the budget.

Radio Advertising

At one time, Radio was king of the airwaves, and while television and online advertising have taken on that role, radio can still play a key role in a marketing managers advertising plan. Radio extends access to consumers beyond the home. It offers a form of entertainment that attracts listeners while they are traveling, in the work place, or just relaxing. It can provide a targeted way to reach the audience and offers a wide variety of formats, including rock and roll, sports talk, news talk, country music, rap music, jazz music, classic rock, and others. Radio also provides up-to-the-minute reports on news, weather, and traffic conditions. Today many professional sports teams will purchase advertising during morning drive of the top sports talk radio stations in their respective markets. In these situations, they are reaching core and potential consumers who start every day on their morning and afternoon drives to and from work listening to the latest updates of their favorite sports teams.

Radio vs. Television

Compared with television advertising, radio is a relatively inexpensive way to reach an audience. Dr. James Lavery, a former professor in the Ohio University Sports Administration program, once referred to radio advertising as "theatre of the mind" because voices, sounds, and music can be used effectively to create moods that would be too expensive to produce in a television commercial.

Radio can provide one of the most basic forms of native advertising. By working with drive time or popular station segments it can integrate the event into the show as part of conversation resulting in the promotion being natural and accepted. Caution needs to be taken with the approach as it can backfire if clear boundaries about what should be discussed are not established in advance.

Radio can also become a personal advertising medium. Joe Tait, the retired radio voice of the Cleveland Cavaliers, had a huge fan base, and by using his voice in radio commercials the Cavaliers connected with their targeted audience. In many of the radio commercials they would take some of Joe's greatest play-by-play calls from the previous season to evoke the emotion of a fan being in the arena seeing the action he would describe.

Radio is one of the most basic forms of advertising.

Reach and Research

While radio can be an effective medium, it does come with some disadvantages. Since most major markets will have multiple stations, the total listening audience for any one station is just a small piece of the total listening audience. With a recent move to satellite radio (e.g., SirusXM), podcasts, and Pandora, the traditional radio audience is starting to shrink.

This is, yet another reason why the event manager must clearly identify their target consumers, the demographic makeup of these groups, and the psychographic preferences that they gravitate to. It is a very good idea for event managers to work with an experienced media buyer that understands the event, the market, and the best stations to invest the event's advertising dollars with.

The mainstreaming of satellite radio has added a new dimension into the media mix. Satellite radio has higher value to events that people travel a distance to attend versus local nightly games. Satellite radio is national in coverage making it cost prohibitive for most events that are not of a national scale or importance. If the event draws 80% of its fans from a 75 mile radius—satellite is an expensive proposition to try to reach a specific audience. If the draw is over a large region or national—satellite is a great option to consider.

As an event organizer, keep in mind that prospective ticket buyers do not listen to the radio all the time. It is important to know when customers are listening. For example, if an event wants to reach a large portion of its audience by advertising during the morning drive when they are commuting to work, the event will have to specify that time period to the radio station when it places its advertising schedule. Two of the most popular times to reach people are during their work commute time with morning (6:00 am–10:00 am) and afternoon (3:00 pm–6:00 pm) drive times. Event managers can expect to pay a premium to advertise during these two drive times because research has shown listening levels are at their highest for the day.

Radio is a personal advertising medium. Station personalities have a good rapport with their listeners. If a radio personality announces an event's commercial, it is almost an implied endorsement.

Since prospective buyers will not be able to automatically recall the commercials, event organizers will need to design a schedule that provides them the opportunity to hear the same commercial four to six times before the message sinks in.

Radio Advertising Glossary of Terms

Knowing the terminology used in the measurement of radio listening is essential to a better understanding of audience estimates. The definitions that follow are generally accepted by the radio industry.

Cost Per Rating Point (CPP) The cost of reaching 1% of the target population. CPP is calculated by dividing the cost of the schedule by the gross rating points. National and regional advertising buyers frequently use this cost efficiency measure, since it can be applied across all media.

Cost Per Thousand (CPM) The relative cost of a schedule of announcements may be calculated by dividing the cost of the schedule by the sum of the average quarter-hour audiences of the announcements purchased.

Frequency The average number of exposures to the commercial or song heard by the average listener, or a frequency distribution revealing the number of persons estimated to have heard the commercial or song one time, two times, three times, four times, and so on.

Format Programming of a radio station aimed at a specific audience such as Country, Adult Contemporary, Urban, Rock, and so on.

Rating The percentage of the population listening to a given radio station during a day part. Ratings apply to both average quarter-hour and cumulative audiences.

Reach The total number of different persons exposed to a commercial or song during a specified day part. Reach can be calculated using a computer for a single station, multiple stations, or across media using formulas generally accepted by the advertising industry.

Share The percentage of people listening to a specific radio station in a particular day part compared with all those listening to radio in that day part. Share answers the question: "What percentage of the radio audience is listening to a specific station at a particular time?"

Time Spent Listening (TSL) The amount of time the average listener spent listening to a radio station during a day part. The estimate may be expressed in number of quarter hours or in hours/minutes. TSL answers the question: "How much time does the average listener spend with this station?"

Source: Arbitron Inc., (www.arbitron.com/radio_stations/tradeterms.htm) and Research Director (www.researchdirectorinc.com/Glossary.htm)

Newspaper Advertising

Every advertising medium has characteristics that give it natural advantages and limitations. Looking through any newspaper will demonstrate that there are some businesses that advertise regularly. Observe who they are and how they advertise their products and services. Events can reach certain types of people by placing their ads in different sections of the paper. Most events will end up advertising in the entertainment or sports section of a paper.

People expect advertising in the newspaper. In fact, many people buy the paper just to read the ads from the supermarket, movies, or department stores. Unlike advertising on TV and radio, advertising in the newspaper can be examined at a person's leisure. A newspaper ad can contain details, such as event ticket prices, charge by phone telephone numbers, online ticketing purchase information, and game times.

There are many advantages to advertising in the newspaper. From the advertiser's point of view, newspaper advertising is convenient because production changes can be made quickly, if necessary. Often, a new advertisement can be inserted on short notice. Another advantage is the large variety of ad sizes newspaper advertising offers. Event promoters may not have a large budget, but they can still afford to place a series of small newspaper ads. Advertising in the newspaper offers many advantages, but it is not without its inherent disadvantages.

Recently, some major daily newspapers have gone out of business, or moved to digital only production. Others are changing their print schedule to come out three to four times a week instead of daily. Another possibility is a combination of reduced print frequency and additional online distribution. Newspapers usually are read once and only stay in the house for a day. The print quality of newspapers is not the best, especially for photographs that event managers might want to capture the true essence of their event. So, simple artwork and line drawings produce the best results. The page size of a traditional daily newspaper is fairly large and small ads can look minuscule. Remember that in the entertainment or sports section, the ad has to compete with other entertainment ads to gain the reader's attention.

Cost and Format

Newspaper advertising is typically sold by the column inch, with most daily newspapers working with a 6-column-wide format. For example, an ad that measures 4 columns wide and 6 inches in height would be the equivalent of a 24-inch ad. If the per column inch rate for the newspaper is $45.00, the ad would cost $1080.00 (24 column inches × $45 per column inch).

Historically, newspaper circulation drops on Saturdays and increases on Sundays, which is also the day a newspaper is read most thoroughly. Create short, descriptive copy for the event ad. Using a less-is-more approach, event managers can develop an uncluttered ad that will increase readership. Do not try to crowd everything possible into the layout space. Including a website and phone number where more information is available is a great strategy to free up space. If the newspaper or an agency helps with the layout, be sure to request a proof of the final version so the event organizers can approve it or make changes before it is printed. Always make sure everyone is satisfied with the ad before it goes to print.

The Dover Way

Mark Rossi, Vice President of Sales and Marketing, Dover Motorsports

In my role as Vice President of Sales and Marketing at Dover Motorsports, a NASCAR track, I am working on our marketing plan on a daily basis and always trying to learn more about our fans. It is true that there are three primary feeder branches to the marketing tree: The first branch is the advertising campaign; the second is the promotional campaign; and the third is the publicity campaign. Each of these main branches has multiple smaller "tactical branches" which grow out from within, based on the marketing strategy. The key to producing a healthy full tree is in this strategy. And you cannot develop a strategy unless you know your fan base. This has to be your first priority, if fact having a solid grasp on your demographics is the key to success for both marketing and sponsorship execution.

For years at Dover, we used a "one size fits all" approach to our marketing. We did not distinguish between "hard core" and "casual" fans when it came to creating our message or our medium. Today, with our new understanding of fans, this has changed. Specifically, we now have a clear distinction between our hardcore and casual fans and the way we communicate with each group is different to maximize attendance.

To learn more about our fans, we have conducted extensive research. To begin, we found that our fans fall into two main categories, "hard core" and "casual" with each having the following characteristics.

Hard Core Fans:

- Have attended before and want to attend again
- Older age group (age 45–54)
- 64% male; 36% female
- Hard working and full time employed
- Large segment of blue collar—construction/maintenance workers
- Median annual income $59,000
- 91% White
- Largely nonurbanites (65% nonurban)
- They plan ahead and need lead time

Casual Fans:

- Open and interested, but need motivation and a reason to attend
- Younger age group (age 18–34)
- Diverse 73% White; 15% Hispanic
- More urban (55% urban)
- Last minute decisions are OK

Then, we researched how our fans consume media in an effort to better target how we reach our fans. We found that magazines, radio, and online were top ways hard core fans consumed media. Casual fans can also be reached through magazines, newspapers, and online but also reported high levels of television viewership (especially Prime Time TV). Hard core fans were less likely to watch TV than casual fans.

Once we had an understanding of media consumption habits, we turned our attention to researching how different types of fans travel and leisure time. This really made us evaluate what, how, where we went to market. The results taught us that our hard core fan is going to plan their trip well in advance and are going to make a weekend of it, while the casual fan is not going to decide until the last minute and he/she is looking for a quick day trip. In our research, we also learned that while our fans consumption of media, and the way they make decisions to attend events are different they do have some key similarities in many "lifestyle" interest.

The similarities between hard core and casual fans are important in marketing as well. Both types of fans are on the go, they get out and visit places (i.e., bars, restaurants, the beach), are mobile, and live an active lifestyle. They also generally love sports and are outdoor focused. In addition to the beach they love camping, fishing, hunting, and other outdoor activities. They consumer a great deal of sports on TV as well.

All of these facts made us re-think the way we go to market. Moving forward, we are changing our marketing message based on which fan base we are targeting (Hardcore vs. Casual). We will market to each at different times with a different media mix, across a different set of DMAs, or designated marketing areas. The message to our hard core fan will target outer markets in a 300 mile radius of the facility while our casual fan efforts will be focused on a 100 mile radius. Each campaign will have a different feel to it. Our Hardcore advertising will be centered on the

▶

facts, heritage, and tradition. The casual fan needs more information. They need to know why Dover is an appropriate substitute for Hershey Park, or a Ravens game, or even a trip to Dewey Beach that weekend.

Sample of Casual Fan Marketing Messages by Age

18–24	25–34	35–54
You've never seen a party like this.	So much to do, we hope you get to see the race.	Your bucket list called, needs you to get to Dover.
Compete with BBQs, tailgates, house parties	Compete with Dorney Park and Six Flags	Play on proximity guilt.

Our advertising budget is about 12% of our gross ticket revenue so it falls within the 10%–15% considered to be standard operating procedure for the industry. What seems at first to be a significant amount of funding becomes less so when you start to consider the many market segmentations that result from the effort to properly market based on our research. Prioritizing each tactic based on its perceived ability to deliver is key at this point. Included into this prioritization is not just the media's ability to deliver an audience, but also the obligations and expectations that sponsors have against our media and its ability to deliver exposure for them as well. All of these have to be thoroughly vetted out before any marketing plan can be finalized.

As illustrated by this example, understanding your market, and differentiating your market into segments takes a lot of time and effort. But, it is worth it when attendance increases and you realize that your efforts have generated new revenue for your organization.

Choosing the Right Media — Nontraditional Media

While television, radio, and newspaper have been the staples for event advertising, it is important to consider other alternatives to traditional advertising formats. Online advertising, outdoor advertising, and direct mail can also produce good results for events.

Digital Advertising

Today, promoters are using digital advertising at an increasing rate to hit target audiences and get the word out about events. Digital advertising utilizes the internet to deliver messages via computer, smart TV, tablets, and mobile devices, just to name a few. It is a rapidly growing platform and can be a very cost-efficient medium. In most cases, the website with the highest traffic in a given market is owned by the daily newspaper. Cleveland Live, www.clevelandlive.com, is a very well read website that redistributes most of the articles contained in *The Cleveland Plain Dealer* and is an effective way to reach an audience that is looking for entertainment options.

Today, when event organizers think of digital advertising, they should not limit their options to banner ads on high-traffic websites. Event marketers need to think about the best platforms to reach their target consumers and explore the wide variety of ways they can acquire, track, and communicate with their target audience. An example might be using tracking cookies for retargeting advertising, search engine marketing, social media campaigns, native and programmatic advertising, as well as boundless opportunities to connect with an intended audience through cross-promotions with tools like email marketing. Many sports venues and recurring events have databases with previous customers who want to stay informed on upcoming events and are always looking for special discounts. These databases allow venues and teams to team-up and email regular newsletters to interested fans about on sale dates and upcoming events. The US Airways Center in Phoenix uses Facebook and Instagram to share information with fans in smaller chunks while also creating a back and forth dialog with them. Dover International Speedway uses content marketing programs and tracking cookies to retarget potential consumers demonstrating an interest in NASCAR racing based on the content that they view online. The consumer then ends up with ticket offers and speedway advertising on their subsequent web pages.

Connecting with an event's past, and prospective, customers via platforms like email, Facebook, Pinterest, and Twitter have many advantages to the event promoter, starting with the ability to distribute information to individuals with a history with the event, venue, or sport. A second benefit is the low cost of engagement. In many cases, if the customer database is built properly, effective marketing can occur with little, or no, additional cost. When an event contracts with a ticketing company like Ticketmaster, the event will receive the right to all names and email addresses of any customers who purchase their tickets online via Ticketmaster. If the event has its own ticketing system and customer relationship management (CRM) system, the levels of detail are only limited by the staff's ability to understand and analyze the data. Today, many live events are incentivizing their customers to purchase tickets online, as it helps build a long-term relationship because the customer's email address is captured. Compared with direct mail, email is much less expensive and allows event organizers to link potential customers back to their website, where organizers can provide additional detail about the event. With targeted offers through email, the event organizers can also measure a direct return on their investment by tracking how many offers are redeemed.

Outdoor Advertising

When most people think of outdoor advertising, they tend to envision billboards along a busy highway; however, there are other forms advertising in this category. Other forms include, but are not limited to, transit advertising (buses, light rail, taxi cabs), wrapped vehicles, delivery truck signage, posters, and electronic displays. Outdoor advertising connects with the audience as an element of the environment and does not have to be invited into a person's home, apartment, or college residence hall. It is part of public domain and represents a form of media that consumers cannot switch off or throw away. As a result, outdoor advertising represents a captured audience that works on frequency, as most outdoor contracts run a minimum of 30 days.

One of the advantages of outdoor advertising for an event promoter is that there is usually plenty of unsold space in most markets. Outdoor companies are open to trade agreements and will provide space in exchange for an equal value of tickets to an event. These companies can use the tickets to entertain paid advertisers without adding money to their travel and entertainment budgets. The event promoters will still need to pay for the price of producing items like billboards, bus cards, and taxi top signage. In some cases, a blend of cash and trade is a good way to extend the event's advertising budget with an outdoor advertising company. The more desirable locations are typically not available for trade, so if the event organizers really want one high-traffic billboard location, they can purchase the unit at rate card and leverage their outdoor reach with other locations.

A great example of impactful outdoor advertising is a marketing campaign run by Ohio University Athletics with their beverage partner, Pepsi. In the small college town of Athens, Ohio University athletics ticketing messaging is on display on Pepsi delivery trucks. The message is located on the back of the truck on the roll-up door. As a result, any vehicle driving behind a Pepsi delivery truck, stopped at a stoplight behind a truck, or even parked near a truck making a delivery is exposed to the message.

Billboards are one form of outdoor advertising.

Having the message on the back of the truck results in longer views as driver are more likely to see the message in front of them as compared with beside them on the side of a vehicle while driving.

When considering outdoor advertising, event managers have to keep in mind some of the disadvantages as well. The event's message has to be short and to the point, as the average reader will only have 3–5 seconds to focus on the message. While event managers might be able to negotiate a rate for 1 month, most outdoor companies will start with a 3-month commitment. Remember that media is one of the most negotiable services, and if the event has cash and tickets to work with, event organizers should be able to negotiate an agreement that benefits both parties.

Direct Mail

What makes direct mail any different than the regular mail someone might receive from a friend or family member? Nothing ... it is just a way that the advertising community describes a promotional offer or message that circumvents the traditional forms of media (TV, radio, and newspaper) that were described earlier in this chapter.

The advantage of direct mail is that it can be very targeted if the event keeps records of individuals who have purchased tickets in the past. Event managers might want to consider an early bird offer by sending a direct mail piece to past purchasers of the event before tickets or entry slots go on sale to the general public. This is a great way to reward fans that have attended or participated in the event in the past and let them know that the event appreciates their continued support. In some cases, the event may even consider a special discount and deadline depending on the overall demand for full-price tickets to the event.

Today, event marketers are using specialized agencies to help designing direct mail campaigns that find likely individuals to target for a direct mail campaign. The generally accepted response rate for direct mail is 1%–2%. But, according to Brandon Steffek (personal communication, March 5, 2015), Director of Sales at Full House Entertainment Database Marketing, "the rate can be double or triple that with quality data, good creative, the right offer, and the type of mail piece." It is becoming increasingly important to develop the right target mailing list. For example, if an event finds that its past sales indicate that a particular zip code represents 25% of its buying audience, it may want to do some additional research within the zip code to find other consumers that match the profile of these past attendees.

The cost of a four-color promotional direct mail brochure can be expensive, and event organizers need to look at the ROI before deciding to use direct mail. As compared with email, where the expense is basically personnel time, direct mail does allow an event to stand out from the clutter if the design of the mail creates excitement around the event.

Direct mail can be specifically targeted to an event's market segment(s).

Additional advice on direct mail:

- Define the target audience and determine who the event wants to reach.
- Determine the offer the event is prepared to make on the campaign.
- Estimate the ROI and use a 1%–2% return rate to be conservative.
- Secure the right mailing list and bring in an outside agency to help determine whom to mail and help the event create an exciting looking mail piece.
- Use clear and concise language with the promotional offer that provides good direction to the audience.
- If event organizers are not prepared to invest in creative services, they may want to eliminate direct mail from their media mix.
- Make sure to coordinate the timing of the mailing with the other forms of media that the event organizers choose for the event.

SUMMARY

From this chapter, students should gain a fundamental understanding of the aspects that are important in creating a marketing plan for events. The event marketing plan includes the production and coordination of all advertising, promotional, and public relations campaigns for the event with the goal of maximizing revenue generation and event attendance. Marketing in sport events has moved from only traditional advertising mediums to now a mix of traditional and new mediums. Event managers and sport executives need to move away from the "one size fits all" approach of marketing and toward market segmentation using different tactics for different fan/customer segments. Students will also understand the terminology and measurements associated with each platform, which better enable event managers to make the right media decisions for their events during the planning process.

Student Challenges

NAME _____ DATE_____

Develop plans around media exposure, advertising, and promotional campaigns for an event. Additionally, create a plan to monitor these activities.

Question 6.1

Develop a basic advertising plan for an existing event in your community. In 250–500 words, list all appropriate advertising outlets including, but not limited to, television, radio, print, outdoor, grass roots, and online. Additionally, indicate *why* each outlet is a good fit for advertising the event. Take notes here and then type up the advertising plan.

Question 6.2

Choose and examine two prospective media partners for the event. Determine how to work with these partners to maximize promotional exposure (e.g., sweepstakes, contests, etc.). Hint: Most events have a local radio station partner at a minimum.

Media Partner #1:
Ideas to maximize promotional exposure:

Media Partner #2:
Ideas to maximize promotional exposure:

EVENT SPONSORSHIP

Jim Kahler and Annie Valeant Brackley

James Kahler is the Executive Director of the Center of Sports Administration at Ohio University. Previously, he helped develop the MBA Sports Business Program at the W.P. Carey School of Business at Arizona State University and was the Senior Vice President of Sales and Marketing for the Cleveland Cavaliers (NBA) and Rockers (WNBA). Mr. Kahler has over 20 years of experience in sales and marketing in sport. He has also served on the NBA's Marketing Advisory Committee and is currently on the Advisory Board for a number of sports business organizations, including the National Sports Forum (San Diego, California), Navigate Research, and In Stadium Advertising (Chicago, Illinois). He also sits on the Board of Directors for US Table Tennis.

Annie Valeant Brackley is currently a Sports Management Instructor at Ohio University. Prior to academia, Ms. Brackley worked full-time as a sports and event planning professional in various business development and marketing roles for the New York Road Runners, Sponsorship Direct, GMR Marketing, ESPN, and the Charlotte Knights. She has also done consulting work for the Southern Ohio Copperheads, Elmira Jackals, National Sports Forum, West Virginia Power Baseball, Charleston Distance Run and the New Orleans Super Bowl Committee.

This chapter provides students with an introduction to the concept of event sponsorships and the key principles associated with sponsorship. Sponsorship has been defined many ways, but for the purposes of this chapter, the International Events Group (IEG) definition will be used. IEG defines **sponsorship** as a cash and/or in-kind fee paid to a property (typically in sports, arts, entertainment, or causes) in return for access to the exploitable commercial potential associated with that property (Ukman, 2014).

IEG was founded in 1981 with the primary goal of helping to establish sponsorship as the fourth arm of marketing along with advertising, publicity, and promotions. Although this chapter will only touch on the broad aspects of sponsorship, event organizers will find IEG to be a useful resource if they are interested in learning more about sponsorships. Visit www.sponsorship.com, for additional information on sponsorships.

According to IEG, worldwide spending on sponsorships was more than $53 billion in 2013, and North America led the world with close to $20 billion spent on sponsorship that year (Ukman, 2014). Events in the United States made up most of this spending with traditional sponsorships in the four major sports leagues (NBA, NFL, MLB, and NHL) and NASCAR. With the recent success of the 2014 Winter Olympics in Sochi and the FIFA World Cup in Brazil, the rest of the world is closing in on this form of marketing.

Sponsorship of sports has continuted to increase over the last three decades.

Reasons Companies Sponsors

Companies have traditionally invested in sponsorship for one of three primary reasons:

- Build brand awareness with a targeted audience
- Capture potential and current customer data
- Increase sales with a targeted audience

Event sponsorship enables companies to achieve each of these objectives while providing an experiential interaction between the product and consumer. A sponsor may strive to fulfill any combination of these objectives, depending on its specific motivation.

Event organizers have the ability to create an atmosphere at their event that allows attendees to interact with a sponsor's product or service, and create a unique experience for their sponsor that traditional advertising (print, radio, television) cannot deliver. This interaction could best be described as **experiential marketing**. Today, experiential marketing in the sport of NASCAR has become part of the live event, with sponsors often competing for the attention of race fans on the day of the event. Some sponsors pay anywhere from $5 million to $35 million annually for a NASCAR partnership (Klara, 2013).

One experiential marketing example, T-Mobile's sponsorship with Major League Baseball (MLB), provides the company a dominant amount of space at the All-Star FanFest, a pregame festival that runs 5 days in advance of the game. The experience for a fan to attend such an event leaves a lasting memory that allows T-Mobile the opportunity not only to build brand awareness, but also increase brand loyalty, as individuals (primarily adults) who attend this event are likely to consider using or switching to T-Mobile. While not everyone can obtain a ticket to the game, almost 115,000 baseball fans in the Minneapolis area attended the MLB All-Star FanFest in 2014 (MLB, 2014).

Fans interact with sponsors at ancillary events, such as fan interactive events, even if the fans can't attend the main event.

So how can T-Mobile use its sponsorship with the All-Star Game and MLB to increase sales? In this case, T-Mobile acquires the right to exploit, on a commercial basis, the logos of MLB and the 2014 All-Star Game. T-Mobile would then have the right to build special displays in various retail outlets across the United States. In addition, T-Mobile can provide fans with the opportunity to meet MLB players and legends at FanFest, participate in various on-site baseball clinics, and charge their mobile devices on-site. T-Mobile customers also get the opportunity to enter FanFest at a discounted price (T-mobile, 2014). Having the opportunity to utilize special promotions like this would allow T-Mobile's sales team the opportunity to generate special displays and increase sales for a 30-day time period. This example of a sales promotion would allow T-Mobile the opportunity to measure incremental sales in the Minneapolis area over the same period of time from a year ago, when the MLB All-Star Game was being played in Queens, NY. This gives the company the ability to then measure the impact of its sponsorship and increased case sales.

Event Sponsorship and Minor Events

Norm O'Reilly, Ohio University, Professor and Sports Administration
Department Chair, Ohio University

Much of what is written about sponsorship is targeted specifically to those major events, often called mega events, where sponsor interest is high and the reach/impact of the event is significant. However, for the majority of events, sponsorship is a challenging—if not daunting—proposition. In fact, many events achieve very little or no cash sponsorship and only cover a small proportion of the value-in-kind (VIK) sponsorship they seek. This is the reality for 99% of all sporting events.

Take, for example, a location triathlon in a small city that draws 400 participants each year. The event is not on television (except for a few minor spots on local news) and is not streamed online. It has a website. Of the 400 participants, 50% are local and 50% come from outside of town but most from less than a 3-hour drive away. Each year, the race director pursues sponsorship. Over the 10-year history of the event, there have been a few title sponsors, a handful of cash sponsors and some in-kind sponsors/suppliers who provide goods. The race director is quite frustrated and wonders why she can't get more revenue from sponsorship.

Her frustration is not a surprise. In fact, it is the reality facing many minor sporting events. A title sponsor may get some recognition locally and some coverage in the press but does it really lead to any significant business for them? The answer lies in whether they are a corporation whose business is directly related to the event or not. If not, such as a car company, insurance company, bank or technology firm, the chance of them achieving value from a minor event sponsorship is very low. In fact, these types of categories—nonsport organizations using sport to achieve their marketing goals—is normally only successful in mega events with large reach where the event can help the brand attached to new attributes. In minor events, this impact is very limited. Thus, it is sponsors directly involved with the sport (e.g., energy drink, swimwear manufacturer, etc.) who have the only chance of generating a return on investment (ROI) through sales to justify the investment. So, if the swimwear manufacturer purchases the title sponsorship for $5,000 and invests another $2,500 activating that sponsorship, they would need to sell related merchandise for at least $7,500 in incremental profit. This is also very challenging in an event with 400 participants.

So what to do? The recommended approach for organizers of a minor sporting event is to focus on building the event to such a point as its assets have enough value to legitimately attract sponsorship.

Types of Sponsorship

Sponsorship typically falls into the following categories:

- Event (or property) sponsorship
- Venue sponsorship
- Broadcast sponsorship

In **event sponsorship,** a company (sponsor) promises to provide cash or a **VIK** donation to the event or property. In return, the sponsor is promised brand exposure and assets associated with the organization. With an event sponsorship, the sponsor may be targeting the participants (e.g., triathlon or CrossFit event) or the spectators or fan at an event (e.g., NCAA March Madness or Cleveland Browns). The nature of the sponsor's business will play a role in whether or not the sponsor decides to provide cash, VIK, or both. Often times consumer packaged goods companies will provide the event or property with product and very little to no cash. The sponsor's product is adding value to the event and property, and saving event organizers money that it would have had to spend if the sponsor were not associated with the organization. In turn, the sponsor is getting brand recognition.

Venue sponsorship is when a company pays an organization to have its name associated with the facility. The financial commitment of the sponsor will reflect the amount of exposure the sponsor receives at the facility. Sponsors will often sign multiyear agreements and pay millions of dollars to have its name associated with the facility. For example, over the course of 20-years, Citigroup will pay $200 million to have the naming rights to Citi Field, the MLB stadium in Flushing, NY (Sports Business Journal, 2011).

Broadcast sponsorship exists when a company agrees to offset the expenses of a specific part of an event broadcast. Often times when fans watch a sporting event on television, they will notice companies who sponsor a specific segment of the event. For example, the 2015 NCAA March Madness

Tournament on CBS features the "AT&T at the Half." During the half-time report, AT&T will be mentioned multiple times by the sports broadcasters and AT&T branded-images will be present throughout half-time, such as in on-screen graphics, on the front of the desk where the talent sit, on the monitors behind the talent, on the note cards the talent holds in their hands, and many other places.

Pricing and Level of Sponsorships

Event organizers may rely on sponsors for either cash and/or in-kind donations. Both the event organizer and sponsor must come to an agreement on a deal that best fits the objectives of both parties. For example, the event organizers may wish to ask potential sponsors for cash. However, the potential sponsor may not be in a financial position to provide money. Often times, the event organizers will then ask potential sponsors for VIK products and services.

An example of a VIK donation is a snack company providing pretzels for each 5K race finisher. The 5K event saves money by not having to purchase snacks for finishers, and the sponsor gets its product in the hands of potential customers (race finishers). In addition, the hope is that the event organizers provide the sponsor with additional assets such as race entries, course signage, and other possible benefits.

Typically, event organizers carve out different levels of sponsorship based on the money and/or VIK provided by the sponsor. The level of sponsorship dictates how many and which assets will be provided to the sponsor. Sponsorship level examples include: title sponsor, presenting sponsor, principal sponsor, and supporting sponsor. In this case, the title sponsorship would be the most expensive, offering the sponsor the most assets, and the supporting sponsorship would be the least expensive and offer the least amount of assets.

Sponsorship pricing is market driven. An international event that draws viewers from across the world will charge significantly more for a sponsorship than a local event drawing a few hundred people. One-time events are also harder to value in comparison with annual events and a series of events. Event organizers usually benchmark other events similar in size and demographics to come up with a sponsorship value. In addition, organizations will work with their accounting team to ensure each sponsorship agreement reaches a certain profit percentage. The percentage varies. Some properties are more conservative than others.

Sponsorship Activation

According to Brian Gainor, Founder of PartnershipActivation.com, **sponsorship activation** is the marketing activities that a company conducts in relation to its sponsorship, linked to measurable goals and objectives (personal communication, November 14, 2014).

Paying the rights fees or providing VIK at an event isn't enough. Consumers are subjected to thousands of advertisements a day. In order for companies to stay top of mind in the eyes of attendees at sporting events, it is imperative that sponsors provide consumers with opportunities to interact with their products and brand image. Sponsorship activation at sporting events may include product sampling, in-game promotions, on-site interactive displays, and enter to win sweepstakes, to name a few.

IEG.com reports that, on average, sponsors spend an additional $1.70 on sponsorship activation per $1 paid for a sponsorship, meaning this is in addition to the money spent on property rights fees (Ukman, 2014). If a company paid a $100,000 fee for event sponsorship rights, on average, that company will spend an additional $170,000 to activate the sponsorship.

Many international, national, and regional brands hire a third-party expert to handle the sport sponsorship activation. It makes more sense for the sponsor to rely on these experts to get the best bang for its buck in sponsorship activation than to try and develop, execute, and measure the success of a sponsorship activation plan itself. Some third-party companies include: GMR Marketing, IMG Worldwide, Team Epic, The Marketing Arm & HMS Worldwide.

In many cases, it does not make financial sense for a sponsor to hire a third-party expert to handle its activation. Either the event is too small or there may be limited opportunities to activate at the specific event. In these cases, the activation is often handled internally. Most sports properties and event organizations have full-time sponsorship service personnel who are hired to service the sponsorship agreements. Part of that position's role is to help facilitate and assist the sponsor in its activation strategy.

Targeting Sponsors

As event managers look to target potential sponsors for their event, it will become increasingly important to ask one very significant question: What's in it for you? In this case, the "you" is the sponsor and this key question can be referred to as the WIIFY. Individuals trying to sell the sponsorship need to put themselves in the position of the company that they are trying to bring on board as a sponsor. Then they should ask themselves what they might do if they were sitting on the other side of the negotiating table. By doing this, whoever is selling will put themselves in position for success.

Listed below is a series of 22 questions that have been developed to help event managers look for the right sponsors for their event. These questions are what sponsors will be asking themselves as they review countless opportunities for sponsorship.

22 Questions That Sponsors Ask Themselves

1. Does the event line up with the image the sponsor is trying to project?

2. Does the audience (whether audience is a literal audience/spectators of an event or the event participants) at the event meet the target audience of the sponsor?

3. Will the event extend the reach of the sponsor with television coverage?

4. Will event organizers provide the sponsor with the right to bring a retail partner on board? (Example: Would the event allow Coca-Cola to bring in a third-party retailer, such as a grocery store, to create a sweepstakes?)

5. Would the prospective sponsor think enough of the event to convert a portion of their existing advertising to showcase the partnership? (e.g., Coors Light's television campaign that helps to celebrate their sponsorship with the NFL via postgame press conference footage with former coaches.)

6. Will the event receive media coverage?

7. Are the potential hospitality benefits affiliated with the sponsorship attractive to the clients of the sponsor?

8. Is the event willing to place the sponsor's logo in all of its advertising for the event? If so, what is the size of the advertising budget and how many other sponsors will be featured in the advertising? (Note: Be careful that not too many sponsors are included in the event's advertising, resulting in "alphabet soup.")

9. If the event provides the sponsor with the right to capitalize on the event logo, will the sponsor take advantage of that opportunity outside of the four walls of the event?

10. Does the date/timing of the event line up well with the sponsor's promotional calendar, or will it conflict with another event the sponsor is already involved in?

11. Is the event willing to provide the sponsor with exclusivity? If not, be prepared to share the overall plan and the number of competing sponsors that the prospect might see at the event.

12. Does the event have the ability to showcase the products or services of the sponsor at the event?

13. What is the projected attendance at the event and is it believable?

14. Can the sponsor drive incremental sales by being involved with the event?

15. Will the sponsor be able to measure their ROI with the amount of extra visibility obtained through the sponsorship and incremental sales driven through the relationship?

16. How will the sponsor's boss feel about the sponsorship?

17. Does the sponsorship have the opportunity to be a long-term partnership? Has the event offered the sponsor the right to enter into a long-term partnership with first right to renew?

18. Will the event be able to deliver everything outlined in the sponsorship proposal?

19. Will the event organizers provide a recap of the sponsorship after the event concludes that helps to justify the cost?

20. Will the sponsor get lost in the clutter of other event sponsors?

21. Does the sponsorship provide a competitive advantage to the sponsor over their competition?

22. If the event managers were sitting at the desk of the prospective sponsor, would they enter into the partnership?

This list is not necessarily exhaustive, but will help event managers to understand the questions that potential sponsors are asking internally. Reviewing the answers may result in revisions to sponsorship proposals to ensure they are tailored to the specific prospective sponsor being approached. Ultimately, this will help in securing a sponsor.

Sponsorship Sales Process

The most efficient ways a property can start out selling sponsorships is by making a list of categories it would like to fill. A **category** is the group, class, or division that describes a company's business area. These categories may have the potential to create exclusivity for each partner whereby its competitor cannot market at the event. In addition, the categories may offset event expenses. Sample categories include, but are not limited to: automotive, banking, quick-service restaurant (QSR), telecommunications, and health care. From there, the property should make a list of potential sponsors within each category and look to set up a meeting with each of the companies.

It usually takes several meetings before a sponsorship agreement is formed. Depending on the size of the sponsorship, it could take months before an agreement is made. Often times, title sponsorships and other high level sponsorship agreements take multiple conversations to ensure each party's needs are met. Each case is different and it is recommended it be treated as such.

If the sponsor sees enough value in the sponsorship proposal and has the resources to fulfill the agreement, the two parties form a partnership. At this point, the event organization will develop a legal contract (see Chapter 3 for sample contract) between both parties, and a representative from each organization or its lawyers with sign off agreeing to the terms found in the document.

If the event seeking sponsorships is an annual event, the organization may want to consider multiyear partnerships with its sponsors. This ensures revenue and/or VIK for the event in years to come. It also saves money and time when developing signage and other sponsor-branded elements associated with the event. In the sponsor's eyes, multiyear agreements allow the company to plan its budget for the upcoming fiscal years.

The contract agreement will often include a date when the sponsorship renewal process begins. If the sponsor sees enough value in the partnership, and can afford it, the sponsor will likely renew.

Sponsorship deals often take time and several meetings for parties to come to an agreement.

The length and size of the partnership is going to depend on how far in advance the sponsorship renewal period will begin. Some sponsorships look to renew a few years in advance while others are looking to renew just a few months before the event. Each case is different.

In addition, one size does not fit all. The same sponsorship agreement often doesn't work for multiple sponsors. It is important that sponsorship sales personnel tailor each sponsorship proposal to fit the potential sponsor and its business objectives. This requires sales staff to research the prospective sponsor ahead of time, and listen to the company's needs and objectives in the first meeting. Once the organization has a better sense of what the sponsor is looking for, the sales staff can work up a potential sponsorship proposal that will fit both parties' needs.

Executing a successful event and the ability to sell event sponsorships are two different skill sets that young event managers need to understand. In some cases, it may make sense for event managers to hire an outside sales agent to sell their sponsorships. This has been the trend with college athletics since approximately the year 2000, with athletic directors at major universities negotiating guaranteed sponsorships from companies like IMG College (www.imgcollege.com) and Learfield Sports (www.learfield.com) that now represent sponsorship sales for nearly 90 schools and over 100 schools, respectively, across the country. These niche companies provide a specific set of sales skills and focus only on selling and servicing sponsorships as compared with event managers being pulled in many different directions.

Hiring an outside agency typically comes with a price of anywhere from 15% to 25% of the gross total generated through the sale of sponsorships. If the event or organization is big enough, like a major college athletic department, it can require an up-front guarantee from the agency that receives the right to sell sponsorships. This would be the case with the NCAA and its Men's Basketball Tournament when it secured an up-front multimillion dollar guarantee from CBS Sports for the airtime and sponsorship inventory associated with the tournament.

Sponsorship Evaluation

After the event has taken place, it is common for a property to recap the partnership for the sponsor. In this recap, properties will include images and video content documenting the sponsor's affiliation with the event. In addition, properties will attempt to quantify the impact the sponsorship has had on the sponsor's business. Examples may include, but are not limited to: number of attendees at event, number of signs, number of impressions, number of samples distributed, and so forth. In the end, the property's goal is to show the sponsor that the partnership is worth the money and/or VIK provided. Properties look to provide sponsors with a recap soon after the event has taken place. If needed, the property and/or sponsor may hire out a third party to measure the overall effectiveness of the partnership. The end result is trying to calculate the ROI and return on objectives (ROO).

ROI means that the business generated by the sponsorship should be at least equal to or greater than the cost of the sponsorship. Return on Objective (ROO) measures whether or not a sponsorship meets the sponsor's business objectives (Lynde, 2007).

Resources that are commonly used to measure sponsorship effectiveness include: impression numbers (e.g., Nielson Report), sponsor sales, web traffic, email clicks, and social media activity (e.g., Facebook friends, likes, photos, Tweets), among others.

Companies that specialize in helping to measure the effectiveness of a sponsorship include: Navigate Research, Sponsorship Research International (Sri), and IEG.

Conflicts and Risk Management Factors in Sponsorship

Event managers need to be aware of possible restrictions they may encounter when renting an arena or stadium to host an event. It is not unusual for facilities to negotiate exclusive sponsorships with companies like Coca-Cola that include exclusive pouring and signage rights within the venue for the soft drink company. The key for any event manager is to be aware of such provisions with facility sponsors and never promise any benefits that may not be deliverable. For example, Coca-Cola has exclusive pouring rights at the Superdome in New Orleans, LA. However, the NFL's beverage partner is PepsiCo. During the 2013 Super Bowl, Pepsi was forced to get creative in how it promoted and distributed its beverages. It did so by displaying temporary Pepsi signage in and around the stadium, and covering up the Coca-Cola branded items whenever possible, and supplementing it with PepsiCo. products.

It is important that risky promotions such as, "Win $10,000 if you make a half-court shot" or "Buy one, get one free if the hometown wins" be insured. Sponsors associated with these types of promotions purchase a prize indemnity insurance policy for that contest that helps to limit the payout risk. For example, in 2014, Quicken Loans ran a sweepstakes in conjunction with its PGA sponsorship, offering entrants a chance to win $1 million if a golfer hit a hole in one on the 10th hole at the Quicken Loans National PGA Tournament in Bethesda, MD. Had someone won this promotion, Quicken Loans would have been covered under its insurance policy. Instead of Quicken Loans having to come up with $1 million, its insurance company would cover the majority of expenses (Quickenloans.com, 2015).

MetroPCS Orange Bowl Half-Court Shot Contest

Christina Ramos

The Orange Bowl Committee is a nonprofit sports organization that promotes Championship sporting events, related premier entertainment, and other year-round activities to inspire youth, engage the community, and enhance the South Florida economy.

Each December, the Orange Bowl hosts the MetroPCS Orange Bowl Basketball Classic, which is a double-header basketball event featuring four Division I college basketball teams.

With MetroPCS serving as Title Sponsor of the Classic, the Orange Bowl must find creative ways to activate their Title Sponsorship and incorporate the MetroPCS brand into the overall event.

In addition to receiving inclusion in the event logo, event marketing, and media, along with traditional in-arena and in-game exposure, MetroPCS also receives recognition during the MetroPCS Orange Bowl Half-Court Shot contest during each game of the Classic (two total per event). The winner of the half-court shot receives a whopping $25,000.

Each year, the Orange Bowl purchases contest insurance (also called prize coverage or promotion insurance) specifically for the half-court shot promotion. **Contest insurance** protects the sport organization from having to fund the cost of the prize if a contestant wins a promotional contest. The insurance company requires the sport organization purchase a policy to cover the cost of the prize. In essence, contest insurance companies know the odds of winning different types of contests and set the cost of policies based on the likelihood they will have to pay out the prize. The larger the prize and easier the contest, the higher the policy cost. In the case of the Orange Bowl, in more than a decade of hosting this sponsored promotion, no one had hit the shot until 2010.

During game No. 1 of the 2010 Classic, the contestant, attempted the half-court shot and made the basket for $25,000! Watch the video here: https://www.youtube.com/watch?v=mQO-wMP-Hgs. After filing an insurance claim, the prize was awarded and the insurance served its purpose.

Not only were the event attendees inside the arena excited about the winning shot, but the promotion was picked up by several media outlets after the event giving MetroPCS additional event coverage and more branding than they anticipated.

In 2011, the Orange Bowl filed for promotion insurance and prize coverage again per company protocol. During game one of the 2011 Classic, the contestant attempted the half-court shot and also won $25,000. Watch the video here: https://www.youtube.com/watch?v=_OiviDmGaeM. This story also received additional media coverage and press attention providing MetroPCS with even more value to their sponsorship.

Sports organizations must be prepared to host exciting and creative in-game presentations and sponsored promotions in order to exceed sponsor expectations and to keep event attendees captivated. The ability to purchase contest insurance allows sport organizations and events to generate buzz and excitement around large prizes without taking on the financial risk of being financially responsible for paying out the prize. Creative programming and properly executed in-event promotions are key components to successful sports marketing and sports sponsorships programs and campaigns.

Future of Sponsorship

Increasing sales, gaining customer information, and building brand awareness continue to be the top three reasons why companies sponsor events.

Every 2 years, the National Sports Forum (www.sports-forum.com) examines the motivations of companies that sponsor sports. In 2015, faculty from Ohio University, the University of Iowa, and Texas A&M University conducted 57 telephone interviews with some of the largest sports sponsors in North America, including Anheuser-Busch, Coca-Cola, Marriott, Pepsi, and UPS. Below is a list of top item results from the study.

- 89% of sponsors plan to spend as much or more in 2015.
- Traditional advertising (print, radio, television) has become less relevant.
- Sponsors are looking to channel money more effectively through activation and digital marketing.
- 48% of sports sponsorship dollars are spent in professional sports and 25% are spent in amateur sports.

- Collegiate sport sponsorship seems to be the biggest growth in amateur sport spending while culinary type events are on the rise.
- The top five threats to traditional sponsorship include: too expensive, sponsorship clutter, poor servicing, lack of activation, and lack of measurement.
- The top five media for directing sports sponsorship dollars are: social media, digital (websites, emails, banners), on-site promotions (Fan-fest, game-day activities), in-stadium opportunities (video board, traditional signage), and mobile (QR coding, augmented reality).
- The top five items sponsors are looking for in a sponsorship package are: use of marks and logos, access to exclusive content, sponsorship exclusivity, social media opportunities, official product or service status of a property.
- The top five elements that impact the evaluation of a sponsorship: drives traffic, direct sales, allows sponsor to break into new market, spending works within budget, property offers own able assets and items to activate around.
- The ability to create and get access to exclusive content is key for sponsors.
- By 2016, it is predicted that more money will be spent on digital media advertisements than traditional television advertisements.

Sponsorship Best Practices

Reebok CrossFit Games

In 2011, Reebok signed a 10-year deal becoming the title sponsor of the CrossFit Games. The sponsorship has added value, credibility, money, and exposure to CrossFit as a sport and the CrossFit Games. Reebok has developed a specific line of CrossFit branded fitness apparel, seen an increase in sales in its fitness apparel line, and has received exposure to over 100 countries participating in the CrossFit Games. Reebok headquarters even has a CrossFit gym for employees illustrating a true integration between the brands (Urback, 2014).

Courtesy of Alicia Carter

The Reebok CrossFit Games are a great example of a sponsorship that is at true partnership.

ASICS Support Your Marathoner Program

In 2010, ASICS took its sponsorship with the New York City Marathon to the next level with its "Support Your Marathoner" program. The program allowed family and friends of runners to go online, enter their personal information, and submit a written message or video encouraging their loved ones running the 26.2-mile race. The heartfelt messages and videos were displayed on video boards in NYC's Central Park and Times Square days leading up to the race, and along the racecourse on marathon Sunday for runners to see.

The program enabled ASICS to better engage with the runners, their families and friends, and generate over 7,000 potential new customer leads from 17 different countries. ASICS activation allowed New York Road Runners to enhance the marathon experience for its runners and their families and friends, while also generating additional exposure for its brand and the marathon.

The Support Your Marathon program won Promo Magazine's "Most Innovative Communication Strategy Award." The program was promoted on the New York Road Runners website, via email to runners, and at the marathon expo (Asics, 2011).

SUMMARY

Sponsorship is vital to the success of an event. It can serve as a means to generate revenue, decrease expenses, and/or enhance the participant event experience. The most successful sponsorship agreements are long-term partnerships that are able to meet the objectives of both the event organizer and sponsor.

Student Challenges

NAME _____ DATE _____

Question 7.1

Choose a sport event that is of interest to you. Create a list of at least 10 benefits/assets (e.g., in-game promotions, signage, etc.) the event has available to potential sponsors.

Benefit #1:

Benefit #2:

Benefit #3:

Benefit #4:

Benefit #5:

Benefit #6:

Benefit #7:

Benefit #8:

Benefit #9:

Benefit #10:

Question 7.2

Using the same event as in question #1, evaluate the event needs to determine four potential sponsors that are a good fit to provide VIK products/services. Discuss what VIK offerings the sponsor could provide to the event.

Sponsor #1:

VIK Opportunity:

Sponsor #2:

VIK Opportunity:

Sponsor #3:

VIK Opportunity:

Sponsor #4:

VIK Opportunity:

Question 7.3

Make a list of four potential sponsors whose target market aligns with that of the event (participants and/or spectators). Discuss the benefit to each if they choose to sponsor different aspects of the event.

Sponsor #1:

Event/Sponsor Benefits:

Sponsor #2:

Event/Sponsor Benefits:

Sponsor #3:

Event/Sponsor Benefits:

Sponsor #4:

Event/Sponsor Benefits:

Question 7.4

Using the companies identified in question #2 and #3, write two basic sponsorship proposals. Use the space provided to take notes and then type up the proposals. One proposal will be for a VIK sponsorship and one proposal will be for a cash (or combination) sponsorship. Each proposal must be for a different company.

Proposal #1 Notes:

Proposal #2 Notes:

EVENT TECHNOLOGY AND SOCIAL MEDIA

Jackie Reau and Michael Pfahl

Jackie Reau has more than 20 years of experience specializing in strategic communications, social media strategies and sports fan research. She is an Adjunct Professor at the University of Cincinnati and Xavier University where she teaches sports PR and event management, respectively. Reau earned a bachelor's degree in journalism from Ohio University and a master's degree in sports administration from Ohio University. She is also active with Cincinnati Sports Professionals Network, Greater Cincinnati Sports Corporation, and the Reds Community Fund.

Michael Pfahl, Ph.D., is an Associate Professor of Sport Administration at Ohio University. Previously, Dr. Pfahl was on the Management and Marketing faculties in the International Colleges of Yonok College (Thailand) and Bangkok University (Thailand), respectively. He worked in various management and sales positions with the Cleveland Cavaliers and the Cleveland Lumberjacks during his career. Dr. Pfahl was also the Cofounder and President of Players Management, Inc., a sport marketing and athletic representation firm. Current research interests include the convergence of media, technology and sport, environmentalism and sport, and human resource issues in sport organizations. Dr. Pfahl earned a master in business administration from the University of Toledo along with bachelor, master, and doctorate degrees from Ohio University.

The way US sports fans consume sports has drastically changed over the past decade due in large part to social media and the emergence of the "four screen viewer." At any given time, sports fans may interact with a sporting event using four screens: TV, mobile phone, laptop, and/or tablet. According to the most recent Global Sports Media Consumption Report, there are 168 million sports fans living in the United States and they spend almost 8 hours per week watching sports on a device or TV. (Sporting News Media, Kantar Media Sports, & Sport Business Group, 2014). Additionally, smart phone users reach for their phones some 150 times per day for the following functions (in order): messaging, voice calls, check the time, music, gaming and the camera, and other uses. (Social Times, 2013).

Media consumption habits have long been measured by W.A.L or Watch, Attend, Listen. Now researchers are increasingly monitoring how fans use social media to engage with a sporting event, team, and/or athlete. With this in mind, event managers are now considering how to integrate the "four screen experience" with the live experience to convince fans to attend events rather than enjoying the event at home.

Social media is centered on the interactions people have in online and Web-based contexts as they share information and ideas with each other (Newman, Peck, Harris, & Wilhide, 2013; Safko &

Brake, 2009). Of course it would be great if every event had someone dedicated to technology and social media, but many events do not have that luxury. For events unable to have someone dedicated to this area, event mangers can work to find a volunteer, intern, or part-time employee with the skills and interest to take on this role. Event managers should be deliberate in how they use social media in the venue, thinking about Wi-Fi accessibility, content development, content delivery, monitoring of content, promotional opportunities, and sponsor integration. The advent of social media influencers (i.e., members of the public with large social media followings that post about the team/event) and the ability to generate revenue via social media use has also added to the complexity of social media. Related to social media strategy, it is critical for event managers to consistently collaborate with colleagues in social media, marketing, public relations, sponsorship sales, and information technology to ensure a holistic fan experience integrated with the technology fans have come to expect. If sport event planners examine their event in light of these technology issues (before, during, and after events), then they will be able to select and to utilize appropriate technologies for their needs. To borrow an old motorsport term, the event planners will use the right *horses for courses*. For example, Facebook skews toward an older demographic so for an event targeted toward undergraduate college students, a different platform will reach them better.

Creating, disseminating, and evaluating messages about an event are a critical component in any event's marketing and external relations plan, but it is not the sole reason for a comprehensive technology/social media plan. **Information dissemination** refers to the ways in which different technologies can help to promote an event and its message (e.g., marketing plan), in addition to sponsors, partners, and just about anything else sport managers want to have people know about the event. The connectivity aspects of social media also mean that engagement, information sharing, feedback, poll or survey taking, and other in-the-moment engagement opportunities can take place.

This chapter focuses on how event managers can leverage the power of technology and social media to enhance the fan experience, provide a high level of customer service, and generate new revenue. Additionally, the authors provide strategies for handling crisis situations and negative fan experiences through real-time social media use.

Website Engagement

One of the most common information and engagement sources in the world today is a website. A **website** is a portal of information, multimedia, and interaction that allows users access to its contents around the clock and around the world. This may be the first interaction a potential participant or spectator has with the event and will leave a lasting impression. Preparing a website requires as much preparation regarding message and marketing issues as it does technical issues. Please see Table 8.1 for foundational issues in website content development.

Exactly how these elements are organized and exactly what event managers provide in each section will vary by event. However, including each provides a well-rounded user interface that is informational and educational for various stakeholders of the event (i.e., participants, fans, media, potential sponsors, etc.).

In addition to these event-based points, it is important to remember to give the design and layout of the website proper consideration. These design issues are the areas of the website evaluated for ease of use and usefulness to visitors, including people with disabilities (i.e., hearing impaired, visually impaired, etc.). User interaction with the website should encourage exploration while informing and entertaining visitors. As with the foundational website elements described earlier, Table 8.2 shows the key points regarding a user's experience to remember during the Website design process.

Table 8-1.   Website Content Development

Issues	Examples
Event information	History, sponsors/partners/charities, previous year or event information, electronic newsletters.
Attendance information	Registration, admissions, and ticketing information including rules and regulations.
Calendar of events	Relevant days and times of the event program.
Media interactions	Information area for media members.
Multimedia	Interactive points including video, photographs, and others.
Travel and destination information	Travel and direction information including event maps.
Sponsors and/or partners	Sponsors and partners (if charitable event, list partner charities).
Merchandise	Merchandise (if applicable).
Safety and security issues	All relevant safety and security information, forms, etc.
Multicultural awareness	Sensitivity to language and images used at the site.
Contact information	Contact information for key event personnel.
Technical issues	Server location, capacity, and performance
	Technical support types, levels, and contact information.

As shown in Table 8.2, an important aspect of design is evaluative criteria to determine the usability of a website, its interactivity levels, or any other relevant criteria. The evaluative criteria scale is a self-check instrument used by designers (and nondesigners if desired) to establish points of success, failure, strength, and areas for improvement. An example of an evaluative criteria scale used to assess the website is shown in Table 8.3.

By taking a multileveled approach to website design, event planners can maximize the impact of their event and event messages by making a site user friendly and useful. A well-designed website will address spectator and participant concerns in a proactive manner, which should lead to a more pleasant event experience for the participants and more organized conceptualization, development, and execution process for event managers.

Table 8-2.   User Experience Issues in Website Design

Issues	Examples
Aesthetics	Color schemes (e.g., complimentary, contrasting), font sizes (small versus large), images (e.g., photographs, advertisements).
Data collection points	Registration for contests, the event, or information (e.g., text message alerts).
	Manage this carefully, because too much will distract a visitor and too little will leave the event organizers with a lack of participant and/or visitor information.
Multimedia	Presentation and issues related to opening and viewing the files, such as time for a file to load (from click to play).

(Continued)

Table 8-2.　User Experience Issues in Website Design (*Continued*)

Issues	*Examples*
	Information load time for files (e.g., PDF), downloads (e.g., wallpapers), and HTML documents.
Sponsors and/or partners	Placement and utilization of sponsor and partner advertising or images (e.g., top, bottom, left side, right side, skyscrapers, banner ads, above or below the *fold* of the page).
Languages	Making the website available in different languages to reach the broadest possible audience.
User accessibility	Allowing most or the entire website to be read aloud by computer software.
Evaluative criteria	Analytical instrument to assess the success of these and other factors included on the website.

Table 8-3.　Sample Evaluative Criteria Scale

Site layout	Poor	1	2	3	4	5	Excellent
Ease of use	Difficult	1	2	3	4	5	Easy
Experience	Poor	1	2	3	4	5	Excellent
Return to site in future?	Unlikely	1	2	3	4	5	Likely
Usefulness to fans	Not useful	1	2	3	4	5	Useful
Usefulness to media	Not useful	1	2	3	4	5	Useful

Collaboration with Colleagues

Social media is most successful when an organization adopts it from top to bottom. As sports fans' consumption of media continues to evolve toward social media platforms, fans expect sport events and teams to use social media to share information about the event, athletes, venue, and promotions.

A social media effort is activated at its best when there is collaboration among key departments including event management, social media, marketing, public relations, sponsorship sales, and information technology. An event manager will know the venue and how to incorporate realistic yet creative solutions to enhancing the fan experience with an eye toward digital solutions that support social media engagement.

Additionally, the event manager is an asset to the sponsorship sales staff in determining new areas of on-site inventory for exhibits, product display, and signage as well as social media activation areas (discussed later in this chapter) that are visually appealing.

On-Site Connectivity

Sports fans expect high-speed Wi-Fi connection while attending events so they can upload photos, post status updates, check scores of other games, and check their fantasy stats. All too often, sports facilities are not adequately prepared to handle the digital activity of their guests. A 2013 article in

Crain's Detroit highlighted that fans have trouble with mobile devices at games and concerts because, "the buildings are usually not conducive to easily transmitting data signals, and the older technology's capacity cannot handle large crowds in small places" (Shea, 2013, para. 8). People are also increasingly uploading photos and videos during events, which uses even more bandwidth (Shea, 2013).

To put into perspective the burden of smartphone app usage, Rob Todd, founder of Houston-based Molitoris Group, which handles cellular and Wi-Fi installation projects for entertainment venues said, "The typical smartphone has the equivalent drain, on average, of 10 ongoing cellphone calls on a stadium's system" (Shea, 2013, para. 10). Upgrading bandwidth in sports facilities should be a priority for a positive fan experience in addition to a new sponsorship opportunity and fan research collection, but for many venues and events the cost prohibits major upgrades.

In some cases, sponsorship can defray or eliminate cost of infrastructure improvements. The BNP Paribas Open Tennis Tournament featured the best in men's and women's professional tennis and drew a record 430,000 tennis fans over 2 weeks in 2015, making it the largest combined ATP World Tour and WTA event in the world (Rukus, 2015). To achieve the goal of all fans being able to access the BNP mobile app, the tournament had to provide each access to Wi-Fi connectivity (Rukus, 2015). To overcome this challenge, Ruckus Wireless, Inc. partnered with the BNP Paribas Open in Indian Wells to install a "massive high-density, high-capacity smart Wi-Fi network throughout its 54 acre complex" (Rukus, 2014, para. 1). The BNP Paribas Open Mobile App was created as a one-stop, multifunctional online resource that was used during the tournament to provide attendees with all kinds of up-to-the minute information, including: tournament player match schedules; live, up-to-the minute scores of all matches in-progress; match results; player bios, and draw information; plus, live video coverage of matches (Rukus, 2015). The app would have been of no value to anyone if Wi-Fi access had been inadequate. This example demonstrates how an event outside of a tradition venue (i.e., stadium or arena) can achieve a cost effective solution to Wi-Fi connectivity for large numbers of attendees.

Event managers should also consider using unused spaces within the venue to create socially engaging areas to create activation areas for fans as well as sponsors. These areas may include but not limited to: large photo walls to be used a selfie photo opportunities, seating with charger stations in proximity to a revenue opportunity (i.e., concessions, bars, merchandise, etc.) as well as sponsorship zones where fans can interact with social promotions such as Chevrolet's "Follow Chevrolet on Twitter to win a t-shirt" promotion.

These social media spaces are also be a good opportunity to work with the marketing department to collect fan research by offering free connectivity. For example, before fans can connect, they have to answer five questions and provide their email address. The questions may focus on any subject or subjects event managers or others are interested in such as spectator demographics, interests, experience, media consumption habits, and/or sponsor recall.

Innovation in Interscholastic Athletics

Aaron Wright, Instructor, Ohio University

Jeff Walrich, the Athletic Director at Gilmour Academy, a K-12 independent Catholic school near Cleveland, Ohio, was concerned about the involvement of the school's student body as spectators at Lancer athletic events. Despite the competitive success of the program, including the girls' volleyball team appearing in two state finals, student attendance was typically low. This was partly attributed to the high levels of student involvement in athletics and other after-school activities.

Gilmour has an enrollment of about 685 students, and offers 23 sports in an athletic program for grades 6–12. More than 85% of its upper school students (grades 9–12) participate on at least one athletic team, with many participating in all three seasons. Maintaining high levels

▶

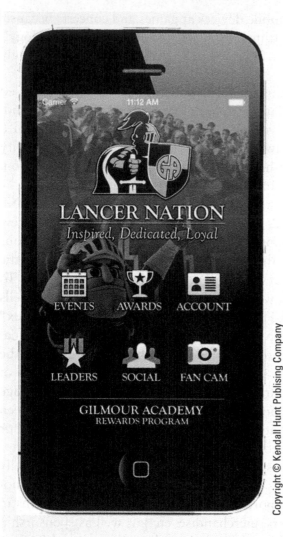

of student attendance at games is a challenge with so many students already participating in athletics and other after-school activities. Jeff began to think about ways to encourage students to attend games when not participating, and to increase engagement and beyond attendance.

Jeff found a possible solution in a smart phone app developed by SuperFanU, a company based in Louisville, Kentucky. The loyalty app uses geolocation to allow fans to "check in" to events and earn rewards determined by the school. The app is customized and branded for each individual school. The app had primarily been used by college athletic programs to increase fan attendance and engagement, particularly for nontraditional sports.

Gilmour Academy became the first high school in Ohio, and third in the country to use the app, which became a critical part of Gilmour's broader Lancer Nation branding strategy. Jeff's primary objective in adopting the app was to increase attendance at athletic events and enhance school spirit. His goal for the first year was to have 75% of students in grades 9–12 download the app.

How it works

At its basic level, using the app is simple: load an event, assign a point value, and set a perimeter around the event with the app's geofencing capability (because the app relies on the user's smartphone GPS, the perimeter can also be drawn around any other schools' athletic facilities). Users "check in" to the event on the app when they are within the established perimeter. Users download the app from iTunes or Google Play, register, and begin using the app immediately. Jeff used a variety of communications early in the school year to encourage students to download the app.

Gilmour Academy students earn points for attendance at designated events, with rewards given for achieving certain point levels: a t-shirt for attending 10 events, "Road Warrior" status for check-ins at away games, and additional digital badges for check-ins for specific sports, and for milestones in increments of 50 points. Users can track their points and compare their ranking using the leaderboard displayed on the app. Attendees are also eligible for in-game contests, including raffles and trivia contests, with Nike school-branded gear and gift cards used as prizes. Jeff uses the app's messaging feature to announce contests and giveaways and increase interest in specific events.

The student with the highest point total at the end of the year wins an iPad, with additional prizes for the top three point totals, point total leaders by grade level, and for faculty and alumni.

Why it Works

The strategy takes advantage of several common consumer motivations. Social motivation, including the need for social interaction and group affiliation, is one category of motivators for sport spectators. High school students attend school sporting events to join their peers in showing their school spirit and supporting their classmates participating in the games.

While this motivation can be enhanced through the use of popular social networking apps, such as Facebook and Twitter, the SuperFanU app has the added benefit of using its rewards system to exploit achievement motives. In spectator sports, fans are typically motivated by vicariously participating in their team's success. Through the SuperFanU app, however, fans can attain their own status that is linked to the achievement levels set by the organization.

The app is an example of gamification, or "turning marketing activities into games where users earn points for their engagement activities" (Kunkel, Funk, & Meuck, 2014, p. 2). The points system for rewards is also similar to customer loyalty programs used for years by a variety of retail businesses, and follows a trend toward developing smartphone apps to deliver these programs. In 2013, a Nielsen survey found that 70% of teens ages 13–17 use smartphones, a number that should only increase (The Nielsen Company, 2013). A 2014 study found that 59% of consumers would be more likely to join a loyalty program that offers a smartphone app. In the same study, 57% of respondents also said they would be more likely to participate in a program that offered exclusivity-based rewards (Graham, 2014).

Results and Future Uses

By March 2015, at the end of the winter sports season, the Lancer Nation app had 492 downloads, with 430 active users, easily beating the goal of 75% of students downloading the app. One of the winter season promotions was for an away girls' basketball game against a rival school, which resulted in attendance of 40 students, a school record for an away regular season game.

The app has additional functionality that Jeff plans to explore in the future. One attractive feature is the ability to sell digital ad space in the app, an important selling point for potential sponsors. Users can also receive digital coupons that can drive traffic to sponsors, or reward check-ins at sponsor locations. The school also plans to expand the use of the app in nonathletic settings, such as college recruiting nights and nonathletic alumni events. This example of a successful integration of an app in interscholastic athletics demonstrates the role innovation can play in this segment of sport and the opportunities available to those interested in the intersection of technology and sport.

Content Opportunities

The term fan is short for fanatic. With that in mind, organizations should embrace social media to share content that will create buzz and engagement with their fanatics, who are also more likely to share this information on their social media networks. Working with the social media coordinator, event managers can provide valuable input on how to creatively use spaces within the venue to create content opportunities for social media. Fans want to see behind-the-scenes activities at the venue such as teams arriving, athletes warming up, pre-event coaches speeches, and event staging.

An emerging trend in sports is the introduction of social media command centers at sporting venues. At the University of Wyoming, nine students work out of the social media command center space called "The Corral" to share content and monitor fan activity during athletic events (Roerink, 2013). A **social media command center** is a dedicated space for staff to manage the organizations social media presence during events. The more informal fan-driven social media suites and dens are discussed in Chapter 9—External Relations. Budgeting space and dollars to this project is relatively inexpensive and is a sponsor opportunity to cobrand the area. At Wyoming, the school invested in three flats screen TVs, two computers with large monitors and decorative branding (Roerink, 2013).

Event managers may want to explore creative spaces for video cameras, outside of the traditional areas dedicated to TV coverage (i.e., field of play). This can even include adding cameras to the equipment of athletes. As video becomes more accessible through cameras like GoPro, there is an opportunity for venues to add more cameras in spaces to allow different viewpoints for the fans. These new vantage points can be used for mobile applications and live streaming as well traditional

'The Corral' is UW's new command station for giving fans and the atheletics department more opportunity to interact on social media. Nine students will work to track any UW sports-related content moving on the web and share it with more fans.

TV broadcasts. During the 2015 NHL All-Star Game, GoPro cameras were attached to the helmets of players. It was the first time that GoPro partnered with a professional league.

In 2015, David Nield reported on the partnership between GoPro and the NHL by writing that, "For the first time, HD GoPro footage can be beamed live as well as captured on a memory card, giving TV producers a new view of the action. As well as showing live shots to the audience, highlights of the captured footage can be used to aid studio analysis of skating, stickhandling, goal scoring, and netminding. In return for all of this technological wizardry, GoPro gets plenty of exposure on the NHL's television and social media channels." (Nield, 2015, para. 4)

Event managers may also want to take a create look at their facilities to determine where to add social media messages to encourage engagement.

In 2012, the University of Michigan painted a social media hashtag on their stadium turf during the annual spring football game. The hashtag #GOBLUE was painted maize at two locations, straddling the 25-yard line on the northeast and southwest sides of the field.

Jordan Maleh, University of Michigan's director of digital marketing stated that the initiative, "will help our athletic department use technology as a competitive advantage to engage and connect to fans, build brand loyalty, grow the digital audience and monitor and listen to what is being said through the digital engagement cycle" (University of Michigan, 2012, para. 4). The University of Michigan athletic department also launched a Tweet Board on the scoreboard to showcase messages on Twitter from fans using the #GOBLUE hashtag (University of Michigan, 2012). Fans that used the hashtag

were also entered into a contest with prizes ranging from VIP seats to gift cards for merchandise (University of Michigan, 2012).

Use Social Media to Enhance the Fan Experience in Real Time

Social media will allow venues to enhance the fan experience in real time as more fans use social media platforms as a new form of a customer service channel.

This fabricated Twitter message is an example of how an event manager can monitor the fan experience via social media. By working with the game-day staff managing social media, the event manager should be alerted to this parking situation to divert additional employees to assist in Lot D. The social media staff should acknowledge in a Twitter response that the team is aware of the situation and is adding staff in Lot D. If the team wants to over deliver, the team president will deliver a beer to the fan's seat as customer service recovery. The latter statement may go over the top but think about the fan loyalty that may be achieved in this situation, which may include a positive social media statement to override the initial negative post.

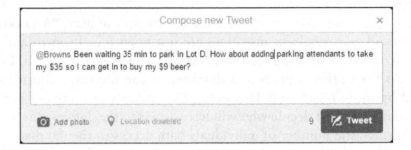

Sporting organizations may also use social media during events to drive sales at concessions and merchandise stands with special codes that are time sensitive. For example, a team may use Twitter to announce a former player is holding an autograph session at half time and taking donations for her foundation. Initiatives that are time-sensitive also allow for better tracking to determine effectiveness.

With all of the potential engagement opportunities at the event, it is possible to allow attendees to demonstrate their excitement for the event creating a sense of community around the event. A first step in the creation of community is the use of user-generated content (UGC). UGC refers to pictures, video, podcasts, and text (e.g., blogs) contributed by individuals for others to see regarding their experiences at an event. The UGC revolution came into its own with the development of YouTube. Today, while technology allows users to upload videos directly to a website or social media platform without needing a link to YouTube, the emergence of a space for people to create, post, and share video content online was an important point in the development of online interactivity. Allowing individuals to post pictures, videos, podcasts, or personal accounts of event experiences not only adds additional educational and entertainment opportunities for visitors to a website, but also provides the posters with an enhanced participatory experience in an event.

Effective UGC areas require that proper evaluation and approval procedures for all submissions (i.e., managed by event staff) are in place for UGC opportunities to remain free from abuse. Fully disclosed terms and conditions should be included as part of any engagement experience, especially anything to do with the registration process. Subscribers should have a clear description of how a person can cancel the subscription at any time. Bombarding individuals with messages before, during, and/or after events should not be the goal of any social media plan.

Knowing the Customer

Creating and managing the data gathered across various technology and social media platforms is a complicated, but potentially lucrative task. A **database** is "a shared, integrated computer structure that stores a collection of end-user data … metadata, or data about data through which the end-user data are integrated and managed" (Rob, Coronel, & Crockett 2008, p. 7). Event managers must make a decision whether or not database construction and management will be done in-house or outsourced. Access by individuals, security concerns, and cost are important considerations when making such a decision.

Databases are useful to event managers because the data collected from various sources, including the event location, can be used in a number of ways. One example is to create an email list for postevent follow-up, marketing, and preparation for the next event. Another example is the way in which database information can be searched or segmented in order to understand who attends and participates in events and how this information can be useful when soliciting sponsors and partners. Such interactivity is important to postevent evaluations of the event and preparations for future events. In relation to payment processing, databases can be used to process payments in groups created within defined parameters (e.g., daily) or as the payments come in (see Chapter 11 Participant Registration for more information).

Database design, then, becomes a crucial issue for event planners. "A good database—that is, a database that meets all user requirements—does not just happen … Proper database design requires the database designer to identify precisely the database's expected use" (Rob, Coronel, &Crockett, 2008, pp. 10–11). As with other aspects of a database, it can facilitate information searches about the data submitted by those registering. However, given security concerns of personal and financial information, the event staff must decide who will have access to the database as well as how often this access will occur. Further, the number of individuals with access to the database at any given time is a critical issue depending on the size of the event, the event staff, and the need for individuals to have access to the information or just reports generated from it.

Some caution must be exercised in relation to utilizing database systems. For mega events (e.g., Super Bowl), expenditures to hire professionals to develop sophisticated database systems are warranted. For smaller events, especially infrequent or one-time events, such elaborate systems are less necessary. In fact, applications such as Microsoft's Excel can be used to handle many database management functions, including preparation of email and regular mail materials via mail merges. Finally, event planners can purchase information from database companies that collect general information about specific groups (e.g., people of a city by zip code). This alternative might be less expensive than creating a database system, but it might also prove problematic because of outdated information and incomplete or inaccurate personal information (e.g., names, addresses).

Keep an Eye on New Trends in Social Media

Social media changes at a fast pace—whether it's a new platform like Instagram a few years ago or the use of Drones to capture aerial video. It is important for event managers to keep current on digital trends and the potential issues associated with new innovation such as safety, security, and licensing.

An example of a social media content trend that turned into a safety issue happened at the 2014 Tour de France when fans along the route were moving onto the road/race course and turning their back to the cyclists in order to take selfies with racers in the background. They ended up too close to the cyclists putting themselves and the racers at risk for collisions. American cyclist Tejay van Garderen

(@tejay_van) to Twitter to scold fans about taking selfies after he crashed into a selfie-taking fan in Stage 2 suffering a minor knee injury by posting the following tweets:

- "...I love the crowds and thank you for your support. But please give us room. Gonna ice my knee now" (2014a).
- "Standing I [sic] the middle of the road with your back turned while 200 cyclists come at you, just to take a selfie. #think #TDF2014" (2014b).
- "A dangerous mix of vanity and stupidity..." (2014c).

The combination of 200 cyclists averaging 25 mph riding along tight European roads crowded by a record setting crowd with estimates over four million spectators is a safety issue even without fans putting themselves in the path of the cyclists (Yuan, 2014).

Again, it's imperative to work collaboratively within the organization to determine these trends and how they can effectively work within the venue.

Other trends in social media may affect equipment gear or a change in equipment gear for promotional purposes. One creative example that drew social media buzz comes from the Columbus Cottonmouths, a minor league team in the Southern Professional Hockey League. The Cottonmouths ran a promotion where the team wore "selfie jerseys" culled from fan photos. The 4-month promotion encouraged fans to submit selfie photos on Twitter or Instagram with the hashtag #snakeselfie in a tribute to their mascot. The photos were used to design team jerseys worn during a March 2015 game that was also designated Social Media Night where fans could use their own social media platforms to engage with the team.

Another trend is to create promotions using social media platforms that combine online and off-line components. Daniel Fleming, an executive at Mellow Productions, Inc (a leading road race production and management company) launched a successful online–offline marketing initiative to promote their upcoming races. A van was wrapped in the company logo and driven around the Mellow Productions market to generate buzz (see photo Example of A Promotions Van). Online, Daniel has posted on the Mellow Productions Twitter and Facebook pages as well as his personal pages letting people know to "Go follow @mellew_runs and if you see the van out & about, take a picture & I'll send you $10 OFF

Courtesy of Daniel Fleming/Mellew Productions

Combination online/offline promotions such as asking people to post on social media if they see this van, engages current and potential customers.

any race registration." This is a tremendous way to connect online and offline promotions using social media as a platform for the online portion. Mellow productions extends their reach with followers looking for the van and then posting photos. These photos make new customers aware of their races and the person posting the photo gets a race discount hopefully resulting in a new participant.

Use Social Media During Crisis Situations

NASCAR was one of the first professional sports organizations to embrace technology to connect fans to the sport with in-car audio and video accessibility as well as live tracking of drivers during races. But a few years ago, NASCAR was challenged by fans when they blocked video of a crash that affected fans.

At the 2013 Daytona 500, a horrific crash on the Saturday of race weekend sent a dozen fans to the hospital while the involved drivers walked away from their wreckage.

The crash was immediately covered by fans using social media who posted videos to YouTube, Twitter, and Facebook. One fan event sent the footage directly to @espn on Twitter within minutes.

This type of response is becoming commonplace as social media has fostered an environment of citizen journalism among sports fans where anyone with a smart phone can capture video or photos and share them directly to news outlets such as ESPN (see Chapter 9 Event External Relations for additional information on public relations). However, fans became angry with NASCAR social media officials was when video footage taken by fans was immediately, and repeatedly after re-posts, taken down on YouTube. Racing fans challenged NASCAR's decision to ban the video in a social media storm of criticism. Staci D. Kramer (2013), a blogger offered a few thoughts on the NASCAR social media situation:

- Set expectations with fans on how you will use social media and engage with fans
- Avoid knee jerk reactions and narrow the parameters for takedowns of social media content
- Be as inclusive and as engaged as possible on all social media platforms
- Give the social media team the power to respond quickly and make sure a high-level exec is available for quick high-impact decisions, especially during events.

Social Media Tips for Event Managers

To begin planning a collaborative social media effort, the following checklist will be helpful:

- Conduct a Wi-Fi audit where staff can test accessibility throughout the facility to determine dead spots and upgrade those areas.
- Determine physical locations in the facility where social media can be leveraged through a social media command center for the organization and/or sponsored areas. This includes exhibit and/or work space, signage, facility grounds, ancillary spaces, and so on.
- Working with the sponsorship sales team, create a collaborative grid or checklist to define all sponsored social media needs at the facility. This may include exhibit space, court or field signage or scoreboard content.
- With the PR and/or social media team, discuss new opportunities for behind-the-scenes content. This may include new camera angles or clubhouse video tours.
- Monitor and manage the social media presence of the event (and teams involved if applicable) beginning months before the event and concluding months after the event. For recurring events, it may be necessary to implement year-round monitoring and management.
- Monitor best practices among other sports organizations by setting a Google alert "sport and social media."

SUMMARY

As discussed in this chapter, it is essential to constantly engage and enhance the fan experience at sports venues and events. Event mangers simply face a battle that pits the event, ticket prices, concessions, and parking against the at home HD TV, comfortable couch, and stocked refrigerator. Effective technology and social media can assist the event managers in coming out on top in this constant fight for fans. The entire event team at a sports venue can work together to build an emotional connection with sports fans with a positive in event experience and consistent connectively through social media platforms. As event organizations continue to evolve into fan-centric organizations, social media platforms provide the opportunity to connect with the team or sporting event in real time so they can share their opinions.

Student Challenges

Question 8.1

You have just become an Assistant Athletic Director for Event and Facility Management at your institution. Choose one venue on your campus and provide at least three recommendations for your sponsorship sales team to activate a social media promotion with a national wireless provider. Considerations should include: space within the facility, Wi-Fi connectively enhancements, signage, and/or opportunities for fan engagement.

Question 8.2

A professional soccer venue is going to create a social media command center in the stadium where up to 12 interns will work during each home game to create content, monitor the teams social media presence, respond to social media posts by fans, and promote the team during live action. What equipment and logistical issues will you need to consider in designing the space?

Question 8.3

You are responsible for a minor league sports team staff is in the process of reviewing all aspects of the sports fan experience to determine any enhancements. Your task is to determine up to five on-site experiences in and outside of your venue where fans may express displeasure and how to mobile staff and resources in real time to solve these issues.

EVENT EXTERNAL RELATIONS

Packy Moran

Packy Moran has 8 years of industry experience in communications and event management at the community, collegiate, and professional levels. He has been involved with executing traveling events for a regional science center, organizing student employees for the opening of an on-campus assembly facility, and responsible for managing the communications and marketing for a family-owned and operated arena and exhibition center. A native of Dayton, Ohio, he has served in several roles in event communications. Mr. Moran was on the sports desk for the *Columbus Dispatch*, was the Director of Communications and Marketing at Hara Arena and Exhibition Center, and served as the Director of Communications and Operations for the Columbus Stars of the United Hockey League and the Premier Development and W-League soccer organizations. Mr. Moran has 6 years of teaching experience in Sport Management and is currently a Lecturer at the University of Iowa.

This chapter introduces the concept of external relations to the framework of event management. At first glance the concepts seem simple. However, when one digs further into the importance of external relations to a successful event, some challenges emerge. As with other aspects of event management (e.g., marketing, sponsorship, ticketing), even if event managers are not directly responsible for the function, they must understand all areas that make the event come to life. Being flexible in channels while staying consistent in message is important in executing a communications strategy. Even with flexibility, there are guidelines event managers and communications professionals can use to help ensure their message is heard, and received as intended. This strategy will evolve alongside the event, but will always be tied to the overall goals, objectives, tactics, and theme.

External relations is defined as the management process concerning the creation and communication of information through media (both earned and paid) to intended audiences (publics) and is akin to communications, but slightly different. During different phases (i.e., conceptualization, development, execution) of the event, the goals of communications will change. While event communications covers the creation of media-focused and straight-to-consumer pieces, the larger concept of external relations considers integrating communication into a management function spanning the entire process or life cycle of the event.

An organized communications system will help maintain positive relationships with distribution channels (i.e., newspaper, television, radio, Internet, social media) and in return help garner cooperation from those media in the event of a crisis. Definitions for paid and earned media are given and their interdependence explained. In-event and participant-based communications can be a point of differentiation for certain groups and should not be ignored. **Brand unity** is the consistent look, style and attitude seen and felt throughout the communications and the event itself. This chapter sheds light on the event communication process, long-term relationship building and planning, and provide instruction on how to perform a media audit and write a press release.

Event Communications

Event managers can discover the common thread in successful event communications in the answer to the following fundamental questions: Why do people want to work in sports? Why does anyone want to spend holidays and weekends at work and maybe make less money than comparable jobs in the financial, medical, and retail sectors?

The answer: Sport creates great stories.

Sport is a sequence of well-planned and managed events. Shared emotional (and sometimes physical) investment is celebrated and the outcome is uncertain and unrepeatable. People gather at an appointed time and place and then people leave when the event is over, never to be relived again. Stories are told about the event, some to a few people, and some to a global audience. Some sporting events are forgotten as soon as they are over, while others raise to such legendary status that people who were not even in attendance claim to have been there. This is why, despite the long hours and the low pay, many still want to join those who help make these events happen.

So, how do event managers set an external relations strategy for a sporting event? While not every sports event has exactly the same process from idea generation to completion, most go through the stages of conceptualization, development (i.e., planning, invitation, and supply), and execution.

As discussed in the prior chapters of this book, event purpose statements, goals, objectives, and tactics are the guiding force in making event related decisions. External relations efforts include the communication processes in publicizing an event and the relationship with the media throughout the event cycle. No one would flier the campus or expect media coverage when having a couple of friends over for a pick-up basketball game, just as one could not expect to fill a gymnasium for a big rivalry basketball game without some contact with the campus and outside media. These paths are chosen during event conceptualization; figuring out the basics of the "why" and "what" will narrow the reasonable options for the "who, when, where, and how."

Event Conceptualization

Event conceptualization from a communications aspect places the organization and event in relative positions to other organizations and events that occur in the same activity, geography, or time-space. Consider various types of basketball as an example. If a person has a gathering to play basketball, it exists in relation to all other basketball games, both on campus and off, both for this game and others before it, as well as everything else that is going on that afternoon. The fact that this basketball game will be played on a custom-designed hardwood court with NBA regulation backboards and breakaway rims may change its position, but it does not change who and what is involved.

The questions of "why" and "what" become central at this point. The "what" is a basketball game with friends played on a great court, but the "why" will determine in what ways one lets others know about the event. Is it a small gathering where calls, texts, Snapchat, or Facebook messages will connect with the right attendees? Is it a local tournament where the number of teams playing determines success? Is it a fraternity fund-raising event, where more attendees are better, but a certain level of player is expected and targeted? All three of these scenarios involve a basketball game, a court, and a communications strategy, but have different goals and ideas as to what makes the event successful.

Just as a youth recreational league, a high school game, and the World Cup are all soccer, it is the "why" (the goal of the event) that determines the "who, when, where, and how" in terms of external communications.

The organization's relative position to other groups and happenings determines strategy. Information provided is about facilitating choices. Hosting a successful event—with the right people there at the right time—includes packaging information in a way that people can make the choice the organizers prefer them to make. "Where do I want to play basketball?" is the question that all three basketball organizers want to help as many people as possible answer in the way most appropriate to reach the goals of all those involved.

Paid vs. Earned Media

There are two main access strategies to media in terms of getting information out to potential consumers: paid and earned. **Paid media** takes the form of advertising, sponsorship, and activation marketing. Paid media can be characterized as media in which the event organizers retain control over the message. Also included in paid media are internally controlled or created pieces for official team or league websites, in-game use (i.e., programs, scorecards, stat sheets, video board spots) or broadcasts controlled by the league or team (radio announcers hired by the team or regional cable broadcasts controlled in-house), and social media. The issue of immediate control makes social media interesting in a discussion of paid versus earned media (see Chapter 8 for additional information on social media). The event managers have control over the initial post, but any sharing, or comments, transition into earned media. For the purposes of this chapter, and because the event manger retains initial control, social media falls into the category of paid media. **Earned media**, on the other hand, goes through an independent editorial source before it reaches the intended audience. A newspaper or online story, a television report, and an ESPN highlight reel are all examples of earned media. The introduction of the intermediary results in the event organizers retaining less control of content.

Event organizers should distribute information to as many people as possible that fit their target market. The goal is volume. Preferably, the communication will reach people who will attend or participate in the event, but ultimately, more people results in more opportunities for revenue and goal attainment. The communication strategy will focus on the number of people expected and the opportunities that exist in that situation. For example, paid media may include social media, fliers, radio ads, newspaper ads, Internet ads, to complement an earned media strategy focusing on sports and entertainment outlets to get information out to the masses. The goal is that those interested will then use word-of-mouth and personal selling to tell their friends, resulting in a large crowd.

To illustrate the above scenario, a fraternity charity basketball tournament will likely flier campus areas, purchase advertising, and put an earned-media campaign in place on campus-specific outlets (i.e., student radio station and/or Internet home page). But a fraternity will mainly focus on more personal distribution techniques. Social media, word-of-mouth, and personal references help to give an air of exclusivity to the event. Even with a fraternity charity tournament, the event's place among the others is important to consider. In this example, using mass media (print, radio, TV) is unlikely, but a message will need to be disseminated that convinces the desired audience (students) to attend. This can be achieved through phrasing personal invitations and referrals in comparison/contrast to events and opportunities competing for the time, attention, and/or money of the audience (i.e., Why the fraternity tournament is a better choice for the weekend than going to watch a movie or to the library to study). In the fraternity charity tournament organizer's case, whom they do not tell is as much a part of the communication strategy as whom they do. Social media is especially valuable in this circumstance, where friends extend the information to their circles expanding with each share.

Sixteen Rules for the Press Release

Packy Moran, Lecturer, University of Iowa

Even in today's social media driven world, the press release is the basic skill needed for media relations professionals. The format and content are varied and determined by the situation, but the fundamentals are the same, just like shooting a free throw or making a golf swing. The 16 rules have been adopted from Mel Helitzer's "The Dream Job" and Dr. Tim Newman (York College of Pennsylvania), and specifically apply to releases sent via mail or fax, but the underlying principles are applicable to all communication with the media.

The digital information age has changed delivery, but not the needs of the receiving outlet based on content or structure. When sending out press releases today, it is just as likely to be seen on the organization's Twitter feed or Facebook page as it is to be sent via email and/or virtual fax. The press release should still be distributed in Word or PDF format. Another way that they may be distributed is by using an FTP or outlet-specific website. The communications department gives access to the media at their request, which allows the communications staff to control access. Regardless of how media access press releases, the format for writing follows these 16 rules.

1. Paper choice: 8 ½ × 11 white paper

   The point: Do not let the medium used to convey the message get in the way of the message itself. In digital communication, this could apply to the file format of attachments. The widest used file formats are Word documents (.doc) and protected data files (.pdf); use anything else sparingly unless specifically requested by a particular media outlet. Balance must be struck between the look of the release and its ability to be used effectively by the outlet.

2. Margins: two inches on the top and one-inch margins on the sides and bottom

   The point: Press releases are working documents. Media members will take notes on the paper if given in printed format, and the ultimate goal is to make the job of the press easier so they can convey the information in as positive a light to the sponsor group as possible. This is important in electronic documents as well, which are often printed at the outlet for ease of use for the reporter and editor.

3. Headers: preprinted information that visually identifies the sponsoring organization and delivers the contact information

   The point: Have a template that works like letterhead. The subtle professionalism will not be lost on your media contacts. The header should include the organization name, address, and several ways to contact (Web site address, email, phone, fax, etc.). While this can be extended to html-coded email headers, be careful of how the information looks to those who pick up their email in environments that do not support html. Perhaps a PDF file attachment of the release with the body copied in the email (and formatted for the text-based email) is the safest bet. Be consistent. An outlet should be able to almost instantly recognize the source of the release.

4. Contact person: include a name, email, and phone number that the media can talk to

   The point: Providing a contact name and number where that person can be reached increases the likelihood of response from the media. They know more information is available, and the gesture of assistance in meeting their deadlines will be appreciated. The follow-up by the contact person is as important as having their information listed. They should be available, at the least during business hours the day the release is sent and the next day. Familiarity with a particular contact person increases the chance for earned media coverage because it provides a known quantity.

5. Release date: use "FOR IMMEDIATE RELEASE" unless embargoed to a specific date

   The point: Old news is *no* news. Most releases (99.7%) are for immediate release, meaning all the information in the release can be used right away. Embargoed releases are sent out to give news outlets a sneak preview of an announcement or an event. The date on the release then signifies when the message can be distributed from their outlet. Hiring a new coach is a good example of an embargoed release, as you want news agencies to be prepared for the press conference, which serves as a formal introduction and place for statements by the organization and the coach. Be specific in whatever medium the release is in as to when the information is to be made public.

6. "Special to" or "Exclusive to": these terms suggest that only the receiver of the release got this information

The point: This is a dangerous but powerful technique that should never be used with "hard" news (hirings, firings, etc.). An organization cannot afford to play favorites amongst the media. This can be used sparingly in terms of feature angles or for pitching personality pieces. Those releases should be sent only to those who have access to the story.

7. Headline: summarize key points in no more than two lines

The point: Just like a newspaper head, the wording should be truthful and emphasize the main points of the release. The font used should be bolded and larger than the body text. A secondary or deck headline can be used if there is a secondary point that can be made quickly.

8. Single space the text of the release

The point: It is a working document and will often be retyped by media members regardless of distribution method; radio or TV will retype into readable copy or into the teleprompter. Single space also allows more information on a single page.

9. The lead: most important information should be stated in the first sentence of the release

The point: Efficiency is important to news organizations. Most will assume that the important information will be in the first couple of lines.

10. The body: inverted pyramid style of writing

The point: Think about each paragraph as a 5-second audio clip. If you had only 10 seconds to give your information, what would be included? 15 seconds? 30 seconds? Specifics and details should be given in subsequent paragraphs; if the news organization wants it, they will find it.

11. Paragraphs: short, but complete

The point: Press release paragraphs include one complete thought. Remember the 5-second example: If the paragraph is reading long, break it up.

12. Subheads: draw attention to the details

The point: Use a subhead if another topic is being covered, or to introduce a table (such as statistics) or a section of supporting quotes.

In the digital age, the next three rules help to let the outlet know they have the entire release.

13. Page numbering: top, center of pages

The point: If a release needs to be longer than one page, number the second page (and subsequent pages) at the top and centered with a convention that will be consistent, such as -2- or {2}.

14. MORE: bottom centered on pages that are continued

The point: The typewritten "MORE" lets the news gatherer know that the release is not just a single page. Most releases are kept to one page.

15. Use ###: bottom centered on pages that are not continued

The point: Acts as the industry's stop sign. Some releases use the old printer's code -30-, or some will change the end key to something that fits their organization, such as *Tigers*.

▶

Finally, a rule that ties a communication skill—press release writing—to the management functions of external relations.

16. Date code

The point: The date code is an internal organization key that allows files to be tracked by release date and media. A typical code will include the numerical date of the release and the modes by which it was sent. "102315fmeWsFbTw" may indicate the release was sent on October 23, 2015 by fax, mail, email, posted to the website, shared on Facebook and linked in a tweet on twitter.

External Relations by Event Type

The four event types listed in Chapter 1, Event Management and the Event Manager, as recurring, traveling, mega, and ancillary events can help to define expectations. Each event type is unique in focus and can occur at every level of size and intensity, but event regularity is only one element in the overall conceptualization of a communication strategy.

Recurring Events

As mentioned before, recurring events are the most common, and therefore provide the most opportunity to utilize communication channels toward an organization's goals. The regularity of a "Third Thursday" event allows a media strategy to let more people know about an event, while adding specific details about each date in order to entice return visits. Any sports team with regularly occurring home games draws similarities—the opponent changes, as does the relative position of the team for championships and postseason chances—but the location and general format of the event is consistent. The promoting group emphasizes differences through news coverage and controlled channels—for example, Web site features on opponents and promotions—but the overall look and feel of the messaging will be consistent. For example, a hockey team may use the same tag line at the bottom of every press release, flier, newspaper ad, Internet ad, and billboard for the duration of a season. The National Hockey League's Columbus Blue Jackets have used "Join The Battle" and "Carry The Flag" in recent years. Logos and recurring slogans are important to unify all of the external outreach around events from the same producers.

Traveling Events

Consistency of messaging and style can also be important to traveling events. While often not within the same **media market**—groups of newspapers, radio, and TV stations that serve a similar geographic area or population, such as the New York City media market—traveling events benefit from consistent messaging used at each stop on their tours. Traveling basketball tournaments can range from the festival-like atmosphere of a Gus Macker or Hoop-It-Up tournament to the selective character of an AAU championship, but each and every branded tournament carries an expectation of what will be communicated and how. The Gus Macker or Hoop-Up will use the commercial enterprise's approach from the "big game" example—mixing fliers, radio, Internet ads, and earned mass media—while the AAU championship will depend on personal invitations and qualifiers from other tournaments. As explained in the Globetrotter example in Chapter 6—Event Marketing, the facility-based communications professional plays a key role in providing the traveling event promoter with information and introduction to the local media market. Traveling outfits are normally on tour for a distinct period of time and dates. They can include concerts, circuses, monster truck rallies, motorsports, family shows (Disney on Ice, Sesame Street Live, High School Musical on Ice, etc.), combat sports, rodeos, and more. To borrow from the Gus Macker Tournament example, the promoter is the Gus Macker Tournament organizer, and the facility is the host. The unity of the branding plays a smaller, but important role in the touring event category as the revenue is created by each individual event. Use of the Gus Macker logo brings certain expectations in terms of quality of management and facilities based on previous events, even though the success of the local event will depend on local circumstances.

Ancillary Events

Ancillary events fit within the scope of the larger events they support. Depending on the event that is the main draw, ancillary events can have their purpose defined by the main event or a specific subsection of that population. A homecoming football game tailgate sponsored by the Chemistry department is an example of an event looking for a subset, while a kids mile run and walk scheduled the day before a major marathon may be looking to attract families instead of just the marathon participant. For a Gus Macker or Hoop-It-Up event, it may be a slam dunk contest, a ball handling demonstration, a 3-point shootout, or a H-O-R-S-E contest. The ancillary events could be additional competitions, or simply to provide entertainment. The type of event and size of the targeted population heavily influence the communication strategy. Understanding the opportunities afforded by the supporting event is key to appropriately situating the ancillary event. Both paid and earned media are available to strike the right mix. The brand unity with the supporting event will depend on the official relationship of the two events.

Mega Events

Mega events provide opportunities for creating and implementing a media strategy of grand scale for a single group of events. Unlike a recurring or traveling event, the mega event is conceptualized, planned, and executed with a single, specific end-date in mind. Logos and graphics are the easiest example.

© shutterstock

A recognizable brand image is important.

Each Olympic Games, Super Bowl, and NCAA Final Four has its own logo (see photo example of branding on a side line chair from 2007 Final Four in Atlanta) that suggests the place and year of the event. These marks act as a unifying symbol for all of the events that happen around, and as part of, the mega event. Communication strategy for mega events often involves an attempt to contextualize the effects or "big picture" of the event. The paid media piece for mega events often falls to the media companies who are capitalizing on the rights fees they paid to carry the sport. The **rights fee** is the payment made by an entity to legally associate with the event. The challenge becomes controlling access and distributing information to the other members of the media who are covering the event for the earned media side. Media's access to facilities and hospitality is often determined by any official relationship with the event, which outlets make the most sense to the efforts of the organization, and existing informal personal media relationships.

News Items vs. Features

Event managers have two main types of stories to offer earned-media producers in dealing with an event: news items and features. These story forms also hold true for in-house paid-media sources, like official event websites, event social media platforms, features on team-controlled broadcasts, and in-event media, such as programs, yearbooks, media guides, and video board productions. **News items** normally surround the event itself and include coverage of what happens at the event, previews of the event, and announcements that the event is going to happen—often by covering a smaller ancillary event related to the main one (e.g., a press conference, weekly coaches show, etc.).

Features are human-interest stories that link back to the event through personalities or elements of the event that are the focus of the story (e.g., a star player on a Final Four team who only began playing basketball at age 14 after moving to the US from Africa). A player on an NCAA Final Four basketball team reading to elementary school kids is a typical feature photo that promotes a positive social message and the team as sponsoring group. Community service projects (i.e., cleaning up parks, visiting a children's hospital, etc.) before college football bowl games are an example of intercollegiate athletic departments meeting several priorities that can be highlighted by the media, including rounding out the student-athlete experience and the involvement of nonathlete students with the program.

After event conceptualization, event managers should be able to answer the "when, where, and who" of the communication strategy as defined by the "what" and the "why" of the event. The question that remains is the "how" of getting the message to those who need to hear it.

Development

Development of the external relations plan is not a solitary process for any one department. Although primarily media strategy will be discussed, it should be understood that buy-in and direction from many departments within the organization is needed to optimize effect. Coordination with other departments prevents disasters caused by misaligned expectations, which often have their roots in an erroneous piece of information put out by a frenzied and unfocused media campaign. In the public assembly facility realm, ticket and security policies are paramount for ensuring everyone (i.e., authorities, patrons, and facility staff) is on the same page. Imagine if a newspaper article stated that bags are allowed at the event, yet the security team is told no bags are allowed. A simple misstep such as this can cause big headaches. In sum, the development phase answers the question of "how" to get the message to the right audience.

Information Sharing

In practice, the communications professional needs to be informed in the decisions that surround the event, and vice versa. Ideally, communications managers should be involved in the decision-making process. The five P's (prior planning prevents poor performance) are as true for external relations as they are for the event manager and athletes. Maintaining the policy decision's original intent through the media's reporting process—regardless of the level of control of the story—is much more likely when the communications professional is involved in the initial decision-making. Familiarity with every aspect of the event is important in offering proper context for paid media and answering any questions from earned media workers. Paid media—social media, print advertisements, radio spots, TV commercials, Internet ads, and so on—have a high level of initial control by the event organizers.

The basic information for an event is the foundation of content for both paid and earned media support materials. The event's external relations staff should have final oversight for each item of paid media before it runs, and should follow up with clippings and **media schedule checks**—a log of when a commercial ran on radio or TV and the rating it received—to make sure the group received what it paid for. Earned media—TV, radio, newspaper, and online news items and public service announcements—is subject to less direct control from the event organizers, but information flow and existing relationships with media members can influence the quality and quantity of transmission of the necessary information. The distribution of controlled social media items through noncontrolled shares and retweets requires the initial post or tweet to have the correct information, or more harm will be done than good. This is true whether the social media post originates from the event organizers or is earned media posted by a media outlet using information provided by the event organizers. Consistency between materials for the two media types is helpful, but allowing the earned media outlets to "do what they do" with the information is key to getting it out through their channels.

Media Audits: Determine the Players, Maintain the Roster

Packy Moran, Instructor, University of Iowa

A **media audit** is the process of determining the content, format, deadlines, and contacts at the entire population of outlets that are active in the media market where the group, and/ or the event, takes place. The audit is a first "scene setting" exercise that a communications professional must perform when taking a new job or launching a new event.

Your audit entries should include:

- Primary media category (TV, radio, newspaper, magazine, web listing, blog, podcast, etc.)

- Contact name and topic area (e.g., Joe Smith—Sports; Terry Green—Education)

- Deadline and report time (e.g., 11 p.m. for morning paper; 11:15 for 11:25 sports report; continuous for web updates; etc.)

- As many contact options as possible (phone, fax, email, mail address, twitter, website, etc.)

- Notes on preferred method for contact and information

Consider this when compiling your initial media audit:

- Each outlet may have multiple formats in which they deliver content to their audiences. Newspapers and local television compete directly on the web with video content. Delivering ready-to-use information in multiple web-enabled formats (print, audio, video) will increase the chances the content is used.

- Media outlets appreciate being asked for their preferred format for releases. It saves them time in transferring content before distribution. Individual media members may have preferences based on how they work. The easier you make it for a media member to get the information the better your chances that it will be used.

- When considering deadlines remember that multiple formats have reduced the time outlets have to process incoming information. Balance complete information and timeliness. Understand each individual outlet's time restraints. Does the local news station have a morning, midday, evening, and late newscast? Which broadcasts include sports reports? What about feature stories on local events?

- Differences in events will call for different editorial contacts at various outlets. A sports writer may be very interested in a college football game, while a linebacker reading to elementary school children as part of his student teaching will intrigue an education beat reporter. The more specific you can get in your contacts the better.

- Don't forget nontraditional media. Bloggers, superfan tweeters, and YouTube celebrities might be the most important contacts one has for certain events.

▶

The following are helpful in maintaining a media audit:

- Use a Web search engine for daily alerts from key word searches including the event and group names; archive as many stories and sources as possible. Google News and RSS feeds make this very easy today.

- Include Web resources and editors affiliated with more traditional media outlets (i.e., newspaper Web sites, TV Web sites, etc.).

- Keep a list of bloggers and influential social media users who mention/cover the events. Add them to your regular media advisory lists.

- Make regular contact with key constituent outlets.

- Update media audits fully every 3 months.

External Relations as a Management Function

Being familiar with each outlet—TV and radio station, magazine, newspaper, Internet, community post, and so forth—and their particular information schedule on both the paid and earned side of the desk is the only way to put a successful strategy in place.

For recurring events, such as a team's home season or a series of annual flat shows (e.g., home show, boat show, etc.), event organizers purchase paid media plans weeks, if not months, before the event dates. Delivery of the ad follows closer to the date of publication or broadcast. Overseeing production of paid media is important because the lessons learned can be directly applied to assisting news media in doing their job at the event site. A communications director should have a basic understanding of media production—lighting, sound control, delivery systems, and a familiarity with the venue in order to manage the organization's advertising and help the news media craft the best possible image of the event. For example, at an outdoor basketball tournament or a road race, white signage looks great, but it doesn't show up well on television. If the event managers anticipate television coverage or are targeting it, choosing black signage will help in the promotion and branding of the event via broadcast media.

This also comes into play for earned media with special emphasis on social media. An effective social media campaign will interact and amplify traditional media by sharing and encouraging interaction with other media being produced during the run up to the event.

Communications managers must be able to facilitate the information created by the event as well as document it for future publicity. Statistical record keeping and archiving are important for communication teams to consider because core constituencies (avid fans, participants, sponsors, etc.) and key partners (leagues, governing bodies, etc.) rely on locally collected information. A long view of the calendar is also needed to make sure production schedules hit deadlines for media guides, yearbooks, and game programs that the event produces—often with an up-to-the-day statistical insert in a program.

Courtesy of Michael Stephens

Print materials communicate important information and serve as souvenirs.

Processes for participant-based events can eventually be turned over as internal operations, but until the event day, participants are an external public, and interact with the event through media managed by the communications team. Everything from event presentation to details on parking and logistics must be communicated through a managed medium. Continuing the race example, runners' bibs and timing chips are internal to the event, whereas a time clock is external as it communicates to an external audience (runners are both internal and external to the race). The transfer of the runners' information from the timing chips and ultimately reporting of the runners' times is an important operations function to communication function handoff. Runners expect to have access to their time quickly, earned media seeks results, and archival records of the event all rely on chip times.

The takeover of the smart phone has seen several innovations in the event information arena. Micro-mobile sites, QR coding, and specialized applications are starting to replace printed materials, but the types of information and the paginated format has remained the same. Event managers should be aware of the technologies available in this area and then need to choose technology integrations that fit with expectations of key stakeholders (i.e., participants, media, sponsors, etc.).

One example of how to integrate a QR-reader into event operations and external relations occurred in 2012. The Columbus Dispatch partnered with Flare Code to create a QR-reader based microsite for smartphones that pulled together all of the coverage for the 2012 Memorial Tournament as it happened. The final result is still available by scanning the code.

The mobile Memorial

The Dispatch's coverage of the Memorial Tournament this year includes a special Flare Code mobile presentation that brings our stories, blog posts, Twitter feeds, videos and other tournament information to your smartphone. Scan this code to get started. (You can get a free QR code reader in app stores.)

Courtesy of Gary Kiefer, Managing Editor

Ancillary and traveling events will have the general media pool (i.e., local media vs. national attention) dictated to them in reference to the event and facilities to which they are related. For these events, communications strategies should also consider the input of the sponsors. Traveling events often seek advice and support from facility communication professionals and lean on existing media relationships with the event venue. Similarly, ancillary events fit within the larger picture of the main draw for the schedule and media positioning—both paid and earned. A road race or basketball tournament that is held in conjunction with a college football bowl game will earn placement and reach as promotion for the larger event. It will function as a separate event, but will also benefit from the brand and coverage of the build up to the larger game.

Mega events become more complex. While a central theme or logo ties a series of events together, communications strategies will be as diverse as the groups sponsoring the events. In mega events, protecting the main identity and themes of the primary event is a principal concern. One misstep can cloud an otherwise successful event. The NCAA Final Four, for example, is likely to have partners policing and enforcing approved use of their logo. Enforcement will encompass the local community, areas surrounding the event site, as well as nonplace-bound areas such as online. Fliers and T-shirts will be destroyed, cease and desist orders mandated, and the potential for lawsuits can result from unauthorized use of a logo.

Development involves communication among all departments helping to plan the event to ensure everyone is on the same page. A successful development phase allows all involved to be able to answer the question of "how" information is being communicated. In the world of mass media and instant information, it helps to be aware of as many media outlets as possible.

There is more to the development phase than individual event strategy. There are also invitation and supply elements of event management communications. The basketball metaphor can help again. Calling to mind the pick-up game and tournaments, each group planning a basketball event had a different target group to attend their event. Inviting everybody to every basketball event does not make sense, but understanding how to reach more, and different types, of people will help event communications professionals assist in reaching the overall event goals. The target audience is the result of the invitation process when it comes to external relations.

Invitation

The invitation is a balance of space issues and expediency for sponsor groups. For some events, working press space will be at a premium, while other events will not have an access problem. **Working press space** refers to functional space dedicated to members of the media where an immediate story

is expected from their outlet. It can include both front-of-house seating areas and boxes and the back-of-house technical areas with interview space, outlets, and grounded cable connections as well as space to write. Official **media credentials**, sometimes called a press pass, are issued from the event organizer to designate who can access those working press spaces as well as to identify working press to the participants. Media credentials are a privilege, and a revocable one at that. The event organizers should use press passes for their greatest good, while maintaining fairness and avoiding political problems. Occasionally issues arise if there is real, or perceived, unfairness in how media credentials are allocated (i.e., competing outlets receiving differing numbers of credentials). The event management staff should reserve the right to determine criteria for credentials. Not every TV station is a competitor to a network affiliate, nor every newspaper the largest daily in the area. Space issues may cause choices to be made as to which media outlets can be accommodated. When the number one team in the country comes to a rural campus for a football game, it would not make sense for the school to exclude its local paper from the press box for three people from the metropolitan TV station 90 minutes away, regardless of how much it is perceived that coverage from the TV station

© shutterstock

For large events, the press should have a designated area where they can work and submit their stories.

may suffer because of it. Quantity and frequency of coverage must be balanced with opportunities to reach the most people when making decisions. Although these discussions occur for each event regarding credentials and access, usually more invitations are extended than are used.

Press passes differ from complementary tickets, in the expectation that some form of news story will be created from the media member's attendance at the event. Reminders that the press area is a working area should be made via announcement in the area and in writing. The Baseball Writers Association of America has specific rules and encourages local oversight of the press box by chapter members (BWAA Constitution, 2007).

In addition to having a quality work environment with media on site to cover the event, appropriate supplies and resources are also helpful to improving the chances of continuing media coverage.

Supplies and Resources

Access to supplies and resources in the working press space is also an issue to consider. Event managers regularly reserve certain places, resources, or experiences for select media when planning the allocation of space and access for an event. *ESPN the Magazine* may be granted exclusive access to locker room pregame and halftime observation, or *Runner's World* magazine may have exclusive access to shadow the race director of a major marathon on race day in conjunction with writing a story for the *Runner's World* website.

The minimum level of service required is the opportunity for media perform their job in an efficient manner, determined by the nature of the medium (i.e., TV, radio, print, Web, etc.) and the schedule of their production (i.e., instant, morning, afternoon, weekly, etc.). Communications professionals consider the timing of the media member's product as well as its potential reach in making these decisions. Most working press areas offer the best views first to those broadcast journalists who are presenting the game live, next to print journalists with the most subscribers and quick turnarounds (dailies, blogs, etc.), and finally to the rest of the media (radio news, magazine writers, weeklies, etc.). Recently, press areas for the nonbroadcasters have been removed from areas immediately adjacent to the field of play so those areas can sold to fans willing to pay top dollar for premium locations.

Seating is only one access issue that needs to be considered. Interview space and behind-the-scenes access is also a resource that communications professionals help allocate. The rise of social media has created a new class of "citizen journalists." The Cleveland Indians were amongst the first to create a **"Social Suite"** or **"Social Media Den"** to provide facilities, mainly charging stations and higher-speed Wi-Fi, as well as direct access to front office personnel for those not with traditional media, but influential on social media due to number of followers or readers. This differs from the concept of a social media command center (discussed in Chapter 8—Event Technology and Social Media) as the social suite is more informal and caters to fans compared with a social media command center where the content is an extension of the event organization. The Indians have expanded the program to a #TribeLive space in a hospitality area down the left field line and a family friendly area near the in-stadium playground. Applications for access are available on the team website (Cleveland Indians, 2014).

The communications professional needs to work with the facility and the event operations, as well as sales and marketing departments, to protect the access of more traditional media members whose outlets have proven reach for the event's messages. Press conferences (both pre- and postevent), partner announcements, and other ancillary events that have had a history of exclusivity have an allure to sales-focused executives who are looking to turn revenue without adding expense. The lead-up events must have their original function maintained: communicating information to media members who control and program the sources that reach key publics.

Another consideration brought on by the acceleration of media content—video on demand and other interactive Web features—is the relationship between in-house sources and more traditional independent sources. Broadcast resources are often at the center of this conflict. Game transmissions of professional sporting events are often the property of the league and teams. But local television and radio outlets, as well as video elements of other resources, will want to produce clips and original content around the event. Balancing these relationships through pool services should help every group meet their needs. **Pool services** are defined as a single photographer or videographer (e.g., the Associated Press or the broadcast rights holder) with limited access (defined by time or place) whose work, most often video and photographs, is made available to other working press. This practice provides a controlled high quality image for the event producers and significantly streamlines the media outlet's process for getting b-roll video or photographs to accompany print stories.

Proper planning and invitation goes a long way toward success for an event's media and communication needs, but some needs arise in reaction to things that cannot be anticipated. Successfully adjusting to these unexpected events is the key to thriving during their occurrence and is part of event execution.

Execution

Event execution in external relations encompasses a realistic and detailed schedule, division of duties by skill set, time, and place, and the limiting of duties for the supervisor in order to provide troubleshooting are all keys to success. Challenges, expected and unexpected, may arise from the nature of the event being conducted. People like sporting events because of the element of the unknown; it is the source of the cliché "That is why they play the games."

Event Day Responsibilities

As discussed above, communications professionals have to manage both the internal collection of information and its immediate dissemination to the earned-media people who need it, all while making sure both operations can function without getting in the way of the core activity—the event itself.

Careful data collection is a core component of the event day role for communications professionals. Career milestones and team records should be carefully recorded and updated as part of the process. Having these records and contextualizing facts about the event and the participant is a part of the expectation of the media on event communication professionals. But, not everything is as predictable as game statistics. Being prepared for, and reacting to, uncertainty is also part of the allure of a career in sport communications. Every event has the potential for something memorable to occur; a fantastic single-game performance or some sort of disaster can strike without warning. The response of the communications staff can make or break how the event is perceived when the unexpected happens.

While the broadcasts and media may be the primary responsibility for the communications professional during the event, several other reactive pieces to an event can add to—or often prevent detracting from—the experience of the attendees. Returning to the basketball metaphor, attendees are often pleasantly surprised by added touches such as free water bottles, gifts, promotional items, or product samples. These are examples of structured ways to enhance experience. Events provide ample opportunities to do this from the mass effort (i.e., a scoreboard and video screen) to the more personal (i.e., scorecard or miniprogram giveaway). The participant-driven event provides chances as well, such as race timing systems in running races, tracking of runners online or via text messages, or presentation-sized pledge boards at fundraising events.

These information touches are becoming an expectation of event consumers and participants. In today's digital information age, personalized mailings, emails, and mobile device programming all are commonplace. Often the key to activating a sponsorship is found through tagging a brand to a piece of information and delivering it in a measurable and actionable way to the attendee in a digital format. A more traditional activation would be a coupon on the bottom of a free program sheet, while the tech-savvy activation is to tag a mobile highlight package with a UPC code for a discount in-store. A communications professional has an opportunity to affect not only event experience, but also the financial bottom line through "outside the box" thinking in both online and more traditional message delivery formats.

Crisis Communications

The defensive contribution the communications professional can make is in coordinating efforts in an emergency situation. Often the external relations worker will be looked to as the spokesperson during, or immediately after, a crisis at an event. A crisis situation ranges from an injury to a player or an ejection of a spectator, to a building evacuation or an event cancellation. As mentioned above, planning for the contingencies is the key to managing them.

Communications professionals must have direct access to decision makers to be able to ask the questions that constituencies (like the media or others) will need to have answered in a crisis situation. For example, a contact for a representative of the governing body or rights holder is needed, as event cancellation and rescheduling planning is often not determined on-site. Good communications personnel will have contacts with local police, fire, and EMT units, and will coordinate with event managers, facility supervisors, and local authorities to ensure an immediate and unified response to unanticipated negative situations (see Chapter 17—Event Safety and Security for more information). Certain scenarios, such as building evacuations, should be practiced for operations and communications staff to understand their role in the emergency. Relationship management that began in the event conceptualization phase will pay off during a crisis. A professional keeps bridges strong before the storm.

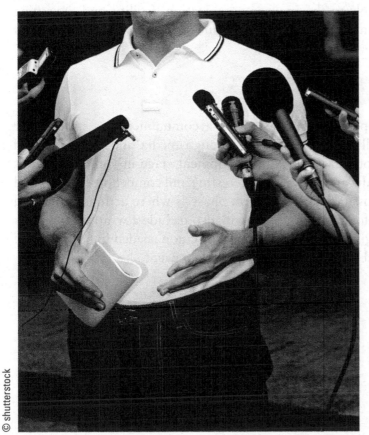

© shutterstock

Designated staff should be trained and prepared to speak to the press if a crisis occurs.

Technology is changing the way people choose to communicate in an emergency as well. A noncellular emergency system is a good idea for large events where the disruption of cell service in an emergency, from either over use or structural damage, is a strong possibility. Second, the collection of spectator cell phone numbers is an important piece of business data for recurring events. Signing up for a text system of alerts is an excellent way to populate this list. Finally, facilities are upgrading their in-event cell and Wi-Fi structures. The continued growth of distributed antennae networks (DANs) will hasten the need for moving more communications into smart phone friendly formats.

Nonnatural disasters—things brought on by human error or frailty—can have similar effects to weather or fire on an organization. Planning and management of those instances can therefore be handled in like manners: prepare, practice, and maintain relationships. In sport, there is nothing more heart-wrenching than a life-threatening injury occurring on a large stage. A detailed plan, including who will act as a spokesperson, where and how sensitive medical information will be released, and a chain of command to make decisions on the postponement or cancellation of the event, can increase efficiency and minimize the crisis environment surrounding a major injury.

Wrap Up

After an event, a careful recap should be performed. One of the many parts in the recap will be the amount and type of the media coverage the event received. Internal relationships with front-line personnel are equal in importance to those with external constituencies for picking up on what is or is not working. Comments about auxiliary items like information-based giveaways (i.e., programs, roster sheets, or fan guides), public address and scoreboard satisfaction, and event-specific details can often be gleaned from front-line staff who were with the consumer throughout the experience. Talking to people in the organization and in the building also saves time and expense compared with surveys.

The communications office should keep a scrapbook of media coverage: newspaper and Internet articles, electronic media Web site coverage, and so forth. The binder (or electronic file) can also contain video footage from the event itself, as well as copies of stories run about the event. Paid media schedules and **fulfillment paperwork**—the copies of the traffic logs that show when the commercials actually ran on air—are also useful to include. Some media professionals use the time of TV or radio earned media multiplied by the "rate card" cost for the time to determine a value of the coverage. The **rate card** is the publicly available or retail price that an outlet charges for its commercial time. The same technique can be used with "column inches" in the newspaper or magazine. Internet sources are more difficult to judge, but **page view counts**—the number of times the content is loaded into a browser—are often available from the page's publisher.

Media reports from events can be valuable to the sponsor organization, facility, and governing body. They should be kept and reviewed with strategic goals in mind, and should be a source of changes in tactics.

SUMMARY

This chapter explains the process of developing and implementing a communications strategy for a sports event. How details of an event will be communicated through media and on-site should be considered during the initial event conceptualization. The development stage in communications strategy involves a mix of paid and earned media and providing interesting and compelling background information of the event as thoroughly as possible. The execution phase is where actions associated with the event will test the results of the development stage, and will also include a wrap-up to justify future efforts. The technology is always changing, but the types of information needed to be successful will always be tied to the purpose and desired outcomes of each individual event.

Student Challenges

NAME _____ DATE _____

Choose a sporting event that occurred in your area over the previous few weekends. Identify and research the media that covered that event. Then, develop the communications strategy to reach each outlet and their audiences with information about the event.

Question 9.1

Conduct a media audit (using Web resources only) for the media market where the event took place. List five outlets including at least one TV, one radio, and one newspaper source. Indicate the contact most likely to handle the event's press release.

For "time of production/update" think about the following: When does information need to be provided to fit the outlet's regular schedule? What time are their newscasts? When do they publish? Is the schedule different for their studio news program and their Web site? Is there a difference between the newspaper's printed copy and their Web copy?

Outlet #1:
    Type of media:
        Time of production/update:
        Contact information:

Outlet #2:
    Type of media:
        Time of production/update:
        Contact information:

Outlet #3:
    Type of media:
        Time of production/update:
        Contact information:

Outlet #4:
    Type of media:
        Time of production/update:
        Contact information:

Outlet #5:
    Type of media:
        Time of production/update:
        Contact information:

Question 9.2

Write three press releases for the event. One should be aimed at TV, another radio, and the third newspaper or online newspaper. Consider the details most important for each type of media outlet and how to convey understanding and support of their needs in the release. Please refer to the **16-Step Guide to Writing a Press Release** contained in this chapter.

EVENT TRAVEL PACKAGES AND SPORTS TOURISM

Roy Edmondson

Roy Edmondson is the Director of Sports Business Development for the Anaheim/Orange County Visitor and Convention Bureau and President of Sports Tourism Consulting. He has worked in the sports industry for over 22 years including roles with ESPN (Disney's) Wide World of Sports, National Hockey League, Royal Sports International, Aviator Sports Complex, Myrtle Beach Convention & Visitors Bureau, and San Jose Convention & Visitors Bureau. He received his bachelor degree from Florida State University. Roy currently is a Board Member for the National Association of Sports Commissions.

What is sports tourism? The first guess most people make is that it has something to do with putting together groups of people to watch sporting events. Although, that is a part of sports tourism it is just a small part. Cities, counties, and states around the United States and globally employ people specifically to bring sports tourism to their destination to help drive economic impact.

In the 1990s, communities started to realize that sporting events other than the Super Bowl, NCAA Final Four, and Olympics were generating money back to the host city when hundreds of families would stay overnight to participate in soccer, hockey, baseball, softball, and basketball tournaments. These families needed to stay in hotels, eat in local restaurants, buy gas, purchase souvenirs, and might even enjoy a local attraction between games.

Sports tourism is important to destinations for many reasons. Imagine a hotel located in a community that is strong with corporate industry. The hotels are filled Monday through Friday with business people coming from around the world for business meetings. What happens to the hotel over the weekend? Unless the hotel is lucky enough to be in a popular tourist destination or host a lot of family reunions or wedding parties, the chances are that most hotels are at a very low occupancy. Then one weekend, the hotel is sold out, the local restaurants, that usually just service locals, are now filled with athletes and their families. The community takes notice and wants to know "How do we get more of these here?" Sports tourism is born!

Convention and Visitors Bureaus and Sports Commissions

A convention and visitor bureau (CVB) is a nonprofit organization that attracts various events, tourism, and business to the local area. It is typically funded through a bed or business improvement tax. A **room tax** is a tax on hotel rooms levied by the state government. A **bed tax** is an additional tax levied on hotel rooms by the local municipality. These taxes are common because it is out of town guests who pay and not local residents. For a long time, CVBs employed staff that focused on corporate, association, SMERF (social, military, educational, religious, and fraternal), international, and tour groups (e.g., bus tours). When sports travel started to be recognized, CVBs were the natural organization to lead this charge for the destination. Over the last 20 years, the number of CVBs that employ a full time sports tourism professional has grown to over 500 in the United States alone.

As the idea of utilizing sports to bring money to the local economy became popular, cities began to add sports commissions. **Sports commissions** exist specifically to attract sports events to the area and assist in hosting the events. Unlike CVBs, there are many different ways sports commissions are funded and many different purposes under which they operate. Sports commissions are generally funded through differing combinations of tax dollars, memberships, fundraising, grants, CVB support, and sponsorship. Typically, a city forms a sports commission when one of the following occurs: (1) the destination is hosting a sports event that requires a local organizing committee; (2) a sports event is coming to the destination that requires fundraising beyond the dollar amount the CVB is willing to contribute; (3) the destination has started hosting enough sports events that is warrants the dedication of multiple staff; or (4) the city is following a trend of the industry. Many rights holders like the fact that they are dealing with an organization that is solely dedicated to sports. Some planners feel that these organizations understand their business and their needs better.

Other than how they are funded and that sports commissions' are dedicated to the sports industry, the most common difference between CVBs and sports commissions is the size. A CVB will typically have one to two staffs dedicated on the sports tourism efforts and a sports commission could have anywhere from 3 to more than 10 depending on the size of the market and number of annual events. There is also a trend that sports commissions are starting to create their own events. This saves on bid fees, dependence on rights holders and others, branding, and is a source of self-funding. In most cases, if an event requires a local organizing committee, the sports commission will take the lead. There are many cities across the United States that have both a dedicated CVB staff for the sports market and a sports commission. The strength of the formal and informal partnership between the CVB and sports commission can impact the success of event in the area.

Securing Events

Recruiting sporting events to a destination, as in most instances of business, has a lot to do with relationships. The people who make the decision of where to take their event want to be confident that their event will be successful and the commitment that was made by the destination will be met. Rights holders will talk to other events if they are considering to go to a destination where they have never been and if the event is a success, it is a safe bet that the next time there is an opportunity to come back, that city will be at the top of the list. When one sits back and thinks about the size of the sports event industry, it is small compared with some other industries, but it is a fast growing area of sports where it is common to be connected to another person by only two degree of separation or less. Reputation is key, and once it is damaged, it is hard to regain that trust.

Conferences

Rights holders and destinations will also attend several conferences throughout the year. These tradeshows bring CVBs, sports commissions, and rights holders together to facilitate discussion about what events are up for bid, the hosting requirements, and what cities can offer to potential events.

The biggest mistake that is repeatedly made is cities wasting their time and money bidding on events that they have no real possibility of attracting. For example, the NCAA is not going to consider holding the men's basketball Final Four in Panama City, FL. At the tradeshows, destinations/cities should do their homework prior to any meetings to make sure they have the capability to host the event. If they don't, they should not plan the meeting so the rights holder can meet with cities that meet the bid and hosting requirements.

There are currently three main tradeshows throughout the year with several other midsize to smaller conferences plus two international conferences. The first large tradeshow is hosted by the National Association of Sports Commissions (NASC, www.sportscommissions.org) and is usually in March or April. It is followed by the CONNECT (www.connectsports.com) conference in August and the TEAMS Conference (www.teamsconference.com) in November. Additionally, Sports Travel magazine and the websites of the above conferences provide up to date information on the sport tourism industry.

Each city/destination will have its own method of determining what events to attempt to secure, but the most important factors for a city to consider are:

1. Venue Availability—Does the destination have the required space to meet the events' needs during the time frame requested?
2. Housing Availability—Does the destination have the required number of overnight accommodations (hotel rooms/motel rooms/camp sites) to host the event?
3. Philosophical Fit—Does the event match with the mission and vision of the organization?
4. ROI—Does financial and time investment give the sports commission and community the return on the investment?

Contemporary rights holders have become business savvy and they understand their events have substantial value. But, some rights holders overestimate the value of the event. This can occur because a previous host destination over compensated to bring an event to their area (e.g., the event filled down time, a local influencer wanted the event brought in, the destination wants to build brand awareness, etc.). Because of this over compensation by one locale, the rights holder may have the expectation that every year any city will give them the same as the previous one.

The opposite could also be true, just because one destination is willing to pay a lot more, their event may not be better off. If the rights holders choose a destination that their participants are not excited about, or has a history of poorly hosting event, then they could see a significant reduction in revenue. For example, registrations will be lower which will reduce entry fee revenue, merchandise revenue, room rebate revenue, gate revenue, and so on. It might also cost more than anticipated to travel staff to the destination. These reduced revenue items in addition to increased expenses may negate any additional revenue picked up on the front end, such as from room rebates.

Housing Packages/Travel Packages

Housing packages, or travel packages, generate revenue for an event in a couple of different possible ways. Housing packages are based on the number of hotel room nights and/or rental car days booked by participants and spectators. Travel packages are based on a fee in the package that goes to the event. At one time, airline tickets were included as a revenue item in travel packages. In the past two decades, airlines have stopped paying a commission for ticket sales. Most events are not going to have their own travel department. They will often contract with a travel partner to perform the booking functions, even with online booking. The travel partner will negotiate with hotels and reserve a block of rooms around the event date(s). The travel partner will negotiate rates with the hotels, airlines, and car rental companies and will be responsible for the block of hotel rooms reserved for the event. The travel partner will have deadlines in their contracts that allow them to drop a certain percentage of rooms from the block by specified dates if they are not selling as anticipated. Depending on the terms of the contract, they may have to pay a penalty. This is called **attrition**.

How do the event and the travel partner make money from these packages? The travel partner negotiates rates with various hotels, choosing hotels in different price ranges and star rating ranges to appeal to a variety of budgets. The travel partner makes its commission from the room rate they have negotiated with the hotel, usually 10% of the event's published room rate. The travel partner and rights holder will negotiate the amount of the commission that each group receives. The 10% commission may be split 50/50 or 60/40 (in favor of the travel partner). Another way to look at a 50/50 split of the commission is to say that the rights holder is earning 5% of the commission.

Event managers work with the travel partner to assist the travel partner in determining how many people the event managers think will be attending the event. This is one of the reasons it is important to track attendance and bookings for events. This number may come from past data or from booking numbers taken from a comparable event. CVBs and sports commissions can be helpful in obtaining this data from past host sites for the event organizers. For a first year event that will be repeated, a rights holder may want to pay for a survey that will provide data on the attendees and determine how many are "booking around" the travel packages, or making travel arrangements on their own. This information can also be collected at the event registration/check-in.

Event organizers may package the entry fee to the event with tickets to local attractions (depending on location), hotel room nights, or special events tickets and require that an individual or team purchase the package in order to enter the event. This is known as **package-to-compete or stay-to-play**. Forcing participants to purchase a package may seem like an easy revenue stream, but it can cause ill will and may backfire.

Another way to build a package involves simply inserting a fee that reverts back to the rights holder and the travel partner receives the commission for the rooms and/or they may also build in their own fee. Payments from the travel partner to the rights holder are made at various stages throughout the booking period (monthly or quarterly) or after the event, depending on what was negotiated between the parties.

Room Nights

There is a difference between rooms booked or sold and room nights. Simply using the term rooms will tell how many rooms have been sold or are occupied, but not for how long. The term **room nights** refers to how many total nights' stay were sold for an event. This is an important figure to know because it affects economic impact in the area and can provide leverage for event managers in securing free rooms, discounted rooms, commissions, hotel sponsorships, and/or additional services from the hotel based on the number of anticipated room nights. Room rebates to an event and/or sports commission are based on room nights. A **room rebate** is a dollar amount per room night booked at host properties that is given back to the event rights holder as part of an agreement for bringing their event to a host city.

Let's use the example of a basketball tournament for girls in Miami that will bring in teams from around the Southeast. The tournament will begin on Thursday evening and continue with games on Friday, Saturday, and Sunday. The championship game will be held on Sunday afternoon at 4:30 pm. For simplicity's sake, assume there are 40 teams in the tournament, that each team has two coaches and twelve players on its roster, and that each coach and player/family on the team will book one room each.

40 teams × 14 people(12 players/families and 2 coaches) = 560 rooms sold

When teams travel, though, they are going to have different travel schedules. A team driving from Orlando may choose to arrive the day the tournament starts and leave Sunday night, even if they make it to the championship game. A team driving from Charlotte, however, may drive to Miami on Wednesday and would then need a hotel room that night. For the return trip, they may decide to stay overnight on Sunday and drive back to Charlotte on Monday. Let's look at an example for each of these teams and assume for the example that all of the teams, players, and coaches behave the same.

Orlando team: arrives Thursday and checks out of the hotel on Sunday, which amounts to a three-night stay (Thursday, Friday, and Saturday).

14 people (rooms) × 3 nights = 42 room nights

Charlotte team: arrives Wednesday and checks out of the hotel on Monday, which amounts to a five-night stay (Wednesday, Thursday, Friday, Saturday, and Sunday).

14 people (rooms) × 5 nights = 70 room nights

In this basic example, assumptions about the number of rooms, length of stay, and uniform behavior patterns of the team members were made. For real events, these numbers and behaviors are going to vary even among individual teams. Some are going to arrive early or stay extra days for vacation, some families will need more than one room, and some athletes may travel with another athlete's parents, and so on.

To show the difference between rooms and room nights at the macro level, let's take our example showing the static total number of rooms booked and make an assumption that every team will stay three nights.

40 teams × 14 people = 560 rooms booked/sold

40 teams × 14 people × 3 nights = 1,680 room nights

While the event participants may only occupy 560 hotel rooms in the Miami area, the event has booked 1,680 hotel room nights. As demonstrated, slight alterations in the team travel can significantly alter room nights. The event schedule can help increase room nights, but event managers should be cautious about creating a schedule that puts an undue hardship on traveling teams. The critical concept with room nights is that event managers must be aware of how many room nights the event is generating within the community and at each local hotel.

Adding a room rate to these formulas would also show the revenue that the hotels are making from the event. Using a room rate of $140/night, the hotel would have revenues of $5,880 from the Orlando team and $9,800 from the Charlotte team. If the average room rate for all of the hotels with packages is $120/night, local area hotels would make $201,600 for this event (1,680 room nights, $120/night). Numbers like these provide a strong selling point for communities to host sports events, especially during times that are slow for hotel bookings.

Measuring the Success of Events

Just as events became more aware of their value, destinations have also become smarter about how to choose and measure an event. Historically, destinations measured the success of an event on the total room nights the event generated, and many destinations still use this method. It seems very logical—a destination wants to invest in an event that brings the most people to stay overnight in its hotels and spend lots of money while they are in town. The problem, though, is how does a destination know where they are all staying? Event organizers will typically secure hotel room blocks with various properties and direct their participants to stay at these locations. In exchange, the planner would get back a rebate, usually in the $5–$15 range per night per room. With the boom of the internet and travel sites, participants have become smarter about how to find the cheapest place to stay. Now the rights holder doesn't get a rebate, the destination doesn't know where they are staying or how many actual room nights have been used. Many cities will only meet the planners' requirements if they meet the room nights that are stated on the RFP.

Many events have gone to a new model using one of the following three types: stay-to-play, call-to-save, or incentive-to-stay model. The stay-to-play model, as noted earlier, requires participants to stay at the hotels blocked by the planner if they want to compete in the event. With this model, the registration fee is built into the hotel package price and it is the *only* way to register for the event. The call-to-save model requires participants to call either the rights holder or a third party housing agency prior to arrival to confirm where the participants are staying. The opportunity here is to offer a great deal that participants will want to purchase. At the very least, the event can hopefully determine where participants are staying. The incentive-to-stay model offers a different entry fee for participants who stay in host properties or a higher entry fee for participants who don't stay in host properties. This way, participants who want to use points to book a hotel or are loyal customers of a certain hotel chain that isn't offered in event packages can stay where they like and still register. The idea is that the additional registration amount will cover the amount the sports commission and rights holder would lose by the participant staying somewhere other than a host property. Cities have also started measuring the success by the number of participants. They require the event to provide not only the number of participants, but also the numbers of participants that live within a certain mile radius that could drive to the destination. Then cities plug those numbers into an economic impact calculator to generate a number indicating the event's relative success.

Economic Impact

Currently, there are two main organizations sports commissions use for sports economic impact calculations—the NASC, mentioned earlier, and Destination Marketing Association International (DMAI, www.destinationmarketing.org). Economic impact is the new money entering a region resulting in a change in regional output, earnings, and employment (Humphreys & Plummer, 1995). An economic impact calculator will ask questions related to the event and based on hours and hours of research and surveys, it will calculate a number. The real question is what do these numbers mean? It depends on who one asks and how good the data is that was entered. These calculators also apply an economic impact multiplier. An **economic impact multiplier** is a certain number that is entered in economic impact calculations because it assumes the money generated from the event will be circulated throughout the community several times. The theory is that family "X" comes into town and buys dinner at the local restaurant. The waiter or waitress who received the tip from that family uses that money at the local bar, the bartender then buys a pizza after work, and the pizza delivery guy buys groceries. So that $10 tip is suddenly calculated as $50 in an economic impact calculator that uses a multiplier.

Some destinations prefer not to use any calculator and use a direct impact formula instead. A direct impact formula is usually calculated by a local university or third party company that will do hundreds of surveys of visitors to the destination. They find out how much money visitors spent on food, hotel, gas, rental car, souvenirs, attractions, tips, and so on. and determine the average amount spent per night per person. Although this method seems the most logical, there are still drawbacks. How does a destination know exactly how many people are coming with every participant? Also, the spending habits vary among sports, age groups, and even by gender. It is well understood, for example, that amateur young girls (~8–12 years old) bring the most spectators while men's softball may not bring many people with them at all. It is also documented that certain sports spend more money than others.

There is no right and no wrong answer to the question of whether to use economic impact or direct impact calculations. Whatever method the organization decides to use and feels comfortable presenting to the public and media, is the method best for that destination.

Sports tourism has seen a big boom with the increase in travel sports. According to a 2001 NASC/Ohio University Study, the sports travel industry has grown 6.5% since 2010 and event growth has increased 10.5% since 2010. The same study found that visitor spending in 2011 alone was over $7.68 billion. Sports tourism has also been determined to be generally recession proof. Few parents will tell their 12–year-old daughter they can't go to the National Championships when there is no guarantee of qualifying next year. Families usually find a way to make it to the event. Every year rights holders and destinations are becoming smarter and more aware of the impact this industry has on tourism dollars and there is no decline in sight.

SUMMARY

Sports travel and tourism are booming areas of the sports industry. As students begin internships and jobs, it is important to be aware of the basic philosophy behind sports commissions. Travel/housing packages are essential aspects to understand because they financially impact both event rights holders and sports commissions. Having knowledge of these areas will be valuable for students working in any area of event management.

Student Challenges

NAME _____ DATE _____

Question 10.1

Research to find out if your city or nearest city has a CVB and sports commission. Determine the main contacts at the CVB and/or sports commission. Research to find out what sports events the city has bid on and hosted in the last 3–5 years.

Question 10.2

Review the Boys' or Girls' Junior National Championship bid manual for USA Volleyball, which can be found at: http://www.teamusa.org/USA-Volleyball/Events/Indoor/USAV-Bid-Documents

Complete the bid packet to host either the girls' or boys' championship in your city. (If you are in a country outside the United States, assume this is your country's volleyball NGB and they have the same requirements OR find the bid documents for your country's volleyball NGB.)

*You may not meet all of the requirements. In those situations, please just indicate in your assignment where you had created your own information. You **do** need to track down real data on hotels related to number of rooms and amenities. You **do not** need to secure group rates for the hotels or provide a contract. Any/all requested attachments in the RFP must be completed. The critical component of this exercise is to go through the process of generating a bid.

EVENT REGISTRATION FOR PARTICIPANTS

Roy Edmondson

Roy Edmondson is the Director of Sports Business Development for the Anaheim/Orange County Visitor and Convention Bureau and President of Sports Tourism Consulting. He has worked in the sports industry for over 22 years including roles with ESPN (Disney's) Wide World of Sports, National Hockey League, Royal Sports International, Aviator Sports Complex, Myrtle Beach Convention & Visitors Bureau, and San Jose Convention & Visitors Bureau. He received his bachelor degree from Florida State University. Roy currently is a Board Member for the National Association of Sports Commissions.

Often an afterthought, but most definitely one of the most important aspects of participant-driven events, is registration. The registration form (online or paper) will contain all critical information pertaining to the event. If this information is incorrect or incomplete, it can lead to endless amounts of frustration for event managers and participants. For purposes of registration, a **participant** is anyone taking part in a sports event. This includes everyone associated with a team taking part in a sports event who will be on the field of play (including, but not limited to, players, coaches, statisticians, athletic trainers, managers); volunteers; participants in promotions; and so on. In the following examples, "participant" may refer strictly to athletes and coaches, but event managers should remember that, generally, other groups are included in the term "participant." On-site registration is the first face-to-face contact between participants and the event. If everything runs smoothly and all information necessary has been provided, then the participants' first experience is a pleasant one, and that will go a long way. It is almost certain that if the experience with registration is bad, then it will take a long time to recover and possibly even cost the event future business.

When to Start?

The most important factor in determining when to disseminate registration information is to understand the sport and its customers. Each sport is different as to when participants determine in what events they will take part. For example, many travel hockey teams will decide in early fall what tournaments they will play for the entire season (September–April). This way, they can include any tournament entry fees in the player team fee once players have been selected for the team. On the other hand, many summer basketball teams are not even formed until late spring, so to have registration out any earlier does not make sense. The most important thing is to have all the event information confirmed before releasing anything. Once information is communicated to the public, it is impossible to fully take it back. Sending out bad information will make event managers look unorganized and unprepared.

Online Registration vs. Paper Registration

Even most small events today can use online registration without it being a huge financial strain on the budget. There are some small ones, though, that may still consider having paper registration. To determine which direction to go, there are two very simple formulas to use: (1) cost of man hours re-entering all the information into a database multiplied by the number of events run over the course of 2–3 years, divided by the cost of creating an online registration system, or (2) the cost of man hours re-entering all the information in the database, divided by the cost of outsourcing registration to a third-party online company. There are additional factors that could be involved in making the determination, such as whether the event will be using electronic registration on-site. How much time is spent processing payments? Does the customer base have access/ability to use computers? At the end of the day, the world is continuously moving to online everything, whether via computer or handheld device, and this saves time, money, and the environment!

Online Registration

If an event does not have the capital to create its own online registration system, using an online registration company, such as Active.com, is a great alternative. Online registration is a route that many events now select. (Remember to use the formula presented when computing cost analysis.) For a nominal fee, there are a number of companies that will handle all of an event's online registration needs. Depending on the registration company and the pricing packages it offers, an event may be charged a flat fee per transaction or the fee may be setup as a percentage of the registration amount. The process is often seamless to the point that participants are not even aware they have left the event's website. When an event does use another company for online registration services, it is important to ensure that the event is still the owner of the participant list and information, not the registration company. This way the event has access to the list for promotion of future events. Additionally, make sure the agreement with the registration company does not allow the company or its partners to use the participant list in any way and/or sell the list to any third party.

© Shutterstock

Online event registration is now routine, event for small events.

With online event registration being very common on sites such as Active.com, there are many additional benefits for both events and participants. In many cases, potential parties can use already existing social profiles to register for events. Offering people the ability to register by using their Facebook or Twitter or other social profile makes it easy for them. All the data the event likely wants (e.g., address, phone, etc.) will not be gathered at that point, but that will be collected when people actually register for an event and enter their payment information. At this stage an event could also offer a link to a National Governing Body (NGB) site if participants need to purchase a 1day membership in order to compete in an event.

Online registration systems can also make it easier by allowing a person to enter multiple participants at one time and only enter payment type for the entire group. This is especially helpful for team sports competitions, corporate team races, etc.

Online payments have changed the way charities receive money, and online registration is an easy way to promote and help charities. Many events have a charity or charities they support. Online registration makes participant giving as simple as clicking two check boxes—clicking "yes," they want to make a donation to a specific charity, and checking next to a box with a specific monetary amount.

Registration Form/Page

An event's registration form should be a "no-brainer" when participants begin to complete it. This is not the place to leave participants scratching their heads. Perception can become reality. If an individual or team perceives that an entry form is unprofessional or lacks information, they can make the leap to believing that the event will have those same characteristics and will be running the same way. Basic information that needs to be included on a registration form includes:

- Date
- Time
- Location
- Fee
- Rules
- Waiver/Release
- Divisions or age brackets
- Awards
- What is included in the registration/entry fee?
- Spectator information (costs, viewing, parking)
- Facility rules (cameras, external food & beverage, etc.)
- Cancellation policy
- Refund policy
- Required membership information (e.g., NGB affiliation)
- On-site registration/Check-in/Packet pick-up times and what they need to bring (e.g., ID, birth certificates, etc.)
- Local hotel/attraction/restaurant information (for events with out-of-town participants)
- Weather policy
- Number of games guaranteed
- Forfeit policy and/or mercy rule
- Tie-breaking policy

- Any deviation from NGB rules
- Protest policy
- Cooler policy
- Contact information for questions

The more information included, the better the participants are informed and the less time is taken out of event managers' days so they can focus on what is most important: getting the maximum number of participants for the event!

Confirmation

All athletes who register (whether on paper or online) should receive a confirmation of exactly what they registered for, how much they paid, and a reminder of the time of site check-in and what they need to bring to check-in. This is another extremely important process that is often overlooked, but the better the communication to participants, the smoother the process and the less likely there will be issues or confusion during the event.

On-site Registration/Check-In

How long should on-site registration and check-in remain open? Each sport is accustomed to different policies, so again, it is important to know the market. Many sports provide team captains/individuals a very small time frame. Other events allow a much longer period of time so that participants do not have to make an extra trip, but can arrive just before the start of the event or their first game. For events like marathons and triathlons, check-in will often open a few days before the event, in conjunction with an expo. These advance days also enable participants coming from out of town to arrive early and rest. In the case of triathlons, it also enables participants to check in their equipment at the transition location(s) and go on a course preview. Generally, the rule of thumb should be to make it as easy for the customer as possible. Why make participants come a night early if they do not have their first game/event until the next afternoon? Participants become frustrated if they feel an event is forcing them to spend extra money on travel packages. Event managers need to weigh the benefit of requiring participants to arrive early with the potential downside of them being so frustrated that they do not attend the event the following year.

On-site registration is often uses as a check-in phase and for distribution of event materials.

Sometimes staffing of registration becomes an issue if the person overseeing the registration is one of the event managers. Event managers cannot be in two places at once, and trying to both manage an event and run registration is not a good idea. It is highly recommended that event managers always dedicate at least one staff member to registration until all participants have checked in. If an event starts on a Friday afternoon or Saturday morning, make sure to schedule check-in to allow enough time for all teams competing in the first event to complete registration and have 45–60 minutes prior to their first game/event. For example, a soccer tournament using 12 fields has first games at 4 pm on Friday. It takes 10 minutes for each team to complete registration and the event has two dedicated registration staff.

$$12 \text{ fields} \times 2 \text{ teams} = 24 \text{ teams} \times 10 \text{ minutes} = 240 \text{ minutes} / 2 \text{ staff} = 120 \text{ minutes}$$
$$+ 60 \text{ minutes prior to first game} = 180 \text{ minutes.}$$

Using this formula, registration should start at 1:00 pm. Another good policy is to open registration 30 minutes earlier than the time posted. This is known as a **soft opening**. Soft openings allow guests who arrive early the feeling that they have been rewarded, and it will also cut down on the typical rush at the start of check-in. This will also allow some time to work through any possible kinks before the majority of participants arrive.

Staff

This is simply a numbers-driven factor. If event managers are limited in the number of people they have, then the previous formula should be used. If they have access to volunteers or a large staff, then the proper way to calculate would be by the following method:

Take the number of participants needing to register, times the time needed to register, divided by the total hours planned for registration to be open.

$$\frac{\text{Number of participants needing to register} \times \text{Time needed to register each participant}}{\text{Total hours planned for registration to be open}}$$

For example, a basketball tournament has 48 teams and registration is from 4:00 pm until 8:00 pm and the check-in process takes 15 minutes per team.

$$48 \text{ teams} \times 15 \text{ minutes} = 720 \text{ minutes} / 240 \text{ minutes(total registration time)} = 3 \text{ staff}$$

OR

$$\frac{48 \text{ teams} \times 15 \text{ minutes} = 720 \text{ minutes}}{240 \text{ minutes (total registration time)}} = 3 \text{ staff}$$

Using this example, event managers would use no fewer than three staff, but it is highly recommend to increase by one to two dedicated staff for registration and at least one additional staff member to answer general questions. If an event is allowing on-site registration, then depending on the expected volume, they can use the same formula. Another good recommendation is to increase staff, especially if the event can use volunteers, for the start of registration. The opening times are the busiest and event managers can always let people go if they are not needed, but they can almost never get extras to start.

Location

On-site registration/check-in should be held in a location that can accommodate the proper number of staff, expected volume, proper power, ample ingress and egress, and be convenient to the participants. One thing that is important about the location is that there should be a separate entrance and exit if at all possible. Having one entrance/exit tends to form unnecessary backup and could disrupt the flow. Registration/check-in is typically held where the event is being held, at a host hotel, or at a local sponsor's location (restaurant/attraction/retail store). For almost all circumstances, hosting registration indoors or under significant cover is most desirable. Hosting outdoor registration/check-in introduces too many variables event managers cannot control and could make for a very messy time. Rain, wind, lightning, lack of power, lights, secured storage, are all concerns that event managers could find outdoors, but very rarely are issues indoors.

Flow

Event managers do not want participants to draw upon the analogy of an amusement park where they waited far too long for a ride that lasted 30 seconds and then walked away, vowing never to return. To avoid the same pitfalls, ensuring the proper flow of event registration/check-in is fundamental. If event managers expect to have 10 people in line at any given time, they should have a queue that fits four times that amount. This serves two purposes: (1) if there is an unexpected backup, they are prepared to have participants wait in an orderly fashion, and (2) when the participants walk in, go through a line and walk right up to the front, they feel like they must have missed the rush and are pleasantly surprised at how quick the process is. Make sure participants do not have to walk back and forth through a long queue unnecessarily. Adjust the queue to accommodate the flow; otherwise, people will be ducking underneath and possibly knocking down stanchions or hurting themselves, which is not good for anyone (see Figure 11.1 for queue set-up diagrams). Event managers should also have a separate line for any on-site registrations, since this process will typically take longer than simply checking in already registered participants. Those who have already completed their registration should not have to wait for those who are registering at the last minute. Finally, try to set up registration/check-in so that participants only make one stop. Having multiple stops can only cause confusion and add the potential for participants to miss a step.

Check-In

When conducting a large registration, it is best to sort check-in materials alphabetically. By using an alphabetical sort, event managers can divide each station with an equal number of participants. Each station does not have to have every single participant's information. The smaller the number of teams or participants that are entered, the easier it becomes to have multiple stations, all of which can check in any participant versus breaking participants down by designated groupings.

Exchange of Information

When participants arrive at check-in, all necessary information is exchanged. Staff/volunteers should collect any and all waivers, money due, local contact information, and more. Before completing participants' check-in information, ascertain how many people are in their party, how many hotel rooms they have booked, and how many nights they are staying. This information can all be used by the local sports commissions and convention and visitors bureaus (CVBs) to conduct a post-event economic impact analysis, which can result in receiving supporting funds for the event in the future.

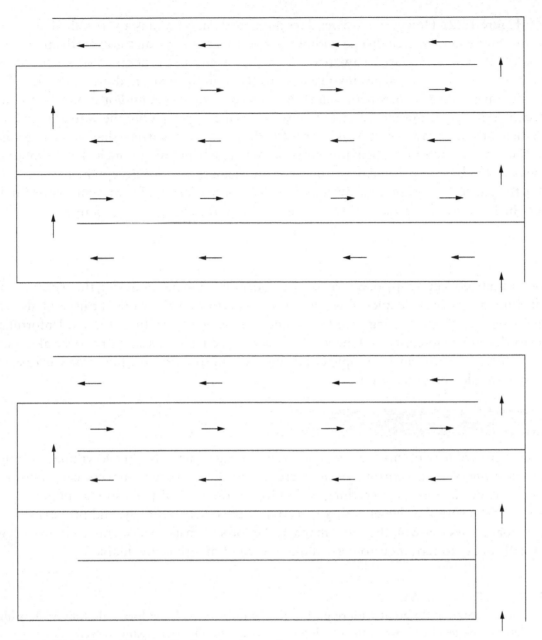

Figure 11.1 Adjustable Event Registration Queue Setup.

Participants should also receive all information relating to the event, if they have not already, such as schedules, captains' meeting information, rules, and gift/goodie bags. If anything of value is given, participants should sign a form acknowledging that they have received the item(s). This is a good way to control inventory and to make sure event managers can verify if someone comes back and says they have not received something important.

Waiver

Every participant should sign a waiver. A parent or guardian must sign for participants under 18. A **waiver, or release of liability,** is "a contract in which the participant or user of a service agrees to relinquish the right to pursue legal action against the service provider in the event that the ordinary negligence of the provider results in an injury to the participant" (Cotten, 2007, p. 85). A waiver by no means is security that an event will never be sued if someone should unfortunately get hurt during the event (**Figure 11.2**). However, a waiver does mitigate damages and is a very valuable piece of paper in those circumstances. One challenge with waivers is that the laws that govern them are at the state level, thus event managers must be aware of the requirements and general enforcement of the waiver in their state. Make sure all parties involved are included in the waiver, along with release for use of participants' images in photo, video, online, any social media type, and/or any as yet undeveloped future technology that the event may use. Consult a legal expert to write the waiver in order to make sure it adheres to state laws. Also make sure if collecting paper waivers that no changes have been made to the waiver, such as participants crossing out statements with which they do not agree. The waiver was drafted for a particular reason and any changes are not acceptable. It is a very simple choice for the participant: sign the waiver as-is, or do not participate. Event managers do not want to be calling the lawyer in the middle of registration to see if the change is acceptable.

IDs

It is a good idea to collect a copy of all participants' identification pieces during the registration process. This will eliminate any future questions regarding a player or participant's status, and also show that the event is serious about making sure the competition is being conducted fairly. Unfortunately, not every person/team has integrity and, believe it or not, some teams actually try to sneak a player onto their roster after registration is complete. Having this information on file makes it easier to solve protests that are filed by other teams.

SUMMARY

Every year there are new events created, and event managers have to do everything possible to keep their past customers. In a sporting event, there is very little event managers can control over the duration of the event. Almost everything is decided on the field of play, so it is important for event managers to make sure the elements they can control are efficient, timely, and professional. Even if a team/participant does not win, the event managers' efforts to ensure an organized event will go a long way and will equate to repeat customers, and the word of mouth is invaluable.

Figure 11.2 Sample Participant Waiver.*
Be aware that each **State is different** with respect to their requirements for enforceable waivers. **It is highly recommended to seek legal counsel in the development of any specific participant waiver.**

First Name: _____ M.I. _____ Last Name:_____

Date of Birth: _____ Gender (M/F): _____

Emergency Contact:_____ Phone Number:_____

Email:_____

Event Information

Event Date(s): July 15, 2017

Event: Fun Run ABC

Event Host: The City of XYZ and Fun Run Inc.

Sport Type(s): walking, jogging, running, and any other activities associated with the Fun Run

Please Read Carefully Before Signing

(**Adult**—18 years of age or over; **Minor**—under 18 years of age)

In consideration of my and/or my child or ward's participation in the Sport Type(s) and Event referenced above and any related activities (collectively, the **"Event"**), wherever the Event may occur, I agree to assume all risks incidental to such participation (which risks may include, among other things, muscle injuries and broken bones). On my own and/or my child or ward's behalf, and on behalf of my and/or my child or ward's heirs, executors, administrators and next of kin, I hereby release, covenant not to sue, and forever discharge the Released Parties (as defined below) of and from all liabilities, claims, actions, damages, costs, or expenses of any nature arising out of or in any way connected with me or my child or ward's participation in the Event and/or any such activities, and further agree to indemnify and hold each of the Released Parties harmless from and against any and all such liabilities, claims, actions, damages, costs or expenses including, but not limited to, all attorneys' fees and disbursements up through and including any appeal. I understand that this release and indemnity includes any claims based on the negligence, action or inaction of any of the Released Parties and covers bodily injury (including death), property damage, and loss by theft or otherwise, whether suffered by me or my child or ward either before, during or after such participation. I declare that I and (if participating) my child or ward are physically fit and have the skill level required to participate in the Event and/or any such activities. I further authorize medical treatment for me and/or my child or ward, at my cost, if the need arises. For the purposes hereof, the **"Released Parties"** are City of XYZ and Fun Run Inc. and their respective parent, subsidiary, affiliated or related companies; the Event Manager referenced above, all Event sponsors or charities, and each of their respective parent, subsidiary, affiliated or related companies; Affiliate #1, Affiliate #2, and Affiliate #3; its Board of Supervisors; and the officers, directors, employees, agents, contractors, subcontractors, representatives, successors, assigns, and volunteers of each of the foregoing entities. I further grant the Released Parties the right to photograph and/or videotape me and/or my child or ward and further to display, use and/or otherwise exploit my and/or my child or ward's name, face, likeness, voice, and appearance forever and throughout the world, in all media, whether now known or hereafter devised, throughout the universe in perpetuity (including, without limitation, in online webcasts, television, motion pictures, films, newspapers, and magazines) and in all forms including, without limitation, digitized images, whether for advertising, publicity, or promotional purposes, including, without limitation, publication of Event results and standings, without compensation, reservation or limitation. I further authorize distribution by the Released Parties of my contact information, including my email address, to third parties for promotional purposes, or for any other purpose whatsoever, without compensation, reservation or limitation. The Released Parties are, however, under no obligation to exercise any rights granted herein. This Waiver and Permission Form shall be governed by the laws of the State of XYZ, and any legal action relating to or arising out of this Waiver and Permission Form shall be commenced exclusively in the Circuit Court of the First Circuit in and for Blue County, State XYZ. State XYZ (or if such Circuit Court shall not have jurisdiction over the subject matter thereof, then to such other court sitting in such county and having subject matter jurisdiction), and I specifically waive the right to trial by jury. I certify I am 18 years of age or older and, if I am executing this Waiver and Permission Form on behalf of my child or ward, the information set forth above pertaining to my child or ward is true and complete.

Date _____

Signature of Participant (if over 18) or Parent (if Participant is under 18) or Court

Appointed Guardian:_____

Print Name of Participant (if 18 or over) or Parent (if Participant is under 18) or Court Appointed Guardian:_____

Student Challenges

NAME_____ DATE_____

In this challenge create a registration form and determine the setup of the registration/packet pick-up area.

Question 11.1

Produce a registration form that contains all of the information that needs to be collected from participants. If the event is not participant-driven, please use a 20-mile charitable bicycle race in the community as an event to create a participant registration form.

QUESTION 11.2

Draw a diagram detailing the setup and flow of registration/packet pick-up for the chosen event. If the event is not participant-driven, please use a 20-mile charitable bicycle race with an expected 1,200 cyclists as an event to create a registration diagram. Half of the participants generally preregister while the other half will need to register on-site. Determine the number of staff needed based on the opening time of registration/packet pick-up and the estimated time it will take to manage each person/team through the process.

CHAPTER 12

EVENT TICKETING

Robb Wade and Landon Huffman

Robb Wade, Ph.D., attended undergraduate and played varsity hockey at Queen's University in Kingston, Ontario. Upon completion of that degree, he attended Ohio University where he earned a master's in sport administration as well as a Ph.D. While at Ohio University, he managed the ice arena, the golf course, and a facility that was used for academics during the week and during home games. He played hockey as a graduate student and then later coached and was the Academic Advisor for the Bobcat hockey team. Dr. Wade completed an internship with the Colorado Rangers professional hockey team and upon graduation from Ohio University worked as the Ticket Manager for the Ohio University Department of Athletics. He later moved to North Carolina State to become the Director of Ticket Operations for Wolfpack Athletics. During that time, he coached minor hockey in the Raleigh Youth Hockey Association. After 6 years in the ticket office, Dr. Wade moved into a teaching role at NC State in the Department of Parks, Recreation, and Tourism Management. He is currently the Director of the Professional Golf Management Program.

Landon Huffman, Ph.D., is a Visiting Assistant Professor of Recreation and Sport Management and Clinical Research Associate for the Bureau of Religion, Spirituality, & Sport at the University of Tennessee in Knoxville, TN. He earned his Ph.D. in Sport Management from the University of Tennessee, Knoxville and graduated with both his bachelor's and master's degrees in sport administration and a minor in coaching education from the University of North Carolina, Chapel Hill. Landon has taught a broad range of courses including sport marketing, sport finance, organization and administration of sport, intercollegiate athletics, ethics in sport, and sociology of sport. His experiences in the sport industry include working in intercollegiate football operations, sport marketing, event operations, compliance, academic advising, and student-athlete development.

This chapter discusses important concepts in ticketing and how ticketing fits into the overall event management process. There are a number of important issues to be considered that relate to the organization, sale, and distribution of tickets for various events. For some events, there might be one or more staff members specifically responsible for ticketing, and the role of the event managers may be minimal. In the case of other events, however, the event managers may wear multiple "hats" and also be the ticket manager. In either scenario, it is important for event managers to have a thorough understanding of the ticketing process and the decisions made along the way.

Due to logistics, ticketing is mainly a topic in traditional spectator-driven events held in traditional sport venues. However, there are some events in non-traditional venues that do ticket the event. Ancillary events, such as a concert associated with a NASCAR event or a fan fest linked to a championship game are two examples of events that are commonly ticketed.

Ticketing an event is a more in-depth process than many people realize. There are questions related to seating arrangements, ticket format, design, sale, and price that have to be addressed for any ticketed event. This chapter will address these topics and others, as well as discuss the role of the customer, how the venue impacts ticketing, premium tickets, parking, credentials, special interest groups, and reconciliation.

Ticketing Basics

A ticket is considered a limited contract between the sport organization and the spectator. The money the spectator paid for the ticket means that he or she is afforded the rights and privileges associated with the purchase of that ticket. Specifically, a **ticket as a limited contract** means that the ticket buyer

Some tickets are still in paper form, but today's events provide many other options for ticket types.

receives the right to attend the event and the organization has an obligation to provide the event as advertised and promoted.

The ticket holder is also owed the ability to observe the event in a safe and enjoyable environment. The person attending the event is not guaranteed a victory for his or her team or a result that he or she might find favorable, but the ticket holder does have the right to expect to see the teams that were advertised and to witness the event. The ticket buyer also has the right to voice his or her opinions about a team's or player's performance. Again, this could be in a positive or negative manner.

The ticket is also a **revocable permit**. This means that the organization reserves the right to take the ticket back from the purchaser (usually with a refund) if he or she is interfering with the enjoyment of others. These concepts go together, in that to ensure that the majority of patrons can exercise their right to see and enjoy the event, others may have to have their tickets revoked. Often, when alcohol is served at events, there are instances where security and/or police must get involved to remove spectators from the venue.

Ticket holders also have the right to know what to expect when they get to their assigned seats. If an obstructed view seat was sold without telling the purchaser that the view of the playing surface was not clear, this would limit the visibility and enjoyment of the event for the spectator. Some refund or accommodation (e.g., relocating the spectator) should be made for spectators that are not able to see and enjoy the event. This has nothing to do with liking the performance, and everything to do with accommodating the guests so they can see the show free from major impediments.

There may be some situations, which involve a change in the event after tickets are bought. This is more common in entertainment events. A high-profile team could, however, get snowed in and become unable to travel to the event, and the event organizers might have a local team substitute for them. This changes the event, and ticket holders requesting refunds should receive them (or a ticket to the rescheduled event if applicable). There are some sports, however, where schedule changes are likely. In these cases, the information must be clearly spelled out at the time of purchase, and preferably on the ticket itself. Baseball is commonly rained out and games are cancelled or rescheduled, sometimes multiple times in a season. It must be clear what the ticket holders' rights are in a rainout situation. If a rainout is called before the game even starts, is that different than a game that postponed or cancelled after the fifth inning? What about if it is a double header where one ticket is used for both games and the second game is cancelled?

The ticket as a limited contract and a revocable permit are both important concepts. Event decisions might have to be made at some point with this in mind. If a traveling show cancels at the last minute, ticket managers must have the money available and a plan for refunding to all of the customers.

The Customer

Most, if not all, sport professionals are familiar with the service industry phrase, "The customer is always right." While that is an admirable and somewhat functional motto under which to operate, it may not always ring true. What about the instance in which the customers want a refund because their seats were further away from the action than anticipated? How about the customer who arrives late and wants a refund on his ticket because he missed the beginning of the game? What should be done about a ticket holder that wants money back because she arrived for a game intoxicated, used profanity, disrupted others, and had to be asked to leave? In each of the preceding scenarios, there is a risk of angering the ticket holder and possibly losing business.

Loss of business means loss of revenue. As is the case with any business, the cost to the organization of attracting new business is about five times greater than the cost of retaining current customers. In other words, it is much more cost efficient to keep the current customer base than it is to continually have to go into the market in search of new ticket buyers. What does this have to do with the three scenarios previously mentioned? The answer is that while these customers were not "right," they are still an important part of the business equation, as they are still adding to the bottom line for that particular event. Quite simply, they are still customers.

Front of house personnel, such as ticketing staff, play an important role in setting customers' first impressions.

For many events, the primary contact spectators have with the organization is the ticket office, ticket takers, parking attendants, ushers, concession, and merchandise staff. These groups with face-to-face contact with the public are known as the **front of house** staff. This is in contrast to **back of house** employees such as the public address announcer, the scoreboard operator, operations personnel, truck dock employees, and even the event managers in some circumstances. Supervisors, such as the ticket manager, must ensure the front of the house staff understand and appreciate their valuable role in conveying the desired image for the entire organization. In most cases, game day workers are part-time employees or volunteers who should not be expected to know this on their own. So, it is the responsibility of the event managers to provide these members of the team with all of the necessary tools and information to be helpful and knowledgeable when approached by patrons.

Although each event and facility is different, it is likely that paying customers will be one of the most important revenue streams for the event. There may also be sponsors, television contracts, boosters, and advertisers that all contribute to the bottom line of the event. In many cases, however, the people purchasing tickets are the most important and largest stream of revenue that the event can realize. For that reason, the ticket buyers must be considered when making decisions about the ticketing process. For the purpose of this book chapter, a new motto will be adopted. Rather than saying the customer is always right, decisions and conversation will be based on a different phrase: "The customer is not always right, but the customer is always the customer."

The Facility

The size and configuration of the facility will dictate much of the decision-making about ticketing. Basic facility information will be obtained in the feasibility portion of event conceptualization. This will include how many seats there are, the availability of accessible seating, and premium seating options. Early in the process, event managers will also work with the venue on specific set-up information for the event. As event development progresses, the venue information needed to make ticketing decisions becomes more specific, such as knowing about any obstructed-view seats. For venues that are constructed specifically for the event, there is usually more flexibility in creating the appropriate seating. However, there is also more work involved, since the venue is being created from scratch.

It is particularly important that those who may respond to media inquiries or that have direct interactions with participants be knowledgeable about the facility regarding seating and beyond. Having the entire sport organization or event management team on the same page (e.g., giving consistent answers to questions about seating), will help to ensure the same message is conveyed by all. Plus, administrators, coaches, promoters, and members of the press will for this, and a host of other information, expect answers quickly. Moving forward in the ticketing process, educated decisions can be made related to pricing, point-of-sale locations, date of on-sale, and use of technology based on the venue constraints.

Seating Configurations

Event managers who work within a traditional sport venue may have the opportunity to work with and for a number of different entities, acts, promoters, agents, teams, and sports. For example, college campuses may host numerous athletic events as well as indoor concerts at the basketball arena, outdoor concerts at the football stadium, and cross-country meets on the golf course. In addition, on-campus venues may host various post-season competitions and tournaments at both the conference and national level. For each and every one of these events, the seating configuration might be different. There could be a concert, basketball game, hockey game, and graduation all within the same week. Event managers working in this type of facility must know the different possible configurations, and how each will change the opportunity to sell tickets. Once the configuration is established, then it must be decided whether seats will be reserved only, general admission only, or a combination. In some venues, the option of having some general admission, standing-room-only tickets might be available.

Venues have different seating configurations for different types of events, such as sports competitions, concerts, speakers, political rallies, etc.

Reserved Seating

Reserved seating is very common in sports. The ticket holder is assigned, or chooses, a specific seat in the venue for the event. There is little confusion for ticket holders in reserved seating scenarios, as the seat is essentially "theirs" for the event. Often there is also a prestige associated with getting "good seats" in the venue that can be leveraged into charging higher prices for the reserved seats that are considered "the best" and in greatest demand.

Reserved seating models will require an usher at each entry point to a reserved section. Therefore, for many events, there simply may not be enough available staff for a reserved seating arrangement, or it may cost more to staff the event than can be realized in financial gain. A local youth basketball game would not use reserved seating because it just would not make sense. However, if the Harlem Globetrotters were performing in a 2,000-seat local area, reserved seating would be an important component to the ticketing strategy. The demand for the Globetrotters will probably exceed capacity with effective marketing techniques, so the market for reserved seats would be strong. Unless the layout of the venue makes it impossible, any event with high demand should have some reserved seats as part of the seating arrangement.

General Admission

Along with configurations, there may be events that are better suited to an arrangement that calls for all seats to be **general admission**. This means that seating is open and patrons with a ticket are able to sit in any unoccupied seat, but they are guaranteed a seat. There are a few inherent problems with general admission seating that should be kept in mind. This type of seating is, for all intents and purposes, first come, first served. The first people in the door and to the seats get their preferred seats. These could be closest to the stage, the field, or center court. In any of these cases, it is likely that a number of people want to be first to the seats, and therefore, there could be some pushing, shoving, running, and possibly even some violence. Plus, when people are not bound to one specific seat, they tend to spread out and leave unused seats in the venue. If a group of three attends an event with general admission seating, they will probably leave one seat between them and the next group or couple which will then go unused, since very few people attend events by themselves.

General admission seating also does not give consideration to the loyal fan, large donor, or season ticket holder. Part of the reason people purchase season tickets or contribute significantly to sport organizations is to choose the seats they want. For season ticket holders, it means they can sit in the same seat for every contest and not have to worry about getting to the venue hours in advance of the start of the contest to claim their seat. General admission seating eliminates that option. It may mean that some of the best supporters and biggest donors are relegated to the seats in which nobody else is willing to sit.

Staffing for general admission is less than for reserved seating, because there is less concern with access control. Since spectators are able to choose their seat, there is no need for ushers in each section.

General admission seating works well for low-demand events where there is little risk of spectators becoming aggressive while trying to obtain seats. A recurring event such as women's volleyball at an NCAA Division II institution may draw a few hundred people in a venue that could seat a few thousand. In that scenario, general admission seating should be adequate, as even loyal supporters will have access to quality seats since the demand is generally not high.

Festival Seating

Festival seating refers to a ticketing process where no seats are assigned and people stand to experience the event in a large open area. Festival seating is common for concerts where there is a wide-open area close to the stage in which people are admitted. Ticket holders generally rush toward the stage to get the best possible view of the act, which can result in pushing and shoving in the crowd. An example of an event where festival seating might be used is at an outdoor concert prior to a championship basketball game. Often, these concerts are held in a downtown area that has been fenced or roped off for the concert and that does not have any seating.

It might seem like festival seating would not require very many staff, but often the opposite is true. There is risk associated with a large group trying to move forward toward the stage, and a lot of security is needed to ensure people act in an orderly fashion.

Standing Room Only

The final type of seating arrangement is **standing room only (SRO)**, and is defined as a ticket to enter the venue with access to specific areas where there are not seats, but where the event can still be viewed. Although not a new phenomenon in sport, few venues have adequate areas for standing-room tickets, and there can be problems with the fire marshal if standing-room tickets impede the ingress or egress of other patrons. Generally, if standing-room-only tickets are sold, it is in addition to other types of tickets. Different from festival seating, standing-room-only tickets could be anywhere in the venue where patrons can gather without seats to view the event. In a few venues, there might be areas designed for this purpose, such as picnic areas, patio areas, or balconies.

Combination Seating Arrangements

It is possible to have a combination of general admission and reserved seating. Based on the configuration of the facility, a portion of the seats can be reserved while others are general admission. This is commonly done, for example, by making end zones general admission and sideline seats reserved, or by making the upper level general admission while the lower level is reserved.

Finally, it is worth mentioning here that there is also a financial consideration when looking at seating arrangements. Reserved seats will command a higher selling price than general admission. Many fans are willing to pay for the privilege to sit in a desirable seat and know it will be available when they arrive at the venue. However, other fans do not mind the crowds in a general admission area. They would rather spend less money, arrive early to get a seat, and take their chances on where that seat might be.

Accessible Seating

Another essential consideration is ensuring accessible seating, which is reserved seating for individuals with physical differences and appropriate accommodations are provided. For instance, according to the Americans with Disabilities Act (ADA), athletic events and venues, in general, are required to provide at least 1% of seating for wheelchair seating locations. Similarly, the wheelchair seating locations must include an adjacent companion seat (which is traditional/conventional seating in nature). In addition to the 1% of seating for wheelchair seating locations, another 1% of all fixed seats are required to have

© Shutterstock

In the United States, the Americans with Disabilities Act (ADA) mandates venues meet certain seating requirements for guests with disabilities.

removable armrests to accommodate individuals with a physical difference who prefer to use a fixed seat rather than a wheelchair seating location.

Furthermore, routes to the public areas, including the ticketed location, must be accessible, which includes ramps and curb cuts. Another legal requirement according to ADA is that accessible seating must be dispersed throughout the athletic venues, including being offered on all levels, so individuals with a physical difference have a variety of choices for admission prices and sight lines comparable to conventional ticket options. For additional information regarding ADA requirements pertaining to ticketing for athletic venues, please contact the Department of Justice ADA Information Line at 1-800-514-0301 or visit http://www.ada.gov/.

The Ticket Manifest

A **ticket manifest** is needed for all ticketed events, and identifies how many seats are in each row and section of the venue. Generally, the manifest is "built" within a ticketing software program (e.g., Ticketmast, StubHub, Paciolan, NeuLion, IMG Tickets) and is used to set prices, print tickets, and keep track of how many and which tickets are sold. However, the information entered must be accurate. It is a major problem if the ticket manifest is not the same as the actual venue, because nonexistent seats could be sold or the event could miss out on potential revenue.

For some events, this is simple, because the venue does not change much from one event to another. In other cases, the venue will be new to the event managers, or it will be altered for the event. For example, a college wrestling meet may use only one or two mats and might not need all of the existing floor space available. In this case, it might behoove all involved to add floor seating to the setup. This will increase capacity, allowing for more tickets to be sold and move the spectators closer to the action. This alteration in the normal seating configuration requires that the event managers, if not serving as the ticketing director, work closely with those in tickets to ensure that they are aware of the available seats.

The Seats

For all events, the seats must be checked prior to the event. In traditional sports venues or for recurring events, this might occur at regular intervals prior to, and during, the season instead of before each event. When checking seats, the event managers are ensuring all seats are in good repair, are numbered, and do not have an obstructed view. This involves having someone sit in every seat, and although not glamorous, it is an important task. If there are seats that are damaged or missing, these should be replaced or repaired as quickly as possible. The labeling of seats is also important, as keeping up on maintenance contributes to a positive event environment. Imagine a situation in which the season opener rolls around and a major sponsor of the event arrives to find his or her seat broken. The time to remedy the problem is not at half time of the game; it is before the customer knows the problem exists.

Recognizing if there are seats with obstructed views is often part of this process. In many venues, the ticketing staff is well aware of seats in which a pillar, wall, or other obstruction is between the spectator and the competition area. There will also be times when media presence creates obstructed views for some spectators, as TV cameras are often set up in front of existing seats. For non-traditional venues or unique setups, obstruction might not be as obvious. Obstructed view seats can be **killed**, which simply means the seat is removed from the ticket inventory for the event. The other option is to sell obstructed-view seats at a discount. In this case, it must be made clear to customers that there is an obstruction prior to their buying the seat.

Lessons Learned in Ticketing

Robb Wade, Director, Professional Golf Management Program,
North Carolina State University

After spending 11 years as a ticket manager, I have a list of lessons I learned the hard way. In 1987, and then again from 1993 to 2003, I was involved in ticketing for a professional hockey team, as well as at two different universities. At one of these universities, major events were a regular occurrence. There were some situations we could have handled better. As a result, I learned a great deal about ticketing and event management, and want to share a few short examples about my experiences. As you read these, consider how closely the operations of the event mesh with ticketing.

Seating Configurations

On campus, we had an old basketball facility that rarely got used since the team had moved into a new facility. In an effort to continue to use the venue, we contracted with an artist to perform in the building. The facility could accommodate 13,000 people for a basketball game. When a stage was added at one end blocking seats, the seating capacity shrank considerably.

The feeling from our standpoint was that it made the most sense to make all seats reserved. What we did not realize was that this particular group was famous for having a mosh pit directly in front of the stage. Unfortunately, nobody on our staff was familiar with the group, we did not do our own research, and the promoter did not tell us about it. So, on the day of the concert, we set the facility with all reserved seats in all locations.

As the concert was about to begin, the band realized what was happening and expressed to us that it could potentially be a very bad situation if the seats were not rearranged allowing for a mosh pit. One hour before the doors were supposed to open and in a panic, we were removing chairs from the floor to create the mosh pit. As it turned out, the event was a success and the fans never even knew there was a problem before the concert. However, by doing our own research and asking the right questions of the promoter, we would not have had to change plans and scramble at the last minute.

Projecting the Right Image: Parking

For football game days, we were fortunate to have an excellent parking situation around the football stadium. With about 5,500 assigned parking spaces for donors, it was critical that each person parked in the correct spot. In fact, an error in parking in the wrong spot resulted in their car being towed. As you can image, we had to hire a lot of people to staff parking entrances and help direct people to their assigned parking spaces. It would not seem like parking would fall under the ticket office's purview, but it did. In my case, the ticket office was heavily involved in parking because passes had to be issued for each of those 5,500 spots, similarly to the ticketing process.

For the fans who came to every game, they knew and understood the process because they were used to it. But for visitors who were unfamiliar with a game day on campus, it could be a nightmare. Imagine their frustration when they arrived at the stadium and asked the parking attendant for directions, and the attendant had none to give. Imagine my frustration when the attendant who did not have the information was also wearing a hat or t-shirt supporting our biggest rival or the team that we were scheduled to play on that particular day. The experience for those interacting with our parking attendants was negative and needed to be fixed.

As much as I would have loved to rely on the parking attendants to remember our verbal instructions, it just did not seem to be working. So, the resolution was fairly straightforward. We decided to post signs at each aisle of parking spaces. Each parking lot attendant was given a map that showed the numbers of each spot that were located in each row. Each parking attendant was given a hat and golf shirt from our institution and was expected to wear it each and every time they came to work. There was a cost involved in outfitting all of these people and printing off all of the material, but in the end it was better to present the right image to all of our customers and start their event experiences off in a positive way.

▶

Two Concerts, Two Different Strategies

We had a rare chance to host two major outdoor concerts in our football stadium within a short period of time. The two shows were very different. The first was a country concert that featured George Strait and seven additional acts. The other concert was Jimmy Buffett. That particular summer, ours was the only outdoor stadium concert that Jimmy Buffett was going to perform. From an event management standpoint, these two shows could not have been more different.

All indications were that the country show would be a very successful concert and that tickets were very likely to sell out. The decision was made to outsource ticket sales so that they could be purchased around the country immediately as they went on sale. This was just as online ticketing was becoming popular, but many people still were buying tickets through ticketing outlets instead of online. As most of us know, a service charge generally applies when a ticket agency is used, and can vary from minimal to substantial. Therefore, a group of people wanting to purchase tickets for the show could be faced with "service" or "convenience" charges of $10 per ticket. However, those who purchase tickets at the venue do not pay the service fee.

The country show was a daylong event. That particular day was extremely hot and humid. The promoters and the facility staff had to work together to acquire and setup mist tents to keep people cool. The concession stands sold every bottle of water they had midway through the afternoon. In addition, alcohol was also being sold at a somewhat alarming rate. The combination of all of these factors led to a number of tense situations. Problems included everything from patrons wanting the tower of speakers on the field to be angled differently to complaints about long restroom lines.

The Buffett show could not have been more different. This particular show was an evening show. Since we have a relatively good parking situation at our stadium, it meant that the Parrotheads, or loyal Buffet followers, spent much or most of the day on campus preparing for the show. As the show opened up, so did the skies. It was as close to a torrential rainstorm as there could be. It rained from the start of the show to the end. We did not experience a single problem that night. In fact, most people stood up in the rain and sang along to every song.

These two shows were both revenue sources for the department. Both concerts sold out and had very large crowds in attendance. Both, however, created a very different set of circumstances for the staff members involved in working the two concerts.

Football Bowl Game Ticketing

Our ticket office had a situation in which our football team was going to a bowl game, which was very exciting but also created a lot of work in the ticket office. As a result of the short turnaround time between receiving the bowl invitation and the actual game, we decided not to mail any tickets, and instead had tickets available for pick up at the game. There was one particular customer that ordered tickets and picked them up. A few weeks after the bowl game, we received a notification that he was disputing the charges, saying that he did not receive the tickets. We were able to produce the envelope that the customer had signed when he picked up the tickets as confirmation of receipt.

On a side note, we did not play very well in that particular bowl game and ended up losing by quite a bit. There were a number of fans who were very disappointed with the performance and quite vocal about their feelings. It is possible that this particular patron was so upset by the game that he was trying to figure out a way to get out of having to pay for the tickets. In this case, we had a system in place that did not allow him to do that and allowed our ticket revenue to remain the same.

The Rival Game

In my first year in the ticket office, our team boasted one of the greatest players the conference has ever had. In fact, in this player's final year, we set attendance records at eight of the nine conference away games. As you can imagine, home games were also very popular.

I clearly remember the game that we played against our archrival. People were begging for tickets and going to any means to attempt to secure them. Our office sold every possible ticket that we could. One week before the game was played, we were completely sold out. There was not a single ticket to be found at any location in the building.

Three days before the game, the call came. The president of the university needed four more tickets for some members of the Board of Trustees. Needless to say, the president's office was not impressed with my explanation. I managed to save my job, but I learned a valuable lesson about games being sold out. There was never a game from that point on that I did not have a small stash of tickets hidden away somewhere for emergency situations. For an event that is very popular, any tickets that I held thereafter would be sold as the event approached.

The Tickets

There are a number of considerations related to the actual tickets, and many of them evolve along with technology. Decisions about the type of ticket needed, ticket design, ticket printing, and security are all part of the ticketing process.

Types of Tickets

The type of ticket refers to whether the tickets will be punched, collected, stubbed, scanned, or whether some other method will be used to denote that the ticket holder has entered the facility. Event managers need to decide if it is important to know how many and which tickets were used prior to deciding on the ticket format. For some types of tickets, information can be gathered about which tickets were used, while other formats do not even allow for an accurate count of spectators. Another consideration is whether any part of the ticket will be used for sponsor advertising. A coupon for a local fast food restaurant printed on the ticket is a great idea, but not if tickets are collected as spectators enter the facility.

Punching Tickets

Punching tickets is the simplest way to indicate whether a ticket was used. It is simply using a hole punch or ink stamp to indicate the ticket has been used. However, it does not allow the organization any record of which tickets were used for the event.

Collecting Tickets

Collecting the tickets will allow for reconciliation of how many tickets were used, but cannot be used for reserved seating events. If the ticket is collected, the spectators are not left with anything denoting their seat as they walk into the venue.

Stubbing Tickets

Stubbing refers to creating a perforated section on the ticket when printed that is torn upon entry to the facility. If the tickets are going to be stubbed, then the seat location must be printed on both the torn and retained portion of the ticket. This will allow for the spectators to have the information needed on their part of the ticket, and the organization to be able to reconcile exactly which tickets were used for that event.

Scanning Tickets

To scan tickets, the event or facility must have the equipment to do so. This includes the scanners for the gate workers, and the technology infrastructure that allows the information gathered by the scanners to be communicated back to the ticket office. The scanners are efficient because they allow the ticket office to keep track of which tickets were used. Scanning also eliminates the hand counting of thousands of ticket stubs. Once a ticket is scanned, it is invalidated. If a fan tries to pass the ticket through the fence to a friend, the friend will not be able to enter because the scanner will recognize the ticket as already being used.

For scanned tickets, barcodes, RFID (Radio Frequency Identification) embedded chips, or magnetic strips are used, with barcodes being more popular at this time. Often, for season tickets, the ticket looks similar to a credit card. The spectator then does not have to worry about keeping track of multiple paper tickets for the entire season. Paper tickets can be scanned using a barcode as well, and one big advantage to using this method is that ticket purchasers can buy their tickets online and print them at home. They can also email tickets to someone else, who can then print the ticket and attend the event. This method eliminates people needing to meet in person to transfer tickets, or using will call to leave tickets for someone. It is extremely convenient.

Even more advanced is the ability to scan tickets directly from a cell phone or PDA. In this case, the spectators are able to use their ticket account online or open an email with their ticket attached on their cell phone or PDA. The ticket can be scanned directly from there, and no paper ticket is ever printed. Whether paper, plastic, or electronic, the scanning of tickets is becoming very popular.

Ticket Design

Ticket design can be simple and inexpensive or detailed and expensive. There are a number of considerations when the time for designing the tickets arrives, such as how much information to include, whether or not to sell advertising on the tickets, and what the graphic should look like. In general, the front of the ticket should at least provide information on the opponent or name of the event, date, time, place, and price. It is also helpful to include entry gate information for venues with multiple entrances. Legal disclaimers and the ticket refund policy are often printed on the back of the ticket, along with any coupons or advertisements from sponsors.

A major part of ticket design is image. Every time customers receive a piece of correspondence, walk into the facility, interact with staff or look at their tickets, they are forming an opinion about the organization. The ticket design is an opportunity to make a positive impression on the customer. There is also a difference when printing single-event versus season tickets. Season ticket designs can include pictures of players, coaches, facilities, or mascots. Single-event tickets are typically less expensive and feature a less complicated design. They are designed more for functionality than flair.

If the ticket is for a one-time only or special event, there is a good possibility that the customer will want to save the ticket as a memento of the event. Given this, it is important to design a ticket, which the person can be proud and display. Events that fall into this category would include a Super Bowl, the Master's, many concerts, the opening or closing of a particular facility, or a night in which a particular athlete or coach is being recognized. There are many other examples—the important factor is that it is going to be a memorable night that will never be repeated, and the ticket should reflect that.

It is critical that the information on the tickets is accurate. Once ticket proofs have been created, have at least three other people look at every bit of information provided on the tickets to ensure accuracy. In some cases, information will be left vague or incomplete on purpose. For example, if there is a chance that game times could change or be altered for any reason (primarily television), then it makes sense to leave the time as "TBA" and announce it when it has been finalized. It is easier to leave information off the ticket and inform customers at a separate time than it is to tell customers a wrong time and then try to reach each and every one of them to inform them of a change.

If communication about a time change is needed, information must go out to every ticket purchaser, all media outlets, and be posted on the website. Despite all of these efforts, it is likely that some people will not get the message and will show up at the wrong time. Needless to say, this leads to hard feelings, disappointment, and, in some cases, loss of revenue if the situation is not handled properly.

Trends

Technology trends move at an incredibly fast pace, and forward-thinking organizations often take advantage of various trends to expand services and experiences for fans. One such technology trend is **augmented reality (AR)**, which is when technology is used to superimpose computer-generated images, sound, video, and/or GPS data onto a real-world view, such as something being viewed through a camera phone. For the 2012 season, the Philadelphia Eagles used AR with their season tickets. When ticket holders hovered their phones over the ticket, they could see highlights, player messages, stats,

Augmented reality is a current ticketing trend among sports teams.

© Shutterstock

and other information (Laird, 2012b). Earlier that year, after their win in Super Bowl XLVI, the New York Giants used AR that enabled fans to take pictures with the Lombardi Trophy and wearing the championship ring from any of the Giants' four Super Bowl wins (Laird, 2012a). Teams and events will get more creative as this technology becomes more commonplace. The Royal Challengers Bangalore of the Premier Cricket League in India used an AR browser with its tickets in 2013 to provide traffic updates, taxi information, parking information, team store access, a 3D view of the stadium, and other features (Laird, 2013). Other AR technologies—such as Google Glass—are going to have an impact on how spectators view and interact with events. Good event managers should keep abreast of new technology and think about how it can impact various areas of their events.

Charity contributions in non-traditional ways have become commonplace in the last several years, and some have even gone viral. TOMS shoes allows buyers to contribute to charity through its "buy one give one" philosophy of selling shoes while the ALS Ice Bucket Challenge in summer 2014 was a huge success that raised over $100 million for the ALS Association. In events, some races are offering runners the opportunity to forego their race T-shirt and have the race donate it to a homeless shelter instead. With tickets, the trend is to offer an option for online buyers to contribute to certain charities during the same transaction as buying tickets.

Ticket Printing

Depending on the type of event and availability of resources, ticket printing is either done prior to the event as hard ticketing, as customers purchase tickets, by the customers themselves, or a combination of these. For small and midsize events, hard printing or printing as tickets are purchased is most likely. The combination approach is common for larger events, as it is able to meet the needs of the most people.

Hard Ticketing

There may be certain events for which all tickets are printed in advance. This practice is known as **hard ticketing**. It has the advantage of giving the ticket seller complete control of the ticket inventory. The sellers can distribute the tickets in the manner and method that they determine, as they are the sole source of obtaining tickets. The disadvantage of hard tickets is keeping records of purchases, and that customers can only get tickets from one entity. A lack of computerized records means that the seller must make other arrangements to keep sales records, assign seat locations, and distribute sales receipts.

Printing As Purchased

For those venues with access to ticket software or that outsource their ticketing to a company such as Ticketmaster, printing can be done in house. In this case, a customer can order a ticket in person, on the phone, or online. The ticket manager can then print the ticket immediately. The software automatically recognizes the specific ticket has been sold and adjusts the available inventory accordingly. This allows for multiple places to be selling tickets at the same time, as the system is networked together to ensure that no duplicates are sold. The computerized records are much more convenient for the ticket manager than hard ticketing, and the ticket office will have the ability to generate a variety of reports related to when, where, and how tickets were sold.

Print Tickets at Home

Having customers print their own tickets at home is certainly the cheapest method for the organization once the technology infrastructure is set up. However, there are still many people that do not want to do this. Some customers want to talk to someone in ticketing as they choose their seat, and others like having a well-designed paper ticket to keep as a reminder of their experience as opposed to something from their home printer.

Besides cost savings in printing and box office staff time, printing at home allows more flexibility for customers. As discussed previously, the customer can electronically send tickets to someone else if they are not going to use the tickets, and might not even have to print tickets at all, and instead simply use their cell phones to display the barcode for scanning at the event.

Combination Ticketing

To ensure the needs of all customers are met, a combination plan usually works best. If finances and time allow, it is preferred to give customers the option of printing their tickets at home or contacting the box office to purchase their tickets.

While sports professionals may prefer electronic ticketing to other methods, there may not be a choice. For example, when a college athletic team gains a berth into a post-season contest (basketball tournament, football bowl game, etc.), the school often receives hard tickets from the venue. It is still possible to keep computer sales records. One possible solution is to build the facility (or part of it) into the computer and assign the seats as they are sold. It is almost like creating a partial ticket manifest for another facility. Another option is to put the sales through the computer and put a note in each customer's record as to the seat location. In conjunction with this, it may also be prudent to draw the sections, rows, and seats that are to be assigned and to write names of patrons on the chart as the seats are sold. The main reason to keep such records is to have backup information if there is a dispute over charges, or if customers happen to lose their tickets before the contest and have not written down their seat locations.

Cost

There is also a cost associated with the printing of tickets. In some places, this can be of little or no consequence, but in some smaller operations, this can be a major concern. The cost of printing tickets varies greatly depending on the design, type of ticket, the number of tickets being printed, and the company that does the printing.

For those that do not have an unlimited budget, a possible revenue source to cover the cost of the tickets is to obtain a ticket sponsor. In other words, it may be possible to approach a local or national company and offer them the chance to obtain thousands of contacts with potential customers. Often, the ticket backs (or space on the paper from home-printed tickets) may be sold as part of a larger package of advertising by the marketing staff of the organization. When customers print tickets at home, there is even more space for advertising and there is no cost to the organization in printing.

The most likely people to advertise on tickets are those businesses that can put an ad on the ticket that will generate business. Restaurants such as McDonald's or Pizza Hut are a natural fit because they can potentially generate business immediately after the event if they print a coupon on the ticket. Automotive supply stores and supermarkets also commonly use tickets as advertising.

The reason that companies enjoy this type of promotion is that they are able to track their return on investment (ROI). They can count up the number of tickets that get redeemed during the course of the season and, in that way, can get a direct measure of the effect of their sponsorship. Keep in mind that if the ticket manager is selling sponsorships, there needs to be frequent communication with anyone else selling sponsorships to ensure a coordinated effort.

Ticket Security

Another element that should be mentioned is there have and always will be a certain segment of the population that will try to gain access into events through some sort of illegal and/or immoral means. This may include anything from using counterfeit tickets, to lying about lost or stolen tickets, to giving false information about being left tickets by someone, to simply trying to make up a story to convince a person of authority to allow them to enter the event. While it is very difficult to eliminate this problem, steps can be taken to reduce these occurrences. Computer ticketing systems are very important in these efforts. The ability to search for customers, seating locations, credit card numbers, and mailing addresses can decrease the issues.

It can be important to have a system to identify reprinted tickets. There are occasions when customers lose or forget tickets. They will usually contact the ticket office and ask for reprints. Some entities charge the customer a fee to reprint the tickets in an attempt to encourage responsible handling of the tickets. When tickets are reprinted, they should be marked in some way. If the original set of tickets was lost and/or stolen and two sets of people show up at the seats with the same tickets, it may be difficult to ascertain who, in fact, is entitled to the seats. Reprints can be marked with a stamp, initials, a hole punch, or any other kind of defining mark. The idea is that the usher in that section must be able to make a quick determination of the rightful owners of the seats.

There are many new security features that can be used in the formatting of tickets to prevent counterfeit tickets from being reproduced and sold. The Southeastern Conference (SEC) printed holograms on tickets to help ticket takers identify a ticket in question. The SEC also offer mobile stations on-site outside of venues as a service for fans to confirm the validity of tickets offered on the secondary ticket market prior to purchasing. These efforts are meant to reduce counterfeit tickets as well as boost security and fan satisfaction. At the 2006 FIFA World Cup, organizers used high-tech methods to ensure tickets could not be reproduced or transferred. Each ticket was embedded with a chip that was able to link to a computer database containing the spectators' names, addresses, nationalities, and even their passport numbers. Only the purchasers of the tickets were allowed to use the tickets, which caused some controversy since there was no way to transfer tickets to a friend or family member. However, this system served a secondary purpose, in that if there was trouble from anyone in the stands, they could be easily identified and found.

Pricing

The price of the tickets is typically not decided by the ticket office or by event managers alone. However, savvy event managers will realize that input from ticketing specialists is important when choosing the price points. Bear in mind that the organization wants to maximize profits and fill every seat. The promoter, coach, or sport organization wants people in every seat. In order to sell the maximum number of tickets, it is imperative to find the price point that is attractive to the most people and will motivate them to buy tickets.

Certain events will sell most, if not all, of the tickets at just about any price. Games against an archrival, play-offs, championships, and popular musical artists and entertainers will have fans eager to obtain tickets. However, the majority of events will not sell out. Look at a simple example of selling tickets for an event.

Imagine a concert in a building being put on by a group that was popular 20 years ago and has had a resurgence in popularity in recent years. For the sake of argument, say the promoter and the facility have allowed the event managers to determine the ticket price. The venue has 10,000 seats and all tickets will be the same price. There is a core group of fans that will show up regardless. If 5,000 tickets are sold at $40, there will be a guaranteed income of $200,000. Alternatively, the event managers may decide to sell tickets for only $20. At that price, all 10,000 seats would have to be sold to make up the same gross dollar amount that would have been realized at the higher ticket price.

Logic and a bit of conservative budgeting dictate that it is not likely that all 10,000 tickets will be sold, but that there may be some people who would like to go but are not willing to pay $40 for the show. Therefore, the decision that might be made in this case would be to find a price range closer to the middle ($30), and hope to sell 8,000 tickets. This would mean a gross revenue of $240,000. In this example, the correct price, combined with the appropriate marketing strategy, led to an increase in revenue of 20%.

If the tickets do not have to all be the same price, the options for pricing are endless. Two or more different prices could be charged, depending on where the seats are located in the venue. Maybe $40 for lower-level seats and $30 for upper-level seats is appropriate. If there were 4,000 lower-level seats and 6,000 upper-level seats, gross revenue would jump to $340,000. This is a greatly simplified example, but it does illustrate the point that price is important. The prices cannot be dictated by what people think events are worth, so much as they are governed by what people are willing to pay. Ticket departments can also offer bundles, which include multiple tickets and concessions, which may be appealing to families.

More advanced ticket pricing strategies are also creeping into the sport industry from other industries, such as the airline industry. One example is the concept of dynamic ticket pricing. Essentially, dynamic ticket pricing is when the price of tickets fluctuates according to real-time market demand using algorithms based on supply and demand. Let's consider Major League Baseball games. Ticket prices could fluctuate depending on the day of the week, time of day, weather, and/or opponent. For example, if there is inclement weather then the prices can be adjusted to a more affordable price to maximize the number of tickets sold. If the opponent is the best team in the league or has a superstar then prices can be inflated because there is more demand and fans are willing to pay more to attend the game. Another similar example is the option to upgrade to another seat at the point of purchase or even during the competition! One such company is PogoSeat, which interfaces with ticketing software and allows fans to purchase seat upgrades. Organizations can optimize unsold inventory, particularly premium seats, like upgrading to first-class seats on a flight.

On-Sale Date

The **on-sale date** for tickets is simply the date the tickets are available for purchase, and is determined by a couple of factors. The first is whether it is a one-time event, or part of a season package. In the case of many ticketed athletic events, each event is part of a season, which means several events in the same venue. The consideration here is to maximize profits by selling the most possible tickets. The best way to do this is to use individual events to drive sales for all events.

Take, for example, a college football season. Depending on the year, the season probably consists of eleven games. In this example, that breaks out into six home games and the rest of the games on the road. Among the six games are two that are likely to sell out easily. There are three others that are against reasonably well-known opponents, and one game that will be difficult to sell out. With those thoughts in mind, how would a decision be reached as to when to put single game tickets on sale?

An excellent approach is to obtain a calendar and mark down dates when everything should happen. The calendar should include all pertinent dates, including when renewal forms will be mailed, when the forms are due back in the office, when tickets will be mailed, and when tickets will go on sale. The dates should be based on the date of the first home contest and be built backward. The premise here is that the popular games drive the sales of all the games. The marketing strategy is to inform fans that the only way to see the one or two marquee games is to buy a full-season ticket package.

In terms of the timeline, the only thing to sell for the first period of time is full-season packages. If tickets are not sold out at the deadline, the next thing to do is to put together a mini-plan or partial package. In the example, this package would be built to include the most popular game, the least popular game, and one of the other three games. The second package would include another popular game and the other two games that will be decent sellers. When putting together these packages, the most important factor is to look at the popularity of the opponent. A secondary factor is to look at the dates of the contests. Avoid selecting and packaging the games that are too close together on the calendar. The ideal schedule would allow each package to have one game at the beginning part of the season, one in the middle, and one toward the end. This way, when people are looking at a calendar and making plans, they can plan to come to the venue and attend the events.

Unless it is a mega event, athletic events are typically most attractive to supporters that are within a 100-mile radius. Ticket sales can generally be handled by the office that handles that responsibility for the team or venue. There are some occasions and events that have more of a nationwide following. Examples could include championship games, professional tennis tournaments, and concerts. There may be a chance to host a concert in a facility that features a nationally known act. In this case, consider using a nationally known ticketing company to assist in ticket sales.

Outsourcing Tickets

Ticketmaster is one of the most well-known companies used by organizations to outsource ticketing. Keep in mind that there are some costs involved with using such a company. In addition to the service fee, there is also an option to have tickets mailed to the customer. This can be done through any of the normal shipping/mailing options that are available. This service also dictates an additional fee. The fee can be as small as $1 if the tickets are to be sent through the regular mail, or as much as $20 if the customer would prefer to have the tickets delivered the next day. Communication is very important here. The last thing that the customer wants is to purchase four tickets for $40 each, and then look at a credit card statement and see a charge for more than $200. It is important to disclose any and all charges that will appear on the credit card and make sure that the customer agrees to the specified charges.

A customer who claims charges were not authorized can cause a substantial problem for the ticket operation. A customer that does not agree with charges may contact the credit card company and inform them that the charges are being disputed. The credit card company will then contact the vendor, in this case the ticket office, to inform them of the dispute. The company that charged the card then has a certain period of time to prove that the charges were justified or can be explained, and that the service or good (i.e., the tickets) were in fact delivered or picked up and used. The problem then becomes proving that the customer knew what they were being charged and that they actually used the tickets. It is imperative to have an effective system in place for both taking orders, tracking mailed tickets, and/or checking identifications for tickets being picked up at the venue, as well as having the customer sign for tickets that are picked up.

Even when customers are interacting with a third party such as Ticketmaster, they still associate their interaction with the third party as an extension of the team, venue, and event. Therefore, the ticket manager and event managers must be confident that the outsourcer will represent the organization well and provide excellent customer service prior to any agreement.

A relatively new phenomenon is for sport organizations to outsource their ticket sales operations. While the sport organization makes all decisions regarding the amount, price, and type of tickets sold for an event, the third party is hired to sell the tickets. For example, IMG Learfield Ticket Solutions partners with intercollegiate athletic departments and earns commission for the revenue they generate through creative ticket-selling strategies. In this example, athletic departments choose to hire a third party extension of their ticket operations because of the return on investment of hiring trained, professional staff whose primary skill set revolves around sales.

Premium Tickets

Premium seating encompasses a variety of seats. Luxury suites, party suites, club seats, loge boxes, field-level seats in baseball, courtside seats in basketball, and any other special section of tickets with enhanced amenities fall into the category of premium seating. For the purposes of this text, the various types of premium seating will be grouped together for discussion.

Premium tickets can be handled in a variety of ways. In many facilities, they are sold for every event in the building. The customer purchases the rights to the particular seats for a specified time length (e.g., 1 year, 3 years, 5 years, etc.)—these are known as a **personal seat license** (**PSL**). Once the rights to the seats have been purchased, the customer still must pay for the tickets to each event. There might even be a requirement that the customer must purchase seats for certain events. For instance, the patron may be required to buy tickets for all basketball and hockey games that take place in the building. In addition to those, the customer would also have first right of refusal for any and all other events in the building. Premium seat holders would be given a deadline, and if the tickets are not purchased by that point, the tickets are made available to other ticket buyers.

Some venues do not sell premium seats if their owners do not use them for events. This means that during concerts or other types of shows, these seats may go unused. It can be disconcerting and frustrating to both promoters and building managers to look around and see empty seats during major events, but that is the contractual agreement in place with the customers.

The customers that sit in these seats represent key revenue streams for the organization. Even though most professional sport leagues require some sharing of luxury suite revenues, it is still considered a key ingredient of an organization's financial prosperity. Spectators pay a substantial amount of money (often $100,000–$300,000 for a luxury suite per year) for the right to buy the tickets to the various events. In addition to the annual fee, the tickets that they do purchase are often much more expensive than the tickets that other customers purchase.

The event managers may or may not be involved in the servicing of premium seats. However, it can never hurt for those associated with the organization to take time to get to know patrons that are key accounts for the organization. Providing first-class service is critical in premium seating. Often, premium seats account for a substantial portion of overall ticket revenue.

Special Interest Groups

There is another group of people that must be kept in mind when deciding on seat locations. For lack of a better term, these will be called special interest groups. This group includes, but is not limited to: student booster groups, players' families and guests, prospective intercollegiate athletes, school or local officials, league officials, promoter's group, major donors, and facility staff. All of these groups will require tickets for seats. Some of them will be paid for, while others will be complimentary.

Depending on the group, they do not necessarily need to be in the best seats possible, but they should be in reasonably good locations. Furthermore, they must be located in seats to allow them to view the contest or event from a reasonable vantage point while not displacing customers and donors that may have paid substantial amounts for tickets.

In some cases, the locations of these tickets may be dictated by an outside agency. For example, a facility that hosts an NCAA Basketball Regional will have the locations of many groups outlined specifically in the tournament manual. Ticket locations for all of the participating teams, bands, NCAA officials, and contestants are among those that are outlined for the host facility. This is an important factor because all of these seats must be held when tickets go on sale. Once the tickets are sold and have been delivered, there is no way to get the tickets back or alter seat locations without having a public relations problem and, most likely, people demanding a refund of their money.

Parking

A source of revenue for event and facility managers that was overlooked for a number of years is the money that is generated through the sale of parking spaces during an event. Depending on the number of spaces available for use and their proximity to the facility, these can translate into substantial amounts of revenue for the event.

Parking Plans and Passes

There are a couple of approaches that can be taken with regard to parking spaces. When dealing with a particular sport season, it may be advisable to issue parking passes for all contests to be played at the facility during the course of that season. These can be charged automatically, but more likely the customer who purchases the season tickets will be given the option to purchase a season parking pass.

The parking pass that is sold can be for any available lot, for a general area, or for a specific spot. Football is traditionally a sport that is associated with tailgating before and, sometimes, after the games. There are some football fans who like to enjoy their pregame festivities with the same people each and every game. For that reason, it may be advisable to number every available parking spot and to assign each customer to a specific spot. While there may be some added expense and labor in terms of numbering all of the spaces, there may also be an opportunity to charge a premium price for people to have the opportunity to be able to arrive at any time before or during the game and know that their spot will still be available.

In other cases, the parking situation can be handled much as the tickets for the event are handled. Those that want the "best" seats are willing to pay a premium price. Such is the case with parking. Those customers that want the best possible parking spaces may be willing to pay a little extra to park close to the facility. The parking areas could be broken down into categories such as platinum, gold, silver, and bronze. The per-game prices for these categories might be $30, $20, $10, and $7, respectively. When making a purchase, either prior to or on the day of the event, customers could be given the option of which area they prefer to purchase.

An additional option for parking is to charge a set amount for every vehicle that enters the parking lot. No spaces would be reserved and the cars that arrived earliest would be able to park in the spaces closest to the facility. While this idea may not seem as appealing as the previous two examples, it may have the potential to generate the same or greater net profit. The reason is that this type of general parking requires a minimal amount of staffing. The only staff required are the attendants who collect the money when the cars enter and a few to help direct traffic to the available spaces. In the first two cases, there are people needed to sell passes, to check passes at the different areas, and possibly tow trucks and vehicle movers to move cars out of spots that are not assigned to them.

There is one scenario that guarantees revenue from parking. Most stadiums and arenas have some number of reserved parking spaces for various groups. Average fans are left to fend for themselves in looking for a place to park. Some venues will build an additional fee into the ticket price and allow fans to park on a first come, first served basis. It is basically a general admission parking pass. This eliminates the need for parking attendants to take money on the night of the event. It also generates instant revenue on every ticket that is sold. While it is a reasonable idea in principle, there is one inherent problem. The problem is there may not be enough parking spaces for all the cars that may come to the game. However unlikely, what would happen if 10,000–12,000 fans all drove their cars to the game and there are only 8,000 parking spaces at the arena (which, by the way, is an unusually large number)? The headache of returning money to people would pale in comparison to the public relations nightmare that would face the venue. Also, regardless of who made the decision, the people that would hear all the complaints and listen to all of the cursing would be the ticket takers and people in the ticket office, since they would be the first people the angry customers would encounter upon entry into the facility. A side note regarding this system of parking: This system may allow for greater concession profits and merchandise. If patrons want to get the best parking spots, they are likely to arrive at the facility quite some time before the beginning of the contest. Logic dictates that the longer people are in the facility, the more likely they are to spend money on food, beverages, and souvenirs.

Considerations

There are a few additional considerations to be kept in mind when making parking decisions. From an event management perspective, one main objective is to get patrons into the parking lots, into the facility, and into their seats as seamlessly as possible. This means parking attendants must be able to perform transactions quickly. These transactions become substantially easier and more expedient if the price for parking does not require the attendant to make too much change. For example, a parking fee of $6 probably means that the majority of the customers will require some change. If the customer pays with a $20 bill, the attendant must count out the required number of bills. It may not seem like a large amount of time, but imagine a situation where 1,000 cars are entering a particular gate. If each transaction takes 15 seconds as opposed to 10 seconds, the customers at the end of the line are waiting a long time to give their money.

A problem that could arise based on the price of the parking pass is having enough change. In the previous example, with a $6 parking pass, any customer that does not have exact change is going to require at least four $1 bills and, possibly a $10 bill as well. Each attendant would have to have a significant number of $1 bills to be able to make all of the required change.

It is important that there be some sort of accounting system for the parking on the day of the event. While unfortunate, it is possible that there may be an occasional parking attendant that tries to take advantage of the system. The cars that pull in and pay for a parking pass should receive some sort of ticket or pass to be displayed in their vehicle. These tickets should be seen by the attendant helping to direct the traffic. A missing ticket could signal an issue with a person collecting money and not turning it in to the event managers.

The event managers must also keep traffic flow in mind. It is not enough to simply accept parking money and expect people to get in and out of the parking lots without some guidance. The people bringing in the revenue from the parking passes also have a responsibility to direct traffic in and out of the lots safely and efficiently.

Credentials

The event managers must make sure that everyone has access to the areas where they need to be. Equally, if not more importantly, the event managers must make sure that people are not in areas where they do not belong. Careful consideration should be given to which people will receive which credentials. There are clearly some people that need to have access to any and all areas within the facility, while there are others that only need limited access—despite what they might think or say.

The most critical areas for access include the playing surface or area where the contest is taking place, any areas where money is being handled, the locker rooms, the officials' area, and any areas where food and beverages are being prepared. Beyond that, there are areas where most people need not be, regardless of whether they are ticket holders or workers.

Credentials must be easily seen and easily differentiated. The most common practices for designing credentials are to make them different colors or to print a large number on the credential. In other words, a person with a green credential or with a hangtag with a large number "1" on it has access to all areas. Each different level of access would have a different

Well designed credentials help in the organization and security of events.

color and/or number associated with it. After the credentials have been designed and made, sample boards are constructed and placed strategically through the building. **Sample boards** have exact replicas of credentials, tickets, and parking passes on them, and provide an easy reference guide for staff. All staff should be charged with helping to keep people out of designated areas where they do not belong, and sample boards help with this.

Keep in mind that the more important or high profile the event, the more elaborate the scheme will be to try to gain access. There have been numerous examples of people trying to beat the system and gain entrance into sold-out games or restricted areas. These include such scams as dressing up as a member of the janitorial staff, concession staff, or a police officer, printing false league official credentials, or even dressing as a member of the team. Also, some people will arrive at certain areas without any credentials and attempt to talk their way into restricted areas. Some of these people will have legitimate excuses, while others will be completely fabricating a story. The bottom line is that the people entrusted with security of certain areas will have to use their judgment and make the best possible decision under the given circumstances.

Reconciliation

Each organization and each facility will have a different way to reconcile event receipts. The computerized ticketing systems allow for sales records to be generated on a daily basis. Further, depending on the system, it is possible to see which outlets are selling which tickets, how many, in which price category, and how quickly they are being purchased. Complimentary tickets should also be carefully accounted for as part of reconciliation. One thing that is an absolute is that receipts must be reconciled at the end of each business day. In the case of major venues with a professional team as a tenant, this could involve reconciling income from as many as 10 or 12 different upcoming events on any given day. Once the total receipts have been counted, they must be broken out and deposited in the appropriate accounts.

As a rule, this does not take long, but there are times when issues arise. Cash on hand may be inaccurate, or credit card charges might not match those reported in the daily activity journal. This can be a frustrating and difficult situation to work through, and makes it even more important that everyone who has a responsibility to ring in sales is diligent and accurate with all that they do. Extra care and caution during the sale will lead to more accurate reports and more satisfied customers and administrators.

Non-traditional Sport Venues

For events in non-traditional venues, event managers must examine where seats are needed, establish how many are needed, and decide if ticketing is appropriate. It can be very challenging to control access for spectators to a roadway, waterway, or park where an event is being held. Even golf courses have found that controlling access given the amount of space used is a challenge. However, renting seating is expensive, so the costs and benefits must be examined before ticketing decisions are made. Before any decisions are made, the event managers must know if there is a market for tickets, whether the physical layout of the venue would allow for access control, and if there are options other than selling tickets available to generate revenue.

Think about the sheer number of staff that it would take to control spectator access to any sort of cycling race. Plus, it is more likely than not that the price of admission would drive spectators completely away from an event such as this unless it was a major international event or Olympic qualifier. Many of these types of events have their goals and objectives based in being participant driven, and therefore selling tickets might move the organization further away from the purpose of the event.

There may be other ways to generate revenue that would be more cost effective and make more sense instead of ticketing the entire event. One option is to ticket the start and finish of a race, and another is to create exclusive areas along the course (e.g., Viewing Zones) where amenities such as food and drink are provided for those wanting to purchase a ticket to enter the area. The most common option is to not ticket the event, but to make sure concessions and/or merchandise are available for spectators throughout the course. When this is done, fans may be more willing to spend money on concessions if they have not had to pay for a ticket.

The Secondary Ticket Market

The **secondary ticket market** refers to the reselling of tickets after the first purchase. Reselling of tickets is an ongoing concern in the industry. While there are some sellers that offer a valuable and legitimate purpose, there are many who simply undermine the process and can adversely affect the event and the price paid for tickets. At some point in the recent past, the name of these entrepreneurs changed from "scalpers" to "ticket brokers." New ways have been devised to sell game tickets at a substantially higher price than face value.

For example, let us imagine that a fan had an ample supply of money and wanted to go to the Super Bowl. Further, for the sake of this example, suppose that the Super Bowl was being held in a state in which it is illegal to sell tickets for anything more than $2 above face value. A person wanting to sell two tickets that are worth $250 each could not legally charge more than $504. The seller would have to sell a lot of tickets to make a profit. What, then, would allow them to realize profits of thousands of dollars? The answer is quite simple. They would not sell tickets to the Super Bowl. They might sell a hat or a jersey with the logo of one of the participating teams proudly displayed. This souvenir might be priced at $5000. The added bonus is that along with the new piece of gear, the seller would toss in a couple of Super Bowl tickets! It can be a difficult proposition to dissuade people from reselling tickets.

© Shutterstock

With technology, the secondary ticket market now looks very different than just a ticket scalper standing outside a venue.

Nonetheless, many sport organizations and professional leagues have partnered with StubHub to benefit from the secondary ticket market. StubHub provides a marketplace for individuals to sell and buy tickets. StubHub earns a percentage commission when the ticket is sold and charges a fee to the buyer when purchasing the ticket. When sport organizations partner with StubHub, they agree to share a portion of the revenue earned from commissions and fees in exchange for being promoted as the exclusive secondary marketplace for fans.

A more recent occurrence is the use of websites such as Groupon (www.groupon.com) and Living Social (www.livingsocial.com) to sell tickets. Sports teams—especially those having trouble filling seats for various reasons—have used these to offer deep discounts, sometimes more than 50% off the usual price. Using these sites enables teams to, hopefully, fill seats a relatively short time before a game and possibly reach a buyer who may not have ever attended a game at the full ticket price.

Incremental Revenue and Breakage

Incremental revenue is revenue that is generated through "up selling." For example, a team might send a loyal fan a $5 coupon for the merchandise store, knowing that the cheapest item in the store is $20. The fan does not want to waste the $5 gift and ends up spending $40 at the next game on merchandise. The team generated $35 that they would not have without the $5 coupon.

This applies to ticketing in that many teams are using the bar coded season tickets on which to "load" these small gifts. The advantage of loading money on the ticket is that there is an electronic record for the team of when the money was spent, how much was spent, and on what. That information is then used in future marketing efforts.

This concept can go a step further where the price of the ticket is increased to account for some in-stadium spending money for the purchaser. In this case, a fan decides to attend an NFL game. The normal ticket price is $85, but the price that the consumer pays is $100 per ticket. Built into the ticket price is an extra $15 that acts like a credit. When the patron arrives at the facility, she can obtain $15 worth of concessions, souvenirs, or anything else that might be for sale.

The added price is not optional, and if the credit is not used that night, there is no refund and the customer may not "save" it and use it at a later game. The difference in the amount that the customer pays and the amount he spends is known as **breakage**. The team or venue receives this "free" money the customer did not spend. Both incremental revenue and breakage strategies are beginning to be commonplace in ticketing strategies.

The Unexpected

The more events that event managers have an opportunity to work with and around, the more unique situations they will experience. There will come a time when computers and ticket printers will stop functioning at the absolute worst possible time. It could be before the biggest game of the season, the start of the play-offs, the on-sale date for a major concert, or the doors opening for a WWE event. Some of these problems are impossible to anticipate while others can be expected. Some simple steps to prepare to handle a technology crash include:

1. Have a printed list of season ticket holder seat locations available.
2. Have an additional laptop computer available to connect to a network.

3. Have additional ticket stock and possibly a ticket printer and an extra set of tickets.

4. Print a set of tickets with no dates or event on the ticket. Take care to ensure that every seat is printed, and that if there are changes to the seating, the back-up tickets are adjusted accordingly. The tickets can be locked away in the back of a closet, and the hope is that they will never be used.

If there ever is an occasion to use anything mentioned above, everyone involved in administering the event will be glad that someone had the foresight to address the potential problem. Hoping for the best but planning for the worst will prepare the ticket manager and event managers for many of the foreseeable problems that could occur in ticketing.

SUMMARY

One of the goals of event managers should be to know as much as possible about what everyone else involved in the event contributes to the process. Especially in ticketing, event managers and the ticket manager must communicate and work hand-in-hand throughout the entire event management process. By working together, all decisions about ticketing will take into account other aspects of the event that the ticket manager may not be aware of.

A ticket manager who is able to provide exceptional customer service, make the ticketing process as easy as possible for customers, and provide options for customers will contribute significantly to the overall success of the event. Customers often interact primarily with the ticket office prior to arriving at the event site, so the ticket office sets the stage for what is to follow in the minds of customers.

Student Challenges

NAME _____ DATE _____

In Challenge #12, evaluate existing ticketing companies as well as potential companies for the ticketing needs for a spectator driven event of your choice. If you can't think of an event, use a beach volleyball pro tour event as the event for these questions. Then, set up a parking and credential access plan for the event.

Question 12.1

Research two ticketing companies that provide ticketing services to events and facilities. Use the event you identified above and generate a list of services each company provides and then list the pros and cons of each company.

    Ticket Company #1 Name:
    Services Provided:
    Pros:
    Cons:

    Ticket Company #2 Name:
    Services Provided:
    Pros:
    Cons:

Question 12.2

Create a ticket pricing strategy for the event, identified above. Explain how the pricing strategy was developed and why the strategy works for this event. Assume that you are the local event organizer and have the right to set ticket prices.

Question 12.3

Create a credential and parking pass plan (e.g., how many different types of access are needed for credentials and why, how will the parking lot be restricted, what will be charged, and why). Identify the various groups in the plan, and create/design the credential and parking passes.

Question 12.4

Create a list of at least (10) different things that could be included in an augmented reality (AR) feature for the event.

EVENT DOCUMENTS

Michelle Wells

CHAPTER 13

Michelle Wells is a Visiting Instructor of Sport Studies at Guilford College in Greensboro, NC. She began teaching undergraduate students in 2008 and has taught event management, sports marketing, sports communication, sports law, and international sports. Prior to teaching, Michelle worked in event management for various organizations, including ESPN (Disney's) Wide World of Sports, Disney's Animal Kingdom, and New York Road Runners. She has managed and/or worked over 200 sports and entertainment events throughout her career. She received her bachelor's degree in business administration (marketing) from the University of Florida and a master's degree in sports administration and facility management from Ohio University.

Information is the key to the success of any project. The documents used to communicate information will be a foundation in the planning process. Being able to use Microsoft Excel for the organization (and budgeting) of an event is important. There are many types and varieties of event management software that can help in creating planning documents, but for the vast majority of events, Excel is sufficient and helps to control costs.

For all events, planning documents are vital, but they are especially so if an event does not have a permanent venue. Items can sometimes slip through the cracks. During an event held in a permanent venue, small items can often be easily fixed. For example, if a table is forgotten, the venue likely owns more and can provide them. For an event held elsewhere, getting additional equipment can be more difficult. The planning documents covered in this chapter include:

- Planning Timelines
- Day of Timelines
- Checklists
- Call Sign Lists
- Equipment Lists
- Fast Facts
- Staffing Positions/Call times
- Diagrams/Maps/CADs/Google Earth
- PA Scripts
- Parking Passes

- Credential Boards/Ticket Boards
- Credential Pick-Up Procedures
- Awards Protocol
- Appearance Guidelines
- Media Information
- Communication Procedures

Planning Timeline

Planning timelines are used to set up and track detailed tasks by functional area. They ensure that event managers can account for each detailed item, who is responsible for specific items, and whether the event is on schedule. By filling in a completion date as well as a due date, event managers can use this information the following year (or for the following event) to evaluate if the planning timeline

Table 13.1 Sample Planning Timeline

Event Date November 13, 2016

Days Out	Date Due	Task	Functional Area	Task Owner	Date Completed
−240	18-Mar-16	Initial course drive-thru	Events	Smith	
−1	12-Nov-16	Final pre-event course drive-thru	Events	Smith	
−150	16-Jun-16	Signage creative design first draft	Creative	Davis	
−75	30-Aug-16	Signage creative design final selection	Creative	Davis	
−45	29-Sep-16	Course split timing mat locations tested for interference	Timing	Ross	
−45	29-Sep-16	Exact course split timing mat locations noted on drive-thru and map	Timing	Ross	
−8	5-Nov-16	Course split timing mat locations marked with spray paint	Events	Thompson	
5	16-Nov-16	Recap report template sent out	All	Thompson	
10	23-Nov-16	Recap reports due back	All	Thompson	

dates were realistic. A common format for a planning timeline is shown in Table 13.1 and it is easy to create in a spreadsheet program such as Microsoft Excel.

At the top of the planning timeline is the EVENT DATE. If the event is over multiple days, this date will be the first day of the event. The DAYS OUT column lists the standard number of days before the event that the task is due to be completed, and is determined before the timeline is created. In the DATE DUE column, a simple formula will calculate the date based on the number listed in the days out column and the date in the event date cell. TASK is the actual work that needs to be performed. The FUNCTIONAL AREA lets everyone involved know which department is responsible for that task, and the TASK OWNER is the person within that department who is accountable to complete the task. The person responsible for completing that task fills in DATE COMPLETED. Some event managers will also add a COMMENTS or NOTES column to account for any details about that task that may be important to record during planning.

For those not familiar with Excel, it may be helpful to open Excel and go through this process while reading this section. The formula for this task will start in cell B4, the cell location of the first DUE DATE, and assuming that the EVENT DATE is in cell B1 and that the DAYS OUT start in cell A4, the formula would be: =B1+A4. Then, copy the dates exactly like copying any formula in Excel. In the formula, it is important to make sure to put the dollar sign ($) before the letter and also before the number of the cell that houses the EVENT DATE. This ensures that the DATE DUE is being calculated from the same cell each time (EVENT DATE). It "locks" the formula to that one cell (EVENT DATE) as the reference point (Figure 13.1).

If multiple people are working on this document, it is a good idea to have an AS OF date in the header or footer. The AS OF date denotes the last date on which the document was changed. This ensures everyone with access to it is working off the most recent version. If the date feature on Excel's header/footer is used, that date changes each time the document is opened, whether changes have been made to the timeline or not. Thus, the best option is to enter the date manually. As the event gets closer (or even just the deadline for completing the timeline) and multiple changes are being made, it may even be necessary to include a time stamp. It will dramatically help the team's productivity if people can be quickly determine if they're using the most recent version of the timeline.

With seemingly constant changes in technology, it is easy to share these documents, even for teams working in different geographic locations. Google Docs, Google Drive, Dropbox, One Drive, and Box

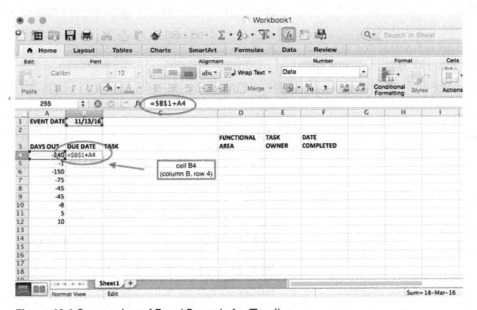

Figure 13.1 Screenshot of Excel Formula for Timeline.

are easy ways for an entire team to be able to share documents if the team is not on the same mapped drive.

Day of Event Timeline

The day of an event involves a flurry of activities. Staff and volunteers report, deliveries are made, signage is set up, and everything that was done has to be undone. A countless number of things happen, and all of them need to be accounted for in one place so that the team managing the event knows what is happening throughout the day. This is where the **day of event timeline** comes into play. Each activity for the day should be on this timeline. Event managers may choose to customize the categories, but a basic setup for a day of event timeline will include most of the same categories as the event planning timeline: TIME, TASK, FUNCTIONAL AREA, TASK OWNER, and NOTES/COMMENTS. Putting each activity as an individual item helps event managers see each activity as it will occur chronologically. Some event managers will create two columns for time: START TIME and END TIME. As an example, let's use some activities related to a band playing on the main entertainment stage, looking only at the TIME and TASK columns.

In the two-column format for time, it would look like this:

START TIME	END TIME	TASK
6:00 am	4:00 pm	generators on site for band on main stage
7:00 am	8:00 am	sound check for band on main stage
9:00 am	3:00 pm	band plays at main stage

The challenge with this format is that people have to search through the timeline for an activity to determine its end time. They may also have to make some assumptions. If the generators are on site until 4:00 pm, does that mean they will be gone at 4:00 pm, or is 4:00 pm when the generator company will start loading out? If they are in at 6:00 am, is that when the company arrives, or when the generators are functional?

The one-column format for time requires more initial entry of information, and sometimes more information in general, but it allows the staff to simply flip through the pages on the event day timeline and check off tasks as they occur. Look at the same example put in a one-column format.

START TIME	TASK
6:00 am	generators arrive on site for band at main stage
7:00 am	generators setup and functional
7:00 am	start of sound check for band on main stage
8:00 am	end of sound check for band on main stage
9:00 am	band begins play at main stage
3:00 pm	band set ends on main stage

START TIME	TASK
3:00 pm	rental company arrives for load out of main stage generators
4:00 pm	rental company finished loading out main stage generators

The load-in time, start time, run time, end time, and load-out time are all separate items in this format. With Excel, information can be entered in any order and then sorted very easily. Each functional area can enter its own information in the master document, and the lead event manager can sort the information by time. The information can also be sorted by functional area and printed for staff in each respective functional area or sent to their electronic device. Timeline information should be distributed on a "need to know" basis. For example, certain staff need all of the information from the timeline, but student interns helping at the finish line of a race only need a copy of the timeline related to their position. These position-specific timelines can be set up so they are small enough to fit in a pocket for reference or viewable on a digital device screen.

If detailed activities, such as load in, are starting a couple of days before the actual event, the day of event timeline may need to be expanded. If that were the case, a field for DATE should be added. It may also be best to use a 24-hour clock (see Table 13.2) to avoid any confusion or typos with "am" and "pm" as staff enter their timeline items.

Table 13.2 Sample Day of Event Timeline

Time(24-hour clock)	Task	Functional Area	Task Owner	Notes/Comments
6:00	Generators arrive on site for band at main stage	LOGS	Harris	
7:00	Generators setup and functional	LOGS	Harris	
7:00	Start of sound check for band on main stage	ENT	Black	
8:00	End of sound check for band on main stage	ENT	Black	
9:00	Band begins play at main stage	ENT	Black	
15:00	Band set ends on main stage	ENT	Black	
15:00	Rental company arrives for load out of main stage generators	LOGS	Harris	
16:00	Rental company finished loading out main stage generators	LOGS	Harris	

Checklists

Often, event managers are responsible for managing various areas within an event. Checklists are an easy way to keep track of "to do's." For a large event, the day of event timeline will often suffice as a checklist, although event managers may still want to have a separate checklist for themselves. Some examples of the things that may be on an individual's checklist but not on the timeline may be for the event manager to specifically check in with an area supervisor or to meet a person at a location. They are tasks, however, that should be tracked and documented: (1) in case someone needs to step in and work the area for that person, and (2) for future event planning purposes.

The format of the checklist may vary depending on the preference of event managers. Some may list the items by time, some by task sequence, others may break down the items on the list by functional area, and still others will utilize a combination format (see Figure 13.2). Functional areas for a marathon could be: Entertainment—Main Stage, Finish Line, Awards, and so on. For a college football or basketball game, the functional areas could be: Field of Play (Court), Equipment, Concessions, Custodial, Ushers, Tickets, and so forth.

For recurring events and events in a fixed venue, checklists are essential. It is too easy for event managers to become so familiar with the steps and nuances of their events and/or venue that they check off the tasks in their heads. Even if they do not formally use a checklist and check off the items, they should create and regularly update checklists for the event and/or event type. Checklists preserve the procedures for the organization when event managers leave, they help to train new staff and interns that are hired, and can be vital if ever requested for legal action or other reasons to demonstrate procedures and actions.

Contact Sheets

The footprint of many events will be so large that event managers are going to need to use communications equipment to speak with one another. There are also people that event managers might need to reach who will not be on site at the event. Having documents on hand with the phone numbers or radio channels for everyone allows event managers to contact people quicker.

Internal

It is hard to think of any organization that does not have its internal contact information available via its email system, internal Web site, or even its external Web site. Even with this information readily available, it is still a good idea for event managers to have a printed **call sign list** that they keep with them during their event. This is also sometimes called a **contact list** or **call sign sheet**. If nothing else, it serves as a backup in case they cannot access those other pieces of information for any reason. A call sign list keeps all the information in one place where it is easy to find and access.

The call sign list should include anyone who may need to be contacted for any reason. Different levels of the event staff may have different numbers on their call sign list. For example, event managers at a Division I NCAA school may have their direct supervisor's cell phone and home numbers on their list (and the common list that everyone has), while their boss will probably have the numbers of athletic department staff who are much higher in the organizational chart. Some events will rent communications equipment (e.g., two-way radios and/or cell phones) rather than requiring staff to use their own. In this case, the call sign list should have both the permanent and rented cell phone numbers listed, along with specific radio channels used for different operational areas.

Figure 13.2a Sample Event Checklist.

Checklist by Time or Order of Operation

——— test communications equipment (radios, Nextels) with finish line crew

——— ensure timing mats are set up at finish

——— confirm arrival of main stage entertainment

——— deliver three event jackets to main stage for entertainers to wear

——— verify with timing crew that timing mats are functioning

——— meet and greet the person who will deliver official results to awards stage

——— confirm location of over-sized check for awards ceremony

——— ensure two Sharpie markers are with the over-sized check and that both markers work

——— verify that awards for top three men, women, wheelchair-men, wheelchair-women are at the finish line

——— check awards stand area to make sure it is clear of leaves, debris, and so on

Checklist by Functional Area

Finish Line

——— walk-thru area and greet staff and volunteers

——— ensure timing mats are set up at finish

——— verify with timing crew that timing mats are functioning

——— test communications equipment (radios, Nextels) with finish line crew

——— meet and greet the person who will deliver official results to awards stage

Entertainment

——— walk-thru area and greet staff and volunteers

——— confirm arrival of main stage entertainment

——— deliver three event jackets to main stage for entertainers to wear

Awards

——— walk-thru area and greet staff and volunteers

——— confirm location of over-sized check for awards ceremony

——— ensure two Sharpie markers are with the over-sized check and that both markers work

——— verify that awards for top three men, women, wheelchair-men, wheelchair-women are at the finish line

——— check awards stand area to make sure it is clear of leaves, debris, and so on

Call Sign List

For large events, event managers often need to create a call sign list or event call sign list that is reduced to the size of a credential, is laminated for weatherproofing, and then worn on a lanyard. The font is usually small, and only essential information can fit. The least amount of information a call sign list should include is: name, area(s) each person is working, event cell phone number and/or personal cell phone number (see Table 13.3). If the event team is using two-way radios, include the

Figure 13.2b Sample Event Checklist at Facility.

HIGH FIVE ARENA

EVENT CHECKLIST

Event:_____   *Date(s)*:_____

Contact: _____ *Ph#*: (____)_____ *Fax*:(____)_____

Areas Used: _____

Move In:_____   *Move out*:_____

Event time(s):_____   *Gates open*:_____

Event Status: Tentative _____ Date_____ Firm _____ Date_____

Contracted _____ Date_____ Canceled _____ Date_____

Preceding Event:_____ *Next Event*:_____

Date_____   Date_____

Pre-Event Information: *Date*   *Date*

1. Rental Application   _____   10. Floor plan/diagram   _____
2. File Created   _____   11. Parking Arrangements   _____
3. Cost Estimate   _____   12. EMT's ordered   _____
4. Contract Prep form   _____   13. UPD ordered   _____
5. Contracts: Mailed   _____   14. Palms Ordered   _____
              Rec'd   _____   15. L2 Retract/Extend   _____
6. Insurance: Mailed   _____   16. PPD Scrub L1/L2   _____
              Rec'd   _____   17. Information Sheet   _____
7. Alcohol Request   _____   18. HVAC settings   _____
8. Cancel Classes/Clubs   _____   19. Concessions   _____
9. Staffing Sheet   _____

Event Information:

1. Supervisor leads: *Set/Strike* _____ *Tech(PL)* _____
       Usher _____ *Security*_____
2. Concessions Locations: _____
3. Attendance: Turnstile _____ Drop Count _____ Announced _____
4. Rental fee _____ Event Starts _____ Ends_____
5. Special Considerations _____

Post Event Information: *Date*   *Date*

1. Post Event Information sheet _____   4. Post Event Letter   _____
2. Event Billing form   _____   5. Final Review of File   _____
3. Questionnaire   _____

Event Notes:

```



```

Table 13.3a   Sample Call Sign List Sorted by First Name

Name	Functional Area	Event Cell	Personal Cell	Radio Channel
Ben Langat	Logistics	(555) 555-9999	(123) 555-0000	5
Erin Davis	Aid Stations	(555) 555-7766	(123) 555-3344	7
Hajar Latif	Start Line	(555) 555-3333	(123) 555-4444	1
Jane Smith	Awards	(555) 555-1111	(123) 555-2222	4
Joe Black	Timing & Scoring	(555) 555-7777	(123) 555-8888	6
Maggie Wong	Finish Line	(555) 555-5555	(123) 555-6666	2
Mike Ross	Course	(555) 555-1212	(123) 555-7788	3
Pedro Torres	Timing & Scoring	(555) 555-4433	(123) 555-1122	6
Regan Adams	Entertainment	(555) 555-9988	(123) 555-5566	2

Table 13.3b   Sample Call Sign List Sorted Functional Area

Functional Area	Name	Event Cell	Personal Cell	Radio Channel
Aid Stations	Erin Davis	(555) 555-7766	(123) 555-3344	7
Awards	Jane Smith	(555) 555-1111	(123) 555-2222	4
Course	Mike Ross	(555) 555-1212	(123) 555-7788	3
Entertainment	Regan Adams	(555) 555-9988	(123) 555-5566	2
Finish Line	Maggie Wong	(555) 555-5555	(123) 555-6666	2
Logistics	Ben Langat	(555) 555-9999	(123) 555-0000	5
Start Line	Hajar Latif	(555) 555-3333	(123) 555-4444	1
Timing & Scoring	Joe Black	(555) 555-7777	(123) 555-8888	6
Timing & Scoring	Pedro Torres	(555) 555-4433	(123) 555-1122	6

radio channel each person will be operating on. The reason to include the area the person is working is that events often have people working—both volunteers and paid staff—who likely will not know one another. With the call sign list, if someone has an issue related to a specific area and cannot reach their immediate supervisor, they can call the person on the call sign list who can help them. Excel is often the best software to create the call sign list if event managers are creating it themselves.

Whether the call sign list is on a lanyard or will be in a production binder, it is advisable to list the names alphabetically by first name rather than last name. Especially when volunteers and event day staff are brought in, people often remember other workers' first names, but not necessarily their last. In fact, they may not even know last names. Let's say a volunteer is told, "Call Ted at the finish line and ask if everything is all set up." If a volunteer does not know Ted's last name and the call sign list is alphabetical by last name, it will be cumbersome to search through dozens of names to find his contact information on the list. On the opposite side of a call sign list—or a separate call sign list—list the numbers and names by area. This way, people can find someone working in, for example, Entertainment, if they have a question about that area but do now know who specifically to call.

As discussed in detail in Chapter 18—Event Operations, having the right equipment at the right time can make or break an event manager's response to an unexpected occurrence. The list provided in Table 13.4 is a great starting point to determining the needs of specific events. Event mangers can create their own equipment list that they add and delete from each time the event occurs. It is important that the event equipment list is updated immediately after the event so that the next year everything that is needed is already easily available on the list.

Table 13.4 Detailed List of Equipment

- Air horn
- Barricades
- Batteries (all sizes/voltages)
- Battery Chargers
- Bike rack
- Blowers
- Brooms, rakes, and/or squeegees
- Bullhorns
- Bungee cords
- Cable cutters (small and large)
- Cable mats
- Cable ramps (Bumble Bees and Yellow Jackets)
- Cable ramps add-ons for ADA compliance (WASP ramps: Walkway Access for Special Purposes)
- Calculators
- Carpet (triathlon-specific, but could be used elsewhere, too)
- Cat litter (or VoBAN for spills)
- Chairs
- Clip boards
- Cinder blocks
- Computers
- Cones and/or delineator posts (w/bases)
- Coolers (for storage and for dispensing)
- Copier (high speed)
- Cork boards
- Cups
- Dry erase boards and markers
- Dumpsters
- Ear pieces and speaker mics for two-way radios
- Fax machines
- First aid kit
- Flags
- Flashlights and/or headlamps
- Fuel for generators and/or golf carts

- Gator utility vehicles
- Generators
- Gloves (work gloves and rubber gloves)
- Golf carts (four-passenger, eight-passenger, flat-bed/utility)
- Greenery/plants
- Grommets and grommet maker
- Hand carts and/or flat-bed dollies
- Hand sanitizer
- Hand and foot warmers (disposable; for outdoor winter events)
- Hand wash stations
- Heat sheets
- Hoses—fire and garden (along with nozzles, hydrant connectors, and hydrant wrenches)
- Ice
- Laminator
- Lanyards (for credentials)
- L-Poles/signage poles
- Lightning detector (outdoor events)
- Linens (tablecloths, drapes, towels, etc.)
- Misting tents/machines (misters)
- "Office in a Box" (pens, pencils, binders, highlighters, labels, dividers, envelopes, receipt book, appropriate stamps, index cards, Sharpies/Marks-A-Lot [for body marking], three-hole punch)
- Padlocks (combination so they can be opened even if the key is lost)
- Pallet jack
- Pallets
- Paper
- Pennants
- Phones (land line and cell)
- Pipe and drape

- Plywood
- Portable toilets (ADA and regular)
- Portable restroom trailers
- Power strips and industrial extension cords
- Power cords for commonly used electrical devices
- Printers
- Production manuals
- Radios (two-way/walkie-talkies)
- Rain ponchos/rain gear
- Results boards
- Risers
- Rope and/or twine
- Safety pins
- Sand bags
- Scanners
- Score cards
- Shovels
- Shrink wrap and dispensers
- Snow fence and/or scrim
- Sport-specific equipment (soccer balls and goals, tennis balls, etc.)
- Sports fence
- Spray adhesive
- Spray chalk
- Spray paint
- Stages
- Stop watches (minimum of two)
- Storage boxes (plastic/waterproof)
- Storage trailers (sea containers)
- Surveyor's tape

- SWAG (Stuff We All Get)—gifts (T-shirts, hats, etc. for various parties)
- Tablecloths and table skirts
- Tables
- Tape (duct, masking, electrical, scotch, packing, etc.)
- Tents (pop-up and/or vendor-delivered)
- Toilet paper
- Tool kits
- Towels
- Tower lights
- Trailers (for on-site office space and/or storage)
- Trash and recycling bags
- Trash boxes (Duso boxes: foldable wax-coated garbage boxes)
- Trash cans
- Trays (coroplast or wax-coated cardboard sheets used for stacking water cups on tables)
- Umbrellas
- Utility cabinets
- Utility knives
- Velcro
- Visqueen (poly sheeting)—for rain cover
- Wet/dry vac
- Whistles
- Wire
- Wire cutters
- Yard stakes (the stakes that real estate professionals use for putting up yard signs)
- Zip ties (various lengths and widths)

External

In the sports world, many events occur on weekends or after normal business operating hours, and delivery/set up of equipment may occur at a time before normal operating hours. If vendors are on the contact list for the event, such as tent companies or ice delivery companies, event managers should make sure the company provides the name and cell phone number of the driver making the delivery. If it is 6:00 am and a vendor was scheduled to make a delivery at 5:30 am, a call to the office is likely only going to lead to the manager's voicemail, and waiting until 9:00 am when the company opens is likely to severely hamper the event. Frequently, this is not only an organizational issue, but is also important if there are security check-points for deliveries. Even if the delivery is for setup of equipment the day before the event, it will impact the setup schedule and could have a domino effect on the setup of other items. For example, assume the tent and flooring rental company is late. The tents and flooring have to be in place before the tables, chairs, and linens can be set up. The audio-visual company will also have to wait to set up any speakers, rigging, video screens, lighting, and soundboards. The company providing the theming and decor cannot decorate a tent that is not set up. The more complicated the event, the more dominoes that could fall if one vendor is late. Whereas if the event managers have the driver's cell phone number and the vendor manager's cell phone number, they can contact the driver directly to see what the problem is,

Trick of the Trade

There is a very small, but helpful, thing that event managers can do when creating a call sign list that will make it easier to read when on a lanyard. When laminating a two-sided call sign list, format the two sides in opposite directions, meaning the top of the front side of the list will be lined up with the bottom of the back side. When the hole is punched in the list to hook the laminated list to the lanyard, punch it at the bottom of the front side of the list. This way, when a person is looking down at the lanyard, the text will be readable without having to twist the call sign list around, and to see the other side, the person only has to flip the card over vertically rather than twist it around on the lanyard.

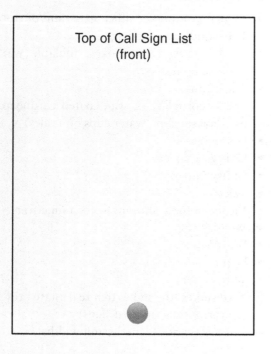

contact the vendor manager to work out a solution (if they cannot work it out directly with the driver), or start adjusting the day's schedule. At a minimum, the event managers can start notifying other vendors of the situation so they can schedule around the delay.

Fast Facts

Fast facts documents are just what the name implies—a fast way for staff and volunteers to find pertinent facts about an event. The information listed will be common questions that participants and spectators are going to ask about an event, and not everyone working the event will know the answers (see Table 13.5). Fast facts are useful prior to the event for front of house staff, which is anyone in direct contact with patrons and that routinely speaks to the public. Instead of front of house staff having to say, "I don't know," they should be able to find the answers to the most common questions in the fast facts. The information on this document should be information that anyone in the public can see. This is not the place to put sensitive or confidential information such as personal contact numbers or emergency protocol. Assume one of these will be left lying around and will be picked up by a member of the general public.

Table 13.5   Sample Fast Facts*

Fast Facts	Race Schedule for Sunday	First Aid	Lost and Found
2016 RUN THE WORLD MARATHON November 13, 2016 Event Managers: Hajar Latif and Maggie Wong	6:00 am —buses begin departing 6:30 am—first runners arrive at start 8:00 am—runners move to start line 8:40 am—wheelchair athletes start 9:00 am—race starts 9:20 am—last runner crosses the start line 10:00 am—male wheelchair winner estimated to cross finish 10:10 am—female wheelchair winner estimated to cross finish line 11:15 am—male winner estimated to cross finish line 11:30 am—female winner estimated to cross finish line	Spectators needing first aid can go to any of the red tents for assistance. Tents are located on both the north and south sides of the race finish line. For athletes needing assistance, medical staff will be in the finish and post-finish areas and will be wearing red shirts and red hats.	Found items can be turned in to any staff or volunteer member in a blue shirt or jacket or taken to the **Information Tent** next to the ticket kiosk on the corner of Lark St. and Watt St. Lost items can be picked up at the **Information Tent** next to the ticket kiosk on the corner of Lark St. and Watt St. **Results** All results will be posted on the event Web site by 10:00 pm Eastern time the day of the race.
Tickets Tickets for the two seating sections closest to the finish line (both north and south sides) are sold out. Spectators wanting to purchase tickets for other seating areas can purchase them at the kiosk on the corner of Lark St. and Watt St. beginning at **6:00 am on race day.** The kiosk will be open until 12:00 pm. After 12:00 pm, seating is first-come, first-served.	**Awards** The awards ceremonies will begin at 12:00 pm at the awards stage, which is located behind Bleacher 3. Male and Female top three places will be presented first (12:00–12:15) Male and Female wheelchair first place winners only will be presented next (12:15–12:25) After awards are presented, athletes will pose for photos in the awards area and then be escorted to the media room for interviews.	**Statistics** There are over 20,000 runners participating in the 2016 Blueprint Marathon. The event has runners from all 50 states and 17 countries. The race sold out 2 days after registration opened. 8,500+ volunteer shifts are needed throughout the week to produce the Blueprint Marathon. This is the 14th year for the Run the World Marathon.	**Volunteers** Volunteer sign-in and sign-out is located at the Volunteer tent on the corner of Watt St. and Bank St. Unfortunately, all of our volunteer positions are full and we cannot take day-of sign-ups for volunteers. Only those already registered and confirmed can volunteer. To sign up to volunteer for next year's race, go to www.rtwraces.com/volunteers.

*By using the layout shown in this table, the Fast Facts can be folded once horizontally and then three times vertically to create a pocket-sized information sheet.

For printing, if the fast facts can be folded so staff can carry the document in their pockets, they will be more likely to hold on to it and utilize it. If an event has the budget for fast facts to be professionally produced and printed, this document can be created to look more like a marketing piece, but it is not necessary just to create a functional document. It can simply be produced in Excel and printed on 8.5"×11" standard size paper or on 8.5"×14" legal size paper. If event managers produce and print the document themselves and it is a multiple-day event, they can re-work the document and print new ones each day. This will allow event managers to add any new items that staff members were asked on the first day of the event. Each day's fast facts could be printed on a different color paper to help avoiding confusion as to which version is the most up-to-date. After printing the fast facts, then it is easy to copy any maps/diagrams onto the second side of the sheet.

If event managers are not sure where to start with information that should go on the fast facts, some of the most common items include:

- Schedule: opening and closing times; competition start times
- Tickets: prices; where they can be purchased; whether they are required or not for all areas
- Parking Information: parking lot locations; drop off locations; disabled parking areas
- Media Information: If the event is on the radio or television, list which station and if it is live or delayed; location of media entrances and work areas
- Lost and Found: where to turn in lost items; where to collect lost items; the hours of operation
- First Aid: location(s) of first aid personnel; times first aid will be open
- Restrooms: locations; wheelchair accessible restrooms
- Concessions: locations; payment options; ATM location; types of food offered
- Results: where they can be viewed; how soon after an event they will be posted on site; the Web site address for results
- Statistics: how many people or teams are entered; how many states and/or countries are represented; what is the capacity of the venue, and so on.
- Maps/Diagrams: inside the foldout is a great place to put a diagram(s) of the event layout

Staffing Positions/Call Times

No matter how much planning is put into an event, plans cannot be properly executed without people. People are the backbone of an event and what allow the carefully thought-out plans to be fully executed (staffing is discussed in Chapter 14). Sometimes, inexperienced event managers can overlook this fact. Many of the people working an event will not be involved in the detailed planning. What is second nature to the event managers may be brand new information to the staff. This is why it is important to provide this information to them.

The staffing schedule and call times should ideally be completed 2 weeks in advance, sooner if possible. If the event is being held in a union venue, staffing needs may need to be submitted even earlier, depending on the requirements of the union's collective bargaining agreement (CBA) with the venue. Producing documents detailing the schedule of the staff and volunteers enables event managers and the managers of other functional areas to make sure there are no gaps in coverage. They can see what areas are covered, at what specific times, and how many people are scheduled to work each area. If there are any gaps in coverage, they can be caught early and corrected. An example of a staffing position document is shown in Table 13.6

Table 13.6   Sample Staffing Positions

2016 Run the World Marathon Staffing and Volunteer Positions		
Position	*Contact*	*Description*
Ushers	Elliott Suarez	- check tickets and credentials at bleacher access points
		- direct spectators to their bleacher section
		- serve as crowd control at the finish area
		- answer general questions from guests
Medal Distribution	Jane Smith	- unpack and unwrap medals and hang on medal racks
		- clean up area of all trash and breakdown boxes before finishers arrive
		- distribute one medal to each finisher by placing the medal around the runner's neck (not handing it to them)
		- pack up remaining medals at the end of the event and stack boxes
Post-Finish Water Station	David Keter	- set up tables for water distribution
		- unpack bottled water and place on tables
		- clean up area of all trash and breakdown boxes before finishers arrive
		- distribute one bottle of water to each finisher
		- clean up area of discarded bottle caps and bottles
		- place bagged garbage in dumpster in the post-finish area

Diagrams/Maps/CADs

Diagrams are useful in many different areas. They can be employed to show equipment for logistics, staffing/volunteer placement, signage placement, participant flow, and more. When it comes to diagramming event details, **CADs (computer-aided design/drawing)** provide the ultimate detail for events and are great because the information is to scale. The downside is that they usually require an expert to create them. If the foundational information does not already exist, such as the layout of the state park the event may be using, the foundational CAD will have to be created. CADs are intricate and complex. Learning to use the software to create them is often time consuming and expensive. It is not a skill that can be picked up in a short time period. Hiring someone to create CADs can also be expensive.

There are other options event managers can utilize for creating diagrams. In the ideal scenario, event managers want diagrams that are to scale, but it is not a requirement. For smaller events it is not always possible or economical. For those situations where general layout is the biggest need, easier options are PowerPoint and Google Earth. With PowerPoint, event managers can use the drawing tool to create diagrams of event areas. These can be very detailed, but event managers need to note that the diagram is not to scale. With the option of saving the diagrams as PDF files, the documents are easy to share without worrying about someone making unauthorized changes. Google Earth is another tool that can be added to event managers' toolboxes. Google Earth can help show exactly where equipment, for example, needs to be placed, where a start and finish line will be set up, and any number of other things by using drawing tools on satellite photos. Rural areas may not be as easy to map. Often, the satellite pictures for rural areas are not available or are not clear at the level of zoom that is available for metropolitan areas. A word of caution on Google Earth is that some of the satellite images can be dated (up to a few years old) and thus not be as accurate as needed.

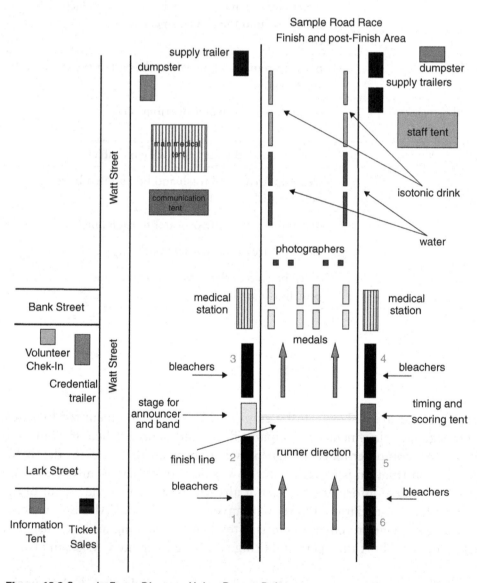

Figure 13.3 Sample Event Diagram Using Power Point.

Public Address/Video Board Scripts

Public address or PA scripts should be written and distributed to announcers in advance of the event. The **PA script** includes the specific details of what is being said when. For events in permanent venues, there is often a person who regularly serves as the announcer. For events where an announcer is less familiar with the script, it is helpful to give her plenty of advance time to review the announcements. Figure 13.4 shows a very short example of a PA script for a road race. If there are any tricky names, make sure to provide a pronunciation key. Write out the announcements exactly as they should be read. Do not abbreviate the event name or any other names. Make sure to include sponsor names where appropriate, and provide instructions on how often the announcements should be read. Some sponsor agreements may contain specifics about how many PA reads are required, and the event managers should ensure this is executed per the sponsor contract.

In addition to sponsor reads, other information that patrons or spectators need to know should be included in the PA script. Examples include where concessions are located, good sportsmanship information, how to exit the facility, and when the next event is being held. Finally, emergency announcement information should be printed on the back page of the PA script (or posted in the PA booth/area) in the event it is needed. If an emergency situation should occur, the PA announcer has the correct announcements readily available instead of having to wait for the announcement to be communicated (see Figure 13.4 for a sample).

For events using video board displays, oftentimes the PA script is combined with a video board script which contains information on which graphic, sponsor advertisement, or public service announcement is shown when. This will ensure that a sponsor graphic will be shown on the video board, at the same time the PA announcer reads the sponsor announcement. The technician responsible for the video board will have all of the graphics and video clips preprogrammed and ready to go on event day, but the script will dictate what is shown and when.

Figure 13.4 PA Script (short sample).

2016 RUN THE WORLD MARATHON
PA SCRIPT (short sample)
NOVEMBER 13, 2016

7:00 am–4:00 pm   Announcer(s) On-Site

The following announcements should be red regularly throughout the day. Each one should be read at least five times each hour (approximately every 12 minutes), interspersed with the announcer's banter, general race info, and calling out runner names via their bib numbers that pop up on the computer. Each announcement may be read individually (i.e., the entire list doesn't have to be read at once) throughout the hour.

Sponsors

This is the 14th annual Run the World Marathon. The organizers would like to thank the runners and their families for coming out and participating in this great race.

Once again, we are serving Gatorade to our runners on the course to help them refuel. Gatorade is the official thirst quencher of the Run the World Marathon. "Gatorade ... Is it in you?"

We want to thank the Costco Wholesale for providing the bananas for runners during and after the race. If you would like to sign up for a Costco Wholesale membership, simply visit Costco.com or your local Costco store.

Aquafina bottled water is available at fluid stations on the course and the finish line today. "Fresh and pure, Aquafina is the perfect companion for happy bodies everywhere." Make sure to stay hydrated today. "Aquafina ... for happy bodies."

<u>Spectator Info</u>

Ladies and Gentlemen, if at any time you need of first aid today, there is a spectator first aid tent on both sides of the finish line area behind each set of bleachers. Again, spectator first aid is located behind each set of bleachers in red tents should you need it today.

Lost and found is located on the west side of the finish line—that's the side over here by me—right next to this stage.

Parking Passes

Parking can become a complex aspect of event operations. As such, the creation of parking passes can take up a lot of time for event managers because the passes must be easily identifiable, different for each parking area, communicate other information to patrons, and not easily copied.

Parking passes should be large enough so they can be identified when put in the window of the vehicle. If there are different parking areas, it may be wise to have the passes in different colors. Utilize both sides of the pass and put the directions and/or a map on the back for the driver. A couple of ways to help prevent people creating counterfeit passes by copying them is to number them and/or to have a hologram put on them when they are made. The parking staff should have a list of the numbers and the names associated with the passes. If the passes are issued to one person and are not transferable for the owner's friends or family to use, the staff should have the vehicle description and license plate number as well. This may be harder for repeat events because people may simply drive different cars each time. These are also added security measures for large events to track who has access to certain areas. For large events, local law enforcement will likely request this list in advance, which also means that event managers have to create, produce, and distribute parking passes according to that requirement.

Make the job of the parking staff as easy as possible. Create a sample board or document that shows what all of the parking passes look like and which lot(s) they allow the person to access. This information should be reviewed at the pre-event staff meeting and also included in the production binder (see Figure 13.5).

Figure 13.5 Sample Parking Pass—Front.

Credential/Ticket Boards

Credentials and tickets allow access to areas of an event. Credentials are usually for staff and may also be given to VIPs and/or media to access certain areas. As with parking passes, credentials should be numbered and/or have a hologram where security is tight. There should also be a list of which credentials are given to specific people or groups. For smaller events and areas of an event where security is not as tight, numbering and holograms are probably not necessary.

There are companies whose entire business is geared around creating access control and credential plans. For intricate events, it may be necessary to consult with one of those companies. These companies can offer security measures such as printing credentials on site with photos on them, RFID chips on the credentials to track them at access points, and many other high-security measures. For the types of events covered by this text, let's consider three very simple methods of determining how to assign credential types and access. (1) The credential type or color can indicate the group to which the person belongs (e.g., staff, VIP, volunteer, medical, vendor, etc.) and then the access code can specifically indicate where they are allowed access. For example, purple credentials indicate staff, green credentials indicate volunteers, red credentials indicate medical, and the codes on the credentials indicate where they can gain access. If it is a road race, AA could mean all access to all areas; FA could mean access to all areas of the finish, F1 could mean all areas of the finish except the finish line proper; S1, CA, and F1 could mean access to all areas of the start except the start line proper, all access to the course, and access to all areas of the finish except the finish line proper. Again, the color of the credential would indicate the group to which the person belongs. (2) The type or color can indicate the area and the access code can specifically indicate where they are allowed access. This method works better if people are not crossing over to multiple areas. For example, let's say that the finish area is indicated by a yellow credential and the start is indicated by an orange credential, then the specific codes to allow a person to access areas is put on each credential. If people are at both the start and finish, such as sponsors, for example, they may require multiple credentials to access areas. The person may have a finish credential with FA and a start credential with S1, as an example. (3) For an event such as a college football season, each game may have a different color. The parking passes, tickets, and credentials would all be color-coded for that game. Game one may be the red game, game two the pink game, game three the yellow game, and so on. Everything for that game would be the same color, but the access granted would be letter or number coded onto it. For events similar to a college football game, this often works best because it allows ticket holders to pass on their tickets, parking passes, and credentials to another person without having to get them back for access to the next game. For the staff working the college football season, their credential may be striped, indicating that it is good for all of the games that season.

Sample boards should be created and posted at access points showing staff which specific credentials and tickets will enable access at that point. As defined in Chapter 12, Event Ticketing, sample boards have exact replicas of credentials, tickets, and parking passes on them, and provide an easy reference guide for staff. It can also be created in a document format and distributed to staff in those areas. This is something that should be reviewed at the pre-event staff meeting and should also be included in the production binder. Figure 13.6 shows a sample credential board and Figure 13.7 shows a sample ticket board.

Production Binders

Many events carve up the responsibilities for supervision of functional areas during an event. Staff and volunteers who have not worked on planning the event may also be brought in to work. In

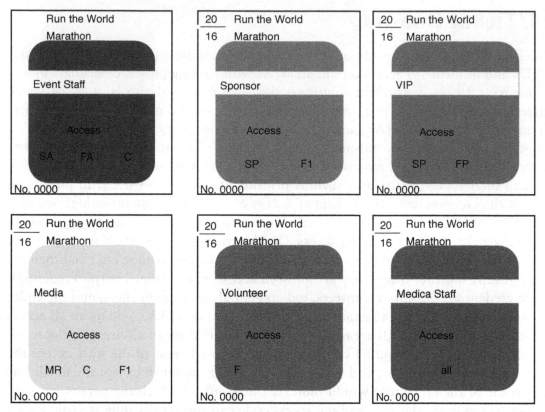

Figure 13.6 Sample Credential Board.

order to facilitate the integration of information from various functional areas for all of these people, event managers create production binders. A **production binder** is a book or collection of detailed information (e.g., parking maps, event day checklists, fast facts, staffing positions, maps and diagrams, etc.) about the event that staff can carry with them during the event. The binders are distributed to staff so they will have most of the information about the event if they need to look up details, especially in areas they do not manage. The documents covered in this chapter are often the ones collected and put into production binders.

Emergency Plans

Emergency plans are something event teams need to create, but something they hope they never need to put in action. This topic is covered in greater detail in Chapter 17, Emergency Planning and Medical Management. Event managers need to consider major scenarios and then develop a plan to account for what actions will be taken. For major scenarios, event managers may be able to name a few of the potential situations, but will never be able to come up with everything (dangerous weather, terrorist action, complete power loss, natural disaster, etc.). It is important for the plan to include actions that will be initiated in any major situation. This should be discussed, finely honed, and the response practiced with the appropriate staff members and with city or municipal authorities. There will be results of many scenarios, though, that may be the same, and to some extent, event managers can plan for those results. For example, if a road race has to be stopped midrace due to lightning, what is the best point (or points) geographically to do this or to try to re-direct people? Is it an area that has public transportation close by? If not, is it an area where buses can easily reach? Is there a plan in place to easily get transportation to that location to return runners to the finish area? Is there adequate room

Ticket for first game –BOYS' Game –is PURPLE

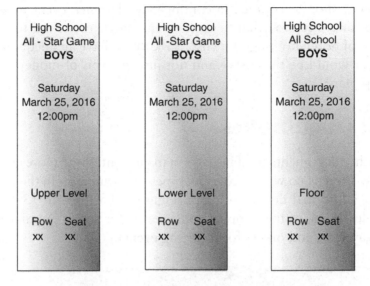

Ticket for second game –GIRLS' game –is RED

Figure 13.7 Sample Ticket Board.

to store backup supplies (e.g., bottled water for runners) in that location in case the race has to be stopped?

In any emergency situation, communication is going to be paramount. The plan for how communication will be handled, who will be in charge of communication, and who will be authorized to speak to the media should all be worked out in advance. Event managers renting venues and/or working with city agencies for their event will also need to partner with the venue and the city to answer these same questions.

Related to crowd management, "What If" sessions (Chapter 16—Safety and Security) are a key to planning for a variety of situations. Alternate scenarios need to be developed and reviewed in detail. It is helpful to come up with the four or five most likely scenarios and work out the specific elements of each, what actions will be taken, and who will be responsible for each one. For the relevant staff members, it is important to go over these few scenarios and the action plans in great detail. Maps and diagrams of alternate routes or locations have to be created and fully understood by everyone involved. Staff should be able to immediately go into action and lead their teams without having to think or ask what should be done. In contingency planning, event managers may have to spend money to prepare for a situation that never happens. What they need to ask themselves is what the opportunity cost is of doing nothing. If it costs $50,000 to have an adequate backup plan, that is a lot of money, but what would be the costs—and not just in terms of money—if something happens and there is no backup plan?

Additional Documents

There are many other documents used in event management, some more common to different types of events than others. There is no way to cover all types of documents. In the following pages, though, are examples of many additional document types (Figures 13.8 through 13.14) for fictitious events that can serve as samples. Some of the samples were created for a very popular marathon, some for a low media profile mega event, and others for recurring events.

SUMMARY

There are many tools that event managers have in their tool bags. Tools that facilitate information sharing are some of the best ones. Planning documents vary in purpose and complexity. Event managers change the format dependent on their personal taste or the event they are working. There is rarely only one right way to do something. It is the same with planning documents. Using one particular format is not nearly as important as the information that is conveyed and the timeframe in which it is distributed.

Figure 13.8 Sample Awards Protocol.

AWARDS PROTOCOL
2016 RUN THE WORLD MARATHON WEEKEND
The Awards Team of the 2016 Run the World Marathon Weekend will be responsible for the following:

- Awards will be presented for all official races held during 2016 Run the World Marathon Weekend.
- Awards will only be given to the athlete who won the award. (e.g., a spouse or child will not be able to receive an award for an athlete)
- An Awards Team member must check the bib number of the participant against the registration information for confirmation of name, age, and gender.
- The awards stage is located behind Bleachers 3 (see diagram).
- The awards ceremony will be consistent from presentation to presentation.
- The Awards Team will record the awards presented and those records will be submitted electronically to the VP of Operations at the end of the event.
- Members of the Awards Team will be set up at a table near the awards stage where athletes can pick-up their earned awards if they are not able to attend their awards ceremony.
- The Awards Team will provide the following items at each ceremony:
  - Announcer(s) and PA equipment for the presentations (small PA system to project in the immediate area only and not interfere with the overall finish line PA system)
  - Award stands for each presentation

- Backdrop behind the award stands
- A record of all awards presented
- The Awards Team will submit a written report (electronic) to the VP of Operations within 2 days of the final event. The report will include a list of all awards distributed and the names associated with those awards; a list of all awards not distributed or picked up and the names associated with those awards; and all supporting documents.
- Any awards not distributed or picked up will be packaged and mailed out to the individuals by the Awards Team within 10 days of the final event.

Figure 13.9 Sample Awards Procedures.

PROCEDURES FOR AWARDS PRESENTATIONS

The awards table will have two volunteers plus the event awards representative to ensure the ceremony runs smoothly. The announcer will ask the winners before each presentation to meet at the awards table. One of the volunteers will place the awards (medals, trophy, etc.) on the tray, making sure the correct awards are ready for presentation. The other volunteer will have the sign-in sheet for each award recipient to sign verifying that they received their award. Both the sheet and the awards will be included in the box(es)/envelope(s) marked for that particular event. If an award winner does not show at the table, ask the announcer to make a second announcement and if still a no-show, proceed with the ceremony. Put the signature sheet and any unclaimed awards back into the box(es)/envelope(s). Each table will also have an envelope of extra awards in case not enough were put in the original box(es)/envelope(s). Obtain a signature from every participant who receives an award.

When the Awards Team and table are ready, communicate to the announcer to begin the ceremony. The volunteer securing signatures will lead the group out to the awards stand. This person will line up the winners in this order: 2-1-3. The volunteer will walk behind the awards stand from left to right with the first person stopping at the farthest step (see below).

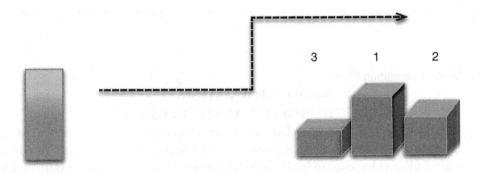

The volunteer will then walk behind the athletes and award stand to be in a position to lead the group back off the platform to the awards table.

The second volunteer who organized the awards on the tray will follow the group out to the awards stand with the medals on the tray. The Awards Team member (or dignitary) presenting the awards will follow the entire group.

The announcer will begin reading the script when the group is lined up behind the awards stand. Allow time after the awards are given for applause and pictures.

The volunteer who led the group in will lead the group out of the area with the second volunteer and presenter then following and walk back to the awards table area.

AWARDS CEREMONY ANNOUNCEMENT

Ladies and Gentlemen, please direct your attention to the awards presentation area.

We will be presenting the awards for the _____(event) _____(male, female, team) _____(age group).

Presenting the awards will be _____.

The third place finisher is _____(name) from _____(city/state/running club, if applicable) with a time of _____.

The second place finisher is _____(name) from _____(city/state/running club, if applicable) with a time of _____.

The first place finisher is _____(name) from _____(city/state/running club, if applicable) with a time of _____.

Let's give a big round of applause to all our award winners!

Thank you.

This concludes our awards ceremony for _____(event).

SIGNATURE PAGE FOR AWARDS

I, _____(print name) do certify that on this _____day of _____, 2016, I competed in the Run the World Marathon. On the above date, I placed in an award receiving status and received my award at the awards ceremony (or pick up location).

_____

Signature

Note: The signature page should be a separate sheet that each individual signs upon receipt of his or her award. It can be an individual page per person or have space for all category recipients (e.g., women 40–45) to sign on one page

Figure 13.10 Sample Media Information Sheet.

MEDIA INFORMATION
2016 RUN THE WORLD MARATHON WEEKEND

During Run the World Marathon Weekend, the Media Relations team credentials news media, runs the on-site media workroom, publishes results to the media, distributes news releases, and coordinates the shooting and release of official photos and/or video clips to local, national, and/or international media outlets. They are located in the Media Trailer, which is next to the Communications Trailer.

The Media Relations contacts for Run the World Marathon Weekend are Jamal Taylor and Aiko Kawaike.

Media Credentials for journalists who already registered for a credential online can be picked up from the Credentials trailer, which is located next to the Volunteer Check-In tent on the corner of Watt and Bank Streets. Online requests for credentials can be submitted until Friday at 5:00 pm. If journalists want to request a credential after Friday at 5:00 pm, they should call Jamal Taylor or Aiko Kawaike at the Media Work Room.

The Media Work Room is located in the large free-span tent near the finish line. **Phone numbers for the Media Workroom are (xxx) xxx-xxxx or (yyy) yyy-yyyy.**

Media Work Room Hours of Operation:

Wednesday	12:00 pm–5:00 pm
Thursday	12:00 pm–5:00 pm

Friday	7:30 am–5:00 pm
Saturday	7:30 am–6:30 pm
Sunday	5:00 am–4:00 pm
Monday	7:30 am–1:00 pm

Results will be posted on our website www.rtwraces.###.

Figure 13.11 Sample Credentials Information.

CREDENTIALS INFORMATION
2016 RUN THE WORLD MARATHON WEEKEND

Anyone working the Run the World Marathon (staff, volunteers, media, etc.) or attending the functions (sponsors, VIPs, etc.) must have a credential. Credentials can be picked up at the Credentials trailer, which is located on Bank Street near the corner of Watt Street, next to the Volunteer Check-In tent.

What do I need to pick up my credential?

Anyone picking up a credential must have a current, government-issued ID in order to pick up his/her credential.

Can someone else pick up my credential for me?

No. Each person will have his/her picture taken on site for the credential.

How long will it take me to get my credential?

It will depend on the line that is already there. Allow at least 30–60 minutes for credential pick-up. It is better to come early in the week, if possible, to avoid the lines that will inevitably be at the Credentials trailer during the weekend.

How do I know where my credential will allow me to go?

On the back of each credential is a map indicating which credential code is required for access to each specific area.

What if I lose my credential?

You will need to return to the Credentials trailer to inform them of the lost credential (they have a protocol for reporting the lost credential to Security). If your credential is not found, they will print another credential for you, but you will be charged a lost credential fee of $50.

What if they don't have my name in the system when I go to pick up my credential?

Names were given to the Credentials staff, 2 weeks prior to the event by area supervisors. If your name was not on the list they initially received, you will need to step outside and call your direct contact and he/she will help clear up the situation. The staff at the Credentials trailer cannot add people into the system without approval from an area supervisor.

Figure 13.12 Sample Appearance Guidelines.

APPEARANCE GUIDELINES

Uniforms

- Shirt—Event issued polo shirt(s) only. Must be tucked in and wrinkle free.
- Shorts—Dress or golf style. Acceptable length is from the top of the kneecap to three inches (3") above the top of the kneecap. Khaki color is preferred. Denim, elastic waistband, running, cut off, spandex, basketball/gym, or short shorts are not permitted.
- Trousers—Dress, golf, or cotton twill. Trousers must be neatly pressed and creased. Khaki color is preferred. Denim, yoga, warm up, or elastic waistband trousers are not permitted.

- Shoes/Socks—Shoes should be an athletic or dress style. Athletic shoes should be white, low top, with no apparent logos or ornamentation (e.g., no blue swoosh on white shoe; must be white on white) and must be worn with white socks. Dress shoes should be worn with coordinating socks for men and trouser socks or hosiery for women. Sandals, cowboy boots, flip flops, Crocs, open toe, or open heel shoes are not permitted.
- Hair—Should be combed neatly in a natural, professional manner.
- Sunglasses—Should be of neutral color with conservative frame and no contrasting logos. Eyes should be visible through the lenses in order to make eye contact with participants and spectators (e.g., no severe colors or mirrored lenses).
- Hats—Event issues baseball caps or plain white baseball caps (no logos or verbiage) may be worn. Straw panama hats may be worn by both men and women, but the band cannot have any logo or verbiage on it.

Front of House Guidelines

- Eating or smoking is not permitted when working front of house where participants and spectators are.
- No chewing gum or candy is allowed in the front of house area.
- Water bottles are allowed. A bottle of water will be provided at the beginning of each shift for those who do not bring their own.
- The event credential should be worn at all times during the shift and should be kept where it is easily visible. (e.g., outside a zipped jacket if it is cold)

Figure 13.13 Sample Communications Outline.

COMMUNICATIONS OUTLINE
Venue Communication Center
"xyz" Multisport Event

<u>Philosophy</u>

The Venue Communication Center (VCC) is the hub for all <u>operational</u> communications within the venue. The VCC serves the entire event and is the "One-Stop-Shot" for information and communications. It does not handle questions related to competition (Sports Information Desks), Results (Results Room), or the event owner (*fictitious third-party multisport rights holder*).

<u>General Description</u>

The VCC manages communication in support of the event by:

- Monitoring radio transmissions on select channels.
- Receiving and directing calls for on-site venues (*hub of 8 sports/venues*) and off-site venues.
- Being the default/primary reception point for incoming calls.
- Maintaining an event incident log for internal purposes only.
- Escalating appropriate communications to the necessary management personnel.
- Gathering off-site incident reports.
- Monitoring off-site venue operational milestones (e.g., Event Manager arrives at location, competition starts/ends, closing of venue)

In general, the VCC manages and distributes information for the event but the VCC does not make operational decisions.

One of the vital roles of the VCC is informing all other groups that need to know about a given situation. Most often, this will be the Senior Management Team, the medical team, the rights holder, and media team. Key functional areas would also be notified as necessary.

The VCC will utilize a variety of communication means in disseminating information depending upon the content, length, and the number of people involved. They will utilize radio transmission, cell phones, texting, email, and hard line phones, and faxes.

The VCC will work closely with medical staff in tracking medical situations for participants and guests. The medical team will relay to the VCC any information related to medical transports or situations which resulted in an incident report.

<u>Dates/Hours of Operation of VCC</u>

- Fri   15   9:00 am–to 6:00 pm
- Sat   16   9:00 am–6:00 pm
- Sun   17   6:00 am–8:00 pm
- Mon   18   6:00 am–8:00 pm
- Tues   19   6:00 am–1:00 am
- Wed   20   6:00 am–1:00 am
- Thur   21   6:00 am–1:00 am
- Fri   22   6:00 am–1:00 am
- Sat   23   6:00 am–1:00 am
- Sun   24   6:00 am–1:00 am
- Mon   25   6:00 am–1:00 am
- Tues   26   6:00 am–10:00 pm
- Wed   27   6:00 am–10:00 pm
- Thur   28   6:00 am–10:00 pm
- Fri   29   6:00 am–10:00 pm
- Sat   30   9:00 am–5:00 pm
- Sun   31   9:00 am–5:00 pm

<u>Types of Information the VCC will have</u>:

(Event staff should keep VCC apprised of any changes not reflected on the event's internal website):

- Cell phone, fax, and radio contact information
- Checklists
- Venue Lists—including staffing, phone/fax numbers, address, directions, and so on
- Radio Call Sign List
- Directions to venues and all special events organized by the Organizing Committee
- Fast Fact Sheets
- Online maps of local area
- CAD drawings of the venues
- Organizational charts
- Description of functional area responsibilities
- "What If" scenarios that were reviewed in team meetings
- Evacuation plan
- Incident reporting policies and procedures

Event Phone Three

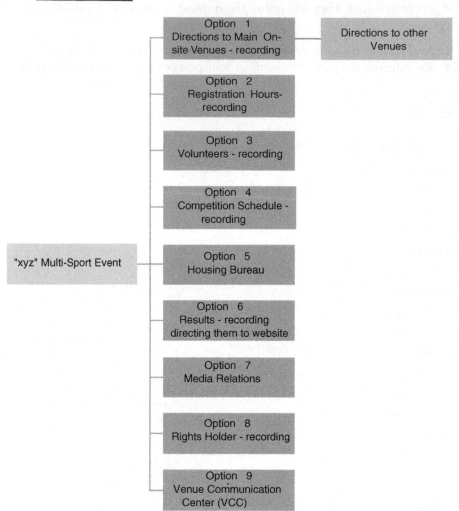

Student Challenges

In this challenge, construct three different planning documents related to the event.

Question 13.1

Draft a planning timeline for an event beginning at least 3 months before the event and encompassing at least eight different functional areas (e.g., logistics, marketing, staffing, entertainment, etc.). Take notes here on the functional areas, the event start date, the tasks for each area, and the number of days out (days before) the event that the task will need to be completed. Using this information, create a version in Excel with the full details as described in this chapter (see Table 13.1, Planning Timeline, for an example).

Question 13.2

Sketch a diagram of the setup of the event's field of play (FOP). Then, using the drawing tool in PowerPoint, create an electronic diagram.

Question 13.3

Create a Fast Facts for the event. Make a list below of the 8–10 information items that should be included on the Fast Facts for the event. Select from this list when completing the final document in Excel.

Information Item #1:

Information Item #2:

Information Item #3:

Information Item #4:

Information Item #5:

Information Item #6:

Information Item #7:

Information Item #8:

Information Item #9:

Information Item #10:

EVENT STAFFING

Colleen McGlone, Heather Lawrence, and Kelley K. Walton

Colleen A. McGlone, Ph.D., is a Professor of Recreation and Sport Management at Coastal Carolina University. She earned her doctorate from the University of New Mexico in Sport Administration in 2005 with a minor in exercise science research. Dr. McGlone's research involves hazing in collegiate athletics, legal aspects of sport and recreation, institutional liability and organizational culture, as well as leadership in sport environments. She has worked with several sport organizations and has been involved in numerous event management endeavors, including founding and implementing nonprofit fun runs, organizing community events, managing sport operations for a nationally ranked National Collegiate Athletic Association (NCAA) baseball team, coordinating media relations for the NCAA regional tournament (men's and women's), as well as coordinating professional conferences. Additionally, she has managed both minor league baseball and minor league hockey events.

Heather Lawrence, Ph.D., is an Associate Professor of Sports Administration and AECOM Professor of Sport Business at Ohio University. She earned her Ph.D. from the University of Florida, and also received bachelor's and master's degrees from Florida. Dr. Lawrence primarily teaches in the area of event and facility management. In addition to her role at Ohio University, she has led event and facility courses in Spain, China, and Dubai. Prior to beginning her academic career, Heather worked in various administrative positions within intercollegiate athletics at Southeastern Louisiana University and the University of Florida. Her sport industry responsibilities have included working in NCAA compliance, facility management and construction/renovation management, event management, and general administration.

Kelley K. Walton, JD, SPHR, is an Instructor for the Department of Sports Administration at Ohio University. She holds a bachelor of science degree from Eastern Michigan University and a juris doctor from Capital University Law School. Prior to joining Ohio University, Ms. Walton served as the Director of Human Resources for the Columbus Blue Jackets of the National Hockey League. She is an Attorney and Consultant specializing in career counseling and human resources consulting in the sport industry. She is the author of *Prepare for Opportunity: A Practical Guide for Applying for a Job in Sports*. Her research interests include best practices in human resources management, legal issues affecting the sport industry, and recruitment and selection in the sport industry. In addition to her role as Instructor, Ms. Walton provides significant administrative support to the Professional Master of Sports Administration program, which is a master of sports administration degree offered in a primarily online format for working sport industry professionals.

The structure of the sport organization responsible for the event will dictate much of what is needed with respect to event staffing. There are some sport organizations that host hundreds of events per year, while others may convene only to host one event every few years. Thus, the organizational structure will impact the staffing needs of the event, the availability of staffing, the role of event managers in staffing decisions, and the resources and expertise available to event managers.

Event managers understand that some level of staffing is needed at all events. While the event manager is responsible for the overall operations of the event, other individuals need to be available to ensure the needs of the participants and spectators are met. The options for staffing events are many. However, figuring out how many workers are needed, where they are needed, and for how long, are at the core of the challenges associated with staffing an event. Event managers can rely on event staffing companies, use local agencies (EMT, police, fire, etc.), hire part time workers, use volunteers or volunteer groups, provide academic credit or practical experience to college students, or use any combination of these. There are advantages and disadvantages to each type of worker that will be discussed in this chapter.

Beyond obtaining event staff, event managers must be skilled in leadership and motivation as they lead their event staff during what are often long events. There are also organizational skills that can help event managers to effectively manage their work teams. Oftentimes the event manager also is responsible for hiring, training, and evaluating the various workers for their specific positions, and needs to know basic employment laws. Leadership, management, and legal aspects in this chapter will be discussed specific to the time period leading up to, and during an event.

Staffing Basics

Knowing who is responsible for what is critical. An event or venue contract will specify, in detail, which entity is responsible for providing staff, which entity decides how much staffing is needed, and who is paying for the staff. Medium to large sports venues often either outsource event staffing or have a pool of workers to pull from to provide staffing services. Thus, the contract might indicate that staff will be scheduled by the venue, but the expense charged to the renter. There are smaller venues, and nontraditional venues, where event managers will need to establish staffing levels and secure personnel independently from the venue. These are pieces of information that event managers must have early in the event process so the budget can be developed accurately and everyone involved can understand the staffing expectations.

Once it is clear whether the facility or the event is providing the staff, then the type and volume of staff need to be determined. The type of staff refers to the various positions that need to be filled during the event. The level of expertise and knowledge needed to fill a position can vary greatly from someone involved in ensuring the restrooms remain stocked to a customer service representative that must be educated on all aspects of the event. The volume of staff will depend on many factors including the type of event, the location, the venue size and type, the anticipated crowd, and the budget. Even if the venue is wholly responsible for staffing, event managers should be aware of, and involved in, the staffing decision making. If the venue does not schedule enough staff to successfully handle the event, event managers will be vicariously at fault for this failure because they should approve all staffing plans.

Types of Staff

Human resources, or the people who work for an organization, can make or break the event. Even if all else goes well, the way staff handle each situation will impact the satisfaction levels of stakeholders (participants, spectators, vendors, sponsors, entertainers, etc.). Think about how a team that has a losing record year after year is still able to fill the stands. It all revolves around creating a positive experience, in which staff is a critical element. To that end, understanding the various roles of the event management staff is important. This section focuses on event day staff since other positions are discussed in other chapters (e.g., volunteer management, ticketing, safety and security, marketing, and sponsorships). The event managers need to treat each event day staff member in a respectful manner regardless of their role, as it will help them envision how they should interact with spectators and participants. It is usually these individuals that are creating an experience with the consumers. If the person giving directions, registering participants, or parking cars is not friendly and professional, it sets the tone for the customer's overall experience at the event.

The Importance of Customer Service

As discussed in Chapter 12—Event Ticketing, the customer is critical to the success of any organization, sport or nonsport. For many sports events, the largest source of revenue is either ticket sales or participant registration fees. The customers that either purchase tickets or participate in the event should feel like their needs are being met before, during, and even after the event.

An organization's customer service philosophy should become a part of the everyday atmosphere. For managers, it is necessary to communicate the customer service expectations and train full-time, part-time, and volunteer workers on those expectations. It is much more expensive for an organization to obtain new customers than it is for the organization to keep their current customers.

There are two categories of workers involved with the event: front of house and back of house. **Front of house** staff is in direct contact with spectators, such as ticket takers, box office personnel, ushers, concessionaires, and merchandise sales people. **Back of house** staff is generally working behind the scenes and has responsibilities, such as setup, teardown, and taking care of a lot of the "nuts and bolts" of making the event happen.

© Shutterstock

Ticket windows are an example of front of house staff.

Front of House Staff

Contact with the front of house staff is the first encounter that spectators have with an event representative. This group can quickly influence a person's experience. Good customer service does not take a lot of effort on the part of staff. It may involve solving a problem for someone or doing something to make the experience more pleasant, such as alleviating lines. Simply interacting with patrons is another way to increase customer service, and it can be as simple as smiling when talking to people. A 2–3 sec interaction with a customer can make a big difference. Front of house staff might ask a child wearing a Patriots #12 jersey how many touchdown passes she thinks Tom Brady is going to throw today, and the child will associate an interest in her with the event for years to come. People want to be treated with respect and treated as individuals. While spectators realize they are one of thousands in attendance, acknowledging them with a simple "Welcome to the game," and "Thanks for coming, see you next time," makes them feel as if they are important, and can go a long way in giving them a memorable experience.

Back of House Staff

Back of house staff does not have the direct interaction with spectators that front of house staff have. However, depending on the event, they could have significant interaction with participants. Participants often turn to the closest event day staff member when they need something. For participant-driven events, that staff member is usually related to the operations of the event. The interaction between the participants and the back of house staff should be as customer service oriented as those taking place between front of house staff and spectators. Back of house staff also have an impact on customer service through the regular performance of their jobs, even when participants or customers do not come in contact with them. The event managers should ensure that back of house staff understand how important they are to creating a memorable, first class event. For example, when they view the event as a whole, it makes sense that it is important the bleachers are wiped down before games, or why a field should be well prepared. As such, event managers must emphasize the role back of house staff in creating an excellent event experience for everyone.

Regardless of whether workers are front of house or back of house, they generally fall into a few categories: part-time employees, volunteers, students/interns, and contracted services. There are advantages and disadvantages of each that are discussed in the following sections.

Part-Time Employees

When event staff is hired, they are most frequently hired as part-time employees based on the nature of events. Since many events only last a short time or only exist during certain seasons, it is difficult to hire many full-time employees. Part-time employment has many pros and cons. Part-time work allows for a greater work force than hiring all full-time people. There are many times when help is needed at peak times and requires a lot of staff, but peak hours may only be 8 hours a week. Part-time employees can get the job done and do not come packaged with the same compensation considerations of full-time employees. In addition, a lot of people like part-time work because it offers a chance to be involved in the event without compromising their other endeavors. Furthermore, part-time employment allows individuals to test the waters of event management to see if it is a viable career option and they can see what other types of opportunities and positions may be associated with event management.

Volunteers

Sports and recreation events often rely on a strong volunteer force. A **volunteer** is typically defined as an individual who takes on a task or duty with no expectation of monetary benefits. In fact, the entire event day staff could be made up of volunteers! Most people volunteer because they support the event

Volunteers are often used for sports events.

or the cause, or because they want to give back to the community or sport organization. Volunteers can help in any area and can be used before, during, and after the event.

Volunteers should be supervised similarly to other employees, but may need closer attention, as they may not be as familiar with all the logistics of the event. Good volunteer training will overcome this potential obstacle. It is also important to remember the event may rely on volunteers, so volunteers should always be treated in a courteous and friendly manner, with their efforts recognized. A thank-you letter, providing event memorabilia, announcing the volunteer group names during the event, providing a thank-you dinner, or having a post-event party may go a long way in letting volunteers know they are appreciated.

The role of volunteers in events is so critical to most events that an entire chapter (see Chapter 16) is dedicated to finding, hiring, and managing volunteers.

Students/Interns

The use of interns is also a way to help staff the event. Usually, student interns are energetic and eager to get involved and help. Interns are students interested in event management looking for experience and it is important to note that they may not fully understand or have the complete skill set to do all of the tasks at hand. They, like volunteers, will need to be trained in the areas they will be assigned to work. When using interns, it is important that they receive an education while they work. This may not be formal education, but they need to gain experience in event operations and should be assigned work tasks that help them meet their goals and that add to their educational foundation. Interns should be asked to do more than basic tasks, and an explanation of why each task is important and how it fits into the overall event operations plan will be beneficial. By utilizing interns, event managers are able to capture and use a specialized work force in a variety of areas (e.g., broadcasting, media relations, merchandise sales). In addition, these interns have knowledge in areas where some volunteers, or even part-time employees, may not be as proficient or skilled. When relying on interns, be prepared to also complete formal evaluations for students earning academic credit for their role with the event.

Contracted Services

In some cases, event managers need to hire specialized services through a contractual agreement. These types of specialized services include, but are not limited to: officials, medical personnel, and vendors. In most cases, these contracted services will be set up as an independent contractor arrangement. **Independent contractors** are people or businesses that provide products or services to another person or business based on the terms of a contract. They do not work on a regular basis as employees do.

Officials

Depending on the type of event, officials may need to be hired. The duties assigned to officials include keeping time; officiating the game; or verifying distance, place, or statistics. Officials may be hired as an employee or an independent contractor. Most officials are paid as contractors who are hired and directly contracted for their services by the event organization or league.

Medical

Event staffing should include a medical emergency plan and staff. Event managers need to make sure staff is trained in emergency first aid and CPR/AED (automated external defibrillators). Medical personnel must also be aware of how to access additional medical assistance from outside the event if needed. Some events will need more medically qualified staff than others.

© Shutterstock

Medical staff are an essential part of most sports events.

In addition, some event insurance policies will require a certain number of qualified medical caregivers on site throughout the event. This will be detailed in the contract.

Vendors

When considering vendors, event managers need to decide which vendors are needed. For example, event managers must choose whether or not to procure their own concessions and merchandise inventory or bring in outside vendors to provide it. Either way, the staffing needs should be fully understood prior to the event. If the event is using vendors, the contract should detail how the area will be staffed and by how many people. In addition, whether the staff will be paid or volunteer, as well as who is responsible for compensation, needs to be addressed. When contracting the services of vendors or setting up vending and concessions, the walk-thru is critical to ensure the venue layout will be able to perform as needed. It can be upsetting to a vendor that needs a power supply to find out there is not an accessible electrical outlet. A careful walk-thru will avoid this and other potential problems.

Another area to keep in mind when vendors are used is to ensure that whatever equipment will be provided by the venue is detailed in the rental contract, and that work orders are done well in advance to ensure that all equipment is available and on-site at the designated time. If vendors are provided by the venue, event managers need to make sure there is an understanding of who is responsible for staffing, providing the merchandise and food, paying the staff, and understanding how any funds raised through sales will be distributed.

All of the various types of event day staff need their supervisors to provide leadership throughout the event. Event managers will develop their own leadership styles with experience, but there are some simple tips that will help to create a work environment where staffs feel valued.

Staffing Numbers and Cost

There are no clear-cut formulas that apply to all events related to the number of staff needed. As discussed throughout this text, communicating with other event managers that have hosted the event previously is a good strategy to obtain information about expected crowd behavior and staffing needs. All events have a **baseline staffing number**. This number takes into account the minimum number of staff required to accomplish the management of the event. For example, an arena may have eight entrances, but the event could occur with only two of those doors open for ticket taking, one near each parking area. This baseline number of staff is where all staffing plans begin, and then are built from there.

Once information on the expected behavior and size of the crowd is obtained, event managers can begin to add staff to the baseline numbers. First and foremost, staffing numbers must be adequate to ensure the safety of the crowd. Second, there needs to be adequate staff so that spectator and/or participant flow is good, even during the busiest times. Finally, the staffing plan must stay within the established budget, while also providing for the previously mentioned items.

Anticipating the Crowd

Even with proper research, there are some events for which the number of expected spectators and participants are very difficult to predict. Participant-driven events that accept event day registrations, as well as spectator events with event day ticket sales, make it difficult to predict the exact number of participants/spectators until the day of the event. By that time, it is too late to make adjustments to staff, so staffing levels need to be established with high participation and/or ticket sales in mind. Being overstaffed is better than being understaffed. For events in nontraditional venues, participant numbers can be capped based on the number of people that the facility can accommodate, and participants turned away if/when that number is reached. Although this strategy helps control participant numbers, it does not solve the problem of the number of spectators, and it takes revenue away from the event.

Even with proper planning, there are times when an event may be understaffed based on a tremendous spectator turnout, and event managers must recognize it immediately when they are in an understaffed situation. If an event is understaffed, workers will need to be repositioned during the event. For example, registration staff may normally be done working once registration is finished, but they could be asked to help work another area once registration is closed if they are needed. Other workers in less critical areas such as ushering might be asked to cover two sections while one person is moved to assist at the entrance gates. Postevent workers should also be called in early, and police, if they are willing, can help cover certain areas. This can become a serious problem, since many venues are only certified to hold a certain number of people by the local fire marshal. Safety is important all of the time, but with an understaffed event, it is even more critical that event managers are aware of everything going on at the event in case an incident occurs, due to crowd size, that puts people at risk. As with all other times during the event, safety is the first priority.

Safety

Event managers need to understand the safety and security needs of the event, which are discussed in detail in Chapter 16, Event Safety and Security. This includes areas outside the venue as well as inside, and involves positions ranging from security at venue entrances, to crowd managers, to EMTs. Even though some positions will have direct responsibility for safety and security, all those working the event can play a role in keeping the event safe and secure. The event managers should emphasize this with all staff, and provide detailed information on how to identify potential issues, report problems, and respond to guests.

There are only two areas in event day staffing in which industry safety standards exist: ticket taking and crowd management. Crowd management is directly related to safety and will be discussed here. Within the seating bowl in traditional venues, or the spectator area in nontraditional venues, industry standards call for one trained crowd manager for every 250 occupants (City of Cincinnati Task Force on Crowd Control and Safety, 1980). A **trained crowd manager** is defined as someone who has been educated in crowd management techniques, the responsibilities of his or her job, as well as emergency procedures. Not only this guideline that will help to ensure a safe event, but if something were to happen where the event managers had to legally defend their staffing numbers, this is considered adequate for a typical spectator-driven event. Common sense must also prevail. The physical layout of the facility, along with the type of event and anticipated crowd, will help to dictate the number of trained crowd managers needed. An event that serves alcohol, anticipates patrons drinking prior to the event, or has a history of aggressive patrons, needs to increase the number of trained crowd managers.

Unfortunately, numbers of staff in other positions are not as clear-cut. Through experience and communication with other event and facility managers, staffing levels can be established. It is clear that it is always better to be safe than sorry. Even if it costs a bit more, providing adequate staff to ensure the safety of all is critical.

Flow

The movement of spectators through the facility in an orderly and efficient manner requires that event managers understand peak times and have staffed those areas appropriately. **Peak times** are periods in which specific areas will have a surge in spectator/participant traffic. For example, sports that have a halftime will see a rush to concessions during this time. For halftime concessions, workers can be moved from other positions to the concession stands to help. Being prepared for peak times that will occur in the parking lots, participant registration, ticket sales, entry gates, seating areas, merchandise areas, and concessions is part of understanding the staffing needs of the event.

As indicated above, there is an industry standard for ticket taking ratios, and adhering to this ratio can help manage flow at the event entrances. For every 1,000 ticket holders, one ticket taker should be employed (City of Cincinnati Task Force on Crowd Control and Safety, 1980). Beyond just knowing how many tickets were sold, the distribution of tickets will help to ensure ticket takers are placed at the appropriate entrances to meet this ratio. For example, at a regular season college football game, the gates may open 2 hours before the game, but from experience the event managers know that the flow of fans will peak 30 min before kick-off until 15 min into the game. In this scenario, the event managers can staff the gate with one ticket taker from the time the gates open to 45 min before the game, and then increase staffing to the appropriate level given the number of tickets sold from 45 min before the game to 30 min into the game. Strategies for all positions that incorporate the peak and nonpeak times will keep patrons moving efficiently throughout the event.

One strategy to prepare for peak times is to use jump teams. As discussed in the sidebar, **jump teams** consist of event day workers that are available to fill in at a variety of staffing positions throughout the event day. They may be used during peak times, or at other areas when it is recognized that more help is needed. Being prepared for both peak and nonpeak times will keep the flow of the event smooth and the spectators and/or participants content.

Jump Teams!

Michelle Wells, Visiting Instructor of Sport Studies, Guilford College

One of my previous jobs in sports was working for New York Road Runners (NYRR) as the Director of Event Development and Production. NYRR is a nonprofit organization that promotes long-distance running and puts on over 55 road races each year. One of their biggest races (after the ING New York City Marathon) is the NYC Half Marathon presented by Nike.

The inaugural NYC Half Marathon presented by Nike was held in 2006 and had over 10,000 runners. One of the areas I managed at that time was the Volunteers Department. Because this was a new event on a new course, we wanted to make sure we were prepared to address any unexpected staffing needs that may have come up during the race. One of the managers in the volunteer department, Steve Boland, came up with the idea to create what he termed "jump teams" for the event. We created a team for each of the three main areas of the race course—Central Park, Midtown, and Downtown—and staged them in those areas. In the volunteer recruitment information, we assigned 10 slots per jump team, anticipating that seven people would show up on race day. The description posted on the volunteer section of the NYRR Website explained the possible responsibilities of the shift, where volunteers would check in on race day, and the fact that they could end their day at another area of the event.

During meetings, we communicated to other staff that we had formed these jump teams. If a location had a shortage of volunteers at their site or needed someone to perform a previously unanticipated task, the area would let the volunteer managers know how many people they needed, and jump team members would be deployed to that location. The jump team members were given a map that showed the specific locations of the cross streets, subway lines, mile markers, fluid stations, medical stations, entertainment zones, and so forth. If they were directed to go to fluid station #2, for example, they knew where they would be going. Steve had secured a van and driver to transport jump team members to locations that were outside of a reasonable walking distance. The van had an "official vehicle placard" in the window, as other race vehicles did, to make it easier for the van to get through areas near the race course. Being in New York City also provided the possibility of utilizing the subway system if necessary.

▶

These teams were deployed to various areas that needed help, and some were even redeployed to a second area after completing their tasks. The volunteer managers were given jump team lists for all of the areas, and could sign out any of those volunteers no matter where they started or ended their day. For volunteers who liked the idea of being on the go and "fighting fires," this position was appealing and provided something a little different from the usual roles. More importantly for the event, they helped alleviate potential problems that could have developed due to needing additional staff in some areas.

Budget

Deciding upon staffing numbers and paying for event staff is a major undertaking for event managers. Managers that have experience with a lot of events are very good at estimating staffing needs accurately, based on the type of event which allows for the most efficient use of the budget. For new event managers, seeking advice from those with experience will prove worthwhile when trying to determine staffing numbers and preserve the available budget.

The budget number can vary widely, even for specific dates in a traveling event. The hourly rate that a traveling event will pay for part-time staff in New York City will likely be different than the rate it would pay for hourly staff in a city the size of Columbus, Ohio, for example. Federal and state minimum wage requirements will apply, and event managers should become familiar with the rate of pay considered fair in their locale.

Cost restraints will almost certainly come into play with any staffing plan. The balance between providing enough staff to accomplish keeping people safe and providing good flow must be balanced with what the budget can handle. As discussed in Chapter 5, Event Budget, the cost of staff can add up quickly—whether part time or full time. The University of Florida incurs event day costs for home football games of about $250,000 (DiRocco, 2009). This includes security, ticket taking, ushers, concession workers, medical support, clean-up, and other game day services (DiRocco, 2009). Luckily for Florida, their revenue far exceeds their costs associated with home football games. However, for many events, staffing costs can eat up a majority of the revenue, or even exceed revenue generated.

Hiring, Firing, and the Law

Successful events require good employees. Finding and keeping them is not easy, but with the right plan and right execution, it can be done. Event managers acquire the best people for the job by focusing on three key elements: recruiting, selection, and hiring. It sounds simple, but it is not. It can be challenging to hire an event staff because each event is different that requires diverse skill sets for a variety of tasks.

Two tips for hiring event staff are to find people who have positive attitudes and find people with whom you can create a "win–win" situation. People with positive attitudes typically have natural customer service skills that will be enhanced with your training. They also are easy to work with in relation to work schedules and working in groups. "Win–win" situations are those that both sides get something positive out of the situation. If you hire someone looking to gain experience, they will take away more than just a paycheck by working the event.

Recruiting, screening, training, evaluation, and termination are all aspects of staff management that event managers may find themselves responsible for. Legal issues also play a role in how staff is managed, and some of the relevant legal issues associated with hiring and management are also discussed here.

Recruitment/Advertising

When considering recruitment for event day staff, getting an early start on recruiting is optimal. Once event managers know what roles need to be filled, they will be able to identify where to recruit. Some simple potential staffing sources are often overlooked. For instance, the local high school ROTC unit might be a great resource for a local 5K run for traffic control. There are many high school groups that are required to do community service and many are willing to assist local events when given enough lead time to organize themselves. Another place to recruit game day workers is local colleges. Again, different academic majors and groups may need to gain experience in several areas related to their course of study. Church and local community groups (e.g., women's clubs, Kiwanis chapters, retirement groups) are also good sources for staffing. Other examples of possible recruitment sources include the event website, social media, newsletters/websites of partner organizations, and community groups that are associated with the event.

When going to local groups is not enough, or if more specialized help is needed, a job announcement may be very beneficial. A written announcement should be prepared based on the job description and skills needed. Be careful not to leave the description or announcement so broad that the event gets more people who are not qualified than those who are. On the other hand, being too specific may result in not getting any interest. A good job description/announcement will contain the essential skills needed and the minimum qualifications for the position to be filled. For any position requiring training or additional certifications, the requirements should be stated in the posting.

Once the position announcement is written, a decision on where to post it needs to be made. In today's digital age, there are more options than just the local newspaper. If looking for specific skills, sending it to a profession-specific electronic listserv or bulletin board will disseminate the information to the targeted group. If the skill sets are less specific, placing the advertisement in online community news publications, which many cities offer for free or a minimal charge, sending a press release to local television and radio stations, and asking current employees to help get the word out about staff needs, are all options to consider.

Screening

Depending on the size and scope of the event, the selection process may be simple or complex. In either case, selection of staff may involve one or more of the following components:

1. The applicant filling out an application that includes background information and previous employment, and references if desired.
2. Conducting a personal interview (either in person or on the phone).
3. Conducting a background investigation (a criminal background investigation is particularly important when working with children, the elderly, or the disabled and a credit background investigation is particularly important when employees will be dealing with cash or credit card payments).
4. In some situations, having the applicant perform or display their skills by completing some type of performance test.

There are a variety of employment laws that can come into play during the screening process. Many are mentioned in the following section, but human resource professionals and attorneys can provide more detailed legal information specific to hiring.

Training

Training sessions should be built into the event schedule for event staff. Training will vary for each position, because the job functions vary. Every employee needs to know the details of the tasks they will be doing, regardless if it is providing security, taking tickets, ushering, directing traffic, or working in the media center. Each area will have a different set of requirements and may require different use of equipment. Staff in each area should be given directions and training prior to the event getting underway.

Staff will feel more comfortable in their roles if they receive adequate training.

The training should ideally include verbal and written instruction as well as on-site practice. Training and skills that staff receives helps each staff member grow, shows that the event managers care about them, and helps to ensure a successful event. In many cases, it will be necessary to pay for staff training time. This is often overlooked in the event budget and can be a significant cost.

During training, staffs need to be trained on basic functions of the organization. This may include understanding the mission of the organization and the event, understanding how the timekeeping system works (e.g., time cards, time clocks), and the issuance of keys, uniforms, and equipment as needed. Event managers should strive to provide uniforms that staff is proud to wear, but still are obvious that they are associated with an event worker. It is important to provide both men's and women's sizes in uniforms. Organizations do not require men to wear uniforms sized and cut for women, so women should not have to wear men's sized uniforms. It is common for event managers to assume that because men's shirts will also fit women, it is okay to only provide men's sizes. All workers feel better when they are proud and confident in their uniforms, and having shirts that fit well is part of that, so a variety of sizes for both genders should be available for workers.

Other areas in which training is needed include when and how shift changes occur, how to deal with difficult customers (and employees), and what to do if an issue arises that requires security. Moreover, each staff person should know what is to be done in case of a medical emergency, security emergency, or other emergent problem that requires managerial response. A walk-thru should be scheduled to familiarize them with the area, how it will be set up for the event, and their specific location. This will be beneficial when spectators ask for directions or where something is located; all staff should at least be able to point them in the right direction and know where to report to on the event day.

Oftentimes, staff members will require training in order to perform various duties, or they may require refresher training. This could range from updating or acquiring new technological skills, such as new video editing equipment or timing devices, to updating CPR/AED certifications. Other areas, such as security, may require on-site training to familiarize them with the flow of the event, the location of cameras, alcohol policies, and the command center. Many large events require advanced training in managerial concepts or in areas that lead to certification. Examples of these include pyrotechnic certification for firework shows, athletic training, security, crime prevention, and certifications offered by the International Association of Venue Managers (IAVM).

Evaluation

Evaluation of performance is an important aspect of event management, but is sometimes overlooked in the grand scheme of the event. All event staff should be evaluated on overall performance based on the job description. Best practices for evaluations dictate that they should be performed privately in a supportive and collegial way. Time should be set aside to discuss the areas of performance that may need improvement, as well as strengths in performance. In terms of event staff, the focus should be on problems and opportunities (Prosser & Rutledge, 2003). This does not have to take a long time, but should be done in a way that demonstrates event managers' cares about employees. Event day staff should also be given the opportunity to evaluate event managers and the overall operations of the event. These individuals are closer to the action than event managers, and can provide important feedback on many aspects of operations. This can be used to improve the event in the future.

Termination

When considering terminating event staff, event managers need to keep the overall picture in mind. Retaining staff is less costly over time than having to obtain and train new staff. Therefore, if a staff member or volunteer is performing unsatisfactorily, the event manager needs to decide if it is best to try and retrain or remotivate an individual in order to retain the person. A person may need to be let go or dismissed from duties for a variety of reasons, including not performing duties in a professional manner or not completing the assigned tasks. While it is no fun to terminate an employee, it is often what is best for the event and organization. In terminating an employee, make sure the process is in compliance with company policies and state/federal laws. Be fair, be clear, and keep in mind that this is likely a difficult situation for the employee. Terminations are difficult, but if the employee is treated with respect, it can be managed well.

Legal Issues

Although it is outside the scope of this chapter and book to go into detail about all the employment laws that may affect an event, there are a few basic laws, legal concepts, and situations that event managers that hire event day staff need to be informed of. In addition to these, event managers should refer to Chapter 3, Event Contracts, for more information on contract law.

Americans with Disabilities Act

The Americans with Disabilities Act (ADA) prohibits private employers, state and local governments, employment agencies, and labor unions from discriminating against qualified individuals with disabilities in job application procedures, hiring, firing, advancement, compensation, job training, and other terms, conditions, and privileges of employment. The ADA covers employers with 15 or more employees, including state and local governments. In addition to applications in labor law, ADA has a variety of stipulations related to equal access to facilities for people with disabilities (United States Department of Justice, n.d.).

Civil Rights Act of 1964

This act is comprehensive legislation that prohibits discrimination. The goal of the act is to eliminate discriminatory practices in employment and places of public accommodation (Moorman, 2007). It provides the framework regarding many employment laws, including sexual harassment, and discrimination based on race, color, religion, sex (gender), or national origin under Title VII.

Fair Labor Standards Act

Event managers should familiarize themselves with the Fair Labor Standards Act (FLSA), which provides regulations for managing overtime and minimum wage requirements as well as restricts the employment of child workers. "Child labor provisions under FLSA are designed to protect the educational opportunities of youth and prohibit their employment in jobs that are detrimental to their health and safety. FLSA restricts the hours that youth under 16 years of age can work and lists hazardous occupations too dangerous for young workers to perform" (United States Department of Labor, n.d., p. 1). There may also be related state laws on using teenagers for labor purposes, as some have more restrictive policies.

Section 13(a)(3) provides an exemption from the minimum wage and overtime provisions of the FLSA for "any employee employed by an establishment which is an amusement or recreational establishment, if (A) it does not operate for more than seven months in any calendar year, or (B) during the preceding calendar year, its average receipts for any six months of such year were not more than 33-1/3 per centum of its average receipts for the other six months of such year" (United States Department of Labor, 2008, p. 3.)

Another important note concerning the FLSA is the exemption for Seasonal Amusement or Recreational Establishments under the FLSA. The FLSA requires employees in the United States to be paid at least the federal minimum wage and overtime after 40 hours of work has been completed in a standard workweek. The act does provide some provisions for seasonal and recreational establishments and their employees in certain occupations. Specifically, Section 13(a)(3) provides an exemption from minimum wage and overtime provisions of the FLSA for "any employee employed by an establishment which is an amusement or recreational establishment, if it does not operate for more than seven months in any calendar year or during the preceding calendar year, its average receipts for any six months of such year were not more than 33 1/3% of its average receipts for the other six months of such year" (United States Department of Labor, 2008). Some states may have more stringent restrictions so it is important to know that when dealing with State and Federal laws that conflict, the employer must comply with the most stringent provisions set by the state or federal statutes. It is a good idea for managers to be familiar with the employment laws in each state in which their company operates and relevant federal employment laws like the FLSA.

It is important for event managers to be aware of the legal issues surrounding the various types of people who are working an event. There have been several lawsuits brought against sport and nonsport organizations regarding interns and volunteers. In 2014, in *Chen v. Major League Baseball (MLB)*, a U.S. District Court in New York dismissed a case against MLB that was brought by a group of volunteers claiming FLSA violations at a MLB All Star Game.

The main issue argued in the case was not whether the group of volunteers were deemed "employees," which would require certain wage and hour protections. Rather, the case focused on whether the Fan Fest involved was deemed an amusement or recreational establishment that operates for less than 8 months, which has certain exceptions from overtime/minimum wage FLSA requirements. The court determined that the FanFest involved was subject to the exception and therefore not subject to minimum wage requirements. While MLB won that case, there is still some uncertainty surrounding interns and volunteers involved with sporting events. It is important to note that this case was at the trial court level and therefore further appeals may follow.

There was a recent nonsport related case involving interns that has many sport organizations reviewing their intern policies. In short, in 2013, Fox-Searchlight films had unpaid interns working on a movie called *Black Swan*. The interns later sued for compensation under the FLSA arguing that they should have been deemed employees and not interns for the type of work they were doing. The court sided with the plaintiffs (the interns) in initial proceedings and has allowed the case to continue stating that the persons working in these positions are "employees" as defined under the FLSA. This will likely be litigated further in the coming years, but for now, it is important for employers to take note that there are important criteria to consider when determining whether a person falls under the unpaid intern category.

There are six criteria that must be applied when determining whether a person is an unpaid intern:

1. The internship is similar to training which would be given in an educational environment.
2. The internship experience is for the benefit of the intern.
3. The intern does not displace regular employees, but works under close supervision of existing staff.
4. The employer that provides the training derives no immediate advantage from the activities of the intern; and on occasion its operations may actually be impeded.
5. The intern is not necessarily entitled to a job at the conclusion of the internship.
6. The employer and the intern understand that the intern is not entitled to wages for the time spent in the internship.

If all of the factors listed above are met, an employment relationship does not exist under the FLSA and therefore minimum wage and overtime provisions do not apply.

As for paid internships, regardless of the title, those persons are employees and will have the same protections as any other employee would under the FLSA.

It is important to understand that whether a person involved with an event is deemed an intern or a volunteer is not just about what the event wants to call that position. It is about the legal definitions of those terms. An organization cannot just deem everyone volunteers to make sure that they are not required to pay people. There are clear criteria to consider when determining a person's employment or intern status.

The most important thing for event managers to be aware is that there are legal issues surrounding the hiring of interns and volunteers. So far, most challenges to sport organizations have been in their favor due to the amusement or recreational establishment exceptions to the FLSA. The legal landscape is ever changing and should be monitored. Event managers should rely on company policies and legal counsel to minimize legal risk.

Occupational Safety and Health Administration

The Occupational Safety and Health Administration (OSHA) outlines the specific conduct that is required to ensure that a safe work environment is being maintained. There are several areas in which event managers need to be aware of OSHA standards, including noise levels, chemical use, and dealing with blood-borne pathogens.

Volunteer Protection Act of 1997

When volunteers provide their services they may unknowingly be exposing themselves to the risk of being sued or having a legal claim filed against them. Furthermore, event managers need to understand that a sport organization or event can be held liable for not only its own actions but the actions of volunteers, known as **vicarious liability**. When volunteers get sued it not only threatens the ability to put on events but also increases the cost of insurance that accompanies many events. Due to the concerns over the potential legal risk to volunteers, in 1997 the Volunteer Protection Act (VPA) was signed into law.

This act does not completely exempt volunteers from liability and this act does not apply to all volunteers. It applies only to those volunteering for a nonprofit organization, school, or other government agency. However, it does provide some basic protections. In order for a volunteer to be protected under the VPA, the volunteer must be:

- Volunteering for a nonprofit, school, or other government agency
- Acting in the scope of their volunteer duties AND
- Be negligent or accused of negligence (not acting with care that a reasonable person would under the circumstances) (ChangeLabSolutions, 2010).

It is important to note the VPA only applies to unpaid volunteers of a nonprofit, school, or government agency against the clam of negligence and does not provide immunity for gross negligence, misconduct, or indifference. It is also important to understand the VPA will not stop volunteers from being named in a lawsuit so does not prohibit lawsuits against a nonprofit organization or limit the liability of nonprofit organizations for harm caused by volunteers. It is also important to understand while the VPA does offer some limited protection against simple negligence, it does not negate the need for organizations and to have liability insurance.

Worker's Compensation

Worker's Compensation is a series of laws aimed to protect injured workers. These laws provide the framework to deal with an employee that gets injured on the job to ensure he or she receives appropriate care and treatment.

Sexual Harassment

Sexual harassment is a form of sex discrimination that violates Title VII of the Civil Rights Act of 1964. It states:

> *Unwelcome sexual advances, requests for sexual favors, and other verbal or physical conduct of a sexual nature constitute sexual harassment when this conduct explicitly or implicitly affects an individual's employment, unreasonably interferes with an individual's work performance, or creates an intimidating, hostile, or offensive work environment (United States Equal Employment Opportunity Commission, n.d., 2).*

It is important to include sexual harassment training for all employees. Training provides guidelines for employees both in how to act and how to report a sexual harassment incident. Training can help limit company liability and, more importantly, provide a safe work environment. Interns and volunteers are not protected against harassment under Title VII. That does not mean the organization should allow or create an environment where harassment exists for these groups. It simply means that event managers, and other leaders within the organization, should be aware of their responsibilities and the differences between employees and volunteers as far as training needs.

Labor Unions

Some areas of the country have a strong union presence, which impacts all types of events and facilities. A **labor union** is a group formed with the goal of protecting the members' with respect to wages and working conditions. If union labor is involved in the facility, event mangers need to be familiar with the collective bargaining agreement and any wage and/or hour implications on an event. For instance, many unions specify the number of workers needed to load in a certain type of event, while others have strict rules on how many hours union employees can work, or how much of a break is needed between shifts. Using union labor for the setup and teardown of an event is not necessarily better or worse than nonunion labor. However, it can be different, as event managers will lack some of the control they are used to and would like to have when union employees are working.

Event managers need to understand that the local labor unions and their practices will match up with the **National Labor Relations Act**. This law restricts an employer's ability to interfere with employees in the execution of their job duties by offering coercive incentive such as higher pay, better work conditions, or a more comprehensive benefits package in order to sway an employee away from joining a union (National Labor Relations Board, n.d.). Unions are restricted in interfering with organizations by trying to influence personnel decisions such as who to hire, promote, or fire.

As indicated, the concepts addressed are specific to areas that commonly involve aspects of event managers' jobs. There are certainly other legal issues that human resources departments deal with on a regular basis. Event managers that are solely responsible for human resources need to obtain additional information from a qualified professional.

Leadership and Management

Leading a team of event day staff throughout a sport season or for a single event can be more difficult than it seems. With all of the other responsibilities event managers have related to the event, providing quality leadership to event day workers is often not a priority. However, an investment in creating a positive work atmosphere can go a long way to increase overall morale of the group, which will translate into better customer service.

Work Teams

There will likely be some event day workers that exhibit exceptional leadership potential early in the hiring process. Delegating some of the management of event day workers to these people can lessen the load for the event managers, as well as help these exceptional workers to develop further. For example, event managers might choose to have a position called Director of Ticket Takers. The Director of Ticket Takers then becomes responsible for the ticket-taking work team using this strategy. This individual can also schedule ticket takers, provide supervision throughout the event, and respond to customer concerns more quickly than the event managers might be able to do.

Motivation

People have a variety of motivations as to why they might work a sports event. Some may be there exclusively for the paycheck, while others are there because they care deeply about contributing to the success of the event or being a contributing member of the community. These reasons for being there will impact the way event managers should interact with individuals. No motivational strategies will directly result in better performance from all employees, but the goal of motivational strategies is to create an environment that is positive and brings out the best in event day staff.

Event managers need to understand these different motivations and use a variety of strategies to reach as many event day workers as possible. Some examples of ways to create a climate of motivation include:

The Environment

- Provide a nice area for workers with snacks, water, and chairs.
- Make sure worker areas are clean and well kept.
- Ensure staffs have ample time to use the restroom and take breaks.
- Provide meals during long shifts or water during shorter shifts.
- Postcommunications near the staff entry doors or in the area where snacks are offered.

Swag/Gifts

- Purchase T-shirts or other gear as gifts for workers.
- If there is a sponsor give-away, purchase/request extras for event day staff.
- If it is a recurring event, provide tickets to employees and their families for those games they are not working.

Recognition

- Implement "Employee of the Game" or "Employee of the Month" type recognition occasions.
- "Catch" people doing things well and congratulate them at staff meetings.
- Send thank you notes to home addresses of workers to ensure their families also know they are appreciated for the work they do at the event.
- Especially for volunteer groups, include a "thank you" public address (P.A.) read during the event. It will provide good community recognition for their efforts.

Treatmentt

- The "golden rule" applies here: "Do unto others as you would have them do unto you."

There are volumes of published management theory, but in event management, a few simple acts will go a long way in motivating much of the event day staff. Sport is different than other industries because people generally have an emotional attachment to the event. Event managers can use this emotional attachment to their advantage with little cost to the organization. Unsold tickets, sponsor freebies, and treating people well can create an energetic work environment where the event day staffs look forward to getting to work and feel like part of the team.

Game Day Organization

No matter how much planning is put into an event, plans cannot be properly executed without people. People are the backbone of an event and what allow the carefully thought out plans to be fully executed. Sometimes, inexperienced event managers can overlook this fact. Again, many of the people working an event will not be involved in the detailed planning. What is common knowledge to the event managers may be brand new information to the staff. This is why communication is critical.

Call time is the time that staff is expected to be on-site, signed in, and ready to go to work. Call times for events will vary. Generally, events and venues want their staff at their stations and ready to go at least 30 min before doors open. Working backward, this often means that staff members have to arrive at least an hour-and-a-half before the event time. For many events, a call time meeting occurs for all staff. If there is a call time meeting, the call time will be even earlier. During the **call time meeting** (see Sample Call Time Meeting Agenda box), event managers review general information about the event, key issues they foresee that might come up and discuss how to handle the issues, and answer any questions workers have. Topics that might be discussed include such things as:

- It is a big game, and if the home team wins the fans may try to rush the court or field.
- How to handle ADA special seating requests.
- Counterfeit tickets are being sold on eBay, and how to tell what a counterfeit ticket looks like.

This is also a good time to hand out the fast facts and review it with everyone. There should be plenty of time allotted to answer questions from staff. All staff needing uniforms will also receive them at this time. Event managers can address what will happen at the end of the shift or end of the event day. For example, they need to know whether they are supposed to return to an area to check out from their shift on their own, or if event managers will come to their area to release them when their shift is over. Information on whether or not to return uniforms and any specific postevent information is also provided during the call time meeting.

Call time meetings are critical to conveying event specific details to working staff and volunteers.

Courtesy of David Pierce

As with any position, it is important that staff know what they will be doing. People should have a good understanding of what is expected of them on event day. Event managers should write up what each general area is responsible for, as well as review the specific positions that people may hold on that day. For example, ushers should help people find their seat, answer customer questions, and ensure that everyone admitted to their area has a ticket for that section. Clarify the name of the supervisory contact for each area in case a worker has questions, needs a restroom break, or other assistance. Ideally, supervisors should be at the call time meeting so that staff can see and be able to recognize them.

To ensure that the call time meeting runs smoothly and that all event day staff is aware of their responsibilities takes a lot of preparation and planning on the part of event managers. During the event, event mangers should regularly check in with all event day staff to ascertain if they need anything. Providing water, food, and breaks to staff working long shifts will help to keep their energy level high and motivation to work strong. Event day staff should be released as soon as they are no longer needed at their positions. Not only will releasing people save the organization money, but event staff will be frustrated if they are working an area where they are not contributing to the operations of the event. For instance, parking workers may arrive earlier than other staff, and should be released shortly after the event begins. There is no reason to have workers guard parking lots after the vast majority of spectators are parked and inside the venue. There may be a few people that sneak in and are able to park for free with unguarded parking lots. However, it is still cheaper for a few folks to park for free than to pay multiple parking guards.

Leading and managing staff on the event day can be both challenging and fun. Event managers have the opportunity to create good memories and experiences for event staff, just as event staff create memories for spectators and participants. Taking care of event day staff and treating them well does not take much effort, but will reap great rewards in the quality of work the event staff will provide during the event.

Sample Call Time Meeting Agenda

The following is a sample call time meeting agenda for a college softball tournament. If the first game of the day is at 11:00 a.m. and the gates open at 10:00 a.m., this meeting would take place from 9:00 a.m. to 9:20 a.m., with all staff in place at 9:30 a.m.

1. General
    A. Review of schedule.
    B. The officials are the only ones that can call a weather delay/cancellation.
    C. All event staff will receive a meal voucher.
    D. Fast Facts distribution.
    E. CUSTOMER SERVICE IS KEY!
2. Facility
    A. Fields Prep Teams will work between EVERY game.
    B. ADA seating is available in Sections 10, 12, and 14, and extra companion chairs are in the concessions area.
3. Tickets
    A. Spectators must have a ticket. All tickets available at entrance gate.
    B. Tickets are torn at main entrance.
    C. All tickets are reserved seating.
    D. There are no pass-outs (people cannot leave and return on one ticket).
    E. In the event of a cancellation, tickets will be good for the rescheduled game.
4. Programs
    A. Programs are available from the entrance gate ticket area.
5. Credentials
    A. All those entering the field of play must have a credential (no parents allowed on the field).
    B. Example of what credentials look like.

6. Parking
   A. Parking is $5 and is collected as fans enter the lot.
   B. Team buses can park for free. We are expecting approximately 6 buses.
   C. Officials and event day staff (with the parking pass I sent ahead of time) do not have to pay.
   D. Example of what parking passes for teams and officials look like.
7. Safety/Security
   A. City Police are on-site and available if you need help with spectators.
   B. Beer is being sold, so beware of intoxicated spectators. Sales will end during the 5th inning of the last game of the day.
   C. EMTs and ambulances are on-site and are located along the right field fence of Field #1 and Field #3.
   D. Fans must act respectful at all times (police will help enforce this).
   E. In an emergency, listen to the P.A. for instructions.
8. Marketing
   A. There are no promotional contests today.
9. Media
   A. All media should be directed to the press box.
   B. The games are live on FM 99.9.
   C. No television coverage.
10. Concessions
    A. Located in the middle of the complex.
11. Merchandise
    A. Located at the entrance gate.
12. Hospitality
    A. Coaches' hospitality is under the tent by Field #1.
    B. Athlete hospitality is located in each dugout.
13. Other issues for discussion?

Staff Positions

Helping all event day staff to understand their roles during the event is the responsibility of the event managers. Many times, it is a lack of communication that results in people underperforming their jobs, as opposed to them being unable to complete the required tasks. Developing simple job descriptions will help event managers to organize their staffing plan, and also help them to communicate with the event day staff about what their responsibilities entail. Some event day staffing positions require more skills than others, but all should know what is expected of them. Job descriptions should be specific to the event. For example, a police officer at a youth soccer tournament will have a very different role than a police officer at an NBA All-Star Game. The following information was compiled to help event managers in the development of their own job descriptions for event day staff.

Professional Staff

Medical Director: A medical director is often required by the rights holders of an event. Sometimes it is part of the sanctioning requirements, and other times it might be tied into insurance requirements for liability protection. The primary duty of a medical director is to plan for medical coverage for participants, spectators, and staff. This includes arranging for how medical care will be accessed and how care will be given. This person will be intimately involved in all risk management plans, emergency preparedness plans, and emergency responses.

Athletic Trainer: Athletic trainers conduct initial assessments of injuries or illnesses to determine whether athletes should be referred to physicians for diagnosis and treatment. Athletic trainers should be present at most athletic events. Often, elite-level teams and athletes will bring their own athletic trainers to the competition site. For other events, the event managers should work to contract with local athletic trainers to cover the event. Often, athletic trainers are able to direct injured athletes as to whether or not their injuries require emergency care, or if they can seek medical care from their primary care physicians when they return home.

Security (Police, Agency): Event security personnel typically provide a variety of duties including crowd management, security scanning, door monitoring, and protecting access points and barricaded areas. Furthermore, security officers assist with customer relations by providing patrols, assisting with compliance and enforcement of alcohol policies, and helping to direct traffic pre- and postevent.

Video Board/Audio: The video board operator and/or audio editor develops, records, produces, and edits programs, features, and shows imaging. They also might operate the control panel of the radio station during live and taped broadcasts, and other times as required.

Website Design: The Web designer creates and designs the look and feel, graphic elements, page layout, and navigational templates for multiple types of sites, products, and services. This individual helps to shape the visual direction for online sites, products, templates, and graphic elements.

Video Streaming: Those working in video streaming must have specialized technical knowledge. Video streaming involves recording an event using specialized video equipment and converting it into a digital and electronic format for viewing over the Internet.

Nonprofessional Staff

Ticket Taker: The main responsibility of a ticket taker is to ensure that no one is admitted to an event without permission, either by showing proof of paid admission or event credentials. This person may also assist in ticket sales and customer relations.

Usher: Ushers assist patrons by performing duties such as collecting admission tickets and passes from patrons, assisting in finding seats, searching for lost articles, and locating such facilities as rest rooms and telephones.

T-shirt Security: Patrols assigned to monitor an area on foot, or in motor vehicles, as assigned, to ensure personal, building, and equipment security. Informs and warns violators of rule infractions, such as loitering, smoking, or carrying forbidden articles.

Concessions: Concession workers may have a variety of duties, but generally interacting with patrons by selling concession items, processing sales as cashiers, and maintaining inventory controls are the primary tasks.

Gate Supervisor: The gate supervisors oversee their assigned areas. A gate could be an entry area to parking or the main venue. Tasks may vary, but include supervising ticket takers and parking staff, as well as interacting with customers.

Ticket Seller: Ticket sellers are responsible for selling event day tickets. Tasks typically include interacting with customers by helping them to choose seat locations for the event. They may also have to use specific software to process payments and complete ticket sales.

Parking: Parking staff is outside, often located away from the primary venue. They are involved in setting up parking areas and providing traffic direction. For restricted lots, they are responsible for confirming patrons have the correct type and number of passes. In addition to helping people park, some events may need parking staff to sell parking passes, process sales, and interact with customers.

Program and Merchandise Seller: Program and merchandise sellers are responsible for selling a variety of merchandise. Tasks typically include selling programs and merchandise, and serving as cashiers.

Scoreboard Operator: A scoreboard operator requires a basic knowledge of the event operations, game statistics, and technology. The primary responsibility is to keep event statistics up to date in real time for spectators, teams, officials, and the Internet.

Public Address Announcer: A public address announcer typically reads the P.A. script, announces important information, and becomes the voice of the event. The announcer may also assist in marketing and promotions, especially for events with a halftime.

Staff positions and their descriptions may seem obvious to event managers, but it cannot be assumed that all those working the event are familiar with the expectations of each position. Clear instructions, along with adequate training, will ensure that the event day workers will excel in their positions.

How to Conduct Event Management Meetings

Athena Yiamouyiannis,
Adjunct Professor, Ohio University

Event managers are responsible for conducting a variety of meetings. There are internal meetings to figure out what type of staffing is needed; external meetings with staffing agencies, police, and volunteer groups; and event day meetings/call time meetings with staff to ensure pertinent information is communicated. A meeting that is conducted well can be a great forum for productive collaboration and sharing; if done poorly, it may be perceived by attendees as a waste of time. It is up to event managers to conduct internal, external, and event day meetings effectively and efficiently so they are productive for all involved.

The first step in meeting planning is to determine what type of meeting is needed (its purpose). Will the meeting's purpose be solely to share information? Will it be to brainstorm or problem solve?

In event management, one of the primary purposes of conducting meetings is to share specific event details with key individuals who will be managing the event.

The next step is to determine who needs to be in attendance at the meetings. Good event managers will identify the individuals who should be present during the meeting so that they can be informed and/or contribute to the discussions. If an event team is being put together, care should be taken to ensure the team is comprised of the individuals necessary to get the job done effectively and efficiently.

Last, there needs to be a decision as to where should the meeting be held and what resources might be needed at the meeting? A location should be identified, along with any equipment needs and documents, including the preparation of a meeting agenda.

The following is a meetings checklist used by the NCAA staff (NCAA, n.d.) for pre-, during, and postmeeting activities.

▶

Before the Meeting:

1. Determine objectives.
2. Select participants.
3. Determine date and time.
4. Ensure room size and seating arrangements suit group size and activity.
5. Prepare meeting agenda and send to participants before meeting.
6. Collect necessary data.
7. Reserve and set up facilities and equipment.

Starting the Meeting:

1. Be on time (leaders and participants).
2. Confirm objectives and review agenda.
3. Review prior meetings.

During the Meeting:

1. Keep on track with the agenda and items.
2. Encourage sharing of ideas; discourage clashing of personalities.
3. Summarize decisions/conclusions.

Ending the Meeting:

1. Review the action plans.
2. Set date, time, and objectives for the next meeting.
3. End on a positive note—thank participants for their time.

After the Meeting:

1. Prepare and distribute summary/minutes.
2. Follow up on action items.
3. Check on progress.
4. Evaluate leadership methods and effectiveness.
5. Plan the next meeting.

As indicated, the meeting organizer should develop and send out a meeting agenda to attendees prior to the meeting. Oftentimes, the meeting organizer will send out a request for agenda items several days before the development of the agenda, so that new issues/problems that arise can be added to the agenda.

At the meeting, someone should be assigned as the scribe (note taker). The scribe is responsible for drafting the "minutes of the meeting," which is a summary of the key points of the meeting. The meeting minutes should clearly specify what needs to be done, the name of the person(s) who will be held responsible for getting the projects/tasks completed, as well as applicable deadlines. The scribe should have the meeting organizer review the notes, and then send out the minutes of the meeting to committee members, generally within 24 hr of the meeting.

Although meetings may be viewed as tedious by those required to attend, they are necessary. If they are run properly, meetings can be extremely beneficial. They provide an opportunity for event managers to work out some of the details of planning the event. One of the biggest errors that event managers can make, though, is to utilize meetings to try to make all the major decisions for an event. Event managers—both the lead event manager and the ones managing specific functional areas—should be using the time between meetings to work out plans and secondary options to problems. Group meetings are for updating everyone on the progress of these areas and to ensure that there are no unforeseen conflicts with things that have been discussed.

In summary, the meeting forum itself offers a great venue for event managers to get various staff members and constituents on the same page regarding event information and implementation strategies. The use of the meeting planning techniques described above (premeeting preparation, meeting protocol, postmeeting follow up) can be used as a roadmap by event managers to assist in the planning and implementation process. By conducting efficient and effective event meetings with internal and external constituents, not only will communications be enhanced, but staff morale will be higher, issues minimized, and the quality of the event improved.

SUMMARY

As with many aspects of event management, staffing is not glamorous; it is challenging because every event has different staffing needs. The management of human resources can make or break the overall success of any event. As discussed, event staffing is multidimensional and impacts contract negotiation, customer service, security, media, and revenues. Event managers need to be able to make difficult decisions, and direct and understand a variety of situations and personalities, all while keeping a perspective on the entire event. Understanding the differences between the various types of staff, positions, and duties is important. Every member of the event staff, whether front of house or back of house, plays an important role in the event. To the participant and spectator, the event day staffs are representatives of the event and need to provide excellent customer service to ensure the event is a great experience from the beginning to the end for all involved. It is a difficult task to determine, how many staffs are needed and which positions are required for a successful event. The combination of research and experience can help event managers as they try to balance controlling cost with providing adequate staffing levels.

Event managers need to have a basic knowledge of what responsibilities should be assigned in each position, and when specialized training or certification is required. In addition, it is important to understand the basic rules, regulations, and laws that may impact the event staffing and operations, based on the type of staff being utilized. Event managers should rely on human resource experts or attorneys to clarify the specifics of employment law as needed.

Creating a good work environment is also a responsibility of the event managers. By using work teams, providing appropriate motivational strategies, communicating effectively with staff, and running efficient meetings, event mangers will have a group that is ready to go on the event day, and one that feels as if it is a valued part of the organization. This includes learning what motivates staff members, and incorporating a variety of motivational techniques to keep morale high. For many, working sports events are important because of their affinity to the sport or sport organization, but some will be motivated by other things. It is up to event managers to ensure that the needs of their event day staff are met along with those of spectators and participants.

Student Challenges

NAME _____ DATE_____

Question 14.1

Attend an athletic event on your campus. Record all of the different event day positions you observe while at the event. If you observe any areas where event staffs are needed, but not on duty, please also record that information. Create a list of staff positions and any missing positions you identify.

Question 14.2

Choose four jobs that were part of the event you attended. Write detailed job descriptions for each event day positions required to successfully run the event. If the positions are similar to what is provided in the chapter, the descriptions must be significantly expanded to fit the event needs.

Position #1 Title:

Job Description:

Position #2 Title:

Job Description:

Position #3 Title:

Job Description:

Position #4 Title:

Job Description:

Question 14.3

Draft an agenda for a call time meeting that directly reflects the items that need to be addressed for the event you attended. The sample agenda in the chapter is for a softball tournament, but can be used as a guide.

EVENT VOLUNTEER MANAGEMENT

Florence May, David Pierce, and Kathryn May

Florence May is the President and Managing Member of The Registration System (TRS). Flory led the TRS volunteer management system development project in 2000 to support her event planning company. She conceived the software based on 15 years of sport and event management working with host committees including National League of Cities, American Association of Museums, NCAA Final Four, and the Indianapolis Motor Speedway's United State Grand Prix and Indianapolis 500. She served on the Super Bowl Host Committee for Indianapolis. Flory is a national speaker and author on topics including professional event management, volunteer best practices, and top technical trends.

David Pierce, Ph.D., is an Assistant Professor of Sport Management at Indiana University Purdue University Indianapolis. Previously, Dr. Pierce was the Program Director for the Sport Administration program at Ball State University where he served as Event Director for the Chase Charlie Races, a series of community road races organized by his senior-level Event Management class. Participation in the event increased from 100 to 750 during his 4 years as Event Director and became a signature event on Family Weekend. Pierce has published 45 peer-reviewed articles in scholarly journals and given over 60 state, national, and international presentations. He is also set to author *Selling in the Sport Industry*, published by Kendall Hunt. Dr. Pierce earned his doctoral degree in sport management from Indiana University Bloomington.

Kathryn May is a Junior Account Manager and Marketing Coordinator at The Registration System (TRS). Kathryn works on-site with large national events. She has coauthored articles on volunteer management and best practices for the International Festival & Event Association magazine.

While the event staff is working hard behind the scenes executing many of the tasks already described in this textbook, guests will be receiving help from front of house volunteers. A **volunteer** is typically defined as an individual who takes on a task or duty with no expectation of monetary benefits. Regardless of the size of the event, every attendee and participant wants volunteers who are knowledgeable, friendly, and efficient. Ironically, the public face of the event is a group of people that spends a relatively short amount of time each year with the event operations. A successful volunteer program involves many of the same key elements of managing full-time employees such as training, defining position responsibilities, controlling risk, scheduling, communication, and evaluation. Volunteers can be great event assets if the organization focuses on the right preparation for maximum return on the volunteer investment.

This chapter explains how event managers can ensure that volunteer programs are properly positioned to support event operations while simultaneously developing volunteers who can meet superhuman expectations. It will also introduce the members of the volunteer management team and introduce the key steps in the volunteer management cycle, which is outlined in Table 15.1.

Table 15.1 Event Volunteer Management Cycle

Timing	Item	Who
12 months prior	Identify volunteer position descriptions, shifts, and restrictions	Volunteer manager with operations and events staff
10–12 months prior	Create volunteer manual	Volunteer manager with review by chief operating officer/event director
11 months prior	Check volunteer liability waiver form.	Volunteer manager with attorney and insurance company
6–8 months prior	Build online volunteer registration site	Volunteer manager
6–8 months prior	Identify team leaders	Volunteer manager and team leaders
4–6 months prior	Test online registration site	Operations manager, event director, and team leaders
3–6 months prior	Take volunteer online registration site live	Volunteer manager
2–3 months prior	Team leader coordination	Volunteer manager with operations and events staff (Must be coordinated)
1–3 weeks prior	Volunteer training	Volunteer manager
7–14 days prior	Schedule reminder to volunteers	Volunteer manager
Event Day(s)	Event volunteer oversight	Volunteer manager
Shortly after the event	Event volunteer wrap-up	Volunteer manager with team leaders
Shortly after the event	Survey of team leaders and volunteers	Volunteer manager
5–10 days after the event	Thank you to team leaders and volunteers	Volunteer manager
2–4 weeks after the event	Evaluate	Volunteer manager with operations and events staff

The Volunteer Team

Before digging into the volunteer management process, let's meet the members of the volunteer management team. You met the event manager at the beginning of the book. The event manager is responsible for everything related to the event. The event manager relies on the **Volunteer Manager** to coordinate all personnel, procedures, and activities related to managing volunteers. The volunteer manager has oversight over the entire volunteer program. Prior to the event, this means creating position descriptions, developing volunteer schedules, recruiting volunteers, and managing the volunteer database. At the event, the volunteer manager is responsible for event-wide allocation of volunteers, meaning making sure that the right number of volunteers get to the right places and taking corrective action when there are challenges or shortages at any venue or position. After the event, the volunteer manager coordinates qualitative and quantitative data collection and coordinates a wrap-up session with the event manager.

Depending on the nature and complexity of the event, volunteer managers may need to identify **Team Leaders** to take oversight of a team of volunteers at a specific position or venue. The team leader is a volunteer responsible for overseeing specific groups of onsite event volunteers. Team Leaders are located at an assigned venue with responsibility for communicating and coordinating with volunteers in the purview, communicating messages from volunteer manager to volunteers, assessing the performance and taking corrective action toward volunteers at their site, and taking attendance and reporting volunteer shortages or excesses to the volunteer manager.

Courtesy of David Pierce

Volunteers serve a critical role in event management.

The event staff also plays a role in the volunteer management process. It is important that the Volunteer Manager communicate to the event staff that the volunteers are part of the event team and should be treated as such. It is the job of the event staff to coordinate and communicate with team leaders, encourage volunteers, and coach team leaders and/or volunteers if the volunteer responsibilities are not being completed correctly. They need to be friendly, reliable, and supportive. When this occurs, volunteers and event staff mesh to work together as a single team to accomplish common goals, rather than compete as opposing forces. The event staff should also submit postevent reflections to the volunteer manager as part of the postevent evaluation and recap.

Planning

This section and questionnaire provide the opportunity for an assessment of the event volunteer management process. Event managers typically have solid measurements for success in publicity, sponsorship, and ticket sales. However, assessing volunteer management programs may seem less tangible and less familiar to many event professionals.

Timeline

In an ideal situation for a recurring event, the volunteer manager starts working immediately after the event ends to plan the tasks for the next event. A large, complicated event should have 9–12 months of lead-time, while smaller events may only require 3–5 months. The following timeline, which may need to be condensed into a shorter calendar, is a snapshot of the event volunteer management planning cycle.

Assessment

Whether the volunteer manager is new to the position or a seasoned professional, it is important to periodically assess the foundational elements of the event volunteer program. If the volunteer manager is new to the position, these questions are a good starter discussion that will help assess whether the volunteer management program is mature or still in the development phase. If the volunteer manager has been through several event cycles, this assessment may serve as a progress report.

Position Descriptions, Shifts, and Operations Coordination

Many volunteer managers want to start by pulling together the volunteer manual information (e.g., expectations, benefits, uniform details) but save those details for later. Begin by working with the appropriate members of the event staff to plan the volunteer needs for the event. It is critical to work as a team to identify team leaders and volunteer position descriptions. Annual assessment of volunteer needs that include feedback from past volunteers and team leaders will ensure that volunteers are not performing duties that are no longer needed. Once you have worked with the event staff to identify the ways in which volunteers can contribute to the success of the event, you can begin to determine when volunteers are needed to perform those duties and how many volunteers will be needed.

Providing volunteers with duty descriptions will help place the right volunteer in the right role.

The culmination of this process is a master volunteer grid that identifies volunteer roles and shift schedules. Creating an organized master grid allows you to retain a significant amount of information about volunteer needs in one place.

Developing the master volunteer grid on paper is an important step that occurs before inserting this information into an online volunteer management platform. This information is at the heart of what needs to be clearly communicated to prospective volunteers. Examining the content of online registration systems reveal that the following information is critical:

- Volunteer position name with detailed (and honest) position description
- Position restrictions and requirements
- Available position shifts (including date, start/end time, and location for each)

The top responsibility of the volunteer manager is to recruit volunteers who are truly helpful, dependable, and productive. Unfortunately, many volunteer programs operate under the short-term aim of recruiting the most volunteers possible simply to fill slots. The pursuit of sheer numbers without an emphasis on position specifics (e.g., skills, restrictions, schedules) tends to be poor use of organizational resources. Quality is the key. Remember, volunteers are people, not cattle. Not all volunteers will show the same ability to carry out assigned tasks. Recruiting the right people for the right positions on the right days is critical.

Position Descriptions

It is important to clearly define and communicate position requirements (e.g., technical skills, stamina/strength) and expectations (e.g., friendly, mobile, flexible, works well in high-stress situations) to recruit the appropriate people to advance the event purpose and achieve the goals. Some volunteers will be patient with volunteer positions that do not seemingly make an impact on the event, but younger volunteers may be more interested in positions that make an impact and help people directly. Younger volunteers also are most likely to expect good use of their time and talents. Talented volunteer managers will match a volunteer's skills, interests, capabilities, and availability with specific event needs for the most effective utilization of organizational resources.

An example of a realistic position description is presented below:

Position Title: [Greeter]
Position Description: [Greeters will be positioned in pairs outside key entry points to event. Greeters will be trained to assist guests with venue directions, event schedule, ticket purchase details, and other frequently asked questions.]
Position Restrictions/Requirements: [Greeters should be prepared for all weather conditions (e.g., sunscreen, umbrellas/raincoats). Greeters will stand during their entire shift but will receive a 10-minute break each hour from a team leader. Greeters may eat or drink during their 10-minute break, but not in front of guests.]

Shift Scheduling

It is also important to be realistic with volunteer shift expectations. Shifts should be neither too brief nor too long. A typical shift should last between 3 and 4 hours. Volunteer shifts should be coordinated so that times overlap. For example, if the first shift runs from 1 p.m. to 4 p.m., then the next shift should have a start time of 12:30 p.m. to allow for the changeover of volunteers, which may require orientation, training, and/or transportation.

For each event, the volunteer manager needs to determine the minimum and maximum number of volunteer shifts that can reasonably be worked and for how long. Weekend shifts, and those scheduled around the workday, rather than during the workday, will likely be the most popular. Shifts located inside will go quickly if the weather is forecast to be anything but perfect. Longer shifts and those in difficult positions (e.g., weather, heavily trafficked areas) need greater attention to rotations and breaks. Also take into consideration the start and finish times for shifts. Ensure that proper lighting, parking, and security are available if the hours are extremely early or late. Aligning transport with shift start and end times is another consideration. In some cases, volunteers might even need transportation to and from parking areas if they are required to park a long distance from the venue.

Finally, you will want to account for volunteers that do not show up for their assigned shift. While the standard no-show rate for event volunteers is approximately 30%, volunteer managers should annually assess the no-show rate for their specific event in order to accurately plan for missing volunteers. Thus, you will want to recruit more volunteers than you actually need to compensate for no-shows.

Recruiting

It is not uncommon to see four generations of volunteers (and staff) come together in support of events. Volunteers come with a wide variety of motivations, skills, and expectations. Carefully consider the skills, unusual demands, or personal traits required for the volunteer position before filling slots. The goal is to recruit volunteers with the hope that it is the beginning of a long-term relationship between the individual and event and/or team.

Crafting the right message for recruiting volunteers will differ among events.

Up until recently, volunteer managers were telling potential recruits, "This is how you can help." The tune has changed. Now, the message is, "This is how your skills, interest, and social commitment are important to making this event successful." Volunteers want to make use of their practical skills and talents. Volunteer managers must communicate to each volunteer that their time will be valued, productive, and impactful. Commitment is even more likely to occur on one of the many online activities than it is in person.

There is no doubt that recruiting can be difficult. Event and volunteer managers have to constantly look for ways to identify and connect with volunteers who have the skills and dedication the organization is seeking.

Motivation

What motivates people to give their time, talent, and sometimes even treasure to event organizations? Clary et al. (1998) identified six motivations for volunteering.

- **Values function**—The person is volunteering to express or act on important values, such as humanitarianism and helping the less fortunate.
- **Understanding function**—The person is seeking to learn more about the world and exercise skills that are often unused.
- **Enhancement function**—The person is seeking to grow and develop psychologically through involvement in volunteering.
- **Career function**—The volunteer has the goal of gaining career-related experience through volunteering.
- **Social function**—Volunteering allows the person to strengthen social relationships.
- **Protective function**—The individual uses volunteering to reduce negative feelings, such as guilt, or to address personal problems.

Bang and Ross (2009) identified additional motivations specific to sport volunteerism.

- **Community Involvement**—The person has pride in the local community hosting an event.
- **Extrinsic Rewards**—The person is motivated by tangible rewards such as clothing, food, accommodations, and tickets.
- **Love of Sport**—The person is motivated by passion for a particular sport or competition.

If volunteers are satisfied and their motivational needs met, then they will likely return as a volunteer in future years (Farrell et al., 1998). As a result, it is important to understand what motivates volunteers so volunteer managers can create a meaningful experience (i.e., assigned roles, rewards, feedback) that fulfills the volunteers' motivation.

Keep in mind that the motivating factors will change depending on the type of event (i.e., mega event, community event) and volunteer (see sidebar for discussion of age). While exploring research findings based on these factors is beyond the scope of this chapter, it is important for volunteer managers to understand the unique, defining characteristics of their event. What gets everyday people to come out and volunteer for the event? Volunteer managers have found that this can differ widely based on what generation these volunteers fall into. The work of Deal (2006) provides guidance as to the various characteristics of generations:

- The Silent Generation (born 1922–1945). Oldest and most experienced volunteers looking to keep busy. Their sense of respect for authority, patience, and dedication to their jobs serves them well in volunteer positions.
- The Baby Boomers (born 1946–1964). Seeking active retirements that often include volunteer opportunities, especially if they can support a cause that is important to them. They work hard, are loyal, and seek gratification from their work.

- Generation X (born 1965–1980). They may volunteer to organize events and will use their social media presence to promote it. But, they are looking for a balance between their volunteer efforts, work, and personal lives. They like to work with technology, are informal in their work and volunteer style, and are generally independent.
- Generation Y (Born 1981–2002). This group wants to participate, wants a voice in decision-making and planning, are confident, and wants immediate feedback. Having the latest technology is expected, but they have a strong desire to be involved in community service and want to make a positive impact.

This is a lot to handle, especially with large events, but take heart, there are commonalities. Based on 7 years of research, Deal (2006) narrowed it down in her book "Retiring the Generation Gap" to discover what all four generations want from their volunteer experience:

To feel valued	(85%)
Recognition and appreciation	(74%)
A supportive environment	(73%)
A capable workforce	(72%)
To be part of a team	(68%)

Though each generation gives slightly different expectations of what respect means to them, leaders must be trustworthy and give respect. Older individuals, Deal's study clarified, spoke of respect in terms of "giving my opinions the weight I believe they deserve," while younger respondents characterized respect as "listen to me, pay attention to what I have to say." Different generations, however, do not have notably varied expectations of their leaders. Above all else, they must be someone volunteers feel is trustworthy.

Build a Team

Event managers want volunteers to treat event guests well and help make the event run smoothly. Time and energy must be invested into the volunteer experience in order to have happy and engaged volunteer team members.

There are eight fundamental principles to ensuring volunteers have a great experience:

1. Clearly communicate expectations and process
2. Make the volunteer experience well organized
3. Create an upbeat, fun environment
4. Recognize volunteers who work hard, give long hours and set the example
5. Remove volunteers who do not work or set a negative tone
6. Regularly rotate volunteers in stressful and environmentally challenging environments
7. Treat volunteers and colleagues with the same respect and dignity
8. Conduct surveys to ensure volunteers can communicate concerns and recommendations.

Volunteers who have a great experience become part of the event team and are more likely to return for the next event. As a by-product, they are likely to encourage friends, families, and colleagues to join them. Rather than building a group to understand a purpose, the most successful volunteer managers build a family that believes in a purpose.

Registration

Online volunteer registration is rarely a problem for any of the generations. Computer use is nearly ubiquitous.

Just as for event registration, online registration is expected for volunteer registration.

The registration process should be efficient for the volunteers and the volunteer manager. An online system normally provides the benefits of accessible and quick sign up processes for the volunteer while giving the volunteer manager the capability to easily track, communicate, and manage all of the information.

Registration includes two components. First, the volunteer manager must clearly communicate expectations, benefits, and opportunities. Do not understate or sugarcoat event needs or requirements when communicating in person or online. Be brutally honest about the experience volunteers should expect. Make sure volunteers understand if a position is physically challenging, requires an "in charge" personality, will be nowhere near the event action or athletes, or if they will be working in demanding or heavily trafficked areas. Keep in mind that volunteers will confirm through personal interactions and social media whether claims made are authentic. Second, the volunteer will provide contact information, sign the disclaimer/waiver, and register for specific positions and shifts.

Make It Easy

Communication is the key for most aspects of event management and it holds true when managing any number of volunteers. But, it is inevitable that not everyone will listen. The solution is to keep things simple. Whether the volunteer is registering for shifts, setting up the day before, working the event, or signing out for the night, avoid making them jump through hoops. If volunteers are bombarding the event manger with questions, it is a strong indication that the process has a glitch. Additionally, getting volunteers wired into your event's social media campaign should be as easy as one or two clicks. Online registration tools should be integrated with the event website and event/volunteer social media tools. Create seamless opportunities during the registration process for volunteers to become part of the event online and onsite.

Database

There are three components to effective databases: collect, update, and communicate. Data should be collected with an online registration site and organized effectively. The information then needs to be kept up-to-date in one centralized location. Finally, use contact information to regularly stay in contact with volunteers to ensure the database is up-to-date, continuously engage volunteers in other organization happenings, and be ready for the next volunteer cycle.

Security, Screenings, and Background Checks

All organizations should take special care to protect personal information of volunteers. Start by collecting only the required personal information on the registration site. The reality is that no online registration system, online form, or excel spreadsheet is immune from security risks.

Volunteer managers need to carefully consider which registrant information is vital for participation. Are birth dates, driver's license numbers, or social security numbers really needed for all volunteers? Or is that information only needed in order to conduct security checks for a few key positions? Volunteers working in high security areas, managing money, and working in close proximity to VIPs, athletes, or children will likely need background checks at the local, state, and/or federal level. If any security checks are done, make certain the online registration system encrypts or masks sensitive information making it more difficult to suffer a security breach.

Communications

Volunteer managers need to be in tune with the communication methods that best reach their group of volunteers. Whether its email, snail mail, Facebook, phone, Twitter, fax, text, website, or the volunteer registration management system, it is incumbent on volunteer mangers to understand their volunteers' communication preferences. Collecting data through survey responses, analyzing email open rates and shares on social media, and gathering informal feedback through conversation help event managers to understand which communication messages are most effective.

Event volunteer communications used to be largely informative and infrequent, with messages only sent from the event organizer to the volunteer. Today, the communication lines are more fluid and instantaneous.

Updates and Reminders

Updates and last minute changes are transmitted through the volunteer management system in conjunction with email, text, automated phone messages, and social media communication tools. These communications channels are important because volunteers expect to be "in the know" as changes occur. Volunteers want to be able to easily find out if a shift is no longer needed or a volunteer parking lot has been moved to a new location so they do not waste their time in the wrong place or showing up when they are not needed. Managers can now instantly communicate additional volunteer needs or emergency directions.

Many volunteers receive updates and last minute communications through computers and smart phones. They will help spread the word to those who are less "connected." Of course, some volunteers will not read updates regardless of how well communications are drafted or displayed. It is just something volunteer coordinators and event managers need to recognize and be aware of. While some volunteers may not read communications or follow instructions, it is still important to clearly communicate information so volunteers know what to expect. The majority will appreciate the effort to communicate and follow the directions. Well, most of the directions!

Through the authors extensive personal experience, they have found that volunteer managers report that volunteers who get regular updates and reminders are likely to feel a greater connection to the organization. Several of these experts commented on the importance of giving their volunteers an emotional connection to the events. One in particular stated that he likes to send emails on a broad array of event specifics so they knew what he knew. This also helps volunteers feel like a part of the group and increases their level of ownership. The more ownership the volunteers feel, the greater the likelihood that they are showing up for their shifts, working hard, and growing their commitment to events they associate with.

Delivery Methods

Volunteers share their experiences with friends, families, and colleagues. They communicate their excitement (or disappointment) about events and organizations primarily by word of mouth. But this exchange is rarely in person. The traditional face-to-face word of mouth has been replaced with social media and online communications. It is viral, replicating an event's marketing message time and time again and in ways that might be surprising. The majority of volunteers will email links for event websites, online volunteer registration sites, and news articles from local media. They might also post their volunteer photos to event photo sites (like Flickr) or via Instagram, Facebook, or Twitter. The most technologically sophisticated volunteers accomplish all of this on smartphones. The majority of volunteer opportunities to attract and register volunteers happen electronically. Make sure the event is prepared to communicate with them electronically.

According to Pew Research, in 2013 56% of American adults owned a smartphone, 35% have some kind of cell phone that is not a smartphone, and 9% do not own a cell phone (Pew Research Center, 2013a). While seniors are generally positive about email and internet usage, they have been less accepting of smartphones and social networking sites. Only 18% of seniors (65 and over) own a smart phone, and only 27% use social networking sites (Pew Research Center, 2013b). Privacy and security continue to be major concerns. Websites should also be compatible with adaptive software for people with disabilities (i.e., hearing and sight enhancement).

Volunteer Management at the US Figure Skating Championship

Faryn Roy

Director of Events & Operations, Sports & Properties, Inc.

Major sporting events can attract tens or hundreds of thousands of fans over a relatively short period of time. When it comes to planning these events, there is often a small number of full-time employees that are responsible for putting everything into place in the years leading up to the event. However, the Local Organizing Committee (LOC) can extend their reach by putting together a strong team of volunteers. The performance of a volunteer team on-site is crucial to the success of the event. This is a mini-case study in the planning, development, and implementation of a large volunteer team at a major sporting event.

US Figure Skating Championships

The LOC for the US Figure Skating Championships was made aware early on of the importance of volunteers for the event. An 8-day National Championship that was coming to Greensboro, North Carolina and the US Championships required a mix of local and national volunteers.

The Early Phases

With 23 months from the host city announcement to the arrival of the first skaters, the initial inquiries from those who wanted to volunteer began to trickle in shortly after the announcement date. With the LOC not yet in a position to put out the official volunteer application, these emails or phone calls were logged into a spreadsheet for prospective volunteers. In the meantime, the LOC began to develop a preliminary list of volunteer "teams," and researched appropriate "team leaders" for each team.

Volunteer Benefits

Many sporting event volunteers choose these opportunities for the benefits that are offered, as well as the chance to be in the venue for a major event without purchasing a ticket. They are generally very interested in the benefits that will be offered in exchange for the 24 hours of personal time that they are committing.

The US Figure Skating Championships developed a package to help appeal to local citizens. Volunteers were given an event jacket, complimentary parking or shuttle passes, a 20% discount on ticket purchases, and refreshments while volunteering. The LOC determined that a full meal service would not be offered to volunteers for this event. The refreshments included coffee, tea, water and soft drinks as well as chips, cookies, and fruit.

A postevent Thank You Party for the volunteers was hosted by the LOC several weeks after the event. The LOC rented a local movie theater showing a figure skating documentary and volunteers were invited to attend. Over 50% of the group attended and the feedback from them was outstanding. They felt the party was an added and unexpected bonus.

Application Process

Events have the option of using either a digital or a hard copy volunteer application form. For this event, the LOC chose a hard copy application that volunteers could print off of the event website. Components of the application included basic personal information, ranking preferred volunteer functions, a background check, and waiver.

The second component of the volunteer application process was the approach of targeted volunteers to serve on the teams where knowledge of figure skating was necessary. These team leaders were the first that were selected. The team leaders came from figure skating clubs from around the state so that they could assist in recruiting local adult skaters or skating parents to serve on their teams.

As applications were received, they were given a tentative team assignment internally, entered into a database, and emailed a confirmation.

Volunteer Planning

While recruitment continued, the LOC worked on finalizing the volunteer teams and recruiting team leaders. Evaluating areas of need and determining the best distribution of volunteers occurred at this point. The following volunteer teams were established:

Figure Skating Specific: Ice Monitors, Sweeper Monitors, Announcers, and Music

Open to Anyone: Communications, Directional, Doping, FanFest, Greeters, Hospitality, Media Services, Medical, Registration, Volunteer Support, and Wheelchair Escorts

Scheduling

After the various volunteer needs were analyzed and teams were set up, the next step for the LOC was to come up with a daily matrix for each team, determining how many volunteers were needed per location per shift. In general, each team would have three shifts a day were targeted for 6 a.m.–Noon, Noon to 6 p.m., and 6 p.m. to Midnight. An initial draft of a matrix was created for each team and reviewed by US Figure Skating. Each volunteer was assigned to one team, and worked all four of their shifts for the same team. Once each team's matrix was finalized, the LOC was able to determine how many volunteers were needed per team. This step allowed the LOC to begin confirming team assignments with volunteers 6 months prior to the event. Within 2 months of the event, Team Leaders began contacting their assigned volunteers.

Team Leaders

The recruitment of Team Leaders was handled through personal interactions with LOC members. For the skating-related teams, referrals were made of individuals with experience in local skating events. These individuals were then vetted by the LOC to determine their ability to organize and communicate. The other team leaders chosen for this event had all played a key role in other major Greensboro sporting events.

The Team Leaders were given their matrix and an initial list of their team members approximately 4 months prior to the event. Some teams were already filled at this point whereas others still needed significant recruitment. Monthly Team Leader meetings began 4 months prior to the Championships. These meetings included a run-down of volunteer benefits, descriptions of roles for each team, scheduling instructions, communication advice, and a facility tour.

Training

With the last volunteer roles filled approximately 1 month prior to the event, attention was then focused on the training of volunteers. A mandatory volunteer training session was held at the Greensboro Coliseum Complex 2 weeks prior to the event. At this training session, the volunteer handbook was distributed and presentations were made covering the general role of an event volunteer. At the conclusion of the full-group training, each team met separately so that team leaders could go over specifics of their role. For some teams, a venue tour was included to help with venue familiarity.

Conclusion

Recruiting, managing, and planning for a large volunteer force is an event component that requires attention well in advance of the event. Keeping the volunteers happy and giving them a sense of ownership in the event allowed them to put their best foot forward for the athletes, coaches, officials, media, and spectators that called the Greensboro Coliseum Complex home for over a week.

Training

Good training sets the stage for volunteer confidence, competence, and camaraderie. This training should be comparable with an employee job orientation with a lot of enthusiasm. Let's take a look at a few situations that are strong indications of poor preparation by the volunteer manager and supporting team leaders.

Scenario 1: A new event volunteer is trying to assist event participants but gives incorrect directions.

Scenario 2: A volunteer is unclear on his duties. He would like to check with a team leader but has not been introduced to anyone who appears to be in charge.

Scenario 3: A guest asks a volunteer team leader about the event title sponsor. The volunteer has no idea what service or product the title sponsor provides.

Team Leader Training

The team leader is a volunteer responsible for overseeing specific groups of onsite event volunteers. The volunteer manager needs to ensure that team leaders have been thoroughly trained with appropriate check lists, timelines, and communication plans.

Team leaders need to be able to:

- Set clear expectations from the beginning of each volunteer shift
- Coach volunteers who are new or have trouble with the volunteer position responsibilities
- Track the attendance of volunteers
- Report volunteers who are late or no-shows
- Recruit from existing volunteer participants to fill gaps
- Manage problem volunteers
- Distribute volunteer gear and/or tickets and other benefits;
- Implement security and safety measures (i.e., lost child, person with a gun, weather plan etc.)
- Understand the crisis management plan
- Communicate with event leadership staff

Volunteer Training

The event staff has the opportunity to create a well-orchestrated team atmosphere. Volunteer training is the time for newcomers to be instructed on position specifics and introduced to their team. Team leaders and veteran volunteers have the opportunity to share their experience and welcome newcomers. Training is also time for returning volunteers to be reminded of the position specifics and coached on any improvements or changes that need to be made from the previous year. Generation Y and X volunteers (teens to late-40s) will seek training that gives them "event insider" status and a sense of position ownership. The more mature volunteers of the Boomer and Silent generations will look for professionally organized management and clear directions.

There are two types of training: event orientation and position-specific.

Training volunteers for their specific tasks cannot be overlooked.

Courtesy of David Pierce

Event Orientation

Require all volunteers to attend one orientation session before they can begin volunteering. The following is a sample event orientation agenda (Table 15.2).

Table 15.2 Sample Event Orientation Agenda

6:00	Welcome	Warm greetings set the tone.
6:05	Intro of event leadership	The event director should personally set the tone for the training.

6:10	Event mission	Why this event happens. What role does this event plays in the community.
6:15	Event schedule	What is going to happen and when. Changes from previous years.
6:20	Sponsors and partners	Introduce organizations and associated products that make the event possible.
6:25	Volunteer expectations	The importance and role volunteers play in the event.
6:40	Safety and security	The role volunteers play in a safe and secure event.
6:50	Meet your team leaders	Who the volunteers will work with during the event?
7:00	Close	Pick up volunteer gear at the close of training.
7:00	Q&A	Team leader Q&A sessions in small groups
7:30	Conclude for evening	

Standard operating procedures should be covered in training, on the website, and on the volunteer registration system. If expectations are not clearly covered, volunteers are left to make decisions independently, which can frequently cause frustrations. Ensure the following are included:

- *Uniforms.* What volunteers expected to wear. Be clear on color(s), shirts, pants, headgear and shoes. If volunteers are provided with a uniform, that eliminates any confusion over what they should wear. However, if no uniform is provided, volunteers should wear a different color from what the participants are wearing. This makes it easy for those seeking assistance to identify volunteers. However, volunteers should avoid wearing red because red it typically reserved for medical volunteers or personnel.
- *Possessions.* What volunteers can bring on site and whether the event has the capability to secure private items such as purses and/or backpacks.
- *Food.* Whether volunteers will be given any food or drinks, be able to take breaks to eat or drink, if they must provide their own food, and if they can bring it in with them.
- *Parking.* Where volunteers should park, if they have to pay for parking, and if there is a shuttle or shared rides.
- *Help.* When team leaders will check on volunteers in case something has gone wrong and how to contact team leaders directly.

Position Training

Ensure volunteers are comfortable with both the site and the position responsibilities through hands-on training.

- *Venue tour.* Walk through the site.
- *Demonstration.* Show/display position responsibilities. Don't just talk about them. Demonstrate.

- *Review FAQs.* Address the common challenges and the proper answers to questions.
- *Dry-run.* Let volunteers practice to ensure clear understanding.
- *Communications.* Clarify where to take onsite problems or questions.

Planning and training are important because they create expectations for all staff and volunteers. If properly communicated, these preliminary steps will eliminate most of the potential headaches and concerns on site and provide a roadmap for how to manage unexpected challenges.

Onsite Execution

A basic goal of most events is to have an event that, from the perspective of the guest or event attendee, is run smoothly and efficiently with friendly, helpful volunteers. The reality is that problems will occur behind the scenes no matter how prepared everyone is. The degree to which training and preparations have taken place allows problems and crises to be managed behind-the-scenes and out of the view of guests and attendees. The reality is that by the time the event begins, planning and preparation should be done. All of the planning and training should be implemented and become second nature. Then, volunteers are not making things up on the spot or figuring out responsibilities and roles.

© Shutterstock

Event managers work in tandem with volunteer managers to ensure an event's success.

The relationship between volunteer managers and team leaders will play a large role in determining the success of volunteers. Additionally, successfully managing problem volunteers will aid in developing cohesion among the volunteer team. The volunteer manager and team leaders need to work in cooperation to have successful operations onsite. Occasionally a volunteer manager will make the mistake of trying to fill the team leaders' role and vice versa!

Lack of, or poor, communication between the volunteer manager and the team leader is a common challenge. To prevent this situation:

- *Know the plan.* Team leaders must be privy to, and understand, the communication plan.
- *Communicate.* Team leaders left out of the communications loop and not "part of the team" will feel frustrated; they will also be less likely to return in future years.
- *Use the contingency plan.* There must be back-up options if the volunteer manager is unavailable.

Problem Volunteers

Almost every event has at least one problem volunteer and everyone knows who the problem is. Problem volunteers can become a cancer spreading negativity throughout the organization and hurting volunteer retention and recruitment. Therefore, standards must be set and adhered to. Problem volunteers come in three types: unhelpful, disruptive, and risky.

Unhelpful volunteers are physically unable and/or uninterested in helping. Before identifying a volunteer as unhelpful, ensure that they understand their role and attempt to coach them. There are volunteers who sign up for the event benefits (e.g., free admission, food, shirt, parking) and are simply not productive. These volunteers are often irritating and frustrate hard-working volunteers. Team leaders should identify unhelpful volunteers to the volunteer manager as soon as appropriate. These volunteers should not be invited back and, if interest is shown, they can be politely thanked and informed that their services are not needed.

Disruptive volunteers exhibit inappropriate or rude behavior. Volunteers cannot be permitted to put a poor face on the event. Disruptive volunteers need to be removed from their position and dealt with appropriately. The volunteer manager should express concerns about their behavior and make the determination about how to handle them. They might be able to be placed in a position where they can do no harm or they can be released from their shifts and told their volunteer services will not be needed now or in the future.

Risky volunteers are doing something dangerous, illegal, or legally problematic. If a volunteer is perpetrating harassment, theft, violence, and so on, the team leader needs to request immediate assistance from the volunteer manager. The volunteer manager and event director should decide whether security or police should be called and if legal action is appropriate. Under no circumstance should a risky volunteer be permitted to continue in a volunteer role.

Managing Risk

In addition to problems posed by problem volunteers, there are a variety of other risk factors that need to be considered when managing volunteers. Proper risk control can protect an organization, its sponsors, and its affiliates from unnecessary liability. A full discussion of risk management strategies is beyond the scope of this chapter and covered in-depth in the Safety and Security chapter of this text. However, it is worth noting that job perils, site concerns, and basic security precautions are important risk elements to address starting in the volunteer registration process and on the volunteer waiver. Risk concerns should be reinforced in the volunteer handbook and training. Event managers still need to have insurance because not all event volunteers are covered by personal homeowners and motor vehicle insurance.

Evaluation

The evaluation of the volunteer program should include feedback from team leaders and frontline volunteers and recognition of high achievers. Assessing the experience of volunteers allows identification of what went well, what did not go well, and what changes need to be made for the next event. Evaluation can come in the form of in-person wrap-up sessions and/or surveys.

Wrap-Up

In-person wrap-up sessions should take place while the event recollections are still fresh in everyone's mind. This objective discussion should include key staff and volunteer leaders. The volunteer wrap-up is a review of what went right, what can be improved, and recommendations for the future. Table 15.3 provides a sample meeting agenda for the wrap-up session.

Table 15.3   Sample Wrap-Up Meeting Agenda

8:00	Welcome.	Greet everyone and thank them for coming
8:05	Summary of results	What happened?
8:15	Team leader reports	What went well? What didn't go well? Recommendations?
9:00	Summary of lessons learned	Here are the big important points, did I hear you correctly?
9:15	Next steps	Take these recommendations back to event leadership for consideration and, if appropriate, implementation; schedule for next event.
9:20	Recognition	Funny or serious awards
9:30	Thank you	See you again in a few months. Look for update in 30 days

Surveys

Surveys can be completed in two ways. Paper-based surveys can be completed by volunteers onsite at the event or an online survey can be completed after the event is over. Online survey tools (e.g., Survey Money, Qualtrics, etc.) reduce the amount of time needed to manually enter data and can be set up to automatically tabulate results, but onsite surveys typically generate a higher response rate. In either case, providing a forum through which volunteers can evaluate their experience will increase the likelihood that they will feel heard by the event leadership. This assists in their sense of value to the event, and if they did experience anything negative, it is less likely they will share it outside of the event organization environment. While social media tools like Facebook and Twitter provide forums for the volunteer manager to communicate key information, social media also provides volunteers and the public the mechanism to communicate their compliments and complaints instantly to the rest of the world, which can be both good and bad.

Event Audit Report

The results of the in-person wrap-up sessions and postevent surveys should be written down as a specific section of the event audit report. Perhaps the most important element of the report is the set of recommendations for the next event. In the event of staff and volunteer turnover, the next group of event managers will benefit from having recommendations in place.

Recognition of High-achievers

It is the perfect opportunity to recognize team leaders at the wrap-up meeting, but what about recognizing volunteers? Those people who were gracious and helpful under pressure, the public face of the event, and instrumental in helping the event operate smoothly also deserve and appreciate recognition. The recognition for all volunteers may be as simple as a personalized e-mail, handwritten notes, or appreciation certificates. Some volunteer managers develop point systems and reward volunteers with event merchandise or prizes based on total service hours. Event leadership should recognize the high performing super star volunteers at a staff meeting or annual board meeting. Many larger cities have annual Recognition of Service Excellence (ROSE) ceremonies to recognize people who make the community a better place.

There are many potential awards and recognitions. Consider which service standards the event culture values and wishes to reinforce:

- Service excellence
- Service in particularly difficult circumstances
- Service by number of hours and/or days for a single event
- Service by the longest number of years.

What's Next?

Within 30 days after the event the surveys should be completed, wrap-up concluded, and lessons learned presented to the management staff. Now, preparations begin to upgrade and improve as the planning cycle begins (see timeline) for the next event.

Jobs

The job market for volunteer management is not easily defined. In many cases, the role of volunteer manager is included as part of another position within the organization. As a result, the ability to manage volunteers is a competency that almost anyone working in event management should possess. However, a few sport organizations devote an entry-level position specifically to volunteer management. In this case, a volunteer management position is a way to secure a foot in the door of the event management industry. Nonprofit organizations outside of the sport industry are more likely to hire volunteer coordinator positions. As a result, experience working outside of sports could also serve as a gateway to future sport event management positions.

Sample Volunteer Job Posting

Fun Time Events—Volunteer Race Hospitality Manager

Company Description:
Fun Time Events is a not-for-profit corporation with a mission of providing community road racing events that cater to beginner and intermediate athletes.

▶

Fun Time Events is currently seeking a volunteer to serve to manage sponsor hospitality at local races. Individuals with a demonstrated record of providing excellent customer service are preferred.

Responsibilities include

- Coordinate race day sponsor hospitality functions.
- Recruit, and supervise, three additional race day volunteers to assist with hospitality operations.
- Communicate with sponsors pre- and postevent.
- Manage access (credentialed individuals only) to hospitality tent area.
- Provide excellent customer service to race sponsors.
- Be willing to assist in other areas of race operations as needed.

How to Apply

Email resume and letter of interest to fun@funtimeevents.###
Fun Time Events is an equal opportunity employer.

SUMMARY

A successful volunteer program involves many of the same key elements of managing full-time employees such as training, defining position responsibilities, controlling risk, scheduling, communication, and evaluation. The tips, and samples, provided in this chapter will help event managers ensure their event operates as smoothly as possible. Events that are able to create a meaningful and enjoyable experience for volunteers will reap the benefits in the future with volunteer loyalty and interest in future events.

Student Challenges

NAME _____ DATE_____

Question 15.1

Your event management class is managing a 2-day Health and Wellness Festival on your campus. Events included in the festival are a 5K road race, a one-mile kids' road race, health testing and assessments, expert speakers, outdoor movies, healthy foods tasting and demonstration by local farmers and restaurants, cooking demonstrations, product and sponsor expo, and a kids' entertainment area. The event will occur from 9 a.m. to 5 p.m. on Saturday and Sunday. Expected total attendance over the 2 days for all events is 2,000. Based on this situation, create the following deliverables:

1. Volunteer recruitment plan that includes specific messaging and use of communication platforms
2. Master volunteer grid with shift times and locations
3. Realistic position descriptions for at least two volunteer positions in your grid
4. Volunteer training materials that would be used at the volunteer orientation meeting prior to the event
5. Postevent survey to gather feedback from volunteers

Question 15.2

The situations described below are real volunteer management examples where proper preventative measures were not taken. Select two examples below and describe what actions the organization could have taken to prevent the following situations from occurring.

- A volunteer wearing sandals while moving chairs to set up for volunteer training stubs her toe, ripping off the toenail and part of the toe bed. She requires immediate surgery.
- A pregnant volunteer is handing out brochures. She trips over a misplaced box, falls down a short flight of stairs, and goes into labor.
- The festival childcare provider is discovered to be a registered pedophile. A front page news story proclaims that the festival did not screen childcare providers.
- A volunteer gets badly injured during an event. The event organization has insurance, but it does not cover volunteers-only staff. The volunteer sues the title sponsor of the event.
- Well-meaning volunteer invites event guests who unable to find a hotel to stay at his house. Event guests steal money and small electronics.
- Volunteer driver is hit while driving an event car. The driver of the second car is uninsured and, to make matters worse, the volunteer's driver license is expired.

CHAPTER

16

EVENT SAFETY AND SECURITY

Jon Niemuth, Stephen J. Duethman, Ryan Sickman, Steve Terrill, and Drew Berst

Copyright © Kendall Hunt Publishing Company

Jon D. Niemuth, AIA, NCARB, LEED®AP, is the Director of Sports, Americas for AECOM's global practice, responsible for the development and delivery of the firm's integrated offering. In this role, he is responsible for work ranging from strategic planning to the creative vision and work product for a diverse offering of sports clients. Based in Kansas City, Jon engages and coordinates the efforts of AECOM's advanced project delivery approach from initial Economic consulting thru Construction. Mr. Niemuth earned his bachelor of architectural studies, master of architecture, master of urban planning/urban design, and certificate of preservation studies at the University of Wisconsin at Milwaukee.

Stephen J. Duethman, AIA, NCARB, is the Managing Principal of the Kansas City office of Ellerbe Becket. In his role as Project Manager over the past 22 years he has successfully and energetically directed the design of many large-scale professional, civic, and collegiate sports facilities for Ellerbe Becket. Some of his projects include John Paul Jones Arena at University of Virginia, McCarthey Athletic Center at Gonzaga University, and a major expansion and renovation to the Dunkin' Donuts Center in Providence, Rhode Island. Mr. Duethman earned his bachelor of environmental design at the University of Kansas.

Ryan Sickman, PE, LEED AP, Americas Sports Sector Principal for AECOM. Ryan is a former student-athlete bringing experience managing some of the largest, high-profile projects in the construction and collegiate sports industries. He has been responsible for more than 40 projects encompassing campus master plans, football stadiums and training facilities, baseball and softball stadiums, soccer stadiums, and basketball arenas and training facilities. He enjoys moving at a fast pace and solving the many challenges that come with large, complex projects. As a Principal in charge and Project manager, Ryan works hand-in-hand with project teams and clients to ensure that the primary vision and goals are achieved throughout the project. He is also responsible for project oversight with respect to AECOM budget, staffing, and resources needed for on-schedule and on-budget completion.

Steve Terrill, AIA, is the Americas Sports Sector Principal for AECOM. Steve leads the east coast practice for AECOM Sports + Venues out of the Richmond, Virginia, office. With more than 30 years of experience, he has spent the last 15 years specializing in the sports facilities market with a particular focus on collegiate projects. As a planner, programmer, and designer, he has worked on a wide range of new construction and renovation projects, including football stadiums, basketball arenas, indoor tracks, baseball and softball stadiums, football and basketball practice facilities, natatoriums, and tennis facilities.

Drew Berst is the Business Development Manager, Sports Venue for AECOM. Drew's role at AECOM is to manage business development opportunities for the Sports Venue practice. He devises great strategies, creates special client relationships, sponsorships, and manages sports pursuits across the United States. His intuitive and creative nature reveals opportunities that have proven to be great decisions for both AECOM and AECOM clients. Through his 10+ years of experience in business development, he likes to establish project goals early-on, and oversees the execution to ensure achievement and success for every client.

Over the last several decades, there has been an increased emphasis on sport event safety and security design and operation. The events of September 11, 2001, along with the previous World Trade Center bombings and the 1995 Alfred P. Murrah Federal Building bombing in Oklahoma are just a few high-profile tragic incidents in recent years. The plaza bomb at the 1996 Olympic Games in Atlanta followed by the 2013 Boston Marathon bombing illustrated that sport events and venues are not exempt from domestic and/or international terrorism. Even with a high level of security, the possibility of the unthinkable happening must be addressed.

Terrorist attacks and bombings are on one extreme end of security incidents in sport venues. Less severe situations are those such as participant or spectator injuries, unruly fans, earthquake, fire, or a power outage such as the one during Super Bowl XLVII in New Orleans. These are more likely than a terrorist attack to happen during an event, but terrorist activity must be considered. Venue architects, operators, and event managers need to be proactive and vigilant in their efforts related to keeping events and venues safe and secure for spectators and participants alike. Everyone involved in events should be looking for ways to prevent problems before they occur—this is true whether related to security, concessions, or any other operational function of the event. Through these efforts enhanced security is provided to spectators, participants, and employees alike.

Before getting into the specifics of event safety and security, a working definition is needed for what a secure event is. AECOM, a world leader in sport venue design, engineering, and construction defines a **secure event** as an event in a venue (traditional or nontraditional) with an enhanced atmosphere for patrons and participants while providing a certain level of safety and an efficient, direct, and unobtrusive emergency response. In essence, patrons, feel well attended-to, while the level of security intervention is minimized. There is a certain intangible "feel" to events that are secure and it is apparent to spectators and participants that if something does go wrong, event staffs are capable of launching the appropriate response.

This chapter focuses on the measures required to sustain a safe venue as well as discussing risk mitigation processes.

Beyond the basic definition, there are some fundamental aspects and key ingredients for a venue to host a safe, secure, and enjoyable event. Building design, function, and equipment are the first defense against all types of safety threats, while a well-trained staff that reacts appropriately is also crucial. Controlling the venue with respect to spectator management and using technology to protect the building also play roles in how the building functions on event, and nonevent, days. Event managers use risk assessment strategies leading up to the event to plan for possible incidents and minimize the negative impact. This process will guide the creation of an appropriate emergency plan that is understood and communicated to all of those involved in event management (discussed in Chapter 17—Event Medical Management).

Venue Control

Thankfully, the days of treating public assembly venues as windowless boxes that open only for ticketed events are long gone. Today's best, most secure, and enjoyable venues are transparent and connected to the community and neighborhood.

Venues are seen as part of their surrounding community.

This facilitates clear observation of activity within and outside the venue, and allows for the facility to be part of its surroundings. However, the building also must employ proper infrastructure design, equipment, and technology to ensure control over the entire space.

Infrastructure

The best security infrastructure is that which is positive and effective while unobtrusive. **Infrastructure** refers to the aspects of the venue that are at the core of its operation such as the structure, roadways, access ways, lighting, and utilities associated with the venue. Well-designed building security strategies include:

- Site bollards and other physical barriers that impede vehicular attack and direct and isolate safe pedestrian and vehicular flow
- Efficient, dramatic, and energy-efficient lighting makes spaces feel safe while enabling better quality video surveillance
- Hardening of the building envelope (e.g., using materials that can withstand major structural forces), where required, will mitigate progressive structural collapse and injury to patrons from flying glass, and so on, should such an event occur
- Building heating/ventilating/air conditioning (HVAC) systems must be configured with outside air intakes located safely and not accessible to criminal assault

Since control methods may be required in a variety of scenarios and locations, consideration should be given to their appearance and integration with the larger project design. One trend in access, primarily for premium seating customers, is to provide direct access from the individual levels of attached parking garages or adjacent structures (e.g., office building) to specific levels of a facility. While not widespread in its adoption for general entry and exiting of the building, this still is an area that must be considered in security measures.

By reducing accessibility to all utilities (mechanical, electrical, and plumbing), they are less likely to become a target area for chemical terrorism. The position of air intakes and exhaust louvers should be elevated from the ground to prohibit access. A venue could use sensors inside louvers to detect airborne chemicals, but such sensors have cost and reliability issues. All utility lines, including exterior vaults, should be locked and monitored as well. Finally, dual electrical service should be provided when feasible.

Spectator Movement

Access control does not end at the sidewalk or vehicle door. The circulation and approach of event traffic present many different levels for evaluation and analysis of control strategies. Spectator management and entry have evolved significantly in recent years, with the resulting strategies challenging new and existing facilities alike. While the approach to search and control of spectators entering tends to vary both by event type and geographical location, some commonly accepted methodologies do exist.

Entry Areas

Interior and exterior entry spaces must be unobstructed and direct; clear and gracious; and provide a simple sequence. This will allow for multiple lines for patron screening and security checks. Typically, these functions occur some distance back from the venue entry to allow for mitigation of potential concerns. To efficiently manage the associated costs of such measures, newer facilities have limited points of entry and access to single, large entry lobby-type spaces where large populations can gather and multiple functions can occur. Adjacent, secure rooms (holding cells) may be required at mega events to allow for transfer of detainees or to separate individuals requiring special security clearance from the main entry population.

Multiple locations or stations for bag and person/apparel checks should be sequenced and separate from the areas of ticket taking. While event staff typically handle these functions, additional screening via a pass-thru metal detector may be required. Because the cost of these devices and the inabilities of older facilities to handle the multiple power locations can be significant, many facilities have chosen to use hand-held wand devices for both economy and expediency.

Event Gate Entry After 9/11

William D. Squires

President/Founder of The Right Stuff Consulting, Inc. former venue manager (Yankee Stadium, Giants Stadium, ESPN Wide World of Sports and Cleveland Browns Stadium), and past president of the Stadium Managers Association.

September 11, 2001 was one of the most tragic days in the history of the United States of America. Many things changed following the attacks on the World Trade Center. Among them was the speed and ease of entering a sports facility.

Prior to 9/11 bags were permitted into most sports venues and the size of the bag was limited by whether or not it could fit under a seat. Bags were routinely checked for alcohol by event staff inside the gates after the spectator's ticket was torn and they passed through a turnstile.

Following 9/11 the major sports leagues, teams, and the individuals who manage sports venues reviewed security policies and procedures and made the necessary changes to ensure the safety and security of the those individuals attending, working, or participating in the events. The size of bags was limited (i.e., bags should not exceed 12 in. × 6 in. × 12 in. in the NFL) and they were checked for contraband prior to the ticket holder having their ticket scanned and entering the venue.

The safety and security for those attending events in sports facilities has been, and continues to be, a major focus in the event industry. Communicating the policies and procedures with season ticket holders and those who may only be attending a single event is a never-ending task. Every media platform, including social media, is needed to get the word out about safety and security policies, but many people still do not know the policies and procedures.

Pat downs of those entering the facility became the norm and in recent years hand-held magnetometers have been used to screen fans and event staff. Currently, walk-thru magnetometers are being used at ballparks that host Major League Baseball teams and many other sports venues throughout the country are beginning to install these magnetometers.

In 2013, the NFL instituted a policy of limiting the size of purses and requiring the use of clear plastic bags which are no larger than 12 in. × 6 in. × 12 in. to bring items into the venue. The 2015 NCAA Men's Final Four also instituted a similar policy allowing small purses, gallon clear plastic bags, and the same standard 12 in. × 6 in. × 12 in. clear plastic bags into the stadium.

Additionally, in 2014, the NFL encouraged the management of venues hosting NFL teams to establish a secondary security perimeter. The perimeter was to be far from the gates, staffed by Safety and Security personnel, and used to screen the size of bags. The intent was to stop noncompliant bags from being brought into the areas outside the gates where ticket holders are queuing to enter the venue. In the half hour leading up to kickoff there could be thousands of patrons waiting to enter the stadium and the NFL did not want a repeat of what happened at the Boston Marathon (e.g., the tragic bombing near the race finish in 2013). In addition, it would be a poor guest experience to have ticket holders wait in line and then be told by the Safety and Security staff that a ticket holder's bag was too large and that it would not be allowed in the venue.

Ticket holders have the option of returning items to their vehicles if their bags that do not meet the established dimensions, or have prohibited items. Most venues provide storage facilities for fans that do not want to return to their vehicles or may have taken mass transit. These storage facilities should be a safe distance from the venue and queuing areas. It is a standard practice to inspect the contents of the bags or items before they are stored.

The events that took place on September 11, 2001 have changed the way we live our lives. Event and facility managers are continuously evaluating security policies and procedures to ensure the safety of their venue and the safety and security of those who are in the venue on event day. This has to be balanced with ensuring a great event day experience. The role of the venue manager has always been complex and multifaceted, but even more so today.

Communication

One way to help fans understand how to enter the facility is to communicate it to them. Web sites, mailings, and marketing materials can be used to "tell" people where to go, how to get there, and what to expect. From simply providing information on parking to more detailed security information, good communication can alleviate many event day problems and frustrations. For example, an event that will be using metal detectors should explicitly state that in their materials. Event managers should also communicate that it might take some extra time to screen all fans, and that they should plan on arriving early. Fans can then adjust their schedule and plan on leaving some extra time to get through security.

Wayfinding

Multiple points of access for either entry or egress present a variety of operational and design-related issues. Visibility in many forms is important to address. Clear line of sight can improve **wayfinding** within a facility, the ease with which visitors find their way throughout the venue. Well placed, visible entries help people to navigate into the building efficiently.

Sports facilities are typically large-scale structures that can be disorienting for their occupants. The inclusion of glass and views to the exterior, plus other major architectural features of "landmarks" in both concourses and in exit stairs help orient the occupants to the exterior and can assist in the efficient egress in evacuation. The connection to security and wayfinding is that at all times, defensible space must be provided. **Defensible space** refers to using architectural design to diminish or mitigate any tendency toward negative behaviors. No dark corners or places should exist where staff or patrons may feel trapped or lacking in clear visibility or access.

This is also true of nontraditional sport venues. In the creation of a facility for an event, wayfinding and defensible space should be kept in mind. Areas that are considered part of the venue for a road race should be away from heavily wooded areas and provide for ease of accessibility to and from key functional areas of the event.

A facility that is planned to ensure clear line of sight for security (either physical observation or with cameras) will aid in efficient control of a building and its perimeter. Visual obstructions must be minimized or eliminated with thoughtful placement of perimeter enclosure, strategic landscaping, and support structures.

How Building Planning and Design Impact Safety and Security

AECOM

The building design and function are the first defense in protecting against all types of security and safety issues. In most cases, the building is well into the design or already built when event managers get involved. However, decisions made in site selection, planning, and design will impact all events that occur in the venue after the building opens. Thus, event managers need to be familiar with how these factors impact event safety and security.

Urban redevelopment has increased in the last 10 years, with sports facilities being a major catalyst for downtown renewal. With growing concerns about potential security threats and new attitudes toward spectator safety and security, both venue planners and operators are challenged constantly. Among the benefits of developing sports facilities in dense urban settings is the close proximity to live-work-play amenities commonly associated with vibrant city centers. This presents challenges to maintaining realistic safety zones between sports facilities and unprotected public right of ways.

Sports facilities share many of the common operational issues of the surrounding businesses. However, their large scale of structure demands considerations in additional areas and careful management. In addition, venue design and operations must accommodate a variety of events and the collateral implications of the size and demographics of a given crowd. A venue should also be a "good neighbor" or good building 365 days a year, not just during events. To achieve these objectives, certain fundamentals in the building site selection and design must be considered carefully. With proper planning and creative design, potential security issues can be properly mitigated to ensure the continuous fabric of the city development.

Site Selection

When planning a new sport facility, site selection brings many challenges beyond the inevitably large physical size and scale of the building. Specific evaluation of surrounding transportation networks, utilities, and infrastructure is required as part of site evaluation. Transportation access and modes are always a concern, and become even more pivotal as the capacity of the venue increases. Vehicle management is key, not only as this relates to the experience of the fan, but also the collateral impacts event days can and will have on the larger urban context. Architects should evaluate and assign proper importance to the capacity of a road network to sufficiently handle event day traffic and not encumber regional movement. Emergency vehicle ingress, egress, and staging at the facility are an important layer to this evaluation. Event-specific personnel are part of standard event practices (ambulance with EMT, local police, and state patrols). In some cases, additional personnel and vehicles may be necessary in the event of fire, a bombing, structural collapse, or hazardous materials incidents. Venue planners must also consider the capacity of surrounding infrastructure to accommodate this additional loading, as well as potential expedited evacuation.

Site Setback

Facility best practices now include consideration of site safety zone setbacks and associated systems to restrict vehicular proximity to the building and site. **Site setback** refers to the distance between the spectator venue and other structures and/or public right of ways. In urban locations, evaluation of these items is needed. Specifically, designers will examine congruity of the venue with the adjacent development as well as the quality of the environment, while still providing the necessary separation.

Architects must strike a delicate balance between creating a facility design that is seamless with its surroundings versus the "Fort Knox" approach adopted by many early-generation facilities. Planners must identify site locations or building plan configurations that can create safe, operationally functional, and attractive site setback. Meeting these objectives is becoming increasingly challenging as developable sites

Courtesy of Timothy Hursley

Notice the distance between the road and building as well as the barrier created by the

become more scarce, and is often "four sided" versus "one to three sided" locations that back up against other buildings. Each side of the building that is prominently exposed presents a "public face." Thus, each side will require adequate measures for access control and security. The more exposure, the greater the complexity of the security challenges.

Site Context

Site context refers to whether or not the venue site and immediate areas convey a sense of welcoming, safety, and control. To create a welcoming feel, designers should conceive a site in the context of surrounding neighborhoods, whether they are urban, suburban, or a college/university campus.

Architects and building planners can take some specific steps in site context to enhance the feeling of security, and they include:

- Control and segregation of vehicular and pedestrian traffic
- Ample, inviting site and building lighting
- A sense of vitality and activity around the site and within the building
- Music, messaging, and video displays
- A carefully orchestrated arrival sequence, including ample accommodation to perform security screening in an efficient, customer-friendly manner.

These features create a sense of heightened pre-event anticipation, and encouragement of postevent lingering to savor the event. Simply, the goal is "smiles on the way in, smiles on the way out."

Designing an Invisible Perimeter

Efficient movement of game day spectator foot and vehicle traffic, both before and after an event, contributes significantly to the fan experience and safety. This can also reduce operation costs related to security and traffic management. Grand boulevards, wide sidewalks, and active hardscape plazas are visually attractive means for providing sports facilities necessary setback without undermining the game day experience. Additional techniques involving site grade transitions with structured planter beds, landscape features, and decorative bollard-type elements can all work in concert to create a perimeter that is visually pleasing, harmonious with its surroundings, and, most importantly, an effective deterrent to direct facility vehicular approach.

In the years since the establishment of the Department of Homeland Security, many municipalities and institutions have begun a process of staging mock event scenarios centered on the stadium or arena to test and review preparedness plans. The integration of limited open plaza-type areas and broad perimeter circulation can double as effective staging areas for these activities as well. In areas of pedestrian circulation, there are many alternatives to unsightly yellow-painted steel and concrete cylinders. Careful attention to the design of unobtrusive architectural barriers, curb heights, or low-height reinforced walls can all provide similar but more visually attractive methods of security. Where land or adjacent property is present, planning strategies that consider connecting walkways or enclosed bridges can provide the same level of service without introducing similar security concerns.

Parking

Especially in urban areas, existing parking garages in the proximity are commonly associated with sport facilities and deserve attention during planning. Parking garages present a series of challenges to venue security, but are also integral components of venue design. As discussed, efficiency of movement is a primary driver in all facets of sports facility planning and operations. Nowhere is this felt as acutely as parking. Delays in loading or unloading can impact customer event satisfaction.

Courtesy of Timothy Hursley

Parking structure design is an important component in event management and security.

In many cases, premium seating and hospitality clients are the only customers with parking access in close proximity to the venue. Delays in entry or exit from the parking area become a big concern for venue and event managers, since these individuals represent a significant revenue stream. Being as such, careful attention should be given to remove inefficiencies and unnecessary delays for this important client group that represents a significant revenue stream for the venue.

Architects should evaluate the proper balance in determining operational procedures related to parking. While convenience is important, especially for premium clientele, the proximity of a significant number of unattended vehicles to a sports venue is a security challenge. Most of the major professional sport leagues have implemented safety zones in which no public vehicle can park, regardless of existing garage or surface layouts. Security experts recognize unattended vehicles as a threat because terrorists around the world have put explosives in unattended cars and trucks close to high-profile target buildings.

Structural Elements

The integration of sports venues into urban developments also typically requires a higher level of physical articulation than their isolated counterparts to achieve the optimum level of "fit" and interaction within the urban context. The introduction of elements such as exterior ornament, lighting, large changeable signage, and significant expanse of glass creates an energetic exterior that will integrate and complement its surroundings.

Building planners should also integrate these elements into their overall security management plan. Consideration must be given for proximity of glass to both the ground and adjacent roadways, to acknowledge concerns related to both blast and vehicle intrusion. Design of exterior elements should incorporate reasonable redundancy in structure to minimize failure. Redundancy concepts relate to how safely people can evacuate a total, partial, and segmented collapse of a building, and help to isolate structural collapses to the impacted area. In general, modern building codes address this concern through a variety of categories including occupancy type and separation, fire-resistive construction assemblies, and seismic design considerations. However, the designers are responsible for the creating an overall safe solution.

These requirements create structures more responsive to the needs of maintaining building integrity, allowing for safe evacuation. Blast-resistive construction is very specialized in its application and tends to be more expensive than conventional design. There are many opportunities to incorporate similar or component-specific technology to typical commercial construction to gain the related benefits without paying an extraordinary premium.

Involving Experts

Best practices today bring police, fire safety professionals, and security consultants together into the planning and design process early. They help set expectations and specific technical program requirements that are integral to the building and design process. Security consultants, specializing in technology, should partner with the design team to help make buildings safer for the occupants. These professional experts, in collaboration with the architect, focus on detailed work sessions with owners, operators, and tenants throughout the project to ensure security measures are reviewed and developed fully. An example of the value of involving security experts early in the process relates to communication systems and protocols. Together, the local police and fire agencies can work with the architects and security consultants to integrate a direct communication link from the facility to the local public safety office via a secured communication system. To add this type of communication after the building was constructed would be extremely challenging, but in the planning and design process, it becomes part of the overall building design.

Event managers may never be involved in the planning and design of a new facility, but understanding the design features that help provide a secure event is important. From the strength of the building's structure to the placement of hardscape plazas, event managers need to know the entire building before a security or emergency plan can be effectively developed. The concepts that help to make a major venue secure can be transposed on a smaller scale to any sport event or facility.

Command Center

Command centers are essentially the building's "nerve center," and bring the use of security-related technologies to a central location.

Command centers act as a central hub for safety and security services.

All sport facilities, traditional and nontraditional, should have a command center, or an identified area that functions as one, as in the case of smaller outdoor events. A properly designed and integrated command center is the hub of facility security, police, fire departments, and outside emergency responders. It will typically bring all the available technologies of facility monitoring, security video, and audio together into one central location. This enables authorities to give public address announcements, alter directional signage, and send out communications to all the various emergency teams.

The individuals staffing the command center will log and document anything related to safety and security, but they may also deal with other event functions. Deliveries that do not arrive on time, missing equipment, reports of lost items, and staff not at their correct location might all be reported to the command center. All incoming communications to the command center are then routed back out to the appropriate person or entity. To give a nonsecurity example of how the command center might operate, imagine a nonfunctioning timing display at the finish line at a road race. The staff at the finish line can radio to the command center that the timing display is not working correctly, the command center can locate the on-call timing system contact, and they can be dispatched immediately to resolve the problem.

For large venues, there are commonly two additional areas where safety and security monitoring and logistical functions take place. Besides the main command center, there is generally a separate fire command center. This location is equipped with redundant security technology and life safety systems that can be controlled by fire and police officials. Because it must have direct access from the exterior, it is often located near the loading dock area. The second command center is generally located in the upper portions of the seating bowl to monitor and direct staff during a situation in the event seating areas or on the event floor. Both of these areas must have quick and direct access to the main command center.

For nontraditional venues, the command center may be located within an existing fire or police station. In other situations, a mobile command center will be used which is set up one of two ways. A portable building can be used like those on construction sites, or it can be set up similarly to a television production truck in that it has all of the functioning of a command center in a venue, but it is self-contained.

A full-service formal command center may be beyond the scope of some events, but for all events there should be a central location where all communications are directed. Many college sports events will use the area from which the game is being run (e.g., P.A., sound, stats) as the central point of contact for all communications. Often the event managers are in this area, and if they are not, the individuals in the area can find them quickly.

Technology

Players, performers, fans, and VIPs expect sport facilities to protect them from situations and persons who might cause them harm. Technology and involving the right people during planning increases event managers' ability to control and monitor the facility. Proper use of current technology can help monitor and screen spectators, help to separate the public and private spaces in the facility, and improve the efficiency of overall building operations.

Closed Circuit Television Systems/Camera Monitoring

Closed circuit television systems (CCTV) have become common elements that help monitor all public areas, especially the ticket-taking area and the seating bowl. Stationary cameras and those that pan, tilt, and zoom are used to monitor areas and alert building security officials of issues needing immediate attention. Cameras can also document and verify events and identify people for postevent investigations. Some facility managers have seen the benefit of having staff dedicated to documenting events with hand-held cameras in addition to CCTV. With this option, security handling of fans or others is documented if it is ever needed following the event, for clarification of situation or legal action. Other common areas that cameras are used to monitor are parking lots, pedestrian access ways, building perimeter, entrances, ticket windows, lobbies, concourses, specialty clubs, team corridors, entry points, and the truck dock area.

Patron Scanning and Ticketing

Frequently, patrons are now asked to go through metal detectors before their ticket is taken or scanned. This process is best implemented before spectators enter the main lobby of the building. Currently, many arenas are using the exterior entrance doors as the point of screening, and patron tickets are then scanned. If possible, event staff should scan tickets before spectators enter the venue. If security staff wand spectators, they should do it in an area that does not impede the flow of spectators into the venue. This must be integrated with a strategy and location for bag checks. The most effective operations for major events have incorporated a 100-foot safety zone for accomplishing these tasks.

Fan Tracking, Engagement Applications, and Texting

Event managers can use patrons' own mobile devices to help make the venue more secure. Venues and team mobile applications provide direct emergency communication and often venues post a number to which fans can text problems in the venue directly to the command center. These services allow fans to help the team and venue keep everyone safe. For example, since facility staff cannot be everywhere at once, a fan may be sitting next to a rowdy fan that is disturbing all of those around her. Instead of having to leave her seat to find a member of security, the fan can quietly text the command center about the problem, and the text can be logged like any other security concern. Teams report that they may have been missing 40% of the problems prior to implementing the texting systems (Lavigne, 2009). This type of texting service is now a feature that fans expect when they attend major sporting events. Teams have even made the hotline numbers easy to remember with the Ravens using "ASSIST," the Colts choosing "ASSIST," and the Bengals adding some humor with "513-381-JERK" (Chase, 2008). Some teams go beyond security and use texting to address maintenance issues in the venue, to share weather and traffic reports, and other event related information. Allowing fan participation in keeping the venue safe is a relatively new strategy, but one that does not cost much and allows the fans to feel even more part of the event.

Delivery Areas and Truck Docks

Certain venues locate separate rooms outside the arena footprint to allow for screening equipment for mail, bulk packages, and other items needing to be evaluated before entering the facility. This is a big expense, and unless incorporated into the design at the earliest stages, can be cost prohibitive in all but the largest of venues. Even for those facilities that employ this security strategy, some vehicles need access directly to the venue.

All event production requires load in and load out of equipment and supplies. This creates some risk, as trucks often drive up to or into the building. For nontraditional venues, deliveries often occur on the event course, such as water delivery trucks on a marathon course. Technology continues to advance in the area of real-time vehicle scans for explosives and other dangerous substances. However, currently these applications are not typically considered an economically viable solution for sport venues and events.

Instead, a combination of well-placed security stations and related video surveillance and access controls create an effective deterrent. Special care needs to be given to vehicle control, restraint, and inspection in areas where vehicles are engaging with the event levels, or will come in close proximity to back of house operations (e.g., player parking, service vehicles, and event-related support).

During planning, screening and securing entry points into the truck dock area of the arena is a challenge that needs to be addressed, especially in urban settings. One option is to restrict truck access with movable bollards or electronic overhead doors to validate the delivery before the truck drives close to the building. Retractable bollards and restraint systems both go beyond the typical operable gate. The benefits of these flexible systems are that they retract when not needed. A typical day often requires less stringent security than an event day, and flexible devices allow for a variety of different levels of security. In some cases, screening of all packages arriving at the facility occurs. If this is part of the security protocol, tagging of items should also occur to clearly distinguish screened parcels from nonscreened parcels.

Even for events without intricate security systems for deliveries, the areas where delivery trucks will enter or be close to the venue need monitoring. Creating one entry point that is easily staffed by security using removable barricades is sufficient for most events. Separating delivery traffic from spectator and/or participant arrival traffic also helps to keep traffic moving and people safe.

Communication between the event managers and those individuals responsible for monitoring traffic into the delivery area is critical. Event managers will likely have to submit a delivery schedule well in advance of an event. The **delivery schedule** will include the date, time, company, the driver's name, contact phone numbers, vehicle description, and the license plate number of each expected delivery. Additionally, for event days, event managers may issue a required vehicle permit that the driver must have (in addition to all other information) to enter the event site. This puts a lot of responsibility on event managers to be aware of every anticipated delivery prior to the event. For good reason, any deviations from the expected list are likely to incur a delay while event managers work with the security at the truck dock to verify delivery, or security might turn them away and refuse access.

Electronic Access Door Systems

Beyond the standard keyed hardware, a number of devices are used to monitor door access. Venue operators are adding card access readers, door monitors (sensing when a door has been opened or left ajar), key pads, electronically controlled locks, and motion detectors to help secure entries. Beyond entry doors to the facility, monitoring is often necessary for interior doors that separate public and private access (entries to event level, locker rooms, ticketing areas, offices, athletic training areas, etc.). **Biometric scanning** uses individual physiological characteristics such as fingerprints, face recognition, and iris recognition to allow or deny access to doors. Venue managers are discussing the possibility of biometric scanning for sport facilities, but cost and complexity of programming have kept this technology from wide adoption.

As science and technology continues to advance, new systems will become available. Buildings need to be adaptable and flexible in order to embrace future options to secure buildings. Event managers may rely on building operators to implement the preceding security strategies, but they also need to have an understanding of the facility in which the event is being held, and how it operates in relation to building control. Beyond the design of the building and equipment used, there should be crowd management policies in place to create a fun and safe environment for all.

Game Day Management

Managing the event, while keeping safety and security in mind at all times, can be challenging. Being prepared for circumstances that may arise will help to set the stage for a safe and secure event. The "What If" game is commonly used to help all those involved in the event think through and share possible responses to a variety of scenarios. For instance, before a skateboarding event at a local skate park, the facility and event staff can challenge each other to brainstorm as many situations as possible that might happen. It might look like this:

- What if it rains?
- What if nobody signs up to compete?
- What if a crack in the skate park concrete is found that day?
- What if a participant is severely injured?
- What if we expect 300 people and 2,000 attend?
- What if a child falls into the competition area?
- What if the parking lot fills up?
- What if there is a fight between spectators?

These are just a few of the many types of situations that might emerge through playing the "What If" game. The game allows event managers to be proactive in addressing each scenario and communicating to staff the appropriate reaction to the situation. Ideas that surface might also remind event staff of things that could have been forgotten during planning. In the skateboarding competition, thinking through what would be done if the parking lot fills up might remind event managers to secure a secondary parking lot at a neighboring business for the day. No situation is too crazy to consider when playing the game. Crowd scenarios will often come up in this game, and managing a crowd is one of the most difficult parts of any spectator event. This process helps in emergency planning as well (discussed in Chapter 17—Event Medical Management).

Managing the Crowd

Understanding the projected crowd is the first step to managing it effectively. Certainly, a NASCAR event and a cheerleading national championship will have very different types of fans attending. Experienced event managers realize how different types of crowds tend to behave, and will adjust their strategies to the anticipated crowd. Beyond the type of event, the significance of the event is important to grasp. What might normally be a regular NCAA Division I basketball game can become a heated battle where emotions run high when a conference championship or NCAA tournament berth is on the line.

Using existing relationships with other event and facility managers is a good strategy to help understand the type of crowd that will attend the event. Most event managers are happy to share information with others when asked. A telephone call to the previous host of the event can garner important information related to attendees.

Other policies can help in the management of the crowd throughout the event. Some of the security strategies highlighted throughout this chapter also relate directly to crowd management (e.g., improved wayfinding, in-venue texting, communications, etc.). Examples of other, more direct strategies include:

- Creating a Fan Code of Conduct. It sets behavioral expectations for everyone and is communicated in a way that encourages good behavior and sportsmanship.
- Prohibiting fans from leaving the venue and returning, often known as pass-outs. For events that do not sell alcohol, this keeps spectators from drinking outside the venue and then returning to possibly cause trouble.
- Setting aside pregame time for the head coach to speak about sportsmanship and behavior. This can be especially impactful at college athletic events, where the head coach is often held in high esteem.
- Using existing in-event communication channels such as P.A. reads, video board productions, social media, and signage can also set the tone for behavior.
- Establishing family-friendly areas that allow those attending the event with children to be able to separate themselves from other fans who might be a little rowdier.
- Ensuring that the presence of television cameras does not draw the crowd down the seating area, creating the possibility of a crush. Cameras should stay well back from crowds and use strong lenses to capture close-up footage.

Policies such as these help to promote a culture of personal responsibility that is important to overall crowd management. By emphasizing good sportsmanship, supporting the team, and respecting the wishes of the head coach, the message is clearly positive. This strategy is more effective than telling people they cannot do something.

Sample Guest Code of Conduct

Team *Successful Sport Management* is committed to sportsmanship among its coaches, athletes, staff, and fans. Sportsmanship has been defined as the conduct becoming to one participating in sport. Team *Successful Sport Management's* coaches, athletes, staff, and fans believe sportsmanship is playing fairly, acting respectfully toward others, and promoting the interests and good name of Team *Successful Sport Management* on and off the field of play.

It is expected that all persons show respect to opposing teams, game officials, and each other while at Team *Successful Sport Management* events.

The following rules apply to Facility Go Big or Go Home:

- Fans are expected to sit in their ticketed seat and be able to show their game ticket if requested.
- No outside food, drink, or glass containers of any kind.
- No bags or backpacks allowed. Purses are subject to search and could delay entry.

- No umbrellas.
- No video cameras.
- No artificial noise makers.
- Smoking is permitted in designated areas only.
- Foul or abusive language will not be tolerated.
- All signs and banners must be in good taste.
- No oversized stadium seats.
- No throwing of objects from the stands.

Guests that become aware of any safety issues or encounter difficulties with other fans are urged to contact a member of the event management staff. Fans violating any of the above rules or displaying poor sportsmanship are subject to ejection from the stadium, revocation of season tickets, and in some cases, criminal prosecution.

Thank you, and GO TEAM SUCCESSFUL SPORT MANAGEMENT!

Staff

The event managers are responsible for setting the stage for events, and the attitude, appearance, presence, and training of event staff is all part of that. Event staffs have an enormous impact on security and the behavior of the crowd. First and foremost, background checks of all staff are important to protect the safety of all patrons. The type of event will dictate what type of background (i.e., misdemeanor versus felony charges) might disqualify someone from working (see Chapter 14—Event Staffing and Chapter 15—Event Volunteer Management for more information). These decisions should be made on an individual basis with all of the available facts.

Having the correct number of staff is critical to ensuring safety for all. Industry standards call for one trained crowd manager for every 250 patrons. This number should be adjusted based on the results of research conducted about the anticipated crowd. For example, for an important college football game, extra crowd managers are needed in the student section. The number might go to one trained crowd manager for every 150 spectators in this scenario. If alcohol is sold, the number of crowd managers might also be higher. Another commonly used ratio is for staffing the ticket-taking areas. In general, one ticket taker for every 1,000–1,200 spectators should be sufficient. By having the entries identified on tickets, event managers can staff each entrance appropriately, because they know the volume to expect at each entrance.

All front of house staff should embrace the point of view that patrons are treasured guests, whose every need must be catered to—and these staff must be sufficient in number to maintain an obvious presence. Workers need to also be continually trained to be on the lookout for activity that might threaten safety or security. Procedures must be established—and continually, rigorously updated via continuing education—so that reactions are quick and effective in any situation that may compromise safety and security.

Event mangers should empower staff to speak up about safety and security issues. Event day staffs work throughout the venue, and are likely to become aware of safety issues before upper level event managers. The same is true of spectators; they are likely to become aware of safety issues before event staff, but they need to know whom to tell. Messages to spectators should include phone numbers and texting numbers which they can use to report safety and/or security concerns. Using all staff (and event spectators) as part of the security team expands the reach of event managers exponentially.

Internal Communication

Internal communication is often overlooked prior to the event. Event managers should regularly communicate with marketing, tickets, concessions, and facility managers to make sure that all the pieces of the event are coming together. This is critical to safety, because if event managers or facility managers are staffing the game, they need to know how many tickets have been sold and in what areas. If the marketing department decided to have a costume contest for a game close to Halloween, it might be a major problem for security, as masks and costumes conceal the identity of people and are not advised from a safety and security perspective. If the facility and security staff are not aware of this promotion and refuse entry to spectators in masks, there are sure to be problems. Event managers are the ones that close these communication gaps and prevent promotions such as this from moving forward if they pose a risk. Even if it does not seem directly related to safety and security, often small decisions in individual departments will impact overall safety and security.

Communications Equipment

Having adequate communications equipment on the event day is critical to keeping the event safe and secure from start to finish. Cell phones and two-way radios are commonly used by event staff, but using them effectively with a large group of workers can be difficult.

© Shutterstock

Proper communications equipment is critical for event staff and all support staff.

Although it can be costly, communications can mean the difference between life and death in an emergency. There is no excuse for not having appropriate communications equipment.

First, event managers must assess their communications needs before exploring the best type of equipment. How many radios are needed? How many different channels on the radios are needed? How far away from each other could event staff be when needing radio communications? Are there any other local agencies that also need to be on the same frequency for security? For single events, often two-way radios can be rented for the event, and sometimes facilities offer event managers the use of their radios as part of the rental agreement. Answering these questions will help event managers decide on what is needed for the event.

In general, two-way radios communicate directly to one another and can cover a fairly large area. So, an event that is small in nature and only needs coverage at one venue can probably use a few two-way radios with one channel and have adequate communications. The more people using the radios and the larger the geographical area that needs to be covered, the more complex radio operations become. Radio frequencies can be programmed by a communications company in a variety of configurations. The event can have everyone on one channel so that everything said is heard by all, or channels can be assigned by group (e.g., marketing channel 1, medical channel 2, event ops channel 3, etc.). The number of people and diversity of their work drive the structure of the channels involved in the event. If the event is loud, then event managers must provide headsets to ensure communications can be heard. Lapel clip microphones allow for communication without removing the radio from the holster, and extra batteries are a must.

The size of the area that the radios need to cover will dictate whether a repeater is needed for communications, or whether exchanges can be radio to radio only. A **radio repeater** receives a low-level signal and retransmits it at a higher power, increasing the distance the signal can effectively cover. A repeater will most likely be needed for golf events, road races, or just to maintain communication within the locale if staffs are driving to do errands. The radio repeater is placed in a central elevated location of the event, and increases the range tremendously. One note of caution is that the repeater is generally AC power operated and not on batteries. The radios still need to be configured to communicate without the repeater in the event of a power outage. Radios are most critical in the event of an emergency such as a power outage, and losing communication at that time can be catastrophic.

Often, the local police or fire agency will provide one of their radios for key personnel to communicate directly with them. This means that event managers will be carrying an event radio as well as the emergency radio for police and fire. Codes should also be established for emergency situations so that the specific emergency is not broadcast to everyone on the radio. For example, if there is a kitchen fire that can be easily contained, it would not make sense to announce there was a fire. Merely the word "fire" can create a panic. Using a code, such as "code red—contained to kitchen" will alert emergency responders listening in and the command center of the exact nature of the incident. Concurrently, others will go about their business.

Alcohol Sales

For some sports events, alcohol goes hand in hand with the event. Unfortunately, alcohol also can cause problems related to crowd behavior. The combination of exciting sports, large groups of people in a confined area, often hot or cold weather, and alcohol is a recipe for disturbances. Event managers may not be directly responsible for alcohol sales, but they should be aware of policies that can be implemented to minimize alcohol-related disturbances and problems.

The Techniques for Effective Alcohol Management (TEAM) Coalition is a group of "professional and collegiate sports, entertainment facilities, concessionaires, stadium service providers, the beer industry, broadcasters, governmental traffic safety experts, and others working together to promote responsible drinking and positive fan behavior at sports and entertainment facilities" (n.d., 1). The TEAM Coalition trains facility and event employees in sport and entertainment (and provides certification) on how to educate their alcohol sales and services staff. It is a great, cost-effective way to help reduce liability associated with alcohol sales, as well as help to reduce alcohol-related incidents at events.

Ensuring that only those of legal age are able to purchase and/or consume alcohol is difficult. A wristband or hand stamp might be provided to those over 21, but as many people know, wristbands and stamps can be transferred to someone else. Often, venues and events outsource alcohol sales to a third party to transfer a lot of legal liability associated with alcohol sales. Regardless of which entity sells the alcohol, event managers should ensure that vendors have adequate training and good policies.

Most sport venues stop selling alcohol at a certain point during the game, often two-thirds of the way through the game. This slows down consumption by fans toward the end of the game, and gives them time to process the alcohol they have consumed before they drive home. Designated driver programs are becoming increasingly popular at sports events. To encourage people to use a designated driver, that person is given a wristband and often some other benefit, such as a free meal, as a "thank you" for staying sober to drive others home safely.

The exact behavior of crowds cannot be predicted, but the general nature of a group of sports fans can be anticipated based on past experiences of others, research, and the specifics of the event. Event mangers can also use specific strategies to encourage good behavior by fans and create a positive atmosphere. However, even with the best strategies implemented, there is always risk associated with a sports event.

Risk Management

Risk can be defined as "a hazard or the possibility of danger or harm" (Mulrooney & Farmer, 2005, p. 309). Risk associated with sports events cannot be avoided entirely, but it can be managed through the risk management process. The entire process of evaluating risk and using cost-effective strategies to reduce and treat risk is known as **risk management**. The overarching goal of event managers with respect to risk management is to protect life, the building, and the finances of the organization. Since events can vary greatly in their characteristics, risk management needs to be considered separately for each event. The uniqueness of each event will result in different risks that are identified and thus, different treatments of those risks.

There are a variety of frameworks available in which risk can be assessed for a facility and/or event in sport. Mulrooney and Farmer (2005) provide a model that is broad in scope and easily applicable to a wide spectrum of events. They explain the risk management process by breaking it into three stages: recognition, evaluation, and treatment (Mulrooney & Farmer, 2005). There are entire textbooks written on the subject of risk management in sport, so the following is designed to provide an overview of risk management for events and is not intended to be all encompassing.

Recognition

The first step in risk management is to identify all possible risks. Recognition of many risks comes with experience, so new event managers should seek out those with experience when beginning this process. For purposes of description, an example of a simple local summer fun run will be used to illustrate the risk management process. For a fun run, some of the risks might include:

- Severe weather (e.g., significant rain, thunderstorms)
- Minor injuries to athletes
- Major life-threatening injuries to athletes
- Vehicle traffic entering the race route
- Lack of event staff to manage the event
- Not enough concessions prepared
- Terrorist attack

Evaluation

The severity of the loss (financial and otherwise), along with the anticipated frequency of occurrences, can be used to evaluate the risk (Mulrooney & Farmer, 2005). A risk matrix (see Table 16.1) is often used to evaluate risks by noting the frequency across the top row of the chart and the significance of the loss in a vertical column down the side. The risks identified in the recognition phase of this process are then included in the matrix to allow for overall evaluation of each risk. In the case of the local fun run, the identified risks have been inserted in Table 16.1 where appropriate.

Table 16.1 Risk Matrix With Identified Risks

	Very Frequent	*Frequent*	*Moderate*	*Infrequent*	*Very Infrequent*
Very High Loss					Terrorist attack
High Loss				Major life threatening injuries to athletes	Vehicle traffic entering the race route Foodborne illness from concessions
Moderate Loss		Ice accumulation on stadium stairs during winter months		Severe weather	
Low Loss	Minor injuries to participants (i.e., sunburn during summer)		Lack of event staff		
Very Low Loss			Not enough concessions prepared		

Treatment

Once the risks have been categorized appropriately (which will differ by event), event managers can begin to assess how to treat each risk. Commonly used categories in sport to treat risk include avoidance, transfer, and keep and decrease (Mulrooney & Farmer, 2005). A treatment matrix (Mulrooney & Farmer, 2005) (see Table 16.2) provides guidance as to how to treat each risk.

Table 16.2 Risk Matrix—Treatment of Risks

	Very Frequent	*Frequent*	*Moderate*	*Infrequent*	*Very Infrequent*
Very High Loss	Avoid	Avoid	Shift	Shift	Shift
High Loss	Avoid	Avoid	Shift	Shift	Shift

(Continued)

Table 16-2   Risk Matrix—Treatment of Risks (*Continued*)

	Very Frequent	*Frequent*	*Moderate*	*Infrequent*	*Very Infrequent*
Moderate Loss	Shift	Shift	Shift	Shift	Keep and decrease
Low Loss	Keep and decrease	Keep and decrease	Keep and decrease	Keep and decrease	Keep and decrease
Very Low Loss	Keep and decrease	Keep and decrease	Keep and decrease	Keep and decrease	Keep and decrease

Source: Mulrooney and Farmer (2005).

Avoid

If a risk falls into a matrix cell that is labeled "avoid," event managers should not hold the event and avoid the risk completely. In these cases, the risk is too great to those involved to have the event. For the fun run, no identified risks fall into this category. However, for any event that had a credible terrorist threat, the best option might be to cancel the event to avoid the terror risk completely.

Shift

Event managers can "shift" the identified risk by transferring the risk to a third party. Often this is accomplished through insurance. For many risks, event managers can purchase insurance, which will protect the event organization financially if the risk is realized. There may be cases in which shifting the risk is not an option because the insurance is cost prohibitive. In those situations, the risk should then be avoided and the event should not occur.

For the fun run, a terrorist attack is very unlikely, as is vehicle traffic entering the race route. A successful terrorist attack would result in very high loss, while vehicles entering the race route have a possibility of high loss since they could injure one or more spectators or participants. Major life-threatening injuries to athletes are infrequent occurrences that result in high loss, since a person's life would be in danger with these types of injuries. All of these risks can be insured against for the fun run, and then the event can occur with event managers knowing they are protected from these occurrences. Severe weather will result in losses through decreased participation and decreased spectators, which will in turn decrease registration, concession, and merchandise revenue. Weather insurance is available for events, but event managers should conduct their own research on past weather on the event date, as well as anticipated losses, prior to purchasing the insurance. If an outdoor event that does not offer concessions or merchandise is sold out (with no ticket refunds available), then severe weather may have little to no impact on revenue, and weather would be categorized as low loss which would not result in recommended insurance.

Keep and Decrease

The final category of treatment is those cells in which identified risks fall that are labeled "keep and decrease." These risks are minimal enough that it is more cost effective to accept the risk and take steps to decrease the likelihood of it happening than to employ any of the other treatment strategies. In the case of the fun run, minor injuries to participants can be expected since physical activity is involved. The risk to the event can be decreased by using participant waivers (Chapter 8, Participant Registration for Events) or informed consent documents that inform participants of the possibility of injury. A lack of event staff may make the day tougher on those involved, but the resulting loss is low and thus can be decreased through proper planning and communication with those that do sign up to work the event. Not having enough concessions prepared might impact the event a bit financially, but through estimating attendance and participation, as well as keeping an eye on weather, event managers can provide some estimates of concessions needs to the vendor.

Follow Up

As with any management process, risk management needs follow up and continual updating to be effective. The risk management process should be conducted for each event, with the individual characteristics taken into account each time. For one event, bad weather may have little impact, while for another it will cancel the event (e.g., thunderstorm at an open-water swimming event). There is not one risk management matrix that fits all events. It is a process that is tedious, yet imperative to comprehensive safety and security operations. Risk management and emergency planning go hand in hand, as the emergency preparedness plan is the result of identifying possible emergency situations based on identified risks and developing detailed plans of actions. Even with the best risk management, emergencies will happen and emergency planning is necessary.

SUMMARY

Whether the event is big or small, the safety and security of all involved are at the forefront of all decisions related to the event. For major sport venues and mega events, many complex security features are now commonplace. Event managers should be current on how the infrastructure and equipment help to keep the venue and event safe. Smaller venues or nontraditional venues face different challenges in providing a safe and secure event.

Student Challenges

NAME _____ DATE_____

Question 16.1

Visit a sport facility and identify safety and security challenges associated with hosting an event at the facility. Specifically, identify five security challenges that event managers will face given the venue characteristics. Describe how the challenges can be overcome.

Security Challenge #1:

Strategy to Overcome:

Security Challenge #2:

Strategy to Overcome:

Security Challenge #3:

Strategy to Overcome:

Security Challenge #4:

Strategy to Overcome:

Security Challenge #5:

Strategy to Overcome:

Question 16.2

Your Event:

What If #1:

Strategy to Address Situation:

What If #2:

Strategy to Address Situation:

What If #3:

Strategy to Address Situation:

What If #4:

Strategy to Address Situation:

What If #5:

Strategy to Address Situation:

Student Challenge

Question 16.2

Choose an event you have attended or participated in. Fill in the provided risk identification matrix for the event and identify how each identified risk will be treated. Be specific!
Your Event:

Risk Identification Matrix

	Very Frequent	Frequent	Moderate	Infrequent	Very Infrequent
Very High Loss					
High Loss					
Moderate Loss					
Low Loss					
Very Low Loss					

Discuss how you would treat each identified risk:

EVENT EMERGENCY AND MEDICAL MANAGEMENT

Ericka P. Zimmerman and Heather Lawrence

Heather Lawrence, Ph.D., is an Associate Professor of Sports Administration and AECOM Professor of Sport Business at Ohio University. She earned her Ph.D. from the University of Florida, and also received bachelor's and master's degrees from Florida. Dr. Lawrence primarily teaches in the area of event and facility management. In addition to her role at Ohio University, she has led event and facility courses in Spain, China, and Dubai. Prior to beginning her academic career, Heather worked in various administrative positions within intercollegiate athletics at Southeastern Louisiana University and the University of Florida. Her sport industry responsibilities have included working in NCAA compliance, facility management and construction/renovation management, event management, and general administration.

Ericka P. Zimmerman, Ed.D., ATC, CES, PES, is the Director for the School of Health Sciences and Associate Professor at Western Carolina University. She earned her Ed.D. from Marshall University, her master's degree from Indiana State University, and her bachelor's degree from St. Andrews College. Prior to arriving at Western Carolina University, Dr. Zimmerman was the Department Chair and Program Director for athletic training at the University of Charleston (WV) with oversight for the medical care of athletes and the academic preparation of students. Prior to her academic career, Dr. Zimmerman served in a variety of athletic training positions in university and clinics.

Event managers sometimes think of event emergency and medical management as something "someone else should do." However, like many other aspects of an event, the event manager should have an understanding of all of the pieces that go into an effective emergency and medical plan. For some events, the event manager may be the person responsible for developing the emergency preparedness plan (EPP), while for other events there might be resources to hire emergency planning experts to develop the plan. In still other situations, the venue where the event is being held may already have a standard EPP that the event will adhere to. The specifics of medical management are always best left to someone with expertise in the area. Some physicians, emergency medical technicians (EMTs), paramedics, fire rescue/fighters, and athletic trainers have the knowledge, training, and experience to partner with the event manager to create an effective medical management plan. Emergency and medical management could be an entire textbook alone, but the intent of this chapter is to familiarize event managers with the process and content in these areas so they can effectively interact with outside experts in developing the plans.

Emergency Planning

The primary responsibility of any venue management team is to provide an environment where fans can safely enjoy the event. While safety is at the forefront at all times, emergency situations heighten the stakes for event managers and facility operators. Planning and preparation are critical to making the right choices at the right time.

The facility or an outside expert usually does emergency planning, but event managers should be aware of the EPP. The difference between emergency planning and risk management is that emergency planning is related to the reaction of all those involved in the event and facility when an emergency occurs. As discussed in Chapter 16—Event Safety and Security, risk management deals with identifying and treating risks, and does not address reaction to them if they are actualized.

All venues, whether traditional or nontraditional, must have an EPP, which is a document that articulates the policies guiding emergency management and how the organization functions given a specific emergency. The development of a good EPP involves a variety of constituents and will match the level of emergency with the appropriate level of response. Whether the emergency is large or small does not change the planning steps that take place to ensure all involved are ready to handle the situation. Proper emergency planning will also increase the management team's ability to make decisions in a calm and instinctual manner, subverting the potential for confusion and/or accidents.

Emergency Preparedness Plan

Event managers should follow certain steps when developing the EPP. The following guidelines are setup for large traditional sport venues, and can be altered for smaller events. There will be variations depending on the size of the event, size of the venue, location of the venue, and anticipated risks, but three steps provide a general guideline to developing the EPP.

EPP Step One: Assess Risk

The first step in formulating a plan for emergency incidents is developing an understanding of the scale of emergency vulnerability. For large venues and events, this will mean going above and beyond the risk management procedures identified previously and involve sophisticated software analysis. The Department of Homeland Security (DHS) Office of Infrastructure Protection is working to prevent catastrophic events. Owners and operators of sport venues are in the best position to determine the risks to their facilities and how to protect their facilities from such risks. The Risk Self-Assessment Tool (RSAT) is available through the Commercial Facilities Sector of the DHS, and was launched in 2009. RSAT is designed to develop risk information by breaking the data collection and analysis into three distinct areas:

- *Venue Characterization*: Information about the facility, including its major uses, size, and capacity.
- *Threat Rating*: The DHS has divided threats into two categories, man-made and natural. For example, a vehicular bomb is a man-made threat, while a hurricane is a natural threat.
- *Vulnerability Assessment*: This is comprised of input from the user about the facility's security preparedness.

Completing this risk assessment provides the venue operator a clear picture of areas in which the facility is vulnerable. Additionally, the program will highlight the facility's strengths and areas for enhancement. Benchmarking is also done through the software, that compares the facility to others that are similar.

Step Two: Plan Preparation

It may seem obvious, but emergency planning occurs best at times of nonemergency. A well-crafted EPP is a result of joining the skills and thinking of every contributor to the emergency situation. Individuals involved in the process may include:

- The facility management team
- Facility ownership (if separate)
- Event managers (if applicable)
- Building security team
- Local law enforcement
- Emergency medical teams (city or private)
- Local hospital
- Local National Guard command
- City Manager's office
- Facility designer or construction expert

The EPP utilizes all these resources to respond to emergency threats internal to an event (via spectators or fire) and external threats (such as terrorist threats or natural disasters). In an emergency, each support team must have their own coordinated activity and have already coordinated those roles with the facility manager and the incident commander for incorporation into the overall facility plan.

Modern building codes have progressed toward addressing the realities of moving large volumes of people in mass, and at times, in partially blinded conditions. People will become largely reactionary and follow the crowd when confused by an emergency. A facility EPP must anticipate this and work with the inherent building design to match the crowd's natural reaction and movement patters with equal amounts of flexibility and rigidity. Additionally, those with special needs must be taken into consideration with respect to their movement. For example, elevators often do not work in an emergency, so an accessible evacuation route without elevators is needed for those in wheelchairs and with mobility impairment.

The EPP also outlines the close working relationship between those in charge who are able to make determinations with respect to response, including the senior fire official, the senior police official, the facility manager, and the event managers. The plan must outline a clear delineation of responsibilities, authority, and the chain of command so action can be taken quickly in an emergency. Roles to be delineated would include:

- *Incident Commander*: Generally, the highest ranking fire and safety official on-site will assume the role of incident commander. In cases where this individual is not present, this is often designated to the highest ranking police official. This person is typically responsible for overall coordination of operations on-scene of the emergency or disaster. This includes coordination of all forces at the scene such as city and outside agencies.
- *Agency Representatives*: Each responding agency and/or military unit must be coordinated by an agency representative. These persons respond to and coordinate resources through the incident commander.

The EPP will identify contact information for each potential agency including:

a. Stadium management
b. Event manager

c.   Establishing the unified command center

d.   Media operations/public information center

e.   Medical operations

f.   Ambulance staging

g.   Special needs rescues

h.   Helicopter landing operations

i.   Fire unit staging

j.   Police unit staging

k.   Prisoner detention area

l.   Victims inquiry center

m.   Traffic control and monitoring

n.   Volunteer coordination

o.   Morgue

The above is for major facilities and large events. However, other event managers can take these principles and apply them to their own situations. It is always better to be over-prepared than underprepared.

Step Three: Training/Rehearsals

Every facility where large groups of people gather should have in place an EPP and rehearse it on a regular basis. The best planning in the world is useless unless it is communicated, rehearsed, and understood by those needed to execute the plan. The industry standard is to perform major emergency event rehearsals at least once a year. Through incident simulation with all participating agencies, validating communication and chain of authority can occur. This will ensure that the plan will be an appropriate response during an emergency event.

© Shutterstock

Practicing emergency response situations is an important part of training.

Small Events

In general, small events (especially those in nontraditional venues) will rely heavily on local agencies in their emergency planning. Much of the response will come directly from police, fire, and EMTs, with event managers making the contact with them. Imperative to this type of plan is up-front and early communication with these agencies. Months or weeks before the event, event managers should communicate all the event specifics (e.g., location of event, age of participants, number of participants, time of warm-up and competition, on-site medical response such as athletic trainers, etc.). Then, event managers should call the week of the event as a follow-up to ensure the local agencies are aware of the event. Providing this information to agencies will allow the local responders to be aware of the event and be ready to respond to the location if needed. It is common that police and EMTs, if not busy elsewhere, will come to the event if they are aware of it as an act of goodwill.

Command Center Function in Emergency Response

The command center is at the core of good emergency response. Operators must first assess if the emergency can be localized. Monitoring a facility properly and responding to situations is centered in the command center. In an emergency, it also functions as a location for briefings, strategy meetings, and training. Because of its critical nature in the event of an emergency, the command center's location in a facility is crucial. Its location should be close to where local police and fire responders will arrive in an emergency, and at the same time have access to the building's main vertical and horizontal circulation (e.g., stairs, escalators, concourses, and elevators).

As discussed earlier, smaller events may not have a command center, but the concepts are the same. Event managers will still establish a specific location where the control of the event occurs. In an emergency situation, event managers will be the point people for the on-site response, but the situation will quickly be turned over to local emergency response through calling 911 or radio communication with emergency response units.

Whether the event is large or small, documentation is critical when any incident occurs. One of the command center functions is to document, organize, and house information related to incidents that do occur. This documentation is important in the event someone is seriously hurt or the launch of an emergency response occurs. The documentation clearly indicates the details of the situation and whether or not established protocols are followed.

Evacuations

Evacuations, on the surface, seem simple: get everyone out of the building or out of a specific area. There are a lot of variables that can impact an evacuation procedure, and a full evacuation is not always a necessary response in an emergency. Plus, evacuations are inherently risky because they can cause panic among the crowd that can result in injuries. Event managers have to figure out how to effectively move people out of the building (or away from a specific area), where people go once they have been evacuated, how people with special needs are identified and assisted, and if there are any issues with getting all the vehicles evacuated in an orderly fashion.

Evacuations are not as simple as they seem. Even a small outdoor event may pose a challenge if people need to be moved quickly away from an area. Event managers commonly use barricades and/or fencing to establish the venue and take tickets at outdoor events. In an emergency evacuation, people need to be able to exit the area quickly, and barricades and fencing can impede their egress. Additionally, people will generally not be as familiar with the entrances/exits, since they might have been created just for that event. Conversely, in a traditional sports venue, the flow is usually logical. For instance, people are in elevated seats in most arenas and stadiums, and they can see the entire venue. Plus, the stairs generally lead to

© Shutterstock

Getting spectators out of a location is only one part of an evacuation.

a vomitory, which leads to a concourse, and then to exit doors. Outdoors, people may be in a flat area and unable to see where appropriate exits are, which can cause confusion. In all emergencies, but especially in evacuations with limited sight lines, communication with the crowd is critical.

The public address (P.A.) announcements should be used to direct people, and bullhorns should be available as back-up in case the P.A. is not working. All communications need to be prescribed, loud, clear, and calming if there is to be any chance of people following the instructions.

When to Evacuate

There is no single answer to the question of when to evacuate. It depends on the risk to those in the building. Fire, bomb threats, hazardous materials, power outages, tornadoes and hurricanes, and lightning are all common emergencies that may warrant evacuation. In certain situations, it will be more dangerous to evacuate people than to have them stay in the building. For example, at an indoor venue, in the event of severe weather such as a tornado, it is likely power will be lost. Evacuations due to power outages are common. However, if there is the possibility of a tornado, all spectators are safer in a dark solid building than outside in the path of a tornado. Common sense and prior planning must prevail in these situations.

In some circumstances, partial evacuations are the appropriate response. In the case of a partial structural collapse of one section of bleachers, those people need to evacuate immediately, while others should stay in their seats so as to not cause more confusion. Once those that are in immediate danger are secure, others can be evacuated.

For outdoor events, severe weather—especially lightning—is a common reason for evacuations. Many outdoor stadiums and bleachers are metal, which are prone to lightning strikes. Amazingly, some spectators will refuse to leave their metal bleacher seats 80 rows up in a stadium, even when they can see lightning approaching. Clear announcements asking people to evacuate and to seek shelter are a necessity. Event managers are responsible for deciding on an emergency response in these situations, prior to the emergency occurring.

Golf tournaments, obstacle races, road races, and multisport events, all are challenging to evacuate since they are often spread over a large area. It is the responsibility of the event to address severe weather in the EPP. For those in a stadium, a neighboring building can be used as shelter, at a golf course, the clubhouse can be used, and for races—getting people out of the water is the first priority followed by safely transporting athletes to any shelter that has been identified along the course. People might also be asked to wait in their cars until the weather passes.

How to Evacuate

With proper planning and the establishment of an EPP, all those working the event will be prepared to assist in the event of an evacuation. The command center will issue the evacuation order following pre-established protocols, and then staff should know what to do from there based on training and drills. It is essential that all event and security staff know where to go and what to do during an evacuation. For example, consider an evacuation due to lightning at a college football game that has a very limited covered concourse area. People will generally make their way to the covered area, but will be reluctant to move out into the rain to the staging areas or to their cars. This can cause significant crowding in exit areas. Since 20,000–30,000 cannot fit in one small concourse, security must move people along to ensure they exit the stadium. A crowd crush can happen quickly if the front of a moving group stops and the back does not.

Just as in risk management, every facility and event is different, but some general guidelines are provided here for evacuations.

- Only evacuate those sections of the facility that must be evacuated.
- Make sure exit doors are unlocked and any gates/fences are quickly taken down.
- Have multiple pre-established staging areas away from the building where people can seek shelter.
- Announcements related to emergency procedures should be written in advance and posted in the P.A. booth or provided as part of every game script.
- Ensure there is clear communication available (that is battery powered or hooked up to an emergency generator).
- Provide information on rescheduling, refunds, and so forth as quickly as possible via bullhorns or the P.A. system.
- Provide ushers with flashlights for all indoor and/or night events to use to show people how to exit if needed.
- Ensure that a specified number of staff is available to help those with special needs.
- Secure all cash, merchandise, and concessions prior to staff evacuating.
- Media should be provided information as quickly as possible for distribution.
- Identify police that will assist with moving vehicle traffic away from the building.

No event mangers ever want to have to evacuate their venues, but the odds are it will happen—especially with outdoor events. The key is to be prepared so that any evacuation is conducted in a calm and controlled manner by those involved. The EPP will help event managers choose appropriate strategies given specific emergency situations.

Medical Planning: Spectators

The timeless Boy Scout motto of "Be Prepared" is relevant to the task at hand for a facility operator that hosts hundreds of events each year and attracts a wide variety of patrons from all demographics. It is likely some patrons will face physical challenges on a daily basis, and they must be accounted for in the dynamics of each event that occurs. Event managers will face medical emergencies of some sort on a regular basis, and the way they are handled can be the difference between life and death. All fans want to enjoy an entertainment event and feel secure in the knowledge that the event and facility managers will respond in an expedient and professional manner in the event of a medical incident.

Just as athletes have a game plan, so too should event managers whose goal it is to access the site where a medical incident occurs, make the proper assessment as to degree of emergency, provide the proper care, and minimize risk to the victim and facility. Management of information, state-of-the-art life safety features, and proper procedures are the three most important elements in dealing with a medical situation.

Managing the Process

In a facility with tens of thousands of patrons and requisite staff, it is essential to effectively manage the communication and subsequent information that is forthcoming when the call comes in about a medical incident. As discussed, an event should have a command center where communications of all incidents are recorded and handled. As part of any standard operating procedure (SOP), or routine process, "Base" is referenced as a person or small group of personnel who field all medical calls and disseminate information during an event at the command center. Event and facility staff should know to call "Base" via radio or landline for any crisis, medical, or otherwise. The "Base" representative initially logs the time when the call comes in (actual time and time on game clock, if applicable), the individual who made the call, and the nature of the call. This person then advises the necessary medical personnel, again logging in need, who was assigned, and time services were requested. Upon resolution of the medical incident, the individual performing the service is supposed to call "Base" back and advise them of the status/resolution of the situation along with any additional information that might be needed for the event files. This ensures prompt communication to the first aid provider, as well as documentation of the timeline of events.

These logs are relied upon to determine what the initial call was, who made it, and approximate response times. Most importantly, they provide a timeline of each occurrence that may play a prominent role in any subsequent investigation or legal process. As such, all medical incidents should be reported to the facility's risk manager. A listing of risk managers and their contact information should be provided as part of the EPP and command center materials.

Medical Response Equipment

The ability to mitigate any medical emergency rests in large part with the availability of medical and operational resources, equipment, and forms that are provided on-site. A concerted effort on the part of the facility operator(s) and state, county, and/or local jurisdictions to coordinate efforts related to emergency equipment is vital to the ability to respond to all types of emergencies that may occur at any given event. Also, training responders in the proper use of automatic external defibrillators (AED) units, radio communication equipment, and other associated equipment will increase the odds of a successful resolution of a medical incident and mitigate any possible legal repercussions. The following is a sample list of equipment and forms that are needed for effective medical emergency response.

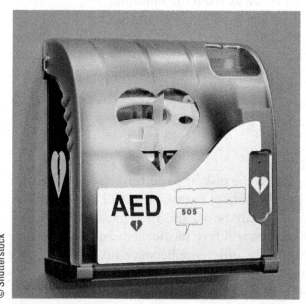

- Fire rescue or first aid/ambulance services
- AED (heart defibrillator) units
- Two-way radio communication equipment
- Communications log
- SOP first aid form
- SOP command base form
- Accident report document

Automatic External Defibrillators (AED) are a common piece of emergency response equipment in venues.

Location of Medical Equipment and First Aid Station

In some venues, the first aid station is located at the end of a hallway, furthest away from the event. Other venues have first aid stations located beside restrooms or concessions. All event staff, not just the event manager, need to know the location of all first aid stations within the venue to appropriately direct an individual with a medical condition. In some instances, an injured spectator is unable to travel to the first aid station; instead, the first responders and medical personnel need to go to the spectator.

Level of First Aid Care and Medical Response

Medical care for spectators falls in line with basic first aid and emergency care and event managers should secure appropriate medical professionals trained in this emergency medical care. The level of spectator medical care may be predetermined by the contract with the group promoting the event; therefore, it is important for event managers to review the contract.

Basic first aid encompasses crutch fitting, blister and small wound care, basic splinting, and ice bag applications. More significant injuries or illnesses, such as a heart attack, heat illness, and seizures, would require advanced medical care. If emergency medical services (EMS) personnel are already on-site they can provide immediate emergency care and stabilization prior to transporting the spectator to a local medical facility. When EMS personnel are not on-site, then the on-site first responders and medical personnel would need to contact EMS to dispatch an ambulance to the venue.

Rendering Assistance

Optimally, first responders will be the first on the scene of a medical emergency, but often the staff member who first arrives on the scene must quickly assess the situation and take steps that do not add further peril for the victim. All staff should be CPR/AED/First Aid certified at a minimum. First responders should be available quickly, and ambulances should be on-site for most events. Only those events with very minimal risk and in close proximity to a hospital (i.e., youth soccer game within 5 min of a hospital) may not have ambulances on-site. Additionally, it is common to have multiple ambulances on-site. In some cases, one set of responders will be focused on participants, ideally in conjunction with athletic trainers, while another is responsible for spectators. For large events, like a college football game, multiple ambulances are needed for spectators. If someone is being transported when another medial emergency occurs, a second ambulance is needed, and often the time needed to call an additional ambulance could put the person at risk.

The most common medical providers utilized as first responders are EMS personnel, which includes EMTs and paramedics. Event managers can also seek other medical professionals educated in first aid and emergency care, such as nurses, physicians, physician assistants, and athletic trainers.

The following procedures are used by the American Airlines Center (n.d.) and provide a good example of steps to be followed to reduce response time and to provide the victim with the best opportunity for further medical assistance:

1. On-scene personnel are to radio Base on command center channel.
2. On-scene personnel advise the location and nature of the incident, and request for first aid response.

    Note: If the incident is life threatening, say so! Radio codes may be used to convey the seriousness of the situation.

    Note: Arena personnel and on-site Fire Rescue must respond to all first aid-type incidents involving guests.

3. Base will repeat the information to ensure that it is correct.
4. Confirm that the information is correct.
5. Render first aid until Fire Rescue and/or Risk Management Arrives.
6. Base will contact First Responders and Risk Management and relay the information.
7. Do not leave the incident scene until First Responders and Risk Management arrive on the scene.
8. Provide any pertinent information to arriving Fire Rescue and Risk Management personnel.
9. Make sure that Risk Management and/or event personnel are completing a written incident report detailing the events and conditions that contributed to the incident. This will include the pre-event condition of the injured person.
10. Once the incident scene is under control by Fire Rescue and Risk Management, leave the area unless requested to stay by Risk Manager or other management.

Transportation to a Medical Facility

In addition to the on-site medical care for spectators, the event manager must identify the mode of transportation for an injured or ill spectator. The most common mode of transportation is through EMS. When contacting EMS to be on-site for an event, event managers need to consider and clarify the following:

- On-call versus dedicated units
- Parking
- Physical location of the EMS personnel (first aid station versus ambulance)
- Cost for services
- Event date, venue location, and arrival/departure time

If EMS personnel are part of the plan for spectator medical care, confirm an ambulance will be present at the venue. When scheduling EMS personnel think about on-call versus dedicated ambulance units. On-call status indicates EMS personnel and equipment, including the ambulance, will be present at the event but remain on-call should their services be needed somewhere else in the city or county. Should the EMS unit receive a call requiring their assistance, they are free to leave the venue. A dedicated unit indicates the EMS unit will remain on-site throughout the entire event and is not subject to a call requiring them to leave the event.

The first aid station may or may not be close to the parked ambulance. Event managers need to clarify if the EMS providers can be physically present at the first aid station or if they must remain with the ambulance unit. When an ambulance is present, whether on call or dedicated, a clear parking location must be established with easy access to the first aid station and the main exit from the venue.

Identify and communicate the length of time the first responders and EMS personnel are needed. Clearly identify an arrival and departure time. For example, if the event begins at 4:00 p.m. and the gates open for spectators at 3:00 p.m., determine if EMS personnel should arrive at 2:30 p.m., 3:00 p.m., 3:30 p.m., or 4:00 p.m.

Example: As the athletic trainer for a football team in the National Championship Football playoffs prepared to travel to a neutral site game, Synita received information on the medical services available for the game. The information included having a dedicated EMS unit and personnel during the game. On the day of the game, the EMS unit and personnel were present outside of the east-end zone. With less than 30 sec remaining in the game, the EMS personnel left the field because it appeared the participants were safe. During the postgame celebration on the field, a spectator suffered a heart attack. It took over

25 min for the ambulance to arrive back at stadium, and access the field as a result of the traffic and number of people in the parking lot and on the field. The event manager can play a role in situations like this by knowing the schedule and holding everyone accountable for the role they play in keeping the entire event safe.

Medical Planning: Participants

Medical care for participants can encompass more than first aid and emergency care. Medical care can also include athlete preparation (e.g., taping, bracing, modalities, stretching); examination, diagnosis, and treatment of injuries and illnesses; and athlete treatment and rehabilitation. Event managers could be responsible for coordinating medical care for participants of an event, such as a triathlon, rodeo competition, or state high-school volleyball tournament. For other events, the organization provides its own medical personnel for the participants. Examples of this include high school, collegiate, and professional sports events. Event managers should not assume a sports team will have an athletic trainer, as many high schools do not employ or utilize athletic trainers (Pryor et al., 2015) and some universities do not employee enough athletic trainers to travel with every sports team. For any event, event managers should contact the organization(s) to determine if medical personnel will be traveling or if the event managers are expected to provide medical care.

Medical Director

When event managers are responsible for providing medical care for participants, the first step is to identify a Medical Director, sometimes referred to as a Medical Coordinator. This is often an individual such as a physician or athletic trainer, or a medical group or organization, such as a sports medicine clinic, who then designates an individual within the organization to be the Medical Director for the event. The ideal medical director is a health care provider with experience providing medical coverage to the specific event or event type occurring at the venue. The two most common providers are athletic trainers and physicians. If an event manager is unsure where to find a medical director, contacting the athletic trainers at a local university, high school, or sports medicine clinic is a good place to begin. Initial contact includes brief information of location, dates, and type of activity; if both parties are still interested then schedule an initial, formal meeting to discuss details.

Athletic Trainers are "health care professionals who collaborate with physicians to provide preventative services, emergency care, clinical diagnosis, therapeutic intervention and rehabilitation to injuries and medical conditions" (Athletic Training, n.d.).

One domain of education is immediate and emergency care, making Athletic Trainers a key health care provider in emergency medical planning for events. Learn more about Athletic Trainers at http://www.nata.org.

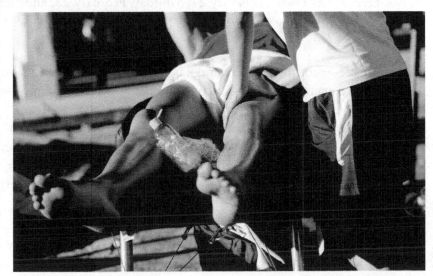

Athletic trainers are one type of medical personnel that may be on site at sports events.

© Shutterstock

Responsibilities

Event managers should have a clear understanding of the responsibilities for the Medical Director and be able to articulate those responsibilities. In most situations, the role of the Medical Director is to coordinate all aspects of medical care, from emergency preparedness plans (EPPs) to personnel to equipment and supplies, and communicate the planning with the event management staff.

Initial Meeting

The best way to develop a mutual understanding of responsibilities for both medical and event personnel is to plan an initial meeting. The initial meeting is a good opportunity to communicate the needs for the event and discuss the timelines. During the first meeting, the following items should be discussed:

- Event details, such as location, date, time, and venue
- Liability insurance
- Supplies and equipment
- Level of medical care and organizational requirements
- Personnel.

Event Details

Share with the medical director the date, time, and location or venue of the event. While sharing this information seems obvious, this is also where some critical mistakes can occur.

> *Example:* The event manager has contacted Sloan Point Sports Medicine Center for assistance in providing medical coverage for the state high-school wrestling tournament, as many of the teams are not traveling with an Athletic Trainer. Sarah, an athletic trainer at Sloan Point Sports Medicine Center, has been designated as the Medical Coordinator for the tournament. During the first meeting, Sarah learns the tournament is the last weekend of February from Friday to Sunday. On Friday, February 20th, Sarah receives a call from the event manager panicked because she is not there and the tournament director will not start the event until an athletic trainer is present. Sarah interpreted the last weekend of February as Friday, February 27, Saturday, February 28, and Sunday, March 1; the event manager meant the last full weekend of February, as in Friday, February 20, Saturday, February 21, and Sunday, February 22.

Specify if pre-event medical coverage is needed; sometimes, this occurs the day of the event and other times the pre-event activities—such as practice or a camp/clinic—may occur in the days leading up to the event.

Clarify arrival times and expectations. If the event begins at 10:00 a.m. and participants arrive at 9:00 a.m., the event manager and medical director should agree upon the arrival time for medical personnel. While the event manager may think 9:00 a.m. is appropriate, the medical providers may need to arrive prior to 9:00 a.m. to set up the medical station(s), especially on the first day of an event.

Liability Insurance

A question often asked by health care providers regards liability insurance or coverage. During the planning, event managers may or may not obtain liability insurance coverage for the event. If liability insurance is purchased, event managers must be certain to find out if the liability insurance policy covers medical professionals or not. This will allow them to clearly articulate a response. The liability insurance provider may request professionals carry their own professional liability coverage or be covered by their employer for such activities. Not all employer paid professional liability plans cover the health care provider for volunteer activities unless it is a requirement of their job. This, too, should be clarified and understood by all medical volunteers.

Supplies and Equipment

Water, cups, and ice are obvious requirements when considering participants on the field of play, but their need goes beyond just that area. Customarily, the event management team provides water coolers/bottles, cups, and for the medical staff. Additionally, they may also need to provide ice chests for storing ice since the ice is used for the water and for injury treatment.

Medical supplies and equipment need to be included in the event budget. In some situations, event managers may ask the Medical Director to provide their own supplies and equipment. For example, EMTs and Paramedics provide supplies and equipment from their transport unit or ambulance. If the Medical Director is associated with a hospital or clinic, the supplies and equipment might also be provided by the clinic in exchange for free advertising (e.g., signage, public announcements, and/or program ads). In many situations, though, event managers will need to provide the medical supplies and equipment for the event. When this occurs, the event manager and Medical Director can partner together to secure necessary supplies and equipment. The equipment manager can identify the budget available for ordering the medical supplies/equipment and the process for ordering. The Medical Director can assist in securing best prices on medical supplies and possibly secure items on loan. Basic supplies (i.e., items for daily use) and equipment (i.e., items that can be used over many years) include an AED unit, wound care supplies, ice bags, and adhesive tape and prewrap to secure bandages, and provide prophylactic taping to joints.

The first year of a repeat event is the most critical to planning, as it is the first year for ordering supplies and equipment. Determine who is responsible for ordering and if supplies and equipment are donated, clarify who is responsible for seeking out donations. If an event has been held for several years, some supplies and equipment may be left over from the previous year or event. However, supplies and equipment stored over a period of time must be inspected to confirm the condition and expiration dates. If an ambulance is on-site, the AED in the ambulance can be used instead of purchasing or borrowing a new unit.

Level of Medical Care and Organizational Requirements

Part of the emergency medical planning is determining the level of medical care to be provided to the participants. An event such as a 3-on-3 basketball tournament might require only basic first aid and emergency medical care. Other events might warrant pre-event coverage to include taping wrapping and stretching, in-depth evaluations, or rehabilitation. Sometimes this information is predetermined by state law or organizational requirements. Event managers need to understand the organizational requirements and state law so these expectations can be clearly communicated to the medical director. This information then allows the medical director to appropriately contact the right type of medical providers to cover the event.

> *Example*: The event coordinator for a local rodeo competition contacted Jody to serve as a medical coordinator for an upcoming competition. The state high-school rodeo association by-laws require an ambulance and EMS personnel to be on-site during competition; however, the event coordinator also wanted athletic trainers present. During the initial meeting, the event coordinator was able to communicate this organizational requirement and the two agreed Jody would coordinate athletic training coverage and the event coordinator would coordinate EMS coverage.

As with spectator coverage, event managers need to think about on-call versus a dedicated unit when scheduling EMS personnel. On-call status often means the EMS personnel may or may not be on-site depending on if they have another call. A dedicated unit will remain on-site throughout the entire event.

While event managers cannot be expected to know all medical requirements established by organizations or state laws, there are resources available to learn more about requirements.

NCAA Health and Safety
- http://www.ncaa.org/health-and-safety

National Federation of State High School Associations
- http://www.nfhs.org/resources/sports-medicine/

State Association With Sports Medicine Sites and Advisory Committees
- http://www.nfhs.org/sports-resource-content/member-state-associations-with-sports-medicine-sites-and-advisory-committees/

National Youth Sports Health and Safety Institute
- http://nyshsi.org/

National Athletic Trainers' Association
- http://www.nata.org

Communication

Proper modes of communication and the chain of command for communicating emergency information should be planned in advance. Event managers coordinate the initial communication plan within the event management team while the medical director will coordinate the initial communication plan within the medical personnel. The two should come together in advance to determine how the two groups will communicate with one another. Items to address include:

- Types of communication, such as two-way radios, walkie-talkies, or cellular devices
- Which medical situations to report to the event manager and when to report them
- Will a command center be used to deploy additional medical personnel or equipment
- Who will speak with media about any medical situation.

An event manager should also communicate with appropriate local authorities, such as the police or fire departments, prior to a community wide event. This responsibility typically falls to event managers unless arrangements have been made otherwise.

On-Going Planning and Timeline

The Medical Director should be involved with certain aspects of the event planning. The Medical Director does not need to be involved in the logo design for marketing or the ticket sales, however, the Medical Director could be invaluable when selecting the date or time, or determining location for water stations and medical tents. For example, a sprint triathlon held in August in Louisiana should begin early in the morning to avoid the hottest and most humid parts of the day, thus decreasing the risk of a heat illness in participants.

Another area of involvement is collection of pre-event medical information from participants. When providing medical coverage for participants, it is important to obtain emergency contact and medical information on each participant. Information should consist of the participants' name, emergency contact name and phone number of another individual in the event of an emergency, and any medical conditions and/or allergies. Some events will post disclaimers or guidelines on their website for engaging in participation.

- Boston Marathon: http://www.baa.org/races/boston-marathon/participant-information/need-to-be-updated/medical.aspx
- Marshall University Marathon: http://marshalluniversitymarathon.com/

Sample Medical Services Timeline

Six months

- Confirm dates, time, venue and event
- Schedule EMS
- Contact local authorities

Four months

- Order medical supplies and equipment

Four weeks

- Confirm medical supplies and equipment have arrived
- Establish EAP

Two weeks

- Conduct final meeting to address any last minute changes or questions
- Reconfirm dates and times with EMS

One week

- Confirm location and set-up schedule of medical station(s)
- Administer mock emergency drill

Event day

- Communicate number of participants
- Evaluate weather forecast

Emergency Preparedness Plans

Prior to the event an EPP (sometimes referred to as an emergency action plan [EAP] or emergency response plan [ERP]) should be created. The Medical Director is the most appropriate individual to develop this plan; however, assistance from event managers' is important. The EPP should be venue specific and provide specific details about locations of emergency personnel, emergency equipment, access to emergency transport/ambulance, means of communication (cell phones, two-way radio). The Medical Director will want to rehearse the EPP, which may include more than just emergency personnel; the event manager and other key personnel should also be included in this rehearsal. The event manager and medical director need to work together to determine the best time to do this based upon the type of event and availability of medical personnel. Mock emergency scenarios at Olympic venues are rehearsed a few days to a week prior to the event. This is an important part of safety and event managers should provide access to the venues for these mock emergency events.

The type of event will determine how early a walk-thru of the venue can occur. The event manager and medical director should determine when this will occur based upon the type of event and when set up occurs. An arena for a high-school rodeo competition may not be set up until 1 or 2 days prior to the event whereas a walk-thru for a college softball game can occur any time.

A comparison of the EPP for participants and the venue's overall EPP should be compared for overlap and conflicts.

Guide for creating an EAP: http://ksi.uconn.edu/prevention/emergency-action-plans/

Postevent Wrap-up

Prior to the event a decision should be made as to the type of postevent wrap up or follow up that should occur. Communicate the expectation with the Medical Director in advance of the event; this meeting could occur immediately after the event or several days after the event. Event managers should consider the type of information important for files and liability insurance requirements. This is a time to also return supplies and equipment and make suggestions for future events.

Other Considerations

Overlap With Participant Medical Care

Aspects of medical care for spectators can overlap with the medical care for participants. It will be important to identify in advance the potential for overlap so services can be coordinated. As in the earlier example, the EMS unit had a dual purpose for the participants and spectators. A local 5K run may request EMS personnel and ambulance at the finish line to provide services for participants and spectators, while an NFL game may have two ambulances—one dedicated to the spectators and one dedicated to the football players.

Other Medical-Related Services

Other medical-related services can also occur during events in which spectators can participate. For example, if an event is occurring in November, which coincides with National Diabetes Month, medical providers, medical vendors, and medical organizations may request to offer free or low cost services to spectators as a means to increase awareness of a disease, condition, or services within the community—such as blood glucose/sugar screening. Other examples of medical-related services include, but are not limited to, massage, blood pressure, vision, body fat percentage, and bone density scans. These medical-related services are not part of the emergency planning for spectators. Event managers must decide if the individual assigned to oversee the emergency planning for spectators should also oversee the medical-related service or not.

Volunteer or Paid Medical Providers

Utilizing medical personnel in a volunteer status can vary from region to region and be influenced by local ordinances, liability insurance, and state licensure laws for the medical providers. This is a topic event managers should research further before making a decision.

Additional Resources

There are many resources used in emergency and medical management, but two of the most valuable pieces of paperwork are the incident report and accident/injury report. In the following pages there are examples of each (Figure 17.1 and Figure 17.2).

SUMMARY

Medical services are part of every event. They should discuss and event managers should make plans regardless of the size of the event, if the event is so small that the plans are to call 911 for all emergencies. The emergency and medical plans should be shared with staff and practiced. There are tools available to assist events and help make them as safe as possible for participants and spectators and help reduce possible liability.

Figure 17.1

INCIDENT REPORT

(Please Print)

DATE: _____ TIME: _____ AM / PM

NAME OF EVENT: _____

LOCATION OF INCIDENT: _____

TYPE OF INCIDENT: _____

PERSON(S) INVOLVED: _____

ADDRESS: _____

CITY: _____ STATE: _____ ZIP: _____ PHONE#: _____

ADDRESS: _____

CITY: _____ STATE: _____ ZIP: _____ PHONE#: _____

_____

DESCRIBE IN ORDER WITH FULL DETAIL THE INCIDENT AS IT OCCURRED:

_____

_____

_____

_____

_____

UNIVERSITY POLICE REPORT TAKEN: ( ) YES   ( ) NO CASE # _____

PICTURES TAKEN: ( ) YES   ( ) NO

WITNESS NAME: _____ PHONE#: _____

WITNESS NAME: _____ PHONE#: _____

COMMENTS BY ANY WITNESS(ES): _____

_____

_____

SUBMITTED BY: _____ DATE: _____

REVIEWED BY: _____ DATE: _____

Figure 17.2

PATRON ACCIDENT/INJURY REPORT

(Please Print)

DATE: _____ TIME: _____ AM / PM

NAME OF EVENT: _____

TYPE OF ACCIDENT: _____

NAME OF VICTIM: _____ SEX: ( ) M ( ) F

ADDRESS: _____

CITY: _____ STATE: _____ ZIP: _____ PHONE#: _____

SOCIAL SECURITY #: _____

_____

BRIEFLY DESCRIBE THE ACCIDENT AS STATED BY VICTIM:

_____

_____

_____

LOCATION(be specific): _____

CONDITION OF AREA:

    Floor: ( ) Wet   ( ) Dry ( ) Other _____

    Lighting: ( ) Bright ( ) Dark ( )Other _____

COMMENTS BY PREPARER ON GENERAL CONDITION OF AREA:

_____

_____

_____

_____

PICTURES TAKEN: ( ) Yes ( ) No

EMS RESPONSE: ( ) Yes ( ) No

TRANSPORTED: ( ) Yes ( ) No

WITNESS NAME: _____ PHONE#: _____

WITNESS NAME: _____ PHONE#: _____

COMMENTS BY ANY WITNESS(ES): _____

_____

_____

_____

SUBMITTED BY: _____ DATE: _____

REVIEWED BY: _____ DATE: _____

Student Challenges
Event Emergency and Medical Management

NAME _____ DATE_____

Question 17.1

You and other students are managing a 40-team volleyball tournament at your university's gym. Create an emergency evacuation plan and handbook for your event. Make certain to use the list of items in this chapter to help with creating this plan.

Question 17.2

Draft an EPP for a youth soccer tournament (outdoor) that includes spectators and participants. In the document make sure to include medical as a category.

EVENT OPERATIONS

Heather Lawrence

Heather Lawrence, Ph.D., is an Associate Professor of Sports Administration and AECOM Professor of Sport Business at Ohio University. She earned her Ph.D. from the University of Florida, and also received bachelor's and master's degrees from Florida. Dr. Lawrence primarily teaches in the area of event and facility management. In addition to her role at Ohio University, she has led event and facility courses in Spain, China, and Dubai. Prior to beginning her academic career, Heather worked in various administrative positions within intercollegiate athletics at Southeastern Louisiana University and the University of Florida. Her sport industry responsibilities have included working in NCAA compliance, facility management, and construction/renovation management, event management, and general administration.

Event operations begin once the event is scheduled, and conclude when the last piece of trash is picked up (and recycled), the lights turned off, and the gates locked. For the spectators and participants, the event experience begins when they leave their homes to attend the event and ends when they return home. Everything possible should be done to make sure the experience is excellent during the entire event experience.

The line between event management and facility management can be fuzzy, so event managers will notice that some responsibilities can fall into either role depending on the specific arrangement between the event organization and the facility staff. When event managers and facility managers work well together, events are generally smoother for everyone involved.

This chapter describes the details of event operations such as facility setup and teardown, procuring and managing equipment, and event flow. It also discusses space management and ensuring each space meets its intended need and is ready for the event. Equipment is used as either a core component to the execution of the event or to support the core function, and may or may not be available from the facility. The flow of the event is the seamless integration between the people involved in the event (i.e., participants, spectators, and officials) and the facility. It is an abstract concept, but event managers can recognize whether the flow is good or not in an instant. People will move in a natural and easy way and the operations of the event become invisible to the spectators if the flow is conceived and executed well. Customer service is also an important aspect of operations that should not be ignored (details about customer service can be found in Chapter 14—Event Staffing).

The Facility

The facility can be broken down into the primary space and the ancillary spaces. The **primary space** is the area of the venue where the main activity takes place. The field is the primary space in a football stadium, and the ice is the primary space in a hockey rink. For nontraditional sport venues, the primary space may have to be created, as in the case of winter mountain sport events, multisport events, and road races. For cycling or running races, the vast majority of the year, the streets used for the racecourse are filled with cars. However, on race day, those same streets become the primary space of the event. For a ski race, the mountain may be open all year to skiers of varying abilities, but during a race week, the course is set up on a particular slope with restricted access so athletes can practice and clear separation between the general ski population, racers, and spectators. As a result, it creates a primary event space on the mountain.

Ancillary spaces are all of the areas that support the primary space. A football stadium has locker rooms, concourses, storage areas, lobbies, press areas, loading docks, offices, restrooms, security areas, merchandise shops, maintenance shops, control booths, concession areas, restaurants, luxury suites, club-seating areas, and maybe even an outdoor gathering place. For a marathon, the ancillary spaces are similar, but may have to be constructed. There could be a participant registration area, staging area, starting line, water stations, restrooms, spectator seating, a command center, broadcast areas, and sponsor hospitality. Event managers are responsible for deciding how each area needs to be set up and function to result in a successful event.

College Athletics: Ancillary Space Setup for Donor Events

Brian Brantley

Director, Tiger Scholarship Fund, University of Memphis Athletics

The lifeblood of most university athletic department's is the annual fund. The annual fund helps fund scholarships for student-athletes, improves facilities, and provides general support for athletic department operations. The development officers in the athletic department or university follow the donor life cycle of identification, cultivation, solicitation, and stewardship (i.e., relationship building and strengthening). All four phases are important in development, but hosting quality events is critical in reaching fundraising goals. These events are often ancillary to a home sport event on campus and understanding the purpose of the event will drive how it is physically set up.

Events are integral to three (i.e., identification, cultivation, and stewardship) of the four phases of the donor life cycle. Success starts with identifying potential donors and home sport events can be used to find season ticket holders who attend every game. In regards to cultivation, an event where current donors mix with new identified donor prospects can helps to turn them from prospects into donors. Current donors can talk about how it is important to give to the athletic scholarship program with the new prospects. Events usually do not occur during the solicitation phase, but events after new donors have given a donation to say thank you and welcome are common. Finally, during the stewardship phase, it is very important to host great events. Stewardship events are focused on relationship building, thanking current donors, and encouraging them to continue giving. Donors also expect to be invited to nice events as a benefit of their support.

For the purposes of explanation, let's focus on a stewardship event that is ancillary to a home basketball game. Below is the process I go through when creating a donor event like this.

- I clearly define the goals of the event. This depends on factors such as current athletic department development goals and needs, the time of year, and available budget.

- I decide whom to invite (i.e., who to steward further). I ask myself if the event is for a few higher end donors who give thousands of dollars and want to have a private reception or if it is an open event open to any donor.

- I then determine what kind of event space is needed. I go back to the event goals and who I am inviting and then decide how much space I need and whether it needs to be a formal space or if something more casual is suitable.

- I decide on the space setup. Do I want to encourage mingling and networking of attendees or is there a formal program where donors will listen to speakers? Is it simply a pregame hospitality area for informal conversation? Is the meal buffet or sit-down service? If the meal is buffet style, the room layout must accommodate people accessing the buffet as compared with a sit-down service dinner where there will be less movement around the room. In general, I choose smaller and more intimate spaces for sit-down dinners with less guests allowing for interaction at each table. Larger gatherings usually are better for an open room setup allowing more movement around the room.

Being aware of the goals of the donor event and the audience attending will drive the answers to the other questions that need answering. Even though donor events are usually ancillary to an athletic event, they are very important to the future of the athletic department. Event managers and development officers need to work together to clearly identify goals for the event, determine the audience or who should be invited, and identify the event area, and determine the appropriate setup for the event. By adhering to these guidelines and knowing as much as possible about the donors, the chances of accomplishing fundraising and development goals are in your favor.

Facility Walk-Thru

A pre-event walk-thru of the facility is an important piece of event operations. A **walk-thru** is exactly what it sounds like, a literal walk around the building or site examining in detail how everything will look, function, and flow for the event. All of the key event and facility managers should be part of the walk-thru, and if applicable, representatives from the rights holder, television, and major sponsors. For big events, multiple walk-thrus will occur at different points of the development process. However, for all events there should be at least one walk-thru during the month prior to the event. Discussions of television camera placement, sponsor activation, hospitality needs, access control, flow, and the event timeline are all part of the walk-thru. Event managers should schedule the walk-thru allowing plenty of time before the event day for any resulting modifications in plans.

Courts, Fields, and Course Specifications

Knowing the correct layout, setup, and specifications for courts, fields, and courses can be complex. There are different requirements depending on the rights holder involved. For example, the dimensions of a basketball court vary from 94' × 50' for professional/college courts to 84' × 50' for high school courts (Athletic Business, n.d.). Imagine being ready to host a high school tournament, only to realize that the professional arena that was rented only has lines for a professional court. This is an issue easily correctable with temporary lines if it is known in advance, but on the day of the tournament, it becomes a very difficult problem. Specifications for most sports are available online from the national governing body (NGB) of the specific sport, but they can also be obtained from the rights holders of the event.

Not only do industry recommendations and guidelines provide activity area information, but some also have guidelines for safety areas between the playing area and spectators. For example, in high school and college basketball, the industry standard is to provide three feet of clear space on the side of the court opposite the team benches, with ten feet recommended (Athletic Business, n.d.).

Setting up and certifying road and waterway courses are even more difficult than dealing with courts. To have a course certified by USA Track and Field, it is recommended that a professional be hired to measure the course (USA Track and Field, n.d.). For participants to be able to compare their race times to other courses and for any record to be set, the race course must be certified (USA Track and Field, n.d.). USA Track and Field provides a database on its Web site of known course measurers to assist event managers in finding someone to measure a course. Specific procedures on how to certify the length of swimming, running, and bicycling courses are usually included in the sanction application and/or bid documents. For events without standards, such as a local fun run, it is up to the organizers to create a course that is fun, safe, and meets the needs of the event.

Even if the distance is not certified, it must be accurate. Wearable GPS units are very common for race participants, so event managers should expect that participants are double-checking distances on their own. An advertised 10k needs to be 10k in distance. All levels of racers enter an event with the hopes of setting personal best times and they rightfully expect the course to be the advertised distance.

Ensuring courts and fields are the correct size and race courses and the expected distance requires up front work to understand the requirements for each type of sport and event as well as diligence in measurement and setup. Safety recommendations and guidelines set forth by professional organizations are important to heed because if something goes wrong and a spectator is injured resulting in a lawsuit, the legal system will look to adherence to industry standards as a guide in assigning fault.

Facility Setup and Teardown

For many event managers, the physical setup and teardown of the venue are the most difficult portions of the event. **Setup** is the process of preparing the venue for the event, and **teardown** returns the venue to the pre-event condition. Needs in these areas will vary depending on the type of venue, type of event, and availability of staff. However, there are some things that are constant. For all events, allowing plenty of time for setup and teardown, making the venue as user friendly as possible, and providing maximum sponsor exposure are important.

Depending on the event and venue, setup could take 5 minutes, 24 hours, or even several days. A rule of thumb is that it takes half as long to teardown as it does to set up. Event staff and volunteers are generally more enthusiastic during setup than during teardown. Many times, people that have worked hard all day are tired, and are ready to go home at the end of the event. Event managers must be clear in their expectation as to who is required to stay for teardown, and use the management strategies discussed in Chapter 15—Event Staffing and Chapter 16—Event Volunteer, to motivate employees and volunteers.

Customer service is at the core of ensuring that the venue adds to the spectator experience and does not detract from it. Making the venue user friendly through good flow is also important and will be discussed later in this chapter. People will remember if they got lost

Multisport events such as triathlons can have complex setup requirements.

between the parking lot and the field, if their seats were soaking wet when they got to the game, or if the gates did not open on time. In the case of facility setup, it is generally good to not be memorable.

Planning for maximum sponsor exposure is the final key point in venue setup. As discussed in Chapter 7—Event Sponsorship, event managers need to make sponsors visible. If there is a live activation, then the event manager needs to set up that area with as much precision and attention to detail as the rest of the venue. Plus, it needs to be in a high-traffic location. If signage is part of a sponsorship deal, then the signs should be placed in the correct locations and be as visible as possible to spectators and media.

Primary Space Setup

The primary event space should receive the most attention during setup because it is the focus of the event. All eyes will be on this area, as will any media presence, so detailed setup according to the pre-established needs of the participants and spectators is crucial. For some events, especially those held in single-purpose venues, there will be little primary space setup. However, for others, there is a tremendous amount of work to be done in creating this area. An ancillary event such as an interactive golf experience and trade show associated with a golf tournament will still have a primary space associated with the interactive golf experience, in that a large area will have to be set up to make the ancillary event a success. There will be vendors arriving, possibly a check-in area to set up, large pieces of equipment and displays to set up, and significant power needs in the area. This is in addition to the golf tournament primary space setup on the course that will probably occur at the same time. So, within one major event (if there are ancillary events associated with the primary event), there can be more than one primary space, and all of them need attention.

Primary space setup could include a changeover. A **changeover** is the process by which the primary space in the venue is converted from functioning for one purpose to another (e.g., flat exhibit space to basketball). Needing a very fast changeover is more common in traditional venues that regularly schedule different types of events on consecutive days. This often falls squarely into the responsibilities of the facility manager, but event managers should be aware of changeover schedules and how long different types of changeovers take to execute for various setups.

There is also an element of participant safety in setting up of the primary space. A soccer field should be checked for holes and other dangerous conditions, just as the area around a basketball court should be checked for sharp corners that could pose a danger to players. Examples of other common setup items for events include the scorer's tables and sideline chairs for basketball; leveling the ice and cleaning the glass for hockey; and installing and checking the touchpads (part of the timing system) and checking the pool chemicals and temperature for swimming. There will probably be sponsor agreements related to signage that must be executed during setup. Ensuring signs are hung in the correct places may seem trivial, but sponsors will notice and be unhappy if they are hung incorrectly.

Warm-up time may be provided to participants in the primary space and needs to be taken into consideration when planning setup. Warm-up is when the athletes get a feel for the environment, so the scoreboards should be on, signs hung, and lighting should be the same as it will be for the event. If a temporary logo needs to be affixed to the basketball court, it should be done prior to all practices so the court is exactly the same during practice as it will be for the game.

For nontraditional sports venues, the setup will be extensive. For example, creating a course, keeping spectators separate from the course, securing the area, and moving the required equipment to the course are all time-consuming activities. It is not unusual for a triathlon starting at 8:00 am to have workers out at 3:00 am setting up. Beyond the primary space, there are supporting ancillary areas that require setup such as medical, registration, transition areas, timing systems, and public address systems.

Organization is Everything!

Dr. Bren Stevens

Director of Athletics, University of Charleston

Dr. Bren Stevens

I completed a 19-year career as the head volleyball coach for the University of Charleston and now serve in the role as the director of athletics for our institution. The University of Charleston is a Division II member of the NCAA, and is also a member of the Mountain East Conference. It is not uncommon to find staff at smaller institutions that wear many hats, and often, head coaches must assume the event manager role for their own games or matches. Trying to solicit help on a game day is like looking for the proverbial needle In a haystack.

Organization is everything to a head coach. An event manager for an intercollegiate sport will help to take a significant burden off of the head coach and his or her staff. This allows the coach to concentrate on the game, the athletes, and ultimately winning. Throughout the years, I have developed my own checklist for the purpose of setting up the gym for a home volleyball match. I am confident that all coaches would rather come across seemingly too organized as compared with the alternative.

I am including a copy of the checklist that we now utilize at the University of Charleston for our volleyball match setup and teardown. It can easily be adapted as a model for almost all other intercollegiate sports. In addition, the event manager should expect to meet with the head coach on the day of a game or match about specifics for the day. Some of the below tasks may be completed by other individuals on campus, but it is the event manager's responsibility to provide oversight for each of the seven areas listed on the checklist.

University of Charleston—Volleyball Match Checklist

I. **Publicity:**

_____Campus advertisement

_____Statistics and talking points

_____Post game media/score calls

II. **Court Preparation:**

_____Properly clean the entire gym floor and surrounding areas

_____Assemble scorer/stats table

_____Set up chairs for team benches

_____Set up the scoring console and test

_____Set up statistical computer and printer and test

_____Set up National Anthem CD or IPhone

_____Place paper stat sheets, pencils, score sheets, libero-tracking forms on scorer's table

_____Turn on gym lights and balcony lights

_____Lock side doors of the gym

_____Clean/lock officials/team locker rooms

_____Dry erase markers and erasers in each of the locker rooms

_____Check bathrooms for cleanliness and toilet paper supply

_____Set up volleyball net system and referee platforms

_____Place balls on to the volleyball court for visitors and home teams

III. **Parking:**

_____Make sure that campus security knows that there is a home match

_____Contact security for assistance with general parking

IV. **Ticket and Program Sales:**

_____Poster that contains ticket prices

_____Money box with change for ticket and program sales

_____NCAA Pass gate list

_____Programs

_____Secure one money taker

V. **Pre-Game Details:**

_____Host to meet and greet visiting teams

_____Host to meet and greet officials and line judges

_____Gather drinks for the officials and table workers

_____Towels and checks for the officials (if applicable)

_____Give the PA script to the Announcer

_____Game details (copies of stats, box scores to visiting teams)

_____Secure one timer

_____Secure one libero tracker

_____Secure one "official" score keeper

_____Secure one PA announcer

VI. **Emergency Medical Care:**

_____Make sure that there is a Certified Athletic Trainer (AT) assigned to the match

_____The AT should place ice, cups, towels, and water coolers for both of the visiting teams and the home team

VII. **Clean-Up:**

_____Put volleyballs and net systems away

_____Unhook scoreboard and put away

_____Lock all doors to the facility

_____Turn in ticket money

_____Put away the PA system

_____Pick up trash around the benches and the scorer's table

_____Send statistical information to the SID

Division II has come up with a strategic plan, which in part addresses the game day environment. The NCAA lists priorities such as:

Priority 3.1: Provide game environments and atmospheres that are competitive, safe, fun, positive, respectful, and entertaining. Oversight: Division II Conferences, Division II Directors of Athletics, Division II Student-Athlete Advisory Committee

Priority 3.2: Enhance and increase the opportunities to strengthen the experience for game day, conference championships and national championships for Division II student-athletes, coaches, officials, fans, and spectators. Oversight: Division II Directors of Athletics, Division II Identity Subcommittee, Division II Championships

Committee 3.1: (NCAA II Strategic Plan 2012–15). http://www.ncaa.org/sites/default/files/2012-15+Strategic+Plan.pdf

The individual that assumes the responsibility of the event manager is instrumental in assisting the NCAA with the associated priorities for their strategic plan. All of us play an important role in making the game day experience positive, and providing organized steps that ensure fluidity and make people feel welcome on our campuses.

All coaches would like to be able to devote more time to the details of coaching, and they will certainly be appreciative of having an event manager that is capable of creating a proper game day atmosphere.

Ancillary Space Setup

Courtesy of David Pierce

Ancillary events such as kids races provide something for the whole family to do on a race day.

Although counterintuitive, the ancillary spaces may take longer to set up than the primary space. The setup of these spaces can be spread over a large area and involve coordinating with various people, waiting at various locations to meet people, and checking-in with people to ensure each area gets set up according to plan. Moving from place to place and meeting up with different people can be very time consuming. To ensure spaces are available to the users when they need them, it is common to set up areas in the order they are needed by all involved.

Parking

Parking lots are the first locations to receive setup attention. Even those working the event need to park, so it is important that procedures are in place to ensure parking lot security and staff are the first to arrive. Barricades, chairs for parking attendants, and parking signage should also be set up early. Some major events will require that parking is staffed the night before the event to ensure cars do not sneak into the lots. One car parked where a media satellite truck is planning to be the next day can cause major problems, resulting in delays for everyone, towing the car, an upset patron, and a frustrated media representative. No matter how much effort is put into securing parking lots, it is likely that cars will need to be moved by tow trucks if reserved lots are being used. Establishing a relationship, or sponsorship, with a towing company before the event is recommended so trucks are available if they are needed.

Weather can also play a role in parking setup. Some events expand their available parking by using grass fields, which creates issues if it rains. Being prepared is key if rain is in the forecast. The heavier the vehicle, the more challenging parking on grass in rain can be. Plywood sheets can be laid end to end to create "lanes" for cars to enter and exit the parking area and avoid it becoming a mud pit.

Tailgating

For events with tailgating, that area should also be set up early. Tailgate setup often includes signage, delivery and setup of portable restrooms, marking tailgate spots, and tent setup. Golf carts are a must for events that have large parking or tailgate areas, as they allow event managers to quickly move from one area to another to deal with any issues that may arise. In the event of rain, severe cold, or snow, event managers can expect that the number of fans tailgating will significantly decrease, and that fans will arrive closer to game time. However, in spring and fall weather, or for events with a lot of meaning to fans, tailgaters will arrive early and sometimes stay late. Therefore, event managers must account for that in their planning.

Participant, Media, Vendor, and Staff Needs

Other facility spaces used by event workers, participants, media, and vendors are set up after parking and tailgating. These groups all arrive much earlier to the event than spectators. For all facilities, this means that worker, media, and participant entrances/registration are open early while the rest of the venue is secured. Also, the security command center (if applicable), locker rooms, participant hospitality, media work rooms, and press row/press box should be open and accessible as early as possible. Members of the media generally set up early and can work for hours after the event concludes.

Communication with all of these groups is important, but ensuring vendors have specific information is especially important. Whether the vendor is a concessionaire bringing in a stand-alone trailer to a snowmobile race, or a charity group collecting money at the event, all should have the same rules. A time prior to the gates opening should be established for all vendors to be set up and ready to open. It can cause significant disruption to the event flow if a vendor arrives late and needs to drive into the event area after the perimeter has been established and gates are open for patrons. Simply transporting a folding table through a crowd of people to accommodate a late-arriving charity group can be dangerous and will interrupt the event flow. Event managers need to be ready to turn away vendors that arrive late and/or do not follow established protocol.

Sponsor, Official, and Spectator Needs

The last wave of setup is those areas used by sponsors, officials, and spectators. Event managers should meet officials in a designated area and escort them to their locker rooms and answer any questions they may have. Weather can also impact setup in spectator areas. For outdoor venues, simple actions such as drying off wet seats or having ponchos for spectators when it rains will help to create a good atmosphere. In hot weather, umbrellas and/or misters can be used to provide a place for fans to cool off.

When the gates open, everything should be "open for business." Concessionaires should have the hot dogs hot, sponsor areas should be established and appropriately staffed, scoreboards should be on, and music should be playing to create the event atmosphere. Once setup is complete, it is not long before teardown begins.

Teardown

Teardown is simply the reverse of setup, and event managers should strive to leave no trace behind. During teardown, the facility is restored to its pre-event condition. This means that every sign and every piece of trash is removed from the site, and all tables, chairs, and other equipment are returned to storage. Some venues may not require this much attention to teardown, but event managers that put in the extra effort in teardown will impress rights holders and venue management. When relying on volunteers, it is difficult to motivate them to stay for teardown. Generally, they have worked a long day and are ready to go home at this point. The management skills and enthusiasm of the event manager will be essential to make sure teardown is as smooth and as quick as possible.

In general, the different groups involved in an event tend to leave in the same order they arrived. Again, the teardown process will take about half as long as setup. The parking lots are the first to be torn down. Midway through the event, barricades can come down and parking staff released. Event staff will also be released in shifts as the game progresses. The ticket taking and gate security areas are generally shut down one-half to two-thirds of the way through the event. Vendors will begin their teardown prior to the conclusion of the event as well. For instance, a temporary concessions setup will probably sell until the last quarter of the event, and then shut down as business winds down. Of course, alcohol sales should stop approximately halfway to two-thirds of the way through the event to reduce the risk of drinking and driving (for additional information see the Techniques for Effective Alcohol Management training at http:// www.teamcoalition.org/). This allows for adequate time for clean-up and financial reconciliation, without losing much revenue in the final minutes of the event.

Teardown generally takes half as long as setup.

Spectators will leave at the conclusion of the event (except luxury suite patrons and barring any unique circumstances), and teardown of any special seating can begin at that time. Participants (unless there are postevent press conferences), the bulk of the event staff, and game officials follow the spectators. Special attention should be given to the safety of game officials. They should be escorted to their vehicles as they exit the facility. The last group to leave is usually the media. The working media area should be available for a few hours after the conclusion of the event so they can finish their work without having to change locations. The event manager should stay until the media have finished working. Usually, during this time, event managers are finalizing all teardown, ensuring the venue is as clean as possible, and that all areas are secure.

A multisport, running, or cycling course will be different than a traditional venue. For a course, teardown will begin immediately after the last athlete has left the starting area. The starting area is torn down immediately, and the teardown team will follow the last athlete, taking down water stations and barricades as the race progresses. As the majority of participants pass the fluid stations on a course, the tables and cups will begin to be consolidated. The number of tables that were set up at the beginning will slowly begin to be reduced, those tables broken down, and the area cleaned, even as the last athletes are utilizing the fluid station. A systematic approach to teardown will keep it from distracting from the main event. Whether the event is in a traditional or nontraditional venue, a good teardown operation will be invisible to the spectators and participants.

Creating and Managing *Green* Events

Michael E. Pfahl

Ohio University, Associate Professor Department of Sports Administration

There are several key points to keep in mind when integrating environmentally friendly practices into the event planning process, no matter the size of the organization or event (see Chapter 4, Event Sustainability for detailed information). While specific events have different levels of environmental planning needs, these keys are applicable across all events. First, an organization's sustainability policy must be integrated into the mission of the event, indicating the planning members' commitment to *green* practices. Once the mission is identified and understood by all constituents, then specific action points can be developed for the overall event plan and the sub-plans that comprise it. Second, like any other aspect of the planning process, the environmental initiatives should have clear implementation, control, and review guidelines developed as part of the overall event management plan. These guidelines must be developed in conjunction with the broader strategy to ensure success. Further, integration helps to foresee complications during the event due to poor planning of green objectives, or to identify potential roadblocks to the success of the green initiatives. Placing the green objectives under the same rigorous criteria as any other aspect of the event plan sends a clear signal as to their importance to the overall event and adds accountability for the event managers. Third, clear and consistent communication of the green objectives to internal and external constituents alleviates uncertainty and encourages individual ownership in the success of the green objectives and overall event. In addition, the external constituents involved in the event are directly encouraged to act in environmentally responsible ways after the event concludes.

In order to accomplish the key points outlined above, a set of *Environmental Levels of Activity* are provided below. These levels are meant to guide event planners toward their desired goals for green planning.

Level 1: Basic Environmental Planning

- Recycle bins for paper, plastic, cardboard, and other materials used during the event
- Goals and procedures to reduce the paperwork associated with the event (internally and externally)
- Moderate environmental language in external relations channels (e.g., press releases, promotional materials) to engage the public in the event's green goals in addition to the event itself
- Commit to environmentally friendly practices as a team; develop an incentive-based reward system for members of the event planning staff and event attendees for their contributions to the green goals
- Obtain any food, beverages, and other materials from local sources (as applicable)

Level 2: Intermediate Environmental Planning (Level 1 plus the following items)

- Partnerships with local community groups to promote green initiatives at the event and to manage the collection and removal of recycled items
- Use of electronic means to advertise and promote the event
- Use Energy Star rated electronic equipment wherever possible
- Utilization of biodegradable or recyclable materials for food and beverages service (e.g., biodegradable cups, utensils, plates)
- Unused food donated to local food banks or charitable/community organizations
- Use of Green Seal cleaning products for event clean-up and removal

Level 3: Advanced Environmental Planning (Levels 1 & 2 plus the following items)

- Paperless internal planning, promotion, and implementation processes
- Paperless registration and dissemination of promotional and other information to external constituents
- Corporate and community partners to promote green initiatives at the event and to manage collection and removal of recycled items

- Activism through placement of advocacy organizations and corporate organizations at the event to promote awareness and behavioral change among participants and the broader community (through media exposure)
- Encourage carpooling by event attendees with possibility of reward (e.g., discounted fee) for such actions
- Use of biodegradable and recyclable materials in any promotional giveaways (e.g., wallet card with environmentally friendly tips included in re-usable gift bag)
- Development and utilization of vendor guidelines including requests (and preference) for vendors with environmentally friendly product offerings.

Event Day Maintenance

Maintenance is not glamorous, but it is critical to a successful event. Event day maintenance does cross over with concepts from setup and teardown. Field, court, and course event day maintenance is often left to a grounds crews and facility management staff. However, all event managers should have basic knowledge of the maintenance requirements for fields, courts, and courses. For traditional sport venues such as outdoor sports-plexes, stadiums, and arenas, it is likely that the event day maintenance will be included in the contract to use the venue. Turf management and field maintenance is a highly specialized area, with many turf managers having advanced degrees in horticulture or related areas. However, savvy event managers will be ready, and willing, to step in and help whenever needed.

The event day maintenance of courses is the most challenging due to the course being used for other functions until the event starts. A racecourse may be open to vehicle traffic until the lead group of runners approaches a specific intersection. Maintenance issues can range from having to fix temporary directional indicators that get inadvertently moved, to having a manhole cover go missing. In 2014 alone, there were two large road races where runners got lost due to signage that had been vandalized, moved, or incorrectly installed. In one instance, some runners took public transportation back to the starting line after borrowing money from a random pedestrian because they were so off course.

Indoor surfaces require minimal attention. Keeping the court clean and dry so it is safe for the athletes is the main concern for indoor courts. It is not the intention of this section to prepare event managers for all possible maintenance issues during an event, but to provide some examples of areas that require attention before, during, and after events.

Natural Grass Fields

Generally, event managers will not be responsible for extensive field maintenance. If the grounds crew does a good job up until game day, there will not be too much to worry about. However, during a multiday event where fields are getting heavy use, or in bad weather, the event managers will want to keep an eye on wear and tear and be knowledgeable enough to help with maintenance. Even after a long day of games when everyone involved is exhausted, taking care of the fields is important to ensure some recovery overnight.

Baseball and Softball

Baseball and softball fields require the most attention of outdoor fields because they are a mixture of grass and dirt. Most coaches and players are also knowledgeable about field maintenance and are used to helping with the fields. Event managers should not exclusively rely on coaches and players, but often these groups are willing to help.

Game day maintenance for baseball and softball will vary with the weather and the number of games being played. If a multigame tournament is being held on a field, relining will take place approximately every third game (or other designated number of games appropriate for the conditions). The time required for this must be factored into the day's schedule. Budgeting for supplies and staff to perform the function is also important. Some common pre- and postgame maintenance tasks include:

Pregame Routine

- Remove tarps
- Mow grass
- Scarify the dirt areas using a spiker
- Drag the skinned areas smooth
- Water the infield area
- Set the chalk lines
- Place pitcher's mat on mound for batting practice
- Set up safety screen for pitcher for batting practice
- Paint/wash bases, pitching plate, and home plate
- Place bases

Postgame Routine

- Remove bases and cover base anchors
- Drag skinned area and baselines
- Recondition mound and home plate area
- Replace, fill, and pack loose divots in turf
- Tarp if needed (The Baseball Tomorrow Fund, n.d.)

Baseball fields do not tolerate rain very well and can become unplayable quickly. In the event of rain immediately prior to or during the game, a rain delay is often called. To combat wet weather, most fields (except youth fields) will have tarps available to protect the infield. Drainage installed in the outfield, the soil composition, and a crown will also help handle the water. A **crown** refers to the slope of the field, and helps drain the field. In baseball and softball, the field slopes slightly away from the baselines to the warning track area to aid in drainage. During a game, the tarp needs to be easily accessible and a "tarp crew" established. Some newer tarps with a lifting and rolling device may only require a few people, but in most circumstances, the players are the "tarp crew" and 15–20 of them are needed. It can take 10 minutes or more to tarp the field and get it protected, so the longer officials and event managers take to decide whether to call a rain delay, the more damage is done to the field. If lightning is a concern, the safety of the tarp crew far outweighs the need to get the field covered. Tarps are either edged with chain, use sand bags, or use spikes to hold them down. It is important that wind is not allowed under the edges, as a blowing tarp allows for water to get to the field. If the game is able to resume, the tarp is removed, drying agents are used where water has pooled on the dirt, and the field is dragged before play resumes. Extra sod, chalk, drying agents, and even green paint to fill in dead spots on the grass should be in the budget and will all come in handy during a long, or multiday, event.

Football, Soccer, Lacrosse, and Field Hockey

Football, soccer, lacrosse, and field hockey fields rarely require much attention from event managers. Besides mowing, striping, replacing large divots, and general field setup, there is little to do pregame if the field is well cared for. Most of these fields will be crowned, with the highest point on the field running down the center of the field from end zone to end zone or goal to goal. Thus, water is propelled toward the sidelines to aid in overall field drainage. If the field is unable to drain as quickly as the rain is coming down, damage to the field can be expected. If any field becomes slippery and dangerous, game delays and/or cancellations are an option.

At some point in the career of event managers, it is likely that painting lines on a field will be required. Many outdoor sports require that the field be lined for both practice and competition. If a grounds crew is available, this task will fall to them. However, event managers should know the basics of how to string and line a field. For natural grass fields, choosing the right paint, preparing the field, and having proper equipment are keys to success. To keep the grass in good condition, water-based paints are preferred (LaRue, LaRue, & Sawyer, 2005). String, small spikes, spray paint, and a field striper are all essential equipment. In some cases, more complex field stripers use pour-in paint as opposed to spray cans. Even a simple soccer field requires specific instructions, attention to detail, and patience to line it correctly. To line a field, the dimensions and layout of the field, string, spikes, a hammer, a tape measure, a paint liner, cans of paint, and a few people are all needed. The outside field lines are measured, staked, and strung first, with the goal boxes and other field markings following. Although the dimensions and layout will change, the principles are the same for painting all natural grass fields.

For those fields requiring more complex logos, call in the experts. Heavy plastic stencils are the most common way to paint a logo on a field, but using a drawing and then creating a scaled grid on the field is also a frequent approach. A projector can be set up and the logo projected onto the field and then painted in as well. Logos can be painted free hand by artistically talented people, but with this method comes a lot of room for error. The majority of outdoor fields are natural grass, so event managers need to be familiar with all aspects of maintenance, especially related to needs during inclement weather.

Synthetic Fields

Synthetic fields have become extremely popular in recent years. They do not require mowing, are more durable than natural grass, can easily handle heavy rains, do not require recovery periods, and the quality continues to improve. However, they do require care. Most new synthetic fields are top dressed with infill that is some combination of sand, rubber, recycled tires, or other plastic material. This material must be evenly spread on the field using small tractors to ensure a level playing surface.

Synthetic turfs do retain more heat than natural grass and can be over 30° warmer than a natural grass field (New York State Department of Health, 2008). Not only is the heat retained within the turf, but it radiates to the playing area, with temperatures in one study at head-level reaching 138°F on a 98°F day (New York State Department of Health, 2008). Watering the field can lower temperatures temporarily, but due to good drainage, the field quickly returns to being hot. Event managers need to account for this increase in heat for summer events on synthetic fields in their emergency medical planning.

Lines on synthetic fields will generally be permanently "painted" through the use of white turf. If temporary lines or logos are needed, removable paint is an option. The application is similar to that for natural grass, but it needs to be tested on a small and out-of-the-way section of turf prior to using it. The paint can be washed away with a solution, agitation from a brush, and light pressure wash. The advent of improved temporary paint products allows synthetic turf fields to be used for a variety of sports, team logos, sponsor logos, and cause related initiatives (i.e., pink ribbon for breast cancer awareness).

Courses

Courses can be maintenance free or they can be a massive maintenance nightmare, depending on the characteristics of the event, the location, and the weather. As indicated throughout this book,

Courtesy of David Pierce

nontraditional venues are more difficult than traditional venues to manage. This can also be true with respect to maintenance. It is helpful if a line is painted (usually blue) on the course of a race several days before the race so that participants can easily see where they are supposed to go. This may require traffic to be shut down for several hours, which will likely require the event organizers to work on the municipality's timetable. Often, painting

Nontraditional events and venues create unique setup and teardown needs.

is completed in the middle of the night when there is less traffic. For cycling races, markings on the road indicating the correct direction to turn at each intersection are common way to mark the route. Given the large area covered by many courses, there is a lot of space that cannot be controlled all the time by event managers. Imagine trying to anticipate road conditions, set up barriers for spectators, and organize a bicycle race on a 100-mile stretch of road. Now, imagine trying to set up and manage that same race while the road is open to vehicles on the same day.

The many unknowns are also what make races a lot of fun to manage; anything can happen. A water main could break 10 miles into the course and flood the road, and it is up to the event managers to make sure they know who to call, and to be there to help resolve the issue before the cyclists arrive at that spot (or re-route them). As for general course maintenance, the course conditions are at the mercy of the weather. Since most events that use a course are endurance related, where athletes are exerting themselves at a high level for long periods of time, the event managers should have a good handle on the expected weather and possible impact on the participants. In heat, extra water and medical personnel should be called in; and in rain, event organizers should be ready for slip-related injuries. In wet conditions, event managers should be especially careful with any banner or chip mats that runners will actually run over during the race. These plastic surfaces can become slippery and dangerous in the rain or even with excessive humidity. During the 2006 Chicago Marathon, the winner slipped on the sponsor logo on the ground at the finish line hitting his head on the concrete. Thankfully, he was not severely injured, but many events now recognize this risk. The video can be viewed here: http://youtu.be/GWheGgqmq0A

With evolving technology, there is also maintenance to go along with timing systems. It is common practice for most races to use timing chips for accurate timing. The chips are worn by participants, and when the athletes pass chip mats spread out on the course in intervals, their time at that point in the race is recorded. In some major races, it takes more than 30 minutes for the back of the pack to cross the starting line. Chip timing allow an athlete's time to accurately reflect their time on the course and not take into account the time it took them to reach the starting line. However, these systems are not without problems. Experts on the timing systems should be on hand to address any issues that may arise. There is little room for error when dealing with timing systems.

Other Surfaces

Indoor surfaces (except ice) are less troublesome than most outdoor surfaces. For wood playing surfaces, a dry sweeper and towels need to be on hand to dry the court and remove any debris. The event managers should also know how to adjust any equipment that is part of the game (i.e., volleyball net, basketball goals, shot clocks, etc.) they are managing. It may sound simple, but often special equipment is needed to do it correctly.

Sports played on ice have specific maintenance needs that are probably beyond the expertise of the event managers. Large and expensive ice resurfacers, such as Zambonis and Olympias, are required to keep the ice clean, at a consistent thickness, and smooth for the athletes. Prior to the event, the ice crew will take measurements of the ice thickness in a variety of areas and then reshape the ice, if needed, to ensure a consistent thickness. It is common to have the edges of the ice rink become thicker than the middle due to the ice resurfacer driver slowing down around the edges (which puts more water on the ice) and driving faster down the middle of the rink (limiting the amount of water put down).

Outdoor hard tennis courts do not require much maintenance during an event unless it rains. In the event of rain, event managers need to have a lot of people ready to work hard to dry the courts as soon as the rain stops. There are specific squeegees made for drying tennis courts, and many should be available for event staff at any tennis event. The goal after a rain delay in tennis is to get the courts dry as quickly as possible so play can resume.

Maintaining all playing surfaces throughout an event allows athletes to perform safely and at their best. Additionally, for natural turf fields, postgame maintenance is crucial to allow for field recovery overnight.

General Facility Maintenance

Besides playing surfaces, event managers should be aware of the entire venue and its maintenance. It would be impossible to mention every maintenance scenario in this chapter. However, once event managers are thinking about the facility as a whole as well as each space individually, they will notice maintenance issues in a timely manner and be able to react to each appropriately. By walking around the venue, and listening to patrons, maintenance issues can be identified and resolved. The types of maintenance issues that might occur during an event are endless, but issues that occur during events such as concession spills, clogged units, overflowing trash cans, and broken seats are all common.

Event managers should have a facility management point of contact that is available to address these types of general facility maintenance issues. Prior to the event, event managers should make sure the facility has trained maintenance personnel either on-call or on-site so that problems that arise can be resolved quickly. Especially for areas that impact the operation of the core event activity (e.g., timing systems and scoreboards) personnel should be on-site and available. Maintenance personnel that might need to be available, depending on event needs and equipment use, include a plumber, electrician (scoreboard, lighting, timing system, etc.), sound specialist, elevator/escalator specialist, information technology specialist, and communications support.

A good maintenance plan, although not a direct responsibility of the event managers, will help the event to run smoothly. The list of items that could need maintenance during an event is endless, but common areas have been addressed here related to playing surfaces and the facility to help event managers plan ahead for maintenance issues they might be faced with.

Managing Events Across Multiple Venues

Mauro Palmero, Ph.D.

Assistant Professor, East Tennessee State University

As an event manager at a major sports complex, I learned how to handle events that were too big for one venue. Among other areas, I was responsible for managing very large boys' and girls' basketball and baseball tournaments that grew larger each year.

My responsibilities included finding venue space, coordinating the logistics of holding multiple and simultaneous events outside facilities we owned, and ensuring that the event was a success. That encompassed: (a) establishing a relationship with schools and private sports venues in the area; (b) reserving dates at each venue; (c) executing contracts for each venue; (d) hiring site supervisors; (e) coordinating equipment and supply delivery to each site; and (f) being the liaison between our client and venues before, during, and after every event. These tasks repeated every year.

The event management process ran on about a 10-month cycle. I began in October for events occurring in July. First, I visited all middle and high schools that had a gym and/or a baseball field, plus any other privately owned sports venue in the region. Then, I met with the client's sport managers to discuss the feasibility of events at each site.

From November to May, I mainly focused on establishing new relationships with sites that had been added from the previous year (the incremental growth in number of teams participating demanded more space every year) and strengthening existing relationships with the schools continuing to be involved. The relationship management process included:

- Negotiation of space usage (i.e., who, what, when)
- Securing equipment and deciding who provided each piece of equipment needed
- Negotiation of rental fees for each school
- Executing rental, insurance, indemnification, and waiver contracts

Simultaneously, I was monitoring all space reserved and making adjustments to reservations based on the needs of the venue and needs of our client. Even with the best planning, scheduling conflicts sometimes occurred because the venues were also hosting other events and/or our client had increasing space needs.

By mid-May, I had most of the venue contracts signed and started working on the logistics of each event. Many details were important for the success of each event. To ensure success (and less headache for me during the events) I ensured the following areas were taken care of:

- Every off-site venue had a copy of our client's insurance policy
- Every off-site venue had an updated schedule they were comfortable with
- Each site director for each venue was contracted (including amount and form of payment) and they were aware of their responsibilities
- Each venue was set to receive the correct amount of equipment at the right time.
- Medical assistance for each venue was contracted and scheduled
- The coordinator of officials had an updated schedule and driving and parking directions to each venue
- Our client had driving and parking directions to each venue to provide to teams and spectators.

By June, I held training sessions for all our staff, event coordinators, and interns assigned to work the summer events. Training included an explanation of daily responsibilities (e.g., checking equipment inventory, contact site director, pickup score sheets, etc.) and what to do (or who to call) in scenarios outside their responsibility area. For example, event coordinators were supposed to call me if it was a venue-related issue, and if it was a tournament-related issue they were supposed to call the client's representative. I also had the event coordinators and other event managers that were returning from the previous season share their experiences and best practices with the newcomers.

By early July, before all events started, I prepared an off-site coverage schedule that determined every event worker's responsibilities and assigned their daily location during the event. Event staff worked on a rotation (opening, mid-day, and closing) to ensure full coverage during the event. Throughout the events, I visited each venue regularly and addressed any issues that occurred. Sometimes, it was merely bringing supplies and updates from tournament headquarters and other times there were issues that needed my attention on-site. I also began the wrap-up process for the July events by paying venue rent and site director salaries.

By mid-August, when the last tournament was ending, I reconciled each event and retrieved leftover equipment from each location. I would also send a "thank you" package (ours and our client's swag) to each off-site venue. Over the course of the summer, I worked 51 days straight and drove over 3,000 miles.

For any event manager, managing simultaneous events at a variety of facilities is a challenge. Having a structured annual process helped to make sure all of the details of event planning got done in a timely manner. Even with all of the hard work and long hours, watching events grow, the athletes have a great experience, and having a satisfied client was a rewarding experience.

Equipment

Equipment can encompass a lot of different items in sport. Basketball goals, an award stand, and even a popcorn popper in concessions are all equipment. The role of event managers is to make sure the appropriate equipment is available, that it works correctly, and that back-up equipment is available for key functions. This all has to be accomplished within the budget. A list of common equipment needed to run an event is provided in Chapter 13—Event Documents.

Capital Equipment

Capital equipment is generally considered to be any piece of equipment costing over $500 with a useful life of 2 or more years (Mull, Bayless, & Jamieson, 2005). This type of equipment is likely owned by the facility and includes items such as basketball goals, portable flooring, staging, concessions equipment, and floor coverings. However, for events at nontraditional sport venues, capital equipment may include scoreboards, timing equipment, and barricades. It is likely that a road race would need to rent this equipment unless it is owned by the host organization, city, or county.

Expendable Equipment

Expendable equipment is less expensive, less than $500, and has a useful life of less than 2 years (Mull, Bayless, & Jamieson, 2005). Because of the shorter lifespan, this type of equipment is replaced as it wears out. Volleyballs, folding tables and chairs, and basketball goal safety padding are all examples of expendable equipment. Facilities may or may not own the needed expendable equipment for a specific event. Any expendable equipment provided by the venue should be carefully examined to make sure it is safe, clean, and reliable. If the facility cannot provide the needed expendable equipment, event organizers will need to purchase or rent it.

Fixed Equipment

Fixed equipment is attached to the facility and could include spectator seating, scoreboards, sound/public address systems, and mechanical systems. Use of this equipment is part of using the venue. Often, fixed equipment is complex and requires someone specially trained to operate it. For example, scoreboard systems vary considerably from facility to facility. The scoreboard operator should be either provided by the facility, or training should be provided by the facility management to a member of the event management team.

Supplies

Supplies are items used on a regular basis that may or may not relate to the core activity of the event. Even if the event is a major football game, supplies such as paper, pens, credentials, and ticket stock will be needed to execute many event functions. Small items, such as greenery and temporary signage, would also fall into the supply category, as these help to create the event atmosphere.

Purchasing Versus Renting

Deciding whether to purchase or rent equipment is often a function of availability, price, and frequency of use. Once it is realized that equipment is needed, event managers should begin researching the equipment. The best scenario is to borrow the equipment from a local sports team or club that already owns the equipment. Another way to obtain equipment is to receive it as a "trade" for a sponsorship. If those are not options, then the cost of buying versus renting should be examined.

If the event is recurring in nature and there is a high likelihood that the equipment will be needed on a regular basis, often purchasing makes the most sense. But, equipment usually takes up a lot space and needs to be stored if it is owned by the event organization. So, storage costs should also be included in the decision on whether to rent or buy. Depending on the location of the event, some equipment might not be available for rent, or it is cost prohibitive to ship the items a great distance for a short rental period. However, in most cases, renting is less expensive than purchasing.

Equipment such as bike barricades (the heavy metal barricades that are used to separate participants from spectators or to create entrance gates) are expensive to purchase. However, because they are very heavy, they are also expensive to rent. Oftentimes, items like this are better to purchase for recurring events (e.g., a small college athletic department needs them for multiple sports and multiple events) because of the transportation costs associated with renting. For a traveling golf tournament, it might be necessary to set up temporary bleacher seating to accommodate the crowd. In this case, renting the seating is probably more appropriate than buying, since it will need to be constructed by representatives from the company and because there is no use for the seating after the event concludes.

Bidding

With respect to equipment, **bidding** refers to a competitive process in which companies are asked to provide service and price information based on criteria set by the event organizers. It is similar to bidding to host an event, but usually much less complex. Many public entities require that purchases/rentals over a certain cost be bid out. Whether it is required or not, bidding is a good practice because the event managers will be able to compare what companies can provide based on set criteria. Event managers need to be clear and detailed in the **request for bid (RFB)**, which is the seeking out of prices on the equipment or service from multiple vendors/suppliers. If the equipment is complex and needs someone with special knowledge to set it up, then the setup should be part of the RFB. Any special costs the company charges for shipping, delivery, or pickup (in the case of a rental) should also be itemized. For equipment being purchased, there should be some expectation of a warranty written into the RFB. Event mangers can do research to see what a standard warranty is for that type of equipment. If the equipment purchased is so specialized that only the vendor selling it can service or repair it, be sure to request standard hourly rates for servicing and/or specific requirements related to service. Also, determining who pays for shipping of the equipment when servicing is needed, what the time needed for repair is, and the limits or exclusions to any warranty are important to know. If the equipment must be delivered on a certain day at a certain time, the RFB should be clear about that expectation. Upon delivery, all equipment needs to be inspected to ensure it is in good working order before delivery is accepted.

Let's use a fictitious youth soccer tournament for an example. The event managers recognize that, because of the location of the tournament and lack of existing restrooms, portable restrooms are needed for both spectators and participants. The event hosts certainly do not want to buy the portable restrooms, but they do need to rent them. A guideline ratio for portable restrooms is one per 75 people for regular portable restrooms, and one per 150 people for ADA units. With 200 participants, 300 spectators, and 50 volunteers, it is estimated that a total of 10 portable restrooms are needed. The regular and ADA units can be combined to arrive at the total needed, and the number of units should always be rounded up when in doubt. The event managers may decide to order six regular and four ADA compliant portable restrooms.

The event managers then write a letter that they will fax to all port-a-potty companies within 150 miles of the event. The letter is specific as to the number of units needed, the drop-off date and time, the location of the units, and the pick-up date and time. If it is a multiday event, the letter will also need to request a cost to have the portable restrooms serviced at the end or beginning of each day. The letter then asks interested companies to respond by a specific date and time with how much they would charge to provide the units. This letter is the RFB. The company that responds with the lowest price within the bid specifications then is awarded the job.

The benefit to bidding is that the companies involved know it is a competitive process and thus will submit the best price possible hoping to win the job. If event managers were to call the first company listed in the phone book, they do not have any leverage to lower the price.

Equipment Storage

The amount of equipment needed for the event will dictate storage needs. For smaller events, it may be that storage is the trunk of a car or a small closet. For others, an entire warehouse might be required to accommodate all of the equipment and supplies. To manage storage needs, special attention should be paid to the specifics of delivery (and pickup, if rented) of equipment. If equipment arrives earlier or later than scheduled, it can cause problems in the order of setup, create storage issues, and generally cause havoc for event managers. The challenge with equipment arriving late is obvious in that it is not available when needed. However, early-arriving equipment can create major storage problems. For most venues, storage is a concern on a daily basis, and the facilities do not have room to store extra equipment prior to an event.

For events with significant storage needs, a rented warehouse or storage unit might be the answer. If the venue is being constructed for the event, there probably will not be any on-site storage. In this case, it is important that the storage is located in a convenient location to the event, is large enough, and is accessible 24 hours a day. Most, if not all, of the items stored will eventually need to be transported to the event location, so the closer it is to the event facility, the better. If large pieces of equipment will be required to be moved, then there needs to be access to a forklift (and forklift operator), pallet jack, or hand cart, depending on the size of the equipment.

Other temporary options for storage are sea containers and tents. Sea containers are large metal boxes traditionally used to transport materials on ships. They can then easily be transferred to the frame of a large truck for over-the-road transport. They can be placed on-site at temporary events. They have the advantage of being able to be locked, and some can include climate control. Tents are inexpensive and easy to use as storage, but have some disadvantages. They require security personnel on-site to ensure that the materials inside are not stolen. If the tent is set up on a soft surface, it may be necessary rent a temporary floor to keep materials from getting muddy if it rains.

Other Equipment Considerations

All equipment should be checked, double-checked, and then checked again immediately prior to use. Oftentimes, equipment will work perfectly when tested the day before the event, but then on event day a problem will occur. Or, the equipment works well in an empty stadium, but once 20,000 people arrive it fails. This is a common scenario with wireless microphones, headsets, and other communications equipment that is sensitive to interference.

Even if a piece of equipment seems to be functioning perfectly, back-up equipment is needed for critical operational functions. Anything related to timing and scoring is critical to event operations. Thus, portable shot clocks, play clocks, game clocks, manual scorecards, stopwatches, and paper and pens for hand scoring and statistics should be available quickly. Ideally, these crucial pieces of equipment and supplies are ready at the first sign of trouble. If the shot clocks go down in the middle of a nationally televised basketball game, the event manager should be able to get the back-up unit from around the corner of the primary space and have it hooked up and working in less time than it takes for a full commercial break. Being ready, staying calm, and handling these types of situations are the mark of great event managers.

Understanding the capital, fixed, and expendable equipment needs as well as the supplies required for the event should begin early in the planning process. Then, when the date of the event approaches, the event manager will check and double-check that the equipment has been bid out and ordered, that there is storage available, that the equipment has arrived intact and operable, that someone knows how to operate it, and that someone is available to fix it on-site if it is critical to the event function.

Event Flow

The **event flow** takes into account the best traffic pattern for the event. Traffic patterns are the literal traffic of car and bus arrival, but also the foot traffic of all involved parties (i.e., spectators, participants, and officials). Keeping in mind people that have disabilities, are not native speakers of the host language, are color blind, unable to read, or have other characteristics different from the majority, should be part of the planning of event flow. Specifically, consideration and attention must be given to the following aspects of flow:

- Quickly getting vehicles to the location
- Getting people to the venue
- Emergency vehicle access
- Putting people in contact with the various areas that will bring in revenue (i.e., tickets, concessions, registration, merchandise)
- Moving people from parking to ticketing
- Purchasing concessions without missing the event

- Participant registration
- Merchandise sales
- Avoiding confusion, cross-traffic, and backtracking in all areas

Good event flow is deliberate and moves people throughout the event experience seamlessly.

Courtesy of Liam Frederick

One of the first questions event managers should ask themselves when reviewing an event is, what is the flow for the event? The flow should be a natural progression from beginning to end. Putting themselves in the place of the various represented groups is a good starting point for event managers. Pretend to be a spectator arriving by car. What is the first thing seen, what is the second? How do I know where to park? How do I know where to go when I exit my car? How do I remember where my car is parked? These are the types of questions that event managers start to ask as they visualize flow and conduct walk-thrus. The flow should be created from the perspective of someone who has never experienced this event before.

The easiest way to conceptualize flow is in a time sequence. Who will be arriving first and how? What happens next? And then what? Let's take the example of a marathon, because it is one of the most complex sports events encountered with respect to flow. For other events, the thought process is the same, it is just less complex. For the fictitious marathon, which will be used to illustrate flow concepts in the following sections, a few assumptions will be made:

1. The start of the marathon is in a location relatively far away from participant arrival and there is no parking at the start.
2. It is a Point A to Point B race, rather than a Point A to Point A, or circuitous, race.
3. The organizers of the marathon will provide transportation to the start for the runners via motor coach.
4. The marathon is very popular, very large, and sold out.

Vehicular Flow

When examining how vehicles will arrive at an event, event managers need to take into consideration how many different types of vehicles are coming in, including emergency vehicles, deliveries, spectator vehicles, participant vehicles, and police, to name a few. How does each group get in and out, and what roadways are available?

Working Vehicles

In the case of the fictitious marathon, vehicles working the event will be taken into consideration first. What access points do they need? Where will they need to deliver equipment and supplies? Will they be coming into the same locations as spectators and participants? If these groups are arriving several hours earlier than spectators and participants, it may not be an issue. However, if there is the possibility of any vehicles needing access while spectators are there, a specific plan for how they are going to enter, where, and what type of access control is at that location needs to be developed. As discussed previously, avoiding all vehicles within the event perimeter once the gates open is preferred. Questions such as what do to if the vehicle enters the wrong area, how do they turn around, and what type of space is available for parking for these vehicles if they need to stay should all be addressed.

A designated emergency lane is probably needed for large events. There may even be a need for multiple emergency access points. For the example marathon, there must be emergency access along the entire route to ensure an ambulance can reach an injured runner quickly. The emergency lane can even be a lane off the side of the road that is grass, but it has to be something that would enable an emergency vehicle to get through, and the emergency responders need to know and accept the plan. If the lane is grass, event mangers need to ensure it can withstand rain and still be passable.

Drop-Offs

In the case of cars dropping off people, a location or multiple locations should be designated where cars can easily get in and get back on the road without crossing traffic. In addition to cars dropping off people, runners are transported via bus to the starting line for the marathon in the example. So, the cars should not disrupt the flow pattern for the buses.

Motor coach buses generally seat anywhere from 44 to 54 passengers. These are quite large and require a good bit of space for maneuverability. What types of considerations should be taken into account as far as their movement? For safety reasons, the drop-off location for the bus should not require it to back up at any time. The bus should come in, drop people off, and then continue in the same forward direction on its way out of the area. Another consideration is to have the drop-off point so that the doors of the bus open toward the event entrance where, in this case, the staging area is for the start of the race. People should not have to get off the bus and go around the front, and definitely not the back, of the bus to get to the event entrance. That is dangerous, slows down egress from the bus, the buses overall, and movement into the staging area. For events with international participants where language might be a barrier, the more natural the flow, the better, so that participants exit the bus and directly continue walking to the next point.

In allowing for this, event managers responsible for managing transportation may need to arrange for and manage what are called "contra lanes," contra meaning "against." **Contra lanes** are vehicle lanes in which vehicles travel opposite the normal direction of traffic. This may be necessary to keep the buses from turning around, so they can swiftly get back to the origination location and pick up additional participants. For example, if the event is near freeway exit ramps, buses could be allowed to drive up what would normally be a down ramp, across the overpass, and then get back onto the roadway in the normal direction via the opposite ramp. Event managers will have to work with the applicable municipal agencies in the event's jurisdiction that control those roads to set up and manage contra lanes. It will also be important to make sure the bus company has trained all of its drivers on the proper route, and that appropriate staff are on-site to direct the flow. Contra lanes could also be necessary for various work vehicles, such as supply and delivery trucks.

Driving In

For this fictitious marathon, participants and/or spectators will not be driving in, but for other events they will be. In that case, what does the parking flow look like? How are cars being parked? Is there parking staff helping people park? Giving people choices can be a bad thing in some cases. Think about large amusement parks. When cars pull in, people are directing them exactly where to park, all the way to the exact parking space. People are not given a choice. Cars go through systematically and it flows well. They may put 20–30 cars per minute through the toll plaza, and can park cars quickly and get people into the park to spend money that much sooner.

Parking must flow well and people need to know where to go based on signage and being able to see staff directing them to park. From there, event managers want to take into consideration things like how are the cars being parked? Are they angle parking or straight-in parking? Which way causes the fewest potential problems for drivers? How are parking areas identified so people can find their car at the end of the event? Disney and other amusement parks do an excellent job of helping customers remember where they park by using visual characters (i.e., the Dopey lot) to identify different parking areas. Event managers also want to remember to take care of certain parking safety issues with flow. Staff can remind people to step in front of their cars and walk to the event to avoid the cars from behind that are continuing to park. From there, what is the flow to the next destination?

Other Vehicular Considerations

For the flow of staff and VIP vehicles, event managers should have very clear and specific directions written and diagrammed that these groups are aware of. Instructions should also include an early arrival time so they are not competing with spectators to enter the parking lots. Encourage staff to carpool or use public transportation as a strategy to eliminating parking issues.

Any security or agency representatives in the parking area need to know about staff and VIP parking. Go over the instructions (repeatedly) with staff and officials on-site. Make sure that everyone has the same, and most up-to-date, directions/maps that are available. It is also essential to generate and distribute parking passes, placards, or other identifiers to vehicles with special access.

No matter how well organized the event is, it is inevitable that there will be late arrivers. Late-arriving spectators are not a big deal; often they can just park themselves. However, late-arriving participants and deliveries are a bigger challenge. In the marathon example, there could be participants arriving late because they did not anticipate how long it would take to get there, or because they did not read all of the instructions provided to them. At this point, a bus transport might not make sense, so a few cars should be available to transport any late runners to the starting area. For deliveries, how are they going to get past the cars that are parking or the buses that are unloading if they arrive late? Is there another entrance? As discussed previously, these situations should be kept to an absolute minimum.

However, there may be times when the event cannot operate without the equipment or supplies that are arriving late. What if the bottled water distributor is late arriving for the marathon? The truck cannot be turned away, but the late arrival must be handled safely so that the driving route intersects participants and spectators as infrequently as possible. Crossing vehicle and pedestrian traffic is dangerous and causes further delay of the delivery and pedestrian movement. Depending on the size of the delivery, one strategy is to have flatbed golf carts available to meet the truck at the event perimeter. Then, the equipment and supplies can be unloaded in smaller quantities, thus causing less disruption to the event flow.

Participant Flow

Participant flow is a major issue for an event such as the marathon in the example. However, for a recurring event such as a baseball game, participants know where they are supposed to be and when, and the flow for them is less of a concern.

For participant-driven events, there are likely two different categories of participants: those people who have registered and only need to pick up their information, and those who are registering on-site. They will all need to go through a registration area, but some may only need to pick up their packet because they registered online, via mail, and so forth. This process can be sped up by having a "packet pick-up only" line for people who have already registered. This will make their event experience begin on a positive note by not waiting in line with those who need to fill out forms and pay. For the fictitious marathon, since it is so large, packet pick-up would take place for several days before the event. No packet pick-up would be available on race day except for extreme circumstances, such as participant flight delays.

For events featuring children as participants, accommodations for parents as pseudoparticipants should also be made. Parents will not want to drop their 7-year-olds off at an arena door and trust they find their way around. Parents should be able to stay with kids until the coach or team is in one place and is functioning as a participant in the event. Then, the parents will flow into the spectator area. Clearly communicated and visible post event meet up locations allow parents to reconnect with kids easily and reduce the chances of a lost child.

Staging Areas

In the marathon scenario, once participants are dropped off by the bus, the best-case scenario is for them to move into the staging area as quickly as possible to avoid a bottleneck at the entrance. The staging area should be a cordoned-off or fenced area where only athletes are allowed. Since this marathon is large and sold out, there may be bandit runners. **Bandit runners** are runners trying to sneak in to run who did not register or sign the waiver. As athletes move into the staging area, event staff should be at the entrance to verify that all runners are legitimate by viewing their bibs (the race numbers on runners' chests).

From a flow perspective, athletes should be encouraged to progress to the farthest point within the staging area. It is similar to the concept of efficiently boarding an airplane. When boarding an airplane, it is best if people move all the way to the back and then fill in the seats moving forward. When people stop at the first seats, others have to wait for them to take their seats in order to go by them. It is the same with a staging area. One way to help encourage runners to go to the back is to give them a reason to go there, such as placing service areas (e.g., refreshments, gear check, or entertainment) toward the back of the staging area. If these service areas are scattered throughout, those in the back should be opened first, and the ones nearer the entrance should have a delayed/rolling opening.

Once participants are in the staging area, they will eventually have to move and load into the start zone. The staging area should be designed to lead runners to the start without them having to go against the traffic or backtrack. Ideally, the flow should be continuous and move in one direction. Backflow will clog things up, aggravate the runners, and slow down the event.

In this scenario, spectators are not allowed at the start. If they were, event managers would need to determine specifically where they are allowed to go and what the flow would be. Should they be kept separate from the athletes? If so, how will they be kept separate and where? Where is the spectator viewing area for the start? What time will spectators be encouraged to move to that area? These additional questions would have to be answered if spectators were to be allowed at the start. Each small change in the event plan changes the flow throughout the event.

Spectator Flow

Spectator flow should be as simple and direct as possible by using straight lines. However, if a winding and bending flow is unavoidable, proper lines should be formed with rope and stanchions. If people start **queuing up**, or creating a line, on their own, they will likely start forming lines that will interfere

© Shutterstock

Proper queues are important for appropriate flow of people.

with other aspects of event flow. Then, event managers will have to make them shift. Once people are already queued and then asked to move, it tends to frustrate and aggravate them. They do not understand why, and are irritated that the line was unanticipated by event management. Be prepared to set up lines and know in advance what type of queue might be needed (or automatically set it up in advance). If it is a long queue, place signs periodically along the way and/or have staff with bullhorns letting people know they are going in the right direction, what is waiting ahead, and how long the wait is.

Generating Revenue through Managing Flow

One of the great advantages of managing flow is that event managers can create the environment of what they want people to see and experience, and in what order. Disney is phenomenal at this. When exiting an attraction at a Disney theme park, the flow moves people directly into a merchandise shop. This is because Disney knows that people are more likely to purchase merchandise shortly after experiencing the attraction. If event managers can create this type of flow at their events, it will result in increased per cap for the event. **Per capita spending,** or "per cap," is the amount of money spent per person during the event.

Keeping Disney in mind, but allowing for the uniqueness of sports events, event managers can locate revenue-generating opportunities in a few prime locations. These areas create excitement because there are crowds, and when others see the crowds, they are naturally drawn to see what is going on. People do not like to feel like they are missing something. Placing revenue opportunities near entrances and exits to the venue will also allow for the event flow to push people to pass by. One cautionary note when placing points of sale near entrances and exits is that it can cause clogs in the flow of pedestrian traffic. By designing the area so that people are led slightly out of the way, congestion can be avoided.

For participants, event registration is the prime location. Every participant must register, so as they flow through registration, consider what the exit looks like. If event managers can get participants to exit through a merchandise location, it could result in more sales. Be aware that if participants are purchasing items before an event, there needs to be an easy way for them to either store items during the event or pick up their purchases postevent.

Signage

One of the considerations with any type of flow is what type of signage is needed. The location of signs is key; excellent information does no good if it is an area where no one will see it. Choosing a color theme for the event and integrating the colors and event logo into all signage will allow it to be easily identifiable to those at the event. Be aware that a segment of the population is **color blind** meaning that they have trouble seeing red, green, blue, and combinations of these colors. For all signage, highly contrasting colors are easier to see (i.e., white text on a black background) as compared with those that are similar (i.e., yellow text on a white background). As event managers are thinking about spectators, they need to put themselves in the place of a spectator that has never been to the venue before and is trying to park, walk to the entrance, buy a ticket, find his or her seat, buy concessions, and finally exit the facility.

Height and clarity of signs are very important. Are the signs visible from a distance? One of the keys to directional signage is height. A vertical height of eight to ten feet is easily visible from a car or for a pedestrian from a distance. If a sign is too low, people walking in front of the signs are going to block them from the view of others. If it is an event where people are going to be arriving at night, make sure the signage can be seen from a car, and that when headlights shine on it, it is clearly readable. Plus, any signs for pedestrians must be lit to be effective at night.

There are also safety precautions with signs. If it is a windy day, what has been done to ensure the sign does not blow down or blow away? Many sign companies have vandal-proof screws available for sign construction. Sports signage is a popular item to steal, and is often found in college residence hall rooms. Ensuring the base of the sign is secure and that vandal-proof screws are holding the sign to the base will act as a deterrent to theft.

Signage should be easy to read and unobstructed.

© Shutterstock

Spectator Signage

Event managers anticipate that people will start to look for signs as they approach an event, whether approaching on foot, via car, or public transportation. To move people to the event location, reassure people as they go through signage indicators that they are headed in the correct direction. This will also keep them from stopping and creating problems with crowd movement. Once people enter the event, it is difficult to get them to read signs because other things catch their attention. However, if there are enough signs, the hope is that at least some of the people will see some of the signs.

Participant Signage

Within a confined space, such as the participant registration area, signs should be clear and plentiful. If there are separate lines for preregistered participants and on-site registration, do the signs clearly indicate that? Event staff can also be assigned to this area to reinforce information on the signs.

Staff can make sure participants know where they are supposed to go, and can speed up registration by reminding participants to "have your ID ready," "already registered? please move to the right," or "think about what size T-shirt you need."

Lighting

Adequate lighting for spectator and participant areas is a responsibility of the event managers and can impact flow. For events where people will be arriving or leaving in the dark, there will need to be tower lights to light the pedestrian areas and vehicle areas. This is a basic safety issue. Not only do people need to see where they are walking and what is around them, but they also need the signage lit so they can read it. If permanent lighting is inadequate, then renting lights is an option, and there are a variety of lighting setups that will ensure a safe environment.

Diagramming Flow

One of the easiest ways to conceptualize and communicate flow is to diagram it. If there is not an existing diagram of the area, make one, even if it is not to scale. Use the diagram to mark locations of staff, signage, where people will be directed, and so forth. Use colors to indicate different types of personnel (e.g., police, staff, volunteers) and arrows to indicate movement direction. Computers make it easy to use different color lines/symbols/icons/objects to designate different groups and their traffic patterns. Or, if the flow changes depending on the time of day, different colors can represent different times of the day. Event managers can then use the diagram to see the traffic flow of the different groups and how the groups will interact with one another.

Once the diagram is created, event managers should walk the event areas repeatedly. Video can even be used to record specific areas if there is limited access pre-event. As discussed earlier in this

---

10 Event Operations Tips

The following list provides some guidelines to help event managers prepare for facility and equipment management during an event.

1. The event experience begins when spectators or participants leave their homes to attend the event, and ends when they return home. Everything possible should be done to make sure the experience is good during the entire event experience.

2. Event teardown takes half as long as setup, and plan accordingly.

3. Operating permits are available on-site in case they are requested by government officials.

4. Limit the number of people that have access (e.g., keys, credentials) for specific areas. The more access, the less secure the area is.

5. Keep rain gear, umbrellas, towels, squeegees, and snow shovels on-hand in case they are needed, and check the weather forecast frequently for outdoor events.

6. For venues without permanent restrooms, research the appropriate number of restrooms needed (include ADA restrooms). (General information can be found from the Federal Emergency Management Agency at http://www.americanrestroom.org/gov/fema/FEMA_SECP39_41.PDF).

7. Concessions should be provided at a ratio range of 1:120 (large concourses and crowded areas) to 1:250 (less crowded areas of the venue (Lamberth, n.d.).

8. Develop relationships with the Fire Marshal and Department of Health representatives prior to the event.

9. If the event will begin OR end when it is dark, provide adequate lighting for safety within the event perimeter as well as in parking and pedestrian areas outside of the event perimeter.

10. Integrate green practices into the event plan.

chapter, walk-thrus are important to help make sure the event does not encounter a situation where the designed flow has to be changed because of unanticipated construction (or something else) that is going to impede the flow. No matter what the agencies/companies/groups say or confirm about the location, event managers should confirm it themselves. As the event gets closer, frequent reviews should take place to ensure that there are no surprises.

Determining the right flow becomes second nature to event managers with experience, and although flow seems like an abstract concept, it begins to make sense when thought of in relation to a specific event. The use of good staff placement, signage placement, point-of-sale locations, and appropriate lighting will all support the main event flow with proper planning.

SUMMARY

There are details related to facility and equipment operations that begin in the development phase of event management and become a reality during execution. On the event day, event managers are the first staff on-site and the last to leave. The tasks associated with operations are not glamorous, but they are crucial to the event meeting the goals, objectives, and tactics. Hours of preparation occur before the event that allows the event managers to be knowledgeable about everything that has to get done. Facility walk-thrus, venue setup and teardown, field and facility maintenance, equipment management, and the overall flow of the event all require careful consideration and each has a list of tasks that fall under the category. Most event managers learn about operations through their own mistakes and successes. However, with proper planning, event managers will be able to complete all of the required tasks, be ready for unexpected situations, stay on schedule and within the budget, and manage an event that leaves participants and spectators satisfied.

Student Challenges

NAME _____ DATE_____

Think about an event in a nontraditional venue and choose one type of event to use as the basis for your responses for the following questions.

Question 18.1

What equipment is needed for the event? List five pieces of equipment needed for the event and conduct research and decide whether the equipment should be purchased or rented. Discuss the rationale for either purchasing or renting each piece of equipment.

Equipment #1-

Equipment #2-

Equipment #3-

Equipment #4-

Equipment #5-

Question 18.2

Create an event day checklist for the setup of the event. This list should include the primary and ancillary space setup needs, as well as specifics as to what time each space should be completely set up. Refer to Chapter 13—Event Documents—for more information on event day checklists.

Question 18.3

Create the flow of the event through text or diagramming. Choose either spectators or participants for your response. A bullet list can be helpful to organize flow in a narrative format. Be sure to integrate strategies to increase per cap spending?

Copyright © Kendall Hunt Publishing Company

EVENT SETTLEMENT AND WRAP UP

John P. Tafaro, Lynda Reinhart, and Heather Lawrence

John P. Tafaro, J.D., received his master's in sports administration from Ohio University in 1977. He spent more than 20 years actively involved in the facility management industry, including close to 10 years as President and CEO of Cincinnati Riverfront Coliseum. He is a graduate of Salmon P. Chase College of Law at Northern Kentucky University, has practiced business law and consulted with or operated numerous business entities in various industries, including sports and entertainment facilities, teams, and attractions. He is the past President of the Cincinnati Bar Association and former Chair of its Sports & Entertainment Law Committee. Mr. Tafaro has been an Adjunct Professor at several institutions of higher learning, and in May 2009 became President of Chatfield College in St. Martin, Ohio.

Lynda Reinhart is the Director of the Stephen C. O'Connell Center at the University of Florida. She began working at the venue as a student in 1994 and joined the full-time staff in 1998. After working her way up the ranks, Lynda was named Director in 2007. At the University of Florida she served as Adjunct Professor for the College of Health and Human Performance where she directed student research on the feasibility of a facility management degree program at UF and taught the facilities management course. She is an active member in numerous organizations including IAVM (International Association of Venue Managers), FFMA (Florida Facility Managers Association), and the GSC (Gainesville Sports Commission) where she has served on and chaired numerous committees as well as served as Board Member for each association. She is a past President of the GSC. Lynda holds a bachelor of science in business administration and master of science in recreational studies, both from UF.

Heather Lawrence, Ph.D., is an Associate Professor of Sports Administration and AECOM Professor of Sport Business at Ohio University. She earned her Ph.D. from the University of Florida, and also received bachelor's and master's degrees from Florida. Dr. Lawrence primarily teaches in the area of event and facility Management. In addition to her role at Ohio University, she has led event and facility courses in Spain, China, and Dubai. Prior to beginning her academic career, Heather worked in various administrative positions within intercollegiate athletics at Southeastern Louisiana University and the University of Florida. Her sport industry responsibilities have included working in NCAA compliance, facility management and construction/renovation management, event management, and general administration.

Event settlement and wrap up are important concepts for event managers to understand. **Event settlement** is a specific process that occurs upon completion of all events. It is a financial transaction in nature, very similar to the closing on the purchase of real estate or the acquisition of a business. **Wrap up** is a general term referring to task completion that concludes the event management process, such as attending to any complaints received, generating sponsor reports, sending thank-you notes, debriefing and paying workers, and completing postevent recaps.

Event managers may or may not play a direct role in the settlement process, depending on the organizational structure of the facility, and whether they manage events as an employee of the venue or represent an outside organization hosting an event in the building. Commonly, settlement is the responsibility of the facility manager. If event managers are directly involved, it is likely they are the event representative settling with the building. Thus, it is imperative that event managers know what transpires during settlement. Regardless of whether or not the event managers are present at settlement, many of the financial components of the transaction are influenced, if not generated, by the work of the event managers.

The settlement process may be managed by the building manager, the facility's chief financial officer (CFO), business manager, or other person of authority. It is this person's responsibility to make sure that all financial consideration is accounted for and properly distributed. First and foremost, the responsible party has a duty to protect the financial interest of his or her facility and its owners, which could be a university or academic institution; a city, county, state or other governmental authority; a fair board; or a private corporation or enterprise. If the staffing model of the facility identifies a CFO, director of finance, or comptroller as the party responsible for conducting the settlement, this individual is the point person in the settlement process, but the facility manager or chief executive is ultimately responsible for what transpires at settlement and should be involved in a supervisory role.

Wrap up may encompass different tasks depending on the event, organization, and people involved. However, differently from event settlement, the event managers will be the responsible party for this task. The overall goal of wrap up procedures is to create a comprehensive event file for the event and to thank all of those that spent time, effort, and money supporting the event. Once the event activities are complete, settlement has concluded, and teardown has finished, many event managers assume the event management process is over. But there are still some important tasks to complete. The importance of relationships is a consistent theme throughout the event management process, and through wrap up, relationships with participants, sponsors, fans, promoters, and the community can be strengthened.

Building Agreement

The settlement process begins with the written building agreement. All buildings have standard agreements or contracts that provide for the staging of an event. Some facilities call them the "Agreement," others are entitled "Contract," some can be termed a "Lease," while still more can be identified as a "License" or even a "Permit." The legal differences of each type of document are best left to another course and another book. Regardless of any name on the top of these documents, they should all contain the same information and set forth the relative duties and responsibilities of each party, specifically, the building and the event sponsor or "promoter." Within this document should be clear direction as to how the revenues are shared and the expenses are divided (see Chapter 3—Event Contracts for detailed information on contracts). Since many events have common financial characteristics, a settlement template form can generally be established using Excel or other software programs capable of doing the required calculations. The specific line items, however, may vary by the type of event.

All events are different, and settlements are distinct and individual business transactions. Most events, however, fall into one of four general categories:

- Rentals
- Copromotions
- In-house promotions
- Multiple performances/anchor tenants

Some events may rent venue space.

The main difference between each type of agreement is degree of risk for the venue associated with the engagement. A variety of documents used by venues to document, track, and ensure clear communication between the event organizer and the facility (see Figures 19.1–19.3).

High Five Arena
PO Box 2000
Athens, OH 45701

This Document Constitutes a Formal Offer to Perform Based on the Information Specified Below.

Offer #	HFA1
Reference #	
Show Status	Submitted

Printed at:	
# of shows:	1

Headliner:

Co-Headliner	N/A
Support	TBD

Show Date:

VENUE: **High Five Arena**

Purchaser:	EMB Group, LLC		Contact:	Chris Rice
Address:	PO Box 2000		Phone:	740-593-xxxx
	Athens, OH 45701		Email:	chris.rice@fakeemail.com

Play Date	09/24/10			Number of Shows	1		
Doors	Opener	Support	Co-Headliner	HEADLINER	Curfew	Run Time
7:00 PM	TBA @ 8PM	TBA	NONE		12am	TBD
On-Sale Date	Pre-Sale	On-Sale Time				
		12:00 Noon				

DEAL INFORMATION - SEE ATTACHED BUDGET WHICH IS PART OF THIS OFFER

MERCHANDISE DEAL	75/25 (90/10 cds)	☒ Artist Sells	☐ Venue Sells

SPECIAL STIPULATIONS Additional Deal Points

- Artist to provide all transportation at their own cost.
- Artists are requested to participate in a backstage meet and greet if requested by the promoter.
- The purchaser has market exclusivity for this performance.
- When a curfew is in effect, the Artist must comply or otherwise be responsible for any costs including penalties or fines associated
- Venue to receive up to 100 comps for promotional purposes.
- Artist to receive 100 comps.
- Should the Artist's rider or requirements cause the show costs to increase above the budget or reduce the sellable capacity, the offer / confirmation may be adjusted accordingly. The Artist's representative is responsible for advising of the rider requirements and other appropriate information and should costs increase, the Fee, Talent guarantee and/or back-end percentages will be adjusted accordingly.
- Artist guarantee will be provided in full on the night of the show in the form of a check payable to the Artist drawn on a High Five Arena account
- Ticket Prices and Scaling are subject to change
- $2 Facility Fee is added onto ticket price, deducted at settlement, and retained by HFA (prices on page 2 reflect this addition)
- HFA and its staff may not purchase alcoholic beverages
- HFA requires all seating be fixed (no open floor)
- Any sponsors must be approved by University. Please note that certain sponsors are prohibited, such as alcohol and tobacco products.
- Settlement will conform to the Performance Offer as confirmed.

Performance Offer Authorization:

_____   _____   _____
Buyer Signature   Date   Management Signature

Figure 19.1 Offer—Cover Sheet.

OFFER PAGE 2   Show Date:

Artist:		Contact:	Chris Rice
Venue:	High Five Arena	Phone:	740-593-xxxx
Address:	PO Box 2000	Email:	chris.rice@fakeemail.com
	Athens, OH 45701		

Printed at:

\# of Shows: 1

Box Office - USD$

180 Endstage	Capacity	Kills	Comps			Available	Price		Gross
P1 --						-	$		-
P2 --						-	$		-
P3 --						-	$		-
One Show	-	-	-	-	-	-	$		-
						Avg. Net			
Total Shows	-	-	-	-	-	-	$		-

Expenses - USD$

Expenses - USD$	Budget - USD$	Comments
Guarantee		
Advertising/Marketing		
Rent		see below under variable costs.
Booking Fee		
Support		
Catering		
Sound and Lights		
Cleaning		
Conversion (set up)		
Furniture		
Electrician(s)		8 hr day (add'l hrs billed as tech sup)
Police		
Forklift(s)		
Ticket Printing		
Insurance		
Riggers		
First Aid		Included in medical
ASCAP / BMI		
Runner(s)		
Spotlight rental		
Other Staff		
Stagehands		(includes tech supervisor)
Stage / Barricade		
Support #1		
Support #2		
Ground Trasnportation		
Telephones - Line Cost		
Internet		
House Staff - FOH		
Towels		
Box Office Staff		
MISC		
Medical Staff		
Total Fixed Costs	0.00	

Potential Show Earnings - USD$

Gross Receipts	$	-
less: Fac. Fee	$	
less: Tax 6.25%		
Net Gross Receipts	$	
Total Expenses (w/out guarantee)	$	-
Promoter Profit	$	-
Net Show Receipts	$	-

OFFER - USD$$

Guarantee		
Vs.% Deal		
Sound & Lights	$	-
Support	$	-
Artist Earnings	$	-
Promoter Earnings	$	-
Promoter Profit		-

Merchandise Deal

Artist Sells	80/20
CD/DVD's	90/10

Break-Even Calculations

Based on:
Avg. Tkt Price
%

Approved By:

Name:

Venue

Signature:

Date:

Variable Costs:

Variable Costs:		%	Min.	Max.
Rent (if Variable)		12.0%		
Credit Cards - Box Office Only		passed to patrons		
Insurance				
Box Office Fee		3.0%		
ASCAP/BMI	0.00			
Ticket Printing				
Total Costs	0.00	15.0%		

Additional Notes:

$2 facility fee deducted and remitted to HFA

Advertising Breakdown

Advertising Breakdown	
Print	
Radio	
TV	
Other	
Total Advertising	$ -

Fee Structure

At the box office & door:
$1 -- up to $10
$2 -- 10.01-20
$3 -- 20.01-$40

Ticketmaster On-Line Service Charges
$2.75 -- up $10
$4 -- $10-20
$5 -- $20-30

Ticketmaster Service Charge (does not include miscellaneous fees such as mail, print at home, credit card)

Figure 19.2 Offer—Estimated Expenses.

Rentals

A **rental event** is one where an outside presenter, sponsor, or promoter (let's use the term "promoter") is fully responsible for producing and staging the event in the venue (see Chapter 3, Figure 3.3, Ohio University Department of Intercollegiate Athletics Facility Rental Agreement). The facility negotiates a rental amount for the venue, which may or may not include building expenses such as staffing, clean up, box office or ticketing services, setup, utilities, and building rent. Rental agreements inclusive of building staff and equipment are commonly referred to as "all-in" deals or house nut. The building rent component can be a flat fee or a percentage of the gate (i.e., ticket receipts), with or without a guaranteed minimum, a cap, or even a sliding scale percentage. Expenses can be quoted as extras, and again be either in the form of a flat fee, on a sliding scale (based on attendance), or at predetermined rates with an overhead factor added or an administrative charge built in.

In all cases on a rental event, it is the building executive's responsibility that adequate rent is charged, regardless of how it is calculated or presented, to protect the financial interest of the venue by covering all expenses and providing a fair return to the building's owners. On a rental, there should be no risk for the venue.

	A	B	C	D	E	F	G	H	I
1	OFFER PAGE 2						Show Date:		
4	Artist:				Contact:	Chris Rice			
5	Venue:	High Five Arena			Phone:	740-593-xxxx			
6	Address:	PO Box 2000			Email:	chris.rice@fakeemail.com		Printed at:	
7		Athens, OH 45701							# of Shows: 1
10	180 Endstage	Capacity	Kills	Comps			Available	Price	Gross
11	P1 --						=B11-C11-D11-F11-F11		=G11*H11
12	P2 --						=B12-C12-D12-E12-F12		=G12*H12
13	P3 --						=B13-C13-D13-E13-F13		=G13*H13
18	One Show	=SUM(B11:B17)	=SUM(C11:C17)	=SUM(D11:D17)	=SUM(E11:E17)	=SUM(F11:F17)	=SUM(G11:G17)	=18/G18	=SUM(H11:I17)
19							Avg. Net	=ROUND(I27/G20,2)	
20	Total Shows	=B18*$I7	=C18*$I7	=D18*$I7	=E18*$I7	=F18*$I7	=G18*$I7		=I18*$I7

	Expenses -- USD$		Budget - USD$	Comments					
23	Guarantee					Gross Receipts		=I20	
24	Advertising/Marketing					less Fac. Fee		=(2*G18)	
25	Rent			see below under variable cos		less Tax	0.0825		
26	Booking Fee								
27	Support					Net Gross Receipts		=SUM(I23:I26)	
28	Catering					Total Expenses (wout guarantee)		=SUM(C64-C23)*-1	
29	Sound and Lights					Promoter Profit		=(I26-I34)*I40	
30	Cleaning					Net Show Receipts		=SUM(I27:I29)	
31	Conversion (set up)								
32	Furniture						OFFER -- USD$		
33	Electrician(s)			8 hr day (add'l hrs billed as te		Guarantee			
34	Police					Vs % Deal			
35	Forklift(s)					Sound & Lights		=SUM(C29)	
36	Ticket Printing					Support		=SUM(C27)	
37	Insurance					Artist Earnings		=IF(I38>I35,I34,I36)*I35,I34)	
38	Riggers					Promoter Earnings		=I30-I38-I29	
39	First Aid			included in medical		Promoter Profit			
40	ASCAP / BMI								
41	Runner(s)								
42	Spotlight rental						Merchandise Deal		
43	Other Staff						Artist Sells	80/20	
44	Stagehands			(includes tech supervisor)			CD/DVD's	90/10	
45	Stage / Barricade								
46	Support #1						Break-Even Calculations		
47	Support #2					Based on:			
48	Ground Transportation					Avg. Tkt Price		=SUM(C64/H19)	
49	Telephones - Line Cost					%		=SUM(I48/G20)	
50	Internet								
51	House Staff - FOH								
52	Towels								
53	Box Office Staff						Approved By:		
54	MISC								
55	Medical Staff					Name:			
56	Total Fixed Costs		=SUM(C23:C55)						
57	Variable Costs:		%	Min	Max	Venue			
58	Rent (if Variable)		0.12			Signature:			
59	Credit Cards - Box Office Only		passed to patrons						
60	Insurance								
61	Box Office Fee		0.03			Date:			
62	ASCAP/BMI		=(0.0026*I27)+(0.003*I27)+(0.0004*I*G20)						
63	Ticket Printing								
64	Total Costs		=SUM(C56:C63)	=SUM(D56:D63)					
65				Additional Notes:					
66	Advertising Breakdown			$2 facility fee deducted and r					
67	Print			Fee Structure					
68	Radio			At the box office & door:					
69	TV			$1 -- up to $10		Ticketmaster On-Line Service Cha			
70	Other			$2 -- 10.01-20		$2.75 -- up $30			
71	Total Advertising		=SUM(C67:C70)	$3 -- 20.01-$40		$4 -- $10-20			
72						$5 -- $20-30			
74	Ticketmaster Service Charge (does not include r								

Figure 19.3 Estimated Expenses with Formulas.

Co-Promotions

In a **co-promotion** or "co-pro", the expenses, revenues, and overall risk are shared between the venue and the promoter. The promoter is typically responsible for expenses associated with the production and staging of the event. This would include costs such as artist guarantee, transportation, performers' payroll, equipment, costumes, depreciation on fixed assets, and all overhead for the attraction (see Chapter 3, Figure 3.2, Harlem Globetrotters Standard Co-Promotion Agreement).

The building is commonly responsible for the expense associated with running the facility during the co-promotion event or events. Typical building expenses could include ticket sellers, ticket takers, ushers, setup, teardown, security, clean-up, supervision, management, utilities, and overhead. Some items can be paid first as shared expenses, or "off the top." This might include advertising expenses, music royalties, event insurance, perhaps union stagehands, taxes, and any bond fee or facility debt retirement use charge. The co-pro agreement should clearly delineate the responsible party for each expense as well as mutually agreed shared expenses.

After the off-the-top items are deducted, there is a negotiated split of remaining revenue. Splits can be fixed at any ratio, for example, 90/10; 80/20; 55/45; or any other combination that totals 100. Splits can also be on a sliding scale, with the bigger share amount often in favor of the party that has a higher cost of doing business, then shifting to a more level arrangement after the parties have recovered their respective costs. A co-promotion split can be as simple as 50/50 split of all costs and revenues or more complicated like: (i) advertising and taxes off the top; (ii) 70% to the promoter and 30% to the building

© Shutterstock

Event managers work with venue personnel on co-promotions.

on the first remaining $200,000; (iii) 60% to the promoter and 40% to the building on the next $200,000; and (iv) 50% each to the promoter and building on all remaining income. This change in split percentage upon reaching certain revenue thresholds can be negotiated as a sliding scale so all parties are satisfied.,

Similarly, the nature of the split can be characterized in actual dollars: (i) promoter gets the first $50,000 (presumably, to cover the costs of the event); (ii) the building receives the next $35,000 (presumably, to pay for the operating costs incurred by the facility); (iii) promoter gets 80% and building gets 20% of the next $100,000; and (iv) the parties split evenly any remaining revenue.

Co-promotions can be structured in any number of ways. If the event is to be a true partnership, then the agreement should be structured to equalize the risk for each party. Everyone should have the same opportunity to make money. Conversely, if the event is not profitable, the loss should also be equally borne.

In-House Promotions

With an event sponsored and staged by the facility, commonly called a **facility promotion** or **in-house promotion,** the building or its owner acts as the promoter and takes all the risks, such as financial, and others. In a market, where one or more promoters actively engage in the trade, the mere fact that an act or attraction is available to the facility may be a red flag that there is undue risk, and the building manager should question why one or more regular promoters have declined an offer to participate. In-house promotions should not be undertaken without substantial, current, and thorough research and a realistic assessment of the revenue potential of the event. Sales history for the contemplated event or similar events should be recent and independently verifiable to be valid. Even if the event does not appear to be financially viable, it may still be a beneficial endeavor for the venue. Community relations, staff training, or as a tactic to secure a future, more profitable event are all reasons a venue manager may choose to promote an event even if they know they will not make money. The key is to know how much of a loss is reasonable for the identified purpose and whether or not the operation can bear the expense.

In the case of an in-house promotion, the settlement will be simpler, and encompass merely the payment of the talent fee to the act, attraction, talent broker, or show producer, which would have been determined well in advance of the event, but could be variable and based on final ticket sales. Other, subsequent accounting and the collection of revenue and disbursement of payments can occur at a later date, but should not be put off for too long. Often, an internal settlement will be conducted for purposes of interdepartmental accounting, budget reconciliation, or postevent evaluation and analysis. As in any case, the settlement of an in-house promotion serves an important purpose in that it shows all income and expenses, so the facility can determine if the event is a financial success, break-even proposition, or an actual losing venture.

Multiple Performances/Anchor Tenants

If a venue hosts a series of events of a similar nature, produced by the same entity and covered under a single rental agreement or contract, there may need to be only one final settlement, or a series of interim settlements may be conducted. Examples of this type of event could be a week-long engagement of a circus, rodeo, ice show or other family show, or a season-long relationship with a sports team, known as an **anchor tenant**, that calls the facility its "home court," "home field," or "home ice."

Regardless, the nature of the transaction is the same. First, all receipts are organized and identified, and all bills gathered with expenses itemized. Then, the balance is paid to the event sponsor, team, or promoter, or an invoice is generated should there be a shortfall in revenue held by the facility.

In the case of a national touring attraction, family show, or sports team, not all of the revenue to be divided may be in the hands of the facility. There may be sponsorship arrangements that fall outside the cash flow parameters of the event, yet the money generated is included in the event proceeds. Ticket revenues from sales through fan clubs, discount sites (e.g., Groupon), or consignment may be remitted directly to the artist. Likewise, a sports team may control its season ticket sales, with the venue entitled to a portion of season ticket proceeds. While these situations are not ideal from the building perspective, they are sometimes unavoidable.

Nontraditional Events

Nontraditional events may or may not occur at a venue, and may or may not include ticket sales as a component of the revenue stream. Instead, these events are participatory in nature, like marathons and other running events, triathlons, or even square-dance or bowling marathons. There is sometimes a charitable tie-in to the event with a recognized nonprofit entity involved in one of many ways, usually as a beneficiary of the net proceeds, or a percentage of the gross revenue, or perhaps even as a commissioned sales agent on sponsorships, or any combination thereof.

With a nontraditional event it is possible there is not a governing building agreement, but a settlement is still necessary and important. Revenues must be itemized and accounted for, and bills need to be paid. The settlement serves as the vehicle by which all such revenue and expenses are identified so that a final determination of profit or loss, or "the bottom-line," can be established. As in the case of a facility promotion, the settlement process for a nontraditional event may not be as time sensitive as for other events, but a speedy process results in more accuracy and quicker accountability from all involved.

Regardless of the type of event, the contractual agreement will set the stage for all that is to follow, including event settlement. The four types of building agreements discussed provide context as to the differences found in each, from those with limited or no risk to the facility, as in a rental agreement, to an in-house promotion where the risk is solely on the building. Generalizations can be made about event settlement based on the type of building agreement, but specifics are limited only by being able to get both parties involved in the contract to agree upon the terms.

Settlement between an event and a venue should occur even for non-traditional events.

An Interview with Renee Musson

Associate Director, Stephen C. O'Connell Center

Renee Musson is integral to the continued success of the Stephen C. O'Connell Center on the campus of the University of Florida. She works with the director as a team, along with other O'Connell Center staff, to attract, execute, and settle the various entertainment events that perform in the building. In this interview Renee provides some insight into the event settlement process.

So the readers understand your building setup, will you describe the Stephen C. O'Connell Center?

The Stephen C. O'Connell Center is a multi-purpose facility that is used for academic classes, recreation, sports, and entertainment events. The 12,000 seat main arena is the competitive home for the University of Florida Men's and Women's Basketball Teams, Women's Volleyball, Women's Gymnastics, and Men's and Women's Indoor Track and Field Teams. The perimeter of the building includes an Olympic-size competition venue that is the home of Men's and Women's Swimming and Diving. Also in the building are a dance studio, gymnastics practice facility, practice basketball court, classrooms, and a weight room.

What are some of the underlying principles by which you operate the building?

The primary use of the arena space is varsity athletic events, but the entire staff is dedicated to fulfilling the mission of the building when attracting, booking, and executing events. The mission statement of the building is:

> The mission of the Stephen C. O'Connell Center is to serve as an academic, athletic, recreational and entertainment facility. In addition, we strive to provide superior service to guests and clients, and training for future leaders while operating the Center's auxiliary as a financially self-supporting entity.

Every decision we make comes back to this mission statement. Although we like to generate revenue through the events we have in the building, we are also aware that we provide a service and entertainment function for the community. So, we will occasionally book an event that will not generate a lot of revenue if it provides a service to the Gainesville area or a learning opportunity for our students.

As a public state facility on a university campus, there are certain rules and regulations that we have to follow in everything we do. If those core principles are compromised by hosting an event, then we cannot host it. For example, we have a rule that prohibits mosh pits in the building. Therefore, if an artist who is known for moshing at their concerts wanted to play at our building, we could not book the performance.

What is the general process for booking events at the Stephen C. O'Connell Center?

The Stephen C. O'Connell Center's primary clients are the University of Florida and University Athletic Association, Inc. (the athletic department at the University of Florida). So concerts, family shows, and flat shows are all booked and scheduled after annual University events (i.e., commencement and career fairs) are scheduled and the athletic schedule is finalized. Sometimes promoters contact us and other times we go out looking for shows to bring to the building. In either case, there are three types of booking:

1. Rental: this is the least risky type of booking. The promoter/artist/performer rents the building and pays all the expenses. They also receive all of the revenue from the show.

2. Co-Promote: a co-promote agreement is where we share the risk with the artist/performer through a predefined split of the expenses and revenue.

3. Promote: a promote booking agreement is risky for us. In this case, we pay the artist/performer and all of the expenses for the show hoping that we sell a lot of tickets and make money through the popularity of the show.

▶

As a side note, we have to be really careful what we book because of our geographic location and market. Located in North Central Florida, we cross markets with Jacksonville, Orlando, and even Tampa. Plus, with many of the potential ticket buyers being students, a lower price point is important to us.

How do you define event settlement?

For us, event settlement is the face-to-face process of accounting for, agreeing upon, negotiating expenses and revenues, and determining how much each party receives for an event.

When does event settlement occur?

Settlement usually begins immediately after the box office closes. So, depending on the show, this could be 30 minutes to an hour into the performance. Then the representative from the act meets with me in the offices to go through the formal settlement negotiations. There is a lot of pressure to complete the necessary calculations quickly and accurately with the show representative looking over my shoulder.

Is the process generally cordial?

In most cases, settlements are quick and painless, as most of the negotiations and issues have been settled as the event day has progressed. However, if the show did not do well, there is more tension because of the possibility of taking a financial loss on the show. If there are disagreements on aspects of the settlement, then Lynda, as the building director, gets involved to resolve them. Good client service is always critical, but it becomes even more important when there is stress and pressure involved. The stronger the relationship is with the client, the easier these types of situations are to deal with as in most situations, good communication throughout the process goes a long way toward eliminating challenges at settlement.

What are some trends in event settlement?

Beyond the developments in the use of technology in the entire management of facilities, there are some other areas in which changes are occurring. Many of the trends are directly related to booking and negotiations and will ultimately impact settlement.

1. Everything is getting complicated. Lots of crazy promotions, Groupon, commission based ticketing, variable pricing, paperless ticketing, VIP packaging and all sorts of other creative marketing efforts are making settlements more complicated. Determining all sources of revenue and being clear in who ultimately receives the revenue has become a very time-consuming task.

2. Flat rate services and complicated rental deals: For a rental booking agreement, the largest portion of the cost to the show is the services provided by the building, and not the rent charged to be in the facility. The cost of security, event staff, forklift operators, and other services used to be charged at an hourly fee to the show. Many promoters are now pushing venues to provide these services at a flat rate versus an hourly rate or are getting really creative with the rental deals. Since the venue then needs to be able to project accurately the cost of the services, complicated deals become more of a financial risk for the venue.

3. Presettlements are becoming more popular. Presettlements are typically requested days in front of the event and involve data collection that might be less than accurate. It is important to get as accurate as possible but to also note on all written documents that the presettlement is based on the information gathered to day and is subject to change based on actual usage.

What personal characteristics and skill sets should someone possess, who is interested in working in event settlement?

Normally you would think someone like an accountant would be a good fit for event settlement, but it is more than just accounting skills that make someone successful at settlement. Bookkeeping, ticketing, and spreadsheet experience are also coveted. Maybe most importantly, the person doing settlement needs to know and understand facility operations. This ensures the building representative has a good understanding of industry terms, what goes on during an event, and can "speak the language" during settlement. Combine operations experience, good business knowledge, customer service skills, the ability to work under a deadline, and you have a great fit for event settlement.

What reports are generated postevent?

There are three categories of reports generated at settlement or after an event: internal reports, settlement reports, and public information. Internal reports contain information that is only for those working in the building or associated with its operations to see (i.e., building management and University governance). Settlement reports are those provided to the promoter at settlement and are also used internally by the venue. Public reports provide information that is shared with media and the public.

Internal Reports

Marketing staff reports: demographics of where tickets were sold and who buyers were.

Accounting reports: sales tax reports and other reports dictated by General Accounting Procedures.

Managerial reports: billed vs actuals and summaries of challenges or exceptions made

Event summary/board: provided to the governing board and includes a summary of the event in memo format.

Event summary/file: for the event file as a general record of the event, its characteristics, and those involved.

Settlement Reports

Ticket audit: indicates how many tickets were sold at each price point.

Financial spreadsheets: expenses and revenues by category and line item.

Building expenses: those expenses that were direct costs to the building.

Pass-through expenses: those expenses that the building paid for, but ultimately were charged to the promoter/agent.

Commissions: special reports are generated when the deal includes various commissions (i.e., group sales efforts are typically commissioned to cover the cost of those efforts).

Complimentary tickets: proof of how many free give-away tickets were used, who used them, and for what purpose.

Public Reports

Boxscore: used to report artist/event, venue, city/state, gross sales, attend/capacity, shows/ sellouts, prices, and promoters in trade publications.

What else should event managers know and understand about settlement?

There are no secrets in event settlement these days. Promoters talk to each other, building operators talk to each other, and artists talk to each other. With the communication channels so open, it is important to treat each show individually.

It is imperative that up-front negotiations and contracts address everything and are solid agreements. As the show approaches, make sure any changes or additions with financial implications are documented in writing. This will lessen any disagreements at settlement. However, not every contingency can be covered, and whoever is sitting in settlement needs to have solid knowledge of both fiscal concerns and operational concerns surrounding an event, should the necessity arise to readdress contracted issues on the day of the event or during settlement.

▶

Can you sum up settlement with five general rules for successful event settlement?

1. Be flexible.
2. Know and understand the mission of the building and why it exists as well as the industry/market as a whole.
3. Know what the cost to the building is to do the show.
4. Communicate, communicate, communicate!
5. Stand your ground and know when it is better to "shut it down" and not have a show than to compromise policy or public safety.

For more information on the Stephen C. O'Connell Center, please visit http://www. oconnellcenter.ufl.edu/.

Marshalling All Revenue

Marshalling revenue refers to identifying, organizing, and accounting for everything related to revenue in an effective way. In the facility management industry there are very few absolutes, so the following presents ideal circumstances, but event managers and those responsible for settlement must be able to acknowledge when a variance from the standard operations will benefit all of those involved. Any variance is most likely to occur in a situation where there is a strong existing relationship with a promoter.

Security Deposit

A security deposit is among the first, and sometimes the most difficult, deal points to agree upon when negotiating a building contract. It operates the same way a security deposit functions in a commercial or even residential real estate setting. When renting or reserving a sports or entertainment facility, nonrefundable money is collected to hold the date and is considered a **security deposit**. The deposit will compensate the building for (i) holding the date and foregoing other income-generating opportunities, public service options, or recreational functions; (ii) to cover all advance costs the building will incur in promoting, producing, and preparing for the event; and (iii) to pay for any and all potential costs should the event cancel, such as security to staff the building on the cancelled date (in case fans arrive not knowing of the cancellation) and ticket refund expenses. (Note: Ticket monies held in trust are not available for this purpose because ticket money must be available for refunds if an event was cancelled.) Likewise, it is the duty of the facility manager to require and collect an adequate security deposit before an event can be announced or tickets can go on sale.

Sponsor Revenue

Some sponsorships are local, some are regional, and others are national. As discussed in detail in Chapter 7—Event Sponsorship, most include a cash component, but many can be in-kind arrangements, where the sponsor supplies goods or services in support of the event with no actual money exchanging hands. A typical in-kind sponsorship can be with a media partner that provides advertising and marketing support for the event in exchange for any number of specific benefits. Benefits frequently include complimentary tickets and/or inclusion in the name or billing of the event. In some cases, the media outlet is promised a share of the event's advertising expenditures or even a percentage of gate receipts. Other in-kind arrangements can include the exchange of equipment, supplies, or other essential goods or services (like dirt for a rodeo or junk cars for a monster jam) for tickets, inclusion in advertising, on-site signage, or anything else of value.

When a sponsorship associated with an event includes a cash component, the final determination of who gets to keep what percentage of the cash needs to be determined at the contracting stage, not at settlement. A fair division of sponsorship proceeds will be determined by whose expenses have been reduced or offset because of the sponsorship and who delivered the sponsor.

Ticket Receipts

Ticket receipts are more often than not the single most significant revenue component of an event that is spectator driven. Therefore, ticket receipts are reported on a separate box office or ticket summary statement. The **box office statement** is often in the form of a computerized report prepared by a third-party ticketing vendor, such as TicketMaster, and will show all tickets sold at each ticket price, and specify the method by which they were sold (e.g., at remote outlets, via phone, on the Internet, etc.). Other valuable marketing reports may be available showing where the event's customers live or where individual tickets were purchased. These reports belong to the venue or client of the ticket company that generates them, and may or may not be shared with the promoter. In any case, beyond the box office statement, these additional marketing reports are outside the scope of the settlement process.

Box office statements show the number and types of tickets sold, as well as where they were sold.

Participant Registration

For participant-driven events, registrations are similar to ticket receipts in that they may be the primary revenue generator. Depending on the type of building agreement, participant registrations may be in the hands of the event organization or the facility. In either case, a careful accounting of income from registrations is needed so that the facility and event managers know who registered, where they are from, and when they registered. A final report of registration numbers in addition to, or in lieu of, a ticket report is common.

Marketing and Advertising

The building may or may not be involved in advertising the event. In the case of a co-promotion, the building is entitled to participate in and approve of all advertising. With an in-house promotion, the building is completely responsible for advertising. In a building rental, the promoter may independently handle all advertising functions, although in today's world of social media, it is rare that the building would not provide some sort of marketing assistance. Regardless of the type of event, the building has a vested interest in assuring that all media outlets are paid. Even though a promoter may bear full responsibility for the payment of advertising bills, if the show leaves town with invoices left unpaid, this casts a shadow on the building, reflects negatively on the business judgment of those involved, and could impair future relationships. It is important to communicate with the media vendors, so they are well aware who is responsible for payment. They should be instructed that invoices, memo-invoices (in the case where final invoices are unavailable), and/or final bills need to be presented to the promoter prior to the event, or final performance in a multiple-performance event, so that money can be reserved for payment at the time of settlement, if still outstanding. The venue manager can often assist with delivering invoices and connecting the parties, but should make it clear that the business relationship is between the promoter and media outlet.

Merchandise

Most, if not all, events bring an array of merchandise for sale to patrons consisting of T-shirts, sweatshirts, other apparel, programs, and perhaps additional novelty items. In exchange for the right to sell this merchandise on facility property, the promoter, rights holder, or artist should be required to pay a fee. The building may or may not provide employees or independent contractors to sell this merchandise, but if labor is provided through the building, an add-on factor for payroll taxes and supervision is warranted. Employees or independent contractors can be paid on a flat rate, an hourly wage, or on commission. The building share of revenue can likewise be negotiated as a flat rate, a per capita fixed rate, or a percentage of sales. The merchandise settlement can be included as part of the overall settlement, or can be a separate and distinct transaction.

Food and Beverage/Parking

Historically, a building's food and beverage sales and parking receipts were not included in gross proceeds to be shared with a promoter; however, promoters and major shows have increasingly been successful negotiating for a portion of this revenue. Anchor tenants, like sports teams playing a full slate of contests, will generally share in this revenue as well. If this revenue is included, it may require a separate settlement or a segregated line or two within the settlement, with different percentages applicable to distinct categories of product sales.

Media Rights

When an event is televised, additional costs will accrue, including higher utility bills and perhaps additional labor and/or security. Also, if television viewership will suppress attendance, and the building is receiving a share of ticket proceeds, then some payment should be required to make the building whole. This fee is often called an **origination fee**. It should be included in the building contract and collected at settlement. The same concept could apply to radio broadcasts, but both the costs of hosting a radio production and its impact on attendance are generally less than television, and the origination fee, therefore, is proportionally smaller.

Taxes/Bond Debt Retirement/Facility Fees

Whether a facility is publicly or privately financed, the cost of construction and development is funded by debt, often in the form of bonds sold to institutional or private investors. Bondholders are generally entitled to some guaranteed revenue stream on all building income in the form of a percentage or fixed fee for each admission or ticket sold. This bond fee, which can sometimes be called an **admission tax,**

facility fee, or **bond charge**, can either be deducted from the price of each ticket and accounted for on the box office statement, which then yields a "net ticket sales" figure that is dropped into the revenue column of the settlement statement or may appear as an additional fee on the ticket, in which case it is handled and accounted for outside of the settlement process.

Preparing Expenses

As settlement approaches, all third-party invoices must be collected and labor reports and equipment lists generated in order to ensure the client/promoter is properly billed. Once the settlement is completed and signed off on, it is very challenging, if not impossible, to seek payment for a missed charge. In the case of touring events, settlement often occurs before the event is over so it is necessary to estimate some of the staffing charges as event staff are still working and the load-out/clean-up has not even begun. The projected figures are called **estimated outs** (see Figure 19.4). The event manager will be responsible for consulting with the tour manager to determine what times the various shifts will end then providing this information to the person in charge of settlement in order to generate the labor reports. The event manager needs to draw on experience and available information to accurately predict the estimated outs. If they are too low, then the promoter will not be billed enough and the building will have to absorb the costs. If they are too high, they will certainly be questioned and challenged by the promoter.

Expense line items should be clearly identified as either facility provided staff and equipment or pass-through charges. Be careful to avoid misrepresenting pass-through charges as in-house costs. Equipment or labor that is supplied by the venue is typically billed at a rate that takes into account necessary overhead above the actual cost. It is well established in almost all businesses that the entity providing services and/or labor is entitled to a marked up or billable rate to include the cost of recruiting, hiring, training, purchasing, supervising, and managing these assets, human or otherwise. **Pass-through charges** are those expenses for which the facility pays a third party on behalf of the renter and then later charges to the renter. An example of a pass-through charge is when the promoter needs extra forklifts and operators to complete the setup for the event. The facility acquires the equipment and then pays for the rental of the equipment. At settlement, the facility might then add an additional percentage fee, say 10%, to the actual cost of the forklifts when billing the renter. The 10% covers the cost and time associated with arranging for the forklifts, scheduling the labor, meeting the rental company for delivery of the forklifts, and ensuring the equipment was picked up as scheduled. Most clients understand that there is a cost to the venue for arranging these services and do not take issue provided the costs are represented accurately and the promoter is fully aware of and agrees to the pass-through charges prior to securing the equipment or services.

Disbursement of Expenses

There are various categories of expense where the building has unlimited liability, and therefore must assure that these items are collected at settlement and paid either concurrently or at a later date. Payroll, payroll taxes, taxes, bond fees, and other governmental charges are examples.

Other expenses could fall outside the scope of the settlement; however, it is in the best interest of the building to make sure the promoter or attraction does not leave town with a host of unpaid bills and obligations. Remember, when the show leaves, the promoter may be gone forever, but the building remains and must do business the next day with the same vendors, who were left holding a worthless receivable. It is in the facility's best interest to seek out those ancillary vendors and protect them if they believe they are at risk for holding an uncollectible bill. These vendors will likely be permanent or long-term building sponsors and clients, such as the local media outlets (TV stations,

Figure 19.4 Estimated Out Sheet.

High Five Arena—Estimated Out Sheet

Expense Estimates—Day of Show for: _____ Reservation Number: _____

RENT DEAL; _____

_____

SHOW END: Estimated End Time: _____

TECHNICAL LOAD-OUT: Call Back: _____ Estimated Time Out: _____

SECURITY STAFF: Estimated Time Out: _____

USHERS STAFF: Estimated Time Out: _____

EVENT COORDINATOR: Estimated Time Out: _____

RECEPTIONIST: Estimated Time Out: _____

RUNNER: Estimated Time Out: _____

SET-UP CREW: Estimated Crew Hours: _____ OR
FLAT @ $_____

CLEAN-UP CREW: Estimated Crew Hours: _____ OR
FLAT @ $_____

ELECTRICIAN: FLAT @ $_____ plus _____ additional hours

UPD—Officer   _____ @ _____HRS/EA

UPD—OIC   _____ @ _____HRS/EA

UPD—Admin   _____ @ _____HRS/EA

PARKING PATROLLERS   _____ @ _____HRS/EA

PARAMEDICS: _____ Hours @ $_____/HR

SPOTLIGHTS: _____ Number @ $_____/ea

CLEAR COM: _____ Number @ $_____/ea

PHONES: _____ Number @ $_____/ea

WIRELESS CONNECTIONS: _____ Number @ $_____/ea

TOWELS: _____ Number @ $_____/ea

FORKLIFTS: _____ Number @ $_____/ea

STAGE: $_____ / NA

STAGE SET/STRIKE: Estimated Crew Hours: _____ OR
FLAT @ $_____

BARRICADE $_____ / NA

POWER DISTRIBUTION $_____ / NA

HEAD RIGGER   _____ @ $_____/ea.

RIGGERS   _____ @ $_____/ea.

RIGGERS (focus/truss)   _____ @ _____HRS/EA

BOX OFFICE: $ <u>800.00 or 3 %</u>   OR Other

_____

What other items need to be on the bill:

_____

_____

Settlement is one of the last business items to occur between a venue and an event.

radio stations, and newspapers), a local hotel, a printer (who may print a local program), a caterer, or even a limousine company. While the building has no obligation to act as a collection agent for these corollary businesses, the settlement process provides a vehicle to make sure local bills are paid. Make sure to alert the promoter or event sponsor in advance that (i) all local bills are to be paid; and (ii) the right to pay any local, uncontested bill at settlement from the settlement proceeds is reserved. See Figures 19.5 and 19.6 for samples of these documents.

Money Held in Trust

Ticket money held in trust is an essential concept and a vital consideration for all event managers. There are always occasions where a scheduled event will never take place. Sometimes inclement weather will force a cancellation. Illness of performers or technical difficulties pertaining to routing could be the cause of a postponement or cancellation. Unfortunately, poor ticket sales can sometimes result in cancellation of an event when the promoter recognizes the event is doomed to fail. When a patron purchases a ticket for an event, the purchase price is paid in exchange for the viewing and experience of

High Five Arena
EMB Group, LLC
Athens, Ohio

The Twist and Flip Extravaganza
Saturday, October 15, 2016
7:00PM

** BOX OFFICE STATEMENT **

	COMP	SOLD	PRICE	GROSS
General Public - P1		6785	$57.75	$391,833.75
General Public - P2		436	$27.75	$12,099.00
Comps	271		$0.00	$0.00
TOTAL	271	7221		$403,932.75
TOTAL ISSUED		7492		
Less 6% Florida Sales Tax on Ticket Sales				($22,864.12)
Adjusted Gross (Less Admin and Sales Tax)				$381,068.63
Less Facility Expenses				($37,745.12)
Less Rent ($19,000 flat for rent and equipment)				($19,000.00)
Less Box Office Charge ($800.00 or 3% of Adj Gross, Cap $3,000)				($3,000.00)
Less Sales Tax				($3,584.71)
Total Expenses				($63,329.83)
Net After Expenses				$317,738.80
Less Advance to Promoter				($5,000.00)
Due to Worldwide Promoters				$312,738.80

_____

for Worldwide Promoters, Inc.

_____

for EMB Group, LLC

Figure 19.5 Sample Settlement—Box Office.

attending that particular event. Until the event occurs, neither the facility nor the promoter has earned anything. The contract between the ticket buyer, the venue, and the attraction is not yet complete. Therefore, the entity holding the money paid by ticket purchasers is holding the money **in trust** for the customer, and is entitled to release these funds for the payment of expenses associated with the event or to the event promoter only after the event has occurred. If the event is cancelled or does not otherwise take place, the ticket purchaser is entitled to a full refund of the purchase price.

Generally, it is unwise to allow a promoter to use ticket trust money in lieu of a security deposit, and giving any promoter or event sponsor an advance on ticket money collected for an event that has not yet occurred is risky. Ultimately, the building is responsible to refund ticket sales to customers and will be liable to those customers regardless of the reason for the cancellation.

Security Interest in Event Equipment/Fixtures

In a commercial lending transaction, a lender, typically a bank, will acquire a security interest in the equipment or fixtures purchased with the loan proceeds. This is known as a **purchase money security interest (PMSI)**. That security interest, however, can extend to other fixed assets beyond those acquired with the money borrowed through the loan. In other words, the borrower may need to add other collateral to induce the bank to make a loan.

EMB Group, LLC
Athens, Ohio

The Twist and Flip Extravaganza
Saturday, October 15, 2016
7:00PM

** BUILDING EXPENSES **

			SUBTOTAL	TOTAL	
CONTRACTED SERVICES					
University Police	71.50 hrs @ $ 69.00 /hr		$ 4,933.50	$ 4,933.50	
University Police - OIC	6.00 hrs @ $ 83.00 /hr		$ 498.00	$ 498.00	
Parking Patrollers	27.50 hrs @ $ 45.00 /hr		$ 1,237.50	$ 1,237.50	
Paramedics (Medical)	5.00 hrs @ $ 210.00 /hr		$ 1,050.00	$ 1,050.00	
		Subtotal Show Staff Charges			$ 7,719.00
HOUSE STAFF					
Security	330.25 hrs @ $ 14.36 /hr		$ 4,742.39	$ 4,742.39	
Security Supervisor	64.25 hrs @ $ 15.13 /hr		$ 972.10	$ 972.10	
Ushers/TicketTakers	148.50 hrs @ $ 14.08 /hr		$ 2,090.88	$ 2,090.88	
Tidy Crew	24.00 hrs @ $ 14.85 /hr		$ 356.40	$ 356.40	
Usher Supervisor	11.00 hrs @ $ 14.85 /hr		$ 163.35	$ 163.35	
Event Coordinator	24.75 hrs @ $ 15.13 /hr		$ 374.47	$ 374.47	
Receptionist	10.00 hrs @ $ 14.85 /hr		$ 148.50	$ 148.50	
Arena Set-up	Flat Rate		$ 875.00	$ 875.00	
Arena Clean-up	Flat Rate		$ 975.00	$ 975.00	
		Subtotal Show Staff Charges			$ 10,698.09
STAGE HANDS					
Technical Crew/Fork Operator	691.75 hrs @ $ 15.46 /hr		$ 10,694.46	$ 10,694.46	
Production Lead	47.75 hrs @ $ 16.23 /hr		$ 774.98	$ 774.98	
Electrician	Flat Rate		$ 300.00	$ 300.00	
Runner	5	@ $ 200.00 each	$ 1,000.00	$ 1,000.00	
Rigger - LEAD	1	@ $ 375.00 each	$ 375.00	$ 375.00	
Riggers	13	@ $ 325.00 each	$ 4,225.00	$ 4,225.00	
Riggers - Overtime/Truss	0	@ $ 40.00 each	$ -	$ -	
		Subtotal Show Staff Charges			$ 17,369.44
EQUIPMENT / SERVICES / PRODUCTION MISC.					
Towels	Inclusive in Rent Deal		$ -	$ -	
Forklift	Inclusive in Rent Deal		$ -	$ -	
Phone	Inclusive in Rent Deal		$ -	$ -	
Power Distribution	Inclusive in Rent Deal		$ -	$ -	
Internet Hookup (hardline)	Inclusive in Rent Deal		$ -	$ -	
Spotlights	Inclusive in Rent Deal		$ -	$ -	
Clear Com	Inclusive in Rent Deal		$ -	$ -	
Stage	Inclusive in Rent Deal		$ -	$ -	
Stage Barricade	Inclusive in Rent Deal		$ -	$ -	
		Subtotal Equipment / Services			$ -
PASS THROUGH ITEMS					
Rental Vans	Per Attached		$ 230.00	$ 230.00	
Rental Van Gas	4	@ $ 60.00 ea	$ 240.00	$ 240.00	
CO2	Per Attached		$ 143.20	$ 143.20	
Ice	Per Attached		$ 105.00	$ 105.00	
Propane	Per Attached		$ 44.00	$ 44.00	
Generator	Per Attached		$ 897.62	$ 897.62	
Overhead on pass through			$ 298.77	$ 298.77	
		Subtotal Pass Through Items			$ 1,958.59
TOTAL BUILDING EXPENSES:					$ 37,745.12

Figure 19.6 Sample Settlement—Building Expenses.

The same concept can apply to a building rental. If the facility is unsure or insecure about the promoter's ability to pay its obligations, it can ask for a security interest in the attraction's assets. Exactly what needs to take place for a valid security interest to be a lien on personal property will vary from state to state and even county to county. An attorney should be engaged to draft the appropriate language for inclusion in the building contract and to advise on other steps required to properly record and protect such an interest. If a facility properly obtains a security interest, it has additional leverage at settlement time by having a legal claim, or encumbrance, on those assets.

Buildings that enter into multi-event agreements with anchor tenants, such as arena football teams, for example, may consider requiring the grant of a security interest in the team's turf field. Minor League hockey teams could be asked for a security interest in the team's equipment or even intellectual property (e.g., the team's name), so if the team folds, the facility owns or at least has a claim against the property, and can use the uniforms, equipment, and team name as a head start in an effort to form a new team. Again, this should only be attempted with the assistance of a qualified attorney.

Other creative collection techniques, all employed to protect the building, include the requirement of a personal guarantee should there be a shortfall of funds available to pay all event obligations to the facility and/or an insecurity provision, which requires the promoter to increase the security deposit should the building reasonably believe there will be inadequate funds available to pay all obligations at settlement.

Event Wrap Up

As with event settlement, some aspects of wrap up may not be a direct event management responsibility. However, there certainly are scenarios when the event managers are responsible for all aspects of wrap up and need to be educated on what those components are. Common postevent wrap up tasks include: (i) completing payroll, (ii) debriefing staff, (iii) examining incident reports, (iv) addressing customer complaints, (v) generating sponsorship reports, (vi) sending thank-you notes and gathering customer information, and (vii) completing postevent recaps. For a sample of type of information included on a post information sheet, see Figure 19.7.

Figure 19.7. Post Event Information Sheet.

HIGH FIVE ARENA (HFA)
POST EVENT INFORMATION

Event: _____   Date(s): _____   Day(s): _____

Gate(s) open: _____   Doors open: _____

Event time(s): _____   Start: _____   Finish: _____

Event Information:

1. Location: _____
2. Administrator in charge: _____
3. Attendance: _____ comps / _____ announced / _____ drop count
4. Seating arrangement: _____   # Box offices open: _____
5. Rental fee: _____
6. Expenses: _____

Concessions Information:

1. Stands open: _____
2. Epic Services gross revenue: _____   HFA gross revenue: _____
3. Epic Services net revenue: _____   HFA net revenue: _____
4. Concessions notes: _____

Ticket Information:

1. Price(s): Student _____   Children _____   Adult _____
     Reserved _____   General Admission _____
2. Gross ticket revenue: _____   HFA gross ticket revenue: _____
3. Net ticket revenue: _____   HFA net ticket revenue: _____
4. Relocates: _____
5. Giveaways/promotions: _____

Parking/Traffic Information:

Accident (EMT)/Incident Information:

Post Event Notes:

Payroll

In most circumstances, the event managers will not do payroll; in fact, it is recommended that a human resources specialist is involved with payroll for any event. Payroll is a complex process involving tax variables, the personal information of employees, and adherence to a variety of regulations. Employee hours worked should be certified by event managers or the specific supervisor responsible for each employee. Then, the time sheets will be submitted to human resources for accurate payment. Checks and balances should be in place at every step of the employee time-keeping and payroll process to ensure accuracy.

Debriefing

The debriefing of staff will be initiated by the event managers. A postevent meeting is an efficient way to share information from the different perspectives of all key staff involved in the event. Individuals serving in event day part-time positions will not be involved in this meeting, but supervisors will be. If any aspect of staffing is outsourced, the contact from the outsourcing agency should also be involved in postevent meetings. Topics of discussion should include details of what went right, what went wrong, what needs to be changed for the next event, and any specific occurrences during the event that warrant further discussion.

Incident and Accident Reports

Incident reports (see Chapter 17, Figure 17.1) are simply statements about any unusual occurrence during the event requiring documentation. These situations range from theft and vandalism to problems with patrons fighting or being unruly, and sometimes ultimately being ejected or arrested. If the situation warrants a police report, the event manager should obtain a copy of the case number and request a copy of the report for the venue's records. **Accident reports** (see Chapter 17, Figure 17.2) are specific incident reports that document anything related to a patron or staff member injury. For an employee injury, worker's compensation paperwork/procedures should be completed to ensure appropriate medical coverage for the employee. All event staff should be encouraged to refer people that need assistance to the appropriate security or medical staff. Medical staff and EMTs should notify the event managers immediately regarding any situations they tend to; however, due to patient privacy laws, they may be prohibited from providing details about the individual hurt and/or the nature of the injury or illness. Therefore, it is critical for a staff member to respond and collect pertinent information. This allows for proper reporting of the incident so it can be examined and documented after the event. Documentation is critical whenever an injury occurs at an event. If the injury occurs due to a venue defect (e.g., loose carpet tile) or operational error (e.g., custodian didn't put out wet floor signs after mopping), there should be further documentation on the corrective actions taken. The event managers must protect the organization from lawsuits by keeping accurate and detailed records of what happened.

Customer Complaints/Concerns

Unfortunately, happy customers generally do not call to thank the event or facility staff. However, those that have an unpleasant experience are not shy in sharing the trouble they experienced. Following an event, it is likely that there are some participant and/or spectator complaints that deserve follow-up. Event managers, who are timely in responding and listening to these complaints and concerns are doing themselves, the event, and the venue a service. Many complaints are valid, and event managers can gather important information related to ways to improve the event experience. Additionally, the event managers can begin to rebuild relationships with the unhappy customers. Remember, unhappy customers will tell many others about their experience. For those complaints that are frivolous, event managers should still lend an ear and do their best to provide a positive response to the customer. By being responsive to complaints and concerns, the event and/or venue will be helping to mitigate public relations damage.

Sponsorship Reports and Acknowledgments

Each sponsor involved in the event should be acknowledged following the event. Depending on the type of event and type of sponsorship, along with the value of the sponsorship, the acknowledgement will vary. Some sponsorship contracts will require detailed return on investment (ROI) reports, while in other situations it may be sufficient to send a nice hand-written thank-you note.

For those sponsorships where an ROI report is generated, the details of what is needed will be discussed during the sponsorship contract negotiations because much of the data needed to calculate ROI needs to be gathered during the event. For example, if a sponsor has provided cash to the event in exchange for space in the program where the sponsor has printed a coupon for their business, they will want to know how many programs were sold, and then they can keep track of how many coupons were redeemed. This will all be included in a report so that the sponsor and the event can evaluate the effectiveness of the sponsorship as compared to the price paid by the sponsor. These reports can get very detailed, and the event managers may need to employ outside expertise to ensure that the information is accurate.

For smaller events where sponsors are involved as an act of goodwill, it may be sufficient to write a thank-you note or stop by in person to thank the sponsor and provide details of the success of the event. Providing photos to the sponsor of their logo integrated into the event is a nice touch that businesses appreciate.

Thank-You Notes and Customer Information Gathering

Everyone likes to be appreciated, so sending thank-you notes to those involved in the event is one way to accomplish this. It is critical to thank volunteer staff in as personal a way as possible. These individuals took time out of their lives to make the event a success and deserve a thank-you note, certificate of appreciation, or phone call from the event mangers. If the volunteer groups are very large, then sending a group thank you to the main contact is appropriate. Other staff also should be recognized for their efforts, but since they are paid for their time, the thank you can be less personal, such as an e-mail to the entire group. It is not feasible for large events to deliver personalized hand-written notes to all participants, but even an e-mail blast thanking participants will be noticed.

These communications are also one way to collect customer data and customer satisfaction information. By collecting as many e-mail addresses as possible during ticket sales or participant registration, event managers can use that contact information for future marketing efforts or to ask for feedback. An online survey can be easily created and sent to various populations to assess the event. Note that customer surveys include patrons, ticket buyers, and participants, as well as the clients or event promotors. Again, this takes time and effort and may not make sense for every event, but surveys are a good way to get valuable information from customers to ensure the success of future events.

Completing Postevent Recaps

Just as event managers prepare documents when they are planning events, they should also create a recap of events that were just completed. This report is for internal use by management and future event managers of the event. Rather than relying on memory, postevent recaps will help in documenting details of the various areas. This is one of the first documents new event managers should read before beginning to work on an event. A postevent recap will include pieces from the other sections, such as debriefing and customer complaints, and will wrap up the overall picture of the event. It often includes, but is not limited to, summary sheets of budget numbers, staffing and volunteers, photographs of the event, complaints, incidents, successes, challenges, and suggested changes.

The Event File

The event file is created so that all pertinent information is stored for future use in one location. The file might be hard copies of documents or electronic, but either way the same information should be included. All of the information needed to create the event file comes from either contracts (Chapter 3), event documents (Chapter 12), staffing (Chapter 13), event settlement, or wrap up. So, there is nothing new to do at this point except to organize and collect the existing information. The following should be included in the event file if appropriate for the event:

Contracts (see Chapter 3 for sample contracts)
Facility rental/promotion contracts
Sponsorship contracts
Game contracts

Event documents (see Chapter 13 for sample Event Documents)
Planning timelines
Event day timelines
Checklists
Contact sheets
Fast facts
Staffing positions/call times
Diagrams/Maps/CADs/Google Earth
PA scripts
Parking pass
Credential/ticket samples
Meeting agendas and meeting notes
Emergency plans

Event Settlement Documents (see the end of this Chapter for sample Event Settlement Documents)
Ticket and/or participant registration reports
Financial reports
The event summary

Wrap up documents (see Chapter 17 for sample Incident and Accident Reports)

Payroll information
Sponsor ROI reports
Incident and accident reports
Minutes from debriefing meetings
Customer complaints/concerns
Postevent recap

Completing a thorough wrap up of the event will strengthen existing relationships, create new ones, and generate positive feelings toward the event. Time and effort spent on sponsor communications and ROI reports will help sponsors justify future involvement in the event or organization, and postevent communications with all personnel help with staff retention.

Having a complete and detailed event file will provide the documentation needed for the future. If the event returns to the facility, all of the finances of the event will be available for reference, ideas for improvement will be noted so they can be implemented, and mistakes are less likely since they will be recorded. Many events will not conduct follow up, therefore, the event that does will also make a mark in the minds of all of those involved as a first-class operation.

SUMMARY

Event settlement is one of the crucial components of a successful sports or entertainment event hosted or staged at any facility. Primarily, the purpose of the settlement is to summarize all income from all sources, pay all legitimate expenses incurred by the event, and to divide any remaining proceeds pursuant to the original contract or lease agreement.

If all revenue and expense items are properly anticipated, accounted for, and verified, and a solid, clear, and executed agreement is in hand, the event settlement should be smooth and simple, with little or no anxiety, argument, or dispute. The parties will then leave the settlement table with a good feeling and be willing to do business together again another day.

Other wrap-up items may seem like common sense, but after a long event it is often a struggle to truly finish the event management process. However, there is significant long-term value in attention to detail in wrapping up the event. By taking time to communicate with sponsors, debrief staff, and create an event file, future events are sure to be improved because there are readily available notes of what went right, what went wrong, and which sponsors were involved. Additionally, all volunteer workers deserve to be thanked for their time, as they will feel valued by the organization and more likely to volunteer at future events. Payment should also be made promptly to staff that are compensated. The event is not truly over until settlement and wrap up are complete, and for many events this process just indicates the beginning of planning for the next event.

Student Challenges

NAME _____ DATE_____

Question 19.1

Choose any event you would like to attract to your campus arena (i.e., sport or entertainment). Brainstorm, a detailed list of the settlement and wrap up tasks that will need to occur to close out the event. Use terms and items specific to the event you are referring to, in other words—do not just copy the list provided in this chapter.

Question 19.2

Using the same event from Question 19.1, what would be the most challenging aspect of event settlement or wrap up for the event? Why?

EVENT RESOURCES (EXAMPLES)

The companies listed here are merely examples. The authors do not necessarily endorse any of the companies listed. Many vendors in these industries are regional, and event managers should search their local area for companies to provide some of these services.

Audio/Video Providers

ACE Communications (www.aceav.com)
Daktronics (www.daktronics.com)
Smart Source (www.smartsourcerentals.com)

Bus Services

Event Transportation Associates, Inc. (www.eventtransportation.com)
Gameday Management Group (www.gamedaymanagementgroup.com)
Mears Transportation (www.mearstransportation.com)

Contest Insurance

K & K Insurance (www.kandkinsurance.com)
SCA Promotions (www.scapromotions.com)
Hole in One, International (www.holeinoneinternational.com)

Ethics Self-Inventory (www.surveymonkey.com/s.aspx?sm=tufJfLstTVJ_2fu0WBN1CpUw_3d_3d)

Event Equipment Suppliers (tables, tents, chairs . . .)

PTG Event Services (Parties To Go) (www.partiestogo.com)
ConTent Party Rentals, Inc. (www.contentpartyrentals.com)
Bedrock Party Rentals, LTD. (www.bedrockpartyrentals.com)
The Tent Rental Company (www.thetentrentalcompany.com)

Event Promotions Management

LEJ Sports Group (www.lejsports.com)
Eventage Event Production (www.eventage.net)

Event Signage

EPS Doublet (www.eps-doublet.com)
APCG Productions (phone: 917-405-4045)
Omni Promotional, LLC (www.omnipromo.com)

Field Maintenance

Carolina Green Corp. (www.cgcfields.com)
Burnside Services Inc. (www.burnside-services.com)

Labor (Part-time/event day)
    Craig's List (www.craigslist.com)

Lighting Services
    United Rentals (www.ur.com)
    On-Site Energy (www.onsite-energy.com)
    Musco Lighting (www.musco.com)

Marketing and Sponsorship Organizations (various types)
    GMR Marketing (www.gmrlive.com)
    HMS Worldwide (www.hmsworldwide.com)
    IEG International Events Group (www.sponsorship.com)
    IMG (www.imgworld.com)
    IMG College (www.imgcollege.com)
    ISP (www.ispsports.com)
    Learfield (www.learfield.com)
    National Sports Forum (www.sports-forum.com)
    Navigate Research (www.navigateresearch.com)
    Nielsen Report (www.nielson.com)
    Octagon (www.octagon.com)
    Partnership Activation (www.partnershipactivation.com)
    Relay Worldwide (www.relayworldwide.com)
    Sponsorship Research International (SRi) (www.teamsri.com)
    Sports Business Daily (www.sportsbusinessdaily.com)
    Sports Business Journal (www.sportsbusinessjournal.com)
    Team Epic (www.anepiccompany.com)
    The Marketing Arm (www.themarketingarm.com)
    Velocity Sports and Entertainment (www.teamvelocity.com)

Media and Marketing Research
    Artibron (www.arbitron.com)
    Nielsen (www.nielsen.com)
    Scarborough Research (www.scarborough.com)
    Turnkey Sports and Entertainment (www.turnkeyse.com)
    Sports Business Research Network (www.sbrnet.com)
    Plunkett Research, Ltd. (www.plunkettresearch.com)
    Team Marketing Report (www.teammarketing.com)

Medical and Safety
    Athletic Trainers
        National Athletic Trainers' Association (www.nata.org)
        Board of Certification, Inc. (www.bocatc.org)
    Emergency Medical Technician (EMT)
        National Registry of Emergency Medical Technicians (www.nremt.org)
        National Association of Emergency Medical Technicians (www.naemt.org)
    National Federation of State High School Associations (www.nfhs.org/resources/sports-medicine/)
    National Youth Sports Health and Safety Institute (www.nyshsi.org)
    NCAA Health and Safety (www.ncaa.org/health-and-safety)

Nurses—American Nurses Association (www.nursingworld.org)

Paramedics—National Registry of Emergency Medical Technicians (www.nremt.org)

Physician Assistants—American Academy of Physician Assistants (www.aapa.org/)

Physicians—American Medical Association (www.ama-assn.org/ama)

State Association with Sports Medicine Sites and Advisory Committees (www.nfhs.org/sports-resource-content/member-state-associations-with-sports-medicine-sites-and-advisory-committees/)

TEAMS Techniques for Effective Alcohol Management (www.teamcoalition.org/)

Merchandise Sales

Zazzle (www.zazzle.com)

CafePress (www.cafepress.com)

Miscellaneous

Bag Tags Inc. (www.bagtagsinc.com)

Event Credentials, LLC (www.eventcredentials.com)

Grainger (www.grainger.com)

Wiki Spaces (www.wikispaces.com)

Online Registration

Active (www.active.com)

Cashnet (www.cashnet.com)

Sports Signup (www.sportsignup.com)

Photography

Brightroom (www.brightroom.com)

Action Sports International (www.asiorders.com)

MarathonFoto (www.marathonfoto.com)

Portable Restrooms

National Construction Rentals (www.rentnational.com)

Mesa Waste Services (www.mesawasteservices.com)

A Royal Flush, Inc. (www.aroyalflush.com)

General Information on Numbers and ADA Requirements

    Federal Emergency Management Agency (www.americanrestroom.org/gov/fema/FEMA_SECP39_41.PDF)

Promotional Products

Brand Marketing Works (www.brandmarketingworks.com)

Barker Specialty Company (www.barkerspecialty.com)

Radios and Wireless Communication

Bearcom (www.bearcom.com)

Event Radio Rentals (www.eventradiorentals.com)

Event Communications, Inc. (www.eventcomm.net)

Road Race/Triathlon Management

New York Road Runners (www.nyrr.org)

Premier Event Management, LLC (www.pem-usa.com)

Track Shack (www.trackshack.com)

Sport and the Natural Environment
Environmental Protection Agency Sport Guide (www2.epa.gov/green-sports)
Green Sport Alliance (www.greensportsalliance.org)
Natural Resources Defense Council (www.nrdc.org/greenbusiness/guides/sports/)

Sports Commissions and Economic Impact
CONNECT (www.connectsports.com)
DMAI (Destination Marketing Association International), (www.destinationmarketing.org)
NASC (National Association of Sports Commissions), (www.sportscommissions.org)
TEAMS Conference (www.teamsconference.com)

Sports Team Travel
Anthony Travel Inc. (www.anthonytravel.com)
American Tours & Travels, Inc. (www.travelgroups.com)

Sustainability (various information)
The American Society for Testing and Materials (ASTM) (previously known as the American Society for Testing and Materials), (www.astm.org/industry/sports-and-leisure-standards.html)
Cost of Sustainability (www.whistler2020.ca/whistler/site/genericPage.acds?instanceid=1967867&context=1967866)
Global Reporting Initiative G4 Reporting Framework and the Event Organizers Sector Supplement (www.globalreporting.org/Pages/default.aspx);
ISO 20121 (www.iso.org/iso/iso20121)

Ticketing
Sales Outlets
> Groupon (www.groupon.com)
>
> Living Social 9www.livingsocial.com)

Software Programs
> TicketBiscuit, LLC (www.ticketbiscuit.com)
>
> Ticketmaster Entertainment, Inc. (www.ticketmaster.com)
>
> Tickets.com (www.tickets.com)

Trophies and Medals
Midwest Trophy (www.mwtrophy.com)
Trophy Depot (www.trophydepot.com)
Wilson Trophy Company (www.wilsontrophy.com)

Weather Information
Apps
> Weatherbug
>
> MyRadar
>
> Intellicast

Lightning Information
> National Athletic Trainers' Association Position Statement: Lightning Safety for Athletics and Recreation (www.nata.org/sites/default/files/2013_lightning-position-statement.pdf)
>
> Korey Stringer Institute: Lightning (ksi.uconn.edu/emergency-conditions/lightning/)

GLOSSARY OF TERMS

Acceptance: Consenting to receive the terms of the offer for the purposes of fulfilling a contract.

Accident reports: Specific incident reports that document anything related to a patron or staff member injury.

Accounting codes (also: chart of accounts): Identification numbers assigned to specific categories (accounts) of revenues and expenses used for record keeping.

Admission tax (also: bond charge or facility fee): Whether a facility is publicly or privately financed, the cost of construction and development is funded by debt, often in the form of bonds sold to institutional or private investors. Bondholders are generally entitled to some guaranteed revenue stream on all building income in the form of a percentage or fixed fee for each admission or ticket sold. This bond fee should be deducted from the price of each ticket and accounted for on the box office statement, which then yields a "net ticket sales" figure that is dropped into the revenue column of the settlement statement.

Advertising campaign: A plan that can utilize all forms of media, including, but not limited to, television, radio, newspaper, outdoor, direct mail, and online advertising to promote ticket sales and/or entry for an event.

Anchor tenant: A team that calls the facility its "home court," "home field," or "home ice."

Ancillary events: Events that supplement and surround the pre-defined core sports events. Examples include a carbohydrate loading dinner the night before a marathon, a tailgate party before the Super Bowl, or a concert after a baseball game.

Ancillary spaces: All of the areas that support the primary space. Examples include the locker rooms, concourses, storage areas, lobbies, press areas, loading docks, offices, restrooms, security areas, merchandise shops, and so on.

Attrition: The shrinkage or reduction in number of hotel rooms to be used. Attrition is different from cancellation, which is the complete annulment of the event or contract. Most hotel contracts have different clauses and terms for these two situations.

Augmented Reality (AR): When technology is used to superimpose a computer-generated image, sound, video, and/or GPS data onto a real-world view, such as something being viewed through a camera phone.

Back of house: Roles in which employees do not regularly engage in face-to face contact with the public, such as the public address announcer, the scoreboard operator, operations personnel, truck dock employees, and even set-up and tear-down employees.

Bandit runners: Runners trying to sneak in to run a race for which they did not register or sign the waiver.

Base: As outlined in the facility's standard operating procedure, base references a person or small group of personnel who field all medical calls at the command center and disseminate information during an event.

Baseline staffing number: This number takes into account the bare minimum of staff required to accomplish the management of the event.

Basic provisions: The section of the contract that lists the fundamental areas for which each party will be responsible.

Bed tax: A tax levied on hotel rooms by the local municipality.

Bidding: A competitive process in which companies are asked to provide service and price information based on criteria set by the event organizers.

Biometric scanning: Technology that uses individual physiological characteristics, such as fingerprints, face recognition, and/or iris recognition to allow or not allow access to an area.

Boilerplate: Detailed standard wording (e.g., insurance, warranty, rules, and regulations) in a contract that remains the same for all clients unless all parties agree to specific changes. Boilerplate can also refer to any section of writing that can be used repeatedly without change. Another example is the company/organization description at the end of a press release.

Bond charge: See admission tax.

Box office statement: A report, often computerized, prepared by a third-party ticketing vendor that will show all tickets sold at each ticket price, and specify the method by which they were sold (e.g., at remote outlets, via phone, on the Internet, etc.)

Brand unity: The consistent look, style, and attitude seen and felt throughout the communications, and the event itself.

Breach of contract: When certain aspects of the contract are not completed, whether intentional or not.

Breakage: The difference in the amount that the customer pays and the amount they actually spend on any packaged purchase (e.g., concessions, parking, merchandise credit, and two tickets).

Budget summary: A one page synopsis showing the total from each segment of the budget (e.g., equipment, labor, marketing) and the grand total of those segments for both revenues and expenses.

Budgeted amount: The expenses and revenues that the event managers project the event will have.

CADs (computer-aided design/drawing): Diagrams created using computer software to show event setup and details in a to-scale depiction.

Call sign list (also: contact list): A record of all parties relevant to the event and all of their contact phone numbers.

Call time: The time that staff are expected to be on site and signed in ready to go to work.

Call time meeting: A pre-event meeting with staff in which event managers review general information about the event, key issues they foresee that might come up and discuss how to handle the issues, and answer any questions workers have.

Capacity: The notion that the parties involved in the contract have the legal right to enter into that contract.

Capital equipment: Any piece of equipment costing over $500 with a useful life of two or more years.

Category: The group, class, or division that describes a company's business area.

Changeover: The process by which the primary space in the venue is converted from functioning for one purpose to another (e.g., flat exhibit space to basketball).

Chart of accounts: See accounting code.

Co-promotion: A contract for an event in which the venue and the promoter share the risk associated with the event and are both responsible for certain expenses usually associated with the production and staging of the event.

Command centers: Essentially the building's "nerve center," bringing the use of security-related technologies to a central location.

Color blind: People that have trouble seeing red, green, blue, and combinations of these colors.

Contact list: See call sign list.

Contract: A legally enforceable promise or set of promises.

Consideration: The details of the contract. Consideration is necessary for the formation and validity of the contract.

Contest insurance: Insurance that protects the sport organization from having to fund the cost of the prize if a contestant wins a promotional contest.

Contingency account: Money set aside in a budget to cover costs that may arise due to an unexpected event or circumstance.

Contra lanes: Traffic lanes closed to allow vehicles to travel opposite the normal direction of traffic in order to speed up the movement of vehicles.

Convention and Visitors Bureau (CVB): An organization, usually nonprofit, that represents an area or destination to promote it and assist in attracting a variety of events, tourism, and business to the local area.

Corkage fee: A charge exacted at a hotel/venue/restaurant for every bottle of beverage (liquor, water, soda, isotonic drink, juice, etc.) served that was not bought on the premises.

Corporate social responsibility (CSR): The ways organizational personnel demonstrate a concern for society through a variety of activities including efforts toward sustainability and caring for the natural environment (Paramio-Salcines, Babiak, & Walters, 2013).

Cost Per Rating Point (CPP): The cost of reaching one percent of the target population. CPP is calculated by dividing the cost of the schedule by the gross rating points. National and regional advertising buyers frequently use this cost efficiency measure since it can be applied across all media.

Cost Per Thousand (CPM): The relative cost of a schedule of announcements. CPM is calculated by dividing the cost of the schedule by the sum of the average quarter-hour audiences of the announcements purchased.

Crown: The slope of an athletic field that helps to drain the field.

Database: "A shared, integrated computer structure that stores a collection of end-user data ... metadata, or data about data through which the end-user data are integrated and managed" (Rob, Coronel, & Crockett, 2008, p. 7).

Day of event timeline: A document created to note and track details of the event day schedule such as time, task, functional area, task owner, and notes/comments.

Defensible space: Using architectural design to diminish or mitigate any tendency toward negative behaviors.

Delivery schedule: A document that includes the date, time, company, the driver's name, contact phone numbers, vehicle description, and the license plate number of each expected delivery.

Design issues: With regard to Web sites, the areas of the Web site evaluated for ease of use and usefulness to visitors, including aesthetics, data collection points, multimedia usage, sponsor images, languages, and user accessibility.

Drayage: The monetary charge for pickup and hauling of containers.

Earned media: Media exposure not paid for by the event organizers and that has gone through an independent editorial source before it reaches the intended audience.

Economic impact: The new money entering a region resulting in a change in regional output, earnings, and employment (Humphreys & Plummer, 1995).

Economic impact multiplier: A certain number ("y") that is entered in economic impact calculations because it assumes the money generated from the event will be circulated throughout the community that number ("y") of times.

Electronic Signatures in Global and International Commerce Act (ESGICA): A law enacted to provide guidance on electronic contracts and electronic signatures.

Emergency planning: The creation and implementation of a plan to address, and minimize, the risk and damage of potential incidents.

Emergency preparedness plan (EPP): A document that articulates the policies guiding emergency management and how the organization functions given a specific type of emergency.

Entertainment and education: The concept that the event planners provide additional experiential opportunities surrounding the event through the use of different technologies, but mainly the Web site.

Environment: Refers to the natural environment.

Estimated outs: The projected financial figures necessary to estimate event expenses prior to settlement. These are most common for touring and entertainment shows.

Event contracts: Similar to game contracts in that the time and place is paramount. Event contracts differ from game contracts in that they often include ancillary event stipulations. An event, in a sporting context, can include a contest, a single special event like the Super Bowl, or multiple events like the Olympics or AAU, Inc. Junior Olympics.

Event management: Event management is the process by which an event is planned, prepared, and produced. As with any other form of management, it encompasses the assessment, definition, acquisition, allocation, direction, control, and analysis of time, finances, people, products, services, and other resources to achieve objectives (Silvers, 2003, para. 2).

Event management software: A package that facilitates different aspects of the event planning process, depending upon the nature of the software.

Event manager: The individual responsible for making the event "come to life," from conceptualization through execution.

Event sanctions: An official approval for the event granted by the governing body associated with the sport (Solomon, 2002).

Event settlement: A specific process that occurs upon completion of all events. It is a financial transaction in nature, very similar to the closing on the purchase of real estate or the acquisition of a business.

Event theme: An idea or topic that helps establish an identity people will associate with the event, and should be a part of every aspect of the event.

Expendable equipment: Equipment that is less expensive than capital equipment (less than $500) and has a useful life of less than 2 years.

Experiential marketing: An atmosphere at the event that allows attendees to interact with a sponsor's product or service, creating a unique encounter for the sponsor which traditional advertising cannot deliver.

Expo: A sponsor and/or vendor display that often ties into a larger event.

External relations: The management process concerning the creation and communication of information through media (both earned and paid) to intended audiences (publics).

Facility contract: See venue contract.

Facility fee: See admission tax.

Event flow: The traffic pattern (people and/or cars) for the event.

Facility promotion: The building or its owner acts as the promoter for an event and takes all the risks, such as financial and others.

Fair Labor Standards Act (FLSA): A law that restricts the employment of child workers. "Child labor provisions under FLSA are designed to protect the educational opportunities of youth and prohibit their employment in jobs that are detrimental to their health and safety. FLSA restricts the hours that youth under 16 years of age can work and lists hazardous occupations too dangerous for young workers to perform" (United States Department of Labor, n.d., para. 1).

Fast facts: A document for staff and volunteers that contains pertinent facts about an event and will list questions that participants and spectators are likely to ask about an event.

Feasibility: Evaluating whether or not the event can be produced successfully.

Features: A form of earned media centered on human-interest stories that somehow link back to the event through personalities or elements of the event that are the focus of the story.

Festival seating: Ticketing process where no seats are assigned and people stand to experience the event in a large open area.

Fixed equipment: Equipment that is part of the facility and could include spectator seating, scoreboards, and mechanical systems.

Flat fee agreement: The facility or city charges the event a set fee for the right to set up and sell products.

Forecast: Showing any positive or negative variances from the original budgeted amount.

Format: Programming of a radio station aimed at a specific audience, such as country, adult contemporary, urban, rock, and so on.

Frequency: The average number of exposures to the commercial or song heard by the average listener, or a frequency distribution revealing the number of persons estimated to have heard the commercial or song one time, two times, three times, four times, and so on.

Frequently Asked Questions (FAQ's): The most common questions that people will have about an event. FAQ's are often listed in a specific section of an event or organization's Web site.

Front of house: Event staff with face-to-face contact with the public, such as ticket office, ticket takers, parking attendants, ushers, concession, and merchandise staff.

Fulfillment paperwork: The copies of the traffic logs that show when the commercials ran on air.

Game contract: A contractual agreement that arranges a contest or contests between two organizations.

Game guarantee: Payment for one team to play another team.

General admission: Seating is open and patrons with a ticket are able to sit in any unoccupied seat, but they are guaranteed a seat.

Goals: Items an organization wants to accomplish with a given strategy and aligned with its purpose.

Governing bodies: Organizations charged with setting the rules for the sports they oversee.

Guerrilla marketing: An aggressive way to market an event that could best be defined as "taking the message to the streets."

Grassroots marketing: Marketing an event on a local and personal level, and a way to get the word out on the event by using a street team or group of volunteers to help promote the event.

Green supply chain: Choosing, or requiring, suppliers, and vendors change their parties to become more sustainable (Mamic, 2005; Sarkis, 2007; Walton, Handfield, & Melnyk, 1998).

Hard ticketing: All tickets for an event are printed in advance.

Human resources: The people who work for an organization.

In trust: Money that is held by the organization, generally ticket money in a sport context, and not spent by the organization. If an event is cancelled, this money is available for customer refunds.

Incident reports are simply a statement about any unusual occurrence during the event requiring documentation.

Incremental revenue: Revenue that is generated through "up selling," such as sending a loyal fan a $5 coupon for the merchandise store knowing that the cheapest item in the store is $20.

Independent contractors: People or businesses that provide products or services to another person or business based on the terms of a contract.

Information dissemination: The ways in which different technologies can help to promote an event and its message (e.g., marketing plan), in addition to sponsors, partners, and other aspects planners want people to know about their events.

Information management: All of the back-end technology employed to plan an event. Examples include the internal work applications, event management software, database structure to handle the information gathered from the event registration section, questions and comments submitted to the staff, and the server that holds the Web site and other event-based information and the benefits of a near-paperless planning process.

Infrastructure: Refers to the aspects of the venue that are at the core of its operation, such as the structure, roadways, access ways, lighting, and utilities associated with the venue.

In-kind advertising: See trade advertising.

Instant messaging (IM): A near-real-time information exchange on a computer or device with Internet access. Organizations can create an IM interface on their Web sites and have staff monitor it, allowing customers to ask questions or even buy tickets.

International governing body (IGB): The international counterparts to National Governing Bodies (NGB's) (e.g., Fédération Internationale de Natation [FINA] for many aquatic sports, and International Federation of Associated Wrestling Styles [IFAWS] for wrestling) that are responsible for international and Olympic playing rules and competitions in specific sports.

Jump teams: Squads of event-day workers that are available to fill in at a variety of staffing positions throughout the event day.

Killed seat: A seat that is removed from the ticket inventory for the event, usually because of an obstructed view.

Labor union: A group formed with the goal of protecting the members' with respect to wages and working conditions.

Legal representation: Internal General Counsel or an outside legal firm that represents an organization's interests.

Legality: See capacity.

Marshalling revenue: Marshalling revenue refers to identifying, organizing, and accounting for everything related to revenue in an effective way.

Measures (also called metrics): The methods used to determine the success of tactics, and subsequently, the goals and the objectives.

Media audit: The process of determining the content, format, deadlines, and contacts at the entire population of outlets that are active in the media market where the group, and/or the event, takes place.

Media center: A special section on the Web site and a centrally located physical site at an event that seeks to provide maximum information to all members of the media.

Media credentials: Sometimes called a press pass, they are issued from the event organizer to designate who can access those working press spaces as well as identify working press to the participants.

Media schedule checks: A log of when a commercial ran on radio or TV and the rating it received—to make sure the group received what it paid for.

Media market: Groups of newspapers, radio, and TV stations that serve a similar geographic area or population, such as the New York City media market.

Mega events: The most complex category of events that often take years of planning prior to the event taking place. Mega events are often international in nature (whether through media exposure, participation, or location) and are easily identifiable to sport consumers because the event is a brand in itself. These events become stand-alone business ventures since many of them have organizing committees composed of full- and part-time personnel dedicated solely to the execution of the event.

Metrics: See measures.

Monetization: Describes the efforts made to utilize Web site space for revenue generation, even if the revenues are not for profit purposes.

National Governing Body (NGB): Recognized by the United States Olympic Committee (USOC) or an international governing organization to oversee a particular sport. Most amateur sports in the United States have an NGB (e.g., USA Volleyball, USA Swimming, and USA Table Tennis).

National Labor Relations Act: A law that restricts an employer's ability to interfere with employees in the execution of their job duties by offering coercive incentives, such as higher pay, better work conditions, or a more comprehensive benefits package in order to sway an employee away from joining a union.

News items: A form of earned media that normally surround the event itself and include coverage of what happens at the event, previews of the event, and announcements that the event is going to happen—often by covering a smaller ancillary event related to the main one (e.g., a press conference).

Objectives: Items connected directly to their explicit, related goals. They are specific and measurable, enabling event managers to determine success.

Offer: The proposal that forms the contract. It is a promise to do something or refrain from doing something.

Offset programs: Initiatives that include buying carbon offset that are linked to renewable energy generation efforts (e.g., through a power provider) that work to balance the emissions from an event with efforts to reduce emissions elsewhere.

On-sale date: The date the tickets are available for purchase.

Opportunity scheduling: Those times during the year where venues and hotels struggle to find occupants.

Organizing committees: These groups play a large role in the bidding, obtaining, and hosting of some events as the local group that puts on the event.

Origination fee: When an event is televised, additional costs will accrue, including higher utility bills and perhaps additional labor and/or security. Also, if television viewership will suppress attendance, and the building is receiving a share of ticket proceeds, then this type of fee may be required to make the building whole.

PA script: Includes the specific details of what is being said when by announcers.

Package-to-compete (also called stay-to-play): Event entry strategy where event organizers group the entry fee to the event with theme park tickets, hotel room nights, or special events tickets and require that an individual or team purchase the package in order to enter the event.

Page view counts: The number of times Internet content is loaded into a browser, which can be tracked by the page's publisher.

Paid advertising: Any time cash is spent in return for the specified form of advertising.

Paid media: Advertising, sponsorship, and activation marketing that event organizers pay for and therefore retain control over the message.

Participant: Anyone taking part in a sports event. This includes everyone associated with a team taking part in a sports event who will be on the field of play (including, but not limited to, players, coaches, statisticians, athletic trainers, managers); volunteers; participants in promotions; and so on.

Participant registration: The act of providing information and/or payment to an event with the expectation of participation and access to all of the rights and benefits associated with event participation.

Partner: Can be a sponsor, but the relationship to the event might be over a longer period of time, carry a higher monetary value, or might just be named differently.

Partnership: Used as a synonym for sponsorship, in that an event organizer should treat a sponsor like a true partner where together both parties can benefit from a successful event.

Pass-through charges: Those expenses for which the facility pays a third party on behalf of the renter and then later charges to the renter.

Peak times: Periods in which specific areas will have a surge in spectator/participant traffic. For example, sports that have a half time will see a surge to concessions during this time.

Per cap: See per capita spending.

Per capita spending (also: per cap): The amount of money spent per person during the event. For example, the per cap for merchandise spending is calculated by taking the total revenue for merchandise divided by the total number of people in attendance.

Per-person fee agreement: Used mostly in merchandise and concession contracts, the event is charged an amount for each person in attendance.

Percentage of gross sales agreement: The event splits its gross revenue with the venue (or city in the case of many nontraditional venues).

Permits: Permission from a city, county, or national governing agency to allow an event to occur. Events that are held outside of a traditional venue will most likely need a permit.

Personal seat license (PSL): A contract between a customer and team or venue where the customer purchases the rights to particular seats for a specified time length (e.g., 1 year, 3 years, 5 years, etc.)

Planning timelines: Documents used to set up and track detailed tasks by functional area. They ensure that event managers can account for each detailed item, who is responsible for specific items, and whether the event is on schedule.

Pool services: A single photographer or videographer (e.g., the Associated Press or the broadcast rights holder) with limited access (defined by time or place).

Premium seating: Encompasses a variety of seats such as luxury suites, party suites, club seats, loge boxes, field-level seats in baseball, courtside seats in basketball, and any other special section of tickets with enhanced amenities.

Primary space: The area of the venue where the main activity takes place.

Processing fee: The amount charged to participants for the right to enter the lottery or other selection process associated with the event. This fee covers the costs to the organization in managing the lottery and entry procedures.

Production binder: A book or collection of detailed information (e.g., parking maps, event-day checklists, fast facts, staffing positions, maps and diagrams, etc.) about the event that can be carried with event staff during the event.

Promotional campaign: Special discounts, giveaways, theme nights, and other publicity strategies that are sponsored by a media outlet and not a part of the paid advertising campaign.

Publicity: Any news coverage for the event that is generated with some type of announcement or interview and is not paid for by the event.

Purchase Money Security Interest (PMSI): In a commercial lending transaction, a lender, typically a bank, will acquire a security interest in the equipment or fixtures purchased with the loan proceeds.

Purpose statement: A short, to-the-point acknowledgment of the overall motivation for holding the event.

Queuing up: When people at an event create a line on their own, often interfering with other aspects of event flow.

Question and answer availability: The different ways in which questions and concerns can be directed to event planning staff, including, but not limited to, information on Web sites, instant messaging, text messaging, and Twitter.

Quid pro quo: A Latin phrase that literally means "this for that." A sponsor will give money, product, and/or services, but expects something in return to benefit the company and provide an effective ROI (Return on Investment) (McMillen, 2003).

Radio repeater: Radio transmission equipment that receives a low-level signal and retransmits it at a higher power, increasing the distance the signal can effectively cover. A repeater will most likely be needed for golf events, road races, or just to maintain communication within the locale if staff is driving out of the immediate event range.

Rate card: The retail price that a media outlet charges for its commercial time. The rates charged vary depending on the time of day or the specific programming on the station. Related to venues, a rate card can also be the rates charged by a venue for rental of its equipment and/or services by a third party.

Rating: The percentage of the population listening to a given radio station during a day part. Ratings apply to both average quarter-hour and cumulative audiences.

Reach: The total number of different persons exposed to a commercial or song during a specified day part. Reach can be calculated using a computer for a single station, multiple stations, or across media using formulas generally accepted by the advertising industry.

Recurring event: An event that happens on a regular basis (e.g., university basketball game or youth soccer game).

Registration fee: The monetary amount that participants pay to enter a competition.

Release of liability: See waiver.

Rental event: An event where an outside presenter, sponsor, or promoter is fully responsible for producing and staging the event in the venue.

Request For Bid (RFB): The letter sent by the event manager to potential vendors seeking out prices on the equipment needed.

Return on Investment (ROI): The calculated amount of income resulting from a expenditures for a sponsorship. The business generated by the sponsorship should be at least equal to or greater than the cost of the sponsorship (Lynde, 2007).

Return on Objective (ROO): Monetary or non-monetary measurements indicating whether or not a sponsorship meets the sponsor's business objectives (Lynde, 2007).

Reserved seating: The ticket holder is assigned, or chooses, a specific seat in the venue for the event.

Revocable permit: The organization reserves the right to take the ticket back from the purchaser (usually with a refund).

Rights fee: The payment made by an entity to a rights holder to legally associate with the event.

Rights holders: Organizations or businesses that control and own the entitlement to an event.

Risk: A hazard or the possibility of danger or harm.

Risk management: The entire process of evaluating risk and using cost-effective strategies to reduce and treat risk.

Room rebate: A dollar amount per room night booked at host hotel property that is given back to the event rights holder as part of an agreement for bringing their event to a host city.

Room nights: The number of total nights' stay sold for an event.

Room tax: A tax on hotel rooms levied by the state government.

RSS feeds: Web feeds that allow people to create links to information sources (e.g., other Web sites) on their Web browser or computer desktop. Whenever an organization or individual adds new content pertaining to that link to a Web site, a hyperlink is created at the individual's browser or desktop indicating new information has arrived.

Sample boards: Displays of exact replicas of credentials, tickets, and/or parking passes used as an easy reference guide for staff.

Secondary ticket market: The reselling of tickets after the first purchase.

Secure event: An event in a venue (traditional or nontraditional) with an enhanced atmosphere for patrons and participants while providing a certain level of safety and an efficient, direct, and unobtrusive emergency response. For the patrons, the feeling is positive and they feel well attended-to, while the level of security intervention will be minimized. The measures required to sustain a safe venue will be focused from a patron service rather than a punitive environment.

Security deposit: Nonrefundable money collected to hold the date when renting or reserving a sports or entertainment facility.

Setup: The process of preparing the venue for the event.

Share: The percentage of people listening to a specific radio station in a particular day part compared to all those listening to radio in that day part. Share answers the question: "What percentage of the radio audience is listening to a specific station at a particular time?"

Shared network drives: Common storage areas that allow individuals to post documents and have them accessed by others who have access to the drive.

Site context: Refers to whether or not the venue site and immediate areas convey a sense of welcoming, safety, and control. To create a welcoming feel, designers should conceive a site in the context of surrounding neighborhoods, whether they are urban, suburban, or a college/university campus.

Site setback: The distance between the spectator venue and other structures and/or public right of ways.

Social media command center: A dedicated space for staff to manage the organizations social media presence during events.

Social media den: See social suite

Social suite (also known as **social media den**): to provide facilities, mainly charging stations and higher-speed Wi-Fi, as well as direct access to front office personnel for those not with traditional media, but influential on social media due to number of followers or readers.

Social media: The interactions people have in online and Web-based contexts as they share information and ideas with each other (Newman, Peck, Harris, & Wilhide, 2013; Safko & Brake, 2009).

Sponsor: An entity that provides cash or in-kind products or services in exchange for an association with or presence within the event.

Sponsorship: A cash and/or in-kind fee paid to a property (typically in sports, arts, entertainment, or causes) in return for access to the exploitable commercial potential associated with that property.

Sponsorship contract: A legal agreement that binds two or more parties to agreed-upon obligations.

Sports commission: An organization, often non-profit, that exists specifically to attract sports events to an area and assist in hosting those events.

Sport governance: "The exercise of power and authority in sport organizations, including policy making, to determine organizational mission, membership, eligibility, and regulatory power, with the organization's appropriate local, national or international scope" (Hums & MacLean, 2004, p. 4).

Standing Room Only (SRO): Tickets to enter the venue with access to specific areas where there are not seats, but where the event can still be viewed.

Stay-to-play: See package-to-compete.

Supplies: Items used on a regular basis that may or may not relate to the core activity of the event (e.g., paper, pens, credentials, ticket stock).

Sustainability: The practices to account for, and as often as possible, to protect the environment in the course of event planning and management operations.

Tactics: The actions used to accomplish the objectives. They can take a variety of forms, but must relate directly to the objectives with which they are connected. A tactic answers the question of how the objective will be achieved.

Team Leaders: Associated with volunteer management, the volunteer manager may assign this role to take oversight of a team of volunteers at a specific position or venue.

Trade advertising (also: in-kind advertising): Any advertising that is secured in exchange on a dollar-for-dollar trade with tickets or something else of value to the event.

Teardown: The process of returning the venue to the pre-event condition.

Terms and conditions: In a contract, the specific details not spelled out in the General Provisions.

Ticket as a limited contract: The ticket buyer receives the right to attend the event and the organization has an obligation to provide the event as advertised and promoted.

Ticket manifest: A representation of the venue layout needed for all ticketed events. The ticket manifest identifies how many seats are in each row and section of the venue.

Time Spent Listening (TSL): The amount of time the average listener spent listening to a radio station during a day part. The estimate may be expressed in number of quarter hours or in hours/minutes. TSL answers the question: "How much time does the average listener spend with this station?"

Trained crowd manager: Someone who has been educated in crowd management techniques, the responsibilities of their job, as well as emergency procedures.

Traveling event: An event that does not occur on a regular basis at a consistent location, but may either occur on a regular basis or at a set location.

Universal design: "The design of products and environments to be usable by all people, to the greatest extent possible, without the need for adaptation or specialized design" (The Center for Universal Design, 1997, para. 1).

User Generated Content (UGC): Refers to pictures, video, podcasts, and text (e.g., blogs) contributed by individuals for others to see regarding their experiences associated with an event.

Venue contract (also: facility contract): A rental agreement for use of a venue/facility that must be in writing.

Vicarious liability: The type of legal liability where a sport organization or event can be held liable for the actions of volunteers and others with official roles with the event.

Volunteer Manager: An event staff position responsible for coordinating all personnel, procedures, and activities related to managing volunteers.

Waiver: Is "a contract in which the participant or user of a service agrees to relinquish the right to pursue legal action against the service provider in the event that the ordinary negligence of the provider results in an injury to the participant" (Cotten, 2007, p. 85).

Walk-thru: A literal walk around the building or site examining, in detail, how everything will look, function, and flow for the event.

Wayfinding: The ease at which visitors find their way throughout the venue. Well placed, visible entries help people to navigate into the building efficiently.

Website: A portal of information, multimedia, and interaction that allows users access to its contents around the clock and around the world.

Worker's compensation: A series of laws aimed to protect injured workers.

Working press space: Functional space dedicated to members of the media, where an immediate story is expected from their outlet. It can include both front-of-house seating areas and boxes and the back-of-house technical areas with interview space, outlets, and grounded cable connections as well as space to write.

Wrap up: A general term referring to task completion that concludes the event management process, such as attending to any complaints received, generating sponsor reports, sending thank you notes, debriefing and paying workers, and completing post-event recaps.

REFERENCES

Agency. (2009, February 25). *NBA veterans find culture class in China league*. China Daily. Retrieved from http://www.chinadaily.com.cn/sports/2009-02/25/content_7511370_2.htm

American Airlines Center. (n.d.). Standard operating procedures. Unpublished document.

Ammon, R., & Stotlar, D. K. (2003). Sport facility and event management. In J. B. Parks & J. Quarterman (Eds.), (2nd ed., pp. 255). Champaign, IL: Human Kinetics.

Arbitron Inc. (2009). *Radio stations: Terms of the trade*. Retrieved from http://www.arbitron.com/radio_stations/tradeterms.htm

Asics. (2011, October 13). Asics expands "support your marathoner" for 2011 ING New York City Marathon. Retrieved from www.asics.com: http://assets.asics.com/page_types/1688/files/20111013_original.pdf?1386146199

Associated Press. (2008, November 17). *UEFA sells Champions League TV rights in China*. Retrieved from http://msn.foxsports.com/soccer/story/8807816/UEFA-sells-Champions-League-TV-rights-in-China

Athletic Business. (n.d.). *Facility specifications*. Retrieved from http://www.athleticbusiness.com/specifications

Bang, H., & Ross, S. D. (2009). Volunteer motivation and satisfaction. *Journal of Venue and Event Management, 1*, 61–77.

Baseball Writers' of America. (2008). *Constitution*. Retrieved from http://www.baseballwriters.org/constitution.html

BC 2010 Olympic bid. (n.d.). Retrieved from http://www.mapleleafweb.com/old/education/spotlight/issue_28/olympic.html

Beck, H. (2008, 19 November). *The real O'Neal puts his cyber foot down*. The New York Times. Retrieved from http://www.nytimes.com

Bishop, G. (2013, February 4). *Out of darkness, springing into action*. The New York Times [online]. Retrieved from http://www.nytimes.com/2013/02/05/sports/football/root-cause-of-super-bowl-power-failure-still-undetermined.html?_r=2

Carter, B. (2013, February 4). *Blackout is a boon for Super Bowl ratings*. The New York Times [online]. Retrieved from http://mediadecoder.blogs.nytimes.com/2013/02/04/blackout-is-a-boon-for-super-bowl-ratings/

Casper, J., & Pfahl, M. (2012). Environmental behavior frameworks of sport and recreation undergraduate students. *Sport Management Education Journal, 6*, 8–20.

Casper, J. Pfahl, M., & McCullough, B. (in press). Intercollegiate sport and the environment: Examining fan engagement based on athletics department sustainability efforts. *Sport & Communication.*

Cecil Soccer. (n.d.). Cecil soccer links page—soccer field measurements. Retrieved from http://www .cecilsoccer.org/links.htm

Changelabsolutions. (2010). *Volunteers and liability.* Retrieved from http://changelabsolutions. org/sites/default/files/Volunteers_Liability_Fact_Sheet_FINAL_%28CLS-20120530% 29_20100727.pdf

Chase, C. (2008, December 19). *Tattletales: NFL teams ask for text messages about rowdy fans.* Retrieved from http://sports.yahoo.com/nfl/blog/shutdown_corner/post/Tattletales-NFL-teams-ask-for-text-messages-abo;_ylt=A0LEVjmgpC5VkqYANQonnIlQ;_ylu=X3oDMTByMG04Z2o 2BHNlYwNzcgRwb3MDMQRjb2xvA2JmMQR2dGlkAw--?urn=nfl,130422

Chen V. Major League Baseball Properties, Inc., et al, No. 1:2013cv05494–Document (S.D.N.Y 2014)

China.org. (n.d.). *Chinese basketball association (CBA).* Retrieved from http://www.china.org.cn/ english/features/2004-2005cba/118959.htm

City of Cincinnati Task Force on Crowd Control and Safety. (1980). *Crowd management: Report of the task force on crowd control and safety.* Retrieved from http://www.crowdsafe.com/taskrpt/ chpt1.html

Clary, G. E., Snyder, M., Ridge, R. D., Copeland, J., Stukas, A. A., & Haugen, J. (1998). Understanding and assessing the motivations of volunteers: A functional approach. *Journal of Personality and Social Psychology, 74,* 1516–1530.

Cleveland Indians, (2014, June 30). *#TRIBELIVE.* Retrieved from http://cleveland.indians.mlb.com/ cle/fan_forum/social_suites.jsp

Collins, A., Flynn, A., Munday, M., & Roberts, A. (2007). Assessing the environmental consequences of major sporting events: The 2003/04 FA Cup Final. *Urban Studies, 44*(3), 457–476.

Collins, A., Jones, C., & Dow. (2014, February 4). *Sochi 2014's direct carbon footprint mitigated before Opening Ceremony.* Retrieved from http://www.dow.com/news/press-releases/ article/?id=6429

Communicaid Group, Ltd. (2007). *Doing business in Australia.* Retrieved from http://www .communicaid.com/access/pdf/library/culture/doing-business-in/Doing%20Business%20in%20 Australia.pdf

Corriher, K. (2007, December 6). *NCAA volleyball tourney a win for the local economy.* Retrieved from http://ohiobobcats.cstv.com/sports/w-volley/spec-rel/120607aaa.html

Cotten, D. (2003). Which parties are liable? In D. Cotton & J. Wolohan (Eds.), *Law for recreation and sport managers* (3rd ed., pp. 66–77). Dubuque, IA: Kendall Hunt.

Cotten, D. (2007). Waivers and releases. In D. Cotton & J. Wolohan (Eds.), *Law for recreation and sport managers,* (4th ed., p. 85). Dubuque, IA: Kendall Hunt.

Crews, D., & Zavotka, S. (2006). Aging, disability, and frailty: Implications for universal design. *Journal of Physiological Anthropology, 25,* 113–118.

Deal, J. J. (2006). *Retiring the generation gap: How employees young and old can find common ground.* San Francisco, CA: Jossey-Bass.

Deeson, M. (n.d.). *Economist says 2009 super bowl will have little economic impact on Tampa.* Retrieved from http://www.wtsp.com/news/local/story.aspx?storyid=73176

DiRocco, M. (2009, April 1). *Numbers don't add up to shift Florida-Georgia game: Some think the annual game ought to be in Georgia despite the tradition.* Florida Times Union.

Retrieved April 5, 2009, from http://www.jacksonville.com/news/metro/2009-04-01/story/numbers_dont_add_up_to_shift_uf-uga_game

Dorman, L. (2008, August 26). *LPGA players required to learn English*. Retrieved from http://www.mercurynews.com/golf/ci_10310954

Environmental Leader. (2010, July 14). *World Cup responsible for 2.7m tons of CO_2 equivalent*. Retrieved from http://www.environmentalleader.com/2010/07/14/world-cup-responsible-for-2-7m-tons-of-co2-equivalent/

Environmental Protection Agency. (2014a). *Green sports*. Retrieved from http://www2.epa.gov/green-sports

Environmental Protection Agency. (2014b). *Regulatory information by topic*. Retrieved, from http://www2.epa.gov/regulatory-information-topic

Epstien, A. (2003). *Sports law. West legal studies*. Clifton Park, NY: Thompson Delmar Learning.

Event. (2014, February 26). *Top 10 qualities that show you are a born event manager*. Retrieved from http://evvnt.com/2014/02/10-qualities-show-born-event-manager/

Event. (2015, January 30). *Rally Australia claims another world first*. Retreived from http://www.rallysportmag.com.au/home/wrc/9295-rally-australia-claims-another-world-first

EventManager. (2009a). *Home*. Retrieved from http://www.sbdatabases.com

EventManager. (2009b). *Download*. Retrieved from http://www.sbdatabases.com/event-manager-software.html

Farrell, J. M., Johnston, M. E., & Twynam, D. (1998). Volunteer motivation, satisfaction, and management at an elite sporting competition. *Journal of Sport Management, 12,* 288–300.

Federal Emergency Management Agency. (2005, March). *Special events contingency planning*. Retrieved from http://www.americanrestroom.org/gov/fema/FEMA_SECP39_41.PDF

Fédération Internationale de Football Association. (n.d.a.). *Previous FIFA worldcups*. Retrieved from http://www.fifa.com/worldcup/archive/index.html

Fédération Internationale de Football Association. (n.d.b.). *TV data*. Retrieved from http://www.fifa.com/aboutfifa/marketingtv/factsfigures/tvdata.html

Fédération Internationale de Football Association. (n.d.c.). *Tournaments*. Retrieved from http://www.fifa.com/tournaments/index.html

Fédération Internationale de Football Association. (n.d.d.). *Contact FIFA*. Retrieved from http://www.fifa.com/contact/index.html

Fédération Internationale de Ski (n.d.). *FIS world ski championships*. Retrieved from http://www.fis-ski.com/uk/majorevents/fisworldskichampionships.html

Fédération Internationale l'Autombile. (2013, June 28). *Creating an environment for change: Introducing an action plan for sustainability, the FIA yesterday put the focus on environmental awareness in sport*. Retrieved from http://www.fia.com/news/creating-environment-change

Fetto, J. (2015, March 6). *One million more ouseholds become cord-cutters last year*. Experian Marketing Services. Retrieved from http://www.experian.com/blogs/marketing-forward/2015/03/06/one-million-households-became-cord-cutters-last-year/

FIFA. (2014). *FIFA and the environment*. Retrieved from http://www.fifa.com/aboutfifa/socialresponsibility/environmental.html

Flash Seats. (2009). *FAQS*. Retrieved from www.flashseats.com

Fontana, A. (2015, February 12). *Two tournaments, two winners of the quicken loans hole-in-one sweepstakes read more at http://www.quickenloans.com/blog/two-tournaments-two-winners-of-the-quicken-loans-hole-in-one-sweepstakes#LFOQbEI7hr9X7sjq.99*. Retrieved from www.quickenloans.com: http://www.quickenloans.com/blog/two-tournaments-two-winners-of-the-quicken-loans-hole-in-one-sweepstakes

Formula 1. (2010). *FIA welcomes Formula 1 emissions programme*. Retrieved from http://www.formula1.com/news/headlines/2010/7/10977.html

Formula DRIFT. (n.d.a.). *Formula DRIFT info*. Retrieved from http://formulad.com/general-info/formula-drift-info.html

Formula DRIFT. (n.d.b.). *Formula DRIFT history*. Retrieved from http://formulad.com/general-info/formula-drift-history.html

Free Teleconferencing and Conference Call. (2009). Retrieved from http://www.freeconferencecall.com/prodfreeconferencecall.asp

Fried, G. (2005). *Managing sport facilities*. Champaign, IL: Human Kinetics.

Gainor, B. (2014, November 14). What is Sponsorship Activation. (A. Brackley, Interviewer)

Gold, S., Seuring, S., & Beske, P. (2010). Sustainable supply chain management and inter-organizational resources: a literature review. *Corporate Social Responsibility and Environmental Management, 17*(4), 230–245.

Goldenberg, S. (2011, November 3). *A run for the money*. New York Post. Retrieved from http://nypost.com/2011/11/03/a-run-for-the-money/National Football League. (2013). *Super Bowl LII Host City Bid Specifications & Requirements*.

Graham, C. (2014, July 23). *Study: Why customers participate in loyalty programs*. Retrieved from TA Technology website: http://technologyadvice.com/gamification/blog/why-customers-participate-loyalty-programs/

Green Events Group (n.d.). *News*. Retrieved from http://www.greeneventsgroup.com/news.htm

Green Sport Alliance. (2014). *About the Green Sport Alliance*. Retrieved from http://greensportsalliance.org/about/on

Griggs, B. (2013, February 4). *The funniest tweets of the #blackout, er Super Bowl*. CNN [online]. Retrieved from http://www.cnn.com/2013/02/04/tech/social-media/super-bowl-funniest-tweets/index.htmlLavigne, P. (2009, November 15). *Fans behaving badly?* Never Fear. Retrieved from http://sports.espn.go.com/espn/otl/news/story?id=4603176

Hagey, K., & Ramachandran, S. (2015, March 17). *Unbundling pay-TV brings new questions*. The Wall Street Journal. Retrieved from http://www.wsj.com/articles/unbundling-pay-tv-brings-new-questions-1426639589

Hart, S. L. (1995). A natural-resource-based view of the firm. *Academy of management review, 20*(4), 986–1014.

Hart, S. L., & Dowell, G. (2011). Invited editorial: A natural-resource-based view of the firm fifteen years after. *Journal of Management, 37*(5), 1464–1479.

Hart, S. L., & Milstein, M. B. (2003). Creating sustainable value. *The Academy of Management Executive, 17*(2), 56–67.

Harte, A. (2005, May 26). *The game that had it all*. Retrieved from http://www.uefa.com/competitions/ucl/news/kind=8192/newsid=304666.html

Helitzer, M. (1999). *The dream job: Sports publicity, promotion and marketing* (3rd ed.). Athens, OH: Ohio University Press.

Humphreys, J. M., & Plummer, M. K. (1995). *The economic impact on the State of Georgia of hosting the 1996 Summer Olympic Games.* Report prepared for the Atlanta Committee for the Olympic Games.

Hums, M. A., & MacLean, J. C. (2004). *Governance and policy in sport organizations.* Scottsdale, AZ: Holcomb Hathaway Publishers.

iCompli Sustainabiltiy. (2014, April 7). *15 things your should know about sustainability report assurance.* Retrieved from http://www.slideshare.net/iCompli_Sustainability/15-things-about-sustainability-report-assurance?qid=ff948b66-2c96-40e1-aade-8536eec0e799&v=qf1&b=&from_search=9

International Olympic Committee. (n.d.a.). *The Olympic games.* Retrieved from http://www.olympic.org/uk/games/index_uk.asp

International Olympic Committee. (n.d.b.). *Beijing 2008: Games programme finalized.* Retrieved from http://www.olympic.org/uk/organisation/commissions/programme/full_story_uk.asp?id=1797

International Olympic Committee. (n.d.c.). *The Olympic movement.* Retrieved from http://www.olympic.org/uk/organisation/index_uk.asp

International Skating Union. (2007). *ISU world figure skating championships 2007.* Retrieved from http://www.isufs.org/results/wc2007/CAT002RS.HTM

ISO. (n.d.). *ISO 2021–Sustainable events. Management system standards.* Retrieved from http://www.iso.org/iso/iso20121

Josephson Institute. (2015). *The six pillars of character.* Retrieved from http://josephsoninstitute.org/sixpillars.html.

Judge, W. Q., & Douglas, T. J. (1998). Performance implications of incorporating natural environmental issues into the strategic planning process: an empirical assessment. *Journal of Management Studies, 35*(2), 241–262.

Kimball, J. (2014, November 20). *New St. Paul Saints goes green with solar energy and water management.* Retrieved from https://www.minnpost.com/political-agenda/2014/11/new-st-paul-saints-stadium-goes-green-solar-energy-and-water-management

Kladko, B. (2008, July 10). *"Show me the money" colleges produce would-be Borases.* Bloomberg.com. Retrieved from http://www.bloomberg.com/apps/news?pid=20601109&sid=avpkYOse_uc4&refer=exclusive

Klara, R. (2013, January 28). *Ever wonder what it costs to get a sticker on a NASCAR car?* Retrieved from www.AdWeek.com: http://www.adweek.com/news/advertising-branding/your-brand-here-146795

Kramer, S. D. (2013, February 23). *NASCAR's social media #FAIL.* Trust But Verify. Retrieved from http://sdkramer.com/2013/02/23/nascars-social-media-fail/

Krause, P. (2008, October 1). *Ticketmaster defeats Cleveland Cavaliers in suit over ticket resale.* Cleveland.com. Retrieved from http://blog.cleveland.com/metro/2008/10/ticketmaster_defeats_cleveland.html

Ladies Professional Golf Association. (2008). *Players.* Retrieved from http://www.lpga.com/players_index.aspx

Laird, S. (2012, May 16). *Giants fans, now you can wear a Super Bowl ring too.* Retrieved from Mashable: http://mashable.com/2012/05/16/giants-augmented-reality-super-bowl-rings/

Laird, S. (2013, April 23). *Augmented reality tickets give sports fans a boost.* Retrieved from Mashable: http://mashable.com/2013/04/23/augmented-reality-sports-tickets/

Lamberth, C. R. (2005). Trends in stadium design: A whole new game. *Implications*, [Electronic version], *4*(6). Retrieved from http://www.informedesign.org/_news/jun_v04r-p.pdf

Larid, S. (2012, July 21). *NFL team enhances season tickets with augmented reality*. Retrieved from Mashable: http://mashable.com/2012/07/21/nfl-tickets-augmented-reality/

LaRue, R. J., Sawyer, T. H., & LaRue, D. A. (2005). Landscape design, sports turf, and parking. In Sawyer, T. H. (Ed.), *Facility design and management for health, fitness, physical activity, recreation, and sports facility development* (11th ed., pp. 220–233). Champaign, IL: Sagamore.

Lawrence H. J., Contorno, R. T., Kutz, E., Hendrickson, H., & Dorsey, W. (2007, May 15), *"Premium seating survey," working paper*. Athens, OH: Ohio University Center for Sports Administration.

Learmonth, M. (2008, July 21). *NBC hedges its Olympic bets: Buy a TV ad, get a Web banner, too*. Silicon Alley Insider. Retrieved from http://www.alleyinsider.com/2008/7/nbc-hedges-its-olympic-bets-buy-a-tv-ad-get-a-web-banner-too

Lehman, P. (n.d.). *The wide world of emerging sports*. Business Week. Retrieved from http://images.businessweek.com/ss/07/08/0823_emerging_sports/index_01.htm?sub=travel

Little League. (n.d.). *Structure of little league baseball and softball*. Retrieved from http://www.littleleague.org/Learn_More/About_Our_Organization/structure.htm

London Legacy Development Corporation. (2012, October 23). *LOCOG and the London Legacy Development Corporation begin Olympic Park handover*. Retrieved from http://www.londonlegacy.co.uk/locog-and-the-london-legacy-development-corporation-begin-olympic-park-handover/

Lynde, T. (2007). *Sponsorship 101: An insider's guide to sponsorships in corporate America*. Lynde & Associates.

Major League Baseball (MLB). (2014, July). MLB all-star game 2014 FAQS. Retrieved from www.mlb.com: http://mlb.mlb.com/mlb/events/all_star/y2014/fanfest/faq.jsp

Mallen, C., & Chard, C. (2011). "What could be" in Canadian sport facility environmental sustainability. *Sport Management Review, 15*(2), 230–243.

Mamic, I. (2005). Managing global supply chain: The sports footwear, apparel and retail sectors. *Journal of Business Ethics, 59*(1–2), 81–100.

Marcus, J. (2014, June 20). *Final figures show insurance softened NYRR sandy losses*. Retrieved from http://www.runnersworld.com/new-york-city-marathon/final-figures-show-insurance-softened-nyrr-sandy-losses

Marketing Charts. (2014, March 17). *Are young people watching less TV?* Marketing Charts. Retrieved from http://www.marketingcharts.com/television/are-young-people-watching-less-tv-24817/

McCarthy, M. (2008, December 18). *A security tool or the "rat line"? NFL targeting the unruly fan*. Retrieved from http://www.usatoday.com/sports/football/nfl/2008-12-18-fan-conduct-cover_N.htm

McClung, D. (2008). *Greenlighting: Sports facilities get energy efficient*. Electrical Contractor: Power and Integrated Building Systems. Retrieved from http://www.ecmag.com/section/lighting/green-lighting

McKinsey Company. (2014). *Is sport sponsorship worth it?* Retrieved from http://www.mckinsey.com/Insights/Marketing_Sales/Is_sports_sponsorship_worth_it?cid=other-eml-alt-mip-mck-oth-1406

McMillen, J. D. (2003). Game, event, and sponsorship contracts. In D. Cotton & J. Wolohan (Eds.), *Law for recreation and sport managers* (3rd ed., pp. 414–424). Dubuque, IA: Kendall Hunt.

Miller, L. K. (1997). *Sport business management*. Gaithersburg, MD: Aspen Publishing, Inc.

Montreal Canadiens. (2009). *Contact us*. Retrieved from http://canadiens.nhl.com/club/page.htm?id=53005

Moorman, A. M. (2007). Defamation. In D. J. Cotton & J. T. Wolohan (Eds.), *Law for recreation and sport managers* (4th ed., p. 518). Dubuque, IA: Kendall/Hunt Publishing Company.

Mueck, T., Funk, D. C., & Mueck, F. (2014, October). *Sport fan engagement through gamification in a digital media environment.* Paper presented at the annual meeting of the Sport Marketing Association, Philadelphia, PA.

Mull, R. F, Bayless, K. G., & Jamieson, L. M. (2005). *Recreational sport management.* Champaign, IL: Human Kinetics.

Mulrooney, A. L., & Farmer, P. J. (2005). Risk management in public assembly facilties. In H. Appenzeller (Ed.), *Risk management in sport: Issues and strategies* (pp. 303–316). Durham, NC: Carolina Academic Press.

Munday, M. (2009). Assessing the environmental impacts of mega sporting events: Two options? *Tourism Management, 30*(6), 828–837.

N.A. (n.d.). *Athletic training.* Retrieved April 7, 2015, from http://www.nata.org/athletic-training

National Association of Sports Commisions (NASC). (2012). Report on the Sports Travel Industry [White paper]. NASC. Cincinnati, OH.

National Association of Sports Commissions and Ohio University. (2011). *2011*

National Cable & Telecommunications Association. (2008). *2008 industry overview.* Retrieved from http://i.ncta.com/ncta_com/PDFs/NCTA_Annual_Report_05.16.08.pdf

National Collegiate Athletic Association. (2009). *I chose division II: Division II strategic plan January 2009 through January 2012.* [Electronic Version]. Retrieved from www.ncaa.org/wps/wcm/connect/resources/file/eb41164f99948fb/Final%2009-12%20Division%20II%20Strategic%20Plan.pdf?

National Collegiate Athletic Association. (n.d.a.). *Composition & sport sponsorship of the NCAA.* Retrieved from http://www.ncaa.org/about/who-we-are/membership/composition-and-sport-sponsorship-membership

National Collegiate Athletic Association. (n.d.b.). *NCAA toolbox—conducting a meeting.* Indianapolis: NCAA.

National Federation of State High School Associations. (n.d.). *About us.* Retrieved from http://www.nfhs.org/web/2006/08/about_us.aspx

National Labor Relations Board. (n.d) *Workplace rights.* Retrieved from http://www.nlrb.gov/Workplace_Rights/i_am_new_to_this_website/what_is_the_national_labor_relations_act.aspx

National Sports Forum (NSF). (2015, January). The 2015 NSF Corporate & Industry Survey Highlight Packet. Retrieved from http://www.sportsad.ohio.edu/nsf-2015-survey/nsf-thank-you/

Natural Resources Defense Council. (2014a). *Guide to composting at sporting venues.* Retrieved from http://www.nrdc.org/greenbusiness/guides/sports/sports-venues-composting.asp

Natural Resources Defense Council. (2014b). *Smarter business: Greening the games.* Retrieved from http://www.nrdc.org/greenbusiness/guides/sports/

New York City Sports Commission & New York Road Runners. (2007). *New York City Sports Commission and New York Road Runners announce economic impact for ING New York City Marathon.* Retrieved from http://www.marathonguide.com/pressreleases/index.cfm?file=NewYorkCityMarathon_071030

New York Road Runners. (n.d.). *About Us: Our impact.* Retrieved from http://www.nyrr.org/about-us/our-impact

New York State Department of Health. (2008, August). *Fact sheet: crumb-rubber infilled synthetic turf athletic fields*. Retrieved from http://www.health.state.ny.us/environmental/outdoors/synthetic_turf/crumb-rubber_infilled/fact_sheet.htm

Newman, T., Peck, J., Harris, C., & Wilhide, B. (2013). *Social media in sport marketing*. Scottsdale, AZ: Holcombe Hathaway.

Nield, D. (2015, January 27). *GoPro's deal with the NHL puts you right in the middle of the action*. Gizmag. Retrieved from http://www.gizmag.com/go-pro-nhl-deal/35793/

Nielsen. (2009). *Profile*. Retrieved from http://en-us.nielsen.com/main/about/Profile

Nike. (2014). *Our sustainability strategy*. Retrieved from http://www.nikeresponsibility.com/report/content/chapter/our-sustainability-strategy

Noble, J. (2007, February 26). *F1 already 'carbon neutral' since 1997*. Retrieved from http://www.autosport.com/news/report.php/id/56953

North American Society for Sport Management. (n.d.). *Sport management programs United States*. Retrieved from http://www.nassm.com/Programs/AcademicPrograms/United_States

NYC.gov. (2007). *Mayor Bloomberg and MLB Commissioner Selig announce 2008 MLB all-star game will be played in historic Yankee stadium in its final season*. Retrieved from http://www.nyc.gov/portal/site/nycgov/menuitem.c0935b9a57bb4ef3daf2f1c701c789a0/index.jsp?pageID=mayor_press_release&catID=1194&doc_name=http%3A%2F%2Fwww.nyc.gov%2Fhtml%2Fom%2Fhtml%2F2007a%2Fpr032-07.html&cc=unused1978&rc=1194&ndi=1

Paramio-Salcines, J., Babiak, K., & Walters, G. (2013). CSR within the sport industry: An overview of an emerging academic field. In J. L. Paramio-Salcines, K. Babiak, & G. Walters (Eds.), *Routledge handbook of sport and corporate social responsibility* (pp. 1–14). New York, NY: Routledge.

Pew Research Center. (2013a, June 5). *Smartphone owernship 2013*. Retrieved from http://www.pewinternet.org/2013/06/05/smartphone-ownership-2013/

Pew Research Center. (2013b, April 3). *Usage and adoption*. Retrieved from http://www.pewinternet.org/2013/06/05/smartphone-ownership-2013/

Pfahl, M. (2011a). *Sport and the natural environment: A handbook for sport managers*. Dubuque, IA: Kendall Hunt.

Pfahl, M. (2011b). Strategic issues associated with the development of internal sustainability teams in sport and recreation organizations: A framework for action and sustainable environmental performance. *International Journal of Sport Management. Recreation & Tourism, 6*, 37–61.

Pfahl, M. (2013). The environmental awakening in sport. *Solutions. 4*(3), 67–76.

Phoenix Open (2014). *2013 Waste management Phoenix open aims to achieve Gold Certification from the Council for Responsible Sport*. Retrieved from http://wmphoenixopen.com/2013/01/2013-waste-management-phoenix-open-aims-to-achieve-gold-certification-from-the-council-for-responsible-sport/

Phoenix Suns. (2009). *Media center: An online resource for Phoenix Suns media partners*. Retrieved from http://www.nba.com/suns/news/media_center.html

Pletz, J. (2010, May 17). *Chicago 2016's final tally: $70.6 M spend on Olympics effort*. Retrieved from http://www.chicagobusiness.com/article/20100517/NEWS02/200038265/chicago-2016s-final-tally-70-6m-spent-on-olympics-effortRice-Jones, G. (2014, February 7). *The economic impact of sporting events*. MHP Financial. Retrieved from http://www.mhpc.com/financial/the-economic-impact-of-sporting-events/2008

Plunkett Research, Ltd. (2008). *Introduction to the sports industry*. Retrieved from the Plunkett Research, Ltd. Database.

Plunkett Research, Ltd. (2008). *NASCAR weathers rising costs*. Retrieved from Plunkett Research, Ltd. Database.

Porter, M., & Reinhardt, F. (2007). A strategic approach to climate change. *Harvard Business Review*, 85(10), 22–26.

Prosser, A., & Rutledge, A. (2003). *Special events and festivals: How to plan, organize and implement*. State College, PA: Venture Publishing.

Pryor, R. R., Casa, D. J., Vandermark, L. W., Stearns, R. L., Attanasio, S. M., Fontaine, G. J., ... Wafer, A. M. (2015). Athletic training services in public secondary schools: A benchmark study. *Journal of Athletic Training, 50*(2), 156–162.

Quinn, J. (2008, November 13). *UK minister's Olympic bid comments cause uproar*. Retrieved from http://usatoday30.usatoday.com/sports/olympics/2008-11-13-289129914_x.htm

Raj, R., & Musgrave, J. (2009). *Event management and sustainability*. Cambridge, MA: CABI.

Research Director. (n.d.). *Glossary*. Retrieved from http://www.researchdirectorinc.com/industry-resources/glossary/

Rob, P., Coronel, C., & Crockett, K. (2008). *Database systems: Design, implementation, & management*. International Edition. Retrieved from http://books.google.com

Rob, P., Coronel, C., & Crockett, K. (2008). *Database systems: Design, implementation, & management*. International Edition. Retrieved March 30, 2009, from http://books.google.com

Roerink, K. (2013, December 1). *Universtiy of Wyoming aims to lasso social media fans with 'The Corral'*. Casper Star Tribune Communications. Retrieved from http://trib.com/news/state-and-regional/university-of-wyoming-aims-to-lasso-social-media-fans-with/article_c6825480-5290-5843-9400-f30a8c886cab.html

Rogowsky, M. (2014, March 18). *Cord cutting; the promise TV viewers keep breaking*. Retrieved from http://www.forbes.com/sites/markrogowsky/2014/03/18/cord-cutting-the-promise-tv-viewers-keep-on-breaking/

Rukus. (2014, May 5). *Rukus smart Wi-Fi is a clean winner at annual BNP Paribas Open tennis tournament in Indian Wells*. Retrieved from http://www.ruckuswireless.com/press/releases/20140505-ruckus-smart-wi-fi-clean-winner-annual-bnp-paribas-open-tennis-tournament University of Michigan. (2012, April 11). *Michigan to paint #GOBLUE hashtag on field for Mott spring game*. M.GOBLUE.COM. Retrieved from http://www.mgoblue.com/sports/m-footbl/spec-rel/041112aaa.html

Rutt, A. (2014, March 26). *Rock and wrap it thrives at Rexall Place*. Retrieved from http://www.nhl.com/ice/blog.htm?id=1125

Safko, L., & Brake, D. (2009). *The social media bible: Tactics, tools, and strategies for business success*. New York, NY: Wiley.

Salt Lake Organizing Committee. (2000). Team 2002 in training. Salt Lake, Utah: Salt Lake Organizing Committee.

Samuel, S., & Stubbs, W. (2013). Green Olympics, green legacies? An exploration of the environmental legacies of the Olympic Games. *International Review for the Sociology of Sport, 48*(4), 485–504.

Sarkis, J. (2003). A strategic decision framework for green supply chain management. *Journal of Cleaner Production, 11*(4), 397–409.

Schaber, G., & Rohwer, C. (1984). *Contracts* (2nd ed.). St. Paul, MN: West Nutshell Series.

Scharfenort, N. (2012). Urban development and social change in Qatar: The Qatar National Vision 2030 and the 2022 FIFA World Cup. *Journal of Arabian Studies*, 2(2), 209–230.

Schmidt, C. W. (2006). Putting the Earth in play: Environmental awareness and sports. *Environmental Health Perspectives*, 114(5), A286–A295.

Schultz, E. J. (2014, January 7). *Forecast: Sponsorship spending will slow in 2014*. Advertising Age. Retrieved from http://www.sponsorship.com/About-IEG/IEG/Forecast--Sponsorship-Spending-Will-Slow-In 2014.aspxSport + Recreation Alliance. (2014). *Engagement with stakeholders*. Retrieved July 31, 2014, from http://www.sportandrecreation.org.uk/smart-sport/communication/engagement-stakeholders

Sharp, L. (2003). Contract essentials. In D. Cotten & J. Wolohan (Eds.), *Law for recreation and sport managers* (3rd ed., pp. 384–392). Dubuque, IA: Kendall Hunt.

Shea, B. (2013, January 13). *Sports fans' techn thirst drains local stadiums*. Craie's Detroit Business. Retrieved from http://www.crainsdetroit.com/article/20130113/NEWS/301139964/sports-fans-tech-thirst-drains-local-stadiums

Show, J. (2008, September 8). Events add spice to fall series. *Sports Business Journal*, 11(19), 8.

Silvers, J. R. (2003). *Event management body of knowledge project*. Retrieved from http://www.juliasilvers.com/embok.htm#The_Definition_of_Event_Management

SocialTimes. (2013, August 26). *The state of digital marketing in sports [Inforgraphic]*. Retrieved from http://www.adweek.com/socialtimes/sports-digital-marketing/489896?red=at

Solaris, J. (2008, April 17). Top 5 qualities of the successful event manager. EventManagerBlog. http://www.eventmanagerblog.com/top-5-qualities/

Solomon, J. (2002). *An insider's guide to managing sporting events*. Chicago, IL: Human Kinetics.

Sporting News Media, Kantar Media Sports, & SportBusiness Group. (2014, May). *Global sports media consumption report*. Retrieved from http://sportsvideo.org/main/files/2014/06/2014-Know-the-Fan-Study_US.pdf

Sports Business Daily (2008). *Sports Business Daily September 12, 2008: NBC touts sale of 85% of Super Bowl XLIII ad inventory*. Retrieved from www.sportsbusinessdaily.com/article/123957

Sports Business Journal. (2011, September 19). Naming rights deals. Retrieved from www.sportsbusinessdaily.com: http://www.sportsbusinessdaily.com/Journal/Issues/2011/09/19/In-Depth/Naming-rights-deals.aspx

Stadium Managers Association. (n.d.). *History* Retrieved from http://www.stadiummanagers.org/index.php/history-of-sma-53/history

T-Mobile Puts Its Network on Show at Major League Baseball All-Star Week. (2014, July 11). Retrieved from www.t-mobile.com: http://newsroom.t-mobile.com/news/t-mobile-puts-its-network-on-show-at-major-league-baseball-all-star-week.htm

Techniques for Effective Alcohol Management Coalition. (n.d.). *Techniques for effective alcohol management*. Retrieved from http://www.teamcoalition.org/about/about.asp

The Baseball Tomorrow Fund. (n.d.). *Baseball field maintenance: A general guide for fields of all levels*. Retrieved from http://mlb.mlb.com/mlb/downloads/btf_field_maintenance_guide.pdf

The New York City Sports Commission. (2008). Annual events. Retrieved from http://www.nyc.gov/html/sports/html/nyc_marathon.html

The Nielsen Company. (2014, December). *The total audience*. The Nielsen Company. Retrieved from http://ir.nielsen.com/files/doc_presentations/2014/The-Total-Audience-Report.pdf

The Nielson Company (2013, September 17). *Smartphone switch: Three-fourths of recent acquirers chose smartphones.* Retrieved, from The Nielson Company website: http://www.nielsen.com/us/en/insights/news/2013/smartphone-switch--three-fourths-of-recent-acquirers-chose-smart.html

The Real Shaq. (2009). *The real Shaq.* Retrieved from http://twitter.com/the_real_shaq

The Volunteer Protection Act of 1997, 42 U.S.C.A.§§ 14501-14505 (West 2010) (Pub. L. No. 105–19), Retrieved from www4.law.cornell.edu/uscode/html/uscode42/usc_sec_42_00014501----000-.-.html

Ticketing. (2009). *Cleveland Cavaliers.* Retrieved from http://www.nba.com/cavaliers/tickets/ticketplans.html

Tsang, G., & Newberry, C. (2008). What do high performance athletes eat for their Olympics diet? Retrieved from http://www.healthcastle.com/sports_olympics_diet.shtml

Ukman, L. (2008). *IEG's guide to sponsorship: everything you need to know about sports, arts, event, entertainment, and cause marketing.* Chicago, IL: IEG, LLC.

Ukman. L. (2014, October). *IEG sponsorship report.* Retrieved from www.sponsorship.com: http://www.sponsorship.com/publications/ieg-s-guide-to-sponsorship.aspx

Union of European Football Associations. (2008, November 18). *China 2009-12 media rights.* Retrieved from http://www.uefa.com/uefa/keytopics/kind=131072/newsid=775377.html

Union of European Football Associations. (n.d.a.). *History.* Retrieved from http://www.uefa.com/uefachampionsleague/history/

Union of European Football Associations. (n.d.b.). *UEFA organization.* Retrieved from http://www.uefa.com/uefa/contacts.html

United Nations Development Programme. (2012, October 9). *UNEP evaluation of South Africa 2010 just 60 per cent of projected figure–other achievements noted in water and waste reduction.* News Centre. Retrieved July 29, 2014, from http://www.unep.org/NEWSCENTRE/default.aspx?DocumentId=2697&ArticleId=9297

United States Department of Justice. (n.d.). *Americans with Disabilities Act questions and answers.* Retrieved from http://www.ada.gov/q%26aeng02.htm

United States Department of Labor (2008). *Wage and hour division: Fact sheet #18.* Retrieved from http://www.dol.gov/whd/regs/compliance/whdfs18.pdf

United States Department of Labor. (n.d.). *The Fair Labor Standards Act.* Retrieved from http://www.dol.gov/compliance/laws/comp-flsa.htm

United States Diving. (2014). *U.S. diving competitive and technical rules.* Retrieved from http://www.usadiving.org/wp-content/uploads/2013/10/Subpart-F-Policies-for-the-Administration-of-Diving-Competitions.pdf

United States Equal Employment Opportunity Commission. (n.d.). *Sexual harassment.* Retrieved from http://www.eeoc.gov/laws/types/sexual_harassment.cfm

University Athletic Association, Inc. (2014, June 23). Florida athletics program take second in 2013-14 Learfield Sports Directors' Cup. Retrieved from http://www.gatorzone.com/story.php?id=28357

University of Pennsylvania. (2013, December 13). *How sports greening is generating new revenue.* Retrieved from https://knowledge.wharton.upenn.edu/article/sports-greening-generating-new-revenue/.

Urbach, R. (2014, May 20). Reebok gets fit with an intense CrossFit sponsorship. Retrieved from www.madisonaveinsights.com: http://www.madisonaveinsights.com/2014/05/20/reebok-gets-fit-with-an-intense-crossfit-sponsorship/

USA Diving. (2007). USA diving competitive & technical rules. [Electronic version]. Retrieved from http://www.usadiving.org/05redesign/resources/rulebook.htm

USA Track and Field. (n.d.). *USATF Course Certification*. Retrieved from http://www.usatf.org/events/courses/certification/

USA Triathlon. (2006). *USAT event sanctioning*. Retrieved from http://rankings.usatriathlon.org/Event_Sanctioning/Event_Sanctioning.htm

USA Triathlon. (2014). *Sanctioned events calendar*. Retrieved from http://www.usatriathlon.org/events/sanctioned-event-calendar.aspx

USA Triathlon. (n.d.). *About sanctioning*. Retrieved from http://www.usatriathlon.org/audience/race-directors/sanctioning.aspx

Vodafone McLaren Mercedes. (2009). *Media centre*. Retrieved from http://www.mclaren.com/mediaroom/media-login.php

Walton, S. V., Handfield, R. B., & Melnyk, S. A. (1998). The green supply chain: Integrating suppliers into environmental management processes. *Journal of Supply Chain Management, 34*(2), 2–11.

Weir. (2013, July 20). *The 2012 London Olympics booster economy by $15 billion, says British report*. Reuters. Skift. Retrieved from http://skift.com/2013/07/20/the-2012-london-olympics-boosted-economy-by-15-billion-says-british-report/

Whistler 2020. (2015). *Does sustainability cost more?* Retrieved from http://www.whistler2020.ca/whistler/site/genericPage.acds?instanceid=1967867&context=1967866

Xinhua. (2008, August 13). *Georgian, Russian volleyballers embrace at Beijing Olympics*. Chinaview. Retrieved from http://news.xinhuanet.com/english/2008-08/13/content_9267520.htm

Yuan, J. (2014, July 9). *Everyone keeps crashing at the Tour de France because so many people are taking selfies*. New York Mag. Retrieved from http://nymag.com/daily/intelligencer/2014/07/selfies-are-causing-crashes-at-tour-de-france.html

Zullo, R. (2005, August/September). *The right moves*. Athletic Management. Retrieved December from http://www.momentummedia.com/articles/am/am1705/rightmoves.htm